Exploring Entrepreneurship

Exploring Entrepreneurship

Practices and Perspectives

Richard Blundel

Nigel Lockett

OXFORD

UNIVERSITY PRESS

OXFORD
UNIVERSITY PRESS

Great Clarendon Street, Oxford ox2 6DP

Oxford University Press is a department of the University of Oxford.
It furthers the University's objective of excellence in research, scholarship,
and education by publishing worldwide in

Oxford New York

Auckland Cape Town Dar es Salaam Hong Kong Karachi
Kuala Lumpur Madrid Melbourne Mexico City Nairobi
New Delhi Shanghai Taipei Toronto

With offices in

Argentina Austria Brazil Chile Czech Republic France Greece
Guatemala Hungary Italy Japan Poland Portugal Singapore
South Korea Switzerland Thailand Turkey Ukraine Vietnam

Oxford is a registered trade mark of Oxford University Press
in the UK and in certain other countries

Published in the United States
by Oxford University Press Inc., New York

British Library Cataloguing in Publication Data

Data available

Library of Congress Cataloging in Publication Data

Data available

Typeset by Laserwords Private Ltd, Chennai, India
Printed in Italy
on acid-free paper by
L.E.G.O. S.p.A.—Lavis TN

ISBN 978-0-19-921155-5

1 3 5 7 9 10 8 6 4 2

Preface: a guide to the book

Aims and approach

We have written this book to help you to explore entrepreneurship in all its complexity and variety. Our approach is based on the view that some subjects, such as medicine, engineering, and entrepreneurship, are particularly well-suited to experience-based learning (Kirby 2004; Binks 2005; Edwards and Muir 2006). The basic idea is that people can learn a lot more if they are able to connect the research evidence and the theory to some kind of direct personal experience. The nature of this 'experience' depends a great deal on what you are studying. For example, a medical student spends time working in different parts of a hospital, while an engineering student might design a new product or test some materials in a laboratory. Providing practical experience is more difficult for entrepreneurship students. However, it is possible to re-create some aspects of a 'real life' experience using new venture exercises, business plan competitions, and computer simulations. In this book, we provide support for all three types of activity. However, experience-based learning is about more than just having an experience. Some of the most important learning happens when practical activity is combined with well-structured reflection. With this in mind, we have designed the book around three related aims:

1. To help you gain essential practical skills and underpinning knowledge, and reflect on the challenges involved in creating an entrepreneurial venture, either individually or as part of a team;

2. To help you develop a deeper understanding of entrepreneurship, as you make connections between your experiences, relevant theoretical concepts, research findings, and the experiences of others;

3. To encourage you to take part in a broader debate about entrepreneurship in the twenty-first century, examining contrasting perspectives on entrepreneurship across a wide range of ventures.

In summary, this book offers a fresh, wide-ranging, and up-to-date approach to entrepreneurship, combining practical relevance with critical reflection. We also hope that it will help you to experience something of the excitement, uncertainty, passion, and sheer hard work that is involved in creating a successful entrepreneurial venture.

Who are we writing for?

We have written this book with three kinds of reader in mind. First, we are writing for students taking advanced undergraduate and postgraduate courses or modules in Entrepreneurship and/or New Venture Creation. We have assumed that most of these readers will already have some background in business and management subjects such as marketing, finance, and operations. However, those with more limited business and management knowledge are supported with concise explanations of key terms and suggestions for further background reading. Second, we are writing for people who are in the process of creating their own commercial or social ventures, or who are considering this option. Our approach is designed to help you reflect on questions that are rarely addressed in 'recipe book' guides to setting up a business. Third, we hope that our book will be a useful resource for people working with social and commercial entrepreneurs (e.g. in regional development, small business finance, or enterprise support organizations), and for anyone who is looking for an accessible review of contemporary entrepreneurship in its various forms.

What does the book cover?

Exploring Entrepreneurship covers practical issues related to the creation of an entrepreneurial venture, together with reviews of related research evidence and more theoretical discussion about entrepreneurship. We also make considerable use of case-based examples, so that you can learn from the experiences of real entrepreneurs as they struggle to create and to develop their ventures. It is worth noting two distinctive features of this book. Firstly, it provides detailed coverage of many different types of entrepreneurship. You will find examples of commercial, primarily profit-oriented ventures and what are often termed 'social' enterprises, where the primary aim is to address a social or environmental challenge, rather than simply to secure a profit. In contrast to most other texts, it also addresses 'anti-social' forms of entrepreneurship, with examples that range from the unethical and environmentally destructive behaviour of legitimate firms to the shady world of organized crime. The argument behind these decisions is simple: entrepreneurial activity is clearly a very powerful force in the world. We think it is important for entrepreneurship students to consider seriously how that power is exercised.

Which aspects are given less emphasis?

Exploring Entrepreneurship has an ambitious agenda, but clearly it is not possible to deal with *every* aspect of entrepreneurship in a single textbook, nor can we cover all of our chosen themes in equal depth. For example, topics that are given less emphasis include: 'corporate entrepreneurship', 'civic entrepreneurship', 'institutional entrepreneurship', and 'entrepreneurial leadership'. The main focus of Chapters 2 to 8 is on the challenge of *creating* a new venture, up to the point where it has secured the support it needs to become established. We do not concentrate on management issues in small *established* businesses (i.e. small business management). Rather than providing general introductions to the main business functions (e.g. marketing, human resource management, and strategy), we consider how these areas of activity need to be adapted in order to address the challenges of new venture creation. For example, Chapter 5 reviews emerging practices in entrepreneurial marketing and Chapter 8 evaluates different options for financing a new venture. Of course, entrepreneurial activity is not just about new venture creation. As any experienced entrepreneur will tell you, the real work begins after the initial 'start-up' phase, when the enterprise is operational. We address this issue in three ways: (1) Chapter 9 features three successful entrepreneurs, who describe their experiences of creating and building their ventures; (2) Case studies in Part One and Part Two of the book illustrate many different kinds of entrepreneurial activity, with some tracing the development of ventures over extended periods (e.g. Case 14.4); (3) Each chapter contains a Guide to Further Reading. Additional information, including a glossary of key terms, advice on preparatory reading, practical checklists, and useful web links, are provided on the Online Resource Centre (ORC).

 online resource centre 'Glossary'; 'Preparatory Reading'; 'Practical Checklist'; 'Web Links'

How is the book structured?

The book opens with a scene-setting chapter (Chapter 1– the many faces of entrepreneurship). The remainder of the book is divided into two distinct but inter-related sections. Part One (Chapters 2 to 9) tackles the main practical activities involved in developing a new entrepreneurial venture. These chapters have a standardized structure, making them easy to navigate. They can be used in various ways, depending on your interests:

- As a stand-alone introduction to entrepreneurship practices, with a particular focus on the process of creating a new venture;

- As a practical, structured guide for students engaged in new venture creation exercises, competitions, or simulations;

- As a resource for prospective entrepreneurs embarking on a new venture.

The co-authors have contributed to both parts of the book, but we each took responsibility for one of the main themes. Nigel drew on his previous experience as an entrepreneur, and a network of contacts, to develop much of the practice-based material that is set out in Part One, and in related sections of the Online Resource Centre. Richard made use of his wide-ranging experience of entrepreneurship and innovation research to assemble the material for Part Two. Both co-authors also acknowledge the major contribution of many colleagues and friends in helping to shape these chapters.

Part Two (Chapters 10 to 15) explores entrepreneurship from several different perspectives. Each chapter draws on some of the latest research evidence, along with the voices of entrepreneurs, researchers, and policy-makers. These chapters can also be used in different ways:

- As a concise, stand-alone overview of contemporary entrepreneurship research and policy-making, with recommendations for further reading;

- As a complement to the Part One chapters, enabling students, prospective entrepreneurs and others to make connections between their practical experience, the experience of others, and relevant research evidence and to help you reflect on your experience.

Chapter 1 contains a more detailed introduction to Part One of the book, focusing on its distinctive approach to entrepreneurial learning. The main themes of Part Two are introduced in Chapter 1 and further developed in Chapter 10.

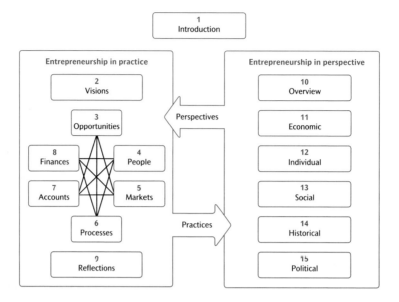

The Online Resource Centre (ORC) contains additional resources. These features, and the overall design of the book, have been carefully designed to provide you with the tools required to explore the worlds of entrepreneurship and new venture creation. Entrepreneurship is an extremely complex, varied, and powerful social phenomenon, and it is well worth exploring in some depth. The best way to embark on such an exploration is to combine your own practical experience with the experiences of others, reinforced by research findings and critical reflection. For students, this often means completing a challenging new venture creation exercise, while also keeping a diary (or log book), and reading about entrepreneurship. This is not an easy combination to achieve. In our experience, students often focus on their new venture creation activity, leaving insufficient time for reading and reflection. It is difficult to balance all three areas, but doing so can lead to some very rewarding, and possibly 'life-changing' personal insights. We encourage you to make the most of this opportunity to explore entrepreneurship and wish you well on the journey.

Richard Blundel
Nigel Lockett
January 2011

References

Binks, M. (2005) *Entrepreneurship education and integrative learning.* Birmingham: National Council for Graduate Entrepreneurship.

Edwards, L-J and Muir, E. (2006) *Tell me and I'll forget; show me and I may remember; involve me and I will understand.* Birmingham: National Council for Graduate Entrepreneurship.

Kirby, D. (2004) 'Entrepreneurship education: can business schools meet the challenge?' *Journal of Education and Training,* 46, 8/9: 510–19.

Acknowledgements

When writing a book of this kind, you are bound to draw on the contributions of many other people. We would like to take this opportunity to thank all the colleagues, friends, and relatives who have helped us in preparing the first edition of *Exploring Entrepreneurship*. It is not possible to name everyone, but we would like to express particular thanks to the following individuals: members of the international panel of reviewers, who provided informed and constructive feedback on the draft chapters; others who provided additional comments on sections of the manuscript, including Sally Caird, Steve Conway, MariaLaura di Domenico, Andrea Moro, Andrew Popp, and Nigel Walton; Haider Ali for his work on the Online Resource Centre, the editorial and marketing teams at OUP, including Hannah Brannon, Claire Brewer, Joanna Hardern, Alice Horrocks, Alexandra Lazarus, and Nicki Sneath; Lawrence Osborn, for copy-editing the manuscript; Gill Clack for proofreading; the 11 entrepreneurs interviewed for the critical incident and narrative cases in Part One – Adnan Awan, Deirdre Bounds, Helen Child, Jonathan Hick, Tim Lockett, Neil Meredith, Lucy Nicholson, Steve Pankhurst, Mark Robinson, Victoria Tomlinson, and Steve Woodford – for telling their personal stories and bringing these chapters alive; Bruce Macfarlane, for sharing his considerable experience as a business angel and venture capitalist; Stuart Riley, for his assistance in interviewing many of these entrepreneurs; Edwin Broni-Mensah, Rajeeb Dey, Lucian Tarnowski, and Hermione Way, for sharing their early experiences as student and graduate entrepreneurs; Matt Smith and Victoria Lennox of the National Consortium of University Entrepreneurs (NACUE), for their valuable assistance; other entrepreneurs and practitioners who contributed directly to the Part Two cases, including Maryam Bibi, Bob Cannell, Colin and Janet Cordner, and Ian Sinclair; the five entrepreneurship researchers interviewed for the 'researcher profiles' cases in Part Two – Boris Blumberg, Mark Casson, Jason Cope, Helle Neergaard, Mary Rose, and Friederike Welter; and other researchers and writers whose work features prominently in Part Two cases and illustrations – Susanne Agterbosch, David Audretsch, Daniel Bornstein, Sylvia Breukers, Steve Conway, Dennis De, Pearce Flannery, Raghu Garad, Francis Greene, Chiara Guglielmetti, Eleanor Hamilton, Hans-Hermann Hohmann, Marcel Hülsbeck, Bengt Johannisson, Oswald Jones, Peter Karnøe, Max Keilbach, Anders Lundström, Hans Landström, Erik E. Lehmann, Alessandro Lomi, Kevin Mole, Bernard Obeng, Eric Osei, Mike Parsons, Andrew Popp, Kate Pritchard, Sarah Robinson, Donald L. Sexton, David Smallbone, Lois Stevenson, David Storey, Richard Swedberg, Angela Tregear, Vadim Volkov, and Fillipo Carlo Wezel. Thanks to current students at the Open University and the University of Leeds, and to our many former students for their contribution over the years. We wish you well in your different ventures and hope you can keep us updated on progress. Lastly, to Beverley, Fay, Sandy, Mhairi, and Georgie (NL), and to Tina, Freya, and Robbie (RB): thanks for your unfailing support, encouragement and inspiration.

Publisher's Acknowledgements

In memory of Jason Cope.

Brief contents

Detailed contents

List of cases

List of figures

How to use this book

Learning Outcomes at the start of each chapter help you to focus your learning, and (in conjunction with the chapter summaries) evaluate your knowledge and understanding of each chapter.

Opening Cases are short 'real-world' examples of entrepreneurship that illustrate specific issues and learning points in the chapter. There are 'points to consider', references and website addresses, providing you with an opportunity for further research and updating.

Case Studies are extended narratives, often based on the lives of 'real world' entrepreneurs and the histories of their entrepreneurial ventures. The cases illustrate issues raised in the chapter and provide material that can be used in practical activities, discussions and research. The Part One chapters include a 'Critical Incident' case. Part Two chapters include a 'Researcher Profile' case.

Ethical Points included in several case studies, highlight an important ethical issue confronting the entrepreneurs and their ventures, and help you broaden your understanding of the issues involved.

Chapter Summaries are 'bullet point' lists which appear at the end of each chapter. They highlight key themes from the chapter and can be used to check your understanding and to link back to the Learning Outcomes.

> **✱ 12.6 Summary**
>
> ➤ Individual-level perspectives on entrepreneurship, using a variety of psychological and behavioural approaches, have enhanced our understanding of entrepreneurship.
>
> ➤ Earlier research focused on the search for distinctive entrepreneurial traits or personality characteristics. These ideas remain popular and influential, but it is important to be aware of their limitations and of subsequent advances in psychological and behavioural research.
>
> ➤ Recent research on entrepreneurial cognition provides some interesting insights in areas such as opportunity recognition. Researchers have also helped to explain cognitive biases can contribute to mistakes and the failure of some entrepreneurial ventures.
>
> ➤ There are three main vehicles for entrepreneurial learning: formal education; informal sources; and learning from direct experiences. People can acquire entrepreneurial skills

Practical Activities are a variety of exercises that can be used by individuals and in team-based settings. Part One activities are designed to improve your understanding of key issues and to provide practical experiences related to the venture creation process. Part Two activities provide opportunities to apply research methods and findings in a more practical way.

> **▶ Practical activities**
>
> **1. My entrepreneurial personality** Re-read the arguments in Section 11.2, and try at least one of the entrepreneurial assessment tests detailed there, or on the companion website. What is your impression of the results? Do they reflect your own assessment? Were there any surprises? If possible, compare the findings with those of a close colleague or friend. (NB If these results suggest a lack of enterprising attributes do not assume that your entrepreneurial journey is over. Instead, review the various limitations of characteristics-based approaches and refer to the discussion on entrepreneurial learning, and how it can transform skills, knowledge, and attitudes.)
>
> **2. Exploring other entrepreneurial lives** Using Cases 11.1 and 11.4 as a guide, find three examples of people talking about the factors that prompted them to act entrepreneurially. This may be establishing a social or commercial enterprise, or becoming an 'intrapreneur' in an existing organization. Compare the accounts, highlighting examples of each of the following: (a) early signs

Discussion Topics at the end of each chapter encourage you to reflect on the techniques, practices, arguments and evidence presented in the chapter.

> **🖥 Discussion topics**
>
> **1.** In terms of finding new ventures to invest in, what might be the differences between a venture investment fund and a social investment fund? What additional criteria would you need to use to determine the social impact of a social enterprise looking for investment? How would you calculate the value of these criteria and measure them?
>
> **2.** Put simply, most of the new jobs created in an economy come from high growth small businesses. What is the role of governments in funding new venture creation and supporting high growth firms? Big companies might get grants for relocating in an area of high unemployment. Should public funds be used to invest in small firms?

Further Reading Guides provide suggestions for additional reading, to help you get a fuller understanding of the topics covered in each chapter.

> **📖 Further reading guide**
>
> The editor's introduction to Swedberg (2000) locates the various strands of social science research on entrepreneurship. Licht and Siegel (2006) review the field from an institutional economics standpoint, while Cope et al. (2007) introduces a special issue on the important theme of social capital. For a review of qualitative approaches in entrepreneurship research, see Neergaard and Ulhøi (2007); for a more quantitative, economics-based approach, see Parker (2009), Research on gender and entrepreneurship is reviewed by Brush (2008), Carter and Bennett (2006), and Greene et al. (2006). For research on ethnicity and entrepreneurship, see Ram et al. (2006), Basu (2008), and Dhaliwal and Adcroft (2007); for a review of migration studies, see Godley (2008). The family entrepreneurship field is summarized in Howorth et al. (2008) and Fletcher (2006). The entrepreneurial networking literature crosses many of the areas discussed in this chapter. Useful reviews of the field include, Conway and Jones (2006), Johannisson (2000) and Ebers (1999), which concentrates on the formation of networks. Pioneering studies include Birley (1985), Dubini

References contain all of the sources cited in the chapter, including those mentioned in the further reading guide and help you broaden your understanding of the topics covered in each chapter.

> **📖 References**
>
> Acs, Z.J. and Audretsch, D.B. (2003) *Handbook of entrepreneurship research: an interdisciplinary survey and introduction*. Dordrecht: Kluwer.
>
> Aldrich, H.E. and Martinez, M.A. (2001) 'Many are called, but few are chosen: an evolutionary perspective for the study of entrepreneurship.' *Entrepreneurship Theory and Development*, 25, 4: 41–56.
>
> Audretsch, D.B., Grilo, I., and Thurik, A.R. (eds) (2007) *Handbook of research in entrepreneurship policy*. Cheltenham: Edward Elgar.
>
> Baumol, W. (1990) 'Entrepreneurship: productive, unproductive, and destructive.' *Journal of Political Economy*, 98: 893–921.
>
> Best, M. (2001) *The new competitive advantage*. Oxford: Oxford University Press.
>
> Blundel, R.K., Spence, L.J., and Zerbinati, S. (2010) 'Entrepreneurial social responsibility: scoping the territory', in L.J. Spence and M. Painter-Morland (eds) *Ethics in small and medium sized enterprises: a global commentary*. Dordrecht, NL: Springer.
>
> Bornstein, D. (2004) *How to change the world: social entrepreneurs and the power of new ideas*. Oxford: Oxford University Press.
>
> Bryman, A. and Bell, E. (2007) *Business research methods* (2nd edition). Oxford: Oxford University Press.
>
> Blumberg, B.F., Cooper, D.R., and Schindler, P.S. (2008) *Business research methods* (2ⁿᵈ European edition). London: McGraw-Hill.
>
> Bygrave, W.D. (1989) 'The entrepreneurship

How to use the Online Resource Centre

To support this text, there is a wide range of web-based content for lecturers and students.

www.oxfordtextbooks.co.uk/orc/blundel_lockett/

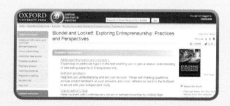

For students

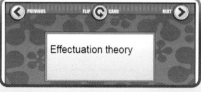

Safer syringes - trying to capitalize on a perceived opportunity

Spring 2002 appeared to mark a turning point for Medisys plc. founded by David Wong in England. The company's flagship product, a retractable syringe had been adopted for sale by Smiths Industries (an FTSE 100 conglomerate) and a well-established player in the medical devices field. Medisys had been formed a few years earlier and one of the key businesses in which it hoped to carve a niche were medical devices that were compliant with the latest healthcare worker safety regulation. This had become a potent issue, in 2001 newly passed legislation in the United States required hospitals to use safer syringes. But Medisys was not the only new competitor in this market. NMT (New Medical Technology), a Scottish company and RTI

Additional Case Studies. In addition to the many case studies included in the text, extra case studies with questions provide the opportunity to apply what you have learnt and analyze real-life examples.

CHAPTER 7

ORC 7.1: Gaining an understanding of business accounts

The prospect of gaining an understanding of business account can seem daunting, but there are a few things we can do to help ourselves:

- **Reading and studying**: you can gain most of the basics by reading introductory books on business accounting, or by attending college courses. Some of the more popular books include: Bookkeeping for Dummies (Barrow and Epstein 2007); Mastering Book-keeping: A Complete Guide to the Principles and Practice of Business Accounting (Marshall 2009); Frank Wood's Business Accounting: v.1 and v.2 (Wood and Sangster 2008); Management Accounting for Business (Drury

Additional Study Materials. You will find reference in the text to additional detail online of a particular topic. This coverage gives you a deeper understanding of interesting aspects of Entrepreneurship.

Blundel and Lockett: Exploring Entrepreneurship: Practices and Perspectives

Social enterprises

www.asho ka.org
Ashoka is a US-based organisation that supports social entrepreneurs around the world through a programme of Fellowships and other initiatives

www.kauffman.org
Kauffman is a major charitable foundation, based in the United States and active in many countries, which encourages research into, and support for entrepreneurship.

Useful Web Links and Exercises. Links to websites relevant to each chapter direct you towards valuable sources of information. You will also find links to the authors' personal blogs.

PREVIOUS   FLIP   CARD   NEXT

Effectuation theory

Flashcard Glossary. Glossary terms presented in an interactive flashcard format to help revise key terms and concepts.

Blundel and Lockett: Exploring Entrepreneurship: Practices and Perspectives

Chapter 01

After reading this chapter you should be able to:

- Appreciate the economic, social and environmental significance of enterprise and entrepreneurship in the twenty-first century.

- Identify different interpretations of the terms 'entrepreneur', 'entrepreneurship', and 'enterprise', including 'social' and 'commercial' forms, and adopt suitable working definitions.

Learning Objectives. Learning Objectives from the book help you evaluate your knowledge and understanding of each chapter.

New Venture Creation Checklists. Checklists which cover the main tasks of developing a new venture provide a useful reference.

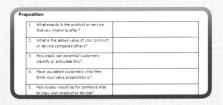

Pre-reading Guide. Suggestions for background reading covering the functional areas addressed in Part One, to help those new to the subject.

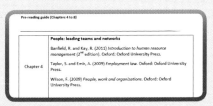

Revision Tips. Advice is provided on how to prepare for a new venture creation assignment and a reflective essay assignment.

Self-test Questions. Each chapter is accompanied by 10 self-test questions that you can complete online. These self-marking questions include instant feedback on your answers and cross-references back to the textbook to assist with your independent study.

For lecturers

PowerPoint® Slides. A suite of fully customizable PowerPoint® slides have been included for use in lecture presentations to save preparation time. Downloadable by chapter and picking out the key points from each topic, these also make a useful class handout.

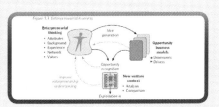

Teaching Notes for Critical Incident Cases. Notes are provided for each of the Critical Incident Cases in Part 1 to help incorporate these cases into your teaching.

Introduction
The many faces of entrepreneurship

The carrying out of new combinations we call 'enterprise'; the individuals whose function it is to carry them out we call 'entrepreneurs'.

Joseph A. Schumpeter, *twentieth century economist*

I'm encouraging young people to become social business entrepreneurs and contribute to the world, rather than just making money. Making money is no fun. Contributing to and changing the world is a lot more fun.

Muhammad Yunus, *academic and social entrepreneur*

Learning outcomes

After reading this chapter you should be able to:

➤ Appreciate the economic, social and environmental significance of **enterprise** and **entrepreneurship** in the twenty-first century.

➤ Identify different interpretations of the terms, '**entrepreneur**', 'entrepreneurship', and 'enterprise', including 'social' and 'commercial' forms, and adopt suitable working definitions.

➤ Recognize the wide variety of ways in which **entrepreneurial activity** is organized, the many different contexts in which it takes place, and the range of goals to which it is directed.

➤ Understand the distinctive approach to studying entrepreneurship that has been adopted in this textbook, the purpose of its two-part structure, and how to make use of various components, including case studies, in order to connect **entrepreneurial thinking**, practice, and reflection.

➤ Explore entrepreneurship in greater depth in the remaining chapters by engaging with entrepreneurial practice, with a particular focus on new venture creation (Part One), and by critically reviewing different research perspectives (Part Two).

Case 1.1 Helen Child: an entrepreneur looks back

Back in 2000, **Helen Child** co-founded a new financial transactions company. In this case, she reflects on the company's first decade, and how she contributed to its success. Helen used many of the skills she gained in her earlier career to grow the new venture. She helped to create a professional and highly motivated team, develop robust information systems, raise equity finance, and manage relationships with strategic partners and customers.

Biography

Helen grew up in the beautiful seaside town of Arnside, in the North of England. She moved there as a young girl when her father was headhunted to run the human resources (HR) department of a large insurance company. She did well at school and planned to go to Warwick University to study as a special needs teacher. However, she then changed her mind: 'I went skiing [and] taught disabled children to ski, for a charity called Back-up. [Then] I came back and needed a job. I was offered a position selling timeshare and realised that the psychology of sales fascinated me. It really intrigued me.' Helen went on to join Yellow Pages, which gave her sales management experience, dealing with large national accounts. Then she moved to Cable and Wireless to join their new Orange mobile phones operation. As she remembers, 'I was always working remotely. I basically lived out of a suitcase for many, many years.' Helen took a four month break from Orange to think about her next career move. She decided to join a large IT consultancy (a 'systems integrator'). It was during this period that she teamed up with work colleagues to develop a new venture, a financial transactions company.

Helen's new venture

In 2000, Helen's team secured funding for their venture: 'We were not a "dot.com", even through we used a lot of information technology, and at this time it was challenging to be raising funds for a new company. Fund raising was very difficult. We decided to go out and win a piece of business that would show all the investors that we had a sustainable business model – so we won a piece of business!' Their first contract was to provide a national building supplies company with credit cards, known as 'trade cards', for their customers. Helen notes that this company is 'still one of our clients – and that tells you a lot about our culture'. They also had to work hard to meet the many regulatory requirements imposed by the UK's Financial Services Authority (FSA): 'We went through a series of FSA hoops, we got through every one first time, to get our licence. Then we got *Mastercard* and *Visa* accreditation. Everybody was amazed that a company of our size could tick all the boxes so quickly.' This was an extremely challenging time for Helen. As she was building the venture, her mother was diagnosed with terminal cancer. Helen split time between her business and nursing her mother: 'I was very blessed with a circle of friends that helped me to keep everything going.' Her founding team consisted of three directors, with Helen taking on the role of managing director. The original idea for the venture came from one of her fellow directors: 'William is like a lot of entrepreneurs, he has hundreds of good ideas before breakfast. It is knowing which of them to harness – I think that is one of my strengths.' Helen explains, 'I also have a lot of ideas but they are always about finding a solution for a problem. For example we have developed an award-winning piece of software that our clients use for their application processing. My ideas are more around that, or new business markets, or new channels to market.'

Building a business in hard times

For Helen's company, the recession of 2008–10 was particularly tough: 'We are in financial services and our clients are retailers, the two worst hit sectors. We are in a "double whammy" [i.e. two problems] and the management team hasn't bolted. They put their shoulder to the wheel and they delivered. So I didn't come in on a Monday morning to a stack of resignations.' This experience reflects one of Helen's original drivers for setting up the company, which was, 'to be the best employer I could.' Helen has also become experienced in raising finance. 'We went out for funding two and half years ago, [then] we did a rights issue [i.e. selling new shares to raise money] last year that brought some more money in. But if you are going to grow a business there is always a working capital requirement. The more working capital we have, the faster we can grow.' Helen also emphasizes the importance of learning: 'I think if you learn from negative experiences – not of your own making – and if you constantly put those sorts of lessons in place rather than ploughing on regardless, you are a better manager for it.' Ethical practice is also important: 'I was brought up with a very strong set of values, that it is how you play the game, it is about being fair. I truly do believe in the strength of a team and collectively you can achieve great things as opposed to one woman trying to do it on her own. Another thing I have learnt is that men play the game very differently from women. Men are very good at big strategic thinking whereas women are probably better at the more tactical implementation. I actually think during these very difficult trading times it is probably the tactical stuff that gets you through!'

Points to consider

1. Can you make links between the events described by Helen Child and the topics addressed in Part One of this textbook (Chapters 2 to 8)?

2. In what ways do you think the success of Helen's new venture can be explained by: (a) individual-level factors (Chapter 12); (b) social factors (Chapters 11 and 13)?

3. What practical lessons about entrepreneurship would you take from Helen's experience?

Source: This case is primarily based on an interview with Helen Child and written by Nigel Lockett.

1.1 Introduction: entrepreneurship in the twenty-first century

1.1.1 The scale, diversity, and significance of entrepreneurial activity

Welcome to *Exploring Entrepreneurship*. The main aim of this chapter is to provide you with a general introduction to entrepreneurship, plus some essential tools and guidance for exploring the subject further in the remaining chapters. The opening case provides an initial insight into the life of one entrepreneur, Helen Child, who created a successful new venture in the early twenty-first century. Throughout the book, you will find many similar cases featuring real-world entrepreneurs, entrepreneurial organizations, entrepreneurship researchers, and policy-makers. *Exploring Entrepreneurship* is concerned with the real world of entrepreneurial practice. It reflects the belief that entrepreneurship is something that can be learnt, from direct personal experience and through the experiences of others. Entrepreneurship has many different faces. By this we mean firstly that it involves all sorts of people, operating in different contexts, engaging in a wide range of activities and creating a variety of organizational forms. In addition, we can use the term 'faces' to refer to the different perspectives on entrepreneurship we discuss in Part Two of the book. Though there is an enormous amount of variety in our subject, there are also some common patterns to discover, and many useful lessons to be drawn from the research evidence.

The rest of the chapter is organized as follows. In Section 1.2, we consider the scope of entrepreneurship as a field of study, and how to define some of its core terms (i.e. 'entrepreneur', 'entrepreneurial', 'entrepreneurship', and 'enterprise'). Section 1.3 takes a closer look at the rich variety of ways in which entrepreneurial activity takes place, and includes some discussion of the differences between commercial and social entrepreneurship. In Section 1.4, we introduce our distinctive approach to studying entrepreneurship, which builds on a combination of practical experience (both direct and indirect), critical reflection and drawing on a variety of perspectives. The discussion is illustrated by three case studies, which report on the experiences of entrepreneurs (Case 1.2), entrepreneurship researchers (Case 1.3), and entrepreneurship students (Case 1.4).

1.2 Scoping and defining entrepreneurship

1.2.1 The 'slippery concept'

So what is it that you are studying? It might be reasonable to expect a textbook to be mapping out the scope of the field at this point, and providing its readers with some clear, unambiguous definitions of the key terms. Unfortunately, things are not that simple. Many years ago, the economist Edith Penrose commented that, 'Enterprise, or "entrepreneurship" as it is sometimes called, is a *slippery concept*, not easy to work into formal economic analysis, because it is so closely associated with the temperament or personal qualities of individuals' (Penrose 1995 [1959]: 33; emphasis added). Today, entrepreneurship researchers, policy-makers, and practitioners are still struggling with this slippery concept, and there is a continuing lack of agreement over the meaning of these terms. So how should we approach the terminology? Clearly, it would be easier if we provided you with one universally accepted definition, but that would also be very misleading. The best approach is to recognize that people may use the same words, yet understand them differently. This is not a major problem because, as we shall discover, the range of interpretations is quite limited. However, it is important to be aware of these differences as you read about entrepreneurship, or listen to people talking about the subject. If you are not sure how they are using terms like 'entrepreneur', 'entrepreneurial', 'entrepreneurship', or 'enterprise', try to check their understanding. If you are still not sure about the definition that is being used, bear this in mind when you interpret their comments.

1.2.2 Key terms: entrepreneur, entrepreneurship, entrepreneurial, enterprise

In this section we review some of the key terminology and give our working definitions of four key terms: 'entrepreneur', 'entrepreneurial', 'entrepreneurship', and 'enterprise'. Each of these words derives from the same source. The French expression *'entreprendre'* is sometimes translated literally as, 'to take between'. In the eighteenth century, English translators began to use the word 'undertaker' to refer to the entrepreneur. In the event, it was the original French expression, rather than the translation, that became established. Though some people prefer alternative terms, such as 'innovator' and 'change agent', the language of entrepreneurship occupies a central place in twenty-first century politics, economics, and popular culture. However, despite the popularity of these terms, and a great deal of effort that has been invested in defining them, there is still no consensus on their precise meaning. Given that the title of this book is *Exploring Entrepreneurship,* we think this lack of precise definitions can be used to our advantage. As a starting point, we are going to introduce some working definitions. However, since these definitions remain open to debate, we encourage you to keep an open mind for the time being. We will be looking at various aspects of entrepreneurship throughout the book, so you can build up a clearer picture of each term as time goes on.

Policy-makers are one of the groups searching for a clear definition of our key terms. The Organization for Economic Cooperation and Development (OECD) and Eurostat commissioned researchers to produce a set of definitions, in order to collect better statistics on entrepreneurial activity in OECD member states and around the world. The research team reviewed the entrepreneurship literature and agreed on the following definitions (Figure 1.1):

Figure 1.1 OECD–Eurostat entrepreneurship definitions

- **Entrepreneurs** are those persons (business owners) who seek to generate value through the creation or expansion of economic activity, by identifying and exploiting new products, processes, or markets.
- **Entrepreneurial activity** is enterprising human action in pursuit of the generation of value through the creation or expansion of economic activity, by identifying and exploiting new products, processes, or markets.
- **Entrepreneurship** is the phenomenon associated with entrepreneurial activity.

Source: OECD–Eurostat (2009: 6).

These definitions are clear and concise. However, for the purposes of this book, we require some broader, and slightly more elaborate, definitions. For example, while we can agree that entrepreneurial activity is about 'enterprising human action in pursuit of value', our definition of entrepreneurs will extend beyond conventional commercial business owners to include the 'social value' generated by social entrepreneurs and social enterprises (NB social entrepreneurship was excluded from the OECD definition because the organization is mainly concerned with commercial enterprise). The following paragraphs review the four key terms, highlighting some of the main differences of interpretation you are likely to encounter:

- **Entrepreneurs** Everyone thinks they know who entrepreneurs are. We all carry around in our minds images of some larger-than-life figures, who have founded several companies and accumulated small (or in some cases, not-so-small) fortunes in the process. Yet the term 'entrepreneur' is used in a number of ways. For example, in North America, it is often applied to anyone who owns their own business. In this interpretation, the 25-year-old multimillionaire Internet tycoon and the 65-year-old, semi-retired owner of a small painting and decorating business can both claim the title, 'entrepreneur'. Another problem with the term is that some people who meet the criteria reject the 'label', while others argue that it only applies to a very small elite of highly successful serial (i.e. repeat) entrepreneurs. Despite these limitations, there is clearly a role for individual entrepreneurs, as people with an identifiable role in founding and developing organizations that generate economic value. For the time being, we can adopt a modified version of the OECD–Eurostat wording as a working definition of entrepreneurs. The modification incorporates the creation of social value that is associated with successful social enterprises:

  > **Entrepreneurs** *are those persons who seek to generate economic and social value through the creation or expansion of economic activity, by identifying and exploiting opportunities for new products, processes, markets, and for meeting outstanding social and environmental needs.*

- **Entrepreneurial activity** What do we mean by 'entrepreneurial' activity? Founding any new small firm or social enterprise can be seen as an entrepreneurial act, but once established the founders of these organizations do not engage in what we would consider to be 'entrepreneurial' activities. They continue to undertake a similar amount and type of work, and may even actively resist opportunities for further growth in the scale or scope of their operations. In addition, they may not actively seek out new contacts to add to the core management team or to the wider network of people and organizations that surrounds their organization. The OECD–Eurostat definition appears to recognize this distinction between entrepreneurship and the ongoing management of an existing small firm. We can therefore adopt the definition, again with a minor modification to incorporate the activity of social entrepreneurs:

  > **Entrepreneurial activity** *is enterprising human action in pursuit of the generation of economic and social value through the creation or expansion of economic activity, by identifying and exploiting new products, processes or markets, and by meeting outstanding social and environmental needs.*

- **Entrepreneurship** As the OECD–Eurostat definition suggests, this word is normally used to describe the activity undertaken by people that we have previously labelled as entrepreneurs. However, entrepreneurship is not simply about the actions of such individuals. Clearly, individual entrepreneurs play a central role in the process. However, as we will see in the Part Two chapters, the entrepreneurship process extends beyond the individual, to involve other levels of analysis. These include teams, organizations, social and inter-organizational networks, and institutions (e.g. rules and regulations, cultural norms). From this perspective, the OECD–Eurostat definition looks rather limited in scope, since it only appears to refer to the activity of entrepreneurs. Our modified definition indicates that entrepreneurship is what researchers have termed a 'multi-level' phenomenon:

  > **Entrepreneurship** *is the phenomenon associated with entrepreneurial activity. It involves a complex pattern of social interactions that extends beyond individual entrepreneurs to incorporate teams, organizations, networks, and institutions.*

- **Enterprise** This term is often found in discussions alongside entrepreneurs, entrepreneurial activity and entrepreneurship. Though this English word is clearly derived from the same French source ('*entreprendre*'), a great deal of time and effort has been spent in attempts to differentiate it from the others. Another complication arises because the meaning of the word 'enterprise' differs depending on whether it is being used as a noun or an adjective. As a noun (i.e. to name something) the word is used to refer to a particular business venture. For example, farmers talk about each of the commercial activities that they engage in, such as raising sheep, growing wheat, or running a farm shop, as a separate enterprise. The term 'SME' refers to **'small and medium-sized enterprises'**. Another use of the noun is in referring to an organization such as Café Direct as a social enterprise. When used as an adjective (i.e. to describe something), the word 'enterprise' has a much broader meaning. Perhaps the commonest use of the term in recent years has been with reference to the 'enterprise culture', which was promoted by countries such as the United States and the United Kingdom in the late twentieth century, and which has since extended its influence around the world (Lewis 2000; Della-Guista and King 2008). This is a topic that we will return to in later chapters. Confusingly, there is also a widespread idea that individuals may be 'enterprising', in the sense of being adventurous, dynamic, taking the initiative, and making their mark on the world, without necessarily being involved in any entrepreneurial activity as previously defined. Examples might include a polar explorer, a performance artist, or a human rights campaigner. To avoid confusion, we are going to restrict our use of the expression 'enterprise' to the following three working definitions:

  > **An enterprise** *is an alternative term for a commercial organization or firm, as in the expression SME (i.e. small and medium-sized enterprise).*

  > **A social enterprise** *is a trading organization that serves a social purpose, and which can take a variety of legal forms, including co-operative, a limited company, and a community interest company.*

  > **The enterprise culture** *is a political project designed to encourage an increase in entrepreneurial activity and a corresponding decrease in the role of the state in regulating and intervening in the economy.*

1.2.3 **The range and scope of entrepreneurial activity**

Throughout this textbook, you will encounter different varieties of entrepreneurship. It is important to recognize that there is more than one way of acting entrepreneurially. As a consequence, the world of entrepreneurship is not exclusive: it is open to a very wide range of people. There are three main sources of variety: the way entrepreneurial activity is organized, the context in which it takes place, and the goals that it pursues:

- **Organization** Entrepreneurial activity can be organized in a variety of ways. The commonest image is probably that of a limited company, with shareholders investing in the business, and the entrepreneurs agonizing about how big a share of their company to 'give away' to the investors. However, many small start-up ventures are unincorporated; in other words, they do not have a separate legal identity. Though they may subsequently be converted into a company, a large proportion of the small firm population will remain unincorporated for the whole of its existence, along with most of the self-employed. A great deal of entrepreneurial activity takes place in existing organizations in the commercial, public, and voluntary sectors. This activity, often termed **intrapreneurship** or corporate entrepreneurship mostly takes the form of a semi-autonomous group (e.g. an internal venture team), operating within the overarching structure of the parent organization. Social enterprises can also be set up in different ways, ranging from small unincorporated organizations operating locally, to more formal legal structures, such as a 'Community Interest Company' (CIC), a company limited by guarantee, or a more conventional limited company.

- **Context** Entrepreneurial activity can take place in many different settings. For example, it might take the form of artisan (i.e. craft) production in a remote rural community in Pakistan's Khyber Pakhtunkhwa region (Case 11.1); applied health research in a regional **cluster** (Case 8.4); or a charity addressing inner city social housing and behaviour needs (Case 7.4). There are also many examples of community-based entrepreneurship, in which the role of the 'heroic' individual entrepreneur is less important than the energy and inspiration that comes from communal action (e.g. Tracey et al. 2005) In each example, it is possible to find some common entrepreneurial features. However, the context is also likely to exert a powerful influence on the kind of activity that occurs, and the potential for growing it into a successful venture.

- **Goals** Entrepreneurial activity can be inspired by the pursuit of some radically different goals. For example, a team of university scientists may be motivated by the opportunity to launch an innovative pharmaceutical product. If the product is successful, it may save or improve the quality of many lives. In addition, the commercialization of their intellectual property may also provide the scientists with considerable personal wealth. In contrast, a group of social entrepreneurs may be motivated by the prospect of using an innovative technology to help empower young disabled people; having decided to adopt a not-for-profit legal form, the founders will have no prospect of creating personal fortunes from their idea, even if it subsequently grows into a large and very successful organization. At the other extreme, there are countless examples of entrepreneurial activity in the world of organized crime, whether it be protection rackets, drugs smuggling operations, Internet pornography, or prostitution. Here, the primary motivation is likely to be financial gain, with some secondary goals such as maintaining influence among powerful local figures (e.g. politicians, police forces) and possibly some attempt at securing community support.

Having discussed some of the key terms and mapped out the scope of the field, it is time to consider how to learn more about entrepreneurship. In the next section, we introduce the distinctive approach adopted in this book.

1.3 Exploring entrepreneurship: our approach

1.3.1 Introducing the two part approach

In Part One of this text, we are focusing on the process of developing a new venture, from the initial generation of an idea/opportunity to the stage when it is converted into a fully worked out venture proposal that can be presented to potential investors, financiers, or sponsors. In Part Two, we look at some of the broader questions about what entrepreneurship is, how it works, and what it can achieve. So why are we taking this approach? We begin by considering the new venture creation activity, which forms the basis for Part One. All new ventures have to go through a process in which a 'raw' idea is refined into a coherent proposal. There is a lot of work to be done, and a lot to learn, in order to maximize the chances that a venture:

- Responds to an attractive market opportunity or real social/environmental need;
- Has the potential to add greater economic and/or social value compared to existing offerings and rival proposals;
- Can be achieved operationally in a cost-effective way;
- Is based around a realistic business model that is capable of attracting the financing required to achieve its growth targets;
- Is being delivered by a capable and credible **entrepreneurial team**, with access to any necessary external expertise.

Creating a new entrepreneurial venture, even for the purposes of an exercise, is a very demanding task. One of the main challenges is to handle, and to integrate effectively, information and resources from several different fields (e.g. marketing, operations, human resources, accounting, and finance). You may have some experience of integrating in other courses (e.g. when analysing a strategic management case study). However, a new venture creation exercise presents you with a much more open-ended challenge. In most cases, you begin with a blank sheet of paper. Your task is to identify a need/opportunity in the outside world and to assemble a working solution in the form of a comprehensive venture proposal that can be defended in front of an audience of potential investors. Your venture proposal will typically be developed by a team of students, and written up as a business plan, possibly combined with a face-to-face presentation or a poster session. You can also complete the exercise working on your own. This will involve more work, but at least there is less scope for argument.

1.3.2 **Part One: can you 'learn' to be entrepreneurial?**

Part One of this book is focused on the practice of entrepreneurship. The focus on practice reflects our belief that entrepreneurship is something you can learn about, through direct personal experience and from the experiences of others. Some people argue, often in very forceful terms, that entrepreneurs are 'born' not 'made'. As entrepreneurship educators, you would not be surprised to hear that we take a different view – to quote the words of a popular management writer:

> *Most of what you hear about entrepreneurship is all wrong. It's not magic; it's not mysterious; and it has nothing to do with genes. It's a discipline and, like any discipline, it can be learned.* (Drucker 1982: 143)

Peter Drucker is correct in arguing against a simple genetic link to entrepreneurial success. However, your prospects of embarking on an entrepreneurial career will be affected to some extent by the place and time you are born, as well as by the people who surround you in your early years. It is also true that you will never become a successful entrepreneur simply by reading a book, or taking part in a new venture creation exercise. There is an ongoing debate about learning and teaching 'for' entrepreneurship (i.e. developing entrepreneurial skills and attitudes) and 'about' entrepreneurship (i.e. understanding of entrepreneurship as a social phenomenon) (e.g. Levie 1999; Kirby 2004). Though this is a useful distinction, our experience is that **entrepreneurial learning** can be deeper and more creative if the two aspects are integrated to some degree. By 2010, more than two-thirds of colleges and universities in the United States were teaching entrepreneurship across all faculties (Whitford 2010). It is widely accepted that a combination of practical exercises, study, and critical reflection can be a good way to open up your thinking about entrepreneurship. And where might those thoughts lead you in a few years' time? Over the years, we have heard from many former students who have gone on to set up their own commercial and social enterprises, and from others who are either working in 'entrepreneurial' roles within existing organizations, or are engaging with entrepreneurs as suppliers, customers, policy-makers, financiers, or consultants. In the closing case, we catch up with four recent graduates in order to find out about their experiences (Case 1.4).

1.3.3 **Part One: chapter structure and contents**

The Part One chapters draw on examples of successful ventures, and feature the voices of real entrepreneurs, talking about their experiences. Chapters 2 to 8 have a standard format. Each chapter begins with a short opening case, which sets the scene for the chapter, followed by two further mini cases, which explore the main chapter themes in more depth. Explanatory text and useful frameworks help draw the key learning points from each case and set these in the context of the chapter. At the end of each chapter, there is a critical incident case, which draws on original interviews with entrepreneurs. In the book, we 'freeze' the action at a critical moment, allowing you to consider the choices open to the entrepreneurs at an important stage of their enterprise's development. In order to find out 'what happened next', you can refer to the companion website. Each Part One chapter builds on the previous one to take you, as a prospective entrepreneur, from an initial vision to a concrete venture. In Chapter 2, we start with an overview of the challenge of turning an entrepreneurial vision into a coherent new venture plan and how it can be expressed as an opportunity business model. Subsequent chapters explore various aspects of that challenge: Chapter 3 – identifying and shaping entrepreneurial opportunities; Chapter 4 – providing leadership; creating teams and networks; Chapter 5 – analysing markets and industries; Chapter 6 – designing and managing operations; Chapter 7 – financial forecasting and planning; Chapter 8 – raising finance. In other words, everything you are likely to need in order to begin the process of exploiting an entrepreneurial opportunity. Opportunity business models will provide you with a structured way of doing this. Put simply, opportunity business models are about the proposition, people, place, process and profit of the new venture or the system of what the venture is about, where it will operate, who will make it happen, how they will do it and all importantly why. That means not just the financial return but the alignment of the venture to wider values as expressed by the entrepreneur, their enterprise and the society at large (Figure 1.2).

Figure 1.2 Chapters 2 to 8: structure and dimensions

Chapter	Title	Opportunity business model dimension	System dimension
3	Opportunities: nurturing creativity and innovation	Proposition	What
4	People: leading teams and networks	People	Who
5	Markets: understanding customers and competitors	Place	Where
6	Processes: controlling operations and technologies	Process	How
7	Accounts: interpreting financial performance	Profit	Why
8	Finances: raising capital for new ventures		

The final Part One chapter (Chapter 9) adopts a different approach. It traces the entrepreneurial journeys of several very successful entrepreneurs. What begins to emerge from these stories is a strong sense of what might be termed 'entrepreneurial thinking', and how it relates to the entrepreneur's background, personal attributes, experiences, networks, and personal values. The reference to 'values' might sound surprising, but throughout Part One we will see how values are at the centre of entrepreneurial activity in the twenty-first century. Of course, financial returns are still important for any entrepreneurial venture, but increasingly we find that enterprises with social purpose or dimension, which is often being driven by the values of individual entrepreneurs.

In summary, Part One provides you with an opportunity to improve your own entrepreneurial thinking by taking you through the stages of idea generation, expressing these as 'opportunity business models,' recognizing which opportunities can be exploited in enterprises and analysing the market context for the new venture. It is imperative to recognize that this is not a one-off process but a continuous cycle of entrepreneurial learning about yourself and your new enterprise (Figure 1.3).

However, the structure of Part One is not meant to imply that entrepreneurship practice can be reduced to a straightforward linear process. It is not simply a series of predictable steps that can be reproduced in any situation – like replicating a formula. In fact, entrepreneurial thinking is essentially a learning cycle (Mumford 1997; Cope and Watts 2000; Corbett 2005). Furthermore, it is a learning cycle that accelerates rapidly as soon as you begin to engage in any kind of entrepreneurial activity. This might also go some way to explaining why successful entrepreneurs can become serial entrepreneurs (e.g. Cases 3.4, 5.4, 9.1, and 9.3).

Books need to be structured in some kind of logical sequence. However, real life – including the practice of entrepreneurship – is not so straightforward. So though it may be necessary to structure our exploration of entrepreneurship in a linear way, the reality (or 'lived experience') of the entrepreneur is rather different:

- **The reader's image** In order for us to explore the subject in a clear and coherent way, that fits academic timetables and also works in book form, we had to set up some logical structures and building blocks (e.g. the chapters covering discrete subjects and the models with their distinct dimensions and drivers).

Figure 1.3 Entrepreneurial learning

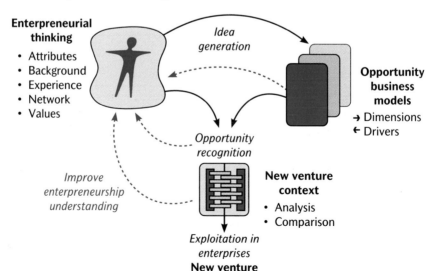

Figure 1.4 An atomic metaphor for entrepreneurship

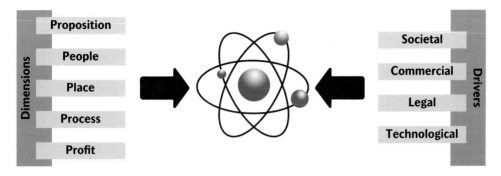

- **The practitioner's image** The practical reality for the 'real-world' entrepreneur is quite unlike the solid and regular building blocks of a textbook. As the cases have indicated, the experience is often much more challenging, and rather like riding a bicycle while simultaneously juggling several plates of jelly.

Entrepreneurial practice involves all of the activities we will discuss in the Part One chapters. Each of these activities influences the others (e.g. marketing decisions affect financing, and vice versa), and they continue to circle around an opportunity that is itself in motion, continuing to evolve as you move towards the creation of your venture. In other words, entrepreneurship is not so much a simple linear process as a series of dynamic, interrelated activities, closer to the traditional image of electrons (dimensions) orbiting a nucleus (vision) that are constantly being buffeted by external forces (drivers) (Figure 1.4).

Our atomic metaphor may still sound rather abstract and remote from reality. In Case 1.2, we return to the 'real world' of entrepreneurial practice to hear from several entrepreneurs about their own experience of entrepreneurship.

Case 1.2 The entrepreneur's story

We spoke to varied group of entrepreneurs to find out about their ventures and how they dealt with a particularly difficult challenge. For this introductory case, we also asked whether they had some advice for anyone following in their footsteps as an entrepreneur. The key themes that emerged included: (a) values and principles; (b) commitment and conviction; (c) partnerships with people; (d) having fun! You can find more about these entrepreneurs in the Part One chapters and the Online Resource Centre:

Helen Child co-founded a new financial transactions company. In Chapter 1, she reflects on the company's first decade of success. Helen used many of the skills she gained in her earlier career to grow the new venture. How have these contributed to its success?

Have a huge amount of energy and a huge amount of drive. You will need to work long hours to make sure that that you deliver at every single level.

Mark Robinson was an experienced manager who became convinced there was an opportunity for a strategy mapping application. In his Chapter 2 he prepares a new venture plan for presentation at a board meeting. How will they respond?

> *How committed are you about it? If you really want to do it and you are passionate about it you will definitely make it but don't be half hearted about it.*

Lucy Nicholson built a successful delicatessen and wanted to expand her business operations. In Chapter 3 she dreams of opening a café or restaurant, providing outside catering services or running a cookery school. When the shop next door becomes vacant what should she do?

> *Can you really commit yourself 110%? Because if you can't it is not the business for you. Keep changing, keep it fresh, and keep it vibrant. Recognizing empowering other people is a fantastic, fantastic feeling.*

Victoria Tomlinson reached a crossroads in her public relations company's development. In Chapter 4 she faces the loss of her biggest customer. Was this an opportunity to downsize, change the way the company worked, or simply sell it?

> *A huge amount of business is about values. We set-up with a number of really core values. Honesty is probably the most fundamental.*

Tim Lockett was the managing director of his own healthcare distribution business. His business strategy was simple: use new technology to provide the most efficient and cost effective service possible. In Chapter 5 he hears rumours that his previous company had lost a big contract and was in difficulties. Should he try to buy it or simply walk away?

> *Everybody says it, but people are the key to your business. If you find the right support staff . . . the right partners, in every sense of the word, who will work with you. People are absolutely fundamental.*

Adnan Awan had grown his office supplies company in just over two years. In Chapter 6 we find out how his small team established strategic relationships with manufacturers, wholesalers, and national carriers. His simple information systems proved to be a barrier to growth and with a large contract available what should he do?

> *Little things make all the difference from any business point of view. Perception is everything.*

Steve Woodford founded and led a 25-year-old charity that provided support to homeless people. In Chapter 7 we find out why he needed to better understand the real impact his organization was having on 'social exclusion' and why they needed to demonstrate value for money. But how could they measure these factors?

> *It is the concept of partnership. There is a different set of values that drives you. Come to work because you feel that you are making a difference, a positive contribution and sometimes . . . it is a bit of fun.*

Neil Meredith had successfully taken his innovative new dental implants venture through nearly 10 years of continuous growth. In Chapter 8 we hear why the investors were keen to strengthen and restructure the board. Was he the right person to lead the company?

> *I respect everybody who works for us and every job that they do. I think that is very important. Having fun and meeting interesting people.*

Jonathan Hick With such a long history of entrepreneurs in his family perhaps it shouldn't be surprising that Jonathan should become a successful serial entrepreneur. In Chapter 9, he reflects on whether his family background was a help or hindrance.

> *Never ever, ever, give up on it. Bring in one or two people who have seen it done it before, either in that sector or a business generally. Listen to their advice and let them help you. You can't do it all on your own.*

Steve Pankhurst simply had a good idea, which after many trials and tribulations, emerged as one of the first commercially successful online social networking communities. In Chapter 9, we see that after just five years it was sold for £120 million. But what motivates him now?

> *I always like to have fun. Don't let it get you down too much. Don't get 'corporate' or the money will take over. Stick to your principles and have fun that is the important thing.*

Deirdre Bounds launched what was to become a highly successful ethical travel company, which she sold just 10 years later for £14 million. In Chapter 9, we find out how the sale of the company fuelled other social, ethical, and charitable activities. What opportunities should she exploit next?

> *Success in any enterprise . . . is down to the would-be entrepreneur. Whatever it is you are going to sell . . . first of all make it unique. Have a really deep and safe conviction in yourself that this will work and you will make it work.*

An explanatory note on the featured cases

Many of the case studies presented in this book, including all those introduced in Case 1.2, are based on personal interviews with the entrepreneurs concerned. In some instances, we have also spoken to other people connected with the organizations and drawn on secondary data sources. Where possible, we have provided links to the organizations' websites and to other useful sources. You are encouraged to visit the websites of the featured organizations, and to search for related media coverage. However, please do NOT attempt to contact any of the featured individuals or organizations directly. Smaller ventures in particular are not in a position to deal with large numbers of student enquiries. If you are researching organizations as part of an assessed assignment, please discuss this issue with your tutor. The Critical Incident cases were written by Nigel Lockett. Other cases were written by Nigel Lockett or Richard Blundel, as indicated. These cases are not intended to illustrate either effective or ineffective handling of management situations. The authors may have disguised certain names, locations, dates, and other identifying information to protect confidentiality.

1.4 Researching entrepreneurship

1.4.1 Part Two: critical reflection and new perspectives

The Part Two chapters and guided further reading are designed to help you to extend your understanding of entrepreneurship as a phenomenon. The idea is to integrate your own direct experience, the indirect experiences of 'real-world' entrepreneurs, and the extensive body of academic research into entrepreneurship. Entrepreneurs often know a great deal about the specifics of their own venture and probably about their own industry. However, there is also something to gain by broadening your perspective. The case for learning 'about' entrepreneurship can be illustrated by a short anecdote. A few years ago, the admissions tutor at a leading business school was surprised to receive an application for their MBA course from a self-made millionaire. At the interview, she could not resist the temptation to pursue the issue further. With a polite smile she said, 'Though of course we're delighted that you will be joining us, to be quite honest, we're not quite sure why you feel the need to study for a management qualification, given your past success.' The millionaire shrugged and replied, 'Well, that's just it. Of course I know *that* I have been very successful, and I have some ideas about *how* I was successful. Now I'd just like to understand a bit more about more about the reasons *why*.' The Part Two chapters explore entrepreneurship from a number of different perspectives. Chapter 10 provides a more detailed introduction to the approach adopted.

1.4.2 The research challenge: handling different kinds of knowledge

People use many different kinds of knowledge to help them engage in, and to better understand, entrepreneurship. As a student, you are likely to be drawing on a wide selection of sources during your studies in search of ideas, evidence, and inspiration. These might include some or all of the following:

- **Business plan guides** and related practical advice (e.g. law, taxation, employing staff), usually found in popular 'start your own business' books and in brochures or downloads from banks and business support agencies. See the further reading guide for examples.

- **News stories,** analysis, and comment about aspects of entrepreneurship found in newspapers and broadcast media, often available via websites. Also coverage in specialist media related to your venture (e.g. *Hotel and Catering Weekly* if you are interested in establishing a restaurant or *Farmers Weekly* if you are considering an agricultural enterprise).

- **Research reports and briefings** produced by government agencies and non-governmental organizations (NGOs) involved in supporting entrepreneurs, often also available via websites. Also industry and market research reports related to your proposed venture.

- **Articles in peer-reviewed academic journals** such as *Entrepreneurship Theory and Practice, Entrepreneurship and Regional Development*, and the *International Small Business Journal*, which are usually available in electronic form.

- **Academic books and book chapters** also contain research findings.

- **Academic textbooks** (and this one in particular!). Also lecture notes, slides, and other supporting materials, which may be available in hard copy or in electronic formats.

- **Documentaries** that feature entrepreneurial activity, which may take the form of films, television programmes, and web-based video clips.

- **Autobiographies or biographies** of entrepreneurs and historical studies of companies and industries, still mostly available in book form (NB short biographies of entrepreneurial founders and short organizational histories can often be found on websites under headings such as, 'About Us').

- **Fictionalized accounts** of entrepreneurial activity in novels, films, plays, and television programmes.

- **Advice and personal anecdotes** from people who are directly involved in entrepreneurial activity, such as guest lecturers, relatives, and friends.

- **Your own personal experience** of entrepreneurial activity, perhaps gained during a youth enterprise competition, from setting up your own entrepreneurial venture, or from observing one as an employee or customer.

The kind of knowledge you will find in these sources ranges from the abstract, wide-ranging and often inconclusive findings produced by academic researchers to the concrete, context-specific, and often very strongly worded advice given by experienced entrepreneurs. Each of these sources can help you to a better understanding of entrepreneurship. Some types of knowledge are going to be more useful than others, depending on your immediate aims. However, in the world of entrepreneurship, it is usually a mistake to ignore either the more 'practical' or the more 'academic' sources entirely. For example, while working on a new venture creation activity (either 'for real' or as part of a business simulation or competition), it certainly makes sense to concentrate on the more 'practical' types of knowledge, such as those found in Part One of this textbook. These activities are usually fairly intense and pressured, so you may think that it is a waste of time to read anything other than a few 'how-to' guides to financial forecasts or marketing plan. Think again! Some of the best new venture ideas we have come across were, at least in part, the product of students pushing themselves beyond the 'safe' territory of the business plan guide. Here is an example of what we mean:

- Members of the student venture team *Smoky Phoenix* gather in the local coffee shop. It is already week five of the project and everyone is feeling depressed. The team has come up with a few venture ideas, but everyone realizes that they are uninspiring – neither innovative nor with much in the way of growth potential. 'Yeah, but who cares?' says Jonas, 'all we need is a "pass"!' At that moment, Sarah, the last team member rushes in and throws a book on the table. It is the biography of a Japanese technological entrepreneur. 'I've got it!' she shouts. 'Got what?' says Jonas, as Sarah collapses on the sofa. 'Look at this . . .', she flicks to the photos in the middle of the book, '. . . these people created the world's first mobile capsule hotel.' Jonas frowns and sipps his double espresso, 'Nah, I don't get it' he adds. Sarah patiently explains her idea: taking the Japanese example as inspiration, the team could create a truly innovative product for the European market, targeting music festivals and other outdoor events. The rest of the team looks convinced, but Jonas is still mumbling to himself: 'I still think we should go with the T-shirts.'

Similarly, when writing a more academically oriented piece of work, such as a dissertation researching an aspect of entrepreneurship or an essay reflecting on your experience while participating in a new venture creation activity, you are likely to focus on academic journal articles, academic books, government reports, and the kind of material that is covered in Part Two of this textbook. These are the best places to locate the concepts, models, and theoretical frameworks that are essential if you are going to structure and make some sense of the empirical evidence (e.g. research findings you have collected for your dissertation or notes from your personal diary that form the raw material of your reflective essay). In these situations, focusing on high quality academic sources is basically a sensible choice. However, it would be unfortunate if, in an effort to appear suitably 'serious', you were to ignore the less formal sources entirely. The key here is to select and apply the different sources in ways that fit with your basic purpose. Consider the following example:

- Katerina is drafting her dissertation in the area of gender and entrepreneurship. She has downloaded more than 60 journal articles, and has a large pile of research monographs on her desk. She has written these up as a rather generic (i.e. unfocused) draft literature review on the subject of public perceptions of female entrepreneurs, but is not sure what to do next. She goes to see Emma, her supervisor: 'OK' says Emma, 'I can see you have done a lot of work here, but how are you going to make it distinctive? Have you identified any useful personal contacts?' Katerina thinks for a moment. 'I haven't been able to secure interviews with anyone, so I don't know what to do.' 'Have you found any other sources of evidence?' asks Emma. 'Well, I did find this discussion thread on a women's enterprise support website . . . but I didn't think it could be used – I mean, it's just a lot of women entrepreneurs stating their opinions.' Katerina shows her supervisor the discussion thread. Emma sits back in her chair and smiles, 'Yes, exactly, and if you treat it in the right way – I mean as raw data that you can analyse – those opinions could be very useful indeed.'

We return to the theme of knowledge in Chapter 10, with a more detailed review of the academic literature and how it can best be used (Section 10.3). By way of an introduction, Case 1.3 offers an insight into entrepreneurship from the researcher's perspective.

Case 1.3 The researcher's tale

We spoke to five leading entrepreneurship researchers to find out about one of their recent research projects. We asked about the reasons why they had selected particular questions, how they had conducted the research, what they saw as the key findings, and what they thought about the current state of their academic field. For this short introductory case, we also asked them whether they had any advice for anyone setting out to study the subject. You will find longer profiles of the featured researchers in the Part Two chapters:

Boris Blumberg is an associate professor based at the University of Mäastricht, in the Netherlands. Boris has used economic research methods to examine entrepreneurship and other areas of organization, including the role of networks. He is also the co-author of a popular textbook on business research methods. In Chapter 11 he talks about his research on credit rationing by finance providers and how this impacts on start-up ventures.

Jason Cope is a senior lecturer at the Hunter Centre for Entrepreneurship, University of Strathclyde, Glasgow, Scotland. Jason's research interests include: how entrepreneurs learn and develop in conjunction with their ventures, the role of critical events and traumatic episodes in stimulating entrepreneurial learning, the socially situated nature of entrepreneurial practice. In Chapter 12, he talks about how entrepreneurs are able to learn from their failures, and what this means for the development of new ventures.

Helle Neergaard is an associate professor at Aarhus School of Business, Aarhus University, Denmark. Helle's research interests include growth, human and social capital, self-efficacy, effectuation, identity and gender, female business owners, leaders and entrepreneurs. In Chapter 13 she discusses her research on women's distinctive approaches to entrepreneurship.

Mary Rose is Professor of Entrepreneurship at the Institute for Entrepreneurship and Enterprise Development, Lancaster University, England. Mary's research interests include innovation and entrepreneurship, path dependency and innovation, leadership succession in business, family firms and business culture. In Chapter 14 she talks about her research on technological innovation and mountaineering, including the key role played by entrepreneurs in the outdoor clothing and equipment trade.

Friederike Welter is a professor based at the Jönköping International Business School, Sweden. Friederike's research interests include: entrepreneurship and small business development and entrepreneurial behaviour in different regional contexts, women's entrepreneurship and enterprise support policies. In Chapter 15 she talks about the role played by entrepreneurship policies in transforming the so-called 'transition' countries of central and eastern Europe.

Our question to the researchers was, 'what advice would you give to someone who wants to explore entrepreneurship in greater depth?' As there was considerable agreement regarding the best advice, we have summarized their responses. Firstly, the researchers emphasized that entrepreneurship is a vast subject, so it is a good idea to begin by getting a broad overview of the main research themes and approaches. Follow up with a more focused review any areas that are of particular interest. You can do this by searching journals and specialist research books. Electronic journals are particularly useful, as they can usually be accessed quite easily, and have the facility to search on keywords. Look out for prominent authors – you will start to see the same names appearing – and take a look at their web pages. These are often a useful source of more recent material, including some conference papers that might be downloadable. Lastly, try to combine your academic study with some direct engagement with 'real-world' entrepreneurs. Look out for any opportunities to meet entrepreneurs at events (e.g. visiting speakers, conferences, exhibitions, and trade fairs), and see if you can make any entrepreneurial connections through your family, friends, and acquaintances.

✱ 1.5 Summary

➤ Entrepreneurial activity is a complex and powerful phenomenon. It has positive and negative impacts on economies, societies, and the natural environment. For these reasons, it is well worth exploring entrepreneurship in greater depth, whether you are an existing or prospective entrepreneur, someone who engages with entrepreneurs, or simply someone who is interested in how the world works.

➤ Entrepreneurship is a slippery concept. The four core terms, 'entrepreneur', 'entrepreneurial', 'entrepreneurship', and 'enterprise' are each open to different interpretations. In order to avoid confusion it is important to: (a) recognize the different meanings that other people attribute to these terms; (b) make your own definitions and assumptions clear.

➤ Entrepreneurial activity can be organized in a variety of ways (e.g. an unincorporated start-up venture, an independent social enterprise, a quoted company). It can also take place in diverse contexts (e.g. a remote rural community, a university science park, a suburban garden shed), and be used in pursuit of radically different goals (e.g. launching a innovative pharmaceutical product, empowering young disabled people, creating a personal fortune for the entrepreneurial founder).

➤ This textbook adopts a distinctive approach to studying entrepreneurship. It encourages readers to develop their own capacity for entrepreneurial learning and critical reflection. The two part structure, and features such as the new venture creation activity, critical incident cases, and further reading guides, provide opportunities for you to integrate learning: (a) from your own experience; (b) from real-world entrepreneurs; and (c) from leading entrepreneurship researchers.

Case 1.4 Student entrepreneurs: where are they now?

When you spend your days developing and delivering entrepreneurship courses, it is always interesting to discover what your students made of the subject. From time to time, we hear from former students who have gone on to set-up their own commercial or social enterprise, and others who have acted as 'intrapreneurs' in larger organizations. In some cases the new venture is based directly on a concept that the student had first developed in class, as part of a new venture creation exercise. However, in most cases, the student project is simply a 'practice-run' for an entirely different venture. To prepare this case, we got in touch with four fairly recent graduates. We asked them to talk about (i) what first got them interested in entrepreneurship; (ii) what ideas they considered at university; and (iii) what suggestions they would give students. Edwin, Rajeeb, Lucian, and Hermione all had different experiences but share the ability to spot and exploit an opportunity, show commitment and determination, have their own values, and also seem to be having fun! They seemed to get a taste for it or, as Lucian described it, 'Entrepreneurship is like the God's Ambrosia – it is the milk that tastes so good nothing quite compares. Once you try it there is no going back – life outside of entrepreneurship just doesn't seem quite so much fun.' Perhaps not surprisingly the share many of these characteristics with the successful entrepreneurs interviewed for Case 1.2.

Edwin Broni-Mensah (www.givemetap.co.uk)

What first got you interested in entrepreneurship?

While at university I was set on entering investment banking, until I was approached by a friend, Alex Ofosu-Adjei, to join be a director in his start-up Origin Signed (www.originsigned.co.uk). This taste of entrepreneurship was enough for me to know that entrepreneurship was fascinating, challenging, and above all so much fun!

What ideas did you consider at university?

The mathematician in me was always coming up with new solutions to problems. My first business idea was to help student entrepreneurs connect better with angel investors using computerized algorithms via the website FreeMyIdea.com. In October 2009 I envisioned an innovative way for people to consume water on the go and have been developing this social enterprise ever since. The enterprise is called GiveMeTap (www.givemetap.co.uk) and enables users of a specially branded (recycled) aluminium bottles to obtain free refills of tap water from a network of cafes and restaurants across major cities – 70% of our profits fund independent water projects.

What suggestions would you give students at university?

University is a wonderful place where so many opportunities are available to students, though they are often not in your face. I would suggest that students hunt for all the schemes, competitions, and networks throughout their universities and most importantly join their respective enterprise society or create one if it does not exist yet. Once you have found these opportunities make sure you 'apply, apply, apply', as most students will not so your chances of success are dramatically increased!

Rajeeb Dey (Enternships.com)

What first got you interested in entrepreneurship?

I stumbled into entrepreneurship by accident. It stemmed from when I was 17 years old and decided to start an organization that would work to give school students a voice in their education. I launched the English Secondary Students' Association (ESSA) and set up www.studentvoice.co.uk. Having established ESSA I realised how fun and fulfilling it is to see an idea to come into fruition and now ESSA employs five people and numerous freelance staff and volunteers and works with thousands of students across England.

What ideas did you consider at university?

I joined the entrepreneurs' society, Oxford Entrepreneurs, in my first year at university and was constantly exposed to fellow entrepreneurial students and high profile entrepreneurs who I invited to come and speak at the society such as Lord Sugar, Sir Stelios, the late Dame Anita Roddick. I was very much thinking about enterprise and being inspired by entrepreneurial people at all times.

What suggestions would you give students at university?

Join your enterprise society, get involved with the committee and start creating your network of contacts early on. Do not underestimate the power of networking or reaching out to well-known people; even though you may be a student you'd be surprised by how receptive so-called 'celebrity' entrepreneurs/business figures can be towards approaches for advice by aspiring entrepreneurs.

Lucian Tarnowski (www.bravenewtalent.com)

What first got you interested in entrepreneurship?

I started my first business selling apples grown in my garden to my neighbours at the age of five. I have known since I can remember that I wanted to run my own business. To me, work is a hobby – it's a lifestyle. While at the University of Edinburgh I decided that I would begin testing the waters of entrepreneurship. I wanted to create something that people wanted, something that was game changing, something that benefited the lives of those that used it.

What ideas did you consider at university?

BraveNewTalent was not, however, my first attempt to start a business. I started by spreading myself very thinly, trying to start numerous different businesses. Later I learnt the importance of focus. While at university I had a difference business idea for every day of the week. Life is so full of opportunities and I wanted to execute on them all! A year after university I dropped all the other business concepts and focused in on BraveNewTalent – it had the most amount of potential. It is such a simple concept but it is surprising that there was nothing that built connections directly between employers and jobseekers.

What suggestions would you give students at university?

University is a great time and place to explore opportunities. Students don't have the same pressures to drive immediate revenue. This is also a unique time for Generation Y – for the first time in history the youngest people entering the workforce are an authority on something that really matters – technology, social media, and the web. We are innovating everything and are therefore in a good position to be starting businesses around the phenomenal change that technology is having in every sector and industry.

Hermione Way (www.newspepper.com)

What first got you interested in entrepreneurship?

My older brother had his own business from a young age, so I am very lucky to have been exposed to the entrepreneurial mind set at a young age, too. I have always been able to grasp concepts quickly and been able to see where innovation can simplify a process or spot where to do something in a different way. Most of my business ideas come from me wanting to solve problems that I encounter in my daily life and thinking 'Why aren't they doing it like that?'

What ideas did you consider at university?

I started my first venture Newspepper.com during my second year of university. The idea was born out of anger and frustration over what my university were teaching me at a time when I was witnessing my industry rapidly changing. I was doing a degree in Journalism and was only being taught newspaper journalism, at a time when newspapers were (and still are) in decline and print was going digital. By the time I graduated my company was earning enough revenue for me to run it full time and I have been in business ever since and am about to start my third venture!

What suggestions would you give students at university?

There's never been a better or easier time to start a business and if you aren't open to entrepreneurship you will be left behind. Graduate unemployment has soared in the recession and the advent of the Internet is having an effect and changing industry across every sector. My advice would be to start a business while at university as you will have the resources and talent around you to start and the risk factor will be much lower at this time than during the rest of your life. I learned more in my first year in business than the entire three years of my degree taught me.

Source: In compiling this case, we are grateful for the assistance of the National Consortium of University Entrepreneurs (NACUE), a grassroots organization that supports and represents university enterprise societies and student entrepreneurs to drive the growth of entrepreneurship in the UK (www.nacue.com).

Practical activities

1. **How entrepreneurial do you think you are?** Complete the questionnaire at one of the websites listed on the Online Resource Centre, or one recommended by your tutor, and obtain the results of the assessment.

 online resource centre 'How Entrepreneurial Do You Think You Are?'

Do the findings reflect your own assessment of your entrepreneurial abilities and/or potential, and that of your friends and family? Do you think you can increase your capacity to act entrepreneurially by studying the subject in this way? Did these results affect your view?

2. **What do the entrepreneurs say?** Conduct a quick search for written accounts in which entrepreneurs talk about their experiences (NB you can use the Further reading guide and web links as a starting point). Select one account and find out about the person's motivations and how these have influenced the kinds of ventures they have created. You can use the following questions as a guide, but feel free to adapt them, or to add your own questions: (a) Why did you want to become an entrepreneur? (b) What kind of activities are you engaged in? (c) Who else is involved

in the venture? (d) What are your ambitions for the future? (e) What lessons have you learned along the way? Summarize your findings in the form of a 1,000 word report or a short presentation.

3. What's happening in your area? Conduct a web search of your city, town or region to identify: (a) five successful entrepreneurial ventures, including a mix of social and commercial enterprises; (b) five organizations encouraging or supporting entrepreneurship and enterprise-related activities, including commercial, public sector, and voluntary sector providers. Prepare a table, with summary information on each organization, including their history and objectives.

💬 Discussion topics

1. Why am I studying entrepreneurship? Based on previous experience, we guess that you are probably starting this exploration of entrepreneurship with one, or possibly several, of the following thoughts in your mind:

- I already consider myself to be an entrepreneur, but think it might be useful to fill some gaps in my experience or to 'test out' a venture concept;
- I definitely want to set up my own business but feel the need to gain some relevant skills and get some ideas for potential ventures;
- I am wondering if I have 'what it takes' to be an entrepreneur, and want to find out in a 'safe' environment.
- I want to know how entrepreneurship links into other subjects, such as strategy and economics (e.g. how it relates to economic growth and competitive advantage);
- I am mainly interested in the social and cultural aspects of entrepreneurship (e.g. the role of gender, ethnicity, family background);
- I am basically critical of entrepreneurship, and see it doing lasting damage to societies and the natural environment.
- To be honest, my main reason for selecting this course was: (a) someone recommended it; (b) it fits my timetable; or (b) there is no exam!

  Spend a few minutes thinking through **your** reasons for studying entrepreneurship, then discuss with others. Is there a common pattern? Do you think your initial motivation might change as you study the subject further? Keep a record of this discussion, and refer back to it once you have completed your course and/or this book.

2. What does it take to be an entrepreneur? This chapter has highlighted the many different qualities that have been associated with 'being an entrepreneur', and the wide variety of activities that have been defined as 'entrepreneurial'. Prepare three lists stating what you consider to be the minimum requirements needed in order for someone to:

- be a prospective entrepreneur?
- act entrepreneurially?
- become a successful entrepreneur?

  After completing your three lists, compare them and see if there are any differences. How did you identify these requirements? Retain your list and review it again, when you have completed most of the book and/or your course of study.

Further reading guide

As you begin to explore entrepreneurship, you will find several different types of reading material, which you may find helpful for particular purposes. First, there are sources of practical information and advice, which can be combined with the information and advice given in Part One of this textbook. For example, Williams (2009) is a well-established guide to setting up a new small business, now published annually, while Yates (2009) is written by a serial entrepreneur and focuses on entrepreneurial start-up ventures. Allen (2007) does a similar job for those with an interest in setting up an ethical enterprise. These books reflect their UK origins to some extent (e.g. rules and regulations), so readers based in other countries may prefer to seek out local publications. Second, there are accounts of the lives of entrepreneurs, and of entrepreneurial ventures. Entrepreneurs' biographies and autobiographies can inform and inspire you. They can also contain useful advice, but do remember who is telling the story. Examples include **Bannatyne (2007)**, **Bounds (2009)**, **Branson (1999, 2008)**, **Caan (2009)**, **Dyson (2003)**, and **Grimson and Mitchell (2008)**. Third, there are introductions to entrepreneurship research. One of the best ways to approach this is through edited collections and handbooks. Of the former, we recommend **Swedberg (2000)**, a collection of classic readings with a very informative introduction. The *Oxford Handbook of Entrepreneurship* edited by **Casson et al. (2008)** covers many of the research approaches introduced in Part Two of this textbook. Another good source are the critical literature surveys, which appear from time to time in leading journals such as *Entrepreneurship Theory and Practice, Entrepreneurship and Regional Development, International Journal of Management Reviews*, and the *International Small Business Journal*. Additional suggestions can be found in the chapter and in other Part Two chapters.

 # References

Allen, P. (2007) *Your ethical business: how to plan, start and succeed in a company with a conscience.* London: ngo.media.

Bannatyne, D. (2007) *Anyone can do it: my story.* London: Orion.

Branson, R. (1999) *Losing my virginity: the autobiography.* London: Virgin Books.

Branson, R. (2008) *Business stripped bare: adventures of a global entrepreneur.* London: Virgin Books.

Bounds, D. (2009) *Fulfilled: a personal revolution in seven steps.* Harlow: Prentice Hall Life.

Caan, J. (2009) *The real deal: my story from Brick Lane to 'Dragons' Den'.* London: Virgin.

Casson, M., Yeung, B., Basu, A. and Wadeson, N. (2008) *The Oxford handbook of entrepreneurship.* Oxford: Oxford University Press.

Cope, J. and Watts, G. (2000) 'Learning by doing – An exploration of experience, critical incidents and reflection in entrepreneurial learning.' *International Journal of Entrepreneurial Behaviour and Research* 6, 3: 104–24.

Corbett, A. (2005) 'Experiential learning within the process of opportunity identification and exploitation.' *Entrepreneurship: Theory and Practice.* 29, 4: 473–91.

Della-Guista, M. and King, Z. (2008) 'Enterprise culture.' In M. Casson et al. (eds) op. cit. (629–47).

Drucker, P. (1982) *The changing world of the executive.* New York: Times Books.

Dyson, J. (2003) *Against the odds: an autobiography.* New York: Texere.

Grimson, L. and Mitchell, A. (2008) *Making it: women entrepreneurs reveal their secrets of success.* London: Capstone.

Kirby, D. (2004) 'Entrepreneurship education: can business schools meet the challenge?' *Journal of Education and Training.* 46, 8/9: 510–19.

Levie, J. (1999) 'Entrepreneurship education in Higher Education in England: a survey.' London: Department for Education and Employment.

Lewis, P. (2000) *The age of enterprise: the emergence and evolution of entrepreneurial management.* Dublin: Blackhall.

Mumford, A. (1997) *Action learning at work.* London: Gower.

OECD (2009) *Measuring entrepreneurship: a collection of indicators* (2009 edition). Brussels: OECD-Eurostat Entrepreneurship Indicators Programme.

Penrose, E. T. (1995 [1959]) *The theory of the growth of the firm* (3rd edition with new Foreword). Oxford: Oxford University Press.

Swedberg, R. (ed.) (2000) *Entrepreneurship: the social science view.* Oxford: Oxford University Press.

Tracey, P., Philips, N., and Haugh, H. (2005) 'Beyond philanthropy: community enterprise as a basis for corporate citizenship.' *Journal of Business Ethics*, 58, 4: 327–44.

Whitford, D. (2010) 'Can you learn to be an entrepreneur?' *Fortune* (22 March).

Williams, S. (2009) *The Financial Times guide to business start-up, 2010* (5th edition). Harlow: FT Prentice Hall.

Yates, J. (2009) *All-time essentials for entrepreneurs: 100 things to know and do to make your idea happen.* London: Capstone.

Part one

Entrepreneurship in practice

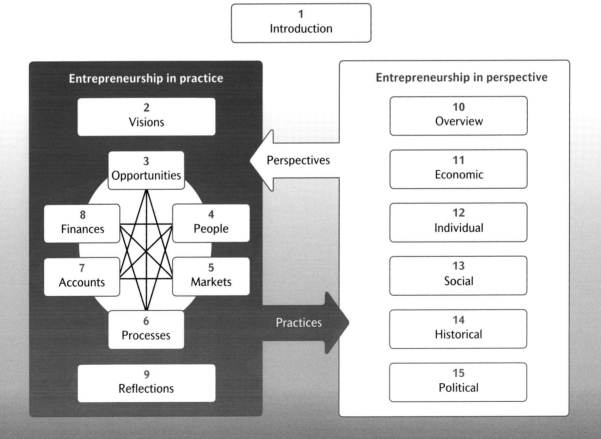

1
Introduction

Entrepreneurship in practice

2 Visions	
3 Opportunities	
8 Finances	**4** People
7 Accounts	**5** Markets
6 Processes	
9 Reflections	

Perspectives

Practices

Entrepreneurship in perspective

10
Overview

11
Economic

12
Individual

13
Social

14
Historical

15
Political

In the next eight chapters (Chapters 2–9), we experience some of the main practical challenges that people face when they attempt to convert a potential opportunity, or simply a 'bright idea', into a viable commercial or social venture – not simply a paper exercise, but something that can work in practice. Chapter 2 considers the different ways that people approach the challenge of creating a new venture. The following six chapters tackle key issues facing any new venture: opportunities, people, markets, processes, accounts, and finances. Importantly, these chapters also include 'Critical Incident' cases based on real entrepreneurs' stories and enable you to step into their shoes. In Chapter 9, we reflect on these issues through the personal experiences of several successful entrepreneurs, highlighting the complex and often unpredictable issues that can emerge along the way. Throughout Part One, there are also many cross-references to relevant material in Part Two of the textbook, and to the Online Resource Centre.

Visions
Creating new ventures

2

Vision without action is a daydream. Action without vision is a nightmare.
Japanese proverb

To be a successful entrepreneur one needs a vision of greatness for one's work. If we dream extravagantly we will be inspired to forge a reality beyond the straight jacket of practicalities.
Sir Ernest Hall, *musician and serial entrepreneur*

Learning outcomes

After reading this chapter you should be able to:

➤ Appreciate the role played by entrepreneurial vision in creating a new venture.

➤ Distinguish between three distinct approaches to shaping an entrepreneurial vision: (a) the emerging vision; (b) the traditional business plan; (c) the entrepreneurial 'opportunity business model' (OBM).

➤ Understand how the entrepreneurial 'opportunity business model' (OBM) can be used to establish the outlines of a venture and to communicate your vision to others.

➤ Identify the dimensions and drivers that underpin an entrepreneurial opportunity, and relate these to the context you intend to operate.

➤ Recognize how the challenge of shaping a vision relates to the themes addressed in other Part One chapters.

➤ Apply these concepts and techniques in order to create your own entrepreneurial venture.

Case 2.1 Electrifying ideas: deregulation lights up new opportunities

In 1989, the UK government passed the Electricity Act that was, over the course of the next decade, to transform a monopoly into a dynamic market supplying electricity to commercial and domestic consumers (http://www.opsi.gov.uk). The intention was to allow customers to purchase their electricity from a range of competing providers, albeit still distributed over the national grid, thereby increasing competitive forces and reducing prices. Intuitively we think of large corporations like E.ON (http://www.eon.com) and Scottish Power (http://www.scottishpower.com) competing in such a large established market rather than smaller providers, let alone new ones. In this case we will explore how individuals created a vision for their new ventures, which were only made possible by the legal driver of deregulation.

The first, **Karen Darby** gained extensive experience in telemarketing by running her own call centre business, Decisions Group, for seven years before selling her share in 1990 (http://www.karendarbydirect.com). She drew on this experience, when deregulation came along, to help consumers understand the promotions being offered by electricity providers. Telesales is all about selling products over the phone but Karen realized that in such a congested marketplace consumers needed advice not promotions. In other words, 'People don't like the idea of being sold to.' (Sunday Times 2004) Her vision was to establish a service company that provided consumers with independent advice on which provider offered the best deal for them. In this way, **SimplySwitch** was born (http://www.simplyswitch.com). Karen's first challenge was to share the vision of her new venture plan with potential investors. She was able to secure £125,000 investment in return for a 35% equity stake and launched SimplySwitch in 2003. In 2006 it was sold for £22 million (Guardian 2007a).

Ethical point Karen now describes herself as a social entrepreneur and believes that a business can both make money and have a social purpose (YouTube 2009). Karen had a clear vision of how she could help consumers and use her experience and skills to develop a new venture in a new market. Interestingly, this intermediary business model has been widely adopted across many sectors and is often underpinned by the Internet. There have been a number of successful comparison websites with http://www.moneysupermarket.com being one of the better-known examples. But what opportunities were there for new ventures actually to generate electricity and supply it, over the national grid, directly to consumers? Surely this was only the preserve of large corporations.

Juliet Davenport faced a particularly difficult challenge. Her vision also involved people changing electricity provider, but she also wanted them to switch to 'green energy'. It was responding to both to the legal driver of deregulation and the societal driver of climate change. In 2002, Juliet became chief executive of an existing renewable energy company, which then began to offer shares to customers, enabling the company to buy a wind farm in Cornwall. The new company, which was re-branded as **Good Energy** (http://www.goodenergy.co.uk), now provides more than 26,000 domestic and business customers with electricity generated by 100% renewable sources. Good Energy employs 50 people and has an annual turnover of over £18 million (€22 million). How did it achieve this breakthrough in such a short period of time? In part, it was because Juliet had a clear vision, saving 1 million tonnes of carbon a year, which she could communicate to investors, independent generators, and customers. The vision is based on a shared set of values, which are closely linked to fighting climate change. As Juliet once described it, 'We see our customers going on a journey, switching to Good Energy is the first part' (YouTube 2007). As a result, many Good Energy customers are also shareholders in the company. The vision is also being spread through a growing community of over 500 independent renewable electricity generators across the UK.

Ethical point There is still much debate about what 'green power' really is and it is sometimes difficult for consumers to compare green credentials (Guardian 2009). How do we know which companies really are green? Good Energy is independently accredited as an Ethical Company (http://www.ethical-company-organisation.org).

Points to consider

1. Deregulation is a good example of a legal driver that is beyond the control of a single enterprise. What other industries have been changed by regulation and deregulation? Try to identify a new venture that has emerged to exploit these opportunities.

2. Environmental concerns are driving many product innovations, such as EcoButton (http://www.eco-button.com). What entrepreneurial opportunities can you identify that respond to this societal driver?

3. What particular challenges did Karen and Juliet face as they created their visions and translated them into new ventures?

Sources: Sunday Times (2004); Guardian (2007a, 2009); YouTube (2007, 2009).

2.1 Introduction

2.1.1 Visions, opportunities, and the entrepreneurial process

This chapter examines the way that **entrepreneurs** shape and realize their visions. Case 2.1 illustrates how two successful entrepreneurs, Karen Darby and Juliet Davenport, were able to articulate personal visions in ways that engaged key audiences. In doing so, they created two highly successful enterprises, SimplySwitch and Good Energy. In both instances, a change in legislation was an initial driver, creating an environment in which these new ventures could flourish. One of the key skills of successful entrepreneurs is being able to identify relevant drivers and to recognize the **entrepreneurial opportunities** that they make possible. Karen had several years' experience of running a telemarketing company and was herself frustrated by the process of changing electricity supplier. Industry deregulation was the catalyst for change, but Karen also had the crucial insight that helping people switch supplier could be a real entrepreneurial opportunity. She also recognized that she was able to bring together the resources required to exploit this opportunity, even though this meant selling an equity share to an investor in order to finance the venture (Chapter 8). Karen's ability to present a convincing vision for her new venture was a critical factor in gaining this investment. So how do you create this kind of vision? Just think for a moment. How would you go about persuading a potential investor to take an interest in your own venture, even though it was not yet trading? Why should other people risk their money on what may be little more than your bright idea? As you begin to shape your vision it is worth keeping these potential investors in mind. Step into their shoes from time to time and ask yourself whether 'that idea' is still of any interest.

The opening case is a good starting point for looking at the **entrepreneurial process** that takes us from idea generation and opportunity recognition to the point where an opportunity is exploited, or converted into a real venture. Figure 2.1 is a simplified illustration of this process, which comprises three distinct but closely related activities. Initially, it will involve you in generating new business ideas (i.e. creativity and **innovation**) and recognizing opportunities that have the potential for exploitation (i.e. evaluation and selection). In practice, there is often a lot of interplay between these activities, which we explore further in Chapter 3. Meanwhile, as a result of these interactions, entrepreneurs are likely narrow down their options, refine their ideas, and organize their resources until they are in a position to engage in the third set of activities, exploiting an opportunity. The end result may be a new commercial or social venture. It could also take the form of a corporate venture that operates within an existing organization.

In this chapter, we concentrate on the first two activities in the entrepreneurial process and look at how you translate your vision into something more tangible. There are broadly three approaches to shaping a vision. We discuss the alternatives and introduce the opportunity business model as a technique that can help you with this task. Understanding the dimensions and drivers for a business idea will allow you (and others) to decide whether you have got a genuine entrepreneurial opportunity that can be exploited.

2.1.2 Entrepreneurial learning

The entrepreneurial process of idea generation, opportunity recognition, and exploitation in enterprises is part of a larger cycle of **entrepreneurial learning**, which we introduced in Chapter 1 (Figure 1.2). The framework provides is reproduced here to show how the opportunity

Figure 2.1 A simplified illustration of the entrepreneurial process

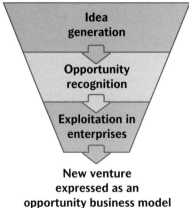

Figure 2.2 Entrepreneurial learning and opportunity business models

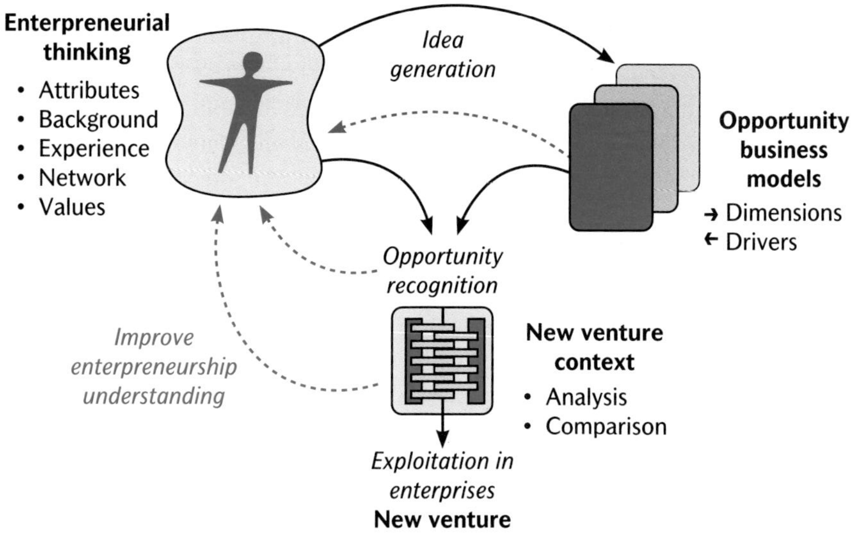

business models fit into the process, as a way of helping entrepreneurs to get a clearer vision of their new ventures. As the linked features of Figure 2.2 suggest, this is certainly not a one-off event. Entrepreneurial learning takes place a continuous cycle, with people learning more about themselves as well as about their new ventures.

This chapter is organized as follows. In Section 2.2 we discuss three approaches to shaping the vision for a new venture: emergent visions, traditional business plans, and business models. Section 2.3 is a more detailed examination of the opportunity business model with examples showing how it can be applied in practice. Section 2.4 shows how the challenge of shaping any entrepreneurial opportunity is addressed in more detail in the remaining Part One chapters.

2.2 Shaping the vision: three approaches

2.2.1 The importance of vision

Having a vision is the key to your entrepreneurial new venture. Without it there is no driving force or sense of direction. However, your vision needs to be backed up otherwise it is pure fantasy. Entrepreneurs and entrepreneurial organizations may convince themselves they have a winning idea but ultimately it is the customer or market who will decide. For example, when they launched their new venture in 1998, the three founders of Boo.com where convinced they had found the solution to the selling branded fashions over the Internet. They also convinced venture capitalists to invest over $135 million in their idea. However, in less than two years the money was spent and the business closed. Failed visions are not the sole preserve of individual entrepreneurs; large corporations can also make mistakes. For example, the idea for handheld personal digital assistant devices (PDAs) was introduced by Apple Computers in 1993, with the launch of the Newton MessagePad. In hindsight, we can see this was the right idea but at the wrong time (i.e. the technology and the market was not sufficiently advanced). Some radical innovations never find their 'right time' while others, including the PDA, relaunch successfully at a later date. It can be difficult to differentiate between crazy ideas that have no future and others that might appear crazy, but which could be the next 'big thing'. Thomas John Watson, president of International Business Machines (IBM), was once famously misquoted to the effect that, 'I think there is a world market for maybe five computers.' Watson may not have made this comment, but at the time (1943), there was a general assumption that the demand for computers was limited; today's huge market for personal computers would have been unimaginable to early industry leaders like Watson. The entrepreneur's initial task is to convert a personal vision into a coherent proposition, and then to articulate (i.e. communicate) it in ways that will attract interest and gain credibility with investors, customers, suppliers, and others (e.g. regulators). This is not an easy task and it often requires considerable persistence in order to succeed. For example, James Dyson's original idea for a bagless vacuum cleaner was rejected by several leading manufacturers. In the end, he decided to set up his own venture and launched what was to become a highly successful range of products (Case 10.4).

➡ **PERSPECTIVES** See section 12.4 for further information.

2.2.2 Introducing the three approaches

One of the main challenges facing any individual or group seeking to create a new venture is to recognize which of their various business ideas can be converted into a real entrepreneurial opportunity. We should not underestimate the scale or difficulty of this task. There are broadly three approaches that you can adopt to shape your ideas for a new venture:

1. Following an emergent vision.
2. Drafting a traditional business plan.
3. Developing an opportunity business model.

In this section, we consider each of these options in some detail, then present an argument for adopting the third option, the entrepreneurial business model, as the most effective way of shaping your vision. In practice, as entrepreneurs you may make use of more than one of these approaches, depending on their circumstances. Though we focus attention on the opportunity business model we also highlight the strengths of the other approaches. Our basic aim is to provide a good balance between the flexibility offered by emergent visions and the logical structure of the traditional business plan.

2.2.3 Following an emergent vision

Many entrepreneurs begin by following their vision without the assistance of a formal business plan. In other words, they adopt a highly intuitive approach, with key strategic decisions often relying heavily on the entrepreneur's 'gut feeling' and previous industry and market experience.

There are many advantages to such an approach, including its flexibility. Even when more formal approaches are adopted, there is no substitute for being close to the market and drawing on your previous experience of a particular product or industry sector. One of the major disadvantages of the emergent approach is that it can be difficult to explain your vision to other people, including potential financiers and partners. These informal approaches are currently attracting a lot of attention from **entrepreneurship** researchers, who analyse them using labels such as **'effectuation'** and 'bricolage' (Section 12.4). They may be appropriate for some kinds of venture, including those that are less growth-oriented and more locally based. Emergent visions can also be effective during the early phases of a venture's development. However, in some situations, including technology-based ventures, this approach is likely to lack the rigour that is required to secure funding and to gain legitimacy (e.g. securing approval from industry regulators). Consider it from the perspective of a business angel or venture capitalist. What is the minimum level of detail and analysis that you would expect an entrepreneur to provide before you agreed to part with a very large sum of money, to be invested in an unproven idea?

➡ **PERSPECTIVES** See sections 12.3 and 12.4 for further information.

2.2.4 Drafting a traditional business plan

One response to the need for clear articulation is to produce a traditional formal business plan. You may already be familiar with the idea of a business plan as they are often created as part of a school or student enterprise activity (i.e. the 'business plan competition'). Banks and investors also require some form of business plan in support of requests for business loans or investment. Business plans for start-up ventures are documents that set out the goals of the venture and how they will be achieved. A typical business plan contains the following sections:

- **Executive summary** Outlines the key features of the venture and may highlight relevant points such as funding required, growth potential, and returns for investors.

- **The business opportunity** Sets out what the venture aims to provide, why there is a demand, and who is involved in the process (e.g. customers, suppliers, partners).

- **Management team** Provides information on key people, often in the form of biographies that highlight relevant skills, knowledge, and experience.

- **Marketing and promotional strategy** Analyses potential market and competition, summarizes **marketing mix**, and explains how products and services will be promoted.

- **Operational strategy** Sets out practical aspects of the venture including key processes, information systems, assets (e.g. premises, technologies), and controls.

- **Financial forecasts** Provide a quantified summary of the other sections, including projected cash flows, profit and loss accounts, and balance sheets.

There is a wide variety of software programs and other services to help you produce your business plan. These include commercial products and others provided at no cost by banks and enterprise development organizations. Accountants also offer support to clients who wish to produce business plans or to calculate their financial projections. The Online Resource Centre provides links to several of these products. We have also included a simple business plan template that can be downloaded and adapted to meet your needs.

 online resource centre 'Business Plans for Start-Up Ventures.

The main limitation of business plans as a way of gaining an understanding of new ventures is that they do not reflect the way that people shape their entrepreneurial visions. Business plans are formal written documents, with a linear structure, in which various aspects of your venture (e.g. marketing, operations) are divided into separate sections. However, when you are thinking through the practicalities of a new venture your mind will often be working in a much more flexible, creative, and holistic way. For example, you might be thinking about the ways that marketing and operational aspects of the venture are interrelated. If you are drafting a formal business plan, it is important to ensure that it reinforces, rather than limits your thinking. When it comes to convincing other people that your venture is worthwhile, it is essential that you and your team need to have a real, in-depth understanding of your vision. In addition, you need to be able to communicate your vision clearly, concisely and with enthusiasm. You can see how this works in practice in the popular television series *Dragons' Den*, where budding entrepreneurs who are seeking finance for their ventures are asked to make short presentations to a panel of investors (i.e. what is sometimes termed an 'elevator pitch'). The applicants face some very tough questioning, which often results in one or all of the investors deciding that they are 'out' (i.e. that they are no longer interested in the venture). Of course, the initial pitch is just the start of the process and any investor would need a lot more information before a contract was signed. However, investors are busy people. They often reject a proposal on the basis of that initial pitch. The key lesson is that unless you are *personally* convincing, your audience is unlikely to invest more time in reading your business plan. Business plans certainly have an important role to play, but in the next sub-section we consider a more dynamic alternative that could help you to shape and articulate your vision more effectively.

2.2.5 Developing a business model

The concept of the business model emerged during the 1990s as a way of understanding and comparing the plethora of new business ideas that developed around the Internet. The concept has since been refined and applied to other kinds of entrepreneurial venture. It offers two important advantages over the other approaches discussed in this section. Firstly, it provides you with a clear and concise way to communicate an entrepreneurial opportunity to potential investors and other interested parties. Secondly, in the process of constructing a business model, you can improve your own understanding of the underlying concept, enabling you to refine it further and build a more convincing case. Back in the 1990s, investors were struggling to make sense of thousands of business plans claiming that their venture was uniquely positioned to exploit the boundless commercial opportunities of the web. The dot-com boom popularized terms such as 'first mover advantage' and 'burn rate' (i.e. the speed at which a venture drains cashflow) (Wolfe 1999; Lewis 2001). It also saw some dramatic failures, including WebVan and Boo.com. In this dynamic and turbulent world, business models offered a way of reaching a shared understanding of the dimensions and drivers of an entrepreneurial opportunity. By identifying these key components, and their underlying assumptions, business models allowed analysts to make comparisons and to identify ideas that were unique or particularly robust. It also became possible to track how business models were changing over time, enabling investors to categorize models and to identify new trends.

A business model can be seen as a working version of the traditional business plan. In essence, it shows how a venture is going to be able to generate revenues and to make a profit from its operations. The model identifies key components and functions of the business, and shows how these relate to its financial performance. Figure 2.3 provides some more detailed definitions from the business and management field. Business models have now become something of a buzzword, but their effectiveness depends largely on how well they are applied. Poorly thought-out business models contributed to the downfall of many dotcoms in the last two decades, and even the most carefully constructed business model is not an automatic guarantee of success.

The business models concept has been refined in various ways. For example, more recent contributions pay greater attention to the role of competition. In one of the earliest contributions, Hamel (2000) created a framework comprising four major components: core strategy, strategic resources, customer interface, and value network, which can be linked to customer benefits and company boundaries. These components were also underpinned by four factors: efficiency, uniqueness, fit, and profits boosters. Osterwalder and Pigneur (2004) reviewed the literature and proposed another business model classification consisting of four main areas of activity:

- infrastructure management (capabilities, partnerships and value configuration);
- product innovation (offering and value proposition);
- customer relationship (customer, channel and relationship);
- financial aspects (cost, profit and revenue).

Figure 2.3 Defining business models

> 'An architecture for the product, service and information flows, including a description of the various business actors and their roles; and a description of the potential benefits for the various business actors; and description of the sources of revenues.' (Timmers 2000: 32)
>
> 'A distinct system of suppliers, distributors, commerce services providers, and customers that use the Internet for their primary business communications and transactions.' (Tapscott et al. 2000: 19)
>
> 'Business models describe, as a system, how the pieces fit together.' (Magretta 2002: 87)
>
> 'The system of components, linkages and associated dynamics, which make commercial advantage of the Internet.' (Afuah and Tucci 2001: 6)
>
> 'A plan or diagram that is used to describe a business idea. How an enterprise competes, uses its resources, structures its relationships, interfaces with customers and creates value and generates profit.' (Barringer and Ireland 2008: 142)
>
> 'A business model describes the rationale of how an organisation creates, delivers and captures value.' (Osterwalder and Pigneur 2010: 14)

Though much of the early work on business models was concerned with new business ideas in the digital economy, the concept has also proved to be highly relevant to understanding new entrepreneurial opportunities in other fields (Chesbrough and Rosenbloom 2002; Hitt et al. 2002; Morris et al. 2005; Osterwalder and Pigneur 2010). This has introduced a broader concept of the entrepreneurial opportunity business model, which describes both the key dimensions and the key drivers that enable new business ideas to be exploited in an entrepreneurial venture. In the remaining sections of this chapter, and throughout Part One of this book, we will be refining this newer application of the business model concept in order to evaluate, select, and pursue entrepreneurial opportunities.

Before considering how opportunity business models can be applied, it may be useful to consider following case (Case 2.2). It shows how a strong vision, if correctly presented, can be used to penetrate established, highly competitive markets in order to bring about positive social change. Sales of bottled water in Western Europe continue to grow at an alarming pace, in spite of the fact that tap water is usually safe to drink. Meanwhile, there are still chronic shortages of clean drinking water in some parts of the developing world. The case shows how two social entrepreneurs shaped their visions to challenge this imbalance in novel ways.

Case 2.2 Water, water everywhere: but not a drop to drink

In the last 30 years sales of bottled water have grown to more than 1.3 billion litres in the UK and to over 9 billion litres in the US. In 2011, this will mean global consumption of bottled water could exceed 175 billion litres. This is of little comfort the estimated 1 billion people in the world who don't have access to safe clean drinking water (WaterAid 2010). Of course, there are many governments and NGOs trying to address this imbalance but what can we, as individuals, do about it?

Let us look at one individual who has a vision to change this imbalance by exploiting the market for bottled water rather than fighting against it. **Duncan Goose**, founder of Global Ethics and One Water (http://www.onedifference.org), set up a new venture, in 2005, to sell ethical bottled water and donate 100% of its profits to installing a specialized water pumping systems called PlayPump (http://www.playpumps.org). He recognized the potential: 'The water market is an absolutely huge market in the UK, worth £1.5 billion' (Guardian 2007b). At one level Duncan's vision is simple: use all the profits from selling water, to people who can afford it, to provide clean water for people who cannot. Clearly, there needs to be more to it than that. In his younger days, Duncan travelled the world; in fact, he was inspired by Ted Simon's motorcycle journey in the 1970s, detailed in his book *Jupiter's Travels* (1979). Duncan is in good company: actors Ewan McGregor and Charley Boorman were also inspired by reading *Jupiter's Travels*. As you can imagine, Duncan has his own adventures, including surviving Hurricane Mike, which destroyed many communities in Honduras in 1998. Duncan recalled, 'What really struck me was to make a difference we did not need a lot of money, just a little money spent in the right way' (Sunday Times 2008). He and his friends identified access to clean drinking water as a major global issue and set about doing something about it (YouTube 2008). One Water was conceived and launched in 2005, just at the same time as Bob Geldof's Live 8 appeal was launched (http://www.live8live.com). Having created a vision and shared it with organizers of Live 8, he faced the challenge of promoting and supplying it to individual consumers. Can you imagine how you would go about persuading retailers and supermarkets, which have shelves full of numerous brands of bottled water, to de-list one and put yours it its place? Indeed, it was very hard work for Duncan, but when Total (http://www.total.co.uk) became the first national stockist in 2006, others started to follow. In their first year, One Water donated £70,000 to charities working in Africa and India. By 2008, this had exceeded £1 million. Then One Difference started expanding its vision to include other humanitarian issues in developing countries, such as HIV through the sale of One Condoms (http://www.onedifference.org/condoms). Interestingly, Duncan has recruited other people to promote his vision, including actors David Tennant and Rebecca Lacey.

Duncan Goose, is not alone in using the sales of water to fund humanitarian projects, **Kate Alcott** created Frank Water (http://www.frankwater.com) in 2005 in order to generate funds for clean water projects in India. Kate had suffered from dysentery caused by drinking dirty water in India. Frank Water not only supplies bottled water but also water coolers to offices. Kate had a clear vision of how each purchase connected to providing clean water in India: 'Every bottled cooler you take on provides an initial 10,000 litres of safe drinking water to Frank Water Projects. Every refill provides a further 1000 litres.'

Do not underestimate how difficult it is to enter a high competitive market, such as bottled water. Even large companies with significant resources can get it wrong. In 2004 Coca-Cola, one of the largest drinks companies in the world, withdrew its bottled water brand, Dasani, from the UK after spending a reported £10 million on launching it (TimesOnline 2004). Perhaps this really does put Duncan's and Kate's achievement into perspective.

Ethical point Duncan earns a salary £6,000 a year from One Water and Kate draws no salary from Frank Water (Sunday Times 2007b).

Questions

1. The societal driver for both One Water and Frank Water was providing clean water in developing countries. What other ways can you think of to achieve this?

2. Look at the websites for both enterprises and see how strongly their vision is presented. If you had to buy a bottle of water from either which would you choose and why?

3. Duncan and Kate use others to promote their vision, such as One Ambassadors and FRANK Champions. How important do you think this is and how successful has each been?

Sources: TimesOnline (2004); Guardian (2007b); Sunday Times (2007b, 2008); YouTube (2008); WaterAid (2010).

Case 2.2 provides two examples of turning a vision into a coherent and compelling proposal for a new venture. Duncan Goose and Kate Alcott had clear visions to help others by selling bottled water. Each of them achieved their visions in different ways, but what they had in common was an ability to shape their vision effectively. They recognized an entrepreneurial opportunity and obtained the resources to turn their ideas into a reality. Both were motivated by more than personal financial gain, which may also have been a factor contributing to their success. Their achievement was to make consumers see a connection between purchasing bottled water in one part of the world and providing clean water in another, where it was most needed. Throughout Part One there are many other examples of entrepreneurs who have been successful in converting their ideas into reality. In the next section, we begin to apply the opportunity business model as a way shaping your entrepreneurial vision.

2.3 Applying the opportunity business model

2.3.1 Introducing the dimensions and drivers

The opportunity business model is a description of the key dimensions (Proposition, People, Place, Process, Profit) and drivers (Societal, Commercial, Legal, Technological) that underpin any new business idea and enable it to be exploited in an enterprise (Figure 2.4). Expressing your vision as an opportunity business model can be an effective way of accelerating your entrepreneurial learning and of developing opportunities into viable entrepreneurial ventures.

In this section, we provide some working definitions of these dimensions and drivers and show how they can be applied in practice. However, before proceeding further it may be helpful to explain why we are adopting this language. Many students on business management courses will have encountered two popular strategic analysis tools, which address a similar set of factors:

- **SWOT (Strengths, Weakness, Opportunities, and Threats) analysis** is used to make connections between external and (environmental) internal (organizational) factors.

- **PEST (Political, Economic, Social, and Technological) analysis** is used to identify different elements in the macro-environment. There are also a number of variations, each with their own acronym, for example, PESTLE (Political, Economic, Sociological, Technological, Legal, and Environmental); PESTER (Political, Economic Social, Technological, Environmental, and Regulatory) and STEEP (Social, Technological, Economic, Environmental, and Political).

Figure 2.4 The opportunity business model

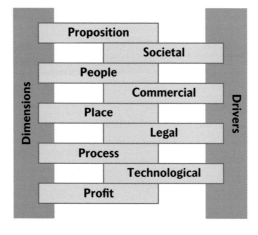

Though these are tried and tested strategic analysis tools, they work most effectively when applied to existing organizations, industries, and markets. It can be difficult to adapt these tools, and to adjust your own approach, in order to analyse entrepreneurial opportunities, and to relate the findings to the practical challenges of creating a new venture. For these reasons, and given the increasing attention being paid to entrepreneurial business models, we will adopt the language of dimensions and drivers throughout Part One (Section 1.3).

2.3.2 Dimensions: the core components of an idea

Dimensions are a way of expressing the different components or elements of the business idea. They help support analysis, structure discussion and enable comparison. The five opportunity business model dimensions express the key components, elements, or building blocks of the business idea:

- **Proposition** What is the core value proposition, as perceived by the customer, of the opportunity? This could be expressed as a mission statement but needs to be clear and concise.

- **People** Who are the leader, management team, and network of advisors, customers, suppliers, and stakeholders? How does social capital and networking support the business opportunity?

- **Place** Where is the market? Who are the customers and competitors? This could involve analysis of market and industry to identify segments and gaps.

- **Process** How is the enterprise structured? What are the key processes and relationships? How will these be enabled and supported? What role does information technology play?

- **Profit** Why do it? What are the real returns? Financials, gross profit, net profit, forecasts, KPIs, and capital required. Is there a social return? This might also include a consideration of the ownership structure and exit strategy.

2.3.3 Drivers: the factors underpinning an opportunity

Drivers are the factors underpinning an entrepreneurial opportunity. Often, one or more driver will apply to each opportunity. For example, an idea for a new road safety product might emerge from a combination of Societal, Legal, and Technological drivers. The four drivers express key factors, influences, or enablers that provide the foundations of a new business idea, and suggest how it might be exploited in an enterprise:

- **Societal** Wider global, social, political, and environmental factors, such as climate change, energy, aging populations, fair trade, and antisocial behaviour.

- **Commercial** Global, national, regional, and local economic and financial factors, such as currency exchange rates, local taxation rates, and the price of oil. What might be the impact on the opportunity if governments introduced a greenhouse gas emission trading scheme?

- **Legal** Legislation, rules, and regulatory requirements. Typically set by governments and consortia. Such as data protection law and trade associations.

- **Technological** New and emerging technologies such as 3G mobile communication networks, public broadband, online social networks, and nanotechnology.

Drivers differ from dimensions in two ways. Firstly, not all drivers apply to every opportunity business model. By considering the most relevant drivers, you can focus more directly on the factors that enable a specific entrepreneurial opportunity. Secondly, it is important to recognize that drivers are usually beyond the direct influence of individual entrepreneurs. Societal, Commercial, and Regulatory drivers are almost always outside your direct control. Technological drivers, such as the broadband Internet, are also effectively a 'given'. An exception would be where a technology-driven venture develops a proprietary technology that they can protect with patents, or introduces a radical innovation that changes the 'rules of the game' (Section 11.3). One way of visualizing drivers in action is to imagine yourself as a surfer, selecting and then riding a series of powerful waves. Like the surfer, your success will depend on a number of factors, including judgement, persistence, and balance. For similar reasons, any attempt to challenge a driver directly (i.e. to stand up against a wave) is almost certain to end in failure.

➜ **PERSPECTIVES** See sections 11.3 for further information.

2.3.4 Applying the opportunity business model

We have argued that the opportunity business model is particularly effective when creating new entrepreneurial ventures. However, in order to illustrate how the model is applied, we have selected an existing organization that will be familiar to most readers. In the following analysis, we explore each element of Apple Computer's digital music business, focusing on its 'iTunes store' business model. Apple's history spans more than four decades, making it an 'old hand' in the highly competitive world of technology. It is also widely recognized as one of the world's most innovative companies (Economist 2007). But what is particularly striking is Apple's expansion since the late 1990s, from its original business in personal computers and operating systems into the emerging field of digital multimedia products and services. How can we make sense of the company's wide range of product and service offerings in this new business, and the drivers that underpin them?

Firstly, we need to consider the *dimensions* of each offering, in this case the online music store iTunes, which was launched by Apple in 2003:

- **Proposition** The core value proposition is to provide access online to music and videos, which can be purchased at a relatively low price. These can be downloaded to either an Apple Mac or Windows PC and then transferred to an iPod, the company's portable media player. How many people do you know who have both an iPod and an Apple Mac?

- **People** Apple is clearly at the centre of this service but requires relationships with the record companies who own the copyright for the music or video. This would not have been a simple task and would have required much negotiation. Apple's strong brand

and high level of customer loyalty would have played a key role in this. Why didn't the record companies simply produce their own online music download service? Perhaps the charismatic CEO, Steve Jobs, was another factor.

- **Place** The Internet has provided consumers with access to seemingly unlimited content. The music industry is a competitive market and perhaps surprisingly, Apple as a new entrant was able to achieve a dominant position in online music sales. Why was Apple able to achieve this?

- **Process** The use of the iTunes store requires an Apple Mac or Windows PC to run the iTunes software through which music files could be downloaded, stored, and copyright protected in a proprietary encrypted file format. Interestingly, this meant that Apple had to develop an application for Microsoft Windows. What might have been the consequences if Apple had not done this?

- **Profit** In this model, a percentage of the sales revenue is shared with the record companies and subsequently the artist. What might be the split between the three parties?

Secondly, we need to consider the *drivers* that underpin the 'iTunes store' business model:

- **Societal** While the growth of the Internet, on which iTunes store depends, is having a profound effect on society, it is not in itself a driver for this business model. What are your expectations of access to music in the future?

- **Commercial** Since the late 1990s the growth of illegal sharing of music files over the Internet has been seen as a major financial threat to the music industry's revenues. The iTunes store represented a much needed legitimate alternative to the industry. Clearly, the industry wanted a commercial solution which could gain the loyalty of artists and consumers alike. Why might this be so important?

- **Legal** In spite of a plethora of copyright law, the sharing of music files continues to pose a threat to the music industry. How many people do you know who still share music files and what would need to change to stop them doing it?

- **Technological** The widespread availability of a near ubiquitous electronic communications platform, the Internet, is a prerequisite to the iTunes store's business model and is clearly outside the control of Apple Computers. However, the company has developed proprietary applications and a file format which gave them a competitive advantage by protecting their intellectual property. How might the growth of 3G mobile networks affect Apple's iTunes service?

Business models usually extend well beyond the boundaries of the organization, and in the case of Apple we can see how the introduction of the iPhone introduced a new set of external partners, telecommunications providers in each of the countries served. These include AT&T in the United States, T-Mobile in Germany, and O2 in the UK. With more than 10 billion songs downloaded (Apple 2010), the success of iTunes store is beyond question. But even the most successful business models need to evolve in response to a rapidly changing world. How might Apples 'iTunes store' model develop in the future? For example, what is the significance of offering videos, movies, TV shows, games, and free radio podcasts? And what are the likely long-term effects on the entertainment industry?

Representing Apple Computer's digital multimedia product and service offerings as an opportunity business model can help us to better understand the entrepreneurial opportunity. In addition, it can support a discussion about what is unique about the model when compared to its competitors. For example, Nokia is a leading manufacturer of mobile telephones. The company also provides a range of products and services that exploit the convergence of the Internet and communications industries. How could Nokia compete with, and differentiate its offerings from, those of Apple? One of the strengths of the opportunity business model is that it provides an analytical framework for this kind of thinking.

Having looked at an established company, our next case examines how the opportunity business model drivers operate in an entrepreneurial start-up venture. Case 2.3 traces the way that a societal driver, in this instance the trend towards safer and healthier food, has spawned a seemingly endless array of entrepreneurial opportunities.

Case 2.3 Food for thought: a simple driver with infinite responses

We all need to eat. However, the desire for safe, healthy, nutritious, and tasty foods goes far beyond this simple human need. There is a great deal of interest in the food and drinks we consume. This interest is often expressed in the form of fashions and trends that can generate new entrepreneurial opportunities. The three entrepreneurs that make up this case illustrate a variety of responses to the basic requirement for food. They also demonstrate the creativity, focus, and determination that are required to be successful in such a competitive market.

1. Babylicious

Sally Preston founded her highly successful business, Babylicious, in September 2001 (http://www.babylicious.co.uk). While bringing up two young children, she became aware of a gap in the market for quality, frozen baby food and used her previous experience as a food scientist, with Marks and Spencer, to develop a range of new products. From day one, Sally had a vision for Babylicious to be a big national or international company, she recalled, 'I never wanted it to be a small cottage industry.' (Startups 2010) Her first large customer was Waitrose, a large UK supermarket chain, with an order for eight varieties of meals to be stocked in 27 stores. Babylicious has subsequently been sold by Asda, Tesco, and Sainsbury's, having had annual sales around £4 million in 2006 (Bridge 2008). Clearly, Sally was able to share her vision for healthy and nutritious baby food with many other parents and build a successful venture around this simple premise. However, while the premise might have seemed simple, putting it into practice was an altogether more complex matter. Consumers demand that food is safe, particularly where children are concerned, and Sally's expertise was also critical in winning the confidence of consumers and investors alike. She recalled that as a trained food technologist, 'I knew how to insure my food complied with all the criteria for traceability, health and safety'. (Sunday Times 2007a)

2. SuperJam

Fraser Doherty, who learnt to make jam from his grandmother, was only 14 years old when he set up his company, SuperJam, selling to church fetes and farmers markets in Scotland (http://www.superjam.co.uk). But surely there were already enough choices of jam – how could Fraser's jam be different from all those familiar, well-established brands? Basically, SuperJam had no added sugar, being sweetened by grape juice rather than sugar. It also contained *superfoods*, such as blueberries. In just four years, Fraser developed a venture from this initial vision. He got the opportunity to pitch his idea to Waitrose when he attended a 'meet the buyer' day. His SuperJam was subsequently launched in the UK by Waitrose and is now sold in a number of leading stores. In 2008 Fraser was producing about 400,000 jars a year (Times 2007) and by 2010 'the jam boy' was reporting on his weekly blog that almost 1 million jars had been sold. Meanwhile, he was continuing to develop export markets and to introduce new product lines, such as marmalade.

3. S&A foods

We can see, from Babylicious and SuperJam, how a relatively simple driver has become a new venture that filled a gap in a seemingly crowded market. However, **Perween Warsi**, who founded S&A Foods in 1986, took her vision to a whole new level (http://www.sa-foods.co.uk). Frustrated by the poor quality of Indian food available in UK supermarkets, Perween built her venture by initially supplying home-cooked samosas to local delicatessens and subsequently establishing her own factory to produce a range of Indian chilled foods. At one point, a larger food company purchased an interest in S&A, but after the parent company went into administration, Perween bought back her company with support from a venture capital firm, 3i. S&A Foods remains family owned and employs approximately 1,400 staff with sales over £100 million. Perween remembers that, 'My vision right from the start was to see the products on the shelves of shops all over the country'. (Times 2008) She has been recognized as a successful female entrepreneur and is one of the wealthiest Asian businesswomen. Perween was awarded an MBE in 1997 and a CBE in 2002 (Dhaliwal 2008).

Questions

1. Food is something all of the above entrepreneurs have in common, but what particular aspect of food distinguishes each of them? Is this factor a 'driver' in their business model?

2. Look at the websites for each company and consider who the most likely customers are. How could they be grouped and described?

3. How did the entrepreneurs' background, experience, or training influence the choice of market?

Sources: Sunday Times (2007a); Times (2007); Bridge (2008); Dhaliwal (2008); Times (2008); Startups (2010).

2.3.5 **Exploring the context**

The three entrepreneurs highlighted in the *Food for thought* case (Case 2.3) are compelling examples of how to create a new venture from a strong vision that is underpinned by a driver. Sally Preston, Fraser Doherty, and Perween Warsi each developed an enterprise to exploit an entrepreneurial opportunity, and each of them has managed to build a business in a highly competitive market. When you read a case study, you have the benefit of hindsight. In other words, we already know what happened. By contrast, the three entrepreneurs had to make decisions without any advance knowledge of the likely outcome. As you explore the context for your own venture, there are a number of questions to consider, such as:

- Can this market accommodate another player?
- Will the customers want our product or service?
- Is there a gap that existing firms are not exploiting?

Once you have expressed your idea in the form of an opportunity business model, the next step is to explore the market and industry (i.e. the context) in which the enterprise will operate. We consider these questions in more detail in Chapter 5, as part of a review of entrepreneurial marketing. In this section, we introduce the main features of the context and relate them to the opportunity business model. Figure 2.5 provides a simplified summary of the opportunity context. It indicates how markets consist of customers (or potential customers) in need of products and services, while industry sectors consist of competitors (or potential competitors) offering products and services. One of the critical requirements in exploiting any new business idea is to gain an understanding of your customers. When you are creating a new venture,

Figure 2.5 The entrepreneurial opportunity context

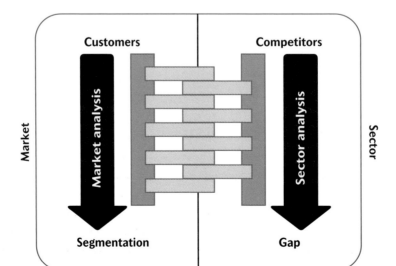

analysing the market and the sector can reveal a market segment that is currently under-served by existing firms. This represents the gap in which your venture is going to operate.

This is only the beginning of the process. As you refine your idea, continued analysis of customers and competitors can help you to maintain your focus. This will enable you to serve your customer segment in ways that satisfy their changing needs while also differentiating your venture from the competition.

2.4 Shaping the vision: a continuing challenge

In this chapter, we have considered the role of vision in the context of new venture creation. We have also looked at the complex relationship between emerging visions and more formal approaches to planning a business. We introduced the concept of opportunity business models as a technique for analysing entrepreneurial opportunities by identifying the key dimensions and drivers that underpin them. The final case in this chapter (Case 2.4), considers a critical incident in the period before a spin-out company was formed. As you read the case, think carefully about Mark Robinson's understanding of his potential customers and likely competitors. Did he identify a gap in the market, and a segment that he could target? Mark is one of ten commercial and social entrepreneurs interviewed for this book (Case 1.2). We will meet the others in the remaining Part One chapters. Together, these interviews will provide you with a variety of insights into the entrepreneurial process. Our final question to each entrepreneur was, 'What is the most important advice you would give to readers of this book?' Mark's response was to highlight the emotional aspects of entrepreneurship:

> *How passionate are they about it? How committed are they about it? Do they really want to do it? Because if they are half hearted about it I would say don't do it. It is like getting into a little boat, a little sailing boat and heading off across the Atlantic Ocean. You have no idea how many storms you're going to get, whether you'll have to bail out, the ship might sink, the mast might get snapped. You are going to feel at times very alone. Those times you have got to say, "No, I want to do this, I want to get to wherever I am heading and I will make it." If however, you prefer to travel as a fare-paying passenger on a cruise liner, where somebody comes and feeds you every day – a big ship that is safe – then that is fine too. But, you know that for some people [life as a passenger] is boring. Yes, so I would say if you really want to do it, and you are passionate about it, you will make it!'*

Each of the remaining Part One chapters builds on the previous one to take you from the entrepreneurial vision, as discussed in this chapter, to the creation of a new entrepreneurial venture. They should also help you to work through the dimensions and drivers of the opportunity business model in greater detail and highlight ways in which the different components of the model interact. In Chapter 9, we conclude Part One by reflecting of the experiences of three very different yet successful entrepreneurs.

✳ 2.5 Summary

➤ The entrepreneurial process can be represented as three linked activities: (1) generating new business ideas; (2) recognizing opportunities; (3) exploitation in enterprises.

➤ The entrepreneurial learning cycle provides a useful practical framework for developing entrepreneurial thinking.

➤ Entrepreneurs can adopt three broad approaches to shaping an entrepreneurial vision: (a) the emerging vision; (b) the traditional business plan; (c) the 'opportunity business model' (OBM).

➤ The opportunity business model is a useful approach that can be used both to shape an entrepreneurial opportunity and to articulate it more clearly to potential investors, partners, and other interested parties.

➤ When expressing an entrepreneurial opportunity as a business model, it is essential to consider the context in which you are operating. This requires research to analyse the characteristics of potential suppliers, customers, and competitors.

Case 2.4 *Critical incident*
Mark Robinson: strategy mapping business

By the end of January 2007, experienced manager **Mark Robinson** had helped his nephew's environmental management company, EnviroManage in London, achieve a good market share. He also became convinced there was an opportunity for the company to provide a generic strategy mapping application and had even developed a software prototype. But the board weren't convinced. Mark was excited about the opportunity for the new application and needed to prepare a new venture plan for presentation at the board meeting in two weeks.

Biography

Mark graduated with a degree in chemistry from the University of York in 1985, just as the first computer chips were being produced by the then fledgling semiconductor industry in Silicon Glen, Scotland. Within just five years in this rapidly expanding industry, he was promoted to departmental manager responsible for 35 highly skilled engineers designing and making microprocessors for some of the world's leading technology companies. It was not long before he was headhunted into international sales by an American company based in Silicon Valley, California. Mark adopted a completely different lifestyle: 'flying about on aeroplanes to visit the US and customers or potential customers in Europe'. After 15 years travelling the world, he was able to bring his own personal vision of opening a high technology factory in the Northwest of England into reality. In 2000, having brought a US and a UK corporation together with the UK government, he made it happen. The operation quickly became really big: 'We went from zero to $25 million in the first year'. However, following changes to the senior management structure, Mark decided to leave the company and look for a new challenge.

EnviroManage

During the late 1990s governments around the world were increasingly expecting companies to comply with international environmental management standards, such as ISO14000. In 1998 Mark's nephew decided to set up a new venture, EnviroManage, to provide environmental consulting services to companies keen to meet these new standards. It soon became apparent that EnviroManage's customers needed a software application to help them manage their environmental practices, and EnviroManage rapidly developed into a software and consultancy company. Within the context of an expanding market opportunity, Mark was soon invited to help his nephew develop the company's sales to large companies. Not surprisingly, given Mark's previous experiences, he quickly won new business with international corporations like GlaxoSmithKline, Vodafone, Orange, and even UK government departments.

EnviroManage rapidly become a well respected market leader in the environmental management sector. Mark had an unusual position in the company. He was not a director. However, being an experienced manager and the uncle of the founder and managing director gave him significant influence within the company. While EnviroManage used the Internet to support its environmental management application, it had a traditional sales model of a large initial licence fee for the use of the software and a small annual charge for maintenance and support.

Application service provision

The Internet has provided numerous entrepreneurial opportunities and many new business models emerged. Some business models, such as online retailing (http://www.amazon.com) and online marketplaces (http://www.ebay.com), even flourished. One of these new sectors consisted of software developers providing access to applications over the Internet, such as simple hosted email (http://www.hotmail.com) and highly complex hosted enterprise applications (http://www.sap.com). These application service providers (ASPs) offered software as a service, also known as hosted applications, on-demand applications, web-based applications, and cloud computing.

One such ASP, which became particularly well-known, was Salesforce.com (http://www.salesforce.com), founded in 1999 by Marc Benioff. In less than 10 years, Salesforce.com became one of the largest providers and specialized in providing its customers with sophisticated customer relationship management (CRM) applications. CRM applications were used to support sales and marketing activities, including telesales, e commerce, sales data analysis, and marketing campaigns. Organizations used these web-based applications rather than just buying the software and installing it on their own computer networks as it took less time, resources, expertise, and money. ASPs reduced costs by hosting and managing software applications centrally and providing access to remote users via web browsers or thin clients. The costs were shared across many organizations, and ASPs rented access to these applications, typically between 10% and 20% of the equivalent purchase price. Perhaps unexpectedly, early adopters were large companies rather than small- to medium-sized enterprises.

Underlying concepts and fundamental truths

Mark had spent much of his working life selling services to chief executives of large international corporations around the world. He had always been interested in the underlying concepts behind a particular issue, opportunity, or problem. 'I have a passion for physics, I have always been that way, I like to look for the underlying concepts and fundamental truths . . . If you can understand the general concepts you can deal with complexity.' He felt that while EnviroManage customers appreciated having an excellent environmental management application they had many other complex issues to deal with. After some time working in his nephew's company, Mark persuaded them to explore the development of a more generic management application, which could map an organization's strategy onto individual objectives and action plan that could be monitored over time.

Mark's previous experience as a manager in a high pressure industry had taught him that motivating individual people was the key to getting things done on time and on budget. Therefore, instead of making the office or factory the unit of analysis, he proposed that it was the individual who contributed to achieving these objectives that were central to any successful performance management system. Mark's belief was that it was 'all about people . . . the smallest atom in the unit needed to be a person not a factory'.

The board of directors consisted mainly of people with a vision to provide environmental management to make the world a greener place. However, after much persuasion and some disagreement within the board, Mark was allowed to build a software prototype of his strategy mapping application. The project used the latest web-based technologies and was designed to be delivered as a service over the Internet paid for on a subscription – in other words, rented not purchased. Perhaps not surprisingly, the prototype project attracted the interest of some of the best programmers in the company. Mark recalled that, 'The two development engineers tended to have a crowd of people around them looking over their shoulders and seeing what they were doing . . . Everyone wanted to get involved.'

Mark and his development team built a software prototype, which captured his vision of linking an organization's highest level mission to actions undertaken by individuals working towards achieving their objectives. This involved establishing a hierarchy of information and linking many objectives to the organization's mission. Mark's vision behind the prototype was for it to:

> Become the world standard for the realization of the strategy of any organization, partnership or community. By realization we mean the creation, planning and agreement of your continuously improving strategy, making it real and visible to all those involved, so that they can view what they need online at anytime via their individually configured dashboards. Using the power and economics of the web to deliver software-as-a-service business model means that there is no software or hardware to buy. One low-cost subscription covers all the people and includes system hosting, support, maintenance, help, backups, and all future enhancements.

The board reaction

Having successfully built the prototype, Mark went back to EnviroManage's board and presented the business plan for taking the new strategy mapping application to market. Some directors had previously expressed concerns about diversifying away from environmental management and even after seeing the prototype did not change their views. Mark believed that some of the directors had never actually met customers and talked to them about their real needs. Some directors viewed the prototype as a cuckoo in the nest, taking resources away from the core activity of environmental management. Furthermore, between authorizing the building of the prototype and presenting the business plan, the company had 'over reached themselves a little bit . . . They had won some fairly large contracts' and overheads had grown but 'it became apparent that it [winning large contracts] was not going to happen every month and we needed to cut back'.

Critical incident

By January 2007 the whole climate had changed. The board suggested that Mark might want to develop a new venture plan for a spin-out company taking the strategy mapping application to market under a licensing agreement with EnviroManage. This would involve taking key developers with him and agreeing which markets could be developed. 'Rather than make people redundant, I got the opportunity to take this prototype off their hands and take some of their staff with me.'

> They wanted to restrict me to the public sector for the first few years so that we weren't treading on each other's toes . . . The public sector is a massive market in the UK.

Mark decided to respond to the opportunity and planned to present his new venture plan to the board of directors in two weeks. He needed to articulate his vision in a way that would convince the board that creating a spin-out company was in both their best interests: 'In a way this could be a win-win because it was all very amicable and it could help them and help me.' In order to achieve this, he needed to think carefully about the motivation for all parties, which market sectors he could negotiate access to, and how to present his vision for the new venture in a way others could understand. He sat down to prepare his case when the phone rang . . .

Source: This case is primarily based on an interview with Mark Robinson and written by Nigel Lockett.

 ## Practical activities

1. Innovation challenge Individually or working in small groups, select any two new or emerging technologies from the list of technological drivers below. Develop a new business idea which uses both technologies and prepare a 10-minute presentation detailing your new business idea using the opportunity business model (Figure 2.2). If you are working in groups, give your

Ten technological drivers	
Broadband wireless in public spaces	Online social networks
Digital multimedia	Radio frequency identification devices
Embedded photonic crystal	Visualization
Hosted business applications	Superimposing computer graphics
Micro fuel cells	Multi-touch interfaces

presentations and follow with a discussion, identifying the strongest ideas and noting any significant weaknesses.

Further details on these emerging technologies and other examples of opportunity business model drivers can be found on the Online Resource Centre.

Online resource centre 'Emerging technologies and other drivers.'
Please visit www.oxfordtextbooks.co.uk/orc/blundel for further information.

2. Business Plan What should be in a business plan? Find three examples of business plans and compare them in order to identify the similarities and differences. Visit the website of a major international bank and see what advice they give for producing business plans?

3. Entrepreneur's perspective Arrange to interview an entrepreneur. Ask them how they came up with the idea for their business. Did they mention their own skills and experience or other people? How much of this is down to luck or being in the *right place at the right time*? What was planned and what emerged? How often do they formally review the venture plan and make changes to the business?

 ## Discussion topics

1. Using opportunity business models carry out a comparison of a successful and an unsuccessful new business idea. Develop criteria for evaluating new business ideas which would be useful for selecting entrepreneurial opportunities.

2. Why does the fashion industry have so many small innovative firms yet the automotive industry is dominated by large international corporations?

3. Compare the drivers for the Sony MiniDisc (http://www. sony.net/Fun/SH/1-21/h4.html) in the 1990s and the Apple iPod (http://www.apple.com/itunes) in the early 2000s. Can you account for their different levels of success?

 ## Further reading guide

There are many step-by-step guides to writing a business plan, including Barrow et al. (2004), Mullins (2006), and Finch (2006). We have also provided links and resources related to business plans on the Online Resource Centre. There is also a wide literature on business models, which are increasingly being seen as strategic analysis and venture generation tools. As we discussed in the chapter, the concept emerged in the late 1990s in response to the proliferation of new Internet-based ventures. Influential sources include Timmers (2000), Amit and Zott (2001), Weill and Vitale (2001), and Currie (2004). The business models literature has generated several useful frameworks, with Professor Gary Hamel becoming a particularly well-respected author in the field: Hamel (2000). By the late 2000s, the original models had been further developed and adapted by authors interested in new venture creation. Recent applications of the concept include Zott and Amit (2007), Barringer and Ireland (2008), and Osterwalder and Pigneur (2010). There are also many online resources available, including an open educational resource on managing the digital economy by Professor Michael Rappa (http://digitalenterprise.org) and a blog about innovative business models by Alexander Osterwalder (http://www.businessmodelalchemist.com).

 # References

Amit, R. and Zott, C. (2001) 'Value creation in eBusiness.' *Strategic Management Journal*, 22, 6/7: 493–520.

Apple (2010) '10 billion song countdown.' Available at http://www.apple.com/itunes/10-billion-song-countdown (accessed 27 May 2010).

Barringer, B. and Ireland, D. (2008) *Entrepreneurship: successfully launching new ventures*. Harlow: FT Prentice Hall.

Barrow, C., Tiffany, P., and Peterson, S. (2004) *Business plans for dummies*. Chichester: Wiley.

Bridge, R. (2008) *My big idea: 30 successful entrepreneurs reveal how they found inspiration*. London: The Sunday Times/Kogan Page.

Chesbrough, H. and Rosenbloom, R. S. (2002) 'The role of business model in capturing value from innovation: evidence from Xerox corporation's technology spin-off companies.' *Industrial and Corporate Change*, 11, 3: 65–73.

Currie, W. (ed.) (2004) *Value creation from e-business models*. Oxford: Butterworth-Heinemann.

Dhaliwal, S. (2008) *Making a fortune: learning from the Asian phenomenon*. Chichester: Capstone.

Economist (2007) 'Lessons from Apple: what other companies can learn from California's master of innovation.' *The Economist* (7 June).

Finch, B. (2006) *How to write a business plan*. London: Kogan Page.

Guardian (2007a) 'There is no point having a load of money unless you enjoy it.' 12 October.

Guardian (2007b) 'Springs and roundabouts.' 22 March.

Guardian (2009) 'We must tackle these false claims for domestic green power tariffs.' 9 February.

Hamel, G. (2000) *Leading the revolution: how to thrive in turbulent times by making innovation a way of life*. Boston, MA: Harvard Business School Press.

Hitt, M., Ireland, D., Camp, M., and Sexton, D. (2002) *Strategic entrepreneurship: creating a new mindset*. Oxford: Blackwell.

Lewis, M. (2001) *The new new thing: a Silicon Valley story*. London: Penguin.

Margretta, J. (2002) 'Why Business Models Matter.' *Harvard Business Review*, May: 86–92.

Morris, M., Schindehutte, M. and Allen, J. (2005) 'The entrepreneur's business model: toward a unified perspective.' *Journal of Business Research*, 58, 6: 726–35.

Mullins, J. (2006) *The new business road test: what entrepreneurs and executives should do before writing a business plan*. Harlow: FT Prentice Hall.

Osterwalder, A. and Pigneur, Y. (2004) 'An ontology for e-business models.' In W. Currie (ed.) op. cit. (65–97).

Osterwalder, A and Pigneur, Y. (2010) *Business model generation: a handbook for visionaries, game changers, and challengers*. Chichester: Wiley.

Startups (2010) 'Babylicious.' Available at http://www.startups.co.uk (accessed 27 May 2010).

Sunday Times (2004) 'How I made it: Karen Darby, founder of Simply Switch.' 22 August.

Sunday Times (2007) 'Best of times, worst of times: Sally Preston.' 18 November.

Sunday Times (2007) 'Do the right-on thing.' 1 April.

Sunday Times (2008) 'How I made it: Duncan Goose, founder of One Water.' 7 December.

Tapscott, D., Ticoll, D., and Lowe, A. (2000) *Digital capital: harnessing the power of the business web*. London: Nicholas Brealey.

Times (2007) 'Teenager's homemade jam to earn him pots of money.' 21 February.

Times (2008) 'How I made it: Perween Warsi, founder of chilled meals company S&A Foods.' 3 August.

TimesOnline (2004) 'Coca-Cola halts European Dasani launch.' 24 March.

Timmers, P. (2000) *Electronic commerce: strategies and models for business to business trading.* Chichester: Wiley.

WaterAid (2010) 'About us.' Available at http://www.wateraid.org (accessed 3 May 2010).

Weill, P. and Vitale, M. (2001) *Place to space: migrating to ebusiness models.* Boston, MA: Harvard Business School Press.

Wolfe, M. (1999) *Burn rate: how I survived the gold rush years on the Internet.* New York: Touchstone.

YouTube (2007) http://www.youtube.com/watch?v=v-OJXRTxrpk (accessed 4 May 2010).

Building low carbon communities

YouTube (2008) http://www.youtube.com/watch?v=oWAG_vGzdtU (accessed 3 May 2010).

One Water: Duncan Goose on ABC Western Australia Part one

YouTube (2009) http://www.youtube.com/watch?v=4MK9aGXJz3Y (accessed 4 May 2010).

The Entrepreneurial Exchange Conference 2009 - Karen Darby

Zott, C. and Amit, R. (2007) 'Business model design and the performance of entrepreneurial firms.' *Organization Science,* 18, 2: 181–99

Opportunities
Nurturing creativity and innovation

3

The entrepreneur believes he [or she] is right, while everyone else is wrong. Thus, the essence of entrepreneurship is being different – being different because one has a different perception of the situation.

Mark Casson, *economist*

Nobody talks of entrepreneurship as survival, but that's exactly what it is and what nurtures creative thinking.

Anita Roddick, *entrepreneur and founder of The Body Shop*

Learning outcomes

After reading this chapter you should be able to:

➤ Identify the principal forms and sources of entrepreneurial opportunity.

➤ Distinguish the different ways that opportunities are recognized, evaluated, and developed into viable business propositions.

➤ Appreciate the role and significance of creativity when creating and pursuing entrepreneurial opportunities.

➤ Appreciate the role and significance of innovation, including its complex relationship with creativity and entrepreneurship.

➤ Apply the principles and techniques identified in this chapter to pursue your own entrepreneurial opportunities in creative and innovative ways.

Case 3.1 A long way from home: from sheep to shop

The fashion industry is full of specialist retailers with each purporting to offer a unique range of clothes that will appeal to a unique group of customers. But how do such niches emerge in what seems like an already crowded market? In New Zealand, merino sheep graze on upland pastures throughout the year and 'ethical wool' from their fleeces is used in high performance textiles prized by many specialist active outdoor and sports clothing companies throughout the world. The Zque trademark, developed by the New Zealand Merino Company, provides a traceable value chain, which includes an accreditation programme that ensures environmental, social, and economic sustainability, animal welfare, and traceability (http://www.nzmerino.co.nz). While home-grown New Zealand companies, such as Ground Effect (http://www.groundeffect.co.nz), use Merino-based fabrics, the market for Merino is worldwide.

Just like the mainstream fashion industry, the active outdoor and sports clothing industry is highly competitive. Many small companies have emerged to meet the needs of customers in this increasing global niche sector. One such company is Howies, which was founded June 1995 by **David** and **Clare Hieatt** in the living room of their London flat (Howies 2010). Initially, they designed just four T-shirts and launched them in a mountain biking magazine – the T-shirts cost £30. The orders came in and the company was in business. During the next decade Howies developed into a leading designer of simple, functional, long-lasting clothes made with a concern for the environment their customers enjoyed so much in mind. In February 2007, after over a decade of independent ownership, the US footwear company Timberland (http://www.timberland.com) acquired Howies (BBC 2007). Let us consider the first two of the three critical stages of Howies story: the decision to start the company (opportunity recognition); the expansion and the move to Cardigan Bay, in Wales (growth); and the sale to Timberland (acquisition). We will also see that cutting through these are the founders' personal ethical values.

Opportunity recognition The identification of the mountain biking sector was a key factor starting the company. The founders and early staff members were passionate about biking, snowboarding, and skateboarding. They knew what their potential customers wanted: something unusual and something different. Initially, Howies sold through shops, with 45 selling their product by the end of 1999, but in 2000 they realized this business model wasn't sustainable; the decision to move into mail order, that is selling from a printed catalogue, was made and the first catalogue was produced.

Growth Space is nearly always an issue for growing firms, and Howies was no different. The company moved to commercial premises in Wales and secured a grant from the then Welsh Development Agency in 2003. Previously, the company was funded by the founders and conventional banking. Howies continued to grow by producing ethically sourced, specialist clothing for outdoor enthusiasts. The mail-order catalogue sales were increasing and were supported by e-commerce sales and the company considered moving back into retail by selling through Selfridges in London and even opening their own shops. By the end of 2005 sales were just over £2 million. Clothes were still promoted as ethically produced, both in terms of manufacturing and the textiles used, including hemp, bamboo, organic cotton (http://www.soilassocation.org), and the Zque-accredited merino wool from New Zealand. The company even moved to the ethical bank Triodos (http://www.triodos.com).

The real challenge is recognizing, of all the things you could do, which are the ones worth investing your time and money in. It is also worth noting that, once an opportunity is recognized and exploited in an enterprise, it has to be constantly reassessed.

Acquisition In early 2007 Howies was acquired by Timberland, the large US-based outdoor clothing company (http://www.timberland.com). The founders of Howies could see that in order for the company to grow to meet ever-increasing demand more working capital was required. The amount of money involved was beyond the reach of conventional funding, such as secured loans. This would either mean raising venture capital or finding a partner with similar values. David and Clare Hieatt felt that for Howies to maintain its values there was only one option. At the time of the acquisition Jeffrey Swartz, President and CEO of Timberland, said: 'We are excited and inspired by the brand potential we see in Howies and are pleased to welcome them to the Timberland family. We look to invest in like-minded brands that are focused on innovation, authenticity and integrity, and Howies encompasses all of these core values.' (BBC 2007)

Ethical point In addition to promoting environmental sustainable material such as Merino wool, hemp, bamboo, and organic cotton, the company uses only 100% renewable electricity from Good Energy (http://www.good-energy.co.uk) for its London store and in 2005 moved to ethical bank Triodos (http://www.triodos.com).

Points to consider

1. With hindsight it is often easy to see the various stages of a company's development. But is it possible for the entrepreneurs who run growing companies to see these at the time?

2. Why would a company, like Timberland, decide to buy a smaller company rather than just develop competing products and brands? Perhaps it is hard for larger companies to be entrepreneurial, or does opportunity recognition become more difficult?

3. The founders of Howies wanted to express their ethical values through their business. Was that important to their customers? Provided sales were growing and the company was profitable did it really matter?

Sources: BBC (2007); Howies (2010)

3.1 Introduction

Our opening case illustrates how David and Clare Hieatt, the founders of Howies, became convinced that they had identified a real opportunity. They began by identifying a promising target market: outdoor enthusiasts, rather like themselves. They linked these potential customers to a fairly novel business idea: retailing well-designed, high performance ethical clothing. Many people get as far as this stage, but go no further; they file their 'pet' ideas away at the back of their minds, or perhaps jot them down in a notebook, and then carry on with their existing lives. The Hieatts were different; they decided to make their dream a reality, and in the process they created what can be termed an **entrepreneurial opportunity**. As we saw, their venture proved to be extremely successful, such that Howies is now a widely recognized, premium international brand with a bright future (see Chapter 9. 'Reflections: learning from entrepreneurs' for first-hand accounts of entrepreneurial opportunities). However, it is very important to remember that *none of this was clear at the outset*. David and Clare had no way of knowing if their idea would really 'fly'. There was a very long journey to travel, and lots of work to do, before those early ideas were transformed into a real, thriving clothing business. For many other budding entrepreneurs (and intrapreneurs, i.e. **entrepreneurship** in larger firms), the story has a very different ending. Opportunities that might once have seemed very attractive turn out to be disappointing or elusive. Seemingly brilliant business ideas and bright, shiny technological inventions often fail to deliver or struggle into life only to collapse when confronted by the harsh, competitive realities of the **markets** and finances.

In this chapter we explore the concept of opportunity, the entrepreneurial opportunity in particular, and try to locate it within the broader **entrepreneurial process**. In doing so, we also examine the closely related roles of creativity and **innovation** as someone's 'bright idea' is evaluated, refined, and developed into a living, breathing entrepreneurial venture.

Opportunities are a familiar feature of everyday life, and we have all had the experience creating, exploiting and, in some cases, missing them. Sometimes the opportunity may be quite insignificant (e.g. the chance to meet a visitor for lunch), while other opportunities may have longer-lasting consequences (e.g. an offer to work abroad). Entrepreneurial opportunities are a particular type of opportunity, which could lead you to create a self-sustaining venture. The process is complex, and is closely related to two other important themes: creativity and innovation. The combination of creativity, innovation, and opportunity recognition can also result in unpredictable, and often surprising, outcomes (Figure 3.1).

Many successful ventures have developed from what would once have looked like an extremely unlikely or unpromising idea. For example, each of the following innovations has appeared in the last 20 years:

- **Products** camera phones, patio heaters, hybrid vehicles.

- **Services** social networking websites, speed-dating, 'free-cycling' unwanted products.

Figure 3.1 Opportunity, creativity, and innovation

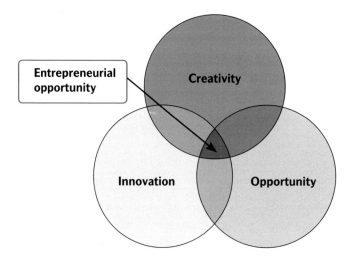

At the same time, there have been some spectacular failures, including the Sinclair C5 (a small battery-powered vehicle), the WebVan (an online grocery delivery service), and Boo. com (an online fashion clothing service). The relationships between opportunity, creativity, and innovation have been the subject of considerable debate among entrepreneurship researchers. Some of these arguments may seem very distant from the 'down to earth' world of the entrepreneur creating a new venture. However, as we shall see, they do have some important practical implications. Here are a few examples, indicating the kinds of questions we are considering in this chapter:

- Where do entrepreneurial opportunities come from?
- Why do entrepreneurs see potential opportunities differently?
- What is the importance of creativity in identifying and developing opportunities?
- How do you nurture creativity in this phase of an entrepreneurial venture?
- Why is invention not the same as innovation?
- What do entrepreneurs contribute to the innovation process?
- How do you communicate entrepreneurial opportunities effectively?

The chapter is organized as follows. In Section 3.2, we explore the concept and sources of entrepreneurial opportunities; in Section 3.3, we consider what creativity means in this context, and how you might make yourself more creative; in Section 3.4, we discuss the relationship between innovation and entrepreneurship; in Section 3.5 we consider how these come together in realizing the entrepreneurial opportunity. Three cases are used to illustrate the concepts and ideas in action: In Section 3.3, the *5-A-DAY* case highlights the link between creativity and innovation; in Section 3.4, the *Passion for chocolate* case illustrates how innovation provides entrepreneurial opportunities; at the end of Section 3.5, in the *Lucy Nicholson* case, we have the chance to consider a critical moment in the entrepreneurial process when an experienced manager identifies an opportunity and has to decide whether to go ahead.

3.2 Exploring entrepreneurial opportunity

3.2.1 A world of opportunity?

The world seems to offer limitless opportunities for the prospective entrepreneur. Yet only a small proportion of these opportunities are converted them into new ventures, and fewer still become successful and sustainable businesses. For example, the transatlantic skies are crowded with airlines competing for business class passengers. How did Richards Branson's Virgin Atlantic emerge and, despite having no track record in aviation, become an established business? At the turn of the new century, the growth of the Internet was creating opportunities for an ever-increasing number of search engines. How did two young technologists manage to develop a new service, which now dominates the Internet – and not just in its original form of searching for content but also as a vehicle for generating online adverting revenues and supplying online applications, such as Google Docs? The world is also full of opportunities for social entrepreneurs (Bornstein 2004; Young Foundation 2007). For example, consider Andrea Coleman who created an innovative new venture called 'Riders for Health'. Andrea realized that one way to improve healthcare in rural Africa was to provide health workers with access to reliable transportation. However, it also reflected her long-standing passion for motorbikes (NB for more information, including a short film by the actor Ewan McGregor, see the organization's website: http://www.riders.org). So how do you turn your interesting ideas into real entrepreneurial opportunities that are capable of supporting an entrepreneurial venture?

If you are a student embarking on a new venture creation exercise, one of your initial challenges is to make some kind of sense of what looks like an infinite number of tempting possibilities. We often see student teams almost paralysed by the amount of information that is 'out there'. So how do you decide which opportunity to pursue? In practice, the opportunities open to any particular entrepreneur, or **entrepreneurial team**, are much more limited than they might at first appear. In this section, we take a close look at entrepreneurial opportunity and try to understand how it works in practice. Our starting point is the rather abstract question: 'Are entrepreneurial opportunities objective or subjective phenomena?' In other words, are they out there in the world waiting to be discovered (objective) or are they in people's minds (subjective)? Bear with us, and you will see why your opportunities are, like those of any entrepreneur, much thinner on the ground than you might at first imagine. With these limitations in mind, we can then consider the best technique for identifying, evaluating, and developing specific opportunities into viable business propositions.

3.2.2 The nature of opportunity: exploiting 'concrete knowledge'

Why do entrepreneurial opportunities exist in the first place? The simple answer is: 'because people know different things about the world'. Some kinds of knowledge are readily accessible to all. Everyone 'knows' what day of the week it is or why it gets dark at night. However, there are other kinds, sometimes termed 'concrete' (or 'local') knowledge, that are only accessible to particular individuals and groups:

> The concrete knowledge which guides the action of any group of people never exists as a consistent and coherent body. It only exists in the dispersed, incomplete and inconsistent form in which it appears in many individual minds . . . (Hayek 1955: 29–30)

From this perspective, entrepreneurial opportunities arise because some people have access to potentially valuable concrete knowledge, which is not available to others (Section 11.3). Here are a few practical examples:

- Due to knowing so much about her local property market, Natalia is able to spot the development potential of an old warehouse that is being put up for auction.

- As Robert has developed an extensive network of suppliers in a specialist area of automobile engineering, he is able to secure first tier supplier contacts with leading manufacturers.

- With experience in both child healthcare and opto-electronics, members of a university research team are able to develop a new surgical procedure.

➡️ **PERSPECTIVES**   See section 11.3 for further information.

Of course, it is not enough to have access to the knowledge. Entrepreneurs need a combination of alertness and vision if they are to identify and exploit opportunities before they become apparent to the rest of us (Kirzner 1973). This idea is also the basis for the old saying, 'Once you can see a bandwagon, it is already too late to jump on it.' Indeed, Foss and Mahnke (2000) argue that entrepreneurship is a 'creative team act . . . which is creatively superior to individual entrepreneurship' and that entrepreneurship research should focus also on the exploitation of opportunities through group as well as individual action. So it is not only the resources an entrepreneur can access that are important but also their concrete knowledge, entrepreneurial team, and, above all, opportunity recognition. This entrepreneurial process is not a single act of an individual but a virtuous and ongoing cycle carried out by an entrepreneurial team in order to recognize, evaluate, and exploit opportunities based on this knowledge (Zahra et al. 2008).

3.2.2 Sources of opportunity: where to start looking

Though we will never be able to spot *every* possible opportunity, clearly it would help if we had a better understanding of the main sources. When you start to speak to successful entrepreneurs or read *their* own accounts of their successful ventures it becomes increasingly apparent that the sources of entrepreneurial opportunity are immensely personal. That is, they experience or perceive something which other people do not. Hundreds of thousands of people have flown across the Atlantic, but it was Richard Branson who experienced a service he was unhappy with and perceived that it could be done differently. This impulse for action, he describes as getting up 'from behind your desk' and seeing for yourself where ideas and people lead to innovation; 'the distinction between innovation and day-to-day delivery is barely noticeable and unimportant' (Branson 2008: 216). Millions of T-shirts are sold everyday, but it was David and Clare Hieatt, the founders of Howies (see Case 3.1) who saw the opportunity to produce ethically sourced and manufactured clothing for outdoor pursuits enthusiasts like themselves. When Geetie Singh opened her first organic gastro pub, the Duke of Cambridge (http://www.dukeorganic.co.uk) in London, it was only after working for many years in the restaurant business and becoming personally disillusioned by the lack of sustainability that she found the determination to change things herself. How many other people have sat in a restaurant and had similar thoughts but done nothing? So we can see that the source of the opportunity is external – a bad flight or an indifferent meal – but its perception is internal (within the entrepreneur). Instead of just complaining they seem compelled to do something about it.

Take the example of Wangari Maathai who founded the Green Belt Movement in Kenya (http://www.greenbeltmovement.org) as an environmental **social enterprise** focused on the planting of trees, conservation, and women's rights. In 2004, Wangari became the first African woman and environmentalist to receive the Nobel Peace Prize for her contribution to sustainable development, democracy, and peace. On receiving the prize she stated, 'If we conserved our resources better, fighting over them would not then occur...so, protecting the global environment is directly related to securing peace...those of us who understand the complex concept of the environment have the burden to act. We must not tire, we must not give up, we must persist.' Clearly, Wangari has a big vision but started in a simple way by focusing on planting trees, particularly indigenous and fruit trees, on farms with women groups as the main implementers. So the source of opportunities may be close at hand and can lead to unexpected consequences.

So where do we start looking? If we reflect on the previous examples the answer has to be within us. We need to experience life, in all its richness, but use our perception to seek out these opportunities – looking for new products, services, markets, suppliers, customers, technologies, and ways of organizing. The drivers that underpin these opportunities, such as climate change and demographics, are all around us, but we have to perceive them in order to see the sources of opportunity. The UK entrepreneur and well-known panel member of the BBC *Dragons' Den*, Duncan Bannatyne is clear that you find opportunities by solving problems, copying, or innovation: 'Ideas for new businesses broadly fall into three categories – those that solve a problem, those that copy another business and those spawned by genuine innovation,' and of these the latter is the most rare (Bannatyne 2008: 38).

In the next two sections, we 'complicate' the question of opportunity in two ways. First, we ask what role creativity has to play in the formation of an entrepreneurial venture, and in the pursuit of entrepreneurial opportunities in particular (Section 3.3). Secondly, we look at the relationship between entrepreneurial opportunity, creativity, and innovation (Section 3.4). It is important to stress, at the outset, that in order to help to explain entrepreneurship we appear to be describing entrepreneurship as a linear process, but do not be deceived. While a single opportunity may form the basis for a new venture, entrepreneurs are constantly pursuing new opportunities (products, markets, suppliers, and ways of organizing) and reinventing existing ones.

3.3 Creativity in entrepreneurial ventures

Creativity is found in many areas of life, including poetry, music, painting, and the performing arts. Many new entrepreneurial ventures are also intrinsically creative, in that they bring to the world something that is somehow new and original. However, **entrepreneurial activity** is not always particularly creative. For example, some successful new ventures simply imitate, or make minor adaptations to, an existing product or service, with the originality coming from other sources, such as using a different supplier, or selling into a new market (Section 5.1). Creativity is a familiar concept, but its meaning can be quite difficult to pin down. A dictionary definition suggests that creativity is the 'power or faculty; ability to create', that is 'involving the use of the imagination or original ideas to create something [new]' (Oxford English Dictionary). Creativity can be studied at many different levels (Henry 2006: ix). It is often explained by looking at cognitive (i.e. thinking) processes within individuals (Section 11.3). However, creativity is also influenced by social factors, such as the interactions between people in an entrepreneurial team (Section 4.2), or the cultures of organizations and geographic regions (Section 12.3).

In *Back to Methuselah*, the Irish playwright, George Bernard Shaw (1921), writes:

Some people see things that are and ask 'why?'
I dream of things that never were and ask, 'why not?'

→ **PERSPECTIVES** See sections 11.3 and 12.3 for further information.

We are all creative in our own way and to varying degrees: decorating our homes, making music, writing a poem, or even just compiling a text message. We all have an innate sense of individual creativity, but what role does it play in the creation of new ventures? Creativity in this phase of the entrepreneurial process is mainly concerned with the ability of entrepreneurs, managers, and firms to generate or invent new business ideas. These ideas might be related to new products, processes, services, or markets, with the first two often being referred to as inventions. However, for many reasons the vast majority of these new business ideas will not be developed beyond this conceptual stage. Of those that can be protected, a few will become formalized in a patent, and of these less than 5% will be commercialized. We can clearly see that the attrition rate is very high, but without creativity we have no innovation and without innovation no entrepreneurial opportunities. The economist Joseph Schumpeter recognized the role of the entrepreneur in finding these 'new combinations' that enable new ventures to form (Section 11.3). He argued that entrepreneurial activity drives a cycle of '**creative destruction**' in which established organizations can become undermined by new entrants if they fail to maintain their innovative drive. Innovation researchers have built on these ideas in order to explore how creativity operates in the context of innovation and entrepreneurship:

The making and communicating of meaningful new connections to help us think of many possibilities; to help us think and experience in varied ways and using different points of view; to help us think of new and unusual possibilities; and to guide us in generating and selecting alternatives. (Tidd et al. 2005: 174)

→ **PERSPECTIVES** See section 11.3 for further information.

Creative ideas have to be both new and appropriate (Henry 2001). But, what does appropriate mean for entrepreneurial opportunities? Of course, being creative is another matter and this will depend on individual characteristics, including ability, mental skill, relevant experience, intrinsic motivation, and the context. Put more simply, creativity is about generating and articulating new ideas, new things, new processes, or new markets. This could be achieved using a range of techniques or even happen by chance – simply being in the right place at the right time with the right idea.

We have seen that creativity is important, but what is the relationship with new venture creation and how do enterprise continue to be creative? The *5-A-DAY* case (Case 3.2), shows how one firm, Innocent Smoothies, responded creatively to the increasing need and desire for people to eat healthily but in a convenient and exciting way. Health experts and governments recognized the need to do something about this; however, we will see how one company emerged to respond to this societal health driver, while large existing companies did not. This can also be seen as an example of Schumpeter's 'creative destruction' in action.

Case 3.2 5-A-DAY: squeezing the most from entrepreneurial opportunities

Everywhere we look, there is an expert ready to tell us what we can and can't eat, what is good for us and what isn't (http://www.5aday.nhs.uk). Sometimes it all seems a bit too much! But there is one message that remains consistent – eating more fruit and vegetables is vital for good health. According to research, the average person is eating considerably less than the recommended five pieces of fruit and vegetables a day (5-A-DAY). This is even lower among young people. So how are entrepreneurs responding creatively to the opportunities that are emerging from this health imperative?

The last decade has seen a huge growth in the fresh fruit-based drinks market (smoothies) in the UK. This trend has largely been led by small entrepreneurial firms, such as The Juice Company founded by Josephine Beach in 1999 (http://www.thebigj.com) and Innocent Drinks founded by **Richard Reed, Adam Balon,** and **Jon Wright** also in 1999 (http://www.innocentdrinks.co.uk). Not surprisingly, both companies have a strong 'look after your health' ethos for their products, but additionally Innocent Drinks has strong ethical values expressed through its commitment to sustainable packaging, carbon footprint reduction, and the Innocent Foundation, which supports building sustainable agricultural communities mostly in countries where Innocent Drinks sources its fruit (http://www.innocentfoundation.org). Clearly, these entrepreneurial individuals had the creativity to invent new drinks based on their own personal values; and they also identified a growing consumer need or demand they addressed by forming companies. By 2008 they supplied the majority of the £280 million smoothies sector in the UK. The smoothies sector was the fastest growing segment of the £1 billion pure fruit juice market in 2008 (Mintel 2008). This entrepreneurial opportunity was successfully exploited not by an existing incumbent, such as Tropicana (http://www.tropicana.co.uk), part of PepsiCo (http://www.pepsico.com) since 1998, or Del Monte (http://www.delmonte.com), but by new enterprises.

Creativity It is potentially quite revealing if we look more closely at Innocent Drinks. The company seems to have maintained its creativity throughout its short history. The product range is increasing from simply smoothies (based on fruit) to drinks including live probiotic yoghurt, foods rich in specific nutrients, and, more recently, portions of vegetables. The company now even produces pure orange juice – seemingly, in direct competition to the large corporates. Interestingly the company also appears to be creative in the way it sources its packaging, claiming that all smoothie bottles are made from 100% recycled plastic, thus showing them to be a resource-efficient business (Innocent 2010a).

Ethical point Innocent Drinks gives 10% of its annual profits go to charity, primarily the Innocent Foundation (Innocent 2010b).

Questions

1. Why was the smoothies market sector exploited by small entrepreneurial firms rather than the larger existing fruit juice suppliers? What was the role of creativity?

2. How would you describe the business model of Innocent Drinks and how does it differ from that of Del Monte? What are the drivers (imperatives) for this entrepreneurial opportunity?

3. What strategy would you recommend for an existing fruit juice supplier wishing to enter the smoothies market sector?

Sources: Mintel (2008); Innocent (2010a); Innocent (2010b).

The *5-A-DAY* case also serves as a reminder of how difficult it is for the incumbent firms to innovate and exploit entrepreneurial opportunities. In some cases, even when large firms successfully innovate, the entrepreneurial managers involved have to operate outside the normal management structures until recognition is achieved; for example, the development of IBM's e-business services and Shell's renewable energy divisions (Hamel 2000). From this, we can see that the recognition and subsequent exploitation of entrepreneurial opportunities in enterprises is vital.

3.4 Innovation and entrepreneurship

3.4.1 What is innovation?

Creativity may be required to identify the new business ideas but how do you select between competing ideas and subsequently develop your chosen idea to the point of exploitation in a new entrepreneurial venture? That is the role of innovation.

Innovation is popularly defined as 'the introduction of novelties; the alteration of what is established by the introduction of new elements or forms'. In commercial terms, it's described as 'the action of introducing a new product into the market; a product newly brought to the market' and the action or process of innovating as making 'changes in something established, especially introducing a new methods, ideas or products' (Oxford English Dictionary).

Innovation, as defined by Porter (1990), 'can be manifested in a new product design, a new production process, a new marketing approach, or a new way of conducting training' and linked to companies achieving competitive advantage. Porter also argues that much of innovation is 'mundane and incremental, depending more on an accumulation of small insights and advances than on a single, major technological breakthrough'. Drucker (2007 [1985]: 17) goes further to link innovation to entrepreneurship as the 'specific tool of entrepreneurs, the means by which they exploit change as an opportunity for a different business or service'. This definition reflects our interest in the role that innovation can play in an entrepreneurial venture. We discuss the broader implications of entrepreneurship, innovation, and economic development in Chapters 11 and 14.

➡ **PERSPECTIVES** See sections 11.4 and 14.3 for further information.

In the context of entrepreneurship, innovation is best thought of as the way in which new business ideas – be they new products, processes, services, or markets – are recognized and developed as potential entrepreneurial opportunities. Clearly it is not a new phenomenon but one that is at the root of human, societal, and economic development. It differs from inventions or new business ideas in one key respect: the attempt to put them into practice, implemented, and, in the view of some, to be commercially exploited (Fagerberg et al. 2004; Parsons and Rose 2009). More recently what has become increasingly important is the ability of firms to consciously, deliberately, and continuously innovate (Christensen 1997; Hamel 2000; Christensen and Raynor 2003; Christensen et al. 2004). It could be argued that is it not the innovation itself that results in an entrepreneurial opportunity but the way in which it is utilized to provide new products, processes, services, and markets, which result in added value to the customer or competitive advantage in markets.

Government and industry alike stress the importance of innovation to both the economy and society. The UK Government Innovation Report (DTI 2003), which defined innovation as the successful exploitation of new ideas, stated:

> *Innovation matters because it can deliver better products and services, new, cleaner and more efficient production processes and improved business models ... for the economy as a whole innovation is the key to higher productivity and greater prosperity for all.*

What types of innovation have been identified? Francis and Bessant (2005) proposed the 4Ps of innovation product, process, position, and paradigm, with characteristic ranges from incremental vs radical, component vs system to product vs service (Figure 3.2). This can be a useful framework to map out ideas for new ventures, and to help identify the type or types of innovation that you may be using.

The concept of innovation has become a powerful metaphor for both entrepreneurs and large firms alike. For example, Hewlett Packard, the international information technology, imaging, and printer provider (http://www.hp.com), recently reinvented its image by moving from 'Hewlett Packard' to 'HP Invent' in order to signify its renewed focus of innovation exploitation. Like many large companies, such as SAP (SAP Labs) and Alcatel-Lucent (Bell Laboratories), it has its own research facilities located in HP Labs across the world (http://www.hpl.hp.com). Indeed one way to determine how innovative a firm is could be to measure the number of new products and services are developed in-house or even what percentage of current sales or profit come from products launched in the last five years. 3M (http://www.3m.com) endeavours to serve its global customers and communities with innovative products and

Figure 3.2 Types of innovation

Type	Changes in	Examples
Product	Product/service offered	Apple's iPod (product) and iTunes (service)
Process	How they are created and delivered	Dell's built-to-order manufacturing process
Position	The way they are introduced to market	Amazon's online store
Paradigm	Underlying business models	eBay's online marketplace
Incremental	Small improvements to product/service	Increased hard disk storage capacity
Radical	New product/service	Digital cameras vs photographic film
Component	Improvement to a part of product/service	Increase in LCD display definition and clarity
System	Improvement affecting all product/service	Introduction of plasma displays
Product	New product	Apple's iPod
Service	New service	Apple's iTunes

Source: Developed from Francis and Bessant (2005).

services. In its Annual Report 2007, entitled 'Leading through Innovation', the company states that, 'without innovation we will not grow' and 'because we are investing both our resources and energy, innovation is again alive and well all across 3M' (2007: 1).

Innovations are not solely based on new technologies. Social innovation involves the introduction of new social practices, activities, or ways of organizing. Examples of social innovation that have been influential in recent years include:

- **Car sharing schemes**, where people find a work colleague who lives locally and share the commuting journey, reducing costs and carbon emissions.
- **Book clubs**, where readers meet up on a regular basis to share their ideas about a book they have been reading.
- **Raves**, where people come together for large, all-night dance parties that are often organized in unusual, and occasionally illegal, locations.

Social innovation is now seen as an important way to tackle economic, social, and environmental challenges. This is creating many new opportunities for entrepreneurs to make a difference by turning new ideas into a reality:

The results of social innovation are all around us. Self-help health groups and self-build housing; telephone help lines and telethon fundraising; neighbourhood nurseries and neighbourhood wardens; Wikipedia and the Open University; complementary medicine, holistic health and hospices; microcredit and consumer cooperatives; charity shops and the fair trade movement; zero carbon housing schemes and community wind farms; restorative justice and community courts. All are examples of social innovation – new ideas that work to meet pressing unmet needs and improve peoples' lives. (Young Foundation 2007: 7)

Technologies often have a role to play in a social innovation, but they are not necessarily the primary source of the innovation. Therefore, what are the sources of innovation? Drucker (2007 [1985]) mentions eight sources for innovation opportunity as part of what he called 'purposeful innovation' (Figure 3.3).

In the case of social innovation, the key to identifying the best ideas is for innovators to get out into the world and in direct contact with people, to ask good questions, and to find out for themselves what needs to be done:

Some of the best innovators spot needs which are not being adequately met by the market or the state. They are often good at talking and listening, digging below the surface to understand peoples' needs and dislocations, dissatisfactions and 'blockages.' (Young Foundation 2007: 22)

Figure 3.3 Sources of innovation

Source	Example
Internal	
1. The unexpected	i) Success ii) Failure iii) Outside event
2. Incongruities	i) Incongruous economic realities ii) Between reality and the assumptions about it iii) Between perceived and actual customer value and expectations iv) Within the rhythm or logic of a process
3. Process need	
4. Industry and market structures	i) Automobile story ii) Opportunity iii) When industry structure changes
External	
5. Demographics	i) Demographics
6. Changes in perception, meaning, and mood	i) Glass is half full ii) Problem of timing
7. New knowledge	i) Characteristics of knowledge-based innovation (convergences) ii) What knowledge-based innovation requires iii) Unique risks (shakeout and receptivity gamble)
Additional	
8. Bright idea	

Source: Developed from Drucker (2007 [1985])

Innovation can be a source of entrepreneurial opportunity in all kinds of organizations, large and small, and in the private, public, and voluntary sectors. However, there are significant differences in the ways that organizations manage the process. For example, in the case of Apple's iPhone and iTunes products (http://www.apple.com), new technologies were developed and exploited within a single firm. By contrast, some large firms choose to obtain their innovations from third parties. Examples include Timberland's acquisition of Howies (Case 3.1) and the Coca Cola Company's 2009 purchase of a minority share of Innocent Drinks. There are also many collaborative, network-based, approaches to innovation in which organizations and individuals work together to develop new ideas (e.g. Seely Brown and Hagel 2006; Conway and Steward 2009) (Section 4.3).

Having outlined some essential features of innovation, we now need to consider how to harness creativity and innovation effectively in order to generate new business ideas. There are a number of important questions to address. For example, how do we identify which ideas have the potential to be genuinely entrepreneurial opportunities? Here, one of the main criteria is whether the resulting venture is going to be 'sustainable'. For some entrepreneurs, this may mean little more than it being financially viable (i.e. in terms of cashflow, profits and capital growth), and therefore capable of providing a return on the initial investment. However, there are also issues related to social and environmental sustainability (e.g. will it provide safe and secure employment opportunities?; will it reduce or minimize environmental impacts?). Today, entrepreneurs need to consider all three elements of sustainability as part of the innovation process. For example, many large businesses are responding to environmental challenges, such as global warming, with innovative technologies. For example, car manufacturers are designing smaller vehicles with more fuel efficient engines, such as Volkswagen's 'Blue Motion' range (http://www.volkswagen.co.uk/bluemotion), while some new ventures are being created to market vehicles powered by electricity (http://www.revaindia.com). There appears to be no shortage of innovation but how do entrepreneurs or entrepreneurial companies decide which ideas are worth developing? What is the role of risk in these decisions?

3.4.2 Linking innovation and creativity

People sometimes find it difficult to make a clear distinction between creativity and innovation (Conway and Steward 2009: 8-10). We tend to think of innovation as beginning with a dramatic burst of creativity, which gives rise to new ideas and inventions (Section 12.3). However, many questions remain. For example:

- How is a creative ideas developed into a fully-fledged innovation?

- Why do so many ideas fail to get beyond the drawing board?

- Can we identify a distinctively 'entrepreneurial' role in this process?

One way of addressing these questions is to picture the entrepreneurial role as a kind of bridge between creativity and innovation. Entrepreneurs translate ideas and inventions into practice, modifying them where necessary and rejecting those that are either technically weak or lacking in credibility. In some cases, the same people manage to occupy the role of the idea generator or inventor and that of the entrepreneur. However, there are also many examples in which the roles are taken by several members of an entrepreneurial team (Section 4.2). Figure 3.4 is a simplified illustration, distinguishing between these roles, and suggesting one of the ways that they might be combined.

Figure 3.4 Creativity, innovation and the entrepreneurial role

Creativity	Entrepreneurial role	Innovation
Generating new ideas	Translating ideas into practice	Realisation of new ideas
After 10 years working in the fashion industry, including some work with an organic cotton supplier, Katherine has the idea of developing a more environmentally-friendly approach to dry cleaning. It could have remained no more than an idea but, by chance, she meets a materials scientist and the pair manage to develop a new cleaning technology. Katherine's idea has now become an invention, but they are not sure how it should be commercialised.	The inventors realise that they need someone else in their team who is capable of championing the idea. They develop a relationship with an experienced technology entrepreneur who has an interest in the natural environment. The entrepreneur helps to evaluate and refine the concept, secure the intellectual property rights, research the market, develop a business model, and build links with suppliers, regulators and other important contacts.	The dry cleaning venture is launched with five directly managed outlets in major cities. The business expands in the home country using a franchising model, and the technology is subsequently licensed for use in other countries. The new venture faces competition from powerful incumbent businesses, prompting a number of operational and strategic changes. However, over a period of time, the venture grows and the technology is widely disseminated.

Source: Fictional illustration drafted by the authors.

From much of the media coverage of new inventions, it might seem that the key lesson is to focus your attention on the most creative new ideas and those with the greatest potential for innovation. However, there is no guarantee that such a combination will end in success. For example, the Apple Newton, a digital personal organizer launched in 1992 met both of these criteria, being highly innovative and displaying a great deal of creativity on the part of its designers. Despite this, the Newton was replaced within one year by a series of alternative products (i.e. MemoPads), which were themselves withdrawn after a few years. In this case, there was a happy ending. A decade later, the company launched a new kind of digital organizer, the Apple iPhone; unlike its predecessors, this innovative product has proved to be highly successful.

At this point, some readers may be wondering if there is any chance of identifying an entrepreneurial opportunity that can support a new venture. However, it may be reassuring to know that many highly creative and innovative ideas emerge from what might be described as 'everyday experiences'. As in the case of social innovations (Section 3.4.1), think about the contact you have with other people, perhaps waiting in a queue in a shop or overcoming a difficulty at work. Also, while watching the news or reading a paper, consider events in their wide context: are there any trends?

3.4.3 Entrepreneurs and innovation

Having considered the sources of creativity and innovation and the relationship between them, we need to identify the role of the entrepreneur in this process. It is often thought that entrepreneurs are the agents, who help to convert an invention into an innovation and then exploit this innovation in an enterprise. In terms of Majaro, they can certainly help to shift things towards the top left corner (Figure 3.4). Innovation generally means taking the idea to market and, in many cases, building a new organization around it that is capable of operationalizing it. Sometimes, the role of inventor and entrepreneur are combined in one individual. James Dyson is a well-known example, but this is not the norm (http://www.dyson.co.uk) (Case 10.4).

Some inventors can become highly influential people without necessarily creating a company to exploit their inventions. Examples include Tim Berners-Lee, the inventor of the World Wide Web, and Linus Torvalds, who helped to develop the Linux operating system (http://www.linux.org). Perhaps more commonly, entrepreneurs and inventors form teams in order to combine their distinctive strengths. For example, Jenny is an engineering design graduate who has invented a simple movement-sensing device, which operates through conventional electrical wiring. One evening Jenny meets Maryam at a friend's party. Maryam is a graduate in marketing with a few years' experience in an international management consultancy and has contacts in a venture capital firm that specializes in new technologies. Together they are able to raise the funds, from family and friends, to develop five demonstrators, which they lend to a local security firm who specialize in large buildings, such as hospitals. The device enables them to monitor movement patterns in the hospital centrally and reduce the number of security staff at night as well as providing a better service to the hospital. Armed with letters of support from both the security firm and the hospital, Maryam and Jenny are able to develop a business plan and raise venture capital funding to start their business.

Chocolate is a favourite treat for many people, but it is also widely available in many different forms, and the industry is well established with a number of large confectionery companies. How can you create an innovation based on such a familiar product? And how can a passion for chocolate provide the basis for a real business opportunity? In the following case, we examine the relationship between creativity, innovation, and entrepreneurial opportunity (Case 3.3).

Case 3.3 Passion for chocolate: new business opportunities from a long-standing love affair

The ever-increasing love affair with chocolate dates back centuries and takes many forms. Today, the industry is dominated by large companies, such as Mars, Cadbury Schweppes (Kraft Foods), and Nestlé (ICCO 2008), yet supports a range of more specialist chocolate confectioners, such as Green & Black's, now owned by Cadbury Schweppes (http://www.greenandblacks.com), Thorntons (http://www.thorntons.co.uk), and Hotel Chocolat (http://www.hotelchocolat.co.uk). In such a well-established and crowded market it might seem difficult to create a new way of exploiting our passion for chocolate. Hotel Chocolat (formerly ChocExpress) was founded in 1993 as a catalogue-based company in the UK (Barber 2010).

- **Creativity Angus Thirlwell** and **Peter Harris** had the idea that some people might prefer to buy and receive delivery of chocolates from the comfort of their own homes. More than that, they might want also to buy specialized chocolates that they could not buy easily from retail shops.

- **Innovation** Sourcing and selecting the best chocolates made from premium wholesome ingredients from specialized chocolatiers from across Europe and offering these as a mail-order service was an innovative idea.

Entrepreneurial opportunity Not only was the idea creative and innovative, customers loved it and kept coming back for more. Over the last 15 years the business has grown significantly yet still retained the founders' ethical principles based on a fair price to cocoa bean growers. Interestingly, Hotel Chocolat has continued to look creatively for entrepreneurial opportunities; it now has over 30 stores in the UK and was awarded Emerging Retailer of the Year by Retail Week in 2007. The company also owns a cocoa plantation in St Lucia and has created an innovative chocolate tasting club. The Chocolate Tasting Club (http://www.chocs.co.uk) offers monthly deliveries of new chocolate selections, which customers then score, creating a loyal customer base passionate about chocolate. Hotel Chocolat is a good example of creativity being applied to business idea generation (i.e. the tasting club), opportunity recognition (i.e. being used to support its existing catalogue-based sales), and exploitation in an enterprise (i.e. developing a complementary brand and new income stream within the main business operation).

Ethical Point Hotel Chocolat has developed what they call a unique ethical approach with cocoa plantations in St Lucia and Ghana (Hotel Chocolat 2010).

Questions

1. Considering how competitive the chocolate market is, why do you think Hotel Chocolat have been able to become established and expand their channels to market?

2. Compare Hotel Chocolat (http://www.hotelchocolat.co.uk) with other catalogue-based companies in the UK, such as Healthspan (http://www.healthspan.co.uk) and I Want One of Those (http://www.iwantoneofthose.com). What are the similarities and differences?

3. What other markets would you recommend Hotel Chocolat to consider developing and why? Who are likely to be their main competitors?

Sources: Barber (2010); Hotel Chocolat (2010); ICCO (2010).

3.5 Realizing entrepreneurial opportunity

We can see from the examples in this chapter that in the context of entrepreneurship, the process of innovation is the generation of new business ideas, through creativity, (*idea generation*) and the subsequent selection and development (*opportunity recognition*) of those with the potential for *exploitation in enterprises*. It is through this entrepreneurial process that entrepreneurs and entrepreneurial managers exploit entrepreneurial opportunities in existing businesses, new ventures, or social enterprises (*enterprises*) in order to add value to the customer or gain competitive advantage in markets (Figure 3.5).

As we warned at the beginning of this chapter, the entrepreneurial process diagram indicates the relationship between creativity, innovation, and the entrepreneurial process, but it is highly simplified and does not reflect the holistic and circular nature of entrepreneurship. Exploiting entrepreneurial opportunities is not a single one-off action but a continuous process of reflection and change. How conscious are entrepreneurs of their engagement in such a process? They often describe their success as being based much more on an intrinsic 'gut feel' rather than the result of a deliberate process. Perhaps this should not be too surprising given the intrinsically people- and team-focused nature of entrepreneurship.

But in all this focus on processes it is important that we remember the importance of serendipity, chance, or just old fashioned good luck. When asked, entrepreneurs will often

Figure 3.5 The entrepreneurial process

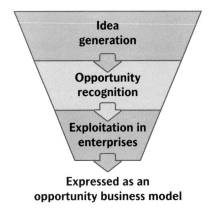

recall a lucky incident or break. For example, Duncan Bannatyne describes in his autobiography how the impetus to start the chain of health clubs came about by accident (Bannatyne 2007: 202). Similarly the late Anita Roddick, founder of Body Shop (http://www.thebodyshop.co.uk), describes how the decision to open a shop was partly born out of her decision not to go back to the 'gruelling business of running a restaurant' (Roddick 2005: 36).

In this chapter, we have seen how innovations can be in products, processes, services, or markets and their exploitation achieved in a wide range of enterprises. And while, quite rightly, this chapter highlighted new technology as a potential source of creativity and innovation, it also considered broader sources of innovation and examples of exploitation in new ventures, existing businesses, and social enterprises. We have defined both creativity and innovation and considered their relationship with the entrepreneurial process.

The final case in this chapter (Case 3.4), provides us with a chance to consider a critical moment in the entrepreneurial process. In this case Lucy Nicholson, an experienced entrepreneur, identifies several entrepreneurial opportunities for her food and catering business that she considers worth pursuing. Entrepreneurship is often about courageous people with ideas, or as Lucy puts it:

> There is a saying that I love that I think is really very true and that is 'being brave doesn't make you live longer but lacking courage means you never live at all' – that is very true. People always say 'You're so lucky!' but I don't think I am lucky. I have made that luck. I have had opportunities and had people who supported those opportunities. But being able to recognize how to empower other people is a fantastic, fantastic feeling.

Lucy also has some personal advice to potential entrepreneurs:

> If somebody was going to go into this kind of business, think very carefully about it. Be really, really careful. Is it really what you want to do? Can you really commit yourself 110% to it? If you can't, it is not the business for you. It is massive. It is your partner, it is your life and you can't just turn your back on it. You have got to keep changing it. Change is very big in this business. Keeping it different, keeping it fresh, and keeping it vibrant.

✳ 3.6 Summary

➤ Creativity, innovation, and opportunity are at the heart of entrepreneurial opportunities. Understand the nature of creativity and sources of innovation that become concrete knowledge and real opportunities.

➤ In the entrepreneurial process, creativity involves the generation of new business ideas, which through the process of innovation are developed into entrepreneurial opportunities that can be exploited in enterprises.

➤ Innovations can be in products, processes, services, or markets. Social innovations involve changes in everyday practices and are often designed to satisfy unmet needs.

➤ Entrepreneurs draw on various sources of innovation, both within and beyond the organization. Some innovations, including many social innovations, emerge as a result of direct personal experiences.

➤ **Entrepreneurial creativity** can be developed through a combination of individual factors, related to psychology and cognition, and social factors, such as the membership of your venture team.

Case 3.4 *Critical incident*
Lucy Nicholson: food for thought

By offering specialist and local food **Lucy Nicholson** had built a successful delicatessen located in the beautiful English Lake District. She wanted to expand her business operations and dreamt of opening a café or restaurant, providing outside catering services, or running a cookery school. In May 2006 the shop next door became vacant, and her landlord offered to buy it and rent it to her. Lucy needed to decide whether this was the right opportunity before someone else brought the shop.

Biography

Lucy was a daughter of a farming family in the heart of the beautiful Warwickshire countryside, and her father ran a successful dairy and milk processing business. By the 1960s he had a fleet of milk carts delivering to 750,000 homes in the Midlands. Lucy joked, 'So I always say I was the daughter of a milkman,' and reflected, 'both my father and my mother were quite entrepreneurial and quite creative as well.' Even though Lucy was surrounded, in one form or another, by business activities she was determined to go to drama school and go on the stage. However, on leaving drama school she took a temporary job in an advertising agency, she recalled: 'What I absolutely loved doing was meeting people and talking about all sorts of different things.' So Lucy never became an actress, and after a successful career in advertising she relocated to Cumbria and started a family. But when her daughter developed leukaemia and required extensive hospital treatment, Lucy decided to reassess her own life: 'I love food. I had also developed an interest in alternative style food that people required on a restricted diet, for example, things like gluten or dairy free.' But it was not just a passion for food that convinced her to open the delicatessen: 'The other thing I was fascinated by was the stories behind the food so I was very interested in why people started their businesses. What drove them, what drove somebody to make fabulous goat's milk cheese.' Lucy had personal values that underpinned her business: 'I do believe firmly that we are custodians for the future. There is a lovely poem that is called "How long is a man remembered for?" He is or she is remembered for as long as somebody holds the memory of their voice, their smile, their laughter, their songs.'

Lucy's specialist grocers

Early on in the life of the delicatessen, Lucy realized that the suppliers of local food were skilled at producing high quality food but had little experience marketing them. She recalled: 'Very often what happens is people who create lovely products are not marketers. Very much like artists they design, draw . . . it is like a baby to them so letting it go is quite hard.' The ability to find, select, and promote high quality food, not just from Cumbria but also globally, soon became a trade for Lucy's Specialist Grocers: 'I realise now over the last few years that yes we have become a brand, yes we are very much in the front of the market place and we trail blaze lots of different things.' This approach attracted customers from all over the UK and more widely. Lucy realized that selling food was increasingly also about good service: 'So people would come in and we would chat about food and different things. Somebody might say I am finding it really hard to get black cardamom pods. That was like a red rag to a bull to me; that is my challenge for the week.'

For Lucy, running a successful business brought its own challenges, including managing finance and building a management team. She recalls: 'Finance is a big headache, massive, and I think people look at you and they have a perception that you are this multimillionaire. What they don't realize is that in order to get to where we have got to and not give up, and there are many times I could have thrown in the towel and thought this is just too hard, I just cannot get through this next barrier, I just want to go away and do something a lot easier.' But, Lucy's determination to succeed was strong: 'I think being in business is massively lonely. I am a sole director so I am a sole trader although it is a limited company. I think it is hugely important to ask for help and it may be women are much better at doing that than men are. My fear of failure is great I wouldn't even consider the F word in terms of business because I can't bear it. I would rather die than let my people, my suppliers, my client, my customers, my staff down.' To help support her, Lucy built a management team she could rely on: 'We have developed the team by recognizing the people that we want to work with rather than those that we don't and understanding the art of delegation. I still like to know what is going on but I have learnt to put the monkey back on somebody else's shoulder. So instead of all the problems being deposited at my door, the team that we have created understand that they bring me solutions.'

Options

Having established her 'Specialist Grocers' as a thriving delicatessen, Lucy felt ready for a new challenge and was not short of ideas: 'I have to learn to harness a lot of that creativity. I would love to just open a business every month with somebody. That would just be my idea of heaven really.' Even though Lucy was not a qualified chef, she considered opening a café, tearoom, restaurant, bistro, outside catering, and even a cookery school. Clearly Lucy had creativity and determination together with experience of managing finance and building strong management teams, which resulted in loyal staff and customers. However, it was her passion for food that underpinned all her ideas. She explored her options and developed plans to take them forward, but how could she decide between them? Each seemed attractive in its own way. Each had advantages and disadvantages.

However, Lucy was not alone: 'I have got a very good business advisor. She is a colleague really, a very good colleague now and she and I have worked together for eight years and that was another good move. So I did have somebody with whom I could bounce ideas off, but actually there were times perhaps when both of us were too creative for our own good and we should probably have had somebody going "Stop!"'

Critical decision

In May 2006, Lucy was approached by her existing landlord for Lucy's Specialist Grocers. She remembers the meeting well: 'The property next door went onto the market in 2006, it was owned by Cumbria Wildlife Trust. My landlords asked me if they bought the premises would I be interested in taking on the lease?'

Lucy recalled one of her favourite sayings: 'I think it is really very true and that is "being brave doesn't make you live longer but lacking courage means you never live at all". You know people always say you are so lucky. I don't think I am lucky, I think I have made that luck. I think I have had opportunities and I have had people who have supported those opportunities and helped but recognizing empowering other people is a fantastic, fantastic feeling."

Lucy and her advisor sat down to run through the options one more time when the phone rang. It was her landlord to say that the estate agent had received an offer on the shop.

Source: This case is primarily based on an interview with Lucy Nicholson and written by Nigel Lockett.

 ## Practical activities

1. Creativity We know that being creative is important for entrepreneurship. Think about creative people you know personally or have read about. What common behaviours do they exhibit? They might be optimistic, positive, passionate, determined, focused, problem solvers, imaginative, but which of these are important to creativity? Imagine you had a sack containing five random objects, says a teddy bear, blank CD-RW, toothbrush, bag of sawdust, and a pair of old shoes. Pick any one of these, and see how many business ideas you can think of in five minutes. Get someone else to do this with the same object and compare your results. Which ideas are the same, which ones are already businesses, and which do you both agree are the best ideas worth exploring further?

2. Autobiography Read an autobiography of a successful business person and prepare a short five-minute presentation exploring three successes and one failure. Try to highlight some of the key characteristics of the person you think have contributed to their success. Are these characteristics unique, or could they be learnt or copied? What have they learnt from failure? Try to compare these with other people's reviews of different autobiographies. What are the differences and similarities?

3. Disruptive technologies Analyse the most recent edition of the *Economist's Technology Quarterly Review* (http://www.economist.com/science/tq) in order to identify disruptive technologies, *innovations*, that could create new products, services, or markets. Consider how long it might take for these to come to market? Research which existing companies are best placed to take advantage of these and investigate their websites and annual reports to see if these disruptive technologies are mentioned.

 ## Discussion topics

1. Discuss what characteristics creative people have and see if you can agree which are the three most relevant characteristics of creativity for entrepreneurship.

2. 3M (http://www.3m.com) are seen as an innovative technology company. How can we make such a judgement? Who might be their biggest competitor and how innovative are they?

3. Is acquisition by a large firm the most likely fate for successful business ideas exploited in new ventures? Compare Green and Blacks (http://www.greenandblacks.com), Howies (http://www.howies.co.uk), and WebEx (http://www.webex.com) with Dyson (http://www.dyson.co.uk) and Dell (http://www.dell.com).

 ## Further reading guide

The suggestions for further reading below are divided into three themes, namely collections of academic research, authored books, and finally biographies and autobiographies. The best collections for innovation and entrepreneurship research are the *Oxford Handbook of Innovation* edited by **Fagerberg et al. (2005)** and the *Oxford Handbook of Entrepreneurship* edited by **Casson et al. (2008)**. These are substantial scholarly works spanning a wide range of issues and themes. Among the most relevant research-based books and texts on innovation are **Conway and Steward (2009)**, **Christensen (1997)**, **Christensen and Raynor (2003)**, **Drucker (2007 [1985])**, **Hamel (2000)**, and **Tidd and Bessant (2009)**. There are many popular books on creativity, and an exploration of this wide subject could begin with **Henry (2001, 2006)**. The list of biographies and autobiographies of successful entrepreneurs and innovators seems ever increasing, but among those worth reading for themes covered in this chapter are **Dyson (2003)**, **Branson (1999)**, and **Bannatyne (2007)**. There are also many relevant articles in journals such as *Journal of Business Venturing, International Small Business Journal, Industry and Innovation, Research Policy, International Journal of Entrepreneurial Behaviour and Research*, and *International Journal of Entrepreneurship and Innovation*.

References

3M (2007) *Leading through innovation, Annual Report 2007*. St Paul, MN: 3M.

Bannatyne, D. (2007) *Anyone can do it: my story*. London: Orion Publishing Group.

Bannatyne, D. (2008) *Wake up and change your life*. London: Orion Publishing Group.

Barber M. (2010) 'Building a brand: Hotel Chocolat', *Growing Business Magazine*, 17 February 2010.

BBC (2007) 'Timberland buys "green" company', 13 February 2007.

Bornstein, D. (2004) *How to change the world: social entrepreneurs and the power of new ideas*. New York: Oxford University Press.

Branson, R. (1999) *Losing my virginity: the autobiography*. London: Virgin Books.

Branson, R. (2008) *Business stripped bare: adventures of a global entrepreneur*. London: Virgin Books.

Casson, M., Yeung, B., Basu, A., and Wadeson, N. (2008) *Oxford handbook of entrepreneurship*. Oxford: Oxford University Press.

Christensen, C. (1997) *The innovator's dilemma: when new technologies cause great firms to fail*. Boston, MA: Harvard Business School Press.

Christensen, C. and Raynor, M. (2003) *The innovator's solution: creating and sustaining successful growth*. Boston, MA: Harvard Business School Press.

Christensen, C., Roth, E., and Scott, A. (2004) *Seeing what's next: using theories of innovation to predict industry change*. Boston, MA: Harvard Business School Press.

Conway, S. and Steward, F. (2009) *Managing and shaping innovation*. Oxford: Oxford University Press.

Drucker, P. (2007 [1985]) *Innovation and entrepreneurship*. Oxford: Butterworth-Heinemann.

DTI (2003) *Innovation report: competing in the global economy: the innovation challenge*. London: HMSO.

Dyson, J. (2003) *Against the odds: an autobiography*. New York: Texere.

Fagerberg, J., Mowery, D., and Nelson, R. (2005) *Oxford handbook of innovation*. Oxford: Oxford University Press.

Foss, N and Mahnke, V. (2008) *Competence, governance, and entrepreneurship: advances in economic strategy research*. Oxford: Oxford University Press.

Hamel, G. (2000) *Leading the revolution: how to thrive in turbulent times by making innovation a way of life*. Boston, MA: Harvard Business School Press.

Hayek, F.A. (1955) *The counter-revolution of science*. New York: The Free Press.

Henry, J. (2001) *Creativity and perception in management*. London: Sage Publications.

Henry, J. (ed.) (2006) *Creative management and development* (3rd edition). London: Sage.

Hotel Chocolat (2010) http://www.hotelchocolat.co.uk/Ghana-ethical (accessed 3 May 2010.

Howies (2010) http://www.howies.co.uk/content.php?xld=112 (accessed 3 May 2010).

ICCO (2010) International Cocoa Organization http://www.icco.org/about/chocolate.aspx (accessed 3 May 2010).

Innocent (2010a) http://www.innocentdrinks.co.uk/us/ethics/sustainable_packaging (accessed 3 May 2010).

Innocent (2010b) http://www.innocentdrinks.co.uk/us/ethics/sharing (accessed 3 May 2010.

Kirzner, I. (1973) *Competition and entrepreneurship*. Chicago, IL: University of Chicago Press.

Majaro, S. (1988) *The creativity gap: managing ideas for profit*. London: Longman.

Mintel (2008) 'Smoothies – UK – October 2008.' Mintel International Group, London.

Parsons, M. and Rose, M. (2009) 'Innovation, entrepreneurship and networks: a dance of two questions.' In Fernández Pérez, P. and Rose, M. (eds) *Innovation and Entrepreneurial Networks in Europe*. London: Routledge (41–60).

Porter, M. (1990) *The competitive advantage of nations*. Chichester: Jossey Bass.

Roddick, A. (2005) *Business as unusual: my entrepreneurial journey – profits with principles*. London: Anita Roddick Books.

Seely Brown, J. and Hagel, J. (2006) 'Creation nets: getting the most from open innovation.' *The McKinsey Quarterly*, 2: 41–51.

Tidd, J. and Bessant, J. (2009) *Managing innovation: integrating technological, market and organizational change* (4th edition). Chichester: John Wiley & Sons.

Tidd, J., Bessant, J., and Pavitt, K. (2005) *Managing innovation: integrating technological, market and organizational change*. Chichester: John Wiley & Sons.

Young Foundation (2007) 'Social innovation: what it is, why it matters and how it can be accelerated.' Oxford: Skoll Centre for Social Entrepreneurship.

Zahra, S.A., Rawhouser, H.N., Bhawe, N., Neubaum, D.O., and Hayton, J.C. (2008) 'Globalization of Social Entrepreneurship.' *Strategic Entrepreneurship Journal* 2, 2: 117–31.

People
Leading teams and networks

4

Never doubt that a small group of thoughtful, committed people can change the world. Indeed, it is the only thing that ever has.

Margaret Mead, *cultural anthropologist*

As a leader, you need courage born of integrity in order to be capable of powerful leadership. To achieve this courage, you must search your heart, and make sure your conscience is clear and your behaviour is beyond reproach.

Konosuke Matsushita, *Japanese industrialist and founder of Panasonic*

Learning outcomes

After reading this chapter you should be able to:

➤ Appreciate how entrepreneurial leadership, teams, and networks can contribute to the success or failure of a venture, and to its overall performance.

➤ Identify significant features of a successful entrepreneurial team.

➤ Understand the processes influencing the development of an entrepreneurial team during the creation of a new venture.

➤ Identify significant features of an effective entrepreneurial network.

➤ Understand the processes influencing the development of an entrepreneurial network during the creation of a new venture.

➤ Apply relevant principles and techniques in order to create your own entrepreneurial leadership, teams and networks.

Case 4.1 I can see clearly now: optical illusions or optical solutions?

The deregulation of the UK healthcare sector over the last two decades has resulted in significant changes to the way that individuals accessed and paid for services. These changes were most noticeable in community-based services, such as general practice and dentistry. Optometry, the care and treatment of the eyes, was no exception. The testing, treatment, and supply of related services experienced increasing competition between both existing providers and new entrants giving rise to fertile grounds for entrepreneurship. It was in this turbulent environment that Trevor Rowley and Jamie Murray-Wells founded their own companies, Postoptics and Glasses Direct respectively.

By 2008 **Trevor Rowley's** Postoptics (http://www.postoptics.co.uk) had 10 years' of experience and had become the UK's largest online supplier of contact lenses and solutions and operated out of purpose-built facilities in York. In 2007, the company was chosen by Boots, the UK's largest retail chemist, to handle its own mail order contact lenses web presence, and Trevor was recognized for his pioneering work with a Future Entrepreneur of the Year award by *Enterprise* magazine. He stated, 'Boots offers one of the most well-known and trusted brands on the high street. We are delighted to be working in partnership with Boots Opticians on this venture, it is a credit to the whole team at Postoptics that our normal working practices have met the stringent demands required by Boots' (Optometry 2007). On 30 November 2008 he sold the company (Rowley 2010).

Clearly, Trevor Rowley was an entrepreneurial leader in an emerging market. After all he had taken his mail-order dotcom start-up and integrated it with a specialist call centre to build one of the country's fastest-growing small firms: expanding at between 20% and 30% per year. In fact, at its peak it held about 90% of the online contact lens and solutions market (BBC 2003). But, did Trevor get there on this own?

Postoptics had not only to build its internal team from scratch but also an external network of opticians and suppliers. The law required that customers needed a recent prescription in order to buy lenses and, after some initial reluctance to collaborate, Postoptics built a network of over 200 opticians. However, Trevor acknowledges that it was his specialist call centre team that provided the company with a unique competence and stated, 'We have a very low churn rate and we aren't wasting all that time recruiting and training people who then leave . . . there's more to it than sitting at a screen reading a script.' Early on in the company's development he decided to appoint an HR manager to lead the development of the call centre. Instead of relying on learning on the job, the company introduced a programme of training and development, which empowered call centre staff. More specifically, this included an induction programme, regular staff appraisals, and reviews of customer feedback. This resulted in an unprecedented staff turnover rate of less than 1%. And, in a sector that was so highly regulated, reputation was everything. Trevor stated, 'Reputation is critical . . . satisfied customers are the best and cheapest form of advertising. And for satisfied customers you need good service' (*Sunday Times* 2004).

Jamie Murray-Wells faced similar growth issues to Trevor when he decided to start his own business, Glasses Direct (http://www.glassesdirect.co.uk), selling glasses directly to consumers. After being horrified at the price of his first pair of glasses on the high street, he put his degree studies on hold and set about finding a glasses laboratory willing to supply him. He launched his business in 2004 and was soon receiving orders for cut price prescription glasses over the Internet. By 2009 he had built the largest online glasses company in the UK, selling a pair every three minutes. But to build his business so quickly was the work of more than one person. Glasses Direct consisted of a team of people committed to quality of service. The first team member was finance manager, Deirdre Walker, quickly followed by office manager, Amy Kent, and several customer service advisors to handle the growing number of sales calls. In 2005, Glasses Direct was featured in *The Sunday Times, The Express, The Mirror,* and *The Daily Mail* all on the same day. As sales continued to grow so did the team. Next to join were two clinical advisors who helped to increase the reputation in the industry and to enhance quality standards for the online business. Just as Trevor had done with Postoptics, Jamie established an external network of dispensing opticians to support his customers. The company continued to grow rapidly, recruited a fulfilment team to run its new warehouse, and Jamie won the Shell LiveWIRE Young Entrepreneur of the Year and the NatWest Young Entrepreneur of the Year for 2005. In 2006, David Magliano joined the team, and the company secured its third round of venture capital funding, launched new services, and received its first shipment of glasses from China. Jamie also won Isambard Kingdom Brunel Young Entrepreneur of the Year. In 2007, a multi-million pound venture investment from Index Ventures and Highland Capital Partners was secured and an experienced senior team was recruited. In the following year, Kevin Cornils, former MD of match.com and buy.at, joined the senior management team (PNE 2008; Glasses Direct 2010).

Points to consider

1. What are the similarities and differences between Trevor Rowley (Postoptics) and Jamie Murray-Wells (Glasses Direct)? Consider their personalities, professional backgrounds, and experience.

2. It would appear that Trevor Rowley focused on developing his own internal team, whereas Jamie Murray-Wells seemed to recruit in expertise. Is this true? What influence did raising investment have on their respective human resources strategies?

3. Both companies developed external networks of optometry professionals. Why was this important to their development?

Sources: BBC (2003); Sunday Times (2004); Optometry (2007); PNE (2008); Glasses Direct (2010); Rowley (2010).

4.1 Introduction

In Chapter 1, we noted some of the typical psychological characteristics and behaviours associated with **entrepreneurs**, and began to consider whether it took a particular kind of person to establish a new commercial or social venture. We also saw that much of the discussion about entrepreneurship, both in the academic literature and more widely in our culture, has emphasized the role played by particular individuals. The entrepreneur is often presented as the hero of the story, an exceptional individual who has single-handedly founded a new business empire, transformed an entire industry, or pioneered a radical social change. For example, consider the following extracts:

> **Muhammad Yunus** is to economic development what Nelson Mandela is to world peace – a revered figure whose Grameen Bank has helped millions of Bangladeshis out of rural poverty by lending them small amounts of money, or microfinance, to set up their own businesses. It has 8 million borrowers, 97% of whom are women, and since 1982 has issued more than $6bn. (Benjamin 2009)

> While he [**Tony Hawk**] was still in high school, he used his winnings to buy a house in Carlsbad, and a few years later, he started his first company (Birdhouse) even though the skateboard industry was tanking at the time . . . at 41, Hawk rules an empire. He is the worlds highest-paid action sports athlete . . . there are Tony Hawk skateboards, bicycles, clothes, shoes, a bestselling autobiography, Jam exhibition tour and a video game series that's a phenomenon unto itself, with worldwide sales topping $1.6 billion since 1999. (Cohn, 2009)

➜ PERSPECTIVES See section 12.1 for further information.

Of course, there may be some truth behind this myth of the heroic lone entrepreneur, but we must be careful not to fall into the trap of oversimplification. We can see from the opening case (Case 4.1) that there is good cause for caution when considering the entrepreneurial activities that can be attributed to the actions of one individual. Clearly, both Trevor Rowley (Postoptics) and Jamie Murray-Wells (Glasses Direct) are both entrepreneurial individuals and could easily be portrayed as hero figures, but on closer examination we can see the danger of oversimplification. In both cases, each built an internal management team (entrepreneurial team) and deliberately developed a number of external professional or supplier networks (entrepreneurial networks). The truth behind this myth is that they are entrepreneurs, but a significant part of their undoubted success can be directly attributed to their leadership skills and ability to create internal teams and external networks.

The evidence to support this observation comes from beyond this opening case. Firstly, there is plenty of empirical evidence to suggest that most new ventures are established by what is sometimes termed the solo entrepreneur, who subsequently becomes the owner-manager of a business. Secondly, some important and influential approaches to studying entrepreneurship, most notably those based on economic principles, continue to focus our attention on the decision-making behaviour of individuals (Casson 1982). However, it is also the case that several people, working closely together as a team, establish new commercial businesses and social sector organizations, for example, the founding of Facebook (http://www.facebook.com) in 2004 by Mark Zuckerberg, Eduardo Saverin, Dustin Moskovitz, and Chris Hughes and also Innocent Drinks (http://www.innocentdrinks.co.uk) in 1999 by Richard Reed, Adam Balon, and Jon Wright. Some teams may be led by a prominent individual, while others consist of more equal partners. In any event, it is unlikely that the team will include someone who has specialized in human resource management (HRM).

Many entrepreneurs lack experience in managing people, so this crucial role is typically covered by a non-specialist during the start-up phase. Furthermore, the performance of entrepreneurial ventures – whether solo or team-based – is also dependent on external sources of skill, knowledge, and experience of another group of people, existing beyond the immediate venture, but who become involved, either directly or indirectly, in its progress. To gain a rounded understanding of entrepreneurship, we need to consider these sets of relationships and how they can be managed effectively.

In this chapter, we begin by considering what it takes to create a successful **entrepreneurial team**. This includes the factors to consider when putting a new team together, and the major challenges of keeping a team working effectively as the venture progresses. While some of the issues may be familiar from previous studies of management teams in existing organizations, we pay particular attention to the issues confronting teams, which are formed as part of the process of creating an innovative, growth-oriented venture. In the second part of the chapter, we turn our attention to the **entrepreneurial network**, the wider cast of actors who operate beyond the boundaries of the venture, but who are drawn upon in various ways. We ask how they are formed, why they are so important, and what can be done to ensure that they provide the kind of support that is needed in order to establish a successful venture. We conclude with some thoughts about the links between individuals, teams, and networks, including the kind of tensions that arise when people try to balance the need to collaborate against their personal ambitions.

4.2 Creating entrepreneurial teams

4.2.1 What is an entrepreneurial team?

New ventures are often based around people working together as members of an entrepreneurial team. There is still considerable disagreement over the definition of this term (Birley and Stockley 2000: 289–90; Cooney 2005: 229–30). Given the focus of this text, we will define the team as comprising two or more people who are actively collaborating in the founding of a venture in which they have a direct financial and/or personal stake. Practical examples of such teams include:

- Six members of a family who relocate to a new country and establish a chain of restaurants.
- Four university-based scientists who convert their discovery in the field of medical genetics into a spin-off venture.
- Three university friends who decide to turn their shared passion for snowboarding into an Internet retailing business.
- A professional couple, who quit their jobs, re-mortgage their house, and use the capital to set up a regional organization to help homeless children.

This pragmatic approach to teams recognizes that we are social beings and intrinsically familiar with working in small groups based on cohesion and continuity (Lewthwaite 2006). Not surprisingly, there are variations in the size and composition of start-up ventures according to the type of product or service being developed. For example, software development appears to have a higher number of single founders than the electronics sector, probable explanations including the range of skills that are needed (i.e. in software development, these skills are commonly found in an individual person, but not in the case of electronics-based ventures) and the amount of capital investment required in the initial stages (Cooper 1998).

In the remaining parts of this section we consider two key issues that arise when you try to create an effective entrepreneurial team from scratch: firstly, *team composition* (i.e. who is going to be in the team); and secondly, *team roles* (i.e. what part are they going to play in the team?). As you read these sections, try to link the ideas discussed to your personal experiences of being in a team, perhaps as a student involved in a group coursework assignment, an employee working on a collaborative project, or a member of a sports team competing against your rivals. It would also be useful to contrast issues applicable to entrepreneurial ventures with those covered on specialist HRM modules, where the focus is more likely to be on large, established organizations. Though some of the issues discussed are specific to entrepreneurial ventures, you should also find some common features in these approaches to dealing with people and organizations. It might also be useful to reflect on what experience and ability many new entrepreneurs have of creating and managing teams. The skills needed to generate new business ideas and recognize which are **entrepreneurial opportunities** might be different from the skills needed to build and motivate the new venture team. Understanding the importance of team composition could be the first step towards achieving this.

4.2.2 Team composition

In some situations, your capacity to select team members may be limited. For example, in the family-based restaurant venture it could be difficult to exclude a close relative, even though that individual might not appear to be the ideal candidate. However, there are usually opportunities during the course of the venture creation process for the founding entrepreneurs to make modifications to their core team. In the case of the medical genetics spin-off venture, the initial team comprised the four university scientists, who had been directly involved in the preceding research programme. The scientists might realize that they lacked certain skills and therefore look for additional team members who had a useful role to play, such as people with experience in intellectual property rights (IPR), finance, and marketing. In self-selected student teams, you often begin by selecting your friends, or at least people you already know, but if you find that there is scope to review team composition, it is well worth making the extra effort. Establishing a new venture is a challenging enough activity without the additional problems that are bound to arise if a team is either unbalanced or in some other way incomplete.

A recent review of the research on management teams has proposed a distinction between the factors influencing entrepreneurial teams during the initial phase of venture creation and those that only become relevant once the venture is becoming established. Future research needs to be clearer about the variables and avoid confusing those that are relevant to venture creation with those that are relevant to venture growth or indeed to mature organizations (Vyakarnam and Handelberg 2005: 246). While agreeing with the general proposition that some factors may become more or less influential as a venture develops, we would suggest that other factors, such as social integration and commitment to task, only become relevant once a firm is growing.

Though it may be relatively straightforward to list a set of issues concerning team composition, our experience suggests that it is much more complex and demanding to apply the underlying principles in practice. In order to help us think through some of these issues in a more concrete way, consider the following worked example.

Creating an entrepreneurial team: a worked example

SquishSquash-Organic children's drinks

Imagine that you have just decided to create a new venture that will manufacture and market a range of organic soft drinks for babies and young children. Your venture is going to operate under the brand name, *SquishSquash*, which you see as capturing the essential characteristics of the product (i.e. enjoyable and natural). You get hold of a blank sheet of paper and begin to list the key requirements for the members of your ideal entrepreneurial team. One way to begin your search would be to identify people who could match your requirements in each of three important areas, namely (i) skills, knowledge, and experience; (ii) tangible and intangible resources; and (iii) shared vision, values, and motivation

Skills, knowledge, and experience

Many ventures demand a wider range of skills, knowledge, and experience than are typically found in a single person, however gifted. New ventures often encounter problems because the solo entrepreneur of the entrepreneurial team is lacking these in one or more of their key areas of activity. In the organic drinks case, your team is going to be involved in both manufacturing and marketing the product. Though there are some degree courses that combine these fields, it is likely that you will need at least one person with a specialized background in the sourcing and processing of fresh produce, including the relevant food hygiene and food safety regulations (an essential requirement!). In addition, you will need someone with the skills required to develop the brand identity, to research the market, and to approach the retail buyers.

Tangible and intangible resources

Tangible resources include a variety of physical assets that are necessary for the venture. Financial capital is perhaps the most obvious tangible resource that founding team members need to bring. Some members of the team may be able to substitute their share of the initial capital for what is sometimes called sweat capital (i.e. when a person contributes their hard work and time rather than their own money). However, someone is going to have to be able to supply initial finance in order to purchase equipment, buy, or lease manufacturing plant, warehousing, etc. (see Chapter 8, 'Finances: raising capital for new ventures'). Intangible resources include a number of things that may be more difficult to specify, but which can be crucially important. For the new organic drinks venture, it will be essential to establish a trustworthy reputation among customers, suppliers, and other external agencies (e.g. food standards regulators). These can be among the most valuable resources to acquire. For example, your food production and marketing people will need to establish their credibility when approaching farmers and major multiple retailers (see Chapter 5, 'Markets: understanding customers and competitors', and Chapter 6, 'Processes: controlling operations and technologies').

Shared vision, values, and motivation

It is difficult to overemphasize the importance of these three factors. Firstly, establishing a shared *vision* for the venture requires that members of the team start out with an essentially similar set of ideas about what they want to create. We saw in Chapter 2 ('Visions') how difficult it can be to create the new venture plan. While there are bound to be differences at the level of the details, everyone in the team needs to be in agreement about the overall aims and the strategic priorities. Returning to the worked example, this means that your team members are able to agree about the kind of product they want to produce, the way they intend to produce it, and the market at which it is targeted. Given the many uncertainties surrounding venture creation, the team will also need to be flexible, adapting the vision where necessary. However, unless there is some degree of consensus in the early stages, it will be difficult to move forward. Fundamental agreements over issues such as the product specification (e.g. Should all the ingredients be organic? Should the fruit be locally sourced? Should preference be given to fair trade produce?) or the target market (e.g. Should it be exclusively for children? Should it be a premium brand?) could be very damaging. In addition, you will find it even harder to convince external audiences, such as prospective financiers, that you are a credible team that is capable of delivering on the investment.

Secondly, members of the team need to begin with a broadly similar set of *values* regarding the proposed venture. In this context, the term 'values' refers to moral principles and standards of behaviour regarding the kind of venture you want to establish and your general approach to the task. Differences over key values for the *SquishSquash* venture might revolve around the importance attached to children's health versus more general environmental concerns, or the desire to change consumer behaviour for the better, versus the need to achieve commercial success. People may also have different standards of behaviour in the way they conduct business dealings, such as negotiating with suppliers or selling to customers. For some, it may be good business practice, to use misleading language in order to get a better price, or to secure a sale; for others such behaviour would be a necessary evil that they would try to avoid, or something entirely unacceptable, that could cause them to abandon the venture. By the time you reach adulthood, these personal values and associated standards tend to be quite firmly established. However, differences in values between team members might only become apparent as the venture develops, particularly in situations where people have not previously worked together. In these cases, it would be worthwhile for team members to discuss their values openly at an early stage.

Thirdly, we need to consider the *motivation* of individual team members. There are two relevant aspects to motivation: the *source* of the motivation (i.e. what are the factors driving this person to take part in the venture?); and its *strength* (i.e. how strongly is the person driven to contribute to the success of the venture?). For example, for Martha (age 23, single) one of the founders of the venture, the primary motivation may be to take control of her life, abandon a boring, poorly paid job and hopefully to become a millionaire in the process. Another member of the founding team, Tariq (age 55, married) may be motivated by the chance to create a healthier food product for his grandchildren, while a third, Jan (age 38, divorced), who is already a successful entrepreneur, may see it as a great opportunity to have some fun with a new venture, and perhaps in the process to rediscover the excitement of earlier times, something that was missing from her life as the owner of several well-established businesses.

Source: This is a fictionalised case written by Richard Blundel.

→ **PERSPECTIVES** See section 12.3 for further information.

As you can see from the worked example, there is a close relationship between vision, values, and motivation. As a consequence, all three need to be addressed as part of the process of building a new venture team. It is a common experience that entrepreneurial teams become so focused on the *task* (i.e. creating their venture) that they lose sight of essential aspects of the *process* (i.e. how they work together in order to achieve the task). We return to these three factors in Section 4.3 when we consider how to manage a growing entrepreneurial team. We have suggested that personal values of team members tend to be quite firmly established and resistant to change. People can also have fairly fixed ideas about the aims and future direction of a venture. However, there is some scope for modifying a person's values and also for inspiring them towards a new vision for the venture. The source and strength of someone's personal motivation can also vary over time, sometimes in response to external factors (e.g. if the venture is received particularly well by potential investors and other audiences) and factors closer to home (e.g. there is conflict within the team, and/or major changes in the personal circumstances of a team member). We have already seen that entrepreneurship is not a one-off process but a continuous cycle of learning about yourself, your **enterprise,** and the new venture team.

4.2.3 **Team roles**

Having considered the basic composition of the new venture team, we can turn to the kinds of roles that team members will play. When considering how an entrepreneurial team might divide up the work, we can draw on a popular approach that was first applied to conventional management teams. The research underlying this approach suggests that team performance can be enhanced by ensuring that you have a well-balanced team. In practice, solo entrepreneurs and members of small start-up ventures have to take on many more roles than their counterparts in larger or more established organizations. However, where there is scope to make modifications to an entrepreneurial team, it may be possible to apply some of these lessons. There are many approaches to understanding team roles. Ranging from three suggested roles of expert, functional and supporting (Lewthwaite 2006) to those originated from a series of experiments involving industrial managers who were attending short courses (Belbin 1981, 1993, 2000). The researchers compared the performance of different teams

Figure 4.1 The concept of team roles: a communication perspective

Team role	Primary contribution	Implied communication task
Chair	Organizes, co-ordinates, and seeks to retain teams focus and involvement.	Monitors and co-ordinates messages between team members.
Team Leader	Initiates, provides leadership, and drives team towards achieving task.	Generates persuasive bilateral and multilateral messages directed at team members.
Innovator	Creates novel ideas and solutions in support of the task.	Synthesizes messages from diverse internal and external information sources.
Monitor-Evaluator	Provides objective assessments of performance in relation to stated purpose.	Analyses primarily cognitive task-related messages within the team.
Team Worker	Encourages other members, fosters team morale, and reduces negative emotions.	Assesses and generates primarily affective, process-related messages within the team.
Completer	Maintains a check on outcomes in relation to project milestones and deadlines.	Analyses primarily cognitive task-related messages within the team.
Implementer	Carries out much of the practical work required to achieve stated purpose.	Receives bilateral messages (i.e. instructions) and avoids distraction from other internal exchanges.
Resource-Investigator	Establishes external contacts to secure resources in support of stated purpose.	Engages in bilateral exchanges of persuasive messages beyond the boundaries of the team.

Sources: Belbin (1993); Blundel and Ippolito (2008: 365).

competing against one another in a series of business games. By measuring psychological and behavioural characteristics of individuals and by experimenting with teams comprising different mixes of people, they were able to isolate eight distinct team roles (Figure 4.1).

The researchers found that the higher-performing teams contained what they described as a balanced combination of these roles, whereas the unbalanced teams tended to perform less well and to display signs of dysfunction. While it is healthy to have some cognitive conflict, such as a constructive task-oriented argument over how to approach some aspect of the venture, it is not helpful to have affective conflict, where the disagreement is focused on individuals and based on personal disaffection (Amason and Sapienza 1997). The notion of a balance between roles suggests that there are several distinct communication tasks to be achieved if an entrepreneurial team is to operate effectively. For example, the Chair's role is concerned primarily with co-ordinating the intense flow of messages between team members, while the Innovator is synthesizing new ideas from a more diverse range of sources, which may extend far beyond the team's boundaries. The Monitor-Evaluator is primarily engaged with cognitive, task-related messages, trying to ensure that the team meets its targets, while the Team Worker is more concerned with the exchange of affective (i.e. emotional), process-related messages, trying to hold the team together and to ensure that everyone is well-motivated.

As the original researchers recognized, it is not easy to form ideal teams in real-world organizations. The task is complicated by a number of practical constraints. For example, you may need to include an individual in your team because she has some essential area of technical expertise, irrespective of any team roles that she might be able to fulfil. Similarly, someone may be an ideal Chair for a team that is lacking this role, yet meet none of the other requirements discussed in the previous section. In a new venture situation, teams are often simply too small to be balanced. A person's ability to fulfil a team role may also be constrained by other obstacles, such as differences in status, cultural factors, or lack of time to devote to the task. In short, teams are always something of a compromise. Rather than aiming for perfection, it is more realistic to aim for a reasonable spread of team roles with the expectation that some of the imbalances can be offset by team members remaining flexible, and being willing to adopt alternative roles in order to cover the gaps. If we take these important limitations into account, two key conclusions about team roles remain applicable to entrepreneurial situations. Firstly, there needs to be some degree of balance in a team: what is needed is not well-balanced individuals but individuals who balance well with one another. In that way, human frailties can be underpinned and strengths used to full advantage (Belbin 1981: 75). Secondly, and perhaps more importantly in this context, team-building should be seen as an *art*, something that can be practised and improved upon (Belbin 1993: 87–95). We develop the theme of team-building in the next section.

4.3 Managing the growing team

4.3.1 Forming, storming, and norming: creating the team

You may already have encountered Tuckman's (1965) widely reported model of team dynamics. This suggests that the developing team passes through several distinct stages of development: forming, storming, norming, and adjourning (Figure 4.2). Though each stage sounds plausible, critics have argued that an ideal-typical model of this kind is unlikely to represent the variety of processes taking place in real organizations. For example, if a venture team comprised people with shared motivation, vision, and values (Section 4.2.3), it might make a rapid transition from forming directly to performing. By contrast, if membership of a venture team introduced pre-existing conflicts (e.g. the team included two former work colleagues involved in a long-standing dispute), it might become stuck permanently at the storming stage. One useful way of reapplying the basic Tuckman model is to consider the patterns of communication associated with the different stages whenever they occur (Blundel and Ippolito 2008: 363). The examples given in Figure 4.2 indicate why it is such a challenging exercise to keep communicating effectively in the fast-changing world of a new venture team. At some points, it may involve intense exchanges between many participants, while at other times it becomes dominated by bilateral exchanges.

The main lesson to take away from the work of Tuckman and from related research on group dynamics is that it is going to require a great deal of skill to manage the dramatic transitions that are bound to take place during the life of an entrepreneurial team. In particular, it is important to recognize the need for different patterns of communication as the venture develops, and to make the necessary adjustments in order to ensure that they occur (Hackman et al. 2000).

Figure 4.2 Applying the Tuckman model to a new venture

Stage	Outline of activity in a new venture	Typical communication patterns within the entrepreneurial team
Forming	Individuals meet, initial attempts at team composition, establishing aims of venture (i.e. task) and ways of working (i.e. process).	Fairly open and multilateral exchanges as people seek an initial indication of each others capabilities and potential roles.
Storming	Disagreements emerge over both task and process issues; some internal conflict and hostility.	Strong bilateral, persuasive communication as members exchange arguments.
Norming	Efforts to resolve differences; venture team reaches agreement over task and process issues.	Greater attention to feedback as team leaders confirm consent and establish roles.
Performing	Team concentrates on achieving its common purpose, while maintaining process dimension.	Bilateral exchanges between team members engaged in delegated roles, with some multilateral communication to ensure activities are co-ordinated.
Adjourning	Focus on completion of task and dissolution of the team.	Combination of intensified multilateral exchanges and some unilateral direction as task is pulled together.

Sources: Tuckman (1965): Blundel and Ippolito (2008: 364).

4.3.2 Team development: from venture creation to venture growth

Having created (forming, storming, norming) the founding entrepreneurial team, which has seen the new venture through the initial start-up phase, it would seem logical that a performing phase would develop. Indeed for the venture to continue, any issues arising from the forming, storming, norming phases will need to have been resolved. Again it is important to reiterate that the entrepreneurial team will be operating within a highly dynamic environment, and its development is unlikely to be linear and progress sequentially through each phase.

We have already acknowledged that entrepreneurs can, all too often, concentrate on creating a vision for their new venture rather than building entrepreneurial teams. In the *Better by design* case (Case 4.2), we will be able to see examples of entrepreneurial leaders who succeeded in overcoming this trap. Both Helen Scanlan (Zuri Design) and Abigail and Thomas Petit (Gossypium) approached this challenge in different ways but both built entrepreneurial teams that shared their vision and the entrepreneurial networks required to bring it into reality.

Case 4.2 Better by design: creating teams and network not just products

When **Helen Scanlan** founded Zuri Design (http://www.zuridesign.com) in 2004, she was driven by a passion for producing African, fair trade, and handcrafted products in order to make a positive and long term impact on the lives of some of Africa's poorest people. But Helen also gathered an early committed team around her. Firstly, Kathleen Scanlan, Overseas Manager, joined on a voluntary basis to help in all aspects of the business including working on market stalls, sourcing products, stock control in Africa, and running exhibition stands. She has since gone on to develop the Zuri Network. Secondly, Julie Scanlan who designed the company's website, managed busy Christmas market stalls, and took part in triathlons to fundraise for the new venture. Additionally, the company readily acknowledges the help received from friends and family.

Interestingly, Helen and her entrepreneurial team were aware of the importance of building a network of producers (Zuri Network), which met their strict ethical and quality standards. Each producer had their own individual story; for example, Zakala Creations, in Kenya, was based in a refurbished workshop and fitted with Internet access. The latter means there is no need to travel through Nairobi's notorious traffic to get their orders and product development. 'The Project is located in Huruma, which is part of Mathare Valley, within the Starehe Constituency. The slum population is approx 8,000 with a very high unemployment rate (approx 80%). The people who live here have many problems including poor housing, lack of basic facilities, including water, roads etc. and lack of education. The drop out from Primary School is very high and few complete their Primary School. (Zuri Design 2010)

Many entrepreneurial teams start much closer to home. Before husband and wife team **Abigail and Thomas Petit** started their new venture, Gossypium (http://www.gossypium.co.uk) in 2000, they visited the cotton fields of Kutch, in western India, in order to find cotton that wouldn't harm the environment or exploit Indian farmers. This led directly to the formation of Agrocel (http://www.agrocel-cotton.com) whose mission is to 'serve the farming community by providing high quality agricultural inputs and guidance all under one roof at a fair price, technical guidance and agricultural output marketing with value addition . . . as well as improving the quality of life of the producers, which has led to the production of organically certified cotton. (Agrocel 2010)

Based on the south coast of England, Gossypium is now a leading brand in fair trade certified organic cotton fashion. 'All our products are designed in-house and we like to think we stand alone, naturally.' In her children's book, *The Eye of the Needle*, Abigail tells the story behind Gossypium and introduces the complexities of both the textiles industry and cotton farming. It raises issues of child labour (Petit 2005). For Gossypium, fair trade means responsibility, sustainability, transparency, agriculture, and textile processing (Gossypium 2010).

Ethical point Not only did Helen Scanlan (Zuri Design) and Abigail and Thomas Petit (Gossypium) form entrepreneurial teams, they were instrumental in forming entrepreneurial networks, consisting of suppliers, based around their ethical values.

Questions

1. Why would Helen Scanlan decide to build an entrepreneurial team so early on in Zuri Designs development? What Belbin roles did Helen, Kathleen and Julie play?

2. What might be the advantages and disadvantages of family-based entrepreneurial teams, like the one created by Abigail and Thomas Petit?

3. Is it significant that both Zuri Design and Gossypium placed so much importance on building their external supplier networks? Was it simply because of their ethical value?

Sources: Petit (2005); Agrocel (2010); Gossypium (2010); Zuri Design (2010).

Figure 4.3 Entrepreneurial leaders, teams and networks

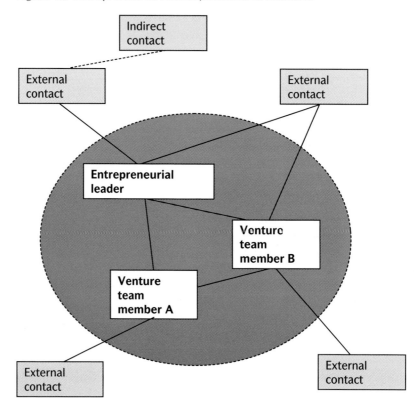

Source: The authors.

The *Better by design* case illustrates the importance of personal linkages in creating entrepreneurial teams. Both Zuri Design and Gossypium required strong internal teams to support their extended enterprises and to guarantee their ethical values were maintained. But in addition, both enterprises relied on networks that extend beyond the boundaries of the venture team. We develop this theme in the following section, by examining the role of external networks in new venture creation (Section 4.4).

We have seen in this section how an entrepreneurial leader can create and develop entrepreneurial teams. In this section we consider how entrepreneurial networks can play a critical role in new venture creation. Entrepreneurial leaders build teams and networks with the later coming directly from their own contacts (primary networks) and also from their team's contacts (secondary networks), see Figure 4.3.

4.4 Creating entrepreneurial networks

4.4.1 What is an entrepreneurial network?

Whether you are acting as a solo entrepreneur or as part of an entrepreneurial team, it is always necessary to make use of existing personal contacts, and to form new ones, in order to secure the services of individuals and organisations that are not directly involved in the new venture. This developing pattern of connections with the outside world is often described as an **entrepreneurial network**. These networks take many different forms, but are likely to include several of the following types of role:

- Suppliers of raw materials, products and services;
- Regulatory agencies;
- Distributors and retailers;
- Customers and end-consumers;

It is clear from the experiences of entrepreneurs, and from the substantial research that has been conducted, that entrepreneurial teams and networks play an extremely important role in the process of creating and developing new ventures (e.g. Aldrich and Zimmer 1986, Birley 1985, Johannisson 2000). Entrepreneurial leaders do not simply create internal venture teams (Section 4.3). They are also responsible for building and making use of a much broader network around the venture. The network may begin with an entrepreneurs' personal contacts, but it is also likely to involve those of other venture team members. Figure 4.3 is a simplified network map illustrating the kinds of relationships that may be involved.

Managing these network relationships can be very challenging, so it is worth spending some time considering the kinds of people you want to involve in your venture, the resources they might bring and the ways that they are likely to interact with one another.

→ **PERSPECTIVES** See section 13.2 for further information.

4.4.2 Creating ventures: the role of personal contact networks

The role of networks in *creating* new ventures is now identified as an important area of **entrepreneurial activity,** and has been the subject of many research studies (e.g. Larson and Starr 1993; Johannisson 1998). One of the early findings was that entrepreneurs rely largely on *informal* sources in their personal contact network (PCN) to mobilize resources before the formation of a venture (Birley 1985: 113). The unique connections between people in the PCN play an important communication role, enabling the entrepreneur to identify opportunities that are not evident to others. At the heart of this network, there are normally a small number of strong ties that provide the entrepreneur with a shelter from the opportunism and uncertainty of the market. For example, one study found that most business owners report between 3 and 10 strong ties, primarily business associates plus a few close friends and family members (Aldrich et al. 1989). The time and energy that entrepreneurs invest in these pre-organizational networks appears to be converted into future benefits for their emerging firms. This includes human capital, in the form of relevant experiences, skills and knowledge, and social capital (i.e. being known and trusted by others). Trust facilitates access to resources, through collaboration, and helps to overcome institutional barriers to entrepreneurial activity (e.g. local political resistance to a proposed development). However, the extensive personal ties used by entrepreneurs often lead to a blurring of business and social life, with mixed consequences. For example, reliance on particular individuals can sometimes lead to sudden, unpredictable, and potentially disruptive structural changes. Furthermore, while all start-up businesses make some entrepreneurial use of their personal networks, most small firms settle down into an established and fairly limited pattern of interactions. By contrast, entrepreneurs continuously develop their networks, with the more or less explicit aim of expanding existing ventures or establishing new ones. To achieve this, they maintain a broader latent network, parts of which are activated when required (Ramachandran and Ramnarayan 1993).

4.5 Managing network relationships

What happens to the entrepreneurial network as the venture develops? Researchers have found that entrepreneurs are active in managing the complex pattern relationships that make up their network. What appears to happen is that the actions of solo entrepreneurs and entrepreneurial teams create a favourable organizing context around the venture, in which it becomes relatively easier to deal with uncertainties and to exploit emerging opportunities (Johannisson 2000: 379). In other words, your network becomes an extension of the venture, providing you additional resources, support, and sources of information. We can simplify the complicated processes involved in entrepreneurial networking into three broad tasks that entrepreneurs need to pursue in order to develop successful ventures: creating new ties; developing existing ties; and reviewing existing ties, pruning them where necessary in order to re-focus resources (Larson and Starr 1993):

- **Creating new ties** This is the task that most people associate with the typical entrepreneur. We can imagine the kind of people who are very confident in social situations, whether it is a business meeting, an international conference, a local sports event, or simply waiting for a flight in an airport lounge. Their networking abilities are displayed in various ways, including: the ease with which they establish friendly relationships with other people; how they are able to discover a great deal about a person in a very short time; a capacity to promote their own infectious enthusiasm for a venture, so that the other person also becomes interested; ensuring that contact details are exchanged (e.g. swapping business cards or email addresses); and, most importantly, following up on any promising contacts. This kind of networking, in order to create new ties, is often seen as a purely individual activity. However, it is also apparent that entrepreneurs create new ties with the help of other members of their core team, who may act as brokers or intermediaries. For example, you have a major design problem with a new product. Another team member introduces you to her brother-in-law, who has a background in product engineering. She acted as the broker. You can then establish a new relationship, and hopefully get some useful advice!

- **Developing existing ties** We have seen that entrepreneurial networks tend to be very extensive, with lots of weak ties that could become more important in the future. Entrepreneurs need to have a capacity to develop these existing ties, which may have remained dormant (or latent) for some time. Developing these ties involves people becoming closer through increasing trust and involvement; this is a process that we have all experienced, in our personal friendships and relationships. In an entrepreneurial setting, you might be renewing contact with an old school friend, now working in a finance house, to provide advice or support for the venture; converting an informal contact made while on holiday into a potential client; or building a much closer relationship with a supplier, which may lead to a formal alliance or merger. In network terms, this process tends to result in weak ties becoming stronger ones, and the related flows along the ties becoming richer in content (i.e. in technical language, multiplex), possibly containing a mixture of information, advice, economic transactions, and friendship. For example, you are running a charity fundraising auction and have been asked to provide a football signed by your national team. You have no personal contacts in the national team but your uncle coaches a local junior club. He offers to speak to the club president who is a friend of the national team coach. In just three steps you can obtain your signed football.

- **Reviewing and pruning existing ties** Networking takes time, effort, and resources. Even the most energetic entrepreneur has a finite capacity to create, maintain, and develop network relationships. Furthermore, there must be a trade-off between the costs involved in additional networking and the alternative uses to which that energy can be applied. As a result, the third networking activity involves a process of reviewing the current pattern of relationships and making any necessary adjustments. In some cases, where there does not appear to be much more to gain from a particular tie, the entrepreneur may decide to either limit or even abandon the relationship.

We are all familiar with social networking via the Internet, with sites such as Facebook attracting millions of users worldwide. Case 4.3 looks at how these technologies can used to support entrepreneurial networks.

Case 4.3 Beyond Facebook: creating online entrepreneurial networks

The extraordinary growth of online social networking websites, such as Facebook (http://www.facebook.com) and LinkedIn (http://www.linkedin.com) took many by surprise, not least the existing Internet companies who were slow to develop their own response. In Chapter 9, we hear the story of Steve and Julie Pankhurst, who simply had a wish to contact old friends. After many trials and tribulations, this idea emerged as one of the first commercially successful online social networking communities: Friends Reunited (Case 9.2). Facebook and Friends Reunited are exemplars of entrepreneurs creating a new venture around the demand for social networking. But can the web be used to promote *entrepreneurial* networking? In this case, we look at three contrasting examples of new ventures that have attempted to meet this need:

The Beat Suite

When **Steve Bainbridge** started The Beat Suite (http://www.beatsuite.com), he recognized the potential of using online creative communities to build a royalty-free music library. The concept seems simple: The Beat Suite provides companies in the creative multimedia, broadcast, and computer games industry online access to high-quality music and sounds to incorporate into their own productions. 'We spend lots of time making sure that our website is in full working order and that every feature is as simple as possible to use – meaning that you get the most convenient online digital music downloading. We have developed a music licensing structure that we feel is fair, convenient and affordable to the various users of production music.' Steve and his entrepreneurial team had a background as music producers, DJs, and composers, which meant that they understood the needs of both the producers and consumers of music and sounds. Music composers submit music tracks to the online music library for producers to access and include in their creative projects. Thus, The Beat Suite acts as a platform that unites the creative networks of composers and producers (Beat Suite 2010).

Creative Networks Portal

The idea of connecting creative communities is not unique to The Beat Suite. The Creative Networks Portal (http://www.creativenetworksonline.com) supports creative professionals in the English West Midlands. While the portal promotes the creative industry and provides information it also supports collaboration between its members. The entrepreneurial team behind the venture has made good use of their prior experience of the creative industry. In essence, the portal supports online information exchange that could lead to physical creative collaborations. The relatively close geographical location of the portal's members makes this type of networking possible. But how could these technologies help when the communities that you want to bring together to create a new venture are literally 'worlds apart'?

Madventure

John Lawler faced just such a challenge when he wanted to create Madventure (http://www.madventurer.com). His vision was to create 'the number one provider of sustainable and ethical projects and challenging adventures worldwide'. What was important to John was to work with local communities in developing countries in order to enable adventurous travellers to have 'life-changing experiences through cultural integration, challenge, education and adventure'. It was John's personal experience as a gap-year student in 1998 that inspired the original idea. He stated, 'Through responsible travel, volunteering and development we all have the opportunity to give back to the fantastic regions we travel to. In our own small way by visiting some of these places and spending time with people, whether it is rural Ghana or mountainous Peru, we can learn so much more than just watching [celebrities on television]. So this year, make it happen and step out of your comfort zone. Take a gap and don't look back.' (ifwecanyoucan 2010). John gained funding from three organizations that support new enterprises: the Princes Trust (http://www.princes-trust.org.uk), Shell LiveWire (http://www.shell-livewire.org), and PNE (http://www.pne.org) to start his venture. He recalled, 'They also taught me how to write a business plan which was needed not only to get these funds but also to put my idea down on paper, which helped in terms of seeing what my vision might look like [. . .] to be a successful entrepreneur you need to ignore all the people who are negative – everything is achievable!' (ifwecanyoucan 2010).

Ethical point John Lawler of Madventure stated, 'In terms of success, we have really made a massive difference in the development of villages in 10 countries and managed to take thousands of young people on gap years and provided life-changing experiences for many of them. We've put thousands of pounds into helping to build classrooms, clinics, toilets, housing and storm drains.'

Questions

1. The Beat Suite succeeded in uniting networks of composers and producers on a transaction platform, which allowed both content and payment to be processed online. Can you think of other examples of this business model?

2. All three examples in this case use the Internet to support online networking. What are the limitations to this approach when building entrepreneurial networks?

3. The Internet is a powerful global communication platform. How could it be used to support internal entrepreneurial teams and external entrepreneurial networks in the future?

Sources: Beat Suite (2010); ifwecanyoucan (2010).

4.6 Top dog or team player? The paradox of collaboration

This chapter has emphasized the importance of effective collaboration with other people, both within a core entrepreneurial team and in a wider entrepreneurial network. But you may be wondering, where does that leave the *competitive* nature of entrepreneurship and, in particular, the view of the entrepreneur as an exceptional *individual*, the top dog who stands out because they have outperformed (or outmanoeuvred) any potential rivals? As we noted in the introduction, it is difficult to establish a successful new venture without the active collaboration of other people. Teams and networks need to be created and developed, since the tasks require a degree of trust and reciprocity between all the people involved. However, it would be naive to imagine that either team-working or networking is going to be free from individual rivalries and power struggles. As we discussed in Chapter 1, among those who are attracted to setting up new entrepreneurial ventures, there are likely to be many people with lively personalities, big personal ambitions, strongly held views about the best way to achieve a particular task, and a very strong competitive drive. If an entrepreneurial team includes two or more people with these characteristics, the combination can be explosive! In extreme cases, it may lead to the failure of a venture, as team meetings descend into continual arguments and internal competition between individuals causes the team to fragment. However, if team members are able to *channel* their energies towards the venture, rather than the satisfaction of their own personal needs, the result can be dramatically different.

As tutors, we have many student venture teams who struggle with precisely this kind of situation. Sometimes the team members simply fail to manage their internal rivalries. Despite our best efforts as external counsellors, the arguments continue and the clash of those with the biggest egos results in the break up of the team. Even if the team survives, it is unlikely to produce a high-quality venture proposal; and prospective investors are unlikely to be impressed if the team presentation is delivered by two opposing camps!

It has been said that there is no limit to what you can achieve if you don't care who gets the credit. For entrepreneurs, a willingness to share credit lies along the 'critical path' to success, simply because the more credit they share, the more people typically will want to help them. (Bornstein 2004: 235).

Importantly, this willingness to share the praise and recognition for achieving something grows out of a person's basic motivation. If an entrepreneur's true intention is simply to make change happen, then sharing credit will come naturally. However, if the true intention is to be *recognized* as having made a change happen, sharing credit may run against the grain. (Bornstein 2004: 235; emphasis in original).

And finally, remember that entrepreneurship is about motivating other people, or as Victoria Tomlinson (Case 4.4) puts it:

> *I have learnt how to motivate other people and that is a huge thrill. For a recent campaign, we had such a short time frame for the clients because they were struggling to get there before the end of the year . . . I said just give me the contract and we will make it happen and we had to go out and get partners involved in this . . . suddenly they were all delivering. So we managed to deliver it in that time scale.*

✳ 4.7 Summary

➤ Entrepreneurship cannot be explained through the actions of individuals alone; we also need to consider the collaborative activity that takes place in entrepreneurial teams and networks.

➤ Entrepreneurial teams can be defined as two or more people who are actively collaborating in the founding of a venture in which they have a direct financial and/or personal stake.

➤ There are several factors to consider regarding the composition of an entrepreneurial team, which can be summarized under the three headings: skills, knowledge, and experience; tangible and intangible resources; shared vision, values, and motivation.

➤ If they are to be effective, teams need to be reasonably balanced and members need to be flexible enough to ensure that a number of different roles are addressed.

➤ Building and developing an entrepreneurial team is an art rather than a science, and it requires practise to deal with the dramatic changes that are bound take place as the venture develops.

➤ Entrepreneurial networks can be defined as enduring patterns of connections between entrepreneurs and other actors, which provide an organizing context for activity.

➤ The personal contact networks (PCNs) of entrepreneurs play an important role in the creation of ventures.

➤ Entrepreneurial networking activity can be broken down into three broad tasks: creating new ties; developing existing ties; reviewing and pruning existing ties.

➤ There is an unresolved tension between the collaborative aspects of entrepreneurial teamworking and networking and the competitive nature of entrepreneurship that emphasizes the competitiveness of individuals seeking to be top dog.

Case 4.4 *Critical incident*
Victoria Tomlinson: network, network, network

At the beginning of June 2004, **Victoria Tomlinson** knew she had reached a crossroads in her public relations (PR) company's development. Fifteen years previously, Victoria had taken the decision to leave the corporate world to set up her own PR company when her then employer, Arthur Young, merged to form Ernst & Young. After years of developing her business, the team, and an impressive client base, she faced the loss of her biggest customer. Was this an opportunity to downsize, change the way the company worked or simply sell it?

Biography

Victoria's early life provided constant challenges. Her father was a test pilot in the Royal Air Force and she moved schools frequently – the most being five schools in two years. She recalled, 'I learnt a lot from this, particularly how to make friendships. I was very shy and realized that the trick was to be interested in other people rather than myself.' Her academic career was not outstanding and she chose some subjects for the wrong reasons, taking A-Levels in Pure Maths, Applied Maths, Physics, and Geography to 'prove I was brainy'. She moved again after A-Levels, joining her family abroad when her father took a two-year contract in Saudi Arabia. She remembers it as 'a great experience'. On her return she completed an HND in business studies and immediately got a job with Plessey Aerospace. 'They recruited one person from our course each year,' she said, 'and it meant I was lucky enough to go in as a graduate trainee with the same terms and conditions as the proper graduates.' After two years she took voluntary redundancy as manufacturing was hit in the late 1970s.

Victoria then considered a number of careers, including Marks & Spencer's management training programme. However, as a woman she could only join if she went in on the HR [Human Resources] side. She wanted store management, so turned it down. She also applied for a job on another Plessey site, still on the contracts side, which had been advertised at £10,000. She was offered the job, but only at £4,000. The manager said she would already be the highest paid female on site and this was as high as they could go. She turned this job down also.

Throughout this period, Victoria also had to deal with having Crohn's disease, an inflammatory disease of the intestines. She joined a peer-support group and soon became involved in the early days of the National Association for Colitis and Crohn's Disease (NACC).

Early years in public relations

Victoria soon found a job with Bradbury Wilkinson, which became De La Rue, selling banknotes around the world. While she was abroad, NACC gave Victoria their public relations brief to handle on a voluntary basis. Victoria recalled she had no experience, 'I knew nothing about PR so asked a number of friends and contacts if they would teach me how to go about this. They taught me about strategies, target audiences and how to design PR campaigns. We did this in the evenings after work and in return I'd cook them supper as thanks.'

After six years at Bradbury Wilkinson, an opportunity came up at Arthur Young to join their start-up marketing and PR team – with the new legislation in 1986, accountants and lawyers were able to promote themselves. Victoria remembers the fast moving environment. 'Suddenly professional firms were recruiting marketing/PR teams. I went in as part of that start up marketing to one of the divisions and within months was handling half the firm's PR. We split the firm into markets and I took on the international banking group and international insurance group among others.'

The culture at Arthur Young was a far cry from Victoria's experience in manufacturing, 'It [manufacturing] was a negative atmosphere, everything was no, with managers and the trades unions playing bluff and double bluff with each other over pay negotiations. There were strikes and nobody respected or trusted each other. When I went to Arthur Young, suddenly people said, Yes, try it. Do something creative. It was entrepreneurial.'

Victoria was promoted again and into new areas. The firm had launched a major culture change initiative, and she was concerned that the focus was only on fee-earning professionals. She came out of a presentation fuming that the people she saw as the grafters were being ignored in plans and training. She walked into the Managing Partners office to ask what was to be done about it.

Perhaps, not surprisingly Victoria was asked to sort it out. She recalled, 'I had a division of nearly 100 people and was given the task of managing culture change for the whole London office of about 1,500 people and was on the management team.' This also provided another chance for learning on the job. 'I needed new skills for this job,' she added, 'as it was a big management task. I asked if I could buy some internal management consultancy time to help me in the role.'

The whole professional services sector was changing, and in 1989 Arthur Young decided to merge with Ernst and Whinney to form one of the Big Four, the four largest international accountancy and professional services firms, including PricewaterhouseCoopers (PwC), Deloitte Touche Tohmatsu (Deloitte), and KPMG. It was time for a change for Victoria as well.

Victoria's new venture

In the same year that Ernst & Young was formed, Victoria decided to leave the company, got married and headed north to Yorkshire. She had been thinking of starting her own business for some time, but had struggled to find the great idea. She recalled, 'I'd spotted the opportunities for recycling very early on, but when I rang a number of paper mills to see what they would pay per tonne, it was peanuts. I couldn't see how to make money from it.'

Once Victoria had moved to Yorkshire it all became urgent. She added 'My husband was concerned I'd be bored and I wanted to show I could sort out my new life. The one thing I had was PR skills which I felt could be packaged with my strong business background. I rang the Yorkshire Post to see what they felt about PR agencies in the region and it seemed there was an opportunity.' She got going quickly, finding a serviced office with a manned phone number and had cards printed. She wrote to everyone she knew in London who had connections in Yorkshire and asked for introductions. She also joined half a dozen networks and attended numerous events.

Victoria also combined starting her business with raising two children.

Unusually for the PR sector, the company built a loyal client base, focusing on business to business, education and public sector, including a large government organization. Naturally, Victoria built her team to support this important client.

The company became recognized for providing both good PR services and partnerships based on mutual trust. Networking became fundamental to their way of doing business – both attracting new clients and helping existing clients with contacts and support. Victoria recalled, 'We help clients and contacts all the time, introducing people who might have mutual business interests. You want to help them but actually it is always repaid in droves. Whatever you give out it comes back ten times over. I think some of this is instinctive – you meet someone and think I know just the person who could help you and so that new network starts.'

Victoria's business background was core to the way they did PR, both in terms of designing campaigns and the client relationship. She recalls one large client who was spending too much money with her company. 'We raised the subject with the client and outlined how they should restructure the PR in-house. It was to our short-term disadvantage but we created a life-long relationship. Clients trust you, come back again and recommend you. A huge number of our clients also become friends.'

Critical incident

However, in spite of all these achievements, the PR contract with the large government organization was lost because of national restructuring. Victoria recalled, 'This had a big impact on the business and demoralising for everybody.' Suddenly, she was faced with some difficult decisions. 'I rarely lose sleep, but I remember a long, dark night when I had to look honestly at every aspect of the business. You look at your own skills – had I lost it? And costs and income – we were going to take a significant dip in profits. Was it still a business worth having?'

Victoria remembered thinking, 'What I really love is the relationship with the clients, operating at senior levels, taking on challenges, finding a solution and making things happen for them.' But how could she achieve this and keep her team? She started thinking about who she knew and who might be able to help her . . .

Source: This case is primarily based on an interview with Victoria Tomlinson and written by Nigel Lockett.

Practical activities

1. Team formation audit Use the guidance in Section 4.2 to identify the requirements of an effective team. You can either base this activity on your own proposed venture, or use one of the following scenarios:

1. You and your partner are 21 years old and both of you have recently graduated with degrees in Fine Art. You have an idea for a new business, based on the use of traditional painting techniques and specialist software that could produce real high-quality customized paintings based on digital images. Your target market consists of top commercial art galleries and large corporations who buy original art.

2. You are an environmental scientist with a technological **innovation** that could help families to reduce their reliance on fossil fuels. You want your idea to have the maximum impact on society, and to be widely available to people, irrespective of their income. You have the support of a wealthy donor, but need some additional expertise in order to establish this social venture.

2. Network audit Use the guidance in Section 4.4 to identify the requirements for an effective network. You can either base this activity on your own proposed venture, or use one of the scenarios from Activity 1 above. Prepare a network map, indicating the main external contacts for your venture (N.B. Figure 4.3 can be used as a model for your map, but you may wish to adapt the presentation format in order to fit your own information). Highlight the connections that you consider to be the most important and note the likely content of the flows between these actors and your venture.

 Discussion topics

1. Teams and team-working

1. Would it be better to create a new venture with a group of close friends, who you have known for many years, or with a group of people you know less well?

2. What are the most important factors you would consider when deciding who to include in your team?

3. Why have you chosen these factors?

4. What do you see as the four biggest challenges in keeping an entrepreneurial team? In what ways (if any) do they differ from those faced by management teams in established organizations? How would you respond to the challenges you have identified?

2. Networks and networking

1. Why might there be a difference between the accounts of famous entrepreneurs, which tend to emphasize their individual achievements, and the evidence on networking and collaboration? Can these contrasting views of entrepreneurship be reconciled?

2. How do you think the networking behaviour of entrepreneurs differs from that of other small business owners? What effect are such differences likely to have on the ventures that they create?

3. Review your own personal contact network, or that of another student/student team prepared as part of the network audit (Activity 2 above). Try to identify another way of connecting members of your PCN in order to create a different commercial or social venture to the one you have already identified. What does this exercise tell you about the role of entrepreneurial networks and networking?

Further reading guide

There is an extensive literature on management teams, but inevitably it is mainly related to the operation of teams in large, established organizations. We have already referred to some of the classic team studies, including Belbin's (1981, 2000, 2003) research on team roles and Tuckman's (1965) early work on team development. Blundel and Ippolito (2008) include a chapter summarizing some of this research, and commenting on communication issues that may influence the effectiveness of a team. Birley and Stockley (2000) provide a useful overview of research on entrepreneurial teams. More recently, the *International Small Business Journal* published a special edition on entrepreneurial teams, with relevant articles including Cooney's (2005) overview, Vyakarnam and Handelberg (2005), Matlay and Westhead (2005), and Clarkin and Rosa (2005). In addition Neergaard (2005) makes a very interesting link between entrepreneurial teams and networking, the two themes covered in this chapter. The networks literature is vast, and can be difficult to navigate. Useful reviews of the field include Nohria (1992), Ebers (1999), which concentrates on the formation of networks, and Penrose (1996), which examines the link between networking and the growth of firms. The entrepreneurial networks literature includes pioneering work that emphasized the role of personal networking, including Birley (1985), Dubini and Aldrich (1991), and Johannisson and Monsted (1997). Research that has questioned the role of networking for many small firms, such as Curran et al. (1993), and studies of networking in particular sectors, such as Brown and Butler (1995), Johannisson (1998), and Jones (2001). Chell and Baines (2000) and Johannisson (2000) provide interesting overviews, plus their own insights into entrepreneurial networks and networking.

References

Agrocel (2010) http://www.agrocel-cotton.com (accessed 3 May 2010).

Aldrich, H.E. and Zimmer, C. (1986) 'Entrepreneurship through social networks.' In D. Sexton and R. Smilor (eds) *The art and science of entrepreneurship*. New York: Ballinger (3–23).

Aldrich, H., Reese, P., Dubini, P., Rosen, B., and Woodward, B. (1989) 'Women on the verge of a breakthrough: networking between entrepreneurs in the United States and Italy'. *Entrepreneurship and Regional Development*, 1: 339–56.

Amason, A.C. and Sapienza, H.J. (1997) 'The effects of top management team size and interaction norms on cognitive and affective conflict.' *Journal of Management*, 23, 4: 495–516.

BBC (2003) Lunch Lesson Seven – Competition & regulation, 28 February 2003.

Beat Suite (2010) http://www.beatsuite.com/page/10 (accessed 3 May 2010).

Belbin, R.M. (1981) *Management teams: why they succeed or fail*. Oxford: Butterworth-Heinemann.

Belbin, R.M. (1993) *Team roles at work*. Oxford: Butterworth-Heinemann.

Belbin, R.M. (2000) *Beyond the team*. Oxford: Butterworth-Heinemann.

Belbin, R.M. (2003) *Management teams*. Oxford: Butterworth-Heinemann.

Benjamin, A. (2009) 'Money well lent.' *The Guardian*, 3 June 2009.

Birley, S. (1985) 'The role of networks in the entrepreneurial process.' *Journal of Business Venturing*, 1: 107–17.

Birley, S. and Stockley, S. (2000) 'Entrepreneurial teams and venture growth.' In D.L. Sexton and H. Landström (eds) *The Blackwell handbook of entrepreneurship*. Oxford: Blackwell (287–307).

Blundel, R.K. and Ippolito, K. (2008) *Effective organisational communication: perspectives, principles and practices* (3rd edition). Harlow: FT Prentice Hall.

Bornstein, D. (2004) *How to change the world: social entrepreneurs and the power of new ideas*. Oxford: Oxford University Press.

Brown, B. and Butler, J.E. (1995) 'Competitors as allies: a study of entrepreneurial networks in the US wine industry.' *Journal of Small Business Management*, 33, 3: 57–66.

Casson, M. (1982) *The entrepreneur: an economic theory*. Oxford: Martin Robertson.

Chell, E. and Baines, S. (2000) 'Networking, entrepreneurship and microbusiness behaviour.' *Entrepreneurship and Regional Development*, 12, 3: 195–215.

Clarkin, J.E. and Rosa, P. J. (2005) 'Entrepreneurial teams within franchise firms.' *International Small Business Journal*, 23, 3: 303–34.

Cohn, G. (2009) 'Tony Hawk carves a new niche.' *Entrepreneur Magazine*, October 2009.

Cooney, T. (2005) 'Editorial: what is an entrepreneurial team?' *International Small Business Journal*, 23, 3: 226–35.

Cooper, S.Y. (1998) 'Entrepreneurship and the location of high technology small firms: implications for regional development.' In R.P. Oakey (ed.) *New technology-based firms in the 1990s*. London: Paul Chapman (245–67).

Curran, J., Jarvis, R., Blackburn, R.A., and Black, S. (1993) 'Networks and small firms: constructs, methodological strategies and some findings.' *International Small Business Journal*, 11, 2: 13–25.

Dubini, P. and Aldrich, H. (1991) 'Personal and extended networks are central to the entrepreneurial process.' *Journal of Business Venturing*, 6: 305–13.

Ebers, M. (ed.) (1999) *The formation of inter-organizational networks*. Oxford: Oxford University Press.

Glasses Direct (2010) http://www.glassesdirect.co.uk/about/story/ (accessed 3 May 2010).

Gossypium (2010) http://www.gossypium.co.uk/catalog/ethicalandeco.php (accessed 3 May 2010).

Hackman, J.R., Wageman, R., Ruddy, T.M., and Ray, C.L. (2000) 'Team effectiveness in theory and practice.' In C.L. Cooper and E.A. Locke (eds) *Industrial and organizational psychology: linking theory with practice*. Oxford: Blackwell (109–29).

ifwecanyoucan (2010) http://www.ifwecanyoucan.co.uk/Entrepreneurs/John-Lawler (accessed 3 May 2010).

Johannisson, B. (1998) 'Personal networks in emerging knowledge-based firms: spatial and functional patterns.' *Entrepreneurship and Regional Development*, 10, 4: 297–312.

Johannisson, B. (2000) 'Networking and venture growth.' In D.L. Sexton and H. Landström (eds) *The Blackwell handbook of entrepreneurship*. Oxford: Blackwell (368– 86).

Johannisson, B. and Monsted, M. (1997) 'Contextualizing entrepreneurial networking.' *International Studies of Management and Organization*, 27, 3 (Fall): 109–36.

Jones, C. (2001) 'Co-evolution of entrepreneurial careers, institutional rules and competitive dynamics in American film, 1895–1920.' *Organization Studies*, 22, 6: 911–44.

Larson, A. and Starr, J.A. (1993) 'A network model of organization formation.' *Entrepreneurship Theory and Practice*, 4: 5–15.

Lewthwaite, J. (2006) *Managing people for the first time: Gaining commitment and improving performance*. London: Thorogood Publishing.

Matlay, H. and Westhead, P. (2005) 'Virtual teams and the rise of e-entrepreneurship in Europe.' *International Small Business Journal* 23, 3: 279–302.

Neergaard, H (2005) 'Networking activities in technology-based entrepreneurial teams.' *International Small Business Journal*, 23, 3: 257–78.

Nohria, N. (1992) 'Is a network perspective a useful way of studying organizations?' In N. Nohria and R.G. Eccles (eds) op cit. (1–22).

Nohria, N. and Eccles, R.G. (eds) (1992) *Networks and organisation: structure, form and action*. Boston MA: Harvard Business School Press.

Oakey, R.P. (1995) *High technology new firms: variable barriers to growth*. London: Paul Chapman.

Optometry (2007) 'Boots chooses Postoptics for its lenses by mail offer.' 12 October 2007.

Penrose, E.T. (1996) 'Growth of the firm and networking.' In M. Warner (ed.) *International encyclopaedia of business and management.* London: International Thompson Business Press (1716–24).

Petit, A. (2005) *The eye of the needle.* Lewes: Gossypium.

PNE (2008) Jamie Murray-Wells, Glasses Direct, http://www.pne.org/casestudies (accessed 3 May 2010).

Ramachandran, K. and Ramnarayan, S. (1993) 'Entrepreneurial orientation and networking: some Indian evidence.' *Journal of Business Venturing*, 8, 65: 513–24.

Rowley, T (2010) http://www.linkedin.com/in/trevorrowley (accessed 3 May 2010).

Sunday Times (2004) 'Opticians focus on HR pays dividends.' 14 March 2004.

Tuckman, B.W. (1965) 'Developmental sequences in small groups.' *Psychological Bulletin*, 63: 384–99.

Vyakarnam, S. and Handelberg, J. (2005) 'Four themes of the impact of management teams on organizational performance.' *International Small Business Journal*, 23, 3: 236–56.

Zuri Design (2010) http://zuridesign.com/producers_intro.asp (accessed 3 May 2010).

5

Markets
Understanding customers and competitors

A customer is the most important visitor on our premises. He is not dependent on us; we are dependent on him. He is not an interruption in our work; he is the purpose of it. He is not an outsider in our business; he is part of it.

Mahatma Gandhi, *spiritual leader and political activist*

In web 2.0 culture, person-to-person connection is key.

John Grant, *marketing practitioner and author*

Learning outcomes

After reading this chapter you should be able to:

➤ Recognize the principal opportunities and challenges faced by entrepreneurs attempting to market a new venture.

➤ Identify the main features of entrepreneurial marketing and how it relates to mainstream marketing approaches.

➤ Appreciate how entrepreneurial marketing practices can contribute to the task of creating and establishing a new venture.

➤ Understand how mainstream marketing approaches might be incorporated for analysis and decision-making in an entrepreneurial setting.

➤ Appreciate how marketing practices connect with themes discussed in other chapters, including leadership, teams, networks, operations, and accounts.

➤ Apply relevant principles and techniques in order to market your own venture.

Case 5.1 More than selling sofas? Made.com

Made.com (http://www.made.com) was launched in 2010 by a 28-year-old entrepreneur **Ning Li**, and a small team based in Notting Hill Gate, London. The start-up raised £2.5 million and has the backing of prominent e-commerce entrepreneurs, including Brent Hoberman and Marc Simoncini, and Profounders Capital, a London-based venture capital fund (http://www.profounderscapital. com). Ning Li was born in Foshan, a city in China's main furniture manufacturing region, and co-founded a related venture in France, called Myfab.com (Butcher 2010). His original vision for the new company, as outlined in his website profile, reflects a personal frustration with existing products and with the underlying structure of the furniture industry:

> After spending a fortune to buy his first sofa for his flat, he turned out to ask himself if the glamour of a chic European middleman brand was really worth the outrageous price and if there is a way to deliver a more affordable price while maintaining the design integrity. Thus, made.com was born. (Made.com 2010)

The profiles of the founding team suggest that the company is developing a distinctive culture. They also indicate the particular combination of talent and specialist knowledge that has been assembled to pursue this vision (Made.com 2010):

- Ning: 'the ideas guy'.

- Julien: 'guardian angel of our operations and supply chain'.

- Chloé: 'probably the most design obsessive person on Earth'.

- Win: 'our art director. Another design fanatic'.

- Andy: 'chief technologist, in charge of the cogs and springs that drive the made.com machine, and the guy that makes sure your purchases are secure and safe'.

- Lodovico: 'the product designer that puts an Italian flavour into our product lines. A religious believer in sustainable design'.

The company has five designers, including Stuart Padwick and Måns Salomonsen, and is inviting others to submit their work. Brent Hoberman suggests that this could create new opportunities for furniture designers to gain market access:

> Made.com is good news for talented designers who struggle to achieve scale production as it will showcase the best new talent to the buying public and generate demand for their products. (Hoberman, quoted in Wray 2010)

The Made.com venture reflects broader socio-economic trends towards 'co-creation' and 'mass customization'. Through the use of Internet technologies, the company is able to connect up previously separated ordering, design, manufacturing, and delivery functions in real time, enabling customers to become directly involved in the process:

- **'Made Labs'** This facility enables registered customers to choose the products that will become part of the company's collection. The proposition is that you can, 'Vote for your favourites and the most popular will be made available to order.' (Made.com 2010)

- **'Being Made'** Once registered on the website, customers are given the option of tracking the progress of their furniture from the point of ordering, through the various production stages, and as it travels to its final destination. At its launch, the company was working with 20 manufacturers. While most were located in the Far East, there were some UK-based firms, 'mostly in the upholstery area' (Butcher 2010).

The business model for Made.com is based on web-enabled interaction between a wide variety of people, including customers, designers, manufacturers, and distributors. It has been designed to encourage active participation in the design and production process, while also minimizing costs. The effect has been described as a transition from retailing to 'me-tailing', with the consumer taking increasing control (Hoffman and Sang 2010: 2). This can create an attractive proposition for customers, while also reducing production costs:

> The website showcases furniture designs and holds public votes, with the most popular designs going into production. Anyone who voted receives a discount in return for their participation in the selection process. Orders are then placed direct with a manufacturer for mass production in container quantities. In theory, there is no unsold inventory and no wastage as the factory only manufactures the exact number of items ordered. (Wray 2010)

The furniture industry is a long-established one, with a complex pattern of larger and smaller firms involved in design, manufacture, and marketing. It has been through many transitions, including the growth in markets for inexpensive, self-assembly furniture during the late twentieth century, led by large international companies such as IKEA, and more recent efforts to bring contemporary designer furniture to a wider market, some of which have proved unsuccessful. Currently, around 80% of the UK's furniture market is sourced from China (Butcher 2010). Made.com has a truly radical ambition, not simply to offer new products to a market, but to alter the structure and practices of an industry:

> Our ambition is to bring original design to as many people as possible by revolutionizing how furniture is sold and how you buy it. By stripping out the middlemen and connecting you with the furniture makers directly we are cutting the cost to you by 50–80%. (Made.com 2010)

Points to consider

1. What are the main differences between the marketing approach adopted by Made.com and that of a conventional 'High Street' furniture retailer?

2. What do you see as the main challenges facing Ning Li and his team?

3. Can mainstream marketing concepts, such as the 4Ps, be applied to this kind of enterprise?

Sources: Butcher (2010); Hoffman and Sang (2010); Made.com (2010); Wray (2010).

5.1 **Introduction**

Marketing is a fundamental issue for any **enterprise**, but for new ventures it can be particularly challenging. The topics addressed by marketing specialists are wide ranging, and include understanding customer behaviour, product pricing, promotional strategies, public relations, relationship marketing, marketing planning, and evaluation. During the twentieth century, marketing became a specialized management function, a profession with its own codes of practice and a field of academic research. Despite this, many **entrepreneurs** get their products to market without any formal training in the subject. So what can we learn from these successes, and from the many less successful marketing efforts? This chapter concentrates on the best ways to apply marketing techniques in an entrepreneurial setting, with a particular focus on creating new ventures. Before beginning our review, it is worth thinking how **entrepreneurial marketing** might differ from mainstream (or 'regular') marketing approaches. The most obvious differences are in the way the process is managed, and in the skills, or competencies, that are required:

> *The management of regular marketing can be characterised by a careful planning process which is informed by market research to guide the selection of target markets and the composition of a marketing mix with which to position products competitively within the marketplace. Consequently, the competencies which it requires include planning, rigour and familiarity with statistics and figures. In contrast, [. . .] the management of entrepreneurial marketing is characterised by intuition, informality and speed of decision making, all of which require different competencies.* (Collinson and Shaw 2001: 763)

The difference between marketing in a corporate setting and an entrepreneurial one is highlighted by the experience of people who have moved out of a large organization in order to establish their own venture. For example, the realities of this transition struck one senior marketing manager a few months after she left her job in a famous name retailer. She was attending her first trade show as an independent entrepreneur, and the most immediate difference was the lack of resources: there was nobody to arrange her travel, book her room, or pay her expenses. Perhaps more significant was the experience of walking into the show without the backing of an established brand. In the past, she could gain easy access to business contacts because of the organization that employed her. Now, she had to rely solely on her personal credibility and skills in persuasive communication. Entrepreneurial marketing involves a distinctive set of techniques and practical competencies that you need to develop, both within your **entrepreneurial team** and through your network relationships, in order for a new venture to thrive.

The language of 'markets' and '**industries**' is sometimes used interchangeably, which can lead to confusion. It is therefore worth clarifying the distinct meanings attached to each of these terms, and how they can be related to one another:

- **Markets** are made up of customers and potential customers, which are sometimes divided up into segments, comprising product and customers that share common characteristics.

Marketers often distinguish between 'business to consumer' (B2C) and 'business to business' (B2B) markets. For example, in the market for furniture, you might identify B2C segments for contemporary design or second-hand 'retro' products, and B2B segments for hotel or office furniture. The main focus here is on commercial markets, but many of the practices discussed are also applicable to social markets. For example, in some countries there are social markets in healthcare and education, with end-users being able to exercise a degree of choice between alternative publicly funded and social sector providers.

• **Industries** (and industry sectors) are made up of competitors offering products or services to these customers. For example, the furniture manufacturing industry is made up of several fairly distinct sectors. Some firms specialize in the manufacture of particular product categories, such as beds, while others serve particular markets, such as flat-pack furniture for home assembly. The terminology of industries and industry sectors is commonly used to refer to commercial enterprises, but can also be applied to social enterprises. Many of these organizations operate in competition – and sometimes in collaboration – with their public and private sector counterparts. For example, there are many social enterprises operating in competitive markets such as sports and leisure, healthcare, housing, and waste disposal.

There are two further introductory points, which are particularly relevant to entrepreneurs in search of new opportunities. Firstly, there are many situations in which one market, or market segment, can be served by more than one industry or industry sector. For example, the market for long-distance transportation of goods is served by the aviation, shipping, and railway industries. These overlaps may seem fairly obvious, and they are certainly not new. What has changed in recent years is the increased blurring of boundaries between different industries and markets. This has been driven by a combination of technological **innovation**, notably the spread of the Internet, and other political, legal, and socio-economic changes. Perhaps the most striking example is the evolution of the mobile phone market. In the 1980s, the first products provided little more than telephone communication without a landline. Since then, the increasing functionality of phones has required the integration of several previously separate industries, including: telecommunications, computing, photography, entertainment, retailing, and advertising. As industries converge, there is often scope for entrepreneurs to broker these 'new combinations'. Secondly, as the mobile phone example illustrates, markets and industries are rarely static. The resulting changes are often another major source of **entrepreneurial opportunity**. For example, if the existing (or 'incumbent') firms in an industry fail to keep pace with the changing demands of their markets, there is scope for entrepreneurial rivals, or potential new entrants to intervene; this is the kind of situation outlined in the opening case, where Made.com is posing a direct challenge to existing players in the furniture industry (Case 5.1). Another example would be the launch of a new technological product, such as the Apple iPad (http://www.apple.com/ipad), or the provision of innovative services such as micro-credit and skills training for women in a remote rural community (Case 11.1). Each of these provides a powerful example of entrepreneurial marketing in action.

➜ **PERSPECTIVES** See sections 10.1 and 11.1 for further information.

The rest of the chapter is organized as follows. In Section 5.2, we introduce entrepreneurial marketing and outline some of the ways it differs from mainstream marketing approaches. Section 5.3 takes a closer look at some of the more widely used entrepreneurial marketing practices, and how they might help in creating and establishing a new venture. In Section 5.4, we revisit some mainstream approaches and see how they might be used in order to analyse markets and make strategic decisions. Finally, in Section 5.5, we review the practical implications of engaging in entrepreneurial marketing, including the implications for leading your entrepreneurial team, building your social networks, and managing other functional areas of your venture, including operations and accounts.

5.2 How do you market an entrepreneurial venture?

5.2.1 Distinctive challenges and opportunities

As we saw in the opening case (Case 5.1), new entrepreneurial ventures face a different set of marketing opportunities and challenges, as compared to their larger and better-established counterparts. The challenges, which we explore further in the next two sections of this chapter, include: lack of resources, lack of legitimacy, and powerful incumbents. However, the founders of entrepreneurial ventures are also well placed to exploit opportunities, due to their inherent flexibility, closeness to customers, and capacity to form new networks. In addition, they are usually seeking to create something that is new, either with respect to the product itself, or the market that is to be served.

Though much of the research on entrepreneurial marketing has looked at commercial ventures, it appears that social enterprises experience a similar set of challenges and opportunities (Shaw 2004; Martin and Thompson 2010). This prompts two questions. Firstly, are mainstream marketing approaches capable of meeting the needs of entrepreneurial ventures? (Section 5.2.2.) Secondly, are alternative – and more effective – options available? (Section 5.2.3.)

5.2.2 Mainstream marketing approaches

During the twentieth century, particular approaches to marketing were developed to meet the requirements of large corporations selling branded consumer goods, including food, household and leisure products in large volumes. The essential tools and techniques of 'fast moving consumer goods' (FMCGs) marketing include marketing research, market segmentation, product positioning, and brand management (e.g. Perreault et al. 2009). Marketers made use of developments in psychology and the social sciences to develop new ways of analysing and exploiting different consumer preferences and behaviours. They applied this knowledge in marketing research, which was used to refine product offerings and advertising messages. Many aspects of the marketing function were quantified and systematized. For example, the effectiveness of mass media advertising was evaluated through the statistical analysis of survey data, with respondents being asked questions that measure 'prompted' and 'unprompted' recall of particular campaign messages. Marketing professionals continue to make use of these mainstream approaches, and we revisit several of them later in this chapter (Section 5.4), to see how they might be applied more effectively in an entrepreneurial setting. However, the dominance of this kind of marketing is increasingly challenged by alternative approaches. These changes in marketing practice are affecting organizations of all kinds, but here we are mainly concerned with the implications for those engaged in **entrepreneurial activity**. The nature and scale of the change is summed up in the following comment on the future of branding, and how it has to move away from practices that were designed for twentieth century FMCG markets:

> *Brands were constructed for ugly industrialized manufacturing businesses (including farming, unfortunately) by adding attractive cultural images, personalities and descriptions. A factory-made fruit pie would become a Mr Kipling* home-baked style *fruit pie. This was a process of communication; an advertising message delivered through mass media. The audience was the passive receiver of this. I say 'was' because many, including myself, have been arguing for over a decade that (except in selected 'image category' preserves such as the perfume market) this model is all but dead. The main reason is growing consumer literacy, marketing resistance and cynicism. People don't trust many companies. Put the two together and you can guess the result.* (Grant 2007: 5)

In a recent example of this phenomenon, the UK's Co-operative Bank achieved a 38% increase in new current accounts during 2009, in the immediate aftermath of the global financial crisis (Kollewe 2010). How did it manage to out-compete the vast international banks that dominate today's financial services markets? The Co-operative Bank, which is part of a larger group, is constituted as a mutual society (http://www.co-operative.coop). This means that it is owned and controlled by its members, rather than by external shareholders. The bank is also part of a much wider co-operative movement that has been in existence for more than a century and which has a presence in many countries worldwide, including: Saraswat Bank, India (http://www.saraswatbank.com); Merkur Cooperative Bank, Denmark (http://www.merkurbank.dk); and Cooperative Bank of Kenya (http://www.co-opbank.co.ke). In the last decade, the Co-operative Group in the UK has built up a distinctive brand image based on its strong ethical credentials. As a mutual, it has been able to engage directly with its customers in its strategic decision-making processes in areas such as investment strategy, product sourcing, and energy use. By adopting an entrepreneurial marketing approach that incorporated operational innovations, the Co-operative Group put substance behind its branding messages. It seems that this combination has enabled the organization to attract a new generation of customers:

> *'We're already seeing a flight to trust,' said Peter Marks, the chief executive. 'People are weary of big business, especially in the financial services sector. They want to feel confident about where they're putting their hard-earned savings.'* (Kollewe 2010)

We can now consider these more recent marketing approaches in greater detail, again with a focus on their potential application in entrepreneurial settings.

5.2.3 New marketing approaches: customer engagement

John Grant is the co-founder of the innovative St Luke's advertising agency (http://www.stlukes.co.uk), and a leading figure in the 'New Marketing' movement. He describes the new marketing approaches as being based on active customer engagement. As in the Co-operative Bank example, this often means that customers become directly involved in the production process:

> *You work together to create ideas, communities, events and lifestyles. It's not a patronising, 'the customer is king' view; it's a new openness, porosity and creative dialogue that can impact product development, retailing experiences and the service – for instance reader reviews on Amazon.com – quite apart from activities which actively engage people – like Nike's* Run London. (Grant 2007: 5)

The new approach extends beyond branding and into other areas of marketing, including customer relations management (CRM) and direct marketing. One of the common themes is the widespread and innovative use of new communications technologies, including social media.

The argument is that, as consumers, we have become more visually literate and have access to much more diverse sources of advertising and other communications. With so many sources of information (e.g. price comparison sites, online reviews, specialist interest blogs), we are much less open to be influenced by/more alienated from the mass market brands. This has created many opportunities for new enterprises. One of the early lessons of marketing effectively in this new arena was demonstrated by *Friends Reunited* (Case 9.2); the secret was to imitate traditional, and therefore familiar, models of social interaction:

> *One of the first successful social networks online was* Friends Reunited. *This didn't seem like joining some weird virtual community. Why? Because it was 'just like a school reunion' (only much better, you could browse what others had been up to and so on).* (Grant 2007: 233)

As the author notes, Facebook worked on a similar principle, taking a face-to-face model that was already well established at universities in the United States, and reinterpreting it as an online community. Other techniques include viral marketing, a form of persuasive communication in which the users of a service are encouraged to forward electronic messages (e.g. emails, texts, or tweets) around their personal contact network. Recent examples include, 'One Difference' (Case 2.2), which used Facebook and YouTube to promote World Water Day 2010 and managed to recruit 250,000 fans. This is essentially an electronic extension of traditional 'word-of-mouth' promotion, but with much greater scope and potential. People have always talked to their immediate circle of friends about favourite bands, clothes, or clubs. Viral marketing enables these interactions to extend beyond your immediate circle of friends, reaching people who would not have been connected in previous times (Scott 2009). 'Buzz' marketing is a similar reworking of a traditional technique. In the past, you might be offered a free or reduced price product (e.g. a meal) in the hope that you would encourage your friends to try it. With electronic media, it is possible to co-ordinate this kind of promotion more tightly, and to encourage the viral spread of promotional messages. While 'word-of-mouth' continues to operate, it has also changed as a result of the new communications technologies and the way they are being used for promotional purposes. Proponents of the New Marketing argue that innovations of this kind can make it easier for less well-resourced initiatives, including new commercial ventures and social enterprises, to have an impact in marketing terms:

> One difficulty is that the projects with the most ambitious objectives tend to be those with the least means, for instance because they are start-ups. However, with web 2.0, word-of-mouth and community there is a much more level playing field for good ideas. (Grant 2007: 13)

While this might sound like good news for the independent entrepreneur, it is becoming less of an advantage as larger and more established organizations begin to learn the lessons of the new marketing, often by acquiring some of the small, entrepreneurial pioneers; for example, *Steve Pankhurst* (Case 9.2) and *Deirdre Bounds* (Case 9.3). So, can entrepreneurial marketing provide a new venture with the kind of advantage it needs to survive and thrive in a competitive marketplace? The next section summarizes some of the more popular entrepreneurial marketing techniques and introduces the distinctive way of thinking about marketing that is often found in successful ventures.

5.3 Exploring entrepreneurial marketing

5.3.1 Techniques and philosophy

As we have noted, entrepreneurial ventures face a number of challenges, including a lack of resources, lack of legitimacy, and powerful incumbents (Section 5.2.2). Many new ventures fail, at least in part, because they are unable to address these challenges, while others find it difficult to expand beyond their initial market niche. Entrepreneurial marketing techniques enable new ventures to grow in more innovative ways (Bjerke and Hultman 2004: 146–51). To do so, they play on the inherent strengths of a new venture. Though these might vary depending on circumstances, they typically include flexibility, closeness to an initial customer base, and capacity to use the personal contact networks of the founders; for example, *Victoria Tomlinson* (Case 4.4). As a consequence, entrepreneurial marketing tends to be based around more informal, personal, and strongly interactive marketing techniques. For example, in the early stages, 'marketing communications' – though this term is unlikely to be used – relies much more on the quality of your personal relationships than it does on a nicely designed advert or brand identity. If the venture is entirely new, the first task for the founding team is to establish their personal credibility with particular audiences. If a product or service is not yet fully defined, the only way of judging a venture is through the knowledge, experience, motivation, and character of the people involved. Therefore, marketing yourself becomes a necessary starting-point, if you are to gain access to potential customers, as well as to the most suitable partners and investors. From these initial contacts, the next step is to refine your social networks in order to serve a number of essential functions. In an entrepreneurial setting, networks are likely to be the main source of market intelligence and one of the most important channels for promotional activity, particularly in the initial stages. Then, as the venture becomes operational, relationships with customers are an increasingly important element. As Bjerke and Hultman (2004: 159) observe, one of the key points to recognize is that 'customer value is subjective.' Given that perceptions of value emerge wherever customers are based, it is essential to remain closely engaged with them throughout the process – an approach to marketing that can be described as the, 'co-creation of customer value' (Bjerke and Hultman 2004: 158–85). This close engagement can be very difficult to achieve in practice, particularly when a process extends beyond the control of the venture team to involve other partners. The difference between deliberate and emergent strategy has long been acknowledged as a distinguishing feature of entrepreneurial marketing (Mintzberg and Waters 1982, 1985). Consider, for example, how customer value is generated in the case of Made.com (Case 5.1). The company is co-ordinating a much wider network or 'value constellation' (Norman and Ramirez 1994), which involves external partners, including the furniture manufacturers and delivery companies. Figure 5.1 summarizes these marketing techniques and provides some illustrations of how they are applied in practice.

Entrepreneurial marketing is not limited to smaller organizations, as suggested in some marketing texts. Larger organizations can also use entrepreneurial marketing techniques (Hills and Hultman 2006: 225). However, as research on corporate **entrepreneurship** (or '**intrapreneurship**') has shown, there are inevitable tensions in such organizations, between the requirements for formalized planning and a desire to encourage more flexible and emergent approaches. Social enterprises may also face some distinctive marketing challenges.

---

 online resource centre 'Social enterprises: a different language?'

In previous chapters, we have discussed the importance of creating a vision and of pursuing entrepreneurial opportunities (Sections 2.1 and 3.2). The entrepreneurial marketing techniques outlined in this chapter show how the founders of new ventures are able to make

Figure 5.1 Entrepreneurial marketing techniques

Technique	Practical example
Establishing personal credibility	Adnan Awan (Case 6.4), Neil Meredith (Case 8.4)
Building and refining social networks	Victoria Tomlinson (Case 4.4), Steve Pankhurst (Case 9.2)
Co-creation of customer value	Tim Lockett (Case 5.4), Deirdre Bounds (Case 9.3)
Co-ordinating value constellation	Steve Woodford (Case 7.4), Jonathan Hick (Case 9.1)

this happen as they gain a deeper understanding of their customer. We can illustrate how these ideas can be applied in practice through a fictionalized account of Michèle Bertrand, a fashion buyer working for a leading women's clothing retailer, located in central Paris.

'Maison des peaux' (episode one): entrepreneurial marketing

In her role as a fashion buyer, Michèle Bertrand spends a lot of time talking to existing customers, attending trade shows, and visiting competitors' stores. She notices that an increasing number of her younger customers are customizing their mobile phones according to the clothes they most like to wear, and in some cases to match a specific outfit. Michèle approaches her manager and suggests that they should consider developing a range of mobile phone 'skins' to complement the next season's range. As a fashion house, they will be able to offer a unique product that cannot be readily imitated by rival firms. Her manager seems unconvinced by the idea, and tells her to focus on her work. Disappointed by this negative reaction, Michèle talks to several friends, including an industrial designer whose work she respects. Their response is completely different. Jaime, the designer, offers to produce designs for three skins, which he thinks will be popular. Michèle asks five close friends to her apartment one evening and invites them to bring two people they think would be interested in these designer skins. The evening is a great success and Michèle decides to develop a range of ten skins targeted at fashion-conscious women and designed to match the summer season's key themes.

Michèle finds a local manufacturer who is prepared to produce her designs in small quantities. She also asks her partner, a web designer, to create a simple website and logo for 'Maison des Peaux'. As a trial promotion, she gives the 15 people who attended the initial evening three skins each. Each night after work she checks for orders and posts them to the customers. In just five weeks she has sold nearly all of her initial stock. Michèle notices that one customer ordered only one design and bought 10 skins at a time. Quite naturally, she assumes it was the design the customer likes. Michèle is getting positive feedback from her customers but decides to conduct some informal market research. She emails all her customers a link to a simple online survey that includes a 'free text' field. Michèle is surprised by the responses. Nearly all of the customers reply and say that they learnt about 'Maison des Peaux' from someone who had already purchased a skin. Interestingly, the customer who bought 10 skins at a time is more interested in the material than the design. He runs a specialist eco-store, which only sells ethical and biodegradable products. By sheer chance one of Michèle's skins was made of ethically sourced latex, rather than plastic. Her customers also confirm that while there were plenty of companies in France selling skins, she has no direct competitors.

Michèle has been using Facebook for a few years to keep in touch with her friends and work colleagues. Encouraged by the response to her online survey she decides to set up a Facebook group for 'Maison des Peaux'. She is surprised that all her customers join and this attracts even more members to the group as news spreads from member to member. Michèle also starts to Twitter and blog about herself and designer skins.

The story of 'Maison des Peaux' is continued in the next two chapters. Having seen promising results from her initial marketing activities, we follow Michèle's efforts to ensure that her new online venture will also work operationally (Section 6.2). In the next section, we take a fresh look at some familiar approaches to marketing to see how they might be redeployed in an entrepreneurial setting.

5.4 Marketing in a new venture context

5.4.1 Using 'mainstream' marketing tools

We began this chapter by highlighting the distinctive challenges and opportunities associated with entrepreneurial marketing. Mainstream marketing concepts were discussed briefly, and we then developed the argument for adopting a more emergent entrepreneurial marketing approach, with several illustrations of its application in practice. However, taking an entrepreneurial marketing approach does not necessarily mean that you have to abandon mainstream marketing altogether. Rather, it is a question of learning from both approaches, and of applying mainstream tools and techniques in ways that meet the needs of an entrepreneurial and new venture context (Hills and Hultman 2006: 223). In this section we discuss a series of marketing-related tasks, highlighting key issues that arise in entrepreneurial settings, and particularly during the launch phase of a new venture. These are summarized in Figure 5.2 as three distinct but closely related areas of activity. The idea is to show how you can combine different tools and techniques in order to: (a) better understand your marketplace; (b) define and articulate their product more clearly; and (c) convince both yourself and other people that you have got the essential foundations for a successful venture.

Figure 5.2 Marketing in a new venture context

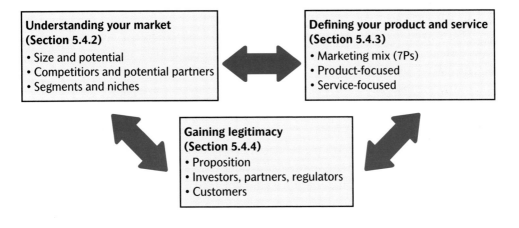

5.4.2 **Understanding your market**

Developing a better understanding of your intended market is an essential and ongoing task, which contributes to the related tasks of refining the product and gaining legitimacy. Mainstream marketing techniques have a role to play, but they need to be complemented by approaches that are better-suited to an entrepreneurial context. Key challenges include a lack of resources and, in the case of innovation-led ventures, new and largely unknown markets.

- **Establishing market size and potential** Calculating the size of a market can be difficult, but it is usually possible to get some idea of its scale, and of recent market trends. One approach is to assemble relevant secondary data sources, and use it as the basis for your own calculations. You can also make use of your own experiences and observations (e.g. spending time experiencing the product or service you are intending to provide), and in talking informally to people involved in the market. The market forecasts may later prove to be incorrect. Despite this, they remain important because they can influence potential investors and others to support the venture. Some markets are intrinsically more attractive than others. They might be larger, faster growing, have greater potential, or be more robust to changes in external conditions (e.g. recessions, changes in fashion or technology). Against this, markets with more opportunities are also likely to attract stronger competition. Therefore, entrepreneurs face a difficult trade-off between entering a new growth market and waiting until it has developed and become more stable.

- **Competitors and partners** There are a wide variety of techniques for analysing industry competitors. These range from the more strategic, such as Michael Porter's well-known 'Five Forces' model (Porter 1985), which provides a high-level overview, to much more detailed analysis of the product offerings of potential rivals. For the more detailed analysis, you may be drawing on local sources, such as telephone directories and published sets of accounts. As we saw with markets, there is also considerable scope for more conducting of informal research. The opening case study of Made.com (Case 5.1), illustrated how 'co-creation' can lead not just to increased customer value (i.e. adding to what was already offered), but something new, which goes beyond previous offerings. However, this was not achieved by the company alone, but through a 'value constellation' (Bjerke and Hultman 2004: 164), comprising consumers, independent designers, manufacturers, and distributors, all of whom are connected using Internet-based technologies. Many ventures succeed with the help of strong partners, while many others have struggled as a result of a partner's incompetence or bad behaviour. As a consequence, it is worth investing time in this area.

- **Market segments and niches** In addition to estimating the size and potential of a market, you also need to consider which part of the market you intend to target. In mainstream marketing, segmentation is a tried and tested process of dividing any market into groups of customers or segments by some differentiating characteristic, such as size, location, or behaviour. For example, the lunchtime sandwich market could be segmented by dietary requirements, such as meat, vegetarian, dairy free, or nut free. In principle, there should be homogeneity (i.e. similarities) within segments and heterogeneity (i.e. differences) between them. They should also be measurable, identifiable, accessible, and large enough to be profitable. This is not an easy task and it requires effort, research, and fine-tuning. There are two main ways of segmenting a market, either based on a particular characteristic or on actual and potential customer needs (Figure 5.3).

---

 online resource centre 'Understanding your market: additional examples and practical applications.'

Entrepreneurs who engage closely with customers can be particularly good at segmenting on the basis of customer need, as they can develop an intuitive understanding. For example, the company Anything Left-Handed (http://www.anythingleft-handed.co.uk) has concentrated on this needs-based segment for more than 40 years, providing a wide range of products and services for a needs-based segment. It is a family business, run by two left-handed people, which also hosts a forum and publishes newsletters for its members. A capacity to understand your customers' needs better than anyone else – in some cases better than they do – can become a powerful source of competitive advantage. In effect, these ventures are creating a distinctive market niche, which is difficult for other organizations to enter. The process can take some time, and the effect is not always obvious to outsiders. For example, the chief executive of Vickers Laboratories (http://www.viclabs.co.uk) explained the company's success over 30 years in the following terms:

> We're almost invisible! We have become embedded in our customers' supply chains and add value to their service offering, which makes it counterproductive to move from us. [. . .] Our markets are deliberately diverse and we are constantly looking for new business that is difficult! Why? Well, we are really a solutions company. Not chemical ones – we solve problems and that draws on our knowledge. (Lockett 2010)

Figure 5.3 Characteristics-based and needs-based segmentation

Characteristics-based:

- Geography: Neighbourhood, province, state, country, region.
- Population density: City, rural, or urban.
- Climate: Continental, dry, temperate, tropical.
- Demography: Age, education, ethnicity, family structure, gender, income, nationality, occupation.
- Psychographic: Activities, lifestyle, interests, or opinions.
- Behaviouralistic: Behaviour towards the product or service.

Needs-based:

- Personal: Based on individual's needs or preferences. For example, Orange has four needs-based 'pay-as-you-go' mobile phone plans: *Dolphin* for 'fun-loving and sociable' customers who prefer to text, *Monkey* for 'music lovers', *Panther* for customers who 'need to stay connected', and *Racoon* where their 'phone is a tool not a toy' (www.orange.co.uk).
- Organizational: Based on the needs of a company or organization. For example, Igloo Thermo Logistics (Case 6.1) emerging in an unstructured third-party temperature controlled distribution sector to provide added value services (www.igloo-thermo.com).

In the next case (Case 5.2), we see how this process operated for an unusual company that has developed a niche in supplying an emerging market for wholefood, organic, and ethically sourced foods. We will see how understanding the needs of small independent retailers is the key to Suma's success, perhaps achieved, in no small part, due to their own innovative co-operative structure, which attracted staff with experience of and similar values to the market sector they served.

Case 5.2 In the niche: how Suma got to know its customers

The publication of Rachel Carson's book, *Silent Spring*, was one of several early steps in the growth of the environmental movement. Carson, a respected marine biologist, drew attention to the potential environmental consequences of the world's growing reliance on industrialized forms of agriculture, and specifically to the artificial pesticide, DDT. In one of the more frequently quoted passages, she warned her readers that, 'Over increasingly large areas of the United States, spring now comes unheralded by the return of the birds, and the early mornings are strangely silent, where once they were filled with the beauty of birdsong.' (Carson 1962: 189) The origins of the organic movement can be traced back further in time, with influential books such as Eve Balfour's, *The Living Soil* (Balfour 2006 [1943]). The movement was led by social ventures, such as Rudolf Steiner's 'biodynamic' approach at Demeter (http://www.demeter.net) and the Soil Association (http://www.soilassociation.org), which worked with farmers, growers, and others to encourage a different approach to agricultural production.

The market for organic food began to grow in Europe during the last quarter of the twentieth century as consumers became more interested in purchasing food that was produced without using artificial fertilizers, herbicides, or pesticides. Demand was fuelled by a combination of health and environmental concerns. The work of accreditation bodies, including Demeter, the Soil Association, Debio (http://www.debio.no), and KRAV (http://www.krav.se), facilitated the growth of the market. On the distribution side, a number of entrepreneurial individuals became involved, and helped to expand the niche. The following account describes how **Reg Tayler** founded Suma, the pioneering wholefoods and organic wholesaler:

> *Reg had already gained some experience of wholefoods in London, and when he moved to Leeds he opened a retail shop,* Plain Grain. *In August 1975, at a meeting attended by all the wholefood shops in the north of England, he proposed they set up a wholefoods wholesaling co-operative in order to supply each other. Reg and friends set up in the back kitchen of a house in Victoria Road, Leeds, from where they sold cereal flakes, dried fruits and brown rice. They soon needed more room, and so rented a lock-up garage nearby – this is where the name 'Suma' was first used for the growing business. At the time, Reg was working as a delivery driver for Jonathan Silver, taking clothes to his chain of menswear shops around the north of England. Reg delivered the wholefood orders in between the 'official' deliveries for his boss, who knew what was going on but turned a blind eye even so. Within a year they needed proper premises, and in 1976 acquired a tiny two-storey warehouse in Wharf Street, Leeds. Lots of stairs had made the warehouse*

unsuitable for storing food, and there's even one particular story of a time when several tonnes of fruit were carried upstairs, resulting in a horrible creaking noise as the ceiling started to collapse! Luckily the day was saved thanks to a little ingenuity and several large pieces of wood used as makeshift 'props'. A retail shop called Beano *was established round the corner and soon became an independent co-operative, separate from the wholesaling side of the enterprise. In 1977, Reg sold the* Suma *business to the then seven employees, who became the founder members of Triangle Wholefoods Collective, trading as Suma (Suma 2010). In 1978 Suma moved into a much larger three-storey warehouse across the road. It seemed huge – the entire stock fitted into one half of the ground floor. However, rapid expansion of the wholefood market meant that by 1986 the whole place was bursting at the seams and* Suma *moved to a larger warehouse. There followed 15 years of steady growth, both of turnover and of the co-operative. Alongside the growth in size there was a corresponding increase in the complexity and sophistication of the business, and the structure of the co-op went through many modifications to manage this change. In 2001,* Suma *moved to 8,000 m² purpose-built premises in Elland, where currently around 150 are employed. (Suma 2010)*

In 2009, Suma was awarded Specialist Wholesaler of the Year (http://www.thegrocer.co.uk). The company continues to specialize in vegetarian, fairly traded, organic, ethical, and wholefood products. Its 'own brand' range of food and household products is sourced ethically and with the environment in mind. Suma has a policy of working with other regional co-operatives, rather than competing to be the largest national distributor. Its status as an employee-owned co-operative also reflects the organization's core values. Co-operative members and employees receive the same net hourly rate of pay, no matter what their job or responsibilities, and they encourage people to work in different areas of the business, which helps them get closer to their customers:

We find that splitting up difficult jobs and doing them with a team is often better than relying on one expert. When people work in more than one part of a business, they understand the 'bigger picture' better. Many Suma customers have experienced this greater understanding. (Suma 2010)

Suma's employees embrace the distinctive ethos of the product range and work to see these values realized. Close relationships with customers enable niche suppliers to build trusted brands that can be difficult for the competitors to overcome. As the organic niche has grown, larger manufacturers have attempted to enter, though most have found it difficult. One strategy has been for corporations to acquire niche companies (e.g. Seeds of Change, acquired by Mars in 1995, and Cadbury's 2005 acquisition of Green and Black's), in order to gain access and experience of its supply chain.

Ethical point Suma has an Ethical Policy, which sets the standards for products, working practices, employment and environment. Practical examples of this policy include: 100% renewable electricity for warehousing and office facilities; reducing environmental impact in product packaging; offsetting CO_2 emissions by tree planting.

Questions

1. Answer one of the following: (a) What factors have influenced the growth of the organic food market? (b) How has the market segment supplied by Suma changed over time?

2. Suma is an example of an organization with a good understanding of its niche, and of the customers it serves. Can you identify and compare two other examples?

3. How can values-based niche organizations survive the growth of their market, and increasing interest from larger and more powerful competitors?

Sources: Balfour (1943), Carson (1962), Suma (2010). Case compiled by the authors with grateful acknowledgement to Bob Cannell, Suma.

5.4.3 Defining your product and service

Having identified the market gap, how can we define the products and services to be offered? The marketing mix is a traditional, but still popular framework that can be used to consider the market positioning of products and services. Though it is primarily a mainstream marketing approach (e.g. Perreault et al. 2009), the marketing mix can be applied effectively to new entrepreneurial ventures. The mix consists of four elements: (1) Product; (2) Price; (3) Place; (4) Promotion. This original list has been extended into '7Ps' in order to make it more relevant to the marketing of services, and their distinctive characteristics such as intangibility. The three additional elements are: (5) People: (6) Processes; (7) Physical Evidence. Each of these elements is considered briefly in Figure 5.4.

5.4.4 Gaining legitimacy

There is convincing evidence that efforts to gain legitimacy make a real difference to the initial survival rates of new ventures (e.g. Delmar and Shane 2004). Legitimacy is a broad term which refers here to the way a venture is perceived by other people and organizations. The core requirement is that you can establish mutual trust between yourselves and those you need to do business with; this is likely to include customers, suppliers, partners, and other influential actors such as industry regulators. Since trust is often built up over time, based on past experience, much will depend on your track record (if any) in related fields. Your personal credibility is also important, especially in situations where you have no track record (e.g. when moving into a new sphere of activity). This is a persuasive communication challenge. In the absence of proof, can you convince people that you and your team are capable of delivering on your claims? Establishing legitimacy can be particularly difficult for innovating organizations, or industry pioneers, compared to new ventures that are mainly imitative, reproducing well-established practices (Aldrich and Fiol 1994: 650). In the early stages, the key tasks are to articulate (i.e. explain) your venture idea in a clear and convincing way, and to ensure that you understand your customers:

- **Articulating the proposition** Demonstrating that your market is growing and robust will increase your confidence and that of investors and lenders. It is also essential to

Figure 5.4 Elements of the marketing mix

Product-focused (4Ps)

- **Product:** Specifications of the goods or services and how these relate to the consumer's needs. This should include some feedback mechanism to determine customer satisfaction. Consider the product life cycle including service and warranty.
  What are the practical benefits offered customers and to what extent do these constitute a unique selling proposition (USP)?

- **Price:** Process of setting the price for a product or service that will generate a return. This may vary depending on the customer or segment. Consider discounting policy.
  What pricing strategy (or combination of strategies) can the entrepreneur adopt: cost-based, customer-based, or competitor-based?

- **Place:** How the product or service is delivered to the customer. This will include the routes or channels to market. For example, retail, direct sales, wholesale, mail order, and online. Place also considers the customer segments to be addressed.
  What is the entrepreneur's route to market? What are the entry barriers? Is direct marketing or licensing feasible? Can a multi-channel approach be taken?

- **Promotion:** Including advertising, sales promotion, public relations, personal selling, and branding. What is the entrepreneurial marketing mix?
  What can the entrepreneur afford? How innovative is the promotional strategy in terms of publicity and PR and Web2.0?

Service-focused (in addition to the '4Ps')

- **People:** Everyone who comes into contact with the customer and can affect the overall experience of your product or service. Even those outside your control, such as retailers.
  What social capital does the entrepreneur possess? Can they sell and negotiate? Can they network?

- **Processes:** Systems and procedures that can impact on the customer experience, for example, information systems, telephones, online ordering, and debt collection reminders.
  Can the service be delivered virtually? What is the scope for process innovation?

- **Physical Evidence:** One of the main challenges of marketing a service or a product with a service element is providing a potential customer with enough reassurance that the stated service will be delivered. This is particularly important for industries like financial services and information systems. Offering free trials or testimonials from existing customers can help. A good reference customer can be invaluable. It might be worth discounting to gain reference customers for new ventures.
  What is the product/service mix? Has sufficient attention been applied to design, styling, and packaging?

show how your venture relates to that market opportunity. The **opportunity business model** (Section 2.2) could be a useful vehicle for explaining your venture idea in a clear, concise, and convincing way. Setting out the drivers of your opportunity business model provides a relatively straightforward way of summarizing the market opportunity, while the dimensions can be used to outline the key components of the venture itself. It is often helpful to illustrate an abstract idea using a diagram. You may also be able to make use of samples, prototypes, or video clips in order to make your product more tangible. It is also important to ensure that you have built a credible team (Section 4.2).

---

 online resource centre 'Practical advice on pitching a new venture idea.'

- **Understanding your customers** It is important to develop your knowledge of the buying process and the various people that are likely to be involved. This understanding can both inform decisions on the marketing mix, and help in establishing trust and legitimacy. When you are developing a new product or service, it is easy to become overenthusiastic and make unrealistic or oversimplified assumptions about your potential customers. It is always worth just pausing for a moment to consider who is making the buying decision. Even in a 'Business to Consumer' (B2C) market, where you are selling directly to the end-user or consumer, other people may influence or control the final decision. For example, while parents and relatives may be the main purchasers of toys, advertisers target the influencers and end-consumers (i.e. children). Similarly, if you were marketing an alarm for use by elderly people in difficulty, the main influencer is likely to be a younger relative (e.g. a son or daughter), since they are more likely to recognize the need for such a device. The differences may be quite subtle and difficult to identify. The situation can be more complicated in 'Business to Business' (B2B) markets. Here, it is very important to recognize the different roles and levels of power being exercised by the various actors in the buying process, each with different roles. Consider the following examples. Firstly, imagine that you have just launched an innovative bandage that reduces post-operative complications for patients convalescing at home. The bandage is given to patients as part of the overall charge for their treatment. The patients' general practitioners (GPs) have much to gain from the new product because it reduces the overall cost of care and improves patient well-being. Here, there is little to gain by promoting the product directly to patients. The customer is likely to be a GP's surgery, the general practitioners are the main influencers, and the patient is the consumer or ultimate user. Secondly, imagine that you have just developed a new software application that can be run on an organization's intranet, enabling staff to monitor their energy consumption in real-time. A typical purchasing team might include the sustainability manager, who is keen to do anything that can help to reduce the organization's carbon footprint (i.e. an 'advocate' role). However, any decision regarding software has to be approved by the information systems manager, who could reject the proposal on technical grounds (i.e. a 'gatekeeper' role). In addition, you will probably need to persuade another senior manager, the budget holder, that there is a convincing business case for the investment (i.e. a 'strategic decision' role).

5.4.5 Bringing it all together: taking a dynamic perspective

Markets change over time. In the traditional markets of the pre-industrial world (e.g. food, craft products), the process of change was often quite slow, though trading conditions could be transformed by unexpected events such as floods, droughts, or conflicts. In many of today's markets (e.g. consumer electronics, fashion, media), the pace of change is much faster, with rapid changes in technologies and consumer preferences. As a result, market gaps can open up, and close down, within a very short space of time. Gaps emerge when existing products and services fail to offer customers what they want. This can result directly from customer demand (i.e. 'pull' factors), or when new products and services create new demand (i.e. 'push' factors). The actions of entrepreneurial individuals and organizations can also create gaps, which encourage further waves of innovation and opportunity. As we noted in the opening section (Section 5.1), it can be difficult for established organizations to adapt quickly to these kinds of market dynamics, opening up new opportunities for nimble and creative entrepreneurial ventures. So the real challenge for entrepreneurs is not only identifying the market segment most in need of their product or service but also in finding the gaps in demand that are not being served by their competitors. This can only be achieved by fully appreciating both your customers and competitors. This means really understanding your customers' needs and your competitors' capabilities, product and service offerings and intentions. The next case (Case 5.3) illustrates how an entrepreneur was able to create a gap in a fast-moving market that was already dominated by some powerful incumbent firms.

Case 5.3 Finding new customers for GPS: the 'buddi' story

Vehicle-based satellite navigation (satnav) has become a huge global market, with European sales exceeding €1.5 billion (£1.2 billion) (Reuters 2010). Competition has intensified, with satnav companies such as Garmin (http://www.garmin.com) and TomTom (http://www.tomtom.com), becoming household names. By using Global Positioning Systems (GPS), satnav devices determine the geographic location of a vehicle by linking to a central database via mobile cellular, radio, or satellite technologies. The position can be displayed on a map in real-time or recorded to identify movements or routes. GPS systems are used in a variety of other B2B and B2C markets, including surveying, agriculture, yachting, mountaineering, and tourism.

So how can an entrepreneur find new market opportunities in a field dominated by such strong industry competition? The story of **Sara Murray** and 'buddi' illustrates how it can be achieved. Sara traces the source of her idea for a new GPS-based tracking product to an incident when her daughter went missing in a large supermarket – the child had gone in search of one of the small trolleys; Sara called the security staff and fortunately her daughter was rediscovered after a few minutes. Though the incident ended happily, it seems that this personal experience remained with Sara. It was reinforced a few years' later when they went on a skiing holiday and her daughter was attending ski school:

> When I used to go on holiday with my daughter, I took to leaving a scrap of paper in her pocket with my number on, just in case. I knew there must be a safer and better way. I found nothing on the internet so I had to invent it myself. (Sara Murray, quoted in Burn-Callander 2008)

Having realized that there must be a better solution to keeping track of children, Sara's initial plan was to find a suitable technology, such as an existing GPS device that could be used or adapted for this market. Having searched the Internet, she located a company in California that appeared to have a suitable product, but she was unable to source it:

> 'I went to try to buy one. They said it wasn't in stock. It's going to be a while.' Then they admitted it wasn't available in Europe. Ms Murray even offered to be their European distribution agent, but the device was set up only to work in US metropolitan areas. 'I decided

to make one myself,' she says. 'I knew the difficult thing would be building the hardware, because I had never done it before.' (Sara Murray, quoted in Waller 2009)

Creating your own electronic device might seem a daunting task, but Sara was already a serial entrepreneur with considerable experience in creating online businesses. She also had some personal capital to invest and a number of high-level contacts who could provide access to the relevant financial and technical expertise. Sara was a graduate of Oxford University, with a first degree in physiology, psychology, and philosophy. After gaining experience in management consultancy and a traditional investment bank, she started her own marketing consultancy in 1992, specializing in the pharmaceutical sector. Seven years later, she created another venture, which provided instant comparisons between insurance company quotations. She later sold the company, which was then re-branded as 'Confused.com' (http://www.confused.com). Now, having been introduced to two engineers, her next challenge was to develop a product that was both technically sound and able to meet the needs of potential users:

'I was completely consumer-orientated. I said, this is what I would like it to do for my child. They were completely technology-orientated. There was a gap,' she admits. 'Most technology companies build technology and look at where they can sell it.' (Sara Murray, quoted in Waller 2009)

The resulting product was branded as the 'buddi' (http://www.buddi.co.uk). It comprises a compact device based on GPS technology. The device, which sells for €359 (£299), plus a monthly service charge, is linked to a website that enables registered users to track the person wearing it via Google Maps. It incorporates a 'panic button' which is linked to a call centre. This facility can be used to contact named individuals and to provide access to emergency services. Though still addressing its original target market, there are other emerging applications. For example, the 'buddi' system is now being used by home-based carers of people suffering with Alzheimer's disease (i.e. dementia), lone workers who may be vulnerable to attack (e.g. social workers making home visits), and even dog owners. These new segments cut across B2C (consumer) and B2B (business) markets, and have the potential to create both social and economic value. For example, by enabling Alzheimer's sufferers to remain at home, you could both enhance an individual's quality of life and reduce the cost of residential care. In her spare time, Sara is a keen sailor and skier. She is also a member of the advisory board of Seedcamp, an initiative that provides mentoring and micro seed funding to the next generation of young entrepreneurs (http://www.seedcamp.com). In 2009, Sarah was awarded 'Best Female Entrepreneur' (http://www.essenceoftheentrepreneur.co.uk) and 'Entrepreneur of the Year' (http://www.nationalbusinessawards.co.uk).

Meanwhile, GPS technologies continue to develop at a rapid pace, creating new market opportunities and encouraging new entrants into the sector. Hundreds of specialist applications (apps) have become available to take advantage of the increased functionality of mobile phones, including Apple's iPhone. Examples include LocoBlog, which allows users to blog and upload images as their location is tracked and displayed on a website (http://www.locoblog.com), and LociMobile, which allows you to track your contacts and display their location on your own phone (http://www.locimobile.com).

Questions

1. In what ways does Sara Murray story illustrate the techniques of successful entrepreneurial marketing?

2. What lessons can you draw from the way that Sara used her background, experience and contacts to establish legitimacy for her 'Buddi' concept?

3. How can a relatively new organization such as Sara's keep close to its customers in such a dynamic and fast-changing market?

Sources: Burn-Callander (2008); Waller (2009); Reuters (2010).

The online resource centre includes a number of checklists designed to help you to identify (or envisage), and to assess potential opportunities. There are also a number of short exercises that will help you identify concrete, practical ways so that your venture can be launched effectively, taking into account the specific characteristics of the market that you are trying to enter.

 online resource centre 'Marketing checklists and practical exercises.'

The closing *Tim Lockett* case (Case 5.4) examines the interconnected relationship between customers, markets and industry sectors. The case shows how Tim identified and pursued a fast-growing market segment, containing customers whose needs were not well served. Tim's strategy was to use new technology to provide the most efficient and cost-effective service possible. Early signs were that his strategy was going to be effective, but much depended on the reactions of the customers and other industry players.

✳ 5.5 Summary

➤ People in entrepreneurial settings, including entrepreneurs attempting to market a new venture, face a number of distinct challenges including lack of resources, lack of legitimacy, and powerful incumbents. However, they are also well-placed to exploit opportunities, due to their inherent flexibility, closeness to customers, and capacity to form new networks.

➤ Marketing practices are now moving away from the industrialized, mass market approaches that developed during the twentieth century, and organizations of all kinds are experimenting with new marketing approaches, including the use of social media.

➤ Entrepreneurial marketing comprises a number of techniques and practices, based on an opportunity-oriented approach to marketing. These approaches tend to emphasize direct engagement with customers, who sometimes become co-producers of a product or service.

➤ Several mainstream entrepreneurial marketing techniques can also be modified in order support the creation of new entrepreneurial ventures. These include market segmentation, market positioning, and the 7Ps of the extended marketing mix.

➤ Strategic analysis has a role to play, but it is important to recognize that there are a number of ways of acting strategically, some of which are more likely to be effective in an entrepreneurial setting.

➤ Effective entrepreneurial marketing requires a strong commitment from the entire team, with core principles such as customer engagement being communicated throughout the venture, including operational and financial areas, as well as its external networks.

Case 5.4 *Critical incident*
Tim Lockett: knowing your customers and suppliers

In 2005, **Tim Lockett** was the managing director of his own healthcare distribution business. In fact, it was his third business. He and his brother had set up their first business in 1998 but they lost control of it after an unsuccessful joint venture with a large medical company. Tim felt that with nearly 20 years' experience in the UK community care sector he knew the market and industry extremely well. He had developed strong relationships with key suppliers and contracts with national care home groups. His business strategy was simple: use new technology to provide the most efficient and cost-effective service possible. His customers seemed to agree, sales were growing, and Tim felt he could put his past behind him. But rumours had started that the old company had lost a big contract and was in difficulties. Should he try to buy it or simply walk away?

Biography

Apart from the first two years of his working life, Tim has always worked for himself. He reflected, 'I was probably inspired by my father, who when he left the army in the early seventies started a family business running care homes. I was, either consciously or subconsciously, influenced by the idea that if you work hard you can achieve goals that you wouldn't necessarily achieve in a normal working environment. I have always wanted to be my own boss.' Tim's working life started after he graduated from university with a business studies qualification. Then in his early twenties he became a management trainee for a big timber importer. Tim recalled, 'I did that for about a year and decided that I wanted to see the world. So, I backpacked for two years through Australia and America.' On his return to the UK, he took up another management trainee role this time in Campbell's, the food company, and quickly became a successful area sales representative. Tim's working life then took a sudden change of direction. He recalled, 'About a year later my brother came up with the idea of starting our own healthcare distribution business. I did think long and hard about the decision because I could see a good career path for me in Campbell's.'

Tim and his brother launched their healthcare distribution business in 1988. Tim recalled, 'We started from scratch! By the mid 1990s we had a turnover of over £5 million, were making profits and making mistakes! It was about then we were approached by one of our suppliers, a large and successful medical company, with a view of setting up a joint venture company. Their objective was to develop the first truly national distributor to the community care sector. We were offered a 50/50 partnership. They contributed a small equipment division plus a significant capital injection and we put in all of our business to form the new company. We saw it as a way of taking the business forward five years in one single step.'

Tim's role was critical to the company. He stated, 'I was the sales director concentrating on generating new business . . . going out there developing relationships with customers . . . I am a great believer in not closing doors. You can lose a customer through no fault of your own. It could just be a change of personnel and somebody wants to make their own mark and so see the need to change suppliers. But as long as you exit with dignity then that leaves the door open in the future.'

But the joint venture didn't develop as planned. As Tim, recalled, 'Unfortunately, these things don't always work out and although we doubled the size of the business, we realised that we had set-up a joint venture with problems built-in. We thought we had done all our due diligence but hadn't understood the business model of their equipment division. We felt like an ocean liner just heading completely in the wrong direction. There were attempts to rectify it but in our first year we lost a significant amount of money. It was almost from that point that I knew the joint venture wasn't going to work.' The large medical company purchased outright control but Tim remained as the sales director for another year.

Out of the frying pan, into the fire

Then in his early thirties, Tim found himself out of a job and was not permitted to work in the healthcare distribution sector for 12 months. He recalled, 'I had negotiated a pretty good contract so my exit payment was reasonable. It gave me time to think. Not surprisingly, after ten years in the one industry, Tim had built up strong relationships with customers and key suppliers. It was not long before he was approached to go back into it. He recalled, 'My first reaction was . . . *I'm not interested*. But they kept badgering me. So, I thought, *"If I am going to do this I have got to do it differently."* I didn't just want to duplicate what we had achieved before.'

Tim knew the care home market was changing rapidly. He saw the move from a small 'cottage-type' industry into an industry that was attracting big corporate investment. Tim commented, 'In 1988, a group might consist of three homes and now the biggest group in the country has over 700 homes. But, this change had only really started in the mid 1990s but it was gathering pace in 2000. So, I needed to offer something that was different and although the product range was similar I wanted to offer quality products across key product categories. I identified key strategic suppliers who were willing to work with me to develop their business in the care home market.'

Having developed his product offering Tim turned his attention to the customer. He recalled, 'The other issue was identifying potential customers who were willing to embrace change in order to benefit from a more efficient service to lower costs. I became increasingly convinced that with the right strategic suppliers and an efficient delivery service I could win the business of the larger group customers.' Tim needed to expand quickly and he remembered how he achieved this: 'Through my network. I had been involved with the business over ten years, people that were regional managers had gone on to become directors or even owners of businesses. I realised quite quickly that I knew a lot of key players within the industry and I simply approached them, explained what I was doing. They were intrigued that I was back in the marketplace. I got an opportunity to talk to people and say, "*If you work with me I will deliver you best quality at the lowest achievable price.*" They could understand that.'

By this time the Internet was beginning to emerge as a real business tool. Tim stated, 'I started to see the Internet as the vehicle that would make a real difference . . . we were in a very competitive industry. You could lose business if you were not competitive enough. So price played a big part.' But how could Tim's business be different? 'I thought, "*How do we differentiate ourselves from other distributors?*" We are not going to replace the driver, the vehicle, the person who picks the goods. The logistics and distribution part of this business – I didn't see being particularly different in ten years. So, what part of our business could we streamline? It was the administrative part. The Internet became the focus of our strategy. We more than tripled our sales but halved our administrative costs.'

Critical incident

Then in 2005, rumours started that the old company had lost a big contract. It was clear that they were running into difficulties. Tim recalled this moment, 'My brother had helped me set up the new business and we decided to contact the legal guy we still knew in the large medical company . . . within 24 hours we were having a meeting with two main board directors . . . in 48 hours we negotiated a stock, assets and goodwill purchase of the old company.'

What about due diligence? Tim and his brother were allowed to walk around the warehouse that evening to view the stock and met the largest customer the following day. Tim knew that it was important to meet this customer. He recalled, 'It was an interesting meeting and it was clear straight away that the service they were getting was appalling . . . they were very close to losing the contract. They had just got a new buyer and whilst I was waiting to see him, this voice said, "*Hello Tim, how are you?*" It was the Managing Director and he remembered me. He had been a manager with another group previously. So, he came over and shook my hand and I knew he would give us a chance to sort it out.'

Tim knew it would be an emotional moment when he and his brother walked through the doors of their old company the following day, almost exactly four years to the day since the original joint venture was dissolved. He sat opposite his brother and said, 'Should we buy our company back tomorrow?' He replied, 'Tim how well do you know this market and industry? It's your decision . . .'

Source: This case is primarily based on an interview with Tim Lockett and written by Nigel Lockett.

 ## Practical activities

1. New product launch: the branding challenge You are responsible for developing a branding strategy to use when launching an entrepreneurial venture based around an innovative product or service. First, select your venture (e.g. it could be one of the following: health food retailer; running shoes; music and arts venue; advice service for young people). Next, outline how you might build a brand image, using: (a) mainstream FMCG-style marketing approaches as introduced in Section 5.2.2; (b) new marketing approaches, as outlined in Section 5.2.3. Highlight the main differences between the two approaches.

2. Understanding customer types The founders of a new venture have developed an educational software application that allows dyslexic students to develop a personal online dictionary of words and phrases they use. These are displayed as a list of predicted words based on the letters being typed. The software application supports multiple word processing packages and the company also produce a free Apple iPhone application. To use the service, students must be at a school that has purchased a licence and installed the software: (a) Who are the customers? (b) Who are the consumers? (c) Who else may be involved in the buying decision? (d) What marketing strategy would you suggest for the software company?

3. From segmentation to practice For each of the following markets, try to identify THREE possible segments based on relevant characteristics and THREE segments based on customer needs. Refer to Section 5.4.2 for guidance. In each case, select the segment that you consider to be most attractive for a new venture. Draft a 300-word outline of the proposed ventures, including your ideas for marketing them effectively: (1) outdoor clothing; (2) mail order cycles and cycling accessories; (3) fresh growing herbs sold to retailers; (4) laboratory equipment.

 ## Discussion topics

1. Finding the gaps What approach would you adopt in order to identify unmet customer needs in ONE of the following areas: home delivered groceries; night clubs; care for the elderly; fairly traded clothing? Would this process also help you in satisfying those needs?

2. Customer perceptions Identify FIVE ways in which the founders of a new service-based venture (e.g. restaurant, sports centre, office cleaning company, opticians, or design consultancy) could get a better understanding of customer perceptions. Which of these would you expect to be: (a) quickest; (b) cheapest; (c) most insightful; (d) least insightful?

3. Entrepreneurs and the new marketing Many of the larger and more established organizations are now adopting 'new' marketing approaches. What can entrepreneurs do to ensure that their marketing efforts remain competitive?

 ## Further reading guide

Marketing is a broad and well-researched field with a wide variety of textbooks, research-based books, and journal articles. Recent marketing textbooks ranging from introductory to more advanced include Dibb and Simkin (2009), Palmer (2009), and Baines et al. (2008). The long-established text by Perreault et al. (2009) follows a more traditional strategic planning approach. Scott (2009) provides up-to-date coverage of social media, including viral marketing and the use of blogs. Bjerke and Hultman (2004) addresses entrepreneurial marketing. Martin and Thompson (2010) includes a chapter on marketing for social enterprises. Blundel and Ippolito

(2008) is a general introduction to organizational communication, including its role in marketing and public relations. The different schools of strategy are described in Mintzberg et al. (2009). Some relevant international marketing journals include *Journal of Consumer Research, Journal of Marketing, Journal of Marketing Research*, and the *Journal of Retailing*. Management and entrepreneurship journals sometimes feature relevant articles on marketing, including the *British Journal of Management, Journal of Management Studies, Social Enterprise Journal, International Small Business Journal*, and *Entrepreneurship Theory and Practice*.

 # References

Aldrich, H. and Fiol, M. (1994) 'Fools rush in?: the institutional context of industry creation.' *Academy of Management Review*, 19, 4: 645–70.

Baines, P., Fill, C., and Page, K. (2008) *Marketing*. Oxford: Oxford University Press.

Balfour, E. (2006 [1943]) *The living soil*. London: The Soil Association.

Bjerke, B. and Hultman, C.M. (2004) *Entrepreneurial marketing: the growth of small firms in the new economic era*. Cheltenham: Edward Elgar.

Blundel, R.K. and Ippolito, K. (2008) *Effective organisational communication: perspectives, principles and practices* (3rd edition). Harlow: FT Prentice Hall.

Burn-Callander, R. (2008) 'Tracking device firm snares £4m in its first year.' *Real Business*, 23 June. Available at: http://www.realbusiness.co.uk/business_woman (accessed 20 March 2010).

Butcher, M. (2010) 'Made.com raises £2.5m to assault designer furniture industry.' Tech Crunch Europe 21 March 2010. http://eu.techcrunch.com (accessed 23 March 2010).

Carson, R. (1962) *Silent Spring*. Boston, MA: Houghton Mifflin.

Collinson, E. and Shaw, E. (2001) 'Entrepreneurial marketing: a historical perspective on development and practice.' *Management Decision*, 39, 9: 761–6.

Delmar, F. and Shane, S. (2007) 'Legitimating first: organizing activities and the survival of new ventures.' *Journal of Business Venturing* 19, 3: 385–410.

Dibb, S. and Simkin, L. (2009) *Marketing essentials*. London: Cengage.

Grant, J. (2007) *The green marketing manifesto*. Chichester: Wiley.

Hills, G.E. and Hultman, C.M. (2006) 'Entrepreneurial marketing.' In S. Lagrosen and G. Svensson (eds) *Marketing: broadening the horizons*. Lund: Studentlitteratur.

Hoffman, J.L. and Sang, R.V. (2010) 'The "me-tail" revolution'. Outlook: the journal of high-performance business, 1: 1–6 (February). Accenture.

Kollewe, J. (2010) 'Co-op profits surge as customers desert UK's bigger banks.' *The Guardian* (18 March). Available at: http://www.guardian.co.uk.

Lockett, N. (2010) 'New Year's resolution: Time to get closer to your customers?' http://www.nigellockett.com/?p=102 (accessed 3 May 2010).

Made.com (2010) 'About us: beautiful furniture doesn't have to cost the earth.' http://www.made.com/about-us (accessed 3 May 2010).

Martin, F. and Thompson, M. (2010) *Social enterprise: developing sustainable businesses*. Basingstoke: Palgrave.

Mintzberg, H. and Waters, J.A. (1982) 'Tracking Strategy in an Entrepreneurial Firm.' *Academy of Management Journal*, 25, 3: 465–99.

Mintzberg, H. and Waters, J.A. (1985) 'Of Strategies, Deliberate and Emergent.' *Strategic Management Journal*, 6, 3: 257–72.

Mintzberg, H., Ahlstrand, B. and Lampel, J.B. (2009) *Strategy safari: the complete guide through the wilds of strategic management* (2nd edition). Harlow: FT Prentice Hall.

Normann, R. and Ramirez, R. (1994) *Designing interactive strategy: from value chain to value constellation*. Chichester: Wiley.

Palmer, A. (2009) *Introduction to marketing: theory and practice* (2nd edition). Oxford: Oxford University Press.

Perreault, W.D., Cannon, J.P., and McCarthy, E.J. (2009) *Essentials of marketing: a marketing and strategy planning approach* (12th edition). Columbus OH: McGraw-Hill.

Porter, M. (1985) *Competitive Advantage*. New York: The Free Press.

Reuters (2010) 'Satnav 2009 unit sales down 12 pct in main-Europe' at http://www.reuters.com (accessed 3 May 2010).

Scott, D.M. (2009) *The new rules of marketing and PR: how to use news releases, blogs, podcasting, viral marketing and online media to reach buyers directly*. Hoboken NJ: Wiley.

Shaw, E. (2004) 'Marketing in the social enterprise context: is it entrepreneurial?' *Qualitative Market Research: An International Journal*, 7, 3: 194–205.

Suma (2010) 'A brief history.' Suma Wholefoods. Available at http://www.suma.coop (accessed 22 March 2010).

Waller, M. (2009) 'Sara Murray: the woman behind buddi, the personal tracking device.' *The Times*, 3 June 2009. Available at http://www.timesonline.co.uk (accessed 20 March 2010).

Wernerfelt, B. (1984) 'A resource-based view of the firm.' *Strategic Management Journal*, 5: 171–80.

Wray, R. (2010) 'Made.com aims to halve designer furniture prices.' *The Guardian*, 22 March 2010.

6 Processes

Controlling operations and technologies

In thinking, keep to the simple. In conflict, be fair and generous. In governing, don't try to control. In work, do what you enjoy.

Lao Tzu, *ancient Chinese philosopher*

No institution can possibly survive if it needs geniuses . . . to manage it. It must be organized in such a way as to be able to get along under a leadership composed of average human beings.

Peter Drucker, *professor of management and author*

Learning outcomes

After reading this chapter you should be able to:

➤ Appreciate the importance of managing operations, technologies, and controls.

➤ Understand the key elements of information systems.

➤ Appreciate the opportunities for gaining competitive advantage from internal systems, customer relationship management, and the extended enterprise.

➤ Understand the role of controls.

➤ Appreciate the importance of electronic communication platforms and the opportunities for gaining competitive advantage.

Case 6.1 Defrosting investors: from hot dragons to chilled food

In 2007, when **Anthony Coates-Smith** and **Alistair Turner**, who had been trading for just over two years, decided to pitch for investment on the BBC's *Dragons' Den* (Series 4: http://www.bbc.co.uk/dragonsden/), little did they realize that their business, Igloo Thermo Logistics (http://www.igloo-thermo.com), would receive an investment of £160,000 for 22.5% of the equity from Richard Farleigh and Duncan Bannatyne (thisismoney 2007). The company's purpose was to deliver chilled and frozen foods from its own distribution centres. Not surprisingly, interest in the company grew after their appearance on television. Anthony commented, 'It sent our sales into orbit. We have doubled our capacity and we are still fully booked' and they recognized that existing suppliers' service levels could be improved, as 'most were not customer focused'. (Telegraph 2007)

By the end of 2009, the company had a high-specification delivery fleet offering high standards in multi-temperature transport. It offered 24-hour services throughout the UK and western Europe. The fleet was operated out of two purpose-built storage and distribution centres in Leeds and London. Each centre offered frozen, chilled, and ambient warehouse conditions as well as operating teams of dedicated customer service and operations personnel. The company prided itself on having years of experience in temperature control, the innovative use of leading edge technology, and an absolute willingness to serve throughout temperature controlled supply chains.

It guaranteed its customers: service, reliability, professionalism, and quality. Testimonials from its expanding customers support these statements. For example, '*They are extremely cost effective, and their levels of communication are outstanding. Their courier service is reliable and extremely professional, they never let us down; [We] used Igloo cold chain weekly for a number of years to transport our vaccines to our clinics around the country. Igloo provides us with a reliable professional service enabling us to tell our patients confidently that their vaccines have been handled safely in transit. An excellent service; I was pleasantly surprised by the friendly staff and attention to detail. The service and standard delivered by Igloo have exceeded my expectations, and I would happily recommend igloo to anyone looking for a first class chill distribution service.*' (Igloo 2010a)

But in order for Igloo to provide such well regarded service, they needed to carefully manage distribution, warehousing, vehicles, and the systems that integrate them.

Distribution Igloo offered services ranging from transporting a single case from A to B to long-term service requiring a tailored solution. Their temperature-controlled distribution service operated on a daily basis throughout the UK and regularly to key European destinations. They provided complete temperature assurance, visibility, and high quality service.

Warehousing Igloo used large pallet storage facilities for chilled, frozen, ambient, and temperate goods at both their Watford and Leeds depots. These were secure managed sites protected by remote monitored CCTV systems linked to red care alarm monitoring. Temperature compliance alerts are linked to auto-diallers that alert staff to any storage facility developing temperature compliance issues. Warehouse personnel were trained in safe operating and temperature control procedures. They picked over of 70,000 items a week.

Vehicles Igloo operated a fleet of over 50 vehicles ranging in size from refrigerated Smart cars to refrigerated 18 ton HGVs. These vehicles offered dual temperature compartments operating temperature ranges between +25 °C and −25 °C. All the vehicles were equipped with temperature monitors and in-cab printers, as well as remote location and temperature tracing through a satellite telemetry system. Conscious of their carbon emissions, the whole fleet was restricted in 2008 to minimize inefficient high speed driving (Igloo 2010b).

The high level of bespoke services enabled the company to offer a special pharmaceutical service. In 2008 they entered into a partnership arrangement with DHL and trialled new innovative technologies, including the DHL Smartsensor, a slimline RFID (Radio-frequency identification) tag that travels with products at case level recording and tracing their temperature throughout transit, uploading this data at RFID control points through the supply chain without the need to open the package, and alerting monitors to any deviation from specification (Igloo 2008).

Ethical point Igloo seemed to be very aware of the environmental impact of their distribution services. However, some distribution companies have gone one step further and sought CarbonNeutral status (CarbonNeutral 2010a). For example, Courier Systems, founded in 1991, is the largest independent courier company in London. They completed over 3,000 consignments every day. The company, like Igloo, also has a focus on quality, customer service, and efficient use of the latest technologies. They had a varied fleet, including bicycles, motorcycles, and vans. In March 2007, they were awarded CarbonNeutral company accreditation, stating, 'Global warming is a serious issue for us all, we have taken the lead by ensuring that all Courier Systems operations are CarbonNeutral and that emissions are reduced in future'. (Courier Systems 2010)

In February 2010, the company announced it had been purchased by Totem, a company backed by the original founders and a new investor. The new investors committed significant funds to development the operation to be, 'at the forefront of temperature controlled logistics and bring additional experience to the senior leadership team'. (Igloo 2010c)

Points to consider

1. How did Igloo Thermo Logistics track its distribution fleet?

2. What role did information systems play in the company's success?

3. Anthony and Alistair making their Dragon's Den pitch (http://www.igloo-thermo.com). What did they do well? What could they have improved? How did the 'dragons' behave?

Sources: Telegraph (2007); Igloo (2008, 2010a, 2010b, 2010b); CarbonNeutral (2010); Courier Systems (2010);

6.1 Introduction

Throughout this book we have considered many challenging and exciting aspects of **entrepreneurship**. But what do the (seemingly ordinary) tasks of managing operations, technologies and controls have to do with **innovation** and entrepreneurship? The answer is simple, 'the Devil is in the details', a favourite saying of German art historian Aby Warburg (1866–1929). When considering your new venture it is important to distinguish between the processes that simply have to be done to a minimum standard from those that could provide you with a real competitive advantage. When considering your new venture think about the things you will have do better than your competitors in order to win new customers, for example, if you were opening a new café in a poplar area of town. Of course, you would have to be in attractive premises that meet legislation for food hygiene standards but how would you be distinctive from and better than your competitors? It might be service, location, decor, or product quality. But, how do you achieve higher service levels than your competitors? Perhaps your staff are better trained, better motivated, or more knowledgeable. So the key is to think about the processes in your new venture that make you different to competitors. We will consider the former shortly, but in the opening *Defrosting investors* case (Case 6.1) we can clearly see that for Igloo to be successful it has to offer a high quality of service. Not just in terms of delivery but also in terms of consistency of temperature controlled delivery. This can only be achieved by attention to detail. Seemingly mundane procedures become of vital importance to success and gaining a competitive advantage. For Igloo, this means investing in accredited quality systems audited by the British Retail Consortium and the technologies and information systems to monitor this. This means that all Igloo's vehicles are equipped with temperature monitors and in-cab printers, along with remote location and temperature tracing through a satellite telemetry system (Igloo 2010a). Much innovation is mundane, incremental, and depends more on the accumulation of small insights (Porter 1990).

This chapter acknowledges that many **entrepreneurs** are successful, at least in part, because of their ability to manage their **enterprise's** operations, the technologies they use, and to introduce the necessary controls required, adding value not cost. We cannot attempt, in this chapter, to cover all the operational, technological, and control issues faced by new ventures. However, we will focus on three cross-cutting themes, which are increasingly becoming sources of competitive advantage, namely, information systems, controls, and **electronic communication platforms**. Some of these rely on the Internet, not just to interact with customers but also strategic partners, suppliers, and service providers.

This chapter is divided into four sections. The next section briefly reviews the basics of operations management. Section 6.3 considers the increasing importance and availability of information systems to support new venture development. Section 6.4 introduces how controls can be used to add value to products and services. Finally, in section 6.5 the significance of emerging electronic communication platforms for gaining competitive advantage is highlighted. New ventures are supported by processes and in many cases it is these processes that provide competitive advantage.

6.2 **Basics of operations management**

Managing operations is concerned with the production of goods and services. It involves ensuring that processes are efficient, use as few resources as possible, and are effective in meeting customer requirements. It can be described in terms of converting inputs (materials, labour, and energy) into outputs (goods and services). However, to be competitive an enterprise needs to add value, as perceived by its customers, by the processes. Any venture will have a wide range of processes that cover everything from legal 'terms and conditions' for customers to 'employment contracts' with staff. Your new venture will have to perform these to a certain minimum standard just to compete in your marketplace. The discipline of operations management has developed over a long period with many of the core processes being well understood (Greasley 2009; Slack et al. 2009).

Let us again consider the example of 'Maison des Peaux', Michèle Bertrand's new venture, introduced in the previous chapter on **Markets** (Section 5.3).

'Maison des Peaux' (episode two): building processes

Michèle's new venture for supplying designer skins for mobile phones is beginning to grow. Fortunately, her employer, a French women's clothing retailer, agrees for her to move to a part-time contract. She now has 30 designs, which she wants to launch in time for the Paris fashion week. Michèle is still running her business, 'Maison des Peaux', from her flat, and her partner continues to develop the functionality on the website. She now has three manufacturers supplying about 10 designs each. But, as the orders continue to grow, so does the amount of information she is collecting. Michèle decides to use a contact management system which can be linked to her website in the future. This is a big step for her but because her partner is a web designer he is able to implement the system.

Michèle can just about cope with running her growing business but is finding it difficult to get the manufacturers to deliver on time and at the right quality. But, Michèle is particularly worried about the one using the ethically sourced latex as recent deliveries have been late. Fortunately, she now has computer records of all orders by each supplier and plans to visit them to discuss future plans. The owner of the specialist eco-store is still her largest customer and wants to have an exclusive design. He is also slow to pay for the goods and this combined with larger amounts of stock is beginning to cause her cash flow problems. Her most reliable manufacturer, which by coincidence is located in Michèle's home town, is interested in helping her to develop her business and if she will provide ethically sourced latex has agreed to manufacturer this range.

Michèle's meeting with her most reliable manufacturer went very well. They recognized the market opportunity for 'Maison des Peaux' and offered to provide funding in return for a 30% share in the company. They also want to manufacture or source all the products in return for taking full responsibility for stock. This would enable Michèle to run the business full time, employ an assistant, and open a small shop in a fashionable area of Paris. Michèle knows the manufacturer and is still friends with the daughter, Aimée who is also a regular customer. Aimée is a journalist for the regional newspaper, and Michèle asks her to take over writing the blogs and tweets for Maison des Peaux so that she can focus on setting up the shop and dealing with the designers.

Setting up the shop is taking much more time than Michèle thought it would. She hadn't appreciated all the legal and planning requirements and even finding the right location at the right price has been slow. At last she finds a shop she can afford. Even though it is very small, she knows it is in the right part of the fashion district and very close to the new Apple and Nokia retail stores. These are yet to open, but a close friend has been involved in negotiating these tenancies on behalf of the property developer.

With a big feature in a national fashion magazine coming out in a month, Michèle just has to recruit the shop assistant and chase the contractors to finish the shop refurbishment. She knows that the article will mention the ethical sourcing of the latex and decides to visit the plantation and arrange for photographs. Michèle has a 'gut feeling' this will be important and also decides to check that all the latex she uses is accredited as ethical. Aimée starts to write blogs and tweets about the trip and build a special section on the website.

Just like any entrepreneur, Michèle is managing a varying number of processes at any one time. These depend on the venture's stage of development, external factors, and of course the market. At times it can feel like you are just dealing with the most pressing matter rather than following a strategy. Just like jugglers keeping a number of plates spinning but continually switching their attention to the one that most needs input.

The cases in this chapter are used to highlight the reality that many different enterprises use multiple processes, which span managing operations, technologies, and controls. We have already seen how Igloo (Case 6.1) used sophisticated systems to monitor temperature and track vehicle locations and were experimenting with RFID (http://www.rfidjournal.com) to provide sealed individual consignment tracking. The next section considers how enterprises innovatively use information systems to manage their operations and develop channels to market, specifically the use of internal systems, **customer relationship management**, and the **extended enterprise**. Case 6.2, '*A Stitch in time*', highlights these for two manufacturing companies. The third section considers quality control, accreditation, and legislation. Case 6.3, '*Entrepreneurial explosion*', moves beyond considering selling products to selling carbon offsetting services and the role the control can play. Not surprisingly, the ability to reassure customers that controls are transparent and auditable becomes vital. The final section considers the opportunity for gaining competitive advantage from new and emerging electronic communication platforms, such as the Internet. The final case, '*Adnan Awan*' (Case 6.4), highlights one entrepreneur's challenge in doing just this.

In the next section we consider the importance of information systems to new venture creation.

6.3 **Information systems**

Even in the 'simplest' of ventures managing information will be a key process. What information will be important to your new venture? Think about the information you need and you generate. What information do you need to run your enterprise, provide customers, or meet the requirements of regulation? In this section we will consider three main aspects of

Figure 6.1 Relationship between information systems

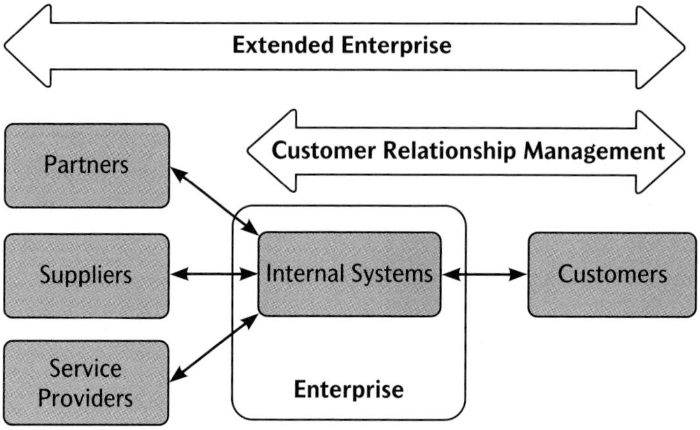

information: (i) internal systems, (ii) customer relationship management, and (iii) the extended enterprise, Figure 6.1. We will discuss the strategic opportunity of emerging electronic communication platforms, such as the Internet, in the final section (6.5) at the end of this chapter.

All information systems should be adequately protected from viruses and hacking. Disaster recovery procedures should be put in place and routinely tested and validated.

6.3.1 Internal systems

In the next chapter, we will look at the role of information systems in accounting and, more particularly, integrated systems that link general, purchase, and sales ledgers with sales order and purchase order processing. In this section, we will take a more general view of the internal information systems used by enterprises.

It is increasingly difficult to imagine any new venture that does not require some form of information system to support its internal systems. Even something as essential as managing contacts, be they customers or suppliers, is increasingly complex. We have seen, in Chapters 4 and 5, how important networking is to new venture creation. As our contact lists expand, both in terms of size and individual contact information, we need to be able to store and retrieve information quickly. It is possible to manage this reasonably well at a personal level with smart mobile phones and entry-level contact management software, such as Microsoft Outlook. The synchronization of devices helps to extend this functionality further. But this will become increasingly difficult to do as your venture expands. More sophisticated contact management applications have emerged to meet this demand, for example, ACT! (http://www. sage.co.uk) and Goldmine (http://www.frontrange.com/goldmine.aspx). Contact management systems need to include the ability to create and manage contact lists, the interactions with the enterprise (appointments, events, and communications), support analysis, and generate and manage tasks. Remember to back up this information regularly. You might be able to rebuild your personal contact list but doing this for an expanding new venture is another matter all together!

Many of the administrative functions of an enterprise can be supported by office automation systems. These help to create, collect, store, manipulate, and analyse office information. All office functions can be improved from typing to filing and from faxing to telephoning. The creation, manipulation, and sharing of documents and spreadsheets can easily be enhanced. There are an increasing number of office productivity tools available, for example, the popular Microsoft Office (http://office.microsoft.com), free open-source OpenOffice (http://www.openoffice.org), and Google's free online document tools (http://docs.google.com).

The need for more specialized information systems will depend largely on the type of enterprise. For example:

- **Manufacturing companies** Manufacturing resource planning (MRP II), including production scheduling, bill of materials, inventory management, material requirements planning, and cost management, for example, Factorymaster (http://www.factorymasterinc.com).

- **Design and manufacturing companies** Computer aided design (CAD), including 2D and 3D modelling. Computer-aided manufacturing (CAM) to control machine tools, for example, TurboCAD (http://www.turbocad.co.uk).

- **Creative media companies** Multimedia applications for creating and editing music, images, film and animation, for example, Logic Studio (http://www.apple.com/logicstudio).

- **Publishing companies** Desktop publishing software (DTP) for designing and printing promotional material, for example, QuarkXPress (http://www.quark.com).

6.3.2 Customer relationship management

A critical aspect of any enterprise is its relationship with customers, which sits within the broader discipline of relationship marketing. Relationship marketing is defined as 'proactively creating, developing and maintaining committed, interactive and profitable exchanges with selected customers (partners) over time' (Harker 1999). This is based on the premise that it is far cheaper to retain an existing customer than it is to win a new one, the economic case for developing such long-term relationships is clear. Reichheld (2001) noted there is a very strong correlation between the loyalty of an organization's customers and its profitability. Customer relationship management (CRM) has emerged as a collective that encompasses the activities required to achieve this. It is defined as the business process that 'addresses all aspects of identifying customers, creating knowledge, building customer relationships and shaping their perceptions of the organization and its products' (Srivastava et al. 1999). Key characteristics of CRM include (Ryals and Knox 2001):

- Adoption of a strong and explicit customer orientation;

- Comprehensive collection and storage of integrated customer information;

- Use of dedicated data analysis software;

- Segmentation of customers by their anticipated life-time value;

- Re-engineering of business processes to deliver customer value;

- Profiling of customers to enable tailored delivery of products and services;

- A strong focus on managing customer, as opposed to product portfolios.

Clearly, implementing a system that can accommodate these characteristics will require a software application that integrates technology, processes, and activities around the customer. It is imperative that any application helps you build strong relationships with customers, add value, and satisfy their needs. In particular, it should help you to:

- Manage the sales process to potential customers (prospects);

- Improve your service to existing customers;

- Make better informed sales and marketing decisions;

- Integrate with your other information systems.

It is about having a 'single view' of a customer across all your channels to market and all your points of contact with them. Think about the information your new venture will generate by interacting with customers. How important will this be to your success? How will you capture, manage, and analyse this information? Compare your intentions with your competitors. Consider the different channels to market and what challenges these will present if you are to have a 'single view' of your customers.

Not surprisingly, a wide range of software applications have emerged to meet this need. The more popular integrated business accounting software packages will include basic CRM functionality, for example Quickbooks (http://quickbooks.intuit.com) and Sage (http://www.sage.co.uk). Specialist applications are also available, including Microsoft's Dynamics CRM (http://crm.dynamics.com) and Sage CRM (http://www.sage.co.uk) and also online versions, including NetSuite CRM+ (http://www.netsuite.com), SageCRM.com (http://www.sagecrm.com), and Salesforce.com (http://www.salesforce.com). These CRM applications should provide a wide range of functionality, including, marketing automation, sales force automation, customer service, customer support, and reporting. We will discuss online social networking, online sales, and e-commerce in more detail in section 6.5.

6.3.3 The extended enterprise

Even the largest corporation does not exist in a vacuum and has to interact with suppliers, partners, and customers. But, for so many new ventures this interaction is at the core of its activities. Any new venture has to extend itself to interact with external organizations. In fact, successful enterprises, out of sheer necessity, can become particularly good at it! In the following case, 'A stitch in time' (Case 6.2), we see how two manufacturing companies, one making workwear and the other making shoes, have done just that. By 2010, James Morley's Blue Autumn was running its sales and distribution operation in Northern Ireland and its manufacturing and accounting operations in Romania. This was only made possible by using an information system, which extended the company's reach across Europe. Interestingly, its largest healthcare customer ordered directly on Blue Autumn's information system. David

Price's Foot Shop Ltd group developed its online customer ordering facilities several steps further. In 2009, the group grew to employ over 110 people and achieved sales of £10 million. Not only had it developed multiple catalogue mail order operations, it used information systems extensively to achieve this. Describing itself as a 'multi-channel marketing company', the group had a 'single view' of the customer across postal, telephone, and online ordering systems.

Your new venture will also interact with suppliers, partners, service providers, and above all customers. How can you configure and manage these relationships in order to gain competitive advantage? Redesigning or reconfiguring the supply chain is an important source of innovation. It seems somewhat obvious to us now, but when Jeff Bezos launched Amazon.com in 1994 the key element of his new venture was to replace high street retailers in the book supply chain and when Michel Dell founded Dell, in 1984, he removed the need for computer resellers.

Case 6.2 A stitch in time: the networked model for entrepreneurship

James Morley founded his workwear clothing company (Blue Autumn) in April 1997. Quite understandably, he located the office and manufacturing plant in Newtownards, Northern Ireland where he lived. His company specialized in the provision of workwear to the healthcare and catering industries (http://www.blueautumn.eu). By 2004, James faced a difficult decision. Due to the ongoing decline of clothing manufacturing in the UK and Ireland, he had to consider relocating his manufacturing operation to a lower cost economy which also had a skilled and committed workforce. Even if he could find this, how would he be able to control the manufacturing at arms length?

The answer came in two parts. Firstly, in April 2004, he made a decision to relocate the manufacturing to Eastern Europe. James stated, 'Our factory is now located in north east Romania, in the city of Iasi. Romania is often referred to as the tailor of Europe. One of the advantages of being in Eastern Europe is the fact we can transport goods from our factory to our warehouse within a 5–7 day period.' Blue Autumn retained its warehousing and offices in Northern Ireland. A key selling point to customers was the quality of service and the suitability of their garments to specialist working environments. They stated, 'Our garments are about styling and quality, we firmly believe that workwear should be manufactured to last and to last staying smart. We are confident that the ranges deliver versatility and comfort, offering you the user first class workwear . . . On reflection you will discover that these attributes put us a stitch above the rest.' (Blue Autumn 2010)

The second part of the solution required Blue Autumn to change information systems from one that operated in a single location to one that would allow for multiple locations, seamless workflows and also provide online ordering facilities to larger customers. The answer came in the form of a hosted information system which employees, both in Northern Ireland and Romania, and customers could access through the Internet.

Blue Autumn's new information system, i-Tr@der, was supplied by Internet Power Systems. The system, operating through a web browser (i.e. Microsoft Explorer), allowed James to manage his business online (IPS 2010). Contacts, emails, task lists, diaries, document filing, accounting, catalogue orders, electronic form orders, order fulfilment, stock, purchasing, and collaborative workspaces were hosted on one system. The company was able to offer both stock and non-stock services with the latter taking between four and six weeks to produce and deliver, upon receipt of order. It promoted a contract service to larger workwear users, such as the UK National Health Service, stating, 'We can supply your requirements in any style, fabric or colour . . . through our Romanian production unit. Romania has become the No.1 location for garment production in the EU due to the quality, the favourable cost structure and the short turn around cycles of its highly developed garment production industry. We can handle the complete sourcing process, from material and trim packs to permanent control of incoming delivery dates and qualities.' (Blue Autumn 2010)

By 2010, Blue Autumn was delivering over 5,000 items of workwear per month with the majority being manufactured to order in its wholly owned Romanian subsidiary, employing then 40 staff. Blue Autumn's largest healthcare customer specified and placed orders online.

David Price, who bought Somerset-based Cosyfeet (http://www.cosyfeet.com) in January 1991, took a different approach to using information systems to develop his business (Cosyfeet 2010). The specialist footwear company became part of David's Foot Shop Ltd group, which employed over 110 people and had sales of over £10 million by 2009. Other specialist companies in the group also included Walktall (shoes in large sizes) and LookAtMyCrazyShoe (fun, funky, functional footwear).

David used information systems to transform his traditional shoe-making business from a conventional mail order company to one that embraced web technology throughout its marketing, sales and distribution. David stated, 'I bought the Cosyfeet business . . . when it was very small . . . We are a multi-channel marketing company. We started really with just Velcro slippers, selling to the elderly in retirement homes. We've now stuck within that niche, and we see ourselves as world leaders really in footwear, socks and hosiery. The four channels we've got are the existing catalogue company, we have about 150,000 customers, wholesale business, so we're selling through 100 or so mobility shops, we have a shop here, and the hub of our business is now increasingly our web business.' (SWFWG 2010)

His confidence in the company's systems was high, 'Yes, we're very good at footwear – we're world leaders at what we do – but actually if we came in to work tomorrow and all our footwear factories had burned to the ground, our core systems and skills would allow us to set up selling virtually any product. So I believe what we're really good at are systems, marketing and transactional websites; which means we are always looking for business opportunities where we can use our knowledge of systems. From my perspective, it has to be niche and the Internet has to be in there somewhere. The old adage that the shoemaker should stick to his last is also very appropriate for us – until now we have stuck to our comfort zone (footwear) but we've started to move into new areas, such as clothing.' David added, 'We're always benchmarking ourselves against other companies and we've come to realise that we're very good at what we do.' (Sanderson 2010)

Points to consider

1. What are the similarities and differences between Blue Autumn and Cosyfeet?
2. Why does David Price describe his group as a 'multi-channel marketing company'?
3. What is the role of information systems in Blue Autumn and Cosyfeet?

Sources: Blue Autumn (2010); Cosyfeet (2010); IPS (2010); Sanderson (2010); SWFWG (2010).

The 'A stitch in time' case (Case 6.2) illustrates the important role various information systems can play in successful ventures. Cosyfeet used a communications system to manage its telecommunications call centre, integrating it with their website and with their main suppliers for credit card payments and deliveries. This means the company could deal with over 2,000 customer telephone calls with a relatively small number of staff. David Price stated, 'It's going to be the heart of what we do when we integrate the web with our call centre, so that people in our call centre can see when our customers are online, what pages they're on . . . We're constantly working on this, and we're quite certain we're at the cutting edge of this type of technology, appropriate for a business of our size.' He added, 'My view on the Internet now is very simply the Internet changes everything. You have to start by thinking Internet first, even though you might be running a chain of shops, you've got to think how people in the future are going to find your shops, do comparison shopping . . . For the most part people are going to do that comparison shopping from the comfort of wherever they access the Internet, which may of course be a handheld thing. You've got to think of it first. It changes everything.' (SWFWG 2010).

However, other entrepreneurs have also used information systems to achieve competitive advantage. For example:

- Alastair Mitchell and Andy McLoughlin: Hurdle, providing secure online workspaces (http://www.huddle.net)

- Ben Black: My Family Care, online booking of carers (http://www.myfamilycare.co.uk)

- Bradley McLoughlin: Trading4u, managing online auctions (http://www.trading4u.com)

- Cabrelli and Miles Latham: Affixxius Productions, producing alternative corporate videos (http://www.affixxius.com)

- Henry Bennett: Island Wall Entertainment, developing mobile applications (http://www. islandwall.com)

- Holly Tucker and Sophie Cornish: Notonthehightstreet.com, selling unusual products online (http://www.notonthehighstreet.com)

- Justin and Louise Bovington: Rivers Run Red, using 3D virtual technology (http://www. riversrunred.com)

- Lisa and Jonathan Wilkinson: t-mac Technologies, providing energy management services (http://www.t-mac.co.uk)

- Sara Murray: buddi, offering tracking services (http://www.buddi.co.uk)

6.4 Controls

For many enterprises, existing information systems, particularly accounting applications, will provide the necessary control mechanisms. However, it is worth exploring two areas where additional controls might be appropriate, namely quality control and accreditation.

6.4.1 Quality control

Quality control can simply be the process by which enterprises manage the production of products and delivery of services to an appropriate standard. Provided customers are happy with the standard achieved then no action is required. However, many organizations are required, by law or an external partner, to demonstrate quality control procedures are in operation and are audited by an independent body. The International Organization for Standardization provides a number of international standards across a wide range of markets and industries, known collectively as ISO standards (http://www.iso.org). These ISO standards specify the requirements for products, services, processes, materials, and systems and for assessment, managerial, and organizational practices, for example, ISO 9001 is a quality policy that sets out the organization's working practices and monitors these for any non-conformances that result in corrective actions. Good quality policies are linked to satisfying customers' needs.

But why would a new venture be interested in informal quality systems if they are not required to use them? The rigour required, for operating formal quality systems, can be of competitive advantage to new ventures because it encourages all staff to focus on the processes required to meet customer needs. Even if formal ISO accreditation is not sought, the discipline of recording non-conformances instils a focus on quality that can identify areas for improvement or corrective action.

When considering your new venture, think about the ways in which quality can be controlled and in particular how you could use it to gain competitive advantage. Do not underestimate the knowledge and expertise required to develop and implement quality control systems but also the possibility that existing enterprises may have entrenched processes that add cost not value. Remember that it is how the customer perceives this value not the enterprise.

6.4.2 Accreditation

In addition to accreditation to ISO quality standards, there are numerous accreditation systems that can impact of a new venture's success. National and international schemes can apply equally to large and small organizations. Accreditation may be voluntary and developed by a trade association in support of its members, by an independent standard body or in response to legislation and applies to all organizations. For example, the provision of care in people's own homes is regulated under the UK's 'Domiciliary Care Agencies Regulations 2002'. In California, the Department of Social Services regulates 'Residential Care Facilities for the Elderly' by setting out the standards required and monitoring procedure. It is imperative to be fully aware of legislation and how to comply.

However, accreditation under voluntary codes can be a source of competitive advantage. Launched in 1993, Investors in People standard is overseen by the UK Commission for Employment and Skills. It is promoted as a highly versatile framework, which 'helps organisations transform their business performance . . . by focusing all our advice and assessment around meeting your organisation's needs. The first thing we do is find out what your performance targets or key priorities are. These then become central to all our work, so we support your business plan and maximise the value you gain from working with us.' (http://www.investorsinpeople.co.uk)

Rabbit Contracting was founded in 2002 specializing in epoxy and polyurethane coating and screed systems (http://www.rabbitcontracting.co.uk). By 2009, it employed six people and operated across the UK on a national basis, particularly in the manufacturing, food processing, and medical sectors. Managing director, Adrian Breeds stated, 'The significant benefits of our engagement with Investors in People have much more than justified our investment. We would definitely recommend it to other small companies in a similar position. We only wish we had known about it five years earlier.' He agreed that, 'without the Investors in People programme Rabbit Contracting would not have still been in business.' The benefits to Rabbit Contracting were (IIP 2010):

- Directors had to establish a vision for the enterprise;
- Directors were better skilled for recruitment and development;
- Performance improved. Turnover increased 39% year-on-year and profitability by 25%;
- Increased quality and repeat customers;
- More completely satisfied customers;
- Returns from investment training and development activities.

In the following case, 'Entrepreneurial explosion' (Case 6.3), we can see how a market has emerged in response to concerns over climate change and in particular production of carbon dioxide. Competitors are vying to provide carbon footprint calculations and verified offsetting schemes. But, what can the organizations gain from voluntarily joining such schemes?

Case 6.3 Entrepreneurial explosion: carbon offset fuels new standards

There has been a dramatic increase in awareness of the issue of climate change. Individuals, companies, organizations, and governments have responded in various ways. The need to do something to help reduce greenhouse gas emissions has resulted in an increasing number of schemes that allow for the offsetting of carbon dioxide produced by human activities. There are two markets for this carbon offsetting. The first operates for large companies, governments, or entities to buy carbon offsets so that they can comply with the limits they are allowed to emit. The second and much smaller voluntary market enables individuals and companies to offset their greenhouse gas emissions from transportation, energy, and other sources. These schemes offer the chance to offset against specific schemes funded by the payments. Typically, these might be renewable energy generation (wind farms, solar power, hydroelectric schemes, and biofuel plants), reforestation, and reduction schemes that replace high carbon producing activities with less harmful ones.

Many innovative and entrepreneurial companies have emerged to exploit this opportunity; for example, Clear, Carbon Footprint, and the CarbonNeutral Company. But how do such companies persuade potential customers that the calculation of their emissions is accurate (their carbon footprint) and the schemes provided will genuinely offset these emissions? Clearly, there is a need for both trust and simplicity, which can only come from robust transparency systems. Consumers need to feel confident in the management, monitoring, and control of schemes and easy access to validated information. Perhaps not surprisingly, governments have been quick to introduce regulations to reassure consumers of the validity of these offsetting measures; for example, the UK government's Quality Assurance Scheme for Carbon Offsetting requires: (i) accurate calculation of emissions, (ii) Kyoto compliant carbon credits, (iii) cancellation of carbon credits within a year of purchase, (iv) clear and transparent pricing, and (v) advice on how a consumer can reduce their carbon footprint (DECC 2010).

The first company to qualify for the scheme was Clear, founded by **Dr Bruce Elliott, Neil Chapman**, and **Ben Hedley**, in 2007. They tried to differentiate themselves by only offsetting using Certified Emission Reductions (CERs) which have been issued every time the United Nations prevents one tonne of carbon dioxide equivalent being emitted through carbon projects registered with the Clean Development Mechanism (CDM) (Clear 2010).

Also accredited by the UK government scheme, Carbon Footprint Ltd, founded by **John** and **Wendy Buckley** in 2005, focuses on businesses looking for carbon management consultancy services. They help these clients to reduce energy consumption and emissions and offset unavoidable emissions through internationally recognized carbon offsetting schemes. John Buckley obtained a degree in Engineering and MSc before working 14 years as a scientist. Wendy Buckley had a PhD in Physics and a background in sustainable energy development (Carbon Footprint 2010). Customers of Carbon Footprint services included Deutsche Bank, Hoover-Candy, IKEA, and Logica.

Interestingly, the CarbonNeutral Company, founded by **Sue Welland** and **Dan Morrell** in 1997 and one of the oldest providers, was not part of the government scheme, choosing instead to be a founding member of the International Carbon Reduction and Offset Alliance (http://www.icroa.org). By 2009 it had contracted more than 4 million tonnes of carbon from 300 projects on six continents (CarbonNeutral 2010a). Customers of the CarbonNeutral Company included Courier Systems, Radio Taxis, and Scandinavian Airlines.

Its schemes include:

- Erbaqu Hydro Power: This generates renewable energy from six run-of-river hydro power plants in China.

- Kotmar Waste Heat Recovery: This captures flue gases at a steel plant to produce clean electricity in Central India.

- Govindapuram Wind Power: This generates renewable energy from wind turbines, which is used to power yarn spinning factories and supply energy to the local grid in India.

- Chindile-Mapanda Reforestation: This establishes commercial forests at two locations in Tanzania. (CarbonNeutral 2010b)

As well as publishing specific schemes, the CarbonNeutral Company worked with the Edinburgh Centre for Carbon Management to help clients analyse their greenhouse gas emissions from their activities (http://www.eccm.uk.com).

Points to consider

1. What is the role of the government Quality Assurance Scheme for Carbon Offsetting? Why did the CarbonNeutral Company not join the scheme?

2. How do Carbon Footprint, Clear, and the CarbonNeutral Company differentiate themselves from each other?

3. Why would an organization want to voluntarily offset and how could they use this to gain a competitive advantage?

Sources: CarbonNeutral (2010a, 2010b); Clear (2010); DECC (2010).

The above case highlights how regulation emerged as the market for carbon offsetting developed. However, convincing potential customers of the added value of voluntarily offsetting goes beyond regulation to understanding their underlying needs. In the next section we will consider how emerging electronic communication platforms provide opportunities for innovation.

6.5 Electronic communication platforms

New technologies are constantly emerging and having an impact on markets and industries – creating opportunities. One particularly significant group of emerging technologies is electronic communication platforms, for example the Internet and 3G mobile networks. The Internet has changed the landscape in many sectors and in many ways. Of course, retailing has changed to accommodate online sales (e-commerce). David Price (see Case 6.2) is adamant that, 'Very simply the Internet changes everything. You have to start by thinking Internet first, even though you might be running a chain of shops, you've got to think how people in the future are going to find your shops, do comparison shopping . . . It changes everything.'

So, it is clear that Internet changes the marketing environment by introducing a new channel or route to market: e-commerce. This is not just the preserve of large companies but can also provide significant opportunities for new ventures and small businesses. For the latter, the Internet is viewed as an important and growing new channel (Lockett and Doherty 2008). However, the Internet, and increasingly 3G mobile networks, is changing not just the channels to market but also the way businesses process and collaborate (often referred to as e-business). Information systems' functionality and capabilities have changed profoundly and dramatically as a result of these new electronic communication platforms. Doug Richard in his 'The Entrepreneur's Manifesto' suggested that, 'true broadband is not 1MB . . . it is 100Mb . . . It is the key infrastructure that will kindle a wave of creative destruction and increased wealth that will match the industrial revolution.' (Richard 2010)

Your new venture may, directly or indirectly, use the Internet for marketing to customer, communicating with suppliers, processing information, or working with key partners. Increasingly, internal information system development is moving to an external development and provision model (outsourcing), driven by the need for lower costs, faster implementation, easier-to-use applications, and effective use of scarce resources (Ward and Peppard 2002). The emergence of hosted e-business enterprise applications is a prime example of a profound change deriving directly from the availability of low cost, ubiquitous electronic communication networks, such as the Internet. E-business is defined as 'the use of electronic communication networks to transact, process and collaborate in business markets' (Lockett and Brown 2005). These hosted applications provide functionality ranging from email to contact management and from sales order entry to financial ledgers with report generators.

Telecommunication, technology, and service companies have emerged or evolved to provide a range of web services and hosted applications designed to exploit existing communication infrastructures. Typically these are known as application service providers (ASP) that: provide a contractual service offering to deploy, host, manage, and rent access to an application from a centrally managed facility, responsible for either directly or indirectly providing all the specific activities and expertise aimed at managing a software application or set of applications (Gillian et al. 1999). This fundamental change in the relationship between user, hardware, and software presents opportunities for new business models for service provision. Typically these hosted applications are offered on a rental or fee basis, rather than the traditional purchase model. The fee normally includes the use of the software and the provision of the processing and storage platforms, but not the provision of the electronic communication networks. One such ASP, which became particularly well-known, was Salesforce.com (http://www.salesforce.com), founded in 1999 by Marc Benioff. In less than 10 years, Salesforce.com became one of the largest providers and specialized in providing its customers with sophisticated customer relationship management (CRM) applications. CRM applications were used to support sales and marketing activities, including telesales, e-commerce, sales data analysis, and marketing campaigns.

The provision of hosted enterprise applications is increasing, particularly in the US, and the potential for hosted services is strong (Lockett et al. 2006). The Internet has provided numerous **entrepreneurial opportunities,** and many new business models have emerged. Some business models, such as online retailing (http://www.amazon.com) and online marketplaces (http://www.ebay.com), have flourished. One of these new sectors consisted of software developers providing access to applications over the Internet, from simple hosted email (http://www.Gmail.com) to highly complex hosted enterprise applications (http://www.sap.com). Organizations use these web-based applications rather than just buying the software and installing it on their own computer networks as it takes less time, expertise, and resources. ASPs reduce costs by hosting and managing software applications centrally and providing access to remote users via web browsers or thin clients. The costs are shared across many organizations, and ASPs rent access to these applications at typically between 10% and 20% of the equivalent purchase price. In Chapter 2, we heard from Mark Robinson (Case 2.4) who built a software prototype of his strategy mapping application. The project used the latest web-based technologies designed to be delivered as a service over the Internet and paid for on a subscription basis.

So, electronic communication platforms are increasingly changing the way enterprises transact and process. However, they also provide a platform for emerging collaborative and interactive online networking services, known collectively as Web 2.0. These include technologies for blogging, forums, RSS feeds and tweets, and wikis, which support the growth of online social networks, such as Facebook (http://http://www.facebook.com) and LinkedIn (http://www.linkedin.com). In Chapter 9, we will hear from Steve Pankhurst who co-founded Friends Reunited (http://www.friendsreunited.co.uk), arguably the first commercially successful online social networking community (Case 9.2). We see how in just five years they took what may in hindsight seem to us like a 'sure-fire' winner from concept through exploitation to eventual sale for £120 million.

Clearly, online social networks can end with a financial return for the service provider, but what use are these to new ventures and enterprises? Duncan Goose, founder of Global Ethics and One Water (http://www.onedifference.org), set up a new venture, in 2005, to sell ethical bottled water and donate 100% of its profits to installing a specialized water pumping system called PlayPump (http://www.playpumps.org) (Case 2.2). The enterprise launched a Facebook group to raise awareness of World Water Day by attracting 250,000 members to the online group (Facebook 2010). Duncan uses Twitter to support this objective (http://twitter.com/duncangoose). Dell Outlet claims that it 'booked more than $3 million in revenue attributable to its Twitter posts' (Twitter 2010a), and the manager of CoffeeGroundz, a small independent coffee shop, used Twitter to extend their relationship with regular customers (Twitter 2010b).

Using Web 2.0 technologies in order to increase your 'virtual footprint' will be an important element in your online strategy. How can blogging, online social networks, and tweeting help your new venture?

This chapter provides insights into the opportunities for gaining competitive advantage through managing operations, technologies, and controls. The final case, 'Adnan Awan' (Case 6.4), is based on interviews with an entrepreneur who is determined to develop his new office supplies company in order to become a national business by establishing strategic relationships with manufacturers, wholesalers, and national carriers. Adnan was confident that the small team of three highly experienced people could win new national contracts. His main worry was changing the basic systems, which the company relied on for telesales and order processing. Adnan knew the Internet could provide lower cost integrated information and telephone systems and that he could not delay this critical decision any longer.

✳ 6.6 Summary

- Managing operations, technologies, and controls are important to running any enterprise but can also provide opportunities for gaining competitive advantage.

- Information systems play a vital role in many new ventures by developing internal systems, customer relationship management, and the extended enterprise.

- Customer relationship management provides an opportunity to achieve a 'single view' of a customer and effectively support multi-channels to markets.

- Controls can support quality and accreditations systems, which in turn can deliver a recognized service standard and provide opportunities for gaining competitive advantage.

- Electronic communication platforms are increasingly important to new ventures, not only in supporting transactions and processes but also collaboration, such as online social networks.

Case 6.4 *Critical incident*
Adnan Awan: a scalable business

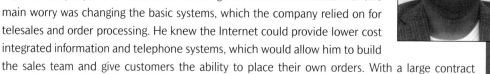

By 2009, **Adnan Awan** had grown his office supplies company to a £350,000 turnover in just over two years. By establishing strategic relationships with manufacturers, wholesalers, and national carriers the small team of three highly experienced people was confident in winning new national contracts. Adnan's main worry was changing the basic systems, which the company relied on for telesales and order processing. He knew the Internet could provide lower cost integrated information and telephone systems, which would allow him to build the sales team and give customers the ability to place their own orders. With a large contract available, Adnan could not delay this critical decision any longer.

Biography

Many of Adnan's close family had started their own businesses. He remembered, 'My father has done it, my uncles, everyone really worked for themselves. My inspiration was my father . . . he came into the country in the late 70s, worked in the mills and then went on from there to set up his own business in textiles. He did very well from it. So it was an ambition I wanted to carry out.'

Adnan gained commercial experience working for one of Europe's largest electronic office supplies (EOS) distributors in the UK. The company supplied a wide range of products, including laser, inkjet fax consumables, storage backup media, paper, filing supplies, and photocopier supplies. Adnan recalled, 'I started work for them at the age of 15 part-time and then full-time when I left school at 16. I then did a bit of college work, went to university to do health and social care but I never finished it.' He added, 'I just got so busy with work . . . I worked from being in the warehouse to credit control, then to customer services and sales then finally to purchasing. I very quickly ended up managing the company's imports and exports . . . I did that for the better part of the last six years. I learnt a lot from this business.' The French-owned company had grown from zero to £120 million turnover within 11 years.

By 2006, Adnan felt that he had reached a senior level where the logical next step would be a position as a director, which would mean taking up an office-based role. His role in purchasing meant that he was constantly travelling all over the world on business and became well respected by the largest manufacturers. Adnan recalled, 'I was 25 at the time and I was earning a fantastic salary. I was earning the same salary as all the directors were. So there was no reason for me to leave my job and sit behind a desk doing nothing. So I decided it was time to move on. I left the company with no real idea of what I wanted to do but realised I had reached my peak there.'

Time for a fresh start

Within just two days of leaving Adnan was offered two separate jobs with Epson and Samsung. But on reflection he felt to go straight back into working for another company was not the right choice. Adnan, said, 'So I turned them both down. Obviously thanked them for the opportunity. Went to Dubai for my holiday . . . came back and sat down and thought, Right what do I want to do?'

Adnan sat down with a close friend from the industry and discussed the possibility of setting up his own company. He recalled, 'We did some research on what was going on in the market and where the demand was. We thought there is definitely a gap in the market.' This would mean, 'exactly the same product range but a different route to market . . . sticking with the product that I knew best – inks and toners.'

Initially, Adnan set up as an online business selling ink cartridges to consumers. He stated, 'You are sat at home, need an ink cartridge for your printer, would log on to the website, place your order and get your product the next day.' This proved very challenging and even with a good website and spending money on online advertising the business was not making a return. He remembered, 'I pulled in a few friends of mine from within the industry and said, I am throwing money at a business at the speed of light and I am not getting a return. They saw that without serious marketing support I was not going to bring in the business.' It was time for Adnan to rethink his business strategy.

An early change in direction

By May 2007, Adnan realized he needed an experienced partner for the business to work. Fortunately, a good friend from his old employer agreed to join him. He said, 'So that is where the new idea came about . . . we sat down and we asked, What can we do with the company? We realised I had a lot of contacts in terms of supplying business-to-business. So we tied up very quickly with the UK's two top suppliers.' He explained, 'In the UK the office supplies market is dominated by two major wholesalers, who supply the 3,500 independent office supplies companies in the UK.'

However, this presented Adnan with a problem. He recalled, 'To deal with these guys you have got to have an expenditure of £10,000 a month, trading accounts, trading history and XYZ . . . we didn't have any of it. We didn't have anything of the sort. So, I picked up the phone to certain people within that business and said, We have got this new office company can you help? Within days we had credit accounts set up, we had a credit limit . . . purely on recommendation!'

Having established the new direction for the company, Adnan turned his attention to sales. He said, 'We had to do telesales to get business. We needed people on the phone to contact customers and say, This is who we are, this is what we do. Are you interested? The biggest problem we had was our pricing structure . . . we had agreements with these two wholesalers but the pricing support wasn't there. They gave us accounts, access to 30,000 different product lines but not enough margins to sell to blue chip companies. To get that we had to tie up with a buying group.' He added, 'Again, through contacts, recommendations and industry knowledge I knew who were the best people to talk to. I approached the largest buying group for our industry with a turnover of £600 million. But they were very picky when choosing their members. Lucky for us, we got in and they gave us membership!'

Now with access to the two largest wholesalers and membership of the largest buying group Adnan knew they had the buying power to compete with anybody. He recalled, 'We started tendering for businesses . . . from very small companies to large corporations. We successfully tendered for 3 or 4 different companies across the UK and won the office supplies business of Europe's largest freight company. We decided that we wanted to be a national business and not a local business.' This approach was not the norm for the industry with most office supplies companies concentrating on local customers.

Competition on a big scale

The office supplies industry was dominated by large international companies, such as Viking, Office Depot, and Lyreco. Adnan knew that market well and stated, 'Most companies in the UK will buy from one of these three companies. Now the independents will go out there to try and take business off these three big boys . . . we make what we call a decent level of margin.'

Adnan said, 'People would talk to us because we had the pricing and we had the experience within our business. We employed a third person with a wealth of experience of tendering with blue chips and co-operatives.' The customer base grew and the product range expanded from electronic office supplies to selling bleach, toilet paper, and fax machines. This gave Adnan more confidence, and even though the turnover of the company was £350,000 they began to quote for large national tenders, in one case being shortlisted for a contract worth seven times their existing turnover. Adnan recalled, 'Perception is everything . . . an example of that is we tendered for the business of a large plc this year. We didn't win . . . I wasn't expecting to win. But the opportunity to actually quote for that business and to be recognised was an achievement. I know today that there are directors of the plc who have seen our letterhead paper, our pricing and I know somewhere down the line my name will be mentioned to them . . . that relationship is there now.'

Critical incident

The company now consisted of a team of three highly experienced and knowledgeable people. Adnan knew that having established the strategic relationships with manufacturers, wholesalers, and national carriers the business could grow quickly. The team knew that to win national contracts they would need to develop their internal information systems considerably. Adnan said, 'We have only got a very basic back-office system . . . basically some software, which gives us invoicing and sales.' They started to search for a new integrated system. Adnan stated, 'We've looked at about half a dozen different systems . . . we want our business to grow in the next three to five years. . . . and stage two . . . is the e-commerce side of the business.' They wanted to integrate both the back-office and sales functions, including e-commerce. As Adnan described it, 'So our customer can sit in their office, anywhere in the UK, place an order and it comes straight off into our distribution centre.' These orders would be dispatched by their wholesaler using a national carrier.

Adnan knew that the Internet would play a vital role. It wasn't just the information systems that needed to be developed. He stated, 'Our telephone system . . . we are probably going to use Internet so that all our calls are routed by the net. Our back-office, e-commerce system and telephone system will be running through it. I wouldn't have to outlay silly money for equipment servers and telephone switchboards. Send it all through the Internet, let somebody else manage it.' He added, 'My job is to run a business, to make a living and to make sure we service our customers . . . by the end of next year I want another three to four people within the business . . . that talent might not necessarily be available nearby so I may have to employ someone in London. And the beauty of the Internet is I can have someone working for the business anywhere in the country. They can log on to a system, sat in London, sort the amount of stock and make a call from our telephone system.'

Adnan knew that once they had found the right system and implemented it, it would, 'open a lot more doors in terms of going out to win new business. The problem we have right now is managing the business we have because our systems don't support it . . . a new system will give us time to go out and win new business and then look for more opportunities. My plan is to take the business from where we are today to a two and half million pound business in three years [2012]. We want to be a national business. It is a dream . . . but then so was everything else and for me if you are not dreaming you are never going to get it.'

Adnan completed at tender for a large national contract and knew he had to make a decision on the new systems soon . . .

Sources: This case is primarily based on an interview with Adnan Awan and written by Nigel Lockett.

 ## Practical activities

1. **Information systems** What information systems will be important for the following enterprises:?

> 1. A manufacturer of sandwiches, which are supplied to over 100 local fuel service stations.
>
> 2. A team of five IT engineers offering next-day on-site repair or replace services.
>
> 3. A social enterprise providing home care to over 200 partially sighted individuals within a 60-mile radius.

2. **Controls** You are launching a new venture, which delivers documents in a busy city centre. You will be offering bicycle, motorcycle, and small van 1-hour deliveries. You decided that all of these would be promoted as carbon neutral. Find two organizations that provide an accredited service. Approximately how much will it cost?

3. **Electronic communication platforms** Review the service offered by NetLedger (http://www.netsuite.com) in terms of functionality and cost. Investigate three other similar providers of hosted enterprise applications in order to identify any difference. Which do you think would particularly appeal to new ventures and why?

 ## Discussion topics

1. **Information systems** Why should a new venture be consider using a customer relationship management system?

2. **Controls** Which is the most used quality system? How do the standards differ for a product and service company? What does accreditation involve?

3. **Electronic communication platforms** What are the requirements for an effective online social network. Visit Facebook (http://www.facebook.com) and LinkedIn (http://www.linkedin.com) and compare the functionality for setting up and developing online groups. What particular features could be useful for the virtual footprint of a new venture? How can blogging and tweeting support this objective?

Further reading guide

The discipline of operations management has developed over a long period with many of the core processes being well understood. Popular operations management books include Slack et al. (2009) and Greasley (2009). These both explore the subject in some detail, including design, planning, control, quality, and challenges. *Operations and Process Management: Principles and Practice for Strategic Impact* (Slack et al. 2008) takes a more strategic view of operations. Business information systems and e-business systems are constantly changing. The core principles are well covered by Chaffey and Wood (2005) and Bocij et al. 2008. Web 2.0 technologies are attracting increased interest with works on blogging by Gardner and Birley (2010), tweeting by Lacy (2009), Robbins et al. (2009), and Thomases (2010), and online social networks by Holzner (2008).

 References

Blue Autumn (2010) http://www.blueautumn.ipsx.org/BlueAutumn/welcome.asp (accessed 3 May 2010).

Bocij, P., Greasley, A. and Hickie, S. (2008) *Business information systems: technology, development and management for the e-business* (4th edition). Harlow, UK: Financial Times/Prentice Hall.

Carbon Footprint (2010) http://www.carbonfootprint.com/aboutus.html (accessed 3 May 2010).

CarbonNeutral (2010a) http://www.carbonneutral.com/our-clients/case-studies/courier-systems/ (accessed 3 May 2010).

CarbonNeutral (2010b) http://www.carbonneutral.com/about-us/our-history/ (accessed 3 May 2010).

CarbonNeutral (2010c) http://www.carbonneutral.com/project-portfolio (accessed 3 May 2010).

Chaffey, D. and Wood, S. (2005) *Business information management: improving performance using information systems.* Harlow, UK: Financial Times/Prentice Hall.

Clear (2010) http://www.clear-offset.com/the-team.php (accessed 3 May 2010).

Cosyfeet (2010) http://www.cosyfeet.com/about_us.php (accessed 3 May 2010).

Courier Systems (2010) http://www.courier-systems.co.uk/environment/carbonneutral.php (accessed 3 May 2010).

DECC (2010) http://offsetting.decc.gov.uk/cms/information-for-offset-providers/ (accessed 3 May 2010).

Drucker, P. (1949) *Concept of the corporation.* New York: John Day Company

Facebook (2010) 'One difference – Facebook.' http://www.facebook.com/onedifference (accessed 25th March 2010).

Gardner, S and Birley, S. (2010) *Blogging for dummies* (3rd edition). Chichester: John Wiley & Sons.

Gillian, C., Graham, S., Levitt, M., McArthur, J., Murray, S., Turner, V., Villars, R., and McCathy Whalen, M. (1999) 'The ASPs' impact on the IT industry.' IDC Corporation.

Greasley, A. (2009) *Operations management* (2nd edition). Chichester: John Wiley & Sons.

Harker, M. J. (1999) 'Relationship marketing defined? An examination of current relationship marketing definitions.' *Marketing Intelligence and Planning*, 17, 1: 13–20.

Holzner, S. (2008) *Facebook marketing: leverage social media to grow your business.* Indianapolis: QUE Publishing.

Igloo (2008) http://www.igloo-thermo.com/pages/news/index.asp?NewsID=37 (accessed 3 May 2010).

Igloo (2010a) http://www.igloo-thermo.com/pages/clients/testimonials.asp (accessed 3 May 2010).

Igloo (2010b) http://www.igloo-thermo.com/pages/services/our-fleet.asp (accessed 3 May 2010).

Igloo (2010c) http://www.igloo-thermo.com/pages/news/index.asp?NewsID=52 (accessed 3 May 2010).

IIP (2010) 'Case studies – Rabbit Consulting.' http://www.investorsinpeople.co.uk/MediaResearch/CaseStudy (accessed 25 March 2010).

IPS (2010) http://www.ipsx.co.uk/IPS_Customers.htm (accessed 3 May 2010).

Lacy, K. (2009) *Twitter marketing for dummies*. Chichester: John Wiley & Sons

Lockett, N. and Brown, D. (2005) 'An SME perspective of vertical application service providers.' *International Journal of Enterprise Information Systems* 1, 2: 37–55.

Lockett, N. and Doherty, N. (2008) 'Mind the gap: Exploring the links between expectations of relationship marketing and reality of electronic-CRM.' *International Journal of e-Business Management*, 2, 2: 19–34.

Lockett, N., Brown, D., and Kaewkitipong, L. (2006) 'The use of hosted enterprise applications by SMEs: a dual market and user perspective.' *Electronic Markets: The International Journal*, 16, 1: 85–96.

Porter, M. (1990) *The competitive advantage of nations*. New York: Free Press.

Reichheld, F.F. (2001) *The loyalty effect: The hidden force behind growth, profits, and lasting value*. Boston, MA: Harvard Business School Press.

Richard, D. (2010) 'The entrepreneurs manifesto.' http://www.schoolforstartups.co.uk

Robbins, A, Comm, J., and Burge, K. (2009) *Twitter power: how to dominate your market one tweet at a time*. Chichester: John Wiley & Sons.

Ryals, L. and Knox, S. (2001) 'Cross-functional issues in the implementation of relationship marketing through customer relationship management.' *European Management Journal*, 19, 5: 534–42.

Sanderson (2010) http://www.sanderson.com/sanim/SuccessStoryCosyfeet,10,4,1041,1.html (accessed 3 May 2010).

Slack, N., Chambers, S., and Johnston, R. (2009) *Operations Management* (6th edition). Harlow, UK: Financial Times/Prentice Hall.

Slack, N., Chambers, S., Johnston, R., and Betts (2008) *Operations and process management: principles and practice for strategic impact* (2nd edition). Harlow, UK: Financial Times/ Prentice Hall.

Srivastava, R., Shervani, T.A., and Fahey, L. (1999) 'Marketing, business processes and shareholder value: An organisationally embedded view of marketing activities and the discipline of marketing.' *Journal of Marketing*, 63: 168–79.

SWFWG (2010) *Cosyfeet in Street* http://www.swfwg.org/case_study/5/case_studies.html?CaseStudyId=1 accessed 25th March 2010).

Telegraph (2007) 'Dragons turn white van men into millionaires.' *The Daily Telegraph* 26 June 2007.

thisismoney (2007) 'Our story, by the Dragons' Den millionaires.' 5 November. Available at http://www.thisismoney.co.uk.

Thomases, H. (2010) *Twitter marketing: an hour a day*. Chichester: John Wiley & Sons.

Twitter (2010a) 'Twitter 101 case study: Dell.' http://business.twitter.com/twitter101/case_dell (accessed 25 March 2010).

Twitter (2010b) 'Twitter 101 case study: Coffee Groundz.' http://business.twitter.com/twitter101/case_coffeegroundz (accessed 25 March 2010).

Ward, J. and Peppard, J. (2002) *Strategic planning for information systems* (3rd edition). Chichester: John Wiley & Sons.

7 Accounts

Interpreting financial performance

Good plans shape good decisions. That's why good planning helps to make elusive dreams come true.

Lester Bittel, *professor of management*

Annual income twenty pounds, annual expenditure nineteen pounds nineteen and six, result happiness. Annual income twenty pounds, annual expenditure twenty pounds ought and six, result misery.

Wilkins Micawber, *fictional character*

Learning outcomes

After reading this chapter you should be able to:

➤ Appreciate the importance of effective financial forecasting and planning for a new entrepreneurial venture.

➤ Understand the key elements of business accounting as they apply to a new venture.

➤ Prepare basic financial statements, including projected profit and loss accounts, balance sheets, and cash flow statements.

➤ Appreciate the value of key performance indicators as a way of managing a new venture.

➤ Recognize the differences between quantitative and qualitative measures of performance, and how these might be relevant to commercial and social enterprises.

➤ Apply relevant principles and techniques of forecasting and planning in order to understand the overall performance of your own venture.

Case 7.1 Beyond outdoor clothing for enthusiasts

Opened in 2001 in the Scottish Highlands, by 2010, **Kate** and **Andy Field's** specialist outdoor clothing company had grown from a single shop to a national chain of 14 stores, each situated in one of the UK's national parks (http://www.nationalparks.gov.uk). Kate and Andy, who are brother and sister, were passionate about combining top quality branded products with high quality customer service. All the staff in the stores were experienced and trained outdoor pursuits enthusiasts. They offered expert advice to their customers who often came back for replacement and additional clothing and equipment. They had a well-earned reputation in the industry for providing good service at an affordable price.

In response to customer demands, they launched a website in 2005 to provide an easy way for their existing customers to order products. Two of the company's store managers, one with a background in IT (Anjam) and the other in fashion retailing (Naomi), volunteered to oversee this project. By 2010, online sales had increased significantly and became greater than any individual store. Anjam and Naomi relocated to Scotland to directly manage the online operations and the new warehouse built next to the first store. This warehouse supplied all their stores and dispatched the online orders.

In 2009, Kate and Andy decided to appoint Anjam and Naomi as directors, and at the beginning of 2010 they held their first strategy away day to discuss the future of the company. They all agreed that the existing 14 stores were well established and not to expand by opening any new stores. However, they needed to find ways of growing sales to help fund the new warehouse and agreed to set a 10% increase in sales for each store and a 20% increase for online sales. The directors realized that their historical success was largely due to building a loyal customer base by providing high levels of customer service in the store.

Total store sales for 2009 could be divided into: waterproof clothing (25%), clothing (30%), footwear (20%), rucksacks (10%), and equipment (15%). For online sales these were: waterproof clothing (30%), clothing (45%), footwear (10%), rucksacks (10%), and equipment (5%). The split between men and women was consistently 60% and 40% respectively for both store and online sales. The profit margin varied depending on the category – with all clothing and rucksacks being 30%, footwear 35%, and equipment 25%. Online margins were 5% less for all categories. For 2009, the total store sales were £2,400,000 and the online sales were £1,200,000. Total store sales had increased by 10% compared to 2008 with no new stores being opened since 2007. However online sales had increased at 20% for each of the last two years. Based on sales reports from the stores and online, Kate had prepared some sales analysis for 2009 and developed a sales forecast for 2010 for discussion (see below).

Kate and Andy's sales analysis

 online resource centre Case 7-1 spreadsheet.xls

Somewhat unexpectedly, Anjam and Naomi reported that the growth of online sales was coming from new customers who had not previously purchased from a store and that their purchasing profile was different from store customers. Naomi explained that the new online customers were purchasing branded clothing, particularly non-waterproof, and that her 'gut feel' was that these were not outdoor enthusiasts but brand conscious consumers with a general interest in outdoor

2009	Store	Online	Total	2010	Store	Online	Total
				Sales growth	10.0%	20.0%	13.3%
Sales (Actual)	2,400,000	1,200,000	3,600,000	Sales (Forecast)	2,640,000	1.440,000	4,080,000
Sales by category (2009)	Store	Online	Total	Sales by category (2010)	Store	Online	Total
Waterproof clothing	25.0%	30.0%	26.7%	Waterproof clothing	25.0%	30.0%	30.3%
Clothing	30.0%	45.0%	35.0%	Clothing	30.0%	45.0%	40.0%
Footwear	20.0%	10.0%	16.7%	Footwear	20.0%	10.0%	18.7%
Rucksacks	10.0%	10.0%	10.0%	Rucksacks	10.0%	10.0%	11.3%
Equipment	15.0%	5.0%	11.7%	Equipment	15.0%	5.0%	13.0%
	100.0%	100.0%	100.0%		100.0%	100.0%	113.3%
Sales by category (2009)	Store	Online	Total	Sales by category (2010)	Store	Online	Total
Waterproof clothing	600,000	360,000	960,000	Waterproof clothing	660,000	432,000	1,092,000
Clothing	720,000	540,000	1,260,000	Clothing	792,000	648,000	1,440,000
Footwear	480,000	120,000	600,000	Footwear	528,000	144,000	672,000
Rucksacks	240,000	120,000	360,000	Rucksacks	264,000	144,000	408,000
Equipment	360,000	60,000	420,000	Equipment	396,000	72,000	468,000
Total	2,400,000	1,200,000	3,600,000	Total	2,640,000	1,440,000	4,080,000
Margin (2009)	Store	Online	Total	Margin (2010)	Store	Online	Total
Waterproof clothing	30.0%	25.0%	28.1%	Waterproof clothing	30.0%	25.0%	28.0%
Clothing	30.0%	25.0%	27.9%	Clothing	30.0%	25.0%	27.8%
Footwear	35.0%	30.0%	34.0%	Footwear	35.0%	30.0%	33.9%
Rucksacks	30.0%	25.0%	28.3%	Rucksacks	30.0%	25.0%	28.2%
Equipment	25.0%	20.0%	24.3%	Equipment	25.0%	20.0%	24.2%
Total	30.3%	25.3%	28.6%	Total	30.3%	25.3%	28.5%
Growth profit (2009)	Store	Online	Total	Growth profit (2010)	Store	Online	Total
Waterproof clothing	180,000	90,000	270,000	Waterproof clothing	198,000	108,000	306,600
Clothing	216,000	135,000	351,000	Clothing	237,600	162,000	399,600
Footwear	168,000	36,000	204,000	Footwear	184,800	43,200	228,000
Rucksacks	72,,000	30,000	102,000	Rucksacks	79,200	36,000	115,200
Equipment	90,000	12,000	102,000	Equipment	99,000	14,400	113,400
Total	726,000	303,000	1,029,000	Total	798,600	363,600	1,162,200
Analysis	Store	Online		Analysis	Store	Online	
Proportion of sales	66.7%	33.3%		Proportion of sales	64.7%	35.3%	
Proportion of gross profit	70.6%	29.4%		Proportion of gross profit	68.7%	31.3%	

Note: full spreadsheet is available on the Online Resource Centre.

activities. In fact, Naomi had got Anjam to include a temporary chat room feature on the website, which had enabled her to chat with some of these customers during their shopping. Andy, who was responsible for purchasing, said that the new 'ethical' brand, introduced at the end of 2008, was selling very well and accounted for 25% of the clothing sales. Furthermore, Andy informed the board that the overseas manufacturer had approached them to become their exclusive wholesaler in the UK. This would mean supplying other small retailers, something they had never done before. They would get an increase of 5% margin but had to agree to supply other retailers at 20% discount. It was estimated that this would only represent 25% of the sales. Time was of the essence as the manufacturer had given them two weeks to decide before they would approach another wholesaler.

The directors discussed many options but narrowed these down to two options:

1. Decline the offer to become the exclusive wholesalers for the 'ethical' brand. This would mean them purchasing off the new alternative wholesaler at a reduced margin of less than 20% rather than 27.9% (30% from store sales and 25% from online sales).

2. Accept the exclusive offer. This would mean an increased margin of 35% from store sales and 30% from online sales on 25% of clothing sales but also £105,000 of new sales to smaller retailers at 20% margin.

Both Naomi and Andy were keen to go for option 2. Naomi also suggested launching an additional website under a new trading name only selling the 'ethical' brand and targeting this at more brand conscious consumers. Kate said they should do more analysis to determine the overall impact on margin and gross profit before making a decision. She was concerned about taking on trade debtors. It was agreed to calculate the new margin and meet the following day to make a decision.

Points to consider

1. Assuming option 2, what will be the margin and gross profit for the clothing category for 2010? (Assuming everything else remains the same.)

2. Assuming option 2, what will be the overall company margin and gross profit for 2010? (Don't forget to include the sales to smaller retailers.)

3. What other information is needed before making this decision? Can it be gathered within the two weeks left before the decision is made?

4. Is Naomi right to develop an additional website under a new trading name? What is the basis for this decision?

5. What could be done to reduce the risk of supplying smaller retailers?

Source: This case was written by Nigel Lockett. It is not based on a real company but draws on the commercial experience of the author.

7.1 Introduction

Having identified an **entrepreneurial opportunity**, reviewed the **markets**, and considered operations we now turn to the vital task of interpreting financial performance. Forecasting and planning are important skills for any **entrepreneur** to have or to develop. In order to construct these forecasts, you may need to make use of historical information, market analysis, and some of your own 'gut feelings' about how the venture is going to operate over specified periods (e.g. daily, weekly, monthly, quarterly, or annually). The financial information produced to support a new venture usually relies on a combination of sources. Some figures may be soundly based in accurate data, while others are based on assumptions and your own 'best guess' of the likely outcome. Financial information is important. It provides evidence to support your decisions about the venture and also helps you to justify those decisions when you present them to other people. As the venture proceeds, you can also compare your previous forecasts with actual performance. This allows you (and others) to monitor your performance. Analysis of this kind can also help you to improve the accuracy of future forecasts.

➜ **PERSPECTIVES** See section 11.1 for further information.

Forecasting can be used in many areas of a venture, for example, predicting customer demand for a product can be used in production planning both internally and through your supply chain and in the production of business plans. However, it is important to keep in mind that all ventures are affected, to a greater or lesser extent, by risk and uncertainty. Though good forecasting can help to quantify risk factors and to highlight areas of uncertainty, it cannot be relied on exclusively.

As mentioned in Chapter 2, one response to this need for articulation is to produce a traditional formal business plan. Business plans are a formal statement, with a set of business goals and objectives. They often include detailed market analysis and financial forecasts. They may have to be produced as a requirement of loans and updated regularly. While there are inherent advantages in spending some time writing business plans, they can be time consuming to produce. The key question to ask is: *If I were investing in the business, what is the critical information I would need and how often would I need it?* (That is, *need* rather than want or like.) Remember that any business plan is out of date as soon as it is printed and that in practice we don't run ventures by following business plans but by reacting to changes in our markets and to operational challenges. But they can provide a welcome opportunity to reflect on previous assumptions and actual versus forecasted performance. In fact, banks, lenders, and investors all seem to place considerable importance in them so they must be important. However, they are simply a formal document that states the **enterprise's** goals and how they will be achieved and often include detailed financial projections and marketing plans.

It can seem difficult to feel any connection between a long document full of positive statements, market analysis, and financial forecasts based on numerous assumptions and your 'gut feel' for an entrepreneurial opportunity you passionately feel is worth exploiting. In the end, it is not the role of this book to provide a step-by-step guide to writing a business plan. If this is what you want you might be better starting with one of the more popular business planning guides, such as *Business Plans for Dummies* (Barrow 2009) or *How to Write a Business Plan* (Finch 2006).

The first challenge presented by the subject of this chapter, *Accounts: interpreting financial performance*, is using often commercially sensitive information to illustrate the principles of business accounting, forecasting, and planning without revealing the identity of the organizations. This is successfully achieved by integrating four anonymous cases that build on each other. The opening case, *'Beyond outdoor clothing for enthusiasts'* (Case 7.1), requires us to analyse sales information and explore the relationship between sales, margin, and gross profit. Case 7.2, *'Cleaning up in business'*, presents a seemingly successful business with good sales, margin, gross profit, and net profit, which faces a cash flow problem. This, all too familiar, problem can be understood by considering the relationship between **the profit and loss** and **balance sheet statements** and the importance of managing these. Case 7.3, *'A recipe for success'*, moves beyond considering trading statements to considering an investment decision. Many enterprises can only trade successfully by purchasing plant and machinery, but this may require money to be borrowed or new investment to be obtained. Understanding the basic elements of return on investment can assist in making these critical decisions. The final case, *'Steve Woodford'* (Case 7.4), is based on interviews with a social entrepreneur whose main focus was not financial performance but the real impact of his charity's activities. This serves to illustrate that entrepreneurs become successful because they understand the importance of managing both finances and other **key performance indicators**. The former uses universally acknowledged principles and practices, but the latter will be unique to the industry, market, and enterprise. We have seen in Chapter 5 ('Markets') how important marketing and industry analysis is to successful enterprise, and this chapter builds on these by recognizing the importance of measuring performance either quantitatively or qualitatively.

We can clearly see, from the opening case, how accurate sales information is important for forecasting the impact of a critical decision. However, whether the company decides to become the exclusive wholesaler for the 'ethical' brand will also be strongly influenced by Naomi's 'gut feel'.

The chapter is organized as follows: In Section 7.2, we identify the accounting information that is required in any new venture and define some key terms. There is also a brief discussion of taxation rules. Section 7.3 reviews the three most important financial statements, the profit and loss account, balance sheet, and cash flow statement. Section 7.4 considers the importance of key performance indicators, including the role of quantitative and qualitative information.

7.2 Accounting for your venture

7.2.1 Importance of business accounting

As an entrepreneur, it is essential that you have a good grasp of business accounting. While it is not essential to be an accountant or to have formal accounting qualifications, it is imperative that you can understand the figures and be aware of your current financial position. The first element to consider is profit: how is your venture going to make more money than it costs to provide the product and/or service? In order to make sensible business decisions, entrepreneurs need to know about the trading performance of their venture and be able to gauge the impact of any changes on its future performance. Financial decision-making is complex and can be affected by unforeseen changes to markets, or by the actions of customers and competitors. However, you should still try to base your decisions on the best available information, and this can only be obtained by adopting good business accounting practices. Commercial and social ventures also need accurate financial information in order to calculate their tax liabilities (Section 7.2.3), and in most cases there will be a legal requirement to submit their accounting statements. For all of these reasons, good business accounting is not simply a 'nice to have' option, but a 'must have' capability within any **entrepreneurial team**. In this section, we focus on profit and taxation. Cash flow, another vital area of accounting, is addressed in Section 7.3.3. We have also provided additional information on accounting and on selecting an accountant on the Online Resource Centre.

---

 online resource centre 'Gaining an understanding of business accounts and choosing an accountant.'

Most new ventures will make use of business accounting software. The function and relationship between the different accounting ledgers and modules is represented in Figure 7.1. At the core of any accounting system will be a sales ledger (with information about customers), purchase ledger (with information about suppliers), and a general or nominal ledger (with summary information about all sales, purchases, assets, and liabilities). It is possible to run a simple business using just these ledgers. However, as a venture grows it will need more complex invoicing and purchasing information, which can be achieved using sales order processing (SOP) and purchase order processing (POP) modules. Some businesses will hold stock and/or manufacture goods for sale, which can be supported by appropriate modules.

Figure 7.1 Simplified relationship between accounting software modules

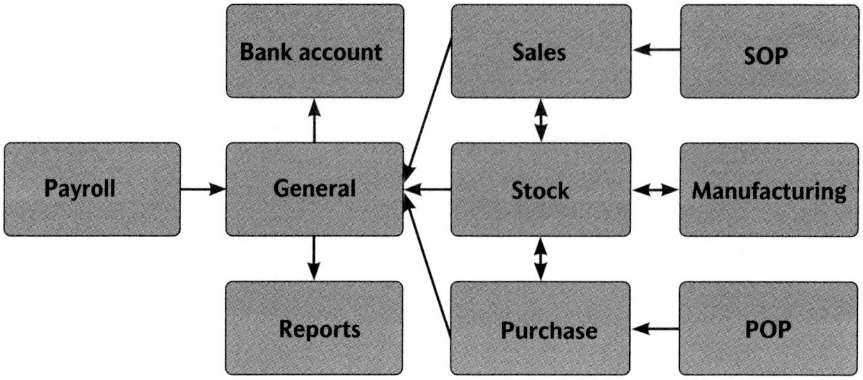

Accounting software tends to be country specific, although some providers, such as Oracle and SAP, provide multi-country, multi-language, and multi-currency applications (http://www.oracle.com; http://www.sap.com). In the UK, popular accounting software packages for small to medium-sized enterprises include Sage Instant, 50, 100, and 200 suites (http://www.sage.co.uk); Intuit's QuickBooks SimpleStart, Pro, and Premier (http://quickbooks.intuit.co.uk); and Pegasus Opera II (http://www.pegasus.co.uk). Choosing and implementing the right accounting software package can be difficult, and mistakes can be both costly and time consuming. Selection depends on the size and complexity of the venture. Unless you are using only entry-level or basic accounting software, it is important that you also choose a good value added reseller (VAR), who will help you install the software and configure it to your needs. Your accountants might have useful advice to give you and may even recommend packages and resellers. There are also an increasing number of online accounting applications emerging, such as http://www.arithmo.co.uk; http://www.clearbooks.co.uk; http://www.ipsx.co.uk; http://www.libertyaccounts.com; and http://www.netsuite.co.uk. The US-based NetSuite was one of the first application service providers. These providers host and maintain your accounting software, which can be accessed via the Internet. Hosted applications are becoming increasingly popular for a wide range of applications. This may also be referred to as cloud computing (Economist 2009).

7.2.2 Profit measures

You are likely to make use of some or all of the following profit measures:

- **Gross profit** A simple measure of profit obtained from the sale of goods and services; also referred to as sales profit.

- **Net profit** A measure of company performance after deducting operating expenses and interest but not taxes.

- **Operating profit** Gross profit less all operating expenses but not interest and taxes; also referred to as earnings before interest and taxes (EBIT). This can be useful for potential lenders or investors because it indicates the likely trading performance without any borrowings and highly company-specific tax calculations.

There are also a number of ways of calculating profitability. These take the form of ratios that compare the profit measure to another figure. Two of the most widely used indicators are:

- **Profit margin** A comparative indicator of profit in relation to sales value, which enables you to compare the profitability of particular product types, customers, time periods. There are several versions (e.g. gross profit margin, net profit margin, operating profit margin).

- **Return on capital employed (ROCE)** An indicator showing the profits earned in relation to the amount of capital invested in the business.

Some **social enterprises** may make use of alternative, but closely related, terminology. Profit and loss accounts are sometimes replaced by 'Income and Expenditure' accounts, and the term 'surplus' may be used in place of 'profit'.

7.2.3 **Taxation**

Having determined your expected and actual profit, it is then important to be aware how tax might affect your venture. Most people accept that we need to pay taxes in order for governments to make the necessary investments in infrastructure and public services. However, even the most responsible taxpayers are unlikely to want to pay more than their 'fair share'. In this section we consider two forms of taxation that you are likely to encounter, Value Added Tax (VAT) and various forms of company tax:

- **Value Added Tax (VAT)** VAT is added to nearly all sales made by VAT-registered businesses at levels set by government. VAT is also known as general sales tax (GST) or just Sales Tax. Typically, it is levied on sales made within a country or trading zone but not on export sales. The UK standard VAT rate is 20%, the reduced rate is 5%, and the zero rate is 0%. Different rates will apply to products depending on their type; for example, televisions are electrical consumer goods and charged at the standard rate (20%); heating fuel is domestic fuel and power and charged at the reduced rate (5%); fruit and vegetables are food and charged at the zero rate (0%). Rates and product types vary by country: in Finland, the standard rate of VAT was 22%, but rose by one percentage point to 23% in July 2010 and, in Sweden, VAT is split into three levels with 25% being the highest rate and applied to most goods and services. An important aspect of VAT is that most VAT-registered companies charge VAT on sales, but they also have VAT added to their purchases from VAT-registered companies. Periodically (often quarterly or monthly), they calculate the net VAT by deducting the VAT charged to them from the VAT they charge to their customers. Normally this results in payments to the government, but for some new businesses and in periods of high investment this can result in payments, or credit against future payments, from the government. It is also important to include VAT in cash flow forecasting. Ultimately, VAT is paid by consumers or non VAT-registered organizations, such as charities and smaller companies with sales below a certain threshold, currently £68,000 in the UK. Certain products are exempt from VAT only when certain individuals buy these products. For example, disabled people buying medical equipment. Each country has its own VAT rules for products and thresholds.

- **Company Tax** As a general rule, profitable companies pay company tax, also known as corporation tax in the UK. Any losses retained from previous accounting periods can normally be offset against profits before the company tax due is calculated. Tax is worked out by taking the 'taxable profits' (net profit (see 7.2.2) plus any depreciation charges already deducted, less any capital allowances and retained losses) and applying the relevant company tax rate, say 30%. Calculating company tax can be difficult and most businesses employ a tax advisor, normally a specialist within their accountants. Even if the rate of company tax remains the same, the rules will often change over time. Governments will typically fine companies that make errors, charging interest on outstanding balances. Many small businesses are not registered as companies, preferring instead to operate as sole traders or partnerships. The advantages of being a sole trader include: easier to start up in business, fewer rules and regulations, the owner has full control, and taxes are calculated after any personal tax allowances have been deducted. However, sole traders have unlimited liability for any debts or claims, and often prefer to change status to a limited liability company (limited company) as they grow and expand their workforce. This is an important decision and needs to be researched carefully and should include taking professional advice from an accountant and solicitor.

Government taxation policies are not fixed, and changes in tax rates and related regulations can have a significant effect on businesses. You may also find yourself encountering new forms of taxation as the venture develops. For example, if you start to export products to other countries, you are likely to be charged an import duty. In some cases, high import duties can have a significant impact on profitability. You are also likely to face a variety of local taxes (e.g. rates charged on your premises and charges for waste disposal services). It can be difficult to keep track of tax changes, or to understand what they mean for your own venture. Though many entrepreneurs produce their own accounting information, they often seek professional advice on taxation. Even when the rules and guidance from government seem clear, they can remain open to interpretation. Differences of opinion over the rules can lead to costly disputes and 'test cases' (e.g. the introduction of IR35 in the UK, and other taxation issues, which are discussed on the Online Resource Centre).

---

online resource centre 'Examples of country specific tax policies: IR35 (UK).'

7.3 Financial statements

7.3.1 Profit and loss

A company's profit and loss statement (sometimes referred to as the 'P&L') indicates the relationship between sales (revenue or turnover), cost of sales, gross profit, operating expenses, interest, tax, and net profit for a specific period (i.e. per month, quarter, or year). This is vital management information for directors, shareholders, and staff and needs to be produced in a timely manner. In other words, quickly enough after a period end so that decisions can be taken to maintain or improve the trading position. There is a standard format for profit and loss statements, which often includes the current and equivalent previous period (Figure 7.2).

Typically, profit and loss statements are simplified so that only key information is displayed. Sales information is the total for the company or business unit rather than by customer type or segment. Expenditure is the total for a particular area, such as administration, rather than sub-divisions, for example office costs, stationery, and postage. For management purposes, the profit and loss statement should indicate the general trading performance and resultant net profit or loss.

At the simplest level the profit and loss statement will include:

- Income – generated by business activities but not interest received.
- Cost of sales – cost of purchased good and manufactured goods (including direct manufacturing overheads and wages).
- Gross profit – income less cost of goods.
- Profit margin (gross profit/income × 100).
- Operating expenses – overhead and staff excluding manufacturing wages.
- Depreciation.
- Operating profit (gross profit less operating expenses).
- Interest.
- Net profit (gross profit less operating expenses and interest).
- Net profit before tax.
- Net margin (net profit before tax/income × 100).
- Corporation tax.
- Net profit after taxes.

The precise structure of profit and loss statements will vary depending on the type of operation. For example, distributors typically invoice for goods delivered and will have stock or inventory, whereas service providers will invoice for staff time and have no stock holding. Stock adds an additional layer of complexity because it must be valued using a consistent method, such as FIFO (first in first out) or average valuation, and must be checked to ensure that physical stock is reconciled with computer stock lists. Manufacturing operations need to account for raw materials, finished goods, and 'work-in-progress' (with the latter including the value of parts used and the estimated staff costs for any partly completed items).

Figure 7.2 Sample profit and loss statement

PROFIT AND LOSS STATEMENT for the year ended 31 December 2010		
Income	£	£
Sales		**6,600,000**
Stock at 1January 2010	700,000	
Purchases	4,900,000	
	5,600,000	
Stock at 31st December 2010	(980,000)	
		4,620,000
Gross Profit		**1,980,000**
Profit Margin		30.0%
Expenditure		
Establishment expenses	160,000	
Administration	370,000	
Selling and distribution expenses	**1,200,000**	
Finance charges	20,000	
Total operating expenses		**1,750,000**
Operating profit		230,000
Net interest	30,000	
		30.000
Net profit before taxation		**200,000**
Net margin		3.0%
Tax	40,000	
Dividends	10,000	
		50,000
Net profit retained		**150,000**

Note: Full spreadsheet is available on the Online Resource Centre.

Depreciation is an important concept, which differentiates profit and loss statements from cash flow statements. Depreciation is simply an allowance based on the value of assets (typically equipment or vehicles), which lose actual value over time. This allowance appears in the profit and loss statement throughout the write-down period but does not appear in the cash flow statement. This is because the asset appears in the cash flow statement when it is purchased – in other words sooner! The asset's actual value is recorded in the balance sheet statement and reduces in proportion to the amount written-down. To make matters more complicated, different types of assets can depreciate at different rates and in different ways. Furthermore, depreciation is not taken into consideration when calculating tax. Perhaps yet another reason to seek professional advice.

7.3.2 **Balance sheet**

A balance sheet statement is a summary of the financial position of the business at a specific date, such as at a month end or the year end. It shows the *balance* between the assets, liabilities, and ownership equity. The difference between assets and liabilities is net worth or net assets or, simply, **equity**. The net worth must equal assets minus liabilities and ownership equity. That is the 'books must balance'. Let us consider each of these in turn:

Assets The value of the company's 'worth' can be expressed in financial terms – the amount it owns or is owed – which includes:

- Cash or 'cash in hand' (petty cash, current bank balance, savings account balance, and any short-term investments).
- Debtors (accounts receivable from credit or trade customers).
- Stock (value of an inventory valued on a consistent basis).

The most easily obtainable or redeemable assets (the most liquid) are listed first.
The total current assets is the sum of cash, debtors, and stock.
Long-term assets are listed subsequently and include plant and machinery (less depreciation since the previous year end), land, property, investments, which cannot be realized in less that one year. The sum of these is the total long-term assets.
Therefore, total assets is the total current assets plus the long-term assets. It is possible to include other assets, such as goodwill, but this is unusual and linked to 'one-off' events; for example, the purchase of a company at a price above its net worth, with goodwill representing the additional amount paid. This goodwill is then 'written off' through the profit and loss, at a rate agreed with your accountant and tax office. Goodwill cannot be introduced spontaneously to increase the asset position of a company. However, land or buildings might reasonably be 're-valued' to improve the strength of the balance sheet.

Liabilities This is the amount a company owes to other entities and includes:

- Creditors (accounts payable to suppliers).
- Accrued liabilities (expenses incurred but not paid for – including products, services, and wages).
- Tax owed (still due – including company tax and employment-related taxes).

The total current liabilities is the sum of creditors, accrued liabilities, and tax owed.
Long-term liabilities include long-term bonds and mortgages, which are not repayable within one year. The total liabilities is the total current liabilities plus the long-term liabilities.

Owners' equity The owner's equity is the difference between the total assets and total liabilities. The ownership equity includes the share capital and retained profit or loss. The share capital can be a nominal sum, such as £100, or a substantial amount. Since the share capital cannot be withdrawn from the company, it can be used to indicate the level of commitment of the founding shareholders. In a new venture the founding directors are normally shareholders.

Figure 7.3 Sample balance sheet statement

SUMMARY BALANCE SHEET as at 31 December 2010		
	£	£
Fixed assets		
Tangible assets	45,000	
Investments	20,000	
		65,000
Current assets		
Stocks	980,000	
Debtors	1,410,000	
Cash at bank and in hand	110,000	
		2,500,000
Total assets		**2,565,000**
Creditors: amounts falling due within one year		(2,200,000)
Net current liabilities		300,000
Total assets less current liabilities		**365,000**
Capital and reserves		
Owners share capital	1.000	
Profit and loss account (including £150,000 for year end 31 Dec 2010	364,000	
		365,000

Note: Full spreadsheet is available on the Online Resource Centre.

The owners' equity provides bankers and investors with an indicator to help determine how much it would be prudent to invest or lend to a company.

The overall balance sheet statement is correct when the total assets = total liabilities + owners' equity (Figure 7.3).

7.3.3 Cash flow forecasting

In the last two sections we have seen how the profit and loss statement and the balance sheet can give us a greater understanding of an organization's financial performance. For the profit and loss statement this is for a particular period, such as monthly or annually, while the balance sheet statement shows the picture at a specific point in time. Both statements provide vital management information, but neither tells us anything about how much money is flowing in and out of the business. This is the role of the **cash flow forecast**, a financial statement that predicts the movement of cash into and out of a venture over a specified period (e.g. weekly, monthly, or quarterly). In the early phases of most new ventures, there is usually a *negative* *cash flow*. Lots of cash is flowing out of the business in order to get it established. You may be spending money on equipment, your initial stock of materials, external advisors, and a variety of one-off purchases that you have to pay for 'up-front' (i.e. at the time of purchase) because suppliers are not yet willing to grant you credit terms. As yet there is no cash flowing back the other way, because until you are ready to trade there will be no cash generated from sales – and even when you are trading, you may have to offer credit to your customers and therefore wait to be paid. As the venture becomes established, your cash flows should begin to balance out. However, the cash flow forecast remains an important tool that can be used to identify periods when you may be short of cash. By anticipating these cash shortages well in advance, you can ensure that you have appropriate sources of funding (e.g. bank loans or overdrafts) in place to avoid a shortfall.

Running out of cash can have a catastrophic impact on any organization, even if it is in an otherwise healthy state. A venture can be highly profitable yet find itself with insufficient cash to continue trading. New and high growth ventures are particularly vulnerable to this problem, which is often described as 'over trading'. There are many reasons for over trading to occur, and they can often occur in combination:

- Having to pay in advance for large amounts of stock to meet increased customer demand.
- Offer extended credit terms to attract new customers.
- Customers delaying (or refusing) payment of their invoices.
- Suppliers requiring immediate payment due to the venture's limited trading record or lack of accounting statements.

The cash flow forecast is based on a number of key assumptions, which vary depending on the type and the period of the forecast. It is best to develop a simple spreadsheet so that you can vary the assumptions to see how sensitive your projections are to any changes. These include:

- Sales forecast – based on a percentage increase or decrease perhaps due to planned marketing activities or contract proposals submitted. Beware of being too optimistic about sales. It is better to report sales above your forecast than explain why you did not achieve them. Accurate sales forecasting builds confidence in your abilities and enables more positive discussions with bank managers and investors.
- Cost of sales – based on predicted profit margin. This might remain fairly consistent or vary considerably depending of mix of sales. What can be done to increase the sales of higher margin products and services?
- Payments received from customers – based on historical performance and expressed as debtor days, for example 60 days. This is a critical area to manage, particularly for new ventures. Keep a close eye on debtors, take up credit references or use credit reference agencies and be prepared to be persistent and firm. Get to know the staff responsible for payments. You have a right to the money for goods or services you have provided. Remember that any bad debt has to be replaced by the equivalent amount in net profit rather than gross profit or sales. Consider offering prompt or early payment incentives to customers but remember to include extra profit margin to compensate for this.

- Operating expenses – based on previous costs and known or expected changes due to price increases or inflation. Be prepared to negotiate with all suppliers but remember that service levels can be just as important as price.

- Staff costs usually make up the largest proportion of operating expenses for organizations. Controlling these costs is vital in maintaining profitability. Employer and employee tax relating to employment and collected by employers is presented after wages.

- Payments made to suppliers – based on historical performance and expressed as creditor days, for example 30 days. Some of your suppliers may offer you early settlement discounts and, provided you have the funds, could increase your profit margin. Try to be fair and consistent with your payments. If you have problems with payments talk to your suppliers and negotiate a payment schedule but be careful to keep to any agreement.

- Interest – based on amount of borrowing and the interest rate charged by lenders and the prevailing national bank base rate. Think carefully about securing loans using your house as collateral. Signing a 'personal guarantee' could also provide lenders with access to all your assets, including your house. Be sure to consider the risks carefully and consult all those concerned, such as your partner. Sometimes there is no option but to give a personal guarantee.

- VAT – many businesses charge VAT to their customers and are charged VAT by their suppliers. In a profitable company this will tend to result in a net VAT owed to the government. These payments should be included in your cash flow forecast. It is important to recognize this important difference compared with the profit and loss statement. Cash flow forecasts include VAT whereas profit and loss statements do not. Usually, VAT is paid monthly or quarterly. Some enterprises, such as charities or businesses with sales below a certain value, are charged VAT by suppliers but cannot charge it to their customers.

- Tax – based on employment derived tax payments and annual company tax calculations related to declared profits are reported separately. The former is included in operating expenses and paid monthly and the latter after net profit before taxes and paid annually.

The cash flow forecast should be based on the past performance and your assumptions. For shorter periods, say a month, some factors such as inflation and interest based rate changes will have limited impact. However, for longer periods these factors need to be considered very carefully. For each period, in your cash flow forecast, subtract the total cash outflow from the total cash inflow. This will result in either a surplus or deficit for that period. Add this total to the opening cash flow balance for the end of each period to give the projected balance. This enables you to see net amount of cash required, or the net surplus generated (Figure 7.4).

The payments received from customers, and made to employees and suppliers, are the lifeblood of any enterprise. Even highly profitable ventures need to manage their sales ledger, purchase ledger, and payroll. In addition to this, it is prudent to establish mechanisms and controls regarding the processing of payments. Over 50% of all small businesses in the UK have been a victim of fraud or online crime (FSBC 2009). As your new venture grows, you may need to delegate part of the authorization of payments to trusted members of staff. Consider what checks and controls you can put in place so that all payments are processed at the appropriate

Figure 7.4 Sample cash flow forecast

CASH FLOW FORECAST for 2011		QTR 1	QTR 2	QTR 3	QTR 4
Cash inflows		Jan-Mar	Apr-Jun	Jul-Sep	Oct-Dec
Sales		1,500,000	1,750,000	1,750,000	2,000,000
Purchases		1,030,000	1,200,000	1,250,000	1,400,000
Opening stock at 31 Dec 2010	980,000				
Closing stock		960,000	950,000	970,000	950,000
Gross Profit		450,000	540,000	520,000	580,000
		30%	31%	30%	29%
Net interest		10,000	10,000	15,000	15,000
Total cash inflows		1,690,000	1,810,000	2,115,000	2,115,000
(Assumes all previous period grosssales received in following period)					
Cash outflows					
Expenditure					
Establishment expenses (VAT)		40,000	50,000	50,000	45,000
Administration (VAT)		20,000	20,000	20,000	20,000
Administration wages		90,000	90,000	90,000	90,000
Selling and distribution expenses (VAT)		150,000	145,000	200,000	190,000
Selling and distribution wages		150,000	160,000	180,000	160,000
Finance charges		5,000	5,000	5,000	5,000
Total operating expenses		455,000	470,000	545,000	510,000
Operation profit		(5,000)	70,000	(25,000)	70,000
Tax paid		40,000			
Dividends paid		10,000			
VAT on sales (20%)		300,000	350,000	350,000	400,000
VAT on purchased and expenditure (20%)		248,000	283,000	304,000	331,000
VAT payments		52,000	67,000	46,000	69,000
Tatal cash outflow		1,689,000	1,843,000	1,999,000	2,121,000
(Assumes all Purchases and expentiture paid in same period)					
cash movement		1,000	(33,000)	116,000	(6,000)
Opening cash balance	110,000				
cash balance		111,000	78,000	194,000	188,000

Note: Full spreadsheet is available on the Online Resource Centre.

time and made to the right person (Section 6.4). This is particularly important in the case of online payments, which provide additional opportunities for fraud, as the cardholder is not present. If you are unfamiliar with cash flow forecasting, it may be worth taking advice from your accountant. There are also several forecasting software applications available, and some of these can be linked to popular accounting software packages, such as the Sage 50 Forecasting module.

7.3.4 When is a venture profitable?

Having reviewed the main financial statements, we should now be in a position to answer this obvious and seemingly simple question. But how do you establish when a venture has become profitable? For a typical trading business, the simple answer might be: when it is selling goods or services at a higher price than it costs to buy them, less any other related expenditure. In other words, once you are able to calculate a net profit for the venture. However, this calculation indicates the current trading position. In the case of a newly established venture, the fact that you are trading profitably in month 12 does not take account of the month-on-month losses incurred in the previous 11 months. The measure that is used to indicate the point at which a venture moves into profit is known as the *breakeven point*. It can be measured as a point in time, and also in terms of activity (e.g. 'our breakeven sales figure is 10,000 units'). The breakeven point is a very important milestone for new ventures, and it attracts a lot of attention from banks and investors. Achieving breakeven can be satisfying, but as we have seen, it does not guarantee that your cash flow is healthy or that you are getting an adequate return on the capital invested in your business. Lastly, it is worth noting that most entrepreneurs are not simply motivated by profit (Hamilton 2000). Other factors, such as increased personal self-esteem and making a positive social impact, can also be important measures of success (Case 7.4).

Understanding the relationship between the profit and loss and balance sheet statements and the importance of managing cash flow is an important skill. In Case 7.2 we see how a seemingly successful business with a good level of sales and healthy profit margins can still encounter serious cash flow problems.

Case 7.2 Cleaning up in business

In 2004, Ludolf founded his cleaning supplies company in Brussels, shortly after leaving his sales role at an international chemical manufacturing company. At only 25 years old, he was the youngest sales manager in the company and many of his colleagues were surprised at his decision to leave and set up his own business. The first three years were very difficult. While Ludolf brought with him all this knowledge of cleaning chemicals and experience of sales, he knew very little about warehousing, distribution, employing people, and running a business. He had to learn quickly, not repeat mistakes twice, and use his intuition on when to trust suppliers and customers. All-in-all it was a steep learning curve. Ludolf's initial strategy was simple: purchase in bulk from large manufacturers, but sell locally to customers who wanted good quality products and high service levels. He was convinced that if he could deliver the product faster than his competition at the same price then people would use him. This worked for the first four years. By the end of 2008 the company had sales of €500,000 at a margin of 20%, gross profit was €100,000 and net profit before tax was €20,000. This was the first year the company made a net profit. All the profit was retained in the company to offset against €30,000 of accumulated losses from previous years.

Just at the end of 2008, his largest customer, a small group of high quality hotels that purchased €200,000 and run by Michèle, announced it had been purchased by a large national chain of 50 hotels, which was focused on more discerning business travellers. His contract was at risk. Initially, Ludolf was hopeful as Michèle was to be employed as the buyer for the national hotel chain, itself going through a period of expansion. Michèle had always been honest with him and explained that while the national hotel chain bought some of the products he supplied they also wanted a cheaper value range and a national delivery service. Their existing supplier had let them down, and Ludolf was given the opportunity to quote for the business. Michèle provided a summary of the products used and a budget based on a margin of 20% for branded products and 15% for the value range.

Ludolf worked hard to analyse the impact this new contract would have on his sales, margin, gross profit, operating costs, and net profit. He produced a forecast for 2009 based on his management accounts for 2008 and the summary from Michèle. With this information, he decided to submit a quotation, which was accepted by the national hotel chain provided that deliveries would start in January. Ludolf managed to speak to his bank manager briefly about the opportunity and estimated that he would need an increase in his overdraft by €25,000 to €65,000. This was agreed in principle provided Ludolf continued to match this with his own capital as equity and produced regular financial statements.

At the end of 2009, after a hectic 12 months of supplying both his existing local independent customers and the national hotel chain, Ludolf faced a number of difficult decisions. Sales to local independent customers had fallen by €100,000, but overall the turnover doubled and resulted in increased margins through greater buyer power. However, the most pressing issue was managing within his overdraft of €65,000 while paying the next month's wages. His bank manager asked to see a cash flow forecast for 2010 before agreeing to increase the overdraft further. She recommended that Ludolf speak to one of the partners of a local accountancy firm. He knew that he had been so busy running the business and had not spent enough time managing his accounts. Ludolf made an appointment to see the accountant and spent the weekend bringing his sales and purchase ledgers up to date. He produced a summary of the profit and loss for 2009 (budget against actual) and projected this forward for 2010. From the profit and loss statement the business looks successful, but he could not seem to stay within the overdraft limit of €65,000 agreed with the bank manager. Ludolf had no more capital of his own to invest in the business so was not optimistic about the bank agreeing to increase the overdraft to nearly €80,000.

Questions

1. What information should Ludolf prepare for the bank manager?

2. Should Ludolf have taken on the contract with the national hotel chain?

3. Is it important for Ludolf to have local customers? What could Ludolf have done to retain sales to his existing customers?

Sources: This case was written by Nigel Lockett. It is not based on a real company, but draws on the commercial experience of the author.

7.4 **Key performance indicators**

In addition to the normal financial statements produced as part of the management or statutory accounts there is other critical information, which can give an indication of how well (or not) an organization is performing. These are known as performance indicators or key performance indicators (KPIs). Typically these indicators have been identified by the organization as being particularly important in achieving some short-term or long-term organizational goals. Some may be internally focused, such as the number of customer orders dispatched within 24 hours of receiving an order, or externally focused, such as the percentage of completely satisfied customers as measured by an annual survey. To be of real value, KPIs need to be measured and reported on regularly so that necessary decisions and action can be taken. Perhaps not unsurprisingly, many new ventures focus only on financial information and neglect other indicators, which can show how they are performing. The specific KPIs required will depend on the nature of the organization, its stage of development, and the priorities of the different stakeholders. Establishing the most appropriate indicators can be challenging but is worth getting right. To measure the wrong KPIs will distract the organization from important areas of concern, but measuring the right ones can increase an organization's overall performance and give all staff easily understood non-confidential indicators. For example:

- An electrical equipment distributor, who supplies electrical contractors both from trade counters (where the customer collects goods) and by delivering to building sites, might be interested in the following monthly KPIs:
  - Number of orders for core product lines completed in full at both trade counters and delivered.
  - Number of picking errors for delivered items.
  - Number of customer product complaints by supplier.
  - Average order value and the number of orders required each week to break even.
- A furniture manufacturer, who makes each item to meet each customer's requirements, which are sold both through independent stores and directly to the customers, might be interested in the following monthly KPIs:
  - Time taken from receiving order to delivery.
  - Value of raw materials wasted at each stage of the manufacturing process. Including the cost of labour.
  - Trends in customer requirements.
  - Number of existing customers that order again and average time between orders.
  - Customer complaints.
- An employment agency, supplying accountancy staff to organizations on short-term contracts, might be interested in the following monthly KPIs:
  - Number of staff available for immediate employment.
  - Average length of contract versus the skill level of the accountancy staff.

 – Average length of contract versus type of organization.

 – Number accountancy staff who become employed by the organization.

The number and type of KPI and frequency of measurement will vary for each organization and sector but some generic principles apply. Performance management systems should include:

- Planning: By understanding current performance we can identify what is important to be measured and why it could improve performance.

- Measuring: Having identified the indicator we need to periodically measure it and report to decision makers.

- Reviewing: Is any action required as a result of the KPI and is it still an appropriate indicator? Do we need to revise the KPI?

7.4.1 Quantitative vs qualitative measurement

There is an understandable attraction to relying on rigorously produced quantitative information when making difficult decisions or predictions. We seem to draw some comfort from them. Quantitative data can be easily manipulated and produce useful insights to help explain what is happening and what might reasonably continue to happen based on declared assumptions. There are relatively well-defined techniques, which people have confidence in. Bank managers and other funders rely heavily on quantitative information, which they can easily relate to their own investment or lending criteria. A good knowledge of spreadsheets can be invaluable. However, quantitative measurement has limitations. Some critical decisions can only be made if we understand both what and why something has happened.

Quantitative measurement can be useful in understanding what is happening, for example, analysis of monthly customer sales for the last 12 months. We can identify increasing and decreasing sales by product types and forecast the impact on future sales. However, this may not provide a complete understanding. Why have some products sold well and others not? We might decide to conduct a customer survey to find out more about their buying decisions. Even this might not indicate why, and we may decide to interview customers to understand their behaviour. These insights can be invaluable.

In the following case, we move beyond considering trading statements to consider an investment decision and begin to understand the basic elements of return on investment and how qualitative information can assist in making these critical decisions (Case 7.3).

Case 7.3 A recipe for success

Growing up in the 50-year-old family food manufacturing business, making traditional pasties, served as a 'business apprenticeship' for Alice. When her parents wanted to retire in 2005, it seemed only natural for her to take over the running of the business. During 2010, she reflected back on her first five years as the owner. Back in 2005, the company made a range of traditional pasties, a pastry case filled with seasoned meat and vegetables, and supplied its own four shops in Cornwall in the south-west of England. The company employed nine people in the factory and office and a further eight people in the shops. As a teenager, Alice worked in the factory during the summer and in the shops at weekends, but she gradually spent more time in the office setting up and running the computer accounting software. In fact, she also helped other local businesses to set up their systems and had recently completed a one-year course in business accounting at a college in London. During this year, Alice noticed the wide variety of fast food outlets, ranging from large international chains to small independent or specialist groups. She spoke to friends and visited the different types to give her some insight into the consumers' buying preferences. She noticed that people liked the predictability and price of the big chains but preferred the atmosphere and personal service of the independent outlets.

During the previous 10 years, before Alice took over the business, the turnover had remained fairly constant at about £900,000 per year with the cost of manufacturing, including salaries averaging £500,000. The cost of running the shops had gradually increased from £300,000 to nearly £400,000 per year. This had resulted in net profits falling from a healthy 10% to just over 1%. Fortunately, the company had no borrowings and owned the factory and the three oldest largest shops. Alice's parents had become increasingly reluctant to make any changes to the business, particularly any that affected the people, most of whom had worked for the company for many years.

In 2005, Alice called a meeting of all the staff and explained that changes would need to be made to ensure the future of the company. She was pleasantly surprised by their reaction. Everyone seemed to know that there was a need for change but were also proud of the company's history and the quality of their traditional 'Cornish Pasty'. She was also aware that, even though she was only 25 years old, people looked to her to make the necessary decisions. Alice desperately wanted to make the right choices but decided to spend her first six months running the business just as it had been before and to deliberately work in each section of the business doing as many different jobs as possible. She also visited all the eight businesses she had helped set up accounting software in, ranging from a fashion retailer to a car repair garage. And finally she joined a regional women's business network, which met every month. She was the youngest person in the network but felt welcomed and, more importantly, that there were more experienced people she could discuss her challenges with.

By the start of 2006, Alice was ready to implement her plan for the business. She decided to leave the factory almost unchanged apart from replacing the old and unreliable baking oven at a cost of £200,000. This was the first investment in the factory for over 15 years, and the news was received very well. The factory staff were all too aware of the problems of the old oven. The new oven had twice the output of the previous one and produced a more consistent product finish. Alice also invested another £100,000 in generally improving the interior of the factory, which looked like a historic building from the outside and appeared on the town's tourist literature. The shops fared less well from the new business plan. Alice decided to close the rented shop and sell the oldest and most profitable shop for £600,000. The decision to close the rented shop was relatively easy as it was loss making and the current manager wanted to retire. However, selling the oldest shop was far from popular with the staff and also her parents. In hindsight, Alice recognized this was an important turning point for her. She had to stand up to the pressure from staff and her parents by asserting her authority as the managing director. But why had she made this decision and was it the right one?

The key to understanding this comes from appreciating Alice's strategy. Her vision for the company was built on both the tradition and quality of their 'Cornish Pasty' – what Alice called their 'brand'. She had a two-stage business plan that would take three years and involve closing two shops, selling the oldest shop, investing in the factory, and redeveloping the two largest shops to include a café and hot food takeout facility. To do this the company would need to use all the proceeds from the sale of the shop apart from £100,000, which would be used as a reserve against any losses. The key was to complete the changes to the factory and refurbishment of the shops in the 4-month 'low season'. The second part of Alice's strategy was to build the 'brand' value of the business. To help do this she employed a public relations company, owned by Colette, another member of the regional women's network. Alice trusted Colette's judgement and valued her extensive experience working for national corporate clients. Rather than advertising their products to potential local customers, they decided to focus on building the reputation by entering food competitions, promoting in regional newspapers, and developing their website with more about the history, vision, and product. By the end of 2009, Alice wanted to be in a position to expand the business by supplying products to other retail outlets. She identified three potential channels, namely:

1. Regional supermarket chain with 20 medium-sized stores.

2. National chain of truck fuel stations, which had recently redeveloped to include facilities to provide hot food to take away.

3. Specialist food wholesaler, which delivered to independent cafes in London.

The factory was nearing 70% utilization and had enough space for another new oven.

Alice had to decide which channels to supply and what the impact on the factory would be. She was very reluctant to borrow money, even to purchase equipment, but she could not supply all the potential new customers without borrowing. To make things more complicated, her most entrepreneurial shop manager had identified a potential new shop for sale at a popular tourist destination nearby and was keen to develop it.

Questions

1. Alice appears to have made a successfully transformation of the business. Why should she consider expanding the operations by supplying new markets?

2. What additional financial information does she need for each of the three options?

3. What qualitative information would be useful and how could it be obtained?

Sources: This case was written by Nigel Lockett. It is not based on a real company, but draws on the commercial experience of the author.

✱ 7.5 Summary

➤ Having a good understanding of business accounting is a critical capability if you are creating and running a new venture.

➤ Financial measures, including gross profit, net profit, and profitability indicators such as profit margins can be used to interpret and to improve your financial performance.

➤ Tax matters: it is essential to understand the tax implications of your decisions and it can sometimes be worth seeking professional advice.

➤ Whether you produce your own financial statements or outsource the task to an accountant, a good understanding of profit and loss, balance sheet, and cash flow statements will help you understand your enterprise.

➤ There are many accounting software packages available. Selecting the right software and the right provider or value added retailer (VAR) are both important.

➤ Key performance indicators, both quantitative and qualitative, can be used to inform your decision-making.

Case 7.4 *Critical incident*
Steve Woodford: more than just numbers

In 2009, **Steve Woodford** knew that the charity he had founded, 25 years previously, to provide support to homeless people, needed to better understand the real impact they were having on 'social exclusion'. As the Chief Executive, he had seen the venture grow to employ over 330 staff and a turnover of more than £12 million. However, funding was getting increasingly harder to win. Steve knew they needed to be significantly more competitive. He also knew that they would have to rigorously demonstrate that they provided value for money and the impact they were having on their clients and customers. But how could they actually measure this?

Biography

Growing up on a farm in rural Suffolk seemed an idyllic way to spend a childhood. However, being the son of a tenant farmer was far from secure, as Steve recalled, 'When I was about six or seven we were forced off the farm'. But his father was nothing if not enterprising, 'He became a teacher and he still grew all the rhubarb for his Suffolk District Council schools . . . I would be employed in the early hours of the morning to go and pick rhubarb or strawberries.' Steve's father had a strong faith and had been a conscientious objector during the Second World War. Perhaps not surprisingly, Steve felt this inspired him and convinced him that he 'wanted to make a difference in the world'.

He decided to go to university and do a social science degree, which included placements with voluntary agencies, local authorities, and social services. Steve recalled one placement in a women's hostel for prostitutes and homeless with mental health problems: 'Being thrust into the centre of

Soho [London] it was fascinating and was definitely a watershed for me . . . the induction process included spending five days living rough in London with no more than 25p and an emergency telephone number. That is not the sort of induction we would be allowed to do these days!' He remembered the resilience of the people and, 'How much people who have nothing are willing to share . . . it is a principle that has stuck with me ever since, that every individual you meet, whatever the circumstances they are in, has almost limitless potential.' Steve finished his degree, working within the probation and prison service in Preston prison and graduated as a probation officer. He worked for three years in the job and recalled, 'A lot of the people I was working with had very few educational opportunities, very disruptive family experiences and there was an injustice about the way that resources were allocated across our society. I wanted to spend my time doing something about creating a better balance, creating more opportunities for individuals who might well have fallen through the net, rather than work for an enforcement agency that tended to "blame" individuals.'

'What I actually did was disappear off to the South of France with a young family and a VW camper van!' Steve recalled. 'When I came back I wanted to be involved in something that changed the surroundings of the individuals . . . I was still very committed to social justice, supporting people to achieve their potential but I believed that was more achievable by providing housing, jobs and education opportunities by which they could pull themselves up.'

In 1978, Steve started running a 10-bed young person's hostel for a voluntary organization in Leeds. He formed two strong partnerships, one was with the Council's housing department, to help get people out of the hostel as quickly as possible and into their own accommodation, and the other with the probation office, so that they could work together to deal with crime related issues. Steve remembered, 'This was very formative, in the sense that the whole way that we work now, 25 years later on, is based on this trust . . . we still operate around partnerships. You can't do everything yourself, you need other people to be involved in providing the resources that your customers need.'

Housing as a building block

'Housing is like a basic building block. Somebody can't have self esteem or certainly any confidence unless they have got some of their basic needs met . . . they need shelter and the chance to make something of themselves. Having said that, my experience has often been that a lot of young people don't necessarily realise what an opportunity that is and will continue to actually make mistakes.' Steve also stressed that, 'One of the things that I have been very keen on, is that people can come back to us. They can fail and come back.'

By 1983, Steve wanted to form a charity to: 'Work out innovative and different ways of trying to solve what was then called "social exclusion". We were looking at homeless people around the city centre who were a nuisance rather than high level criminals . . . it was relatively straightforward to get the commitment from housing, local authority and probation to say, "Well instead of always having these people round a revolving door off into court, or to prison for seven days and out again, why don't we do something more sensible with them?"'

After five years of running the voluntary hostel in Leeds, Steve rejoined the probation service. He recalled, 'I had always vowed I would never go back! . . . but a very visionary senior person within probation basically brought me into the service because he wanted this to happen on a broader basis.'

By forming a separate charity, Steve was able to get new funding. He developed two roles: 'In those early days, I used to play off being a probation officer, firmly in the statutory sector one day, with being a charity the next. Basically, it worked a treat . . . I look back now and it obviously was a business that could deliver added value to key partners as well as impacting on the individuals themselves.'

Steve's new venture

Recognizing that finding innovative ways of solving problems in partnership with others was a new business model that could best be exploited, as a charity or social enterprise, outside of the public sector, was an important moment. Steve recalled, 'The mission in my mind wasn't called ending "social exclusion". It was around creating opportunities for individuals who at that moment had fewer opportunities or who had taken wrong moves in their lives and wanted to get them back on track by collaborating with other organisations.' Steve gave an example: 'The housing department, despite having empty flats, didn't really want to let them out to these guys because they could be a bloody nuisance and upset the neighbours and they would never quite get themselves sorted and they might be drinkers or have other problems. We'd go along to the housing department and say, "*Don't worry. Don't give the tenancy directly to them. Give to us.*" We would sign up the tenancy agreement, we sublet to the individual and gave them the appropriate support to try and help them to make it. If they didn't, we moved them on.'

In 2003, the government introduced a completely new funding mechanism for community services called 'Supporting People'. Steve recalled, 'There was a kind of market before but generally things weren't competitively tendered . . . we had always prided ourselves on high quality service. But we were having to become more competitive by looking at much more rationalisation around overheads, office costs and local management . . . we also had to maintain high level links to strategic networks within the local authorities who were commissioning us. So we had a complete restructure. Like a lot of organisations our management structure had grown organically, I guess it was somewhat out of hand and we just put a line right through it and established our management for the future. We called this our "future-proofing" and the Board provided an allowance of £250k for shedding staff following a rigorous assessment centre process.'

Critical incident

By 2009 and after 25 years in existence, the charity had grown significantly to an annual turnover in excess of £12 million and employed over 300 highly skilled staff. A healthy surplus of £432,000 was generated in 2009, and there were net assets of nearly £2 million. At any one time, there were over 3,000 clients being supported a year with 812 supported tenancies. Steve was also increasingly keen to understand the real impact of their activities, not just the financial ones. Results from the annual customer satisfaction survey showed levels approaching 95% for all indicators. Each year they produced an Impact Report, but Steve knew that this didn't capture the real value or impact of the work they were doing (see below).

 online resource centre Case 7-4 spreadsheet.xls

As part of understanding their performance, they decided to measure services in terms of an hourly cost per customer. Steve stated, 'We knew that there was a target here . . . requiring something like a 15 to 20% reduction in a whole range of our overheads in order to be more competitive and continue to win contracts whilst still maintaining the best quality we could.'

Steve's financial information

SUMMARY INCOME & EXPENDITURE ACCOUNT for the year ended 31 March 2009

Income	2009 (£000)
Net Rents & service charges	3,065
NOMS Together Women Project Funding	1,240
Supporting People Income	6,409
Social Services Care Contracts	483
Voluntary income	82
Investment Income & Other Income	81
Other Contract funding	764
	12,124
Expenditure	
Governance Costs	135
Other Operating costs	11,557
	11,692
Revenue Surplus for the Year	432

SUMMARY BALANCE SHEET as at 31 March 2009	
Fixed Assets	1,134
Current Assets	3,720
Less Current Liabilities	(1,857)
Net current assets	1,863
Net assets	2,997
Funds	
Restricted Income Funds	469
Designated Funds	1,223
General Funds	1,305
	2,997

Note: this spreadsheet is available on the Online Resource Centre.

Steve's annual customer satisfaction survey

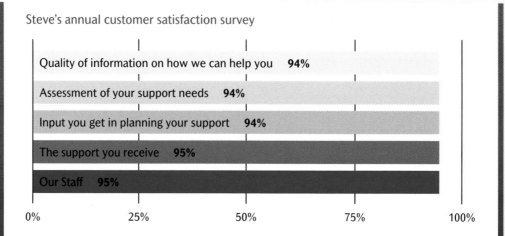

This level of increased performance would have to be supported by cultural change in the organization so a new Resources Director was recruited from industry. The new management team decided that they wanted to bring in outside expertise but realized their needs were unique. Not only did they want to reduce overheads, become more competitive, and bring about cultural change, they also wanted to develop a rigorous system for performance measurement, which showed the impact they were having on their customers. As Steve put it, 'Our impact on ending "social exclusion"'. No other similar organization had developed a way to measure this variable.

The new Resources Director emailed Steve with the idea of working with a local university to help them develop an organization-wide performance management system. A professor from a top business school was due to visit that afternoon to discuss the scope of a project. Steve looked at the email again. The professor asked them to produce a list of key performance measures, both financial and impact. Steve recalled, 'I knew I couldn't delegate this task . . . but what could we actually measure?'

Source: This case is primarily based on an interview with Steve Woodford and written by Nigel Lockett.

 Practical activities

1. Sales analysis For each of the different types of company, namely: grocery supermarket, fashion retailer, petrol station, coal merchant, describe between three and six categories of sales they might make. Discuss the likely difference in sales and profit margin. How might VAT be different for each company and category?

2. Business accounting For each of the different types of company, namely: (i) mail order catalogue company (selling gifts), (ii) management consultancy, (iii) car gear box manufacturer, and (iv) social landlord providing housing for rent, describe the similarities and differences in the following terms:

1. Gross profit
2. Net profit
3. Short-term assets
4. Long-term assets

3. What are the three most popular accounting software packages for small businesses? How much do they cost? What do the systems offer? What training is available?

 ## Discussion topics

1. Key performance indicators Any enterprise needs to manage its finances but there might be other non-financial information that could indicate how well a company is doing. How would you set up the following:

1. An annual customer satisfaction survey for a management consultancy.
2. A system to monitor picking errors in a clothing mail-order company and to calculate the financial cost to the company.
3. A 'total quality' measure which includes five different performance measures for a train operating company.

2. Choosing an accountant You have decided to start your new office supplies company and need to find an accountant. You produce a shortlist of three. One recommended by your new bank manager, one by a family friend and one you meet at a business networking event. You have arranged to see each for one hour before deciding which accountancy firm to appoint. What questions would you ask and how would you differentiate between the answers? What other factors would influence you? Having selected one what else could you do to reassure yourself?

 ## Further reading guide

There are many introductory guides to business accounting and book-keeping, including Barrow and Epstein (2007), Barrow and Tracy (2008), Drury (2009), Marshall (2009), and Wood and Sangster (2008). For advice and further readings on business plan preparation, see Chapter 2 and the Online Resource Centre. The professional accounting associations are another useful source of information. These include the Association of Chartered Certified Accountants (ACCA) (http://www.accaglobal.com), Chartered Institute of Management Accountants (CIMA) (http://www.cimaglobal.com), Institute of Chartered Accountants in England and Wales (ICAEW) (http://www.icaew.com), and Institute of Chartered Accountants in Scotland (ICAS) (http://www.icas.org.uk). For introductions to the use of key performance indicators to manage your venture, see Parmenter (2009) and Eckerson (2005).

References

Barrow, C. (2009) *Business plans for dummies.* Chichester: John Wiley & Sons.

Barrow, P. and Epstein, L. (2007) *Bookkeeping for dummies.* Chichester: John Wiley & Sons.

Barrow, C. and Tracy, J. (2008) *Understanding business accounting for dummies.* Chichester: John Wiley & Sons.

Drury, C. (2009) *Management accounting for business* (4th edition). Florence, KY: Cengage Learning.

Eckerson, W.W. (2005) *Performance dashboards: measuring, monitoring, and managing your business.* Chichester: John Wiley & Sons.

Economist (2009) 'Cloud computing and the tech giants.' *The Economist*, 15 October 2009.

Finch, B. (2006) *How to write a business plan.* London: Kogan Page Ltd.

FSB (2009) *Inhibiting enterprise: fraud and online crime against small businesses.* London: Federation of Small Businesses.

Hamilton, B.H. (2000) 'Does entrepreneurship pay? An empirical analysis of the returns to self-employment.' *Journal of Political Economy*, 108, 3: 604–30.

Marshall, P. (2009) *Mastering book-keeping: a complete guide to the principles and practice of business accounting.* Oxford: How To Books Ltd.

Parmenter, D. (2009) *Key performance indicators (KPI): developing, implementing, and using winning KPIs.* Chichester: John Wiley & Sons.

Wood, F and Sangster, A. (2008) *Frank Wood's business accounting* (two volumes). Harlow: FT Prentice Hall.

Finances
Raising capital for new ventures

8

Pecunia, si uti scis, ancilla est; si nescis, domina – *If you can use money, money is your servant; if you can't, money is your master.*

Old Roman proverb at a tablet found in Verona

The only function of economic forecasting is to make astrology look respectable.

John Kenneth Galbraith, *economist and diplomat*

Learning outcomes

After reading this chapter you should be able to:

➤ Appreciate the role of raising capital and securing investment in new venture creation.

➤ Understand the different types of capital and investment and their sources.

➤ Understand how to obtain different types of capital and investment.

➤ Appreciate the need to consider raising capital and securing investment as part of forecasting and planning.

Case 8.1 Bruce Macfarlane

After a successful career in corporate finance and many years' experience as a business angel, **Bruce Macfarlane** reflects on the first decade of running his hybrid venture capital firm, which manages over £70 million of funds, a portfolio of 20 investments, and a strong syndicate of business angel investors.

Hybrid venture capital firm

'I started in venture as a business angel. Our heritage in this firm is as a group of business angels. What we discovered was, first, that the deal flow was completely haphazard: it depended on somebody hearing of something. Second, everybody was far too busy to do proper due diligence. We all had day jobs and no time to structure the deals or impose proper legals.' Bruce along with his two founding partners decided there was an opportunity to bring business angels together more professionally.

'Our idea was that we would have an engine room of professionals who would track the deals, sift them, structure them, do the due diligence and the business angels would provide the money. But the business angels would also provide additional resources because they would often make their network of contacts available and help the new ventures get into big companies to sell their products. They could also help with strategic input and valuable mentor type capital.

'Now, we manage £70 million and are growing all the time. Whether you are an angel or a venture capitalist, the truth is that you are backing companies at a fragile stage in their development. You are putting in true equity and have to be prepared to help them as they grow. They almost invariably have gaps on their boards and in the management team and their finance function is often weak. They need advice on how to go international, to grow by direct sales or with resellers. These decisions may be a problem for a large company if they go wrong but for a small company can be absolutely fatal.

'We are very cautious about that larger capital that can wipe out the earlier investors. What it means, in our case, is that we are not going to put money into a business unless we can get it to profitability. That is a very good reason for bringing in other investors alongside you. Once a company is profitable its choices of raising more money are much greater. It is a guiding principle for us. We will often come in where there are already existing business angels. Our team tightens up the documentation and drives the company forward. We have standard documentation and shareholder agreements. We actually have a page of "what we expect from management" and "how we want to operate". This is operating on a basis of complete disclosure on both sides so there are no surprises.'

A leap of faith

'The numbers [financials] should tell you how big the market opportunity is and what percentage of it they can realistically win. We have made mistakes: we backed a software business that provided a very clever enterprise solution for mobile phone retailers. The founder had got the software developed very cheaply abroad so the product was priced to sell. What we didn't do properly was assess the market opportunity. The market just wasn't that big. Even if they got 50%

it was never going to be that interesting. You have to get a sense of how big the market is. How do you do this? Some entrepreneurs have come from the market and know it inside out; others, who have not come from the market, go out there and talk to the market. I suspect there are few successful entrepreneurs who started out just with the aim of making a stack of money and then came up with an idea. It is far more likely they had some intuitive experience first. I don't think we have ever backed a business where there is no competitor. There is always some sort of competition.'

Getting a return for your money

'Planning the exit at the outset is essential. We have to have a common understanding of where we are going with the business at the time we invest – we sit down with the entrepreneur and agree the timeline, the likely end buyer and how we can achieve optimal value. The funny thing is that almost all the business plans we see say exit three years down the road but that is usually very optimistic for an early stage business. The average is about five or six years. When we invest in the business we think about exit. In fact, when we write our investment paper, there is a whole section on how we are going to get out and what sort of multiple [return on investment] we can expect to get. Fundamentally, you have to gain the trust of the founder(s). We only succeed and make money if the entrepreneur does. One issue is that the management team is typically diluted as more capital is raised because they do not have the funds to take up their rights. It is essential to keep them incentivised and we ensure that by retaining an option pot for management. Unless it is going to be a really big business you know the entrepreneurs are not going to want to come down much below 10%.'

Looking to the future

'Firstly, I think it costs so much less to start a business today than it did even ten years ago. The barriers to starting a business have come down which is tremendously exciting. You can outsource virtually everything and can focus on what is core to your proposition. Secondly, we don't see failure as a serious problem. We actually like people who have tried and it hasn't worked out. An entrepreneur who is self-aware and has learnt from their experiences is by far the most interesting entrepreneur. We are seeing many more talented young people wanting to join small businesses. I think this is very positive. We are seeing this more than ever before and the quality has definitely been going up.'

Points to consider

1. What are the similarities and differences between business angels and venture capitalists?

2. How has Bruce Macfarlane developed his investment company to include the 'best' elements of business angel and venture capitalist investments?

3. Why would a new venture prefer a trade investor rather than a business angel or a venture capitalist?

Source: This case is mainly based on an interview with Bruce Macfarlane and was written by Nigel Lockett.

8.1 **Introduction**

This chapter considers a fundamental prerequisite to establishing a successful new venture, namely, borrowing capital or raising investment. Without financial resources, a new venture will not be able to obtain the resources and trade to exploit their business idea – no matter how good it is. In this chapter, we will consider the sources of finance, from founders, family and friends, through borrowing from banks to securing **equity** investments. Each is considered in turn, but this should not be seen as a linear process from one point to another. In reality, borrowing capital and securing investment will vary depending on the type of company, growth rate, historical trading performance, balance sheet, market sector, forecasts, existing shareholders, and the aspirations of the founders and directors. Companies may also have multiple sources of capital and investment at any one time, for example, there may be a limited amount of initial capital from the founding shareholders, a loan from a bank to purchase manufacturing equipment, and investment from a business angel. All will have different expectations. The bank will want regular capital and interest payments against a legal contract, whereas the business angel might expect dividends, based on distributing retained profit and growth in their original investment when all or part of the company is sold or floated on a stock exchange. Getting this balance right is critical.

➡ **PERSPECTIVES** See section 11.1 for further information.

So, there are broadly three ways of raising finance for your business: (i) founders, friends, and family (bootstrapping), (ii) debt (borrowing), or (iii) equity (raising investment by selling shares). Debt can be obtained by overdrafts, loans, leasing, and invoice discounting. You will pay interest on debt. Raising equity finance from investors will require selling shares in your business to investors who will make a return through dividends and any sale of shares. Selling shares can change the nature of your business and ultimately lead to you losing control. Because returns for shareholders are linked to the financial performance of the company, it can help reduce the cost of finance and bring in outside expertise. However, some **entrepreneurs** are negative about selling shares to venture capitalists (Delmar 2000).

It is also important to remember that the return from a venture could be both financial and social.

The opening case, '*Bruce Macfarlane*' (Case 8.1), gives the perspective of an experienced business angel, venture capitalist, and investment fund manager. It certainly goes some way to dispel the myth that venture capitalists are only focused on maximizing their returns. His company has limited investment funds of over £70 million. Bruce stated, 'We get up to 800 business plans a year. From these we back only three or four a year, partly due to just simple resource limitations because this is incredibly labour intensive. Not just the sifting through and the due diligence but after we have invested there is an enormous amount of input and hand-holding that goes on with a growing company. A big issue, as a venture capitalist, is missing the deal that is actually going to blow the lights out. Although we are generalists we do focus very much on companies where we think they can grow faster than the niche they are operating in. So we like growth sectors, such as healthcare, technology and financial services. It all becomes part of the DNA.'

There are three further cases in this chapter: The second, *'Three of a kind'* (Case 8.2), considers sources of early funding for new ventures used by three very different companies: an IT communications provider, a fast food business, and an ethical clothing company. Case 8.3, *'The big investment issue'*, investigates the growth of alternative investment funds, which explicitly look for both financial and social returns. The final case, *'Professor Neil Meredith'* (Case 8.4), draws on an interview with a leading medical academic who became the founder of a rapidly growing international dental implants company. Having successfully grown the venture, he now faces the challenges of leadership for the next stage of growth.

The next section considers a number of types of capital for new ventures, namely: **founders, family, and friends** (informal capital), borrowing (formal capital), and equity investment. In the subsequent section three sources of finance (banks, business angels, and venture capitalists) are compared before considering additional capital and investment available to trading businesses (factoring, trade investment, and **flotation**). The final section looks at the possible returns of **enterprise**.

8.2 Types of capital available for new venture creation

8.2.1 Founders, family, and friends

Investment by founders, family, and friends plays a vital and often unrecognized part in new venture creation. A total of $600 billion was invested in 2006 in the 27 countries participating in a GEM study. This compares with less than $40 billion provided by venture capitalists (GEM 2007). The founders of a business will often try to fund their new venture with their own money, on average representing over 60% of the $65,000 start-up capital needed (GEM 2007). This can be attractive because they believe in the business idea and it can show their commitment to other potential investors. Typically, this initial investment will come from savings and borrowing. The latter might be secure on a property or unsecure on a personal guarantee. Credit cards are an important and often unrecognized source of capital, albeit an expensive one. Balancing multiple credit card debt can be challenging but has the attraction of flexibility and easy access.

Dominic List (see Case 8.2) mentions this as a source of his initial funding. As Bruce Macfarlane (Case 8.1) stated, 'The first place an entrepreneur should go to for finance is friends and family, that is the typical route. He should also see his bank manager. We tend to see businesses when they have already been down that route and are looking for their first £1 or £2 million. We are quite clear that we will invest very early on, often pre-revenue. But we would expect to see the individuals put in some of their own money. We would expect to see them have that kind of commitment to growing the business.'

Having exhausted their personal sources of funding, entrepreneurs will often turn to family and friends (Wingborg and Landström 2000; Ebben and Johnson 2006). This is often referred to as bootstrapping. These informal investors will often settle for lower returns than more formal investors, such as business angels (GEM 2007). Bruce Macfarlane (see Case 8.1) states, 'The first place an entrepreneur . . . should go to for finance is friends and family.' This might even be before any bank is approached for loans. It can certainly help the case of bank lending if funds are available from founders, family, and friends.

Ben Taylor's development of an online tool for nightclubs to promote and sell tickets for their events required his father to secure an application for a £15,000 bank overdraft. Six months later, his father also invested £25,000. Ben's business, Fatsoma (http://www.fatsoma.com), was founded in 2006. In three years it had sales of over £2 million and generated a profit. Having an experienced entrepreneur in the family can be an added bonus and provide useful support and mentoring (http://www.smallbusiness.co.uk).

Once this type of very personal capital (founders, family, and friends) is gathered, the new venture may also need to access more formal types of funding by either borrowing capital or raising investments (equity).

There is often an additional source of unrecognized funding for small businesses, which may not be available to new start-ups, namely trade credit. Once a business has a track record, suppliers will look more favourably on providing a trade or credit account.

8.2.2 Borrowing

Banks provide most of the capital borrowed by businesses. They are a vital type of financing for new ventures. As they do not normally take a shareholding or have an equity investment in the business, they require any capital to be repaid and charge interest. This interest might be charged at variable (base rate plus a fixed amount, say 2%) or a fixed rate. A number of variants have emerged in recent years, such as capped rates, which limit the lower and/or higher rates charged. It is important to remember that the bank assesses the risk and their return when calculating rates and each bank will have different policies on this. Banks will normally charge a fee for arranging financing and annually for agreeing overdrafts.

Unsecured borrowing The most used form of unsecured borrowing is credit card debt. Recent US research on new businesses indicates that the majority of small firm borrowing, typically less than $35,000, is on credit cards (Shane 2008). Credit cards are appealing to small businesses because they are easy to use, can streamline payments, are easier to get than bank borrowing, widely accepted, and an anonymous source of funding, which requires no explanation to the lender. However, credit card debt is more expensive than other formal borrowing – averaging around 15%. In spite of this, they remain popular, with nearly 60% of new businesses using them to fund approximately a third of their debt in their first year (Scott 2009).

An overdraft linked to a current bank account facility remains the most popular method of funding trading activities. It is borrowing at a variable rate with an agreed limit. Typically, this limit is agreed each year, and an arrangement fee is charged. It tends to be used for day-to-day expenses rather than purchasing expensive items of equipment or machinery. Once arranged, it is flexible and there is no penalty for not using it. However, the bank can charge for unauthorized exceeding of the overdraft limit, and in some circumstances, banks may want security from business assets.

Some governments provide loan guarantee schemes for small businesses that meet certain criteria, for example, in the US the Small Business Administration offers Express programmes (http://www.sba.gov) and in the UK the Department of Business Innovation and Skills offered the Small Firms Loan Guarantee (SFLG) scheme for over three decades (http://www.berr.gov.uk). It was replaced by the Enterprise Finance Guarantee scheme in response to the 'credit crunch' in 2009. Over the previous decade, the SFLG scheme averaged around 4,500 loans per year. The schemes have been developed in response to perceived market failures, which act as a barrier to small businesses accessing finance. Governments intervene because supporting viable small businesses helps to generally increase productivity and job generation. Recent research supports this view by finding that cost–benefit analysis shows that the overall benefits outweigh the cost to the economy and other economic benefits include growth in sales growth, exports, and jobs. Firms that use this scheme are 6% more likely to export, 17% more likely to use new technology, and 24% more likely to use 'cutting edge technology' than similar borrowing firms (Cowling 2010). However, such a scheme can be bureaucratic and time consuming to set up.

Credit cards do not often require the entrepreneur or small business owner to provide security in the form of company assets or personal guarantees. This makes them popular with borrowers but a cause of concern for lenders, even though the interest rates charged may be higher than secured loans. This is a topical area of **entrepreneurship** research in the United Sates and Europe (e.g. Europe: Hernández-Cánova and Koëter-Kant 2008; Germany: Harhoff and Körting 1998; Italy: Howorth and Moro 2006; Spain: Jiménez et al. 2006).

Secured borrowing Banks make their money by lending to people and businesses. Tried and tested structures and procedures support this activity, which requires the bank to take a calculated risk against the likelihood of making a net return greater than other forms of investment. This net return is based on the difference between the interest payments they receive against the interest payments they make for accessing funds. The return has also to include deductions for any write-offs for bad loans. Banks reduce these write-offs by carrying out credit checks, developing risk assessment methods, and taking securities against assets.

Obtaining a loan secured against assets tends to be cheaper and easier to obtain than equity finance and you retain control of your business. However, banks like to see a track record in business and may require regular financial information.

Typically, borrowing is secured against property. This might be to purchase the property itself or equipment. It can be helpful to link the security to the item being purchased. If the property being used is a home, it is imperative to consult with anyone affected by this guarantee.

Capital equipment, machinery, and vehicles can also be purchased by specialist loans. These include hire purchase (HP) where you own the asset at the end of the agreement and leasing where you might have the option to purchase the asset at the end of the agreement. HP requires the capital value of the item to be depreciated through the profit and loss account but is not allowable against taxes. Leasing, like rental charges, are deductible in full. For enterprise with stock, whether purchased or manufactured, banks may consider lending and taking these as security.

Banks will seek to have 'first charge' over any assets. This means that in the event of a default, the lender will have legal ownership of the asset, and other secured and unsecured lenders will only receive funds if there is a surplus. In practice, these legal charges are most relevant to property-based securities and in the case of receivership government debts must be cleared first.

4.2.3 Equity

Establishing your business as a limited company allows for the sale of equity (shares) to external investors. This could be used to bring in a new director/shareholder, capital, or a 'private equity' investment firm. Private equity funds are invested, in exchange for a stake in your company; with the investors getting future returns that are dependent on profitability or the growth in value. More often than not, they will be looking to invest in growing entrepreneurial businesses. In this instance, the purpose of selling shares is to increase the capital of the firm and possibly bring in new expertise rather than for existing shareholders to make personal gains. There are a number of bodies who can provide this form of investment, such as seed funds, business angels, and venture capitalists.

Case 8.2 brings the different strands of this discussion together in a study of early stage funding and how it worked in practice for three ambitious entrepreneurs.

Case 8.2 Three of a kind? Sources of early stage funding

Raising the initial capital to start a new venture is one of the first challenges an entrepreneur faces. Dominic List, Amina Ansir and Penny Jones each had a good business idea and managed to launch them but raised capital by different means.

When **Dominic List** appeared on Channel 4's Secret Millionaire programme in October 2009, both he and his successful IT company, Comtact (http://www.comtact.co.uk), were exposed to media attention. In the programme he went undercover in Peckham, London, just a few miles from his own flat and saw at first hand the challenges of inner city unemployment. Dominic commented, 'I have been really overwhelmed by the response, I think it has been really great . . . it was a great opportunity to highlight those that are doing a really good job in their community and those who represent a really positive image for their communities . . . I have also been really happy with the responses and it has been really great to get other people offering their support and assistance to both the people that you have seen on the programme but also for other projects that I might be working on as well.' (Channel 4 2009)

When Dominic founded Comtact in 2005 he relied on a combination of credit cards, the remortgaging of his flat, a loan from his father, and the sale of his car. He is an advocate of using family and friends: 'These are the best sources to raise seed capital but [they] also get work done. I had my father's accountant do the accounts for us as a favour.' (Real Business 2009) So he began the business from his own home, using the £100,000 he raised.

Comtact provides converged voice, data, and networking solutions to its corporate customers in order to reduce the telecommunication costs. Perhaps entrepreneurship was in Dominic's blood. His father was a serial entrepreneur starting a range of new ventures, from chip shops and hairdressing to industrial cleaning (Sunday Times 2009). Dominic's advice to new start-ups includes: outsource; work from home or in the car; use a forwarding address; beg or borrow; use non-geographic telephone numbers; use Google Apps; think big (http://www.dominiclist.co.uk). In 2008, Dominic won the IAB Business Entrepreneur of the Year Award (http://www.iab.org.uk).

Ethical point Dominic is increasingly involved in social projects, including Fredericks Foundation (http://www.fredericksfoundation.org), Ilderton Foundation (http://www.ildertonfoundation.org. uk), and Peckham Park Youth Project.

Foreign travel was the catalyst for **Amina Ansir** developing her business idea. It was after graduating from college that Amina first decided to run her own business. During a visit to Canada, she was impressed by the various fast food outlets and their use of automation. When one of her relatives visited her from the United States, she shared her vision to create a venture at grass-roots level by employing a semi-skilled and skilled workforce. This inspired Amina to investigate the potential for opening a pizza takeaway and delivery business in Islamabad, Pakistan, and she launched Pizza Plus in 2006. She borrowed the money to start her business from family friends (Shell Livewire 2010). Initially, she focused on pizza as her main product but soon expanded to offer a wide variety of pizzas, burgers, parathas, salads, and coffees. Amina launched an online ordering for frozen pizzas to cook in the home and deliveries of food to meetings and conferences. Pizza Plus grew to employ 15 staff (http://www.pizzaplus.com.pk).

When, in 2004, **Penny Jones** decided to start the White T-shirt Company (http://www. thewhitetshirt.co.uk), she approached a **social enterprise**, PNE Group, for a start-up loan (PNE Group 2010). She quickly got the money she needed to launch the environmentally friendly White T-shirt Company and after two years secured additional funding from the PNE Group. Penny's business idea was simple yet distinctive, and it helped that she was a former designer and buyer for retailers such as Harrods and Marks & Spencer. Penny produced the 'perfect white t-shirt', which had a 'wearable difference', made from organically grown cotton from Danish Green, a pioneer in the manufacture of environmentally friendly and sustainable textiles. The business has developed a strong online presence and used the Internet and press coverage to promote the brand.

Ethical point Penny's decision to use only Danish Green organic cotton for all her products was to provide her customers with independent certification for the whole production process. It is based on the principles of governing cultivation, ginning, spinning, knitting, weaving, dyeing, printing, cutting, sewing, and recycling (http://www.novotex.dk).

Questions

1. What are the five sources of funding mentioned in the cases? What are advantages and risks of borrowing from family and friends?

2. What might be the next sources of capital for each business and why might these be different?

3. If you were starting a new venture which family members and friends could you approach? What information would you want if a friend asked you for a loan to help set up a new venture?

Sources: Channel 4 (2009); Real Business (2009); Sunday Times (2009); PNE Group (2010); Shell Livewire (2010).

8.3 Sources of finance

8.3.1 Banks

Banks are a vital source of formal finance for small businesses and new ventures. In the UK, during 2008, banks provided over £9 billion in overdraft facilities to businesses, attracted over 500,000 new small business customers, and provided £2 billion of lending to approximately 200,000 small businesses (BBA 2010). During the global credit difficulties, inter-bank lending, which provides the liquidity necessary for business lending, was hard for banks to access. Many national governments intervened to help banks borrow money from other institutions, such as the European Investment Bank (http://www.eib.org). Both national and international banks provide finance to business. However, national banks, such as Lloyds TSB (http://www.lloydstsb.com) and Yorkshire Bank (http://www.ybonline.co.uk) in the UK, tend to be more visible to entrepreneurs and small business owners than international banks, such as Citibank (http://www.citigroup.com). Some banks operate at both a global and a national level, for example, Barclays (http://group.barclays.com and http://www.bank.barclays.co.uk), HSBC (http://www.hsbc.com and http://www.hsbc.co.uk), and Banco Santander (http://www.santander.com and http://www.santander.co.uk)

Choosing the right bank for you can be difficult because their services can seem very similar. However, banking is a service, albeit a rather important one, and requires that you form a relationship. It is worth investing some time meeting with different banks and asking friends and colleagues for their experiences. Some will also be particularly keen to attract new business customers and provide support and advice beyond just banking, such as insurance.

8.3.2 Business angels

When bank lending and other informal sources are insufficient to finance a rapidly growing venture you may decide that the only way to expand your business further is to sell shares to private equity investors. One of the first types of private equity you might want to consider is business angels. These tend to be wealthy individuals who want to invest their own money in high growth businesses. They may also be part of a syndicate with other business angels. In addition to money, they often bring with them experience, skills, and contacts. They will tend to look for opportunities in industries and sectors where they feel they have relevant experience. Typically, they will invest between £10,000 and £750,000 (http://www.bbaa.org.uk). Finding the right business angel can be difficult and is just as much about relationships as finance. In the first instance, it is worth approaching regional business groups, such as the Cambridge Network (http://www.cambridgenetwork.co.uk), or larger business angel networks, such as British Business Angels Association (http://www.bbaa.org.uk) or the European Business Angel Network (http://www.eban.org).

Bruce Macfarlane (Case 8.1) stated, 'In a totally rational market, there should be different classes of investor for each stage of a company's development. In the same way, you might argue, there should be different kinds of management at different stages of a company's development. So if it all worked properly business angels would back the entrepreneur at the very early stage, get the business to a position where it needed a few million pounds, hand it over to a venture capital manager (like us) who would develop it further and, finally, we would hand it over to a late-stage development capital firm who would ready it for IPO or trade sale and replace the entrepreneur with professional management. In reality, it doesn't work like that . . . Business angels sometimes view venture capitalists as red-blooded capitalists who come in and destroy everything. But the advantage of venture capital is that it does bring discipline and an outside perspective.'

Bruce also recalled how difficult and risky investing can be: 'In my early days as a business angel, I backed a business where I ended up losing $100,000 dollars. The founders were healthcare specialists with Harvard MBAs and they [company] had a very good healthcare idea. But their first action was to go to a consulting firm and spend half a million dollars getting advice on the market and a report that wasn't worth anything. There was no money left to get the business going. What you need is a team that have gone out there themselves and worn out their shoe leather in building a proper understanding of their market.'

8.3.2 Venture capitalists

Venture capitalists (VCs) are also a source of private equity capital, but they usually manage larger funds than syndicates of business angels. Venture capital firms usually manage deals of between £250,000 and £2 million (BVCA 2009a). They are also more likely to look for an exit through an initial public listing (IPO) or trade sale to a larger company. In the US, the National Venture Capital Association (NVCA) has over 400 member VCs (http://www.nvca. org); the European Private Equity and Venture Capital Association (EVCA), a non-profit trade association, is based in Brussels (http://www.evca.eu); the British Private Equity & Venture Capital Association (BVCA) has a membership of over 230 private equity venture capital firms with an accumulated total of approximately £32 billion in funds under management and over 220 professional advisory firms (http://www.bvca.co.uk). Members of BVCA have worked with a range of high growth businesses including Adaytum Software, Card Warehouse, Entropic Cambridge Research Laboratory (ECRL), Gala Group, Jungle Online, Landmark Information Group, Luminar, and Permira (BVCA 2009b).

It is important to briefly consider the extent of venture capital funding and the high degree of variation across countries. Firstly, in 2006, venture capital represented only 6% of new venture funding when compared with informal investment (see 8.2.1). Secondly, the relative amount of venture capital invested varies markedly between countries ($8.6 million in US and $1.8 million in G7 countries) as does the percentage of the total funds invested (71% in US; 10% in UK; less than 5% in Canada, France, Germany, and Japan; and only 2% in Italy) (GEM 2007). In other words, venture capital is an important source of finance, but it is not as important as you might expect.

It is difficult to generalize because every deal is different, but usually it takes between three and eight months to raise funding from VCs. Entrepreneurs can be expected to give at least 20% but sometimes considerably more and the exit is expected within three to seven years (http://www.businesslink.org.uk).

Raising finance is not a one-off event. As Bruce Macfarlane (Case 8.1) stated:

For example, we have backed a new company in the dental implant market, a market where there are some giant companies competing. This company invented a much more efficient implant system. But would the big guys squash them before we got them off the ground? The market as a whole was growing at 15/20% a year and they were all enjoying substantial profits. So why would they bother to squash a tadpole? It was a judgement and we correctly surmised they would not bother. When we invested, the management thought a million pounds would see them through to profitability but that was never going to be the case. We weren't certain how much money would be required. Therefore, to hedge our risk, we invited another venture capital firm to come in with us that had a healthcare background, which would be useful. Every time we go into a business we assume we will have to follow our money. These are growing companies that always require more capital and so if we are putting in a million pounds, we have already mentally worked out we are going to have to put in a further £2 or £3 million. There is no doubt though that, regardless of extensive due diligence, every investment is a leap of faith.

The truth is that when entrepreneurs take professional money they have fundamentally lost their complete freedom of action . . . It doesn't matter what percentage we own, the shareholder agreement gives us a veto over all important decisions. That is something one has to understand at the outset of going for professional money. However, they will also get powerful support. We backed a digital media company and the founder was very talented, with a background in digital media, who saw the opportunity to grow a 'lead generation' business. They had to get data on people who would be interested in particular products and then they were able to sell those data lists: for example, a cosmetic company which wanted to target women between 25 and 35 for a new skin cream. It is difficult to generate that data because people voluntarily give their information often for something in return. We were very impressed by this entrepreneur, but he didn't have much of a management team. We said we would only invest if we recruited a finance director, which we did. We also found a chairman and chief operating officer for him.

8.4 **Financing an ongoing venture**

Once you have launched your new venture it is possible to arrange access to the funds tied up with trade customers, a technique called 'factoring' or 'invoice discounting'. Running a high growth company might also attract the interest of trade investors, either from within the sector or those wishing to enter it. Finally, having successfully established a market position and reputation you and your shareholders might decide to 'exit' by selling the business to a trade investor or by some form of flotation.

8.4.1 **Factoring**

Factoring and invoice discounting can provide valuable finance to growing companies who trade with other businesses and offer credit accounts. Such companies will raise an invoice for goods or services and give the customer 30 days to pay it. It is not unusual for this period to become extended to an average of over 60 days. This can result in profitable businesses experiencing cash flow difficulties. The two most common methods of accessing these funds are factoring and invoice discounting.

- **Factoring** In this case, the bank agrees to pay a percentage, for example 80%, of approved debts as soon as they receive a copy of the invoice. The balance, in this example 20%, is paid when the customer settles the full invoice. A small percentage or fixed fee is deducted from this payment. You are still responsible for collecting the debt from your customers who are not aware that you have factored the invoice. Factoring agreements normally have a limit to the total amount you can borrow as well as limits on the age of the invoice, such as 90 days.

- **Invoice discounting** This is similar to factoring but is likely to be offered to younger or smaller businesses. It has one important difference: the bank provides the debt collection service and your customer is aware that a third party is involved. This will probably result in a larger service charge. Historically, this type of finance has been seen as a weakness, but many successful companies have used this service so perceptions are changing.

Factoring and invoice discounting can provide a significant and quick boost to cash flow and can be a valuable source of working capital. It can also prove cost effective with modest charges and interest only being charged on the funds used rather than the total available. You might also be able to use this access to funds to negotiate early settlement discounts with your suppliers. With invoice discounting you will need to consider the reaction of your customers. This type of funding can also be available for new start-ups.

8.4.2 Trade investors

Many high growth companies, particularly in a sector with a history of acquisitions (such as IT and medical) will receive the necessary finance from trade investors, rather than business angels or venture capitalists. Usually, these trade investors will have expert industry knowledge or wish to gain it. The initial investment may be followed by an attempt to acquire the company. These amounts invested or paid tend not to be in the public domain.

Cisco Systems, the large global computer networking company, was founded in 1984 and by 2009 had over 65,000 employees and a turnover of $36 billion. It has a track record of acquiring many smaller high growth companies with technology it was interested in (http://www.cisco.com). For example, in December 2009, it acquired ScanSafe, a UK Internet security service provider (http://www.scansafe.com) founded by two brothers in 1999, for approximately $183 million.

8.4.3 Flotation

Some high growth companies work through several types of financing until they reach the point where a flotation becomes both desirable and profitable. The instances of successful flotation are few and far between. One mechanism for this is an initial public offering (IPO) or initial public stock offering, where a company offers shares for sale on a public platform, such as the NASDAQ stock market founded in the US (http://www.nasdaqomx.com). This is a complex and costly process involving an underwriting firm to manage it.

Founded in the UK, the Alternative Investment Market (AIM) has allowed over 3,000 companies to become traded since its launch in 1995 (http://www.londonstockexchange.com). It provides an opportunity for smaller and growing companies to raise capital. In 2009, the highest value AIM listed companies included Playtech (http://www.playtech.com), KSK Power Ventur (http://www.ksk.co.in), Gulf Keystone Petroleum (http://www.gulfkeystone.com), Coal of Africa Limited (http://www.coalofafrica.com), and Datatec Ltd (http://www.datatec.co.za).

The flotation of high growth companies attracts much media attention. But how does the amount of finance raised compare to other forms of investment? During the whole of 2005 in the US, $8.7 billion was raised by the flotation of 965 companies. However, this is less than 3% of the $300 billion of informal funding (founders, families, and friends) used to fund over 3 million companies over the same period (GEM 2007).

The following example from the recent history of Google illustrates the financing process, from the use of informal sources at the start-up stage (i.e. obtained from the founders, their family, and friends), through venture capital as the enterprise grew rapidly, and finally to flotation (i.e. the 'IPO' or initial public offering):

Financing Google: from start-up to IPO

Google founders Larry Page and Sergey Brin bought a terabyte of storage at bargain prices and built their own computer housings in Larry's dorm room, which became Google's first data center. Unable to interest the major portal players of the day, Larry and Sergey decided to make a go of it on their own. All they needed was a little cash to move out of the dorm – and to pay off the credit cards they had maxed out buying their terabyte of memory. So they wrote up a business plan, put their Ph.D. plans on hold, and went looking for an angel investor. Their first visit was with a friend of a faculty member. Andy Bechtolsheim, one of the founders of Sun Microsystems, was used to taking the long view. One look at their demo and he knew Google had potential – a lot of potential. But though his interest had been piqued, he was pressed for time. As Sergey tells it, 'We met him very early one morning on the porch of a Stanford faculty member's home in Palo Alto. We gave him a quick demo. He had to run off somewhere, so he said, "Instead of us discussing all the details, why don't I just write you a check?" It was made out to Google Inc. and was for $100,000.'

The investment created a small dilemma. Since there was no legal entity known as 'Google Inc.,' there was no way to deposit the check. It sat in Larry's desk drawer for a couple of weeks while he and Sergey scrambled to set up a corporation and locate other funders among family, friends, and acquaintances. Ultimately, they brought in a total initial investment of almost $1 million.

On September 7, 1998, more than two years after they began work on their search engine, Google Inc. opened its doors in Menlo Park, California. The door came with a remote control, as it was attached to the garage of a friend who sublet space to the new corporation's staff of three. The office offered several big advantages, including a washer and dryer and a hot tub. It also provided a parking space for the first employee hired by the new company: Craig Silverstein, now Google's director of technology.

Source: Extracts from http://www.google.com/corporate/history.html reported in GEM (2007).

Most of our discussion has concentrated on the financing of commercial ventures. However, social enterprises also require capital in order to achieve their objectives and to expand the scope and scale of their operations. Case 8.3 looks at how one social enterprise, The Big Issue Foundation, is helping to finance other organizations in order to produce a better return for society and for the environment.

Case 8.3 The big investment issue: Investing for social returns

Increasingly organizations and governments around the world are recognizing the importance of enterprise for bringing about social change. Venture capital funds are beginning to emerge to provide alternative methods for raising capital and making investment. One of the first of these was the Big Issue Invest, which is a specialized provider of finance to social enterprises or trading arms of charities that seek to bring about social and environmental transformation (Big Issue Invest 2010). It is part of The Big Issue group of companies. Big Issue Invest has recently launched a £10 million Social Enterprise Investment Fund, which provides investment from £100,000 to £500,000 in the form of loans, participation loans, and equity to high impact social enterprises with the potential for scaling-up. It can also arrange larger financing with other social finance institutions. Big Issue Invest also has a loan fund, which provides loans to social enterprises or trading arms of charities that have been trading for three years or more and have a turnover of over £250,000. The Big Issue was founded by John Bird in 1991 to help homeless people have the dignity of self-employment through selling.

The ventures accessing the fund are wide and varied. They include Belu Water, Fifteen Foundation, and Training for Life.

Belu Water is the first carbon neutral, bottled water company in the UK. It uses compostable bottles made from corn and invests all surpluses in clean water projects. It supplies leading supermarkets, high-end restaurants, and corporate boardrooms. The CEO, **Reed Paget**, won *The Independent's* 2008 Social Entrepreneur of the Year award. Belu Water seeks to 'create a sustainable balance between people and the planet' by using all the profits from the sale of bottled water to fund clean water projects and to 'create the most eco-friendly bottled water in the world' by being carbon neutral and use a compostable bottle made from corn (Belu 2010).

Fifteen Foundation was founded by **Jamie Oliver** to provide training in the restaurant industry for disadvantaged young people. Fifteen has succeeded in giving young people a transition opportunity to a good career – latest figures show that 75% were still chefing or working in another part of the food industry. The Fifteen restaurants serve food of the highest quality made from the best ingredients in the kitchens where the apprentices learn their trade. Fifteen's philosophy is to help young people learn within the work environment, from experts in the field, surrounded by the produce, equipment, and dishes that they will work with. Gradually, their levels of responsibility increase with increasing skill, and their confidence grows despite the setbacks they may have experienced. Fifteen has restaurants in Amsterdam, Cornwall, London, and Melbourne (Fifteen Foundation 2010).

Training for Life was launched in 1995 by **Gordon da Silva**, an award winning social entrepreneur. It also helps long-term unemployed return to work by gaining entrepreneurial experience within small businesses such as restaurants, gyms, and training centres. Much of this work is done through training or 'Prospect Centres', which help local communities to improve the quality of their lives by addressing their needs, whether through employment, health, leisure, or residential support. Since it was founded it has helped return over 12,000 people, previously long-term unemployed, homeless, or from prison, back to full-time education or employment and created more than 150 new jobs. It has created several Prospect Centres worth about £20 million. As a social enterprise, 100% of the profits are fed back into their charitable work (Training for Life 2010).

Ethical point Interestingly, for personal financing The Big Issue Invest are also developing an alternative credit scoring model, which could help up to 1.5 million low-income people in the UK by providing better informed and fairer credit decision-making. This could allow access to mainstream credit, which should reduce the interest paid by some of the poorest households. The model recognizes that many of these people reliably pay rent and bills and that this is not recorded by the credit reference agencies (http://www.bigissueinvest.com).

Questions

1. Why do social enterprises use alternative funds, like the Big Issue Invest rather than conventional loans?

2. What other social investments are available for social entrepreneurs?

3. Why is there so much interest in social enterprises by governments?

4. Are there any differences in the skills required to be a social entrepreneur rather than an entrepreneur?

Sources: Belu (2010); Big Issue Invest (2010); Fifteen Foundation (2010); Training for Life (2010).

8.5 Securing a return on the investment

8.5.1 First things first: what is the investor looking for?

Before considering the return that investors are likely to require, it is worth reminding ourselves what they see as the essential features of a 'good' business idea. The venture capitalist and business angel Bruce Macfarlane (Case 8.1) has highlighted three key requirements: a strong general proposition, access to experienced people, and an interesting business plan:

- **A strong proposition** 'First of all there is a general proposition. There are plenty of bright ideas out there but it is much easier to have one than to execute it. What makes the difference is somebody's ability to turn that bright idea into a business and deliver it. That is very difficult. In our society, we value people who are very, very clever and we have tended not to value the engineers and the doers. But execution is all important. We need to be sure that the innovative idea also provides a service or product that is needed in the market. We have to understand the market and how they are going to sell to it. What is unattractive is somebody who has a good idea and then just wants money . . . you need far more than that. It has to be a special idea with insight into a particular market need – are they close enough to the market to appreciate the customer's needs?'

- **Access to experienced people** 'What is very attractive is when someone with a good idea brings in somebody with commercial experience who is going to help them commercialize it. We don't expect a fully fledged team (there are always gaps), but you expect the nucleus to be there.'

- **An interesting business plan** 'We tell people that we want to see a business plan before we meet them. The business plan has got to be sufficiently interesting for us to take it to the next stage. We do not have a template. It is probably true to say a well written business plan with a clear outline of what the business is all about and where they are going will receive more attention. Someone has to write a coherent, well thought through business plan with numbers. Of the several hundred we get we then meet about 20%. In the course of a year, we will have whittled down to perhaps twenty plans, on which we are thinking seriously about issuing "heads of terms". I don't think the first formal presentation should be any longer than an hour. The team [company] has to be very concise in an hour and persuade us that it is a compelling proposition. From this very first meeting we'll get a quick sense whether this is something that is worth spending time on.'

In earlier chapters, we have encouraged you to develop an **opportunity business model** as a way of thinking through and articulating your venture idea clearly and effectively (Section 2.3). However, we also recognized that more formal business plans have a role to play, and one of their primary roles is to support a request for finance. It is important that business plans are written with your audience in mind (Blundel and Ippolito 2008; Mason and Stark 2004). In this case, the challenge is to persuade the potential investor that your venture is attractive, and that your **entrepreneurial team** is capable of achieving your operational and financial goals.

8.5.2 The nature of the return to investors

Clearly, entrepreneurs, lenders, and investors all want a return for their effort, finance, and investment. For lenders, this will simply be interest charged on the money borrowed and, for investors, the dividends on shares. But, whereas lenders will want capital repaid over an agreed term, investors will probably be looking for significant capital growth on an equity investment.

However, not all returns are financial. Entrepreneurs could achieve far more personally than money. They may find the challenge of launching a successful business and managing people rewarding as well as enjoy being in control or 'their own boss' as it provides them with an increased quality of life (Hamilton 2000). The aim of most business angels and venture capitalist is not to achieve a personal gain for the founding team but to achieve a return on their investment. Clearly in some cases the interests of the founding team and future investors will be very different. As we saw in Case 8.3, '*The big investment issue*', the returns can be both financial and social. By 2010, there were more than 60,000 social enterprises employing over 800,000 and contributing over £24 billion to the economy. Businesses driven by a social or environmental purpose are attracting talented people from all backgrounds, an indication that non-financial returns can be a powerful incentive (http://www.socialenterprise.org.uk).

In the critical incident case, '*Professor Neil Meredith*' (Case 8.4), we see how an expert in dental implants exploited his academic knowledge to create a successful medical company, which has grown with founder, venture capital, and trade investment. What has he learnt from this experience? Firstly, that 'Venture capitalists are objective business people . . . what you need to continually do is understand your true value to the business . . . you need to be very aware of it.'

Secondly, that, 'The invention is 10% of the product and the product is 10% of the business' – Meredith's law of **innovation**.

✳ 8.6 Summary

➤ Raising finance is a critical element of new venture creation.

➤ Finance for new ventures and growing businesses can come from informal investment from founders, family, and friends. This is often the first source of finance for new entrepreneurs.

➤ Borrowing can be unsecured or secured. Credit cards form the largest element of unsecured borrowing for small firms. Banks play a critical role in providing finance to new ventures and small businesses.

➤ Investment can be obtained from selling equity to business angels and/or venture capitalists. This requires detailed business planning and assessment. It can also be used as a mechanism to gain expertise for the company.

➤ Established businesses can factor their sales invoices to raise working capital.

➤ Trade investors also make equity investments in attractive high growth firms.

➤ The selling of new venture shares on a stock exchanges (flotation) is rare.

➤ Lenders require interest and capital repayment. Investors seek dividend payments and capital growth.

➤ Not all returns from enterprise are financial: social outcomes are increasingly evident.

Case 8.4 *Critical incident*
Professor Neil Meredith: invention, product, and business

By 2009, Professor **Neil Meredith** had successfully taken his innovative new dental implants venture through nearly 10 years of continuous growth. As CEO he had personally negotiated through the maze of getting equity investment to fund this high growth business. Beginning with the founders investment to get early sales, he firstly secured venture capital funding and secondly a strategic investment from a trade investor which helped open up the US market. The company was set for the next stage of development. But was Neil the right person to lead the company? The investors were keen for the restructuring to happen, but Neil had reservations about finding the right person with the right experience who he could work with and the company could afford. A recruitment agency was appointed.

Biography

Neil celebrated his 50th birthday a couple of months ago and remembered his grammar school education in Stockport near Manchester, 'I decided to study dentistry and went to Guys Hospital in 1979 qualifying in 1982. I did a series of hospital jobs in a range of departments. And then, went from Guys Hospital to Glasgow to Kingston. So I rotated around the country quite a lot!' However, in the mid 1980s, Neil decided to go into general practice.

Setting up a new practice in the Isle of Wight was a rare opportunity and Neil recalled, 'It was quite a nice adventure. During that time, I also passed the first part of the fellowship examinations for the Royal College of Surgeons.' This was unusual, but Neil was particularly interested in restorative dentistry: crowns and bridges. In 1987, he studied for an MSc and then went on to undertake a PhD in bio-mechanics at the Eastman and Imperial College, which he completed in 1992.

It was while working at Imperial College that Neil's interest developed in dental implants. He explained, 'We were talking about dental implants with engineering colleagues. Dental implants are pre titanium screws inserted into bone to which the bone fuses directly. One of the difficulties is knowing how well that osseointegration has worked. The implant may fail to fuse and the patient is completely unaware of it, there is no infection. There is no swelling, pain or discomfort but the implant is mobile. In 1993, we developed a technique called resonance frequency analysis, which was attached a small electronic transducer, similar to a tuning fork, to the implant.' Neil had always had an interest in electronics as a hobby, and his technical understanding proved very useful in this process.

Spinning out implants

This interest developed further and Neil moved to Sweden to complete his second PhD, this time looking at resonance frequency analysis. He recalled, 'I came back from Sweden published a number of papers and was coordinator for a European grant of €1.8 million to assess the technical viability of this technique as a clinical diagnostic technique for patients.' By the mid 1990s, Imperial College was encouraging technology transfer, patents were filed, and a spin-off company was formed. Neil soon went to Leeds to become a professor in clinical bio-materials and restorative dentistry. One of the challenges that Neil and his colleagues embraced was that existing dental implant systems were very complex and consisted of up to 3,000 articles. The systems were supplied by six big dental implant companies. Neil recalled, 'You need to be a specialist, not just to place the implant, but to read the catalogues . . . we decided it was an appropriate time for the "common sense implant" . . . we sat down and designed a dental implant system for interest.' They formed the company, located near Leeds, in 1999 in order to protect the intellectual property (IP) and with £50,000 made prototypes to validate their new system.

From prototype to production

It took about 18 months to develop the new dental implant system. The company had no borrowings and no family investment. Early feedback was very positive, and Neil recalled, 'All the clinicians and technicians that saw the system said, "You must do something with it. It is different." It was not crazily different, it was a real evolution. There were some really smart ideas and the combination and design of components resulted in an implant system including instruments and all components of less than one hundred articles but with no clinical restrictions. This meant that the cost of stocking and using the system was lower than the competition and it could be used on all patients.'

However, Neil was concerned not to over-promote the innovation and remembered, 'We just kept it very quiet and I think that it was the right thing to do. Because of the stock as well as development costs and production costs, our intention wasn't to manufacture these articles. There were suppliers around Europe who supplied all the big medical device companies, so there was no need to invest in capital equipment. But there was stock and there was a sales force and setting up the company. Therefore, it needed a significant amount of capital.'

'So I wrote a business plan . . . with no financial training. I read widely and sought advice . . . without question this was the most challenging part. We talked to over 20 sources of funding before finding our VC [venture capitalist]. Getting that first stage of funding is the most difficult thing I have ever done. The due diligence process is very challenging. Very challenging!' In early 2003, the first stage was secured and the new venture set its sights on international markets from an early point. This was an important decision, as Neil recalled, 'The reason is that the UK was a much smaller market than Europe because of the lack of NHS support and the healthcare structure. The number of implants sold in the UK was approximately 10% of those sold in Germany. We had a very clear plan and recruited very talented people for our German and Australian subsidiaries. Most of the people we recruited have been from other companies. . . where professional sales people had had very strong relationships with clinical specialists. These companies started to rely on less technically skilled sales people.'

Neil advised, 'One of the things I would say to entrepreneurs is that it is quite difficult to understand the mechanics and mechanisms of funding. It is worth knowing how VC funds work, what their time constraints are, what their interests are, what their motivation is. I would encourage people to ask questions . . . talk to some of the people a fund has invested in. Do your own due diligence.'

The first sales were in Germany in 2003 and developed rapidly from there. Neil recalled, 'The company grew rapidly and we moved into different markets. Now, Neoss has subsidiaries in the UK, Germany, Sweden, Italy, Australia, New Zealand and, most recently, in the United States. We have seen year on year growth. Our first year sales were £1 million, second year £2 million, £4 million, £8 million, £12 million and this year was over £14 million. Margins of our product are high at over 70% gross margin. It's obviously an attractive product! It is small and easy to sell – you can put £1,000 worth in a jiffy bag!' The company's success has been driven by product and service innovation, yet this is only a small part of the picture. Neil stated that, 'the invention is 10% of the product and the product is 10% of the business'. He calls this Meredith's law of innovation.

Securing a trade investor

Even though Neil was pleased with the growth sales and profitability he recognized that the market opportunity, particularly in the US, was far greater and that the company would need more resources to exploit it. The current investors were very happy with the prospect of bringing a new investment but Neil thought there was an opportunity for this to come from a trade investor. Neil arranged a meeting with a large American medical device company. He recalled, 'They brought some of their people over from America including the senior vice president of the business development and we had a very good discussion.' Interestingly, the medical device company had their own venture fund, which they invested in small companies strategically to understand the market. They had been very impressed with Neil's company and he said, 'You need to come forward with a proposal.' By October, they had come back with an offer.

Neil now had to find ways forward. He either increased the investment by the existing venture capitalist firm or brought in a new trade investor. He understood the former but wanted access to the industrial experience and market knowledge of the latter. How was Neil going to brokerage a deal which kept both parties happy? He knew the existing investors did not want to diminish their influence on the board and recalled, 'Because their agendas are different, their timelines were different, and very often they had views about how it was done . . . our current investors were quite rightly anxious about a trade investor. But I thought it was good to have a very prestigious trade investor . . . for us to have a strategic affiliation. So I was quite up for it but I hadn't got the experience to give our investors the confidence about negotiations.' A specialist advisor was brought in to help work with all parties and facilitate the deal, and by the end of 2005 the investment came in. However, it was not just about money. Neil recalled, 'This was strategic investment . . . we were and continue to be invited to participate in areas of technology development.'

Critical incident

The board expanded to include experienced directors from the venture capital community and a new chairman with a strong medical management background. Neil recognized that his role as CEO had changed and remembered, 'We hadn't really done any research for five years.' Neil had developed strong management skills and gained the trust of the board and investors to lead the company to the next stage of growth. Should he continue to do this or spend more time on product research and development even though his own law – invention is 10% of the product and the product is 10% of the business – suggested otherwise? Perhaps the company could invest in their own R&D capability and Neil could concentrate on the business. He remembered a colleague inviting him to meet with somebody who turned out to be the worldwide chairman of medical devices for one of the world's largest healthcare companies. Neil remembered, 'He had travelled from the US to the UK. We had an excellent discussion and I was deeply impressed with his depth of knowledge and strategic perspective.'

He continued, 'In 2008, we had a very good discussion around the board and everybody felt we should look for a new CEO. We appointed a high calibre, if rather expensive, recruitment agency. We saw a number of prospective candidates . . . I was very open. I believe we can all learn from somebody with more experience.' The investors were keen for the restructuring to happen but Neil had reservations about finding the right person with the right experience, whom he could work with and the company could afford. Everybody was keen to take things forward.

By coincidence, the worldwide chairman of medical devices he had met the previous year had taken early retirement and had moved back to his family home near Leeds – also the headquarters of Neil's company! He got in contact and expressed an interest in getting involved.

Source: This case is primarily based on an interview with Neil Meredith and written by Nigel Lockett.

 ## Practical activities

1. You are approached by a new venture capital fund looking to invest in new technology firms in the emerging area of microgeneration of renewable energy. They have asked you to produce a first-stage assessment framework for them to screen business plans. They expect to receive between 50 and 100 business plans a month and have enough funds for four investments a year.

1. List the five most important criteria you would use and how each could be assessed and ranked. Who should do this?

2. Who should be on the monthly assessment committee, and how much time can they spend discussing each business plan?

2. Interview an entrepreneur about how they raised the funds to launch their new venture and the current sources of finance:

1. Compare types of finance they used before and after the venture was created. Comment on any changes.

2. How much planning and forecasting went into determining the amount of finance required to launch the new venture? Were there any differences between the forecast and reality? If so why?

Discussion topics

1. In terms of finding new ventures to invest in, what might be the differences between a venture investment fund and a social investment fund? What additional criteria would you need to use to determine the social impact of a social enterprise looking for investment? How would you calculate the value of these criteria and measure them?

2. Put simply, most of the new jobs created in an economy come from high growth small businesses. What is the role of governments in funding new venture creation and supporting high growth firms? Big companies might get grants for relocating in an area of high unemployment. Should public funds be used to invest in small firms?

 ## Further reading guide

Making the best case to an investor is difficult and requires you to be able to produce a proposal and be prepared to present this to investors. It will be useful to read some accounts of entrepreneurs who have achieved this and have also become business angels or venture capitalists. These include **Duncan Bannatyne (Bannatyne 2007), James Caan (2008), Rachel Elnaugh (2008), Peter Jones (2008), Deborah Meaden (2009),** and **Theo Paphiti (2009)**. Government support agencies provide online resources related to raising finance, including European Commission (http://ec.europa.eu/enterprise/); UK Business Link (http://www.businesslink.gov.uk); US Small Business Administration (http://www.sba.gov). Banks provide guides on raising finance generally and for their own services, for example, Barclays (http://www.bank.barclays.co.uk/BusinessBanking/); HSBC (http://www.knowledge.hsbc.co.uk). Many associations of business angels and venture capitalists offer guides to equity finance (BVCA 2009a; ECA 2007).

 ## References

Bannatyne, D. (2007) *Anyone can do it: my story.* London: Orion Publishing Group.

BBA (2010) 'Statistics Release: Serial no. 001/10.' London: British Bankers' Association.

Belu (2010) http://www.belu.org/mission.asp (accessed 3 May 2010).

Big Issue Invest (2010) http://www.bigissueinvest.com (accessed 3 May 2010).

Blundel, R. and Ippolito, K. (2008) *Effective organisational communication: perspectives, principles and practices* (3rd edition). Harlow: FT/Prentice Hall.

BVCA (2009a) *A Guide to Private Equity.* British Private Equity & Venture Capital Association (BVCA) publication. http://www.bvca.co.uk

BVCA (2009b) *Entrepreneurs.* British Private Equity & Venture Capital Association (BVCA) publication. http://www.bvca.co.uk

Caan, J. (2008) *The real deal: my story from Brick Lane to Dragons' Den.* London: Virgin Publishing.

Channel 4 (2009) http://www.channel4.com/programmes/the-secret-millionaire/episode-guide/series-6/episode-5 (accessed 3 May 2010).

Cowling, M. (2010) *Economic evaluation of the Small Firms Loan Guarantee (SFLG) Scheme.* London: Department of Business, Innovation and Skills.

Delmar, F. (2000 'The psychology of the entrepreneur.' In S. Carter and D. Jones-Evans (eds) *Enterprise and small business.* Harlow: Prentice Hall (132–54).

Ebben, J. and Johnson, A. (2006) 'Bootstrapping in small firms: an empirical analysis of change over time.' *Journal of Business Venturing*, 21: 851–65.

Elnaugh, R. (2008) *Business nightmares: when entrepreneurs hit crisis point.* Richmond, UK: Crimson Publishing.

EVCA (2007) *Guide on private equity and venture capital for entrepreneurs*, EVCA Special Paper. Brussels: European Private Equity and Venture Capital Association.

Fifteen Foundation (2010) http://www.fifteen.net/thefifteenstory/Pages/allaboutFifteen.aspx (accessed 3 May 2010).

GEM (2007) *Global Entrepreneurship Monitor Financing Report 2006.* http://www.gemconsortium.org.

Hamilton, B.H. (2000) 'Does entrepreneurship pay? An empirical analysis of the returns to self-employment.' *Journal of Political Economy*, 108, 3: 604–30/

Harhoff, D. and T. Körting (1998) 'Lending relationships in Germany – empirical evidence from survey data.' *Journal of Banking and Finance*, 22: 1317–53.

Hernández-Cánova, G. and Koëter-Kant, J. (2008) 'Debt maturity and relationship lending: an analysis of European SMEs.' *International Small Business Journal*, 26, 5: 595–617.

Howorth, C, and Moro, A (2006) 'Trust within entrepreneur bank relationships: insights from Italy.' *Entrepreneurship: Theory and Practice*, 30, 4: 495–517.

Jiménez, G., Salas, V., and Saurina, J. (2006) 'Determinants of collateral.' *Journal of Financial Economics*, 81: 255–81.

Jones, P. (2008) *Tycoon.* London: Hodder Paperbacks.

Mason C. and M. Stark (2004) 'What do investors look for in a business plan? A comparison of the investment criteria of bankers, venture capitalists and business angels.' *International Small Business Journal*, 22, 3: 227–48.

Meaden, D. (2008) *Common sense rules: what you really need to know about.* London: Random House.

Paphitis, T. (2009) *Enter the dragon.* London: Orion Publishing Group.

PNE Group (2010) http://www.pne.org/casestudies/?i=1 (accessed 3 May 2010).

Real Business (2009) http://realbusiness.co.uk/startups/dominic_list_how_to_do_business_on_a_budget (accessed 3 May 2010).

Scott, R.H. (2009) 'The use of credit card debt by new firms.' Kauffman Firm Survey.

Shane, S. (2008) *The illusions of entrepreneurship: The costly myths that entrepreneurs, investors, and policy makers live by.* New Haven, CT: Yale University Press

Shell Livewire (2010) http://www.tameer.org.pk/olive.php (accessed 3 May 2010).

Sunday Times (2009) 'How I Made It: Dominic List Founder of Comtact.' 20 September 2009.

Training for Life (2010) http://www.trainingforlife-city.org (accessed 3 May 2010).

Wingborg, J. and Landström, H. (2000) 'Financial bootstrapping in small business: examining small business managers' resource acquisition behaviour.' *Journal of Business Venturing*, 16: 235–54.

Reflections
Learning from entrepreneurs

9

What is entrepreneurship, after all? Bigness is not the issue. Poor people are the ones who take challenges every day. The guy who sells a hot dog on the street is as much an entrepreneur as anyone else.

Muhammad Yunus, *economist and founder of the Grameen Bank*

The only source from which an entrepreneur's profits stem is his ability to anticipate better than other people the future demand of the consumers.

Ludwig von Mises, *Austrian aristocrat and economist*

Learning outcomes

After reading this chapter you should be able to:

➤ Appreciate the value of an individual entrepreneur's story in helping to understand new venture creation.

➤ Identify common themes to emerge from entrepreneurs' stories and how they highlight both the 'business' and the 'personal' challenges of creating a new venture.

➤ Make use of the entrepreneurial opportunity business model, as set out in previous Part One chapters, to analyse these real-world examples.

➤ Reflect on the entrepreneurial learning cycle, as it relates to the entrepreneurs featured in this chapter.

➤ Make connections between these accounts and your own exploration of the entrepreneurial process.

Case 9.1 Jonathan Hick: birth of a serial entrepreneur

With such a long history of entrepreneurs in his family, perhaps it shouldn't be surprising that **Jonathan Hick** should become a successful serial entrepreneur. But is his past a help or hindrance? Are entrepreneurs born or bred? The roots of Jonathan's success may lie in the past, but his business interests increasingly include international companies in diverse sectors. But his journey has not been easy. In this extended interview, he talks openly about the pressures and rewards of entrepreneurship in the twenty-first century.

Grandfathers: the great and good

'I suppose the entrepreneurial side of me started 150 years ago when my great, great grandfather set up a timber traders business in Bradford called Beacroft and Whiteman. . . . I think somehow some genes have come through from the family. Actually the entrepreneur was probably his son, my great grandfather Charles John Whiteman, who built the business into quite a significant enterprise importing timber from large saw mills.' In fact Jonathan's great grandfather also had an eye for emerging technologies and **innovation**, 'He backed a man who had got certain patents on the cooling tower. Modern cooling towers are concrete shells full of timber; the hot water cools as the steam rides over that timber.'

The family timber business passed down the generations through his grandfather, Ben – who won a Military Cross in the Second World War and sadly died near the end of the war – and finally to his father, Peter. 'My father found himself in the timber trade after national service and was sent to learn the business at Hull.' Jonathan recalled the effect this had on him, 'So Dad became managing director of the whole business in the 1960s and I grew up with a father who went to work on a Saturday. I remember the timber coming on railway lines from the docks, going to Bradford on the railway lines from the sawmills.' He also recalled the intense pressure on his father, 'When people talk about recession, I've seen three of them. The biggest recession ever was in 1973/74 when we had a three day week. The dockers' strike nearly killed us as a business and I remember my father in tears saying we have been in business 120 years and I think this is going to finish us.'

What did Jonathan pick up from watching his father running a group of businesses that, at its peak, employed over 1,000 people? He recalled, 'I am very much a people person and "prince and pauper" [See Mark Twain's novel, of the same name, about two boys, one a prince and one a pauper, who trade places] person. Everybody called my father "Peter", not "Mr Hick", and he knew the names of every single employee. He knew their wives' names and their children's names. Dad always involved me with "we are thinking of buying this company" and "we are thinking of selling this company" and in all the sort of deals that they were doing. You just don't realise what an incredible effect that has on you in terms of firing your interest in business.'

Significant early influences

Jonathan was also influenced by his mother and recalled, 'My mum had come from a fairly poor background. She had grown up in a council house, her father had been a bit of a gambler and

Granny didn't know whether there would be any money this week. So that was very difficult and she [Jonathan's mother] bettered herself through education and became a teacher. Education and hard work were very important to her.' He also recalled, 'I have seen that insecurity, as well as some terrible losses. My grandfather dying, and also losing some friends in my late teens and early 20s – suicide, a friend with a terrible illness that came from nowhere turned out to be pneumonia and another friend who had a very bad car accident.'

Jonathan remembers some early entrepreneurial experiences, 'As a kid I remember at five designing membership cards for a club and bringing people together in a little bit of leadership in classrooms. By eight I would design all the letterheads and we were into transport and shipping and then by the age of 12 I was actually forming companies and doing things.' He recalled one particular enterprise: 'I was selling union jack socks for the Queen's Silver Jubilee. I bought 1,000 pairs [but] they all turned out to be laddered and we got agents in five schools and all wanting their money back. I think I went off sick from school for a couple of weeks!'

But Jonathan was not easily deterred. As he recalls, 'I started a mobile disco when I was 13. That was my first business with Barclays Bank and not only did they lend me the money to buy equipment but they gave me three staff parties. By the time I was leaving school I was selling sweatshirts for the local rugby league clubs – I was the first person to bring huge cut out foam hands in from American football . . . I bought 5,000 of these from a foam manufacturer. We borrowed some walkie-talkies and there were four entrances and eight of us went down to the stadium. One lot started selling at £1.50 at one gate, another £2.50 at another gate. We all walkie-talkied as to how sales were going and within ten minutes found out the best selling price was £1.75.'

Not all of Jonathan's new ventures were successful, he remembers, 'In 1992 I had quite a costly mistake but it was one of the big lessons in life. I had a friend who was big in the fish industry. I was in the marketing and advertising business and we bought in a third friend who was in fish and chip retail. We bought x tons of fish, filleted it and sold it in regular sizes – we called it the Hudson Bay Clipper Company and sold 8,000 portions a week at the peak. But it just became too corporate and we were not listening to what was going on the ground. A national newspaper mounted a campaign against us, for supposedly selling cod in a haddock area, and we had a really hard time of it. Local chippies were saying this big company has come over from Canada and it is going to kill us all and we must all fight together to see them off.'

Building a career in advertising

Initially, at the insistence of his mother, Jonathan went to study Law at university but he did not enjoy it: 'I hated it from day one. It was a massive mistake and I only did two of the three years and failed.' But he knew what he was going to do: 'I had worked in advertising in my holidays for a wonderful man called Richard Milner who had quite a big agency and some international interests.' He was, 'a glamorous man, fired me with enthusiasm for advertising and I worked many school holidays thanks to him . . . I knew I was going back into advertising.'

In fact Jonathan got his first job, after leaving university, in Barrington Advertising, the second biggest outside London. He enjoyed his work and made some key contacts in the industry. Within two years Jonathan and two others bought, 'a 50-year-old advertising agency in Sheffield

. . . we thought we could take on the world and I had a young, aggressive take on the world. By the time I was 25 I was Managing Director.' But after financial difficulties, Jonathan brought in, 'two other guys [investors] who put some cash in and helped stabilise us . . . and then began a very stable period in my life.' However, Jonathan recalled the financial pressure of running a business: 'I did get quite frightened actually . . . a terrible knotting up inside, a general nervousness, an unsettledness, sickness all the time where I really did think I was up against it. I felt it was a terrible failure to owe people money and yet when I look back it was one of the proudest moments.'

The advertising agency worked out really well and Jonathan recalled, 'The father [of the investors] was a great influence on me in terms of discipline, money, board meetings . . . he was totally self taught in business but he was a very disciplined man, a tough cookie . . . he ran sophisticated board meetings.' By his early thirties Jonathan was running a 'very successful business, making good money, employing about 50 people and by this time everything was fantastic.'

Money in the Directorbank

Jonathan began to see the opportunity of working with other enterprises and started to work one day a week for an international business convention organizer. Jonathan recalled, 'I started getting involved with some people in the City . . . I read a story about 3i [private investment company] which had a register of non-executive and executive directors who were looking to invest. I was aware that there was an increase in corporate people wanting to get into management buy-ins because they kept banging on my door and saying "you did one Jonathan, how do I get it?" So I set up a register of people willing to do these management buy-ins. I put an advertisement in the *Financial Times* . . . fortunately there were 267 replies and I never looked back – I think that is probably my proudest achievement.'

In 1998, Jonathan started to build MBi Register, the business that was to become The Directorbank Group. He recalled, 'I recruited a couple of guys from the City – one as chairman one and one as non-exec director to help me. They made lots of introductions into London where I had very few contacts and I just pounded the streets. We created the framework, the base of what became Directorbank, an online database of chairmen, chief execs, finance directors who are immediately available to do private equity deals. The immediate availability is the key thing to look at deals in the private equity space.'

Jonathan Hick (http://www.jonathanhick.com) has interests in a number of companies, including CallUma, which is Europe's leading multilingual traveller support service company (http://www.calluma.com), The Brand Cellar, which preserves and markets established brands (http://www.thebrandcellar.com), Sterling Graphic Equipment, which is Europe's leading hub for the trading of used print machinery (http://www.sterlinggraphicequipment.com), and The Spencer Arms (http://www.spencerarms.co.uk), a thriving village pub near Barnsley, Yorkshire.

Giving back

Jonathan is very open both about his business and the personal challenges he faced, 'Part of my story was having a nervous breakdown six years ago, which was the reason I went on *Secret*

Millionaire to talk about it. They asked me to talk about it for the good of mental health and to break the taboos.'

Jonathan recalled, 'I had quite a lot of business pressure but I had more pressure in my personal life. I divorced two years previously and split up with a girlfriend . . . so yes that took me down to a very bad breakdown. I got out of it relatively quickly but it was very serious.' Because of this profound experience Jonathan agreed to go on *Secret Millionaire*, which he says was 'an amazing experience, very cathartic – but also quite daunting. When you go on to the street undercover, it is almost like you are spying as I walked through the streets of Sunderland.' Channel 4 wanted to focus on mental health issues because there, 'is a massive stigma . . . I helped a wonderful mental health charity called Headline which is a self support group of 150 people. They have a walk in centre in the middle of Sunderland where they all go and talk to each other.'

Source: This case is primarily based on an interview with Jonathan Hick and written by Nigel Lockett.

9.1 Introduction

This final chapter of Part One adopts a different approach to Chapters 2 to 8. It traces the entrepreneurial journeys of several successful entrepreneurs. We can learn from their experience in a number of ways. For example, you see how the entrepreneurs' accounts relate to the various concepts and frameworks we have introduced in the previous Part One chapters. It may also be interesting to compare their reflections on entrepreneurship with your own initial thoughts about the challenge of creating a new venture. These profiles are all based on interviews that we have conducted with 'real-world' entrepreneurs. The chapter opened with Jonathan Hick's story. Jonathan is a serial entrepreneur with over 30 years' of experience of setting up and running a wide range of businesses. He appeared on British television, as part of Channel 4's award winning series *The Secret Millionaire*. The episode was filmed in Sunderland, in the north-east of England, where Jonathan visited local charities and was moved by the important social issues they addressed, such as mental health, alcoholism, and drugs. Jonathan remains committed to supporting many of the groups he encountered there, and is using his entrepreneurial skills to help them achieve their social objectives.

The second case explores a very different story. Steve and Julie Pankhurst simply had a wish to contact old friends. After many trials and tribulations, this personal need emerged as the first commercially successful online social networking communities, Friends Reunited (http://www.friendsreunited.co.uk). We see how in just five years they took what may in hindsight seem to us like a 'sure-fire' winner from concept through exploitation to eventual sale for £120 million. Not many entrepreneurs achieve such financial wealth, but we will see that the same principles and skills apply to many enterprises. Interestingly, since the sale of Friends Reunited, Julie and Steve have established the Happy Charitable Trust to support global ethical causes.

The final case in this chapter tells the interesting story of Deirdre Bounds, who combines 'boundless' entrepreneurial flair with a strong sense of social and ethical purpose (http://www.deirdrebounds.com). We will see how, in 1996, she launched what was to become a highly successful ethical travel company, i-to-i (http://www.i-to-i.com), which was sold just 10 years later for £14 million. Far from slowing Deirdre's social and ethical ambitions down, the sale of the company has fuelled other social, ethical, and charitable activities. She has also developed her profile as a motivational speaker and mentor and published her first personal development book, *Fulfilled*, in 2009.

9.2 The entrepreneurial process revisited

9.2.1 Jonathan Hick and Directorbank

In Chapter 3, we considered a simplified version of the complex set of activities that we called the **entrepreneurial process** (Figure 9.1).

Having worked through the different parts of this process in Chapters 2 to 8, we can now map a *real* entrepreneur's story on to the three phases: idea generation, opportunity recognition, and exploitation. As an example, we can consider the case of Jonathan Hick and one of his companies, Directorbank. As we suggested in Chapter 3, the whole process turns out to be much less linear than the diagram might suggest. In 1998, Jonathan started the MBi Register, the business that was to become the Directorbank. He had been approached by people asking how he had managed to achieve a management buy-in of an advertising agency many years earlier.

- **Idea generation and opportunity recognition** Like many business ideas, Directorbank was born out of the personal experience of the founding entrepreneur and their increasing awareness that this might be an opportunity that could be exploited. Jonathan freely admits that the idea of a register came from reading about 3i, Europe's largest **venture capitalist** company, and connecting that to his own experiences of a

Figure 9.1 The entrepreneurial process

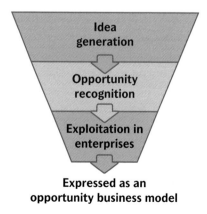

management buy-in, which other people placed a value on. But having a business idea and recognizing a genuine opportunity are two different things. Jonathan is a case in point. He had many business ideas, most of which remained just that. Yet a few went beyond this stage to develop into successful enterprises. Even when Jonathan began to recognize the potential of his idea, he still needed to validate it. The critical moment for him was returning from holiday having placed an advertisement in the *Financial Times* and finding over 250 replies on his doorstep. Not only did Jonathan think it was a good idea, so did many others. The original business idea of matching private **equity** investors with experienced directors who were willing and able to execute a management buy-in was then recognized as an opportunity.

- **Exploitation in enterprises** The next big challenge for Jonathan was to bring together the resources needed to exploit this opportunity in an enterprise. He formed an **entrepreneurial team** from contacts within his already extensive **entrepreneurial network**. Subsequently, Directorbank has since gone on to become a leading management buy-in company and has also expanded internationally.

Of course, what makes Jonathan a particularly interesting entrepreneur is that he has had many business ideas, some of which he has recognized as opportunities and exploited in enterprises. Unfortunately, not all have been successful, such as Hudson Bay Clipper Company. However, Jonathan's successes far outnumber his failures, and he continues to generate new business ideas both from his own personal experiences and increasingly by helping other people to recognize the value of their ideas and obtain the resources to exploit them in enterprises. Particularly striking examples of the latter are CallUma, Europe's leading multilingual traveller support service company, and Sterling Graphic Equipment, Europe's leading hub for the trading of used print machinery.

9.2.1 Steve Pankhurst and Friends Reunited

The following case is an extraordinary example of how a business idea can be converted into a successful venture. The original idea emerged when Steve's wife, Julie, was finding it difficult to track down some of her old friends. In just five years the Pankhursts took their idea from an initial concept through to a fully functioning business that was eventually sold for £120 million (€145 million).

Case 9.2 Steve Pankhurst: with a little help from our friends

In 2000, **Steve** and **Julie Pankhurst** simply had a good idea, which after many trials and tribulations, emerged as one of the first commercially successful online social networking communities: Friends Reunited. In just five years they took what in hindsight might look like a 'sure-fire' winner from concept through exploitation to an eventual sale for £120 million (€145 million). Very few entrepreneurs achieve this level of financial wealth, and even fewer do so over such a short period of time. However, similar principles and skills can be reapplied in other kinds of venture, including social enterprises. Since the sale of Friends Reunited, Steve and Julie have established the Happy Charitable Trust to support good causes.

Information technology rules

Despite having a degree in Mathematics from Imperial College London, Steve Pankhurst did not like computers. Despite this, his first job was as an IT software analyst and software programmer. He quickly gained experience in various industry sectors, including defence, financial pensions, building, and construction, before setting up his own business. Steve recalled, 'I was a programmer moving to analyst, got bored with working for people. I suppose I always had in my mind to work for myself. I met Jason Porter in 1992 and left to do contracting, so we basically set up a little freelance company.' They mostly worked for small companies on marketing systems and procurement systems 'Our company name was VCS which stood for Visual Computing Solutions but the real unofficial name was "very crap software", and in 1992 we started working for a company providing pension solutions for insurance companies.' This was in response to government legislation to regulate the selling of pensions. Steve remembers, 'It turned out to be seven years' work, nearly full time.'

In 2000, Steve and Jason stopped working full time for the pension solutions company and set up the Happy Group. 'Fortunately, we were kept on with a bit of consultancy and he [the owner] invested in us . . . he actually put in seed capital . . . if you think back to 1999/2000 all these Internet companies came up with an idea. People, VCs and banks, were throwing millions at them. We had many ideas, anybody could come to us with an idea and we literally had a pipeline list of twenty. People would come to us because they knew we could do it. Some of the ideas were just embarrassingly bad . . . a lot of people thought they could just make money from advertising . . . this was madness. We'd got £50,000 in the bank to buy servers and to get us going . . . our philosophy was we would spend a maximum of £7,000 . . . the minute we went over £7,000 and it wasn't making any money or wasn't working we'd drop it.' There were more ideas than the seven that could be developed, for example, a singles dating website didn't succeed. However, their Happy party bags idea was 'doing well, but that took a lot of money . . . it is nothing more than a glorified mail order catalogue. So, there is a lot of buying stock, a lot of manual work . . . it also made us realise that we didn't want to do that bit because you had to deal with orders; you had to deal with deliveries, with complaints.'

Yet another idea

Julie Pankhurst was also a software programmer before becoming pregnant and taking a break in her career. Steve recalled, 'She had the school reunion idea and really it was going to be a project for her while she was on maternity leave to learn the new technology that I had learned. It never happened of course because being a mum takes up a lot of time . . . Julie had this nagging idea . . . she wanted to track down old friends . . . I actually thought it was rubbish because I hated looking back . . . I hated school.' Julie kept the pressure on for the reunion website idea to be developed. Steve recalls a critical point, 'I remember it well, she said *I have found the site. My site!* It turned out to be an American version of her idea but not quite. So, that was the changing point for me . . . I did a search around and there were a couple of very, very basic sites in Britain. It made me think, *Hang on a minute! If it is working in America your idea should work over here.*'

'Friends Reunited was very much a backburner project. It was easy to write for me. It took me about a week in my spare time . . . the original version was awful . . . there was nothing to it.' It was difficult to identify how the website could generate any revenue from advertising or subscriptions. Steve recalled, 'We always thought that model [subscription] may work but we weren't sure. We thought, *We need to get 100,000 people on there to make it critical mass so that people have a reason to pay*. But we didn't know how to get there.'

From a small trickle

Steve remembered, 'I just put it live June 2000 . . . within a day or so someone registered . . . within a week ten people had. Julie used to get a few email responses and asked me to do changes, like a message board . . . so it became this little hobby. For the first six months it was nothing more than a hobby but the concept was beginning to take shape . . . then someone emailed us and said, *What a great idea, I have just found someone I haven't seen for thirty years*. That was quite a key point. It made me realise I can put a little bit more time and effort into it and Julie kept on coming up with the ideas . . . Julie was passionate about it.' But, there was still the challenge of increasing the number of users: 'I would find lots of people looking for other people on message boards. I would send a personalised email to them saying, *You are looking for someone? Come to Friends Reunited and see if you can find them* . . . I got it up to about 70 people registering a day through just hard grafting. Just a bit of time every day.'

Then suddenly, 'The Friends Reunited server just died. I looked into it and we had been "website of the day" on the Steve Wright show on Radio 2. Every time we rebooted the server died . . . what the hell is happening? It felt like everybody in the world was trying to connect to our tiny little server . . . you could see hundreds of people trying to access the site. We bought another server . . . Jason worked through the night and got it going.' Steve recalled, 'Well that was January 2001. By February we realised we really could be on to something. We started to get a few local papers contacting us.' But, having built up the number of users, how could they generate revenue to fund the website? Steve remembers, 'We decided to charge £5 to send emails. So you can use the site, find people. The WOW factor was, "My god. There is that person." It seemed harsh to us and to people. But why not £5 a year?'

But why £5? 'We bought two drinks in a pub and didn't get any change out of a fiver! At the same time we took what was a very good calculated risk. We resigned from our consultancy jobs because we thought, *Right. We have really got to go for this*.'

'The first day one person paid. The second day three people paid. The next day five people paid. Then it went ten, fifty, and honestly the amount of money! If I showed you the stats it's scary. We made, I don't know, £2,000 the first month, £10,000 the second, £50,000 the third, £200,000 the fourth, £600,000 the fifth, a million pounds the sixth. It really went like that. It was all a bit of a blur. Within a month we were being called in to do local radio shows. Which is scary as hell. The local press as well, so it was growing . . . We were contacted by a PR [public relations] company . . . they put a plan together and we never really implemented it because events took over . . . then we were contacted by the *Guardian*. Within a month we had been in *The Times, The Sun*, BBC 6 o'clock news.'

All this publicity increased the number of users. Steve recalled, 'It was strange how everything was. It was 24 hour days, 7 days a week. The biggest mistake we made was we didn't delegate. But the problem was it was happening so fast . . . Within two months of my first radio interview, I could do six radio interviews just like that. It almost came natural. Julie was doing the same; we were getting invited to do this, that and the other. We were answering 3000 emails a day. . . we used to do shifts all day long. We had this screen which showed how many registrations that day and how much money. You hit the refresh button and as you refresh every few seconds the money would go up by £50 and then £100 and the registrations were up by 200 every five seconds and Julie and I would just sit there sometimes and say *Oh my . . . God what have we created?* This is brilliant but scary.'

But how long could it continue? 'In 2001, we had two or three customer services people . . . It was just bizarre. You just open the paper and there was a whole page feature on me and Julie and our life and how we had created this thing. But the stress levels were just unbelievable. We were working non-stop, eating badly and drinking to get through the evening. Never going out. Going to sleep worrying.'

'In 2002 we sat down and we thought, *For the next year, we will just go with it. We will do it properly. We are going to recruit ten people.* We recruited a proper customer service manager and a couple of developers.' Steve remembers another key moment, 'We were still growing and I came up with a new idea for Genes Reunited. This was all about building your own family tree and sharing it. My idea came from my cousin who was doing a massive family tree and he put it on the Internet. Somebody, a distant relative from Canada, had also been doing it. So we had done a whole year of hard grafting in 2002. It got better because we had employed people.'

No shortage of suitors

Serious offers to buy the company started to come in. But Steve recounts how this caused problems, 'It distracts you for months while due diligence takes place. So by the end of 2003, we did it all officially. Got in contact with all the interested parties and it took days and days of presenting it. We were making £3 million profit a year and we had 10 million registered users with a lot of them coming back.' In spite of this, no suitor made a serious offer.

Then, Michael Murphy joined the company as the Chief Executive. Steve recalled, 'Michael is brilliant he is a real networker. He is really down to earth . . . he knew all the VCs. His desk was clear and he got other people to do everything. He is brilliant at just getting things done.'

By 2005, 'Profits were £7 million . . . they put feelers out and suddenly it was leaked . . . We had about four/five serious offers and figures that we never ever dreamed about . . . ITV felt right.' Friends Reunited was sold to ITV in December 2005 for £120 million.

Happy?

After the sale of Friends Reunited, Steve remembers deciding to set up a charitable trust, 'Yes, we call it the Happy Foundation . . . We build schools abroad, we are on our fourth now. It is the best thing I do. We get a pile of requests for money, although it is quite hard because you have to reject 99 out of 100 of them. Julie went to see the one in Ghana and had an amazing experience. We visited the one in Peru last year, which was an amazing experience for our children to see the slums and we are just about to start one in Vietnam.'

Source: This case is primarily based on an interview with Steve Pankhurst and written by Nigel Lockett.

How do Steve Pankhurst's experiences map on to the three stages of the entrepreneurial process: namely, idea generation, opportunity recognition, and exploitation.

- **Idea generation and opportunity recognition** We can certainly see evidence of these phases of the process. In this case, Steve and Jason (his business partner) had a structured way of developing and considering new business ideas. They decided to allocate £7,000 of their £50,000 seed capital to develop each idea. Steve stated, 'the minute we went over £7,000 and it wasn't making any money or wasn't working we'd drop it.' The ironic feature of this well-controlled approach was that it did not include the idea of building an online social networking community! However, once they had generated this idea, how did they recognize it as a real opportunity that could be exploited in an enterprise? There appear to be two moments when this happened. The first was in January 2001 when the number of registrations suddenly increased due to unexpected national publicity. The second was a few months later when a £5 registration charge was introduced. The figures were extraordinary. Steve recalled that, 'We made, I don't know, £2,000 the first month, £10,000 the second, £50,000 the third, £200,000 the fourth, £600,000 the fifth, a million pounds the sixth.'

- **Exploitation in enterprises** As the registration money flowed in, it was clear that they had found an opportunity. Simultaneously, it seems that they had established the basic business model for the enterprise. However, this was not simply a matter of happening upon a winning formula. Steve also describes how they built the company through sheer hard work and commitment, up to the point that it was sold to ITV. He had the relevant technical knowledge and, with the income stream from the registrations, he was able to obtain the other resources needed to continue developing the business.

In this section we have reflected on the experience of creating a new entrepreneurial venture. We heard how two successful entrepreneurs, Jonathan Hick and Steve Pankhurst, told their own stories, and we then related these accounts to the three phases of the entrepreneurial process. Hopefully, this provides some new insights into the ways that people generate ideas, how they recognize real **entrepreneurial opportunities**, and how they assemble the necessary resources to exploit these opportunities. In this section, the focus was on the individual entrepreneur. However, in order to fully appreciate the entrepreneurial process we also need to consider the entrepreneurial **opportunity business model**, and its relationship with the new venture.

9.3 Entrepreneurial opportunity business model revisited

In Chapter 2 (Vision), we introduced the entrepreneurial opportunity business model as a way of describing the five dimensions (i.e. Proposition; People; Place; Process; Profit) and four drivers (Societal; Commercial; Legal; Technological) that underpin any new business idea (Figure 9.2). We also used it to explore each element of Apple Computer's digital music business both in terms of the products (iPod) and services (iTunes). Before considering the dimensions and drivers for Directorbank and Friends Reunited, let us refresh our understanding of the elements of the entrepreneurial opportunity business model.

Figure 9.2 Entrepreneurial opportunity business model

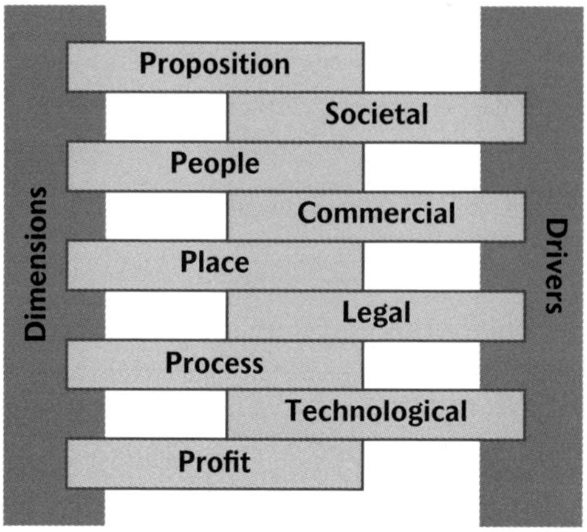

Dimensions are a way of expressing the different components or elements of the business idea. They help support analysis, structure discussion, and enable comparison. The five opportunity business model dimensions express the key components, elements, or building blocks of the business idea: Proposition, People, Place, Process, and Profit:

- **Proposition** What is the core value proposition, as perceived by the customer, of the opportunity? This could be expressed as a mission statement but needs to be clear and concise.

- **People** Who are the leader, management team, and network of advisors, customers, suppliers, and stakeholders? How does social capital and networking support the business opportunity?

- **Place** Where is the market? Who are the customers and competitors? This could involve analysis of market and industry to identify segments and gaps.

- **Process** How is the enterprise structured? What are the key processes and relationships? How will these be enabled and supported? What role does information technology play?

- **Profit** Why do it? What are the real returns? Financials, gross profit, net profit, forecasts, KPIs, and capital required. Is there a social return? This might also include a consideration of the ownership structure and exit strategy.

Drivers are the factors that underpin the entrepreneurial opportunity. Often, one or more driver will apply to each opportunity. For example, there may be a combination of Societal, Legal, and Technological drivers. In addition, drivers are nearly always outside of the direct control of the entrepreneur. The four drivers express the key factors, influences, or enablers that underpin the new business idea, and suggest how it might be exploited in an enterprise; Societal, Commercial, Legal, and Technological:

- **Societal** Wider global, social, political, and environmental factors, such as climate change, energy, aging populations, fair trade, and antisocial behaviour.

- **Commercial** Global, national, regional and local economic and financial factors, such as, currency exchange rates, local taxation rates and the price of oil. What might be the impact on the opportunity if governments introduced a greenhouse gas emission trading scheme?

- **Legal** Legislation, rules, and regulatory requirements. Typically set by governments and consortia. Such as data protection law and trade associations.
- **Technological** New and emerging technologies such as 3G mobile communication networks, public broadband, online social networks, and nanotechnology.

The first three drivers (societal, commercial, and regulatory) are always beyond the control of the enterprise, but they can have a profound effect on the successful exploitation of a new business idea. While most technology drivers, such as the broadband Internet, are normally taken as a given, technology-driven enterprises can develop advantage through developing proprietary technology they can protect with patents. Drivers also differ from dimensions as not all the drivers apply to every opportunity business model. By considering these drivers, you can also focus more directly on the enablers that underpin any entrepreneurial opportunity. As you review this analysis of Directorbank and Friends Reunited, consider whether there may be additional or alternative interpretations of these models.

9.3.1 Directorbank's opportunity business model

Firstly, the *dimensions*:

- **Proposition** Directorbank was initially set up to serve the venture capitalist industry by helping them to identify suitably experienced directors who were interested in joining the boards of businesses funded by private equity investors.
- **People** Jonathan Hick was the founding director but grew the senior management team to the point where he could hand over the chief executive role to another director. As the company expanded internationally, the management team grew to include people with local market knowledge. By providing a matchmaking service Directorbank developed a valuable network of directors, dealmakers, and industry experts. This network became a competitive advantage for the company and made it harder for new firms to enter the market.
- **Place** The private equity marketplace relied heavily on personal relationships: knowing the right person at the right time. The over-dependency on these personal relationships limited both the number of directors exposed to any deal and the number of deals possible. Private equity investors were frustrated by these limitations, and experienced directors were simply hidden from view. Directorbank emerged to meet both the investors' and directors' needs. There was no direct competitor.
- **Process** Directorbank provided a matchmaking service to help investors find the right directors. Initially, this replicated the traditional personal relationships model but quickly expanded to include a more robust and reliable network of directors who were both suitably experienced and willing to join a board of directors. Private equity investors increasingly saw Directorbank as the first point of call for finding directors.
- **Profit** The financial services industry is very familiar with *finders fees* and commissions based on a percentage of transactions. Directorbank was able to negotiate revenue streams from private equity deals.

Secondly, the *drivers* that might underpin this model:

- **Societal** Industrial capitalism has grown to become the dominant economic and social system to support enterprise, creating a demand for people with these capabilities and experiences to occupy senior positions in corporations.

- **Commercial** Private equity is a form of finance for companies, which is not publicly traded on a stock exchange and can be used to support management buy-ins. Typically, private equity investors will buy a majority control in an existing company and introduce new management into the senior team. Any mechanism that supports this process will increase the competition between available financial resources and directors.

- **Legal** None?

- **Technological** Directorbank makes use of electronic databases and web-based communications technologies to provide a distinctive service to client companies.

9.3.2 Friends Reunited's opportunity business model

Firstly, the *dimensions*:

- **Proposition** By 2005, Friends Reunited had grown to support the interactions between an online social network of over 19 million members in the UK. The company expanded its services to members, including Genes Reunited for collaboratively building online family trees.

- **People** The original idea was created by Julie Pankhurst but developed by Steve Pankhurst. He and his business partner initially grew the company without expanding the management team. However, as the number of members grew, it became increasingly difficult to manage. A customer services manager was recruited to build a team. After being unsuccessful in identifying an external partner, a new highly experienced CEO was recruited. Michael Murphy saw the company to the point when it was sold. The real value of the company was not just its revenues but also its active membership of nearly 20 million people.

- **Place** The Internet is a highly innovative and competitive environment. The nearly ubiquitous availability of this interactive open communications platform has led to the development of online communities. In 2000, program technologies that could support these communities were becoming available, but very few had emerged to exploit it. There was very little competition.

- **Process** The Friends Reunited platform provided members the ability to build online profiles with details of the schools, colleges, universities, and employers and make this searchable by people looking to re-establish contact and allowed subscribers to be able to make contact by a double-blind system, which concealed email addresses.

- **Profit** To use the platform to contact other members a £5 subscription was charged. As the number of members grew the costs of operating and hosting the platform also grew, but at a minimal rate. The breakeven point was reached within only a few months. The business became highly profitable.

Secondly, the *drivers* that might underpin this model:

- **Societal** Human beings have a strong intrinsic need to belong to a group in which they can interact with one another and develop a sense of shared common identity. Groups often share interests, values, background, and family. As members of groups disperse, these interactions become harder but the need to belong is still part of human nature. People are becoming increasingly mobile and more dispersed.

- **Commercial** There is a cost to communicating. However, the Internet provides a relatively low cost ubiquitous global communications platform. Once established there is an insignificant increase in cost for further use.

- **Legal**: None?

- **Technological** By 2000, the programming software became available to support the development of database-driven interactive websites.

Before we leave opportunity business models, it is also worth reflecting on the emerging pattern of entrepreneurship in the twenty-first century. How are social, ethical, and environmental factors going to influence **entrepreneurial activity** in the near future, including the kinds of opportunities that are likely to emerge and the business models that entrepreneurs will choose to adopt? Throughout the Part One chapters, we have heard from many different entrepreneurs. Many of them have combined making a profit with conscious attempts to change things for the better, either through their approach to doing business, the products and services they provide, or the ways that they make use of income generated by successful ventures.

---

 online resource centre 'The emerging pattern of entrepreneurship: what does the future hold?'

In this section, we have seen how both Directorbank and Friends Reunited can usefully be explored using the entrepreneurial opportunity business model. In Section 9.4, we continue our exploration by revisiting the **entrepreneurial learning** cycle. Looking back at the entrepreneurs' own accounts, it is easy to see how Jonathan Hick learnt from his experiences. However, he clearly placed a lot of emphasis on his history and stated, 'I suppose the entrepreneurial side of me started 150 years ago when my great, great grandfather set up a timber traders business in Bradford.' Does this suggest that entrepreneurs are born and not bred? (Section 12.1) Could our family history be a more important factor rather than our own experiences? (Section 12.4) The final case, '*Deirdre Bounds*' (Case 9.3), presents an alternative perspective on these issues. Deirdre recalls not being particularly entrepreneurial, commenting that, 'I am a worker but I was never a young entrepreneur. I didn't have great enterprising ideas.'

9.4 Entrepreneurial learning

The previous section provided one opportunity to examine your own **entrepreneurial thinking**. In this section, we return to an earlier discussion on entrepreneurial learning and relate it to the experiences of the three entrepreneurs who are profiled in this chapter. As many of our cases have indicated, entrepreneurial learning is *not* a one-off process but a continuous cycle of learning, both about yourself and about your enterprise (Figure 9.3).

We all start our entrepreneurial learning from a different place and with a unique set of attributes, experiences, social networks, personal values, and backgrounds. As a consequence

Figure 9.3 Entrepreneurial learning

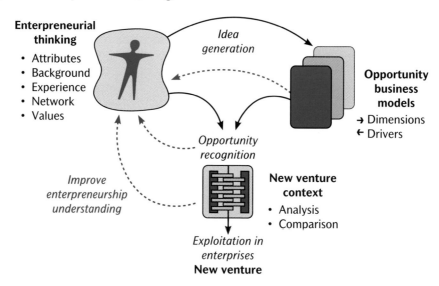

our learning journeys are going to be unique, and it is impossible to predict where they will lead. However, entrepreneurship researchers have studied various aspects of learning, both at an individual level (e.g. personality, cognitive science) and a social level (e.g. family influences, learning through peer support networks). Each of these areas is examined in more detail in Part Two (Sections 11.3, 11.4, and 12.2).

➜ PERSPECTIVES See sections 11.3, 11.4 and 12.2 for further information.

Experience counts in all areas of life, and it is through practical experience that we learn new things and enhance our abilities. Entrepreneurship is no different. Jonathan Hick (Case 9.1) did not start out as a serial entrepreneur, and could not have predicted that he would eventually become involved in such a wide range of international businesses. Steve Pankhurst (Case 9.2) started out as a reluctant software programmer, while Deirdre Bounds (Case 9.3) was a youth worker who became frustrated by the lack of opportunities for the underprivileged young people that she worked with. In some cases, such as Steve Pankhurst's, the learning process was very rapid, as the venture quickly became a reality. In others, the journey can be much longer. For example, in Deirdre Bounds's case it took many years for an entrepreneurial opportunity to emerge and incredible determination to obtain the resources to exploit it in an enterprise.

When embarking on your own entrepreneurial journey, it is important to remember that life is never straightforward. Though each chapter in Part One is linked to the next in a neat, linear sequence, your experiences as an entrepreneur will be far more complex and much less predictable. Another important difference between the textbook and real life is that many of our cases have featured individuals who have made good judgements and often had a fair share of good luck, being in the right place, at the right time, or having the support of the right people. So while the Part One cases have highlighted successes, it is also important to remember that most new ventures fail. Furthermore, whether the enterprise is successful or not, the personal cost to entrepreneurs and their families can be extremely high (Section 12.1). As we noted in

Chapter 1, our aim in this book has been to help you to live with two conflicting metaphors (or images) of entrepreneurship:

- **The reader's image** In order for us to explore the subject in a clear and coherent way that fits academic timetables and also works in book form, we had to set up some logical structures and building blocks (e.g. the chapters covering discrete subjects and the models with their distinct dimensions and drivers).

- **The practitioner's image** The practical reality for the 'real-world' entrepreneur is quite unlike the solid and regular building blocks of a textbook. As the cases have indicated, the experience is often much more challenging, and rather like riding a bicycle while simultaneously juggling several plates of jelly.

Entrepreneurial practice involves all of the activities we have discussed in Part One. Each activity influences the others (e.g. marketing decisions affect financing and vice versa), and they continue to circle around an opportunity that is itself in motion, continuing to evolve as you move towards the creation of your venture. In other words, entrepreneurship is not so much a simple linear process as a series of dynamic, interrelated activities, closer to the traditional image of electrons (dimensions) orbiting a nucleus (vision) that are constantly being buffeted by external forces (drivers) (Figure 9.4).

9.5 Learning from experience

At the end of the previous Part One chapters, we asked the entrepreneurs featured in the Critical incident cases to reflect on their own entrepreneurial story and to provide an incident for you to consider. For this closing chapter, we asked our three entrepreneurs to respond to a rather different question, but one that might be useful to any prospective entrepreneur: 'What is the most important advice you would give to the readers of this book?'

   Jonathan said: 'I think I would probably answer in two parts. *One* if you really do believe in yourself never ever ever give up on it. See it through. But, *two* bring in one or two people who have seen it or done it before. Either in that sector or business generally. Listen to their advice and let them help you. You can't do it all on your own.'

Figure 9.4 An atomic metaphor for entrepreneurship

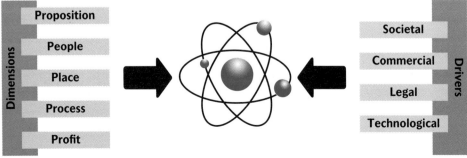

Steve said: 'I always like to have fun. Don't let it get you down too much because it did a bit with us in some respects, and maybe delegate a little bit but always stick to your principles. Don't let corporates and the money take over. Try and stick to your principles and have fun. That is the important thing. That is why I won't do anything else unless it is fun.'

Deirdre said: 'I think the success in any enterprise is very much down to the person. It is down to the would be entrepreneur (or whatever they decide to call themselves). Whatever it is that you are going to sell – service, gadget, website but first of all make it unique. The most important thing is just to have a really deep and safe conviction in yourself that this will work and you will make it work.'

✳ 9.6 Summary

- ➤ Entrepreneurs come in all shapes and sizes, and each has their own unique story to tell. We can learn a lot about new venture creation by studying each entrepreneur's story in order to identify the similarities and differences.

- ➤ The three stages of the entrepreneurial process (consisting of idea generation, opportunity recognition, and exploitation) can be related to a *real* entrepreneur's behaviour and provide a useful framework for organizing new venture creation activities.

- ➤ The entrepreneurial opportunity business model consisting of dimensions (proposition; people; place; process; profit) and drivers (societal; commercial; legal; technological) provides a framework for analysing *real* enterprises.

- ➤ Entrepreneurs are born with a range of attributes but learn from doing. Recognizing that entrepreneurship is a learning cycle is an important step in valuing experience and creating learning opportunities to accelerate personal development.

Case 9.3 Deirdre Bounds: seeing eye to eye

Deirdre Bounds's success in business seems to spring from her boundless energy, enthusiasm, and keen sense of social justice. In 1996, she launched what was to become a highly successful ethical travel company, which she sold just 10 years later for £14 million. However, far from slowing Deirdre down, the sale of the company has fuelled other social, ethical, and charitable activities. She has also developed her profile as a motivational speaker, mentor, and published her first personal development book, *Fulfilled*, in 2009.

Breeding ground for social justice

Deirdre went to a comprehensive school in Liverpool before studying a degree in Sociology and Business Studies in Leeds. Having gained an ordinary degree she left, rather than staying to complete her honours. She recalled that she thought, 'I can't bear academia any more . . . it was the boredom of study. It was the futility of it . . . also I didn't quite fit in with the whole middle class university crowd and I felt very much like I was on the outside looking in . . . Now, if I went to university I would look at it as a place to really expand my mind. I understand the value of education.' Deirdre is the youngest of five children: 'My sister is the eldest. She went first. She is now a teacher. She was kind of a role model for me because all I wanted to do really was get out of Prescott . . . it was just a dead end, no work place . . . My family are Irish and they didn't belong there.'

However, Deirdre didn't recall being particularly entrepreneurial, 'I am a worker but I was never a young entrepreneur. I didn't have great enterprising ideas. I wanted to earn money. I knew the value of money and I suppose I came from a background of lack of money. Just get out and get a job and the way to get a decent job is to get a good education.' However, she also recalled, 'I am a decision maker, once it is made it takes time to get there. When I was eleven, I had a really miserable time at primary school. I had no friends and there were a couple of bullying girl twins and I will never forget they made my life a misery . . . I thought, *Right you are moving now Deirdre and this is your time to make a big mark in this school Get into the top band of the comprehensive school. Just make sure that you do that.* I remember making that decision . . . I became a bit of a leader in the school.'

Looking back, Deirdre remembers struggling to achieve what she wanted, 'I only started my business when I was 29 and before then I had no entrepreneurial skills whatsoever. At the age of 27, I had no money. I was a bit of a floater, doing nothing . . . I was a lost soul. I had ten years where life wasn't kind of going my way and I was a bit rudderless. Really, I didn't know what I was doing . . . I look back now and I think again that lack of direction took me off to Japan as an English teacher.'

The impact of travelling

Deirdre's decision to travel played an important part in helping her find an entrepreneurial opportunity: 'I went to Japan and I met some great people there . . . I travelled around went to Australia . . . I would take a palm coated mini bus to the bus station at six o'clock in the morning . . . the wind howled up the Sydney High Street and I remember standing there, I was 27, I thought, *Is this what my life is, touting for back packers?* . . . but then I was able to turn it around. I made the decision to *do the best that I can*.' She soon continued her travels, 'I worked for a school over in Greece . . . the head teacher ran a massive school. I said, *How do you do it?* She said, *I am not just interested in success, I am interested in successful people and it is just a game*.' Inspired, Deirdre returned to the UK and became a youth worker and stand-up comedian. She recalled, 'People told me I am quite funny and again I just made these decisions . . . I couldn't really work for anybody . . . the best training, for going into very scary situations in business and doing public speaking, was my stand up comedy. Unbelievable, nothing can be as bad as being booed off stage by 300 people! I couldn't work for anyone else, I was too much of a maverick.'

All these experiences had an impact on Deirdre: 'I became kind of fearless after that because I really pushed out and tried different things . . . there were lots of young kids at the youth club saying, *How did you travel?* . . . I looked around and I thought, *These kids are never going to get a chance to take one of these gap year* things. It was very expensive and it was the domain of the middle class children . . . I thought, *Well why the hell not?!*'

Through her own eyes

Deirdre recognized a problem and had an innovative solution. She recalled, 'I know it changed people's lives because I know it changed mine . . . how are they [these kids] going to get this opportunity when there is no avenue for them?' Deirdre went to Leeds Education Department and asked if she could put on a course, 'How to teach English as a foreign language' . . . 'I looked at her and she looked at me and I tried to keep my face straight because I thought I can't believe what I have just said and she said okay . . . I put the courses on in about thirteen schools in Leeds and then decided to put it on at the weekends. Then people started to ask, *Can you get me work placements abroad?* Now I'd become a tour operator!'

Deirdre contacted different schools around the world asking if they wanted English teachers: 'I knew this was a bottomless pit of people waiting for native English speakers. I had been there and so I saw the problem. The proposition to these school owners was too good . . . All they had to do was to provide them with a place to live and a job. I went to India, Sri Lanka and Russia.' However, Deirdre faced her first big challenge – having generated interest she received a visit from a school in St Petersburg: 'They wanted to see my school and I was still in the bedsit in Leeds. By then you become unstoppable, if you really want something. I thought, *Well, okay, you want to come and see my school? Fine* . . . I said, *Yes* . . . I contacted the head teacher of a college in Leeds and said, *I have got these Russians can I borrow your office for a few hours?* It doesn't matter how you are going to do it as long as you commit to it and then you will find a way . . . Somebody somewhere knows that and has connections to do what you want to do.'

Deirdre began to see the value in her network of contacts. She recalled, 'I see things, I am a very big thinker, I am not a details person . . . you know I could see this could become a global phenomenon. Now what did I know about opening businesses across the world? Nothing. But there is always somebody who does. You have a good lawyer or you talk to somebody who has done it, and then you just keep moving towards what you see in your mind's eye.'

A global business with soul

Deirdre recalls. 'I think back now; *i-to-i* is the largest trainer of English as a foreign language [TEFL] teachers in the world; we teach 17,000 people a year. It is the biggest gap year company; it sends about 7,000 abroad to do volunteer projects around the world and I look back and I think, *Yes all these people are "inch by inch" making the world a bit of a better place* . . . It was the value of the company. Honestly, I think *i-to-i* is a great company. It was a very profitable company because it was a very niche company. We were the leaders of the pack. We were not the dedicated followers of fashion. That is what I took delight in.'

The company was very personal to Deirdre: 'Every fibre of me went into that company and that is why it was a success. You know, that is the top and bottom of it. Yes, it was the right place at the right time and a bit of luck . . . At the end of the day, even when I had a great team around me, I had to have the mental stamina to keep the global juggernaut going.' But how did she go about building a 'great' team? 'I had no idea of recruitment policy . . . I just learnt recruitment processes and wrote a decent job spec and 50% of the time it worked and 50% of the time it didn't. I created a team through the pain of recruiting really bad people. In the end I realised what I was not good at. I really had to practise a lot of patience and tolerance with some. Staff are very, very challenging because you can't control it. You can't control people. People will do what they like, when they like, how they like. Now I understand the importance of vision, translating that to the team, having strategic direction . . . one day to the next. How are we going to get buy in [commitment] from the team? How are we going to deliver this? How are we going to get this from general management books? . . . I got approached by someone who wanted to join, so he came in as a project development person and then I made him MD.' Just 10 years later Deirdre sold the company for £14 million.

Personal development and beyond

Deirdre's undoubted business success did not come easily and she remembers, 'The rocky years were between from about 18 to 27 and then I found it . . . quite phenomenal success.' But she also recognizes her strengths: 'I have got a talent I have some source of innate talent . . . I think there are a couple of types of entrepreneurs. There are entrepreneurs who are brilliant dealmakers; they smell a deal . . . I am not that sort of entrepreneur. I am the creator of the concepts and I get things off the ground and I see problems and I see great solutions.'

Interestingly, Deirdre was not deterred by her limited financial experience: 'The importance of just watching your bank balances go up and that was about as much of finance as I knew. I didn't know anything about spreadsheets. I can't use Excel. I am just about at the level now where I can read a balance sheet and read a profit and loss. My mathematics is dreadful. Did that stop me? *No!*'

Commenting of the future, Deirdre said, 'I am about to launch two businesses, including Training for Travel, and my new book is just out. Why do I keep on doing this? I could retire now I have made enough money . . . I have written a personal development book called *Fulfilled*', which is based on her personal story.

Sources: This case is primarily based on an interview with Deirdre Bounds and written by Nigel Lockett.

 ## Practical activities

1. Entrepreneurial process Review each of the cases in the chapter to identify the three stages of the entrepreneurial process, consisting of idea generation, opportunity recognition, and exploitation. Are there any differences between the cases? Can you identify any additional stages or a repetition of any stages or even the entire process?

2. Entrepreneurial opportunity business model: Map i-to-i, as described in the *'Deirdre Bounds'* case (Case 9.3), onto the five opportunity business model dimensions consisting of propositions, people, place, process, and profit. Review the case to identify any drivers that underpin this business idea. How did Deirdre become aware of these drivers? Did these drivers change over time?

 ## Discussion topics

1. What are the values of the three entrepreneurs described in the cases in this chapter? What role have these values played in the development of their businesses? Visit http://www.deirdrebounds.com and watch the short videos. Visit http://www.jonathanhick.com and watch the *Secret Millionaire*

episode (http://www.channel4.com/programmes/the-secret-millionaire/4od#2924011) in which he features. Are values a help or hindrance to success?

2. How is creating entrepreneurial learning opportunities for new venture creation different in a classroom, compared to starting a real enterprise? What can you do to accelerate your own personal development?

Further reading guide

It has never been easier to read about the experience of being an entrepreneur. There are broadly three types of books that tell the entrepreneurs' stories. Firstly, there are autobiographical accounts, which are largely written by the entrepreneurs themselves. Recent examples include **Duncan Bannatyne (2006, 2008), Karan Bilimoria (2007), Richard Branson (2006, 2008, 2009 [1998]), James Caan (2009), Michael Dell (2000), James Dyson (1997), Peter Jones (2009), Gerald Ratner (2008), Anita Roddick (2000),** and **Howard Schultz (1998).** In each of these, it is up to the reader to decide how much of the story is a faithful recollection of events and how much the entrepreneurs' attempt to re-tell history in their favour. Secondly, there are biographies, which are written about an entrepreneur with or without their co-operation or consent. Recent examples include Steve Jobs of Apple **(Young and Simon 2006; Moritz 2009)** and Larry Page and Sergey Brin of Google **(Vis, 2005).** And thirdly, there are books written about a number of different entrepreneurs with some similarities, such as success, race, or gender, and often based on interviews by the authors. Two noteworthy examples are *My Big Idea* **(Bridge 2006)** and *Making a Fortune* **(Dhaliwal 2008).**

References

Bannatyne, D. (2006) *Anyone can do it: my story.* London: Orion.

Bannatyne, D. (2008) *Wake up and change your life.* London: Orion.

Bilimoria, K. (2007) Bottled for business: the less gassy guide to entrepreneurship. Chichester: Capstone.

Branson, R. (2006) *Screw it, let's do it: lessons in life.* London: Virgin Books.

Branson, R. (2008) *Business stripped bare: adventures of a global entrepreneur.* London: Virgin Books.

Branson, R. (2009 [1998]) *Losing my virginity: the autobiography.* London: Virgin Books.

Bridge, R. (2006) *My big idea: 30 successful entrepreneurs reveal how they found inspiration.* London: Kogan Page.

Caan, J. (2009) *The real deal: my story from Brick Lane to 'Dragons' Den'.* London: Virgin Books.

Dell, M. (2000) *Direct from Dell: strategies that revolutionized an industry.* London: Profile Business.

Dhaliwal, S. (2008) *Making a fortune: learning from the Asian phenomenon.* Chichester: Capstone.

Dyson, J. (1997) *Against the odds: an autobiography.* London: Orion.

Jones, P. (2009) *Peter Jones, an autobiography.* Stage 1. BiblioBazaar.

Moritz, M. (2009) *Return to the little kingdom: Steve Jobs and the creation of Apple.* New York: Overlook Press.

Ratner, G. (2008) *Gerald Ratner: the rise and fall . . . and rise again.* Chichester: Capstone.

Roddick, A. (2000) *Business as unusual: the journey of Anita Roddick and the Body Shop.* London: Thorsons.

Schultz, H. (1998) *Pour your heart into it: how Starbucks built a company one cup at a time.* New York: Hyperion.

Vise, D (2005) *The Google story.* New York: Random House Books.

Young, J. and Simon, W. (2006) *Icon Steve Jobs: the greatest second act in the history of business.* Hoboken, NJ: John Wiley & Sons.

Part two

Entrepreneurship in perspective

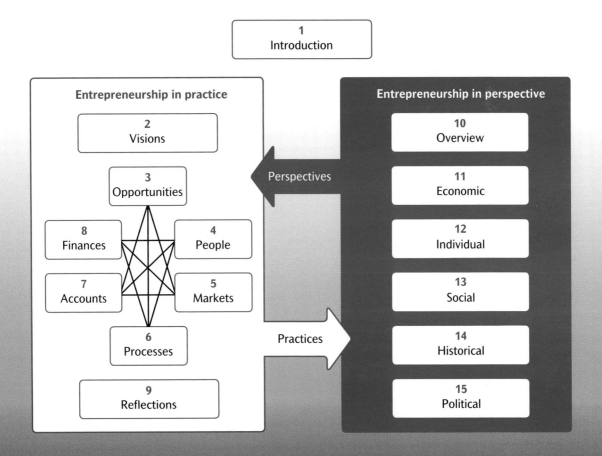

In the next six chapters (Chapters 10–15), we move away from the practical focus of Part One to explore the underlying nature of entrepreneurship: what it is, how it works, and why it is so important. Chapter 10 introduces Part Two and asks why entrepreneurship is still so difficult to define. It argues that, while direct practical experience is extremely useful, we also need to make use of other sources, including research evidence, to gain a deeper understanding of entrepreneurship in all its variety. The following five chapters examine five broad research perspectives: individual, social, historical, and political. Throughout Part Two, we keep in touch with 'real-world' entrepreneurship through practical illustrations, case studies, and activities. There are also many cross-references to relevant material in Part Two of the textbook, and to the Online Resource Centre.

Perspectives on entrepreneurship
An overview

10

[T]he essence of entrepreneurship is a change of state. And a change of state is a holistic process in which the existing stability disappears. When you try to take it apart, it tends to decompose.

William D. Bygrave, *entrepreneurship scholar*

There is always a well-known solution to every human problem – neat, plausible, and wrong.

H.L. Mencken, *twentieth century writer*

Learning outcomes

After reading this chapter you should be able to:

➤ Identify a variety of forms of entrepreneurship found in different contexts around the world, and in other historical periods.

➤ Evaluate the different kinds of knowledge about entrepreneurship that are generated by practitioners, academic researchers, and others.

➤ Outline the leading approaches to entrepreneurship research, and the more common research methods.

➤ Appreciate the relevance of entrepreneurship research for various audiences, including policy-makers, practitioners, and citizens.

➤ Apply these ideas to your own experiences of entrepreneurship.

Case 10.1 Enterprise across two centuries: changes and contrasts

Imagine for a moment that you are a young person growing up in the mid 1980s. The twentieth century is drawing to a close, highly centralized Communist governments are beginning to collapse, and people are talking about a new era in which many more countries will become representative democracies operating under a capitalist, market system. In the autumn of 1989, these dramatic changes are symbolized by the collapse of the Berlin wall and the reunification of East and West Germany. In 1991, the Soviet Union breaks into a number of independent republics. As state Communist regimes retreat, the world is beginning to experience a new kind of globalized free-market capitalism. Governments in the United States, the United Kingdom, and some other countries are paying increasing attention to entrepreneurial activity, as a source of new jobs, economic growth, technological innovation, and international competitiveness. For some, it is a time of great optimism, as market liberalization and the privatization of large state-controlled organizations open up new opportunities. However, there are also plenty of critics of the new enterprise culture. For example, in the world of entertainment:

- 'Opportunities (let's make lots of money)', a 1984 song by the Pet Shop Boys, challenges the notion that beauty and intelligence are all that is required to become fabulously rich. Meanwhile, another hit song of the period, 'Money's too tight to mention' by the Valentine Brothers highlights negative impacts on poorer people.

- Oliver Stone's movie, *Wall Street* follows anti-hero financier Gordon Gecko (Michael Douglas) as he pursues the hostile takeover of a traditional manufacturing firm. Having promised to rescue the company, he strips its assets to make a short-term gain. In a speech to fellow-financiers, Gecko famously declares that, 'greed is good'.

Mobile phones: transforming business in the 1980s

© OUP

Shanghai in the early twenty-first century

© istockphoto.com/Nikada

Despite such critiques, and more active demonstrations against neoliberal governments, such as the 1984 miners' strike in the UK, the enterprise culture project is looking well-established and set to extend its reach around the world.

Thirty years on: the time traveller awakes

Now imagine that you are transported forward a quarter of a century, and find yourself waking up in the year 2011. Your world is transformed and you are still struggling to grasp the sheer scale of the changes that have taken place. How did they manage to make mobile phones so small and televisions so large? Back in the 1980s, entrepreneurs were either marginalized or seen as greedy speculators. Now, they have become central figures, driving economic development around the world. Entrepreneurial activity has already transformed the economies and the industrial structures of many countries, including India, Brazil, and Ireland. China has become the world's major manufacturing centre and also its leading emitter of greenhouse gases.

Back in Europe, vast swathes of the economy, including retailing, entertainment, and communications, are increasingly dominated by large technology-based corporations such as Amazon, Google, Facebook, and Twitter. Why do the names of these companies sound so strange and unfamiliar to the time traveller? Because none of them existed in the mid 1980s; Amazon was the first, appearing as an online book retailer in 1995. Public sector provision is also being transformed around the world, with the opening up of procurement both to commercial providers and to a new generation of social enterprises. University courses in entrepreneurship have also multiplied in the last few years, moving beyond the business school and into arts, science, and humanities faculties. Compared to their 1980s' predecessors, today's graduates are less attracted by management training schemes in large organizations, with many more opting to set up their own commercial or social enterprise. Looking around you, it is easy to spot examples of entrepreneurial activity generating positive outcomes, but there are also signs of how things can go seriously wrong. A few years ago, several aggressively 'entrepreneurial' corporations, including: Enron (United States), WorldCom (United States), Parmalat (Italy), and Barings Bank (United Kingdom), went out of control, with disastrous results for their employees, customers and others as their once-profitable businesses collapsed. These isolated cases were followed by a much more wide-ranging failure. The so-called 'credit crunch' of 2007 has developed into an unprecedented global financial crisis. Several large banks have become insolvent, including Lehmann Brothers in the United States, Northern Rock in the UK, and all the leading Icelandic banks, including Landsbanki and Kaupthing. There is a period of severe economic instability, with increased unemployment and large financial losses. The government 'bail-outs' of the banking sector have stabilized the situation, but at an enormous cost to taxpayers. Though there is still disagreement over the underlying cause of the crisis, it is widely acknowledged that a combination of inadequate regulation, complicated financial innovation, and the reckless pursuit of profit opportunity contributed to the problem (e.g. Stiglitz 2010). There have been a variety of responses to the crisis. For some governments, the answer has been to penalize the more 'entrepreneurial' individuals and organizations in the banking industry by capping employee bonuses or imposing a 'windfall tax' on the industry. For others, the answer is to promote new and different kinds of entrepreneurial activity. For example, in order for Iceland's troubled economy to recover from its over-exposure to the banking sector and to diversify its economy, the government is now considering proposals to promote technological innovation and new forms of entrepreneurship.

Points to consider

1. What do you see as the most important changes in entrepreneurship and enterprise since the 1980s?

2. Why are governments around the world both seeking to promote and to control entrepreneurial activity?

3. You are a time-traveller: given the choice, when (and where) would you prefer to establish your first entrepreneurial venture?

Ethical point New waves of entrepreneurial activity have helped to create livelihoods for millions of people in this period, while others have suffered as a result of financial scandals, corporate collapses, exploitation and environmental pollution. Can entrepreneurial energy be channelled or is it a permanent revolution that is largely out of our control? (NB a sequel by Oliver Stone, *Wall Street: Money Never Sleeps* was released in 2010. For information on the songs mentioned in this case, see: http://www.petshopboys.com and http://www.billy-valentine.com).

Sources: Milne (2004), Stiglitz (2010).

10.1 **Introduction**

In Part One of *Exploring Entrepreneurship*, we concentrated on the main practical challenges that people face when they try to create and build new entrepreneurial ventures. In the Part Two chapters, we take a step back to see how entrepreneurship works, and to examine its role in the wider world. As the opening case suggests, the picture is a complex and rapidly changing one. Entrepreneurs have a dual role in the dynamics of change. From one perspective, they are the agents of change (i.e. the people who make change happen). However, they can also be seen as the beneficiaries of change (i.e. the people who pursue the new opportunities that change brings in its wake) (Case 10.1).

If you are simply looking to set up your own entrepreneurial business, the material covered in Part One could be sufficient, at least for the time being. However, there is a great deal more to learn about entrepreneurship, and much of it has a real *practical* application as well as being interesting from an academic perspective. In Part Two, we are going to explore this wider entrepreneurial landscape, and try to get a flavour of its richness and diversity. Our job is to provide some background information and to guide you towards some of the more interesting destinations. As with any trip into unfamiliar territory, it is worth investing some time before you set off in order to study the maps, plan the route and assemble essential supplies. Chapter 10 is designed to help you with this task, so we recommend that you read it first, before embarking on the other Part Two chapters.

The chapter is structured as follows. In Section 10.2, we begin by sampling some of the varied forms of entrepreneurship that can be found in different contexts around the world. Section 10.3 reviews the types of knowledge that can be used to inform yourself about entrepreneurship, building on an earlier discussion in Chapter 1. In Section 10.4, we introduce the remaining Part Two chapters by looking at their source disciplines, including economics, psychology, sociology, geography, history and policy studies. Section 10.5 considers the practical implications of this considerable research effort for policy-makers, practitioners, and citizens.

10.2 **The variety and complexity of entrepreneurship**

Though it is often presented in a narrow way, entrepreneurship turns out to be an extremely varied and complex phenomenon. This is hardly surprising. If you take a close look, everyday life is full of variety and complexity. For example, in the average vegetable garden, you could uncover many different species of insects busily engaged in complicated webs of activity. Social worlds are equally varied – take a look around your own city centre or university campus and you will find a rich mixture of people, organizational forms, and patterns of behaviour. The Part One case studies reveal something of the diversity of entrepreneurship. In Part Two, we take a more detailed look its *causes* and the *consequences*. To indicate why there is so much variety, we can begin with a short profile describing two out of a multitude of examples of entrepreneurial activity. The cases are fictionalized, but they are based on real examples. **Venture A** is a small, long-established firm making a regional speciality, such as wine or cheese. Following the initial start-up, the owners have managed it as a small family firm, where the priority was to produce a traditional product, make a steady income, and enjoy bringing up their children in the countryside. The daughter of the founders has recently returned home having studied for a degree in marketing and worked for a few years for a marketing consultancy, dealing with some major food brands. She brings new skills, ideas and business contacts, plus some much-needed energy to the business. Following some disagreements with her parents, the daughter initiates a new growth phase in the venture; within a few years it could become a major player within its market niche, building a strong export trade. **Venture B** is an entirely different business. A technology-based start-up, it went through a very turbulent period of rapid growth, culminating in a stock market **flotation** that made the original founders into instant multi-millionaires. However, a few years later, a series of accounting irregularities and a worsening economic situation have left the firm in a serious financial situation, with several stakeholders (e.g. equipment suppliers and customers) being seriously damaged in the process. The main requirement now is to stabilize the business, and to introduce better managerial and audit procedures. The contrasting profiles of these businesses illustrate how entrepreneurial activity is influenced by the context in which it takes place; they also indicate how the nature and intensity of entrepreneurial activity can fluctuate over time (Figure 10.1).

We have already seen that entrepreneurial activity can be found in a wide variety of organizational contexts, and at different degrees of intensity. Furthermore, it can have wildly

Figure 10.1 Entrepreneurial variety: between contexts and over time

Factor	Venture A	Venture B
Core technology	Traditional (artisan food)	High-tech (software)
Size (employees)	Small (10)	Medium (150)
Size (turnover)	Small (€500,000)	Large (€20 million)
Age	More than 20 years	Less than 5 years
Growth rate	Low/steady	High/fluctuating
Leadership	Family firm	Entrepreneurial team
Strategic priorities	Social and commercial	Purely commercial
Organizational form	Private company	Public company
Sector	Food service	Internet security
Geographic location	Rural	Urban
Geographic scope	Local/regional	Global
Economic impact	'Productive' (e.g. promoting innovation)	'Destructive' (e.g. rent-seeking or criminal)

contrasting impacts – both positive and negative – on the wider world. This variability has often led to confusion over what constitutes 'entrepreneurship', both in the popular imagination and amongst academic researchers. For example, for much of its life, the food firm depicted in Figure 10.1 would not have been classified as 'entrepreneurial'. It would be easy to label it as a 'small business', but by looking more carefully, we can distinguish the entrepreneurial phases in its development (i.e. in this case, the period immediately around the initial start-up of the venture, and some years later, when the daughter returned to take control of the business).

Perhaps unsurprisingly, the concept of 'an entrepreneur', referring to an individual person, has also proved difficult to define. As a consequence, it is a category that remains open to a wide variety of interpretations. The term been used to describe all kinds of people who would appear, at least on the surface, to have little or nothing in common with one another. In North America, it is often used to describe any owner-manager of a small, independent business. For many people, influenced by popular media representations of 'celebrity' entrepreneurs, it suggests lavish lifestyles, ostentatious wealth, and political influence. For others, 'entrepreneurs' have entirely negative connotations, associated with illicit activity and exploitation of more vulnerable people. In the following case study, we review three examples of human activity, each of which is described as entrepreneurship. We meet the entrepreneurs concerned, and try to find some common ground (Case 10.2).

Case 10.2 Entrepreneurs: from violence to social innovation?

This case study presents two contrasting examples of activities, both of which have been defined as entrepreneurship. At first sight, you might conclude that the people and the organizations portrayed in the extracts have very little in common. What could possibly connect Alex, the director of a Russian private protection and enforcement agency, with Fábio, the head of a Brazilian local agricultural department? However, if we take a closer look, it may be possible to identify some similarities between these individuals, and the activities they are engaged in:

Violent entrepreneurship: Komkom's 'question solving'

Vadim Volkov has analysed the various forms of violent entrepreneurship that emerged during the process of market building and state building in post-communist Russia in the last decade of the twentieth century. In the following extract, he describes the activities of private protection companies such as Komkom, which are headed by former officers of the KGB, MVD, and similar organizations:

> *What do private protection companies do? Being a type of violent entrepreneurial agency, the private protection company provides the standard set of 'roof' [krysha] services to other business agents and 'solves' their 'questions' – the phrase also frequently used by heads of MVD and KGB-backed companies even in published interviews. These are protection, contract enforcement, dispute settlement, debt recovery, information gathering, and*

sometimes organizational consultancy. For instance, in 1992 the protection enterprise Komkom successfully solved the question of a large debt recovery for the Petersburg branch of Sberbank Rossii, the biggest state commercial bank, and subsequently became its enforcement partner. The work in this field implies competition as well as co-operation with illegal enforcement partners, i.e. criminal structures. According to its director, Alex had a dispute with a Petersburg criminal group over a 'well-known company'. 'On the second day after we settled there they tried to intimidate us by phone. Then [we] set up a meeting (strelka). In the end [they] threw a grenade into our office. But things worked out well in the end, we did not abandon the object'.

Since criminal groups were first to discover this entrepreneurial niche, they also laid down the basic rules and terms of the game, which every newcomer in the field had to take into account. As the head of the Department of Licences and Permissions of the Interior Ministry, Yu Buryak, noted, 'The business of private protection is impossible without relations with criminal structures. I do not mind the strelki, they were and they will be. But I am strongly against what is called the razborki' (violent showdowns). Because of the similarity of functions private protection companies in many ways resemble their criminal rivals. At the same time, the ex-KGB and MVD structures assert their difference in that their service is more reliable, predictable, and has a more competitive price. The charge for debt recovery varies between 15% and 40% of the debt. The claim of a better quality of service rests on the professional experience of the personnel of large private protection companies who are able to use not only violence but also informational and analytical methods acquired during their career in state service. The major emphasis is said to lie not on direct physical protection or intimidation but on the preventive neutralization of potential conflicts and threats. The vice-chairman of the security service of the Association of Russian Banks, A. Krylov, described the methods of legal enforcement partners thus: 'To recover the debt one does not need to resort to violent means – it is sufficient just to demonstrate that you have information that compromises the debtor and the channels for its dissemination.' (Volkov 1999: 750–1)

Social entrepreneurship – Fábio Rosa and the red rice

In this extract, the writer Daniel Bornstein describes one of many projects initiated by the social entrepreneur, Fábio Rosa. The main aim of this initiative was to improve the living and working conditions of rural communities in Palmares, a depressed region in southern Brazil. Rosa had seen a TV interview with Ennio Amaral, a professor who had developed an inexpensive system for supplying electricity to rural areas. He was now working with an electrical technician, Ricardo de Souza Mello, to provide low-cost irrigation using cheap electricity and simple water pumps:

One of the other major problems facing farmers in Palmares was 'red' rice. Red rice is like a weed. Its seeds multiply quickly. If land is continually cultivated, eventually the red rice will destroy the desired rice crops. To inhibit the weed growth, small farmers cultivated only one-quarter of their land each year, leaving the remainder fallow for three years before replanting. Rosa had a better solution. Farmers could flood the fields before planting the rice and keep them saturated while the rice grew. The soil would be deprived of oxygen, preventing the red rice seeds from germinating. The trick would be to preterminate *the domestic rice plants in prepared beds and transplant them to the submerged paddies. Then only the desired rice would grow. In Palmares, this kind of rice farming, known as water seedling, had been impractical. But cheap irrigation changed everything. 'Using the saturation system,' Rosa explained, 'we could multiply the land that each farm could use by a factor of four.' He put it together like an equation: inexpensive electricity + shallow artesian wells + monophase pumps = cheap irrigation. Rosa created a municipal department to train locals in the new rice farming methods and added a credit mechanism so they could take loans to prepare their land, sink wells, and pay for the irrigation. 'Finally,' he said, 'we had a complete system.' After drafting his plan, Rosa travelled to Rio de Janeiro to present it to the Banco Nacional de Desenvolvimento Econômico e Social (BNDES), the $50 billion federal agency responsible for long-term national development funding. 'I showed them the cost structure and they jumped,' he recalls, 'It was like selling sweets to children.' (Bornstein 2004: 24–5)*

Questions

1. Taking each example in turn, prepare a list of the activities, attitudes and values that you consider to be 'entrepreneurial'.

2. Compare the three lists and identify similarities and differences.

3. How might you begin to explain what you have discovered?

Ethical point There are clearly major differences between the ethical status of these two entrepreneurial ventures. This raises various questions. For example: What is the relationship between ethics and entrepreneurship? Is there some kind of minimum level required, even in Alex's business? What ethical issues does someone like Fábio face, in his role as a social entrepreneur?

Sources: Volkov (1999), Bornstein (2004). Case introduction and questions prepared by Richard Blundel.

The rich variety of entrepreneurship is broadly to be welcomed. It is, as the old saying goes, 'the spice of life', with the various types of entrepreneurial activity providing a range of economic and social benefits (e.g. generating wealth and employment, producing useful and desirable products). However, it also leaves students of the subject with some major headaches. Firstly, how do we make sense of such a varied and complex social phenomenon? Secondly, how do we avoid making assumptions or believing popular 'myths' about commercial and social enterprise (Nicholson and Anderson 2005; Reid and Griffith 2006)? And assuming that we do manage to gain some understanding, how can we best influence the pattern of events (e.g. to promote 'productive' forms of entrepreneurship and to discourage the more 'destructive' ones)? People sometimes try to avoid the mental and emotional effort of dealing with variety and complexity. Instead, they revert to crude generalizations and stereotypes, which appear to make things simpler. For example, they might simply assume that entrepreneurial activity can be encouraged by adopting methods that were used successfully in another region, sector, or time period. Occasionally, these simplifications may work, at least as a short-term 'fix'. However, they can also lead to poor decision-making, undesirable outcomes, and a waste of resources. If we want to develop a deeper and more critical understanding of entrepreneurship and the enterprise culture, there are no short-cuts: we have to acknowledge (and deal with) its inherent variety and complexity. To do so, we will need to make use of knowledge from various sources, including academics, industry specialists, and the entrepreneurs themselves. We now return to an earlier discussion regarding these different kinds of knowledge (Section 1.4), and ask how they can best be used to explore entrepreneurship.

10.3 Exploring entrepreneurship: different ways of knowing

In Chapter 1, we introduced some the principal sources and discussed how to make use of different kinds of knowledge about entrepreneurship. The main lesson was to be critical in selecting and applying these sources. Some kinds of knowledge are likely to be particularly useful for *practical* tasks (e.g. preparing a financial forecast as part of a business plan, or developing relationships with key stakeholders), while other kinds of knowledge are more relevant when we are 'taking a step back', and looking at the more *theoretical* aspects of entrepreneurship (e.g. trying to understand why there is more entrepreneurial activity in a particular team of people, organization, or geographical location). The economic sociologist Richard Swedberg has suggested that there are four broad types of knowledge about entrepreneurship, which can, 'with a bit of simplification' be situated along a continuum (Figure 10.2)

The twentieth century political economist, Friedrich von Hayek first used the term '**practical knowledge**' to refer to the kind of specialized local knowledge that an entrepreneur might use from day to day in order to secure a profit (Hayek 1972 [1945]: 80) (Section 11.4). In Figure 10.2, we can see the founders of the biotech start-up and the social enterprise both making use of this kind of knowledge in order to establish their new ventures. Hayek contrasted this with the '**scientific knowledge**' used in economics; an example of this would be the correlation between R&D spillovers and economic growth, which has no immediate practical implications for entrepreneurial practice. His distinction can be used more generally to refer to the kind of knowledge produced by researchers using social scientific methods, including the historians who identified an explanation for the success of a nineteenth century industrial district. While all these forms of knowledge have a purpose, Richard Swedberg argues that entrepreneurship research would benefit from closer links between the more 'practical' and the more 'scientific' ends of the continuum:

> *One conclusion that can be drawn from Hayek's argument is that economics, as well as the other social sciences, need to incorporate some of this 'practical knowledge' into their analyses. By this is not meant that the social sciences should become a depository for all the empirical facts that have ever played a role in successful business ventures – this would clearly be absurd and also make it impossible to produce any science. What it does mean, however, is that if the social sciences are ever to get a better handle on entrepreneurship, they will have to learn to pay more attention to the concrete ways in which entrepreneurs locate and exploit opportunities. This type of knowledge has a certain degree of generality to it; and it is precisely this generality which makes it relevant to the social sciences.* (Swedberg 2000: 10; emphasis in original)

Figure 10.2 Four broad types of knowledge

	Type of knowledge	Examples
More concrete	Practical knowledge of the entrepreneur	• The founders of a biotech start-up know about the technical performance of a new pharmaceutical drug. • The founders of a new social enterprise know about the needs of young disabled people in their city.
	Practical knowledge about entrepreneurship	• The owner-manager of an established Internet service provider knows which providers of venture finance to approach in order to grow her business. • The directors of a co-operative know that it is important to establish effective relationships with their suppliers.
	Social science knowledge with practical implications for entrepreneurship	• Organizational researchers show how entrepreneurs can use social networks more effectively. • Sociologists uncover new evidence of credit rationing affecting new ventures.
	Social science knowledge with no implications for practical entrepreneurship	• Economists identify a correlation between research and development spillovers and economic growth in two countries. • Historians provide a new explanation for the success of manufacturing firms in a nineteenth century industrial district.
More abstract		

Source: Swedberg (2000): 38; by permission of Oxford University Press; examples added

Entrepreneurship researchers need to combine the theoretically informed, research-based evidence generated by academics and the more concrete 'practical' insights of entrepreneurial actors. Otherwise, our understanding of entrepreneurship can easily 'fall between two stools', becoming either too abstract and divorced from reality, or too anecdotal and context-specific. The two-part structure of *Exploring Entrepreneurship* attempts to bridge this gap, with Part One emphasizing the 'practice' issues involved in creating a new venture and Part Two providing the necessary social scientific 'perspective'. The following case (Case 10.3) illustrates some of the practical challenges facing researchers when they attempt to connect the worlds of academic investigation and entrepreneurial practice.

Case 10.3 What's *really* happening? Practical research challenges

With all the research that has been conducted over the years, you might imagine that entrepreneurship researchers and policy-makers would already have a fairly good understanding of their subject. However, entrepreneurship is complex, dynamic, and difficult to define. In this case, a team of researchers is trying to make sense of some dramatic changes taking place in London's black and ethnic minority ('BME') communities, and amongst young people in particular. The team was asked to, 'determine the current position, business development and growth needs and contribution of Black, Asian, Chinese and other minority ethnic-owned businesses to the London economy.' (LDA 2005: 14). Their challenge was to get beneath the surface and find out what was really going on. The case focuses on entrepreneurship in a particular community and location, but it raises issues that will be familiar to anyone studying entrepreneurship. Whether you are interested in Danish rural enterprises, or high technology start-ups in South Africa, there are similar issues to face in designing and conducting research.

Entrepreneurship in BME communities

The researchers found that patterns of entrepreneurship in these communities were changing in a number of ways: 'Traditionally, BME-owned enterprises tended to be concentrated within their own communities and to focus on easily accessible markets and low value products. Although these ethnic markets had growth limitations, the knowledge of and easy access to their communities gave these businesses a distinctive market advantage. This pattern of development led South Asians into the catering, food retailing, clothing and textiles sectors; East Asians into catering, textiles, import and export; African Caribbeans (Black) into personal services (notably hairdressing and beauty), catering, car repair services and small scale construction; and West Asians into textiles, travel, catering and some areas of import and export. However, in the last decade there has been a significant shift by BME entrepreneurs from these traditional ethnic niche markets into more mainstream and international growth sectors. There has also been a major shift in the types, sectors, scale, complexity and diversity of firms owned and run by the people of Asian, Black (African and Black Caribbean), Chinese and other minority ethnic backgrounds.' (LDA 2005: 21)

The changing world of young BME entrepreneurs

The researchers also explored how entrepreneurial activity and potential amongst younger people: 'Enormous generational changes are taking place among BME communities; for instance, second and third generation individuals have significantly different language skills, levels of education and social networks, all of which affect their entrepreneurial behaviour. As with the majority population, those with a family background in self-employment or business ownership are more likely to start and, critically, sustain their own business. Interestingly, they are less likely to stay in the family business and will tend to start businesses at a much younger age than their parents did. Research by *Barclays Bank* suggests that the typical entrepreneur today is younger than those of the last generation. Young entrepreneurs from Black African, Black Caribbean and East and South Asian communities are no different in this respect. They are also increasingly establishing businesses in mainstream and international growth sectors instead of the ethnic niche sectors.' (LDA 2005: 21)

Innovations in information and communication technologies had also opened up opportunities to create new ventures, many of which were operating internationally: 'The researchers identified two distinct ways in which these young entrepreneurs were exploiting their connections with other countries: 'First, their production and development networks have extended deeply into their countries of origin. For example, relatively young Indian IT entrepreneurs with strong links to the IT sector in Bangalore or textiles in north west India are common. Second, their networks extend far into North America. While links with similarly successful South Asians in the USA might be expected, the strength of their financing and technological networks remains surprising. That noted, there is little information available about the ideas and technologies underpinning these ventures. What does exist suggests marked differences from the majority population: although young BME entrepreneurs do not turn to British universities for their research and development (R&D), they use research facilities abroad, and are more likely to collaborate internationally.' (LDA 2005: 21)

The researchers made an important contribution in highlighting these developments and identifying a number of other issues concerning entrepreneurship in these communities. However, as the extracts indicate, there is still a great deal to be explored. Well-constructed research studies can generate valuable findings, but they are also likely to raise new questions.

---

 online resource centre 'Talking to the BME entrepreneurship research team.'

Questions

1. What kinds of evidence would these researchers need to collect in order to answer the following questions: (a) Why is there an increased level of business ownership by BME women?; (b) Why are young BME entrepreneurs using overseas facilities rather than British universities for their research and development (R&D)?

2. Which research methods would you choose to research to help them collect the evidence identified in the previous question?

3. How might the findings of these researchers influence: (a) entrepreneurial activity in these communities?; (b) public policies to support and encourage entrepreneurship?

Ethical point There are many ethical issues to consider when conducting social research, particularly when it involves direct contact with people. For example, researchers need to ensure that their respondents give 'informed' consent (i.e. you need to make them aware of how the research is going to be used, and also give them the option of not participating). It is also important to address issues such as confidentiality.

Sources: LDA (2005); Bryman and Bell (2007); Ram et al. (2006). Written by Richard Blundel with acknowledgements to Eric Osei, London Develoment Agency.

10.4 Entrepreneurship research: perspectives and methods

10.4.1 Five disciplinary perspectives

In this section, we introduce five broad disciplinary perspectives, which have provided some of the most significant contributions to entrepreneurship research. Each perspective is further elaborated in the remaining Part Two chapters:

- Economics (Chapter 11).
- Psychology and behavioural studies (Chapter 12).

- Sociology, human geography and anthropology (Chapter 13).

- Business history (Chapter 14).

- Political science and policy studies (Chapter 15).

The grouping of the perspectives reflects the fact that each shares some common ground in terms of the academic researchers involved, the research methods they tend to adopt and the journals in which they publish. By 'significant contributions', we mean that these perspectives have generated peer-reviewed publications in leading journals, research-based books and reports, and that their research findings and insights have influenced public policy. In some cases, they have also fed into popular understandings of entrepreneurship having been disseminated more widely via educational courses, management books, and mass media coverage. Our introductory comments cover three aspects of each perspective: (a) What kinds of questions does it address? (b) What kinds of research methods does it tend to employ? (c) What kinds of findings does it generate?

- **Economics** Of all the disciplines, economics probably has the best claim to having 'invented' entrepreneurship. Or, more strictly speaking, the pioneers of what we now know as economics were responsible for introducing the term, 'entrepreneur', firstly into the French language in the early eighteenth century, and subsequently into English. At the same time, they provided us with the first definition of the entrepreneurial function (Section 11.1). Over the years, economists have developed two broad strands of entrepreneurship research: (1) a more theoretical and inward-looking strand that tries to specify the function of the entrepreneurial actor within conventional economic frameworks (i.e. how to reconcile the active role of the entrepreneur with the 'invisible hand' of the market); (2) a more policy-oriented and outward-looking strand that examines the relationship between entrepreneurial activity and achieving greater economic growth (e.g. researchers might examine the impact of policies such as deregulation, tax breaks, and support for new ventures). In empirical research, economists often make use of large datasets (e.g. macro-economic measures such as rates of growth, employment, unemployment, interest etc.), which are then subjected to quantitative analysis and modelling. Economics-based research on entrepreneurship has also tended to emphasize the collection and analysis of quantitative data. In addition to macro-economic data of the kind already mentioned, researchers have often relied on individual-level data derived from questionnaire surveys (e.g. a telephone-based survey of a large representative sample of owner-managers). However, economists do also make some use of qualitative data (e.g. from in-depth interviews). The findings generated by economists have, for obvious reasons, tended to focus on the *economic* aspects of entrepreneurship. If non-economic factors are considered (e.g. the role of culture), it is usually in order to evaluate the impact of such factors on economic outcomes. So how should you organize an economy in order to get the most from entrepreneurship? We begin our search for an answer in Chapter 11.

- **Psychology and behavioural studies** The common theme in psychological and behavioural research is that the focus is on *individual* human beings. People are often attracted to these perspectives on entrepreneurship because it relates directly to their own personal experience. Again, there are two broad strands: (a) the first tries to identify what makes people entrepreneurial; (b) the second examines the behaviours associated with being entrepreneurial. The first strand is perhaps most strongly associated with the efforts of psychologists to isolate specific personality 'traits' and 'characteristics'. Though these approaches are now largely dismissed, they remain remarkably influential. Other, more significant work in the first strand includes the work of developmental psychologists on the influence of childhood experiences, and of social psychologists on peer groups and role models. The second strand, which developed in response to critiques of some of the earlier studies, looks at the actual behaviours of people identified as entrepreneurial. One of the more compelling questions raised by such research is whether it is possible to 'teach' someone to behave entrepreneurially – and furthermore, how far is entrepreneurial behaviour a predictor of becoming a successful entrepreneur? Assuming that you were not 'born' an entrepreneur, can you still be 'made' into one – and, if so, how? We address these questions in Chapter 12.

- **Sociology, human geography, and anthropology** Though research at the individual level has produced interesting findings, entrepreneurship is a phenomenon that extends well beyond the minds and behaviours of individual entrepreneurs. The major contribution of sociology, human geography, and anthropology is to examine how entrepreneurship is shaped by larger social forces. For example, a sociologist might examine gender differences in entrepreneurship, including the tendency to underplay the role of women in many accounts of entrepreneurial activity. The geography of enterprise is another important research field, with themes such as **spatial variation** (i.e. why are more new ventures being created in this area?) and clustering (i.e. why do similar enterprises tend to locate close to one another?). Anthropologists may seem an unlikely breed of entrepreneurship researcher but their studies of other cultures, including pre-industrial ones, have revealed interesting insights into the different forms that entrepreneurial activity can take. Social research of this kind adopts a very wide range of approaches, and is often conducted at multiple levels of analysis (e.g. individual, group, organization, local community, region). The use of qualitative data is probably more common, particularly in anthropology, but researchers may also make use of quantitative data in some cases (e.g. industry statistics and social survey data). In much of the work adopting a social perspective, there is a largely uncritical approach to entrepreneurship – the assumption is that we are simply interested in encouraging more of the same. However, there is also some more critical work, which examines its more negative forms and more destructive impacts (e.g. organized crime, environmentally harmful businesses), as well as possible alternatives. We consider these, and other related issues in Chapter 13.

- **Business history** In one of the opening quotations, William Bygrave suggests that entrepreneurship is fundamentally about a 'change of state'. The implication of this is that 'history matters'. In other words, we can only understand entrepreneurship as a process that unfolds over time, and where current activity is influenced, to some degree, by what has happened in the past. In order to grasp the importance of historical perspectives, just think of another process unfolding over time, such as a football match. A 'snapshot' image taken at some point during the game might be interesting, but it would tell us very little about how the game was being played, or where it was going. However, it would also be true to say that reviewing the whole match once it is over is an entirely different experience from that of the players (or the spectators), who are involved in real time, and where the outcome is unknown. In practice, many researchers take some account of the time dimension. Some make limited use of historical methods, while others at least introduce some kind of longitudinal element into their research. However, there is also a distinct tradition of business history research, with strong links to entrepreneurship. Business historians have addressed a variety of questions across the full range of the other perspectives. Their methods are also distinctive, with a particular focus on archive-based research (e.g. investigating early company documents, personal diaries, trade publications, etc.). In Chapter 14 we see how the use of such methods, coupled with the longer-time horizons of the historian, can enhance our understanding.

- **Political science and policy studies** Having started this review of the main disciplinary perspectives with the pioneers of economics, our final chapter comes full circle, with a discussion of politics – or what is sometimes termed 'political economy' – and policy studies. In an echo of the period when Adam Smith, John Stuart Mill, and Karl Marx were writing, there has been a recent trend to examine the connections between the political and the economic aspects of contemporary society. In the late twentieth century, a powerful coalition of economists and political scientists, sometimes referred to as the 'New Right', developed a series of policy initiatives to create more entrepreneurial economies based on a liberalized market model. Today, we are in a rather different environment, in which alternatives to the 'free' market have largely disappeared, yet where the world is faced with enormous social, environmental, and economic challenges (e.g. international terrorism, climate change, the global financial crisis). Policy studies provide us with insights into the sort of intervention that governments have adopted to promote entrepreneurial activity of various kinds. For example, there is a strong strand of research on policies to promote new venture creation in difficult environments, including marginalized communities and post-conflict situations. Political scientists have contributed to research on the role of government in relation to entrepreneurship. This includes a more critical research tradition that challenges aspects of the 'enterprise culture' project, including its negative impacts on certain individuals and communities. In Chapter 15, we examine previous policy initiatives and evaluate their impact on both the 'quantity' and the 'quality' of enterprise in various parts of the world. Building on insights from policy, political science and the other perspectives, we will also raise some questions about the ways that entrepreneurship might develop in the twenty-first century.

10.4.2 Multi- and interdisciplinary research

We have now reviewed the five main disciplinary perspectives on entrepreneurship, noted the approaches they have adopted, and indicated what kinds of findings each has contributed. Each perspective has something to contribute to our understanding of entrepreneurship. As we have emphasized, the perspectives are broad categories, comprising a rich variety of research approaches and insights. However, it is also important to recognize that many of the most interesting studies of recent years have been *multi*disciplinary (i.e. drawing on two or more of the disciplines identified previously), or *inter*disciplinary (also: *trans-* or *neo-*disciplinary, meaning new approaches that have emerged from earlier disciplines) (Zafirovski 1999). Furthermore, there are many overlaps and 'grey areas' within and between disciplines, contributing to occasional 'turf wars' (i.e. intellectual disputes) concerning issues such as the most appropriate methods, theoretical frameworks, and terminology in use. Our approach to these problems is to build each Part Two chapter around a distinctive perspective on entrepreneurship, while also indicating how different disciplines and levels of analysis have been combined in order to pursue specific research questions. Another challenge faced by many people is how to relate academic research, which often seems rather remote and abstract, to your personal experience. We have addressed this issue by introducing a new type of case study for Part Two. In each chapter, you can find one 'Researcher Profile', which presents background information on a leading entrepreneurship researcher, followed by an interview. The profiles are designed to provide insights that are not always available from other sources, such as published articles. Researchers tell us about their reasons for selecting particular topics, the methods they are using, their key findings, and where they see the research area developing in future.

10.4.3 The current state of entrepreneurship research

So what is the current state of entrepreneurship research? The answer is likely to vary, depending on who you speak to and what you choose to read. Some researchers argue that we already know a great deal about our subject, while others are more cautious. Two decades ago, William Bygrave, a former physicist, argued that the field was still in its infancy. As a consequence, he thought researchers should be spending less time on theoretical modelling and sophisticated statistical analysis, and more on basic field research:

> *Unlike physics, which has been central to intellectual thought for more than two millennia, entrepreneurship has barely begun to be noticed. This has important implications for the theory and methods that we use. [. . .] It is rather like biology before Darwin's natural selection theory, or nuclear physics before Rutherford's model. At that stage, the emphasis should be on painstaking observations rather than theory building.* (Bygrave 1989: 12–19)

Since that time, entrepreneurship research has continued to blossom, extending into new academic disciplines and yielding a rich harvest of empirical and conceptual material. One of the major challenges for today's researchers is in making sense of the many different kinds of evidence that are now available. With a few notable exceptions, most studies have been conducted at a single level of analysis (e.g. individuals, firms, **industries**), often reflecting the disciplinary backgrounds of the researchers (e.g. psychology, organization studies, economics). This tendency was noted in an earlier review of the entrepreneurship research field (Low and MacMillan 1988). The authors argued that **multi-level** studies, though limited in number, had demonstrated their potential to provide a richer understanding of the subject, and that more work was needed in this area:

> *The challenge for entrepreneurship research is to increase the incorporation of multiple levels of analysis into future research designs.* (Low and MacMillan 1988: 152)

More than a decade later, a survey of articles published in the leading US and European entrepreneurship journals, revealed that research was still dominated by micro-level analysis, and that integrated approaches still represented a small proportion of published work (Davidsson and Wiklund 2001). While there has been a lot of debate over the relative importance of different research approaches, relatively little progress has been made in integrating them, either empirically or conceptually. Low and MacMillan (1988: 153) also drew attention to the need for 'wide time frame studies' that would allow researchers to pursue causal linkages (e.g. demonstrating how a particular combination of factors contributed to a change in the level of entrepreneurial activity). Since that time, there *has* been something of a shift towards studies that address the process of entrepreneurship, particularly in areas such as **entrepreneurial learning** and growth (e.g. Macpherson and Holt 2007). Process-based research can be distinguished from variance-based research by its emphasis on the complex interactions that generate observed patterns of events:

> *Whereas variance theories provide explanations for phenomena in terms of relationships among dependent and independent variables (e.g. more of X and more of Y produced more of Z), process theories provide explanations in terms of the sequence of events leading to an outcome (e.g. do A and then B to get C).* (Langley 1999: 691)

Researchers have employed various strategies to build or refine process theories. Each has sought to understand 'patterns in events', but their methodologies differ in the extent to which they can probe beyond observed events (i.e. surface-level effects), to explore the underlying causal sequences and mechanisms. For example, population ecology is a well-established approach to studying entrepreneurial activity (e.g. Swaminathan 1995: Staber 1997). It uses a single-level methodology, exploring macro-level processes with aggregated quantitative data (e.g. official statistical datasets recording firm entries and exits) (Section 13.2). There are also approaches that examine entrepreneurship at a more detailed level. These include ethnographic studies (e.g. Fletcher 2006; Ram 1999), who reveal micro-level processes by collecting mainly qualitative evidence through fieldwork (e.g. observing and engaging with a particular group of entrepreneurs) (Section 13.2). There is also a long tradition of **historical research** in entrepreneurship, which has used a variety of approaches, sometimes combining multiple levels of analysis (e.g. studying how an interplay between entrepreneurs, organizations, and institutions has shaped the growth of industrial districts) (Section 14.3). Multi-level studies can provide us with more sophisticated explanations of entrepreneurial activity that take account of interaction between individual-level processes and those identified at higher levels (i.e. the firm, industry sector, and region). Examples of studies include Best's (2001) analysis of the resurgence of entrepreneurial firms and inter-firm networks in the USA, and Jones's (2001) examination of divergent strategies of technology- and content-driven entrepreneurs in the early years of the US film industry. However, this kind of research is difficult to undertake, and there is still plenty of scope for researchers to develop new multi-level research approaches:

> *Despite our advances in understanding the process and context of entrepreneurial activities, we still have a long way to go before achieving Low and MacMillan's [1988: 14–6] vision. They not only suggested a need to study process and context, but also to integrate them*

into a coherent theoretical framework. We would like to go a step beyond their statement and suggest that we also need to empirically *integrate process and context.* (Aldrich and Martinez 2001: 51; emphasis in original)

In summary, we can argue that the entrepreneurship research field is healthy and active, with considerable progress being made in addressing its limitations and extending its scope. The subject is also of central importance, both in terms of economic performance and social well-being (Casson et al. 2006: 27–9). The remaining Part Two chapters feature many examples of research studies that are providing us with fresh insights into entrepreneurship, in all its variety. The potential contribution of research is illustrated in the closing case study 'Deconstructing Dyson' (Case 10.4). It shows how two researchers applied the concepts of social networks and **entrepreneurial networking** in order to reinterpret a well-known entrepreneur's account of his efforts to build a technology-based enterprise. In doing so, they revealed the previously hidden roles played by other key actors, and highlighted important features of the institutional context in which this entrepreneur was operating.

10.5 Practical implications

The findings generated by entrepreneurship researchers can be useful to various audiences, including policy-makers, practitioners, and citizens. In this concluding section, which reappears in each of the Part Two chapters, we consider some of the ways in which research findings are used to improve policy-making and to inform practice.

10.5.1 Improving policies

In the opening case we discussed how governments had adopted the enterprise culture 'project' in an attempt to achieve various economic and social goals by encouraging new waves of entrepreneurial activity (Case 10.1). During its first three decades (i.e. from the mid 1970s to the mid 2000s), the main policy goals were economic growth, reduced unemployment, and increased competitiveness. It is clear that major changes have taken place in countries that have engaged in this project, including some improvements in economic performance. However, in recent years there has been an increasing concern over the effectiveness of policy. At this point, we can indicate three reasons why research is needed in order to make better policy; each of these will be taken up in more detail in Chapter 15. First, analysis of the recent historical evidence suggests that some of the economic achievements of the last 30 years may not be directly attributable to **entrepreneurship policies**, but rather to cyclical trends, and there is also evidence that some of the least 'enterprising' regions have failed to respond to successive policy initiatives (e.g. Audretsch et al. 2007, Greene et al. 2008). Second, we are not well informed about many areas of entrepreneurial activity, making it difficult to know what policies are required in particular circumstances (e.g. encouraging entrepreneurial activity in the communities featured in Case 10.3). Third, there is considerable evidence to suggest that some policies are having extremely damaging effects, however unintended, on the social and natural world. These include increased inequality, the destruction of wilderness areas, and environmental pollution (e.g. Della-Guista and King 2006; Porritt 2006). Fourth, with the increasing interest in social entrepreneurship in the early twenty-first century, some people are beginning to recognize that entrepreneurial activity has the potential to contribute towards a much broader range of positive outcomes, beyond conventional economic measures of profitability and growth. To some degree, this may simply be a matter of changing the 'hearts and minds' of those engaged in entrepreneurship. However, policy tools, including regulations, incentives, and penalties, will also play an important part in efforts to redirect entrepreneurial energy away from destructive, unsustainable activity and towards more constructive and benign alternatives (Baumol 1990; Blundel et al. 2010; Bornstein 2004; Minitti 2008; Parrish and Foxon 2009).

10.5.2 Informing practice

Throughout history, entrepreneurs seem to have managed quite well without the benefit of researchers, and the seemingly endless supply of books, journal articles, and conference papers that they produce. So what does a practitioner stand to gain by engaging with academics? Though some areas of entrepreneurship research have no obvious practical application, there are other areas where research could influence entrepreneurial activity:

> [I]t is totally uninteresting, from the perspective of practical entrepreneurship, whether the activities of the entrepreneur should be understood as restoring an equilibrium (Kirzner) or as disturbing an equilibrium (Schumpeter). To conceptualize entrepreneurial profit as rent on ability, as Mangoldt and Marshall do, is also of minimal interest from a practical perspective. What is much more relevant is to figure out what this 'ability' consists of, how to develop it, and how to spot it. (Swedberg 2000: 21)

In the next five chapters, there are many specific cases where research findings are making a contribution to everyday practice. To take one example, recent research on the financing of entrepreneurial start-ups has been used to inform the work of **venture capitalists** and other finance providers. It also feeds back into practice through education and training programmes, which provided guidance for entrepreneurs seeking to raise capital (Section 11.2 and Case 11.3). Another example is where people are making use of results obtained from studies of entrepreneurial learning and networking to design new kinds of peer support programme for entrepreneurs and owner-managers (Section 12.4 and Case 13.2). The other major contribution is made by entrepreneurship research as a whole, rather than by particular studies. In combination, this large body of research is broadening our horizons. It can provide new insights into people and places we would not otherwise come into contact with, suggest new ways of thinking about the subject, and open up different ways of acting entrepreneurially. But how does all of this knowledge convert into *practical* guidance for an existing or an aspiring entrepreneur? Here are three ways that research can improve your chances of establishing a successful venture:

1. By learning from the research that reports on the experiences of other people, and from other sources such as statistical evidence on firm performance, you can identify common pitfalls and consider alternative approaches to creating an entrepreneurial venture.

2. By making use of research findings and analytical techniques, you can be more selective when bombarded by a mass of information and guidance, including 'recipe book' advice and anecdotes from successful entrepreneurs, which may not be relevant to your situation.

3. By reflecting on the research evidence, you can think more deeply about the kind of venture you really want to establish, what is going to be involved in acting entrepreneurially, and how best to prepare yourself in order to achieve your ambition.

A common theme here is that people need to act in different ways depending on the kind of venture they are trying to establish, the context in which they are operating, as well as their personal vision and values. So, for example, an entrepreneurial art and design student setting up a new craft-based venture needs to develop practices that are relevant to her profession, rather than simply following a standardized approach (Gibb 2007; HEA/NESTA 2007). In the same way, the founders of a new social enterprise need to decide on its legal form, the markets it should serve, and the balance they want to strike between social, economic, and environmental goals (Bornstein 2004; Spear et al. 2009). Research is useful because it can broaden your horizons, helping you to make these important practical choices in more open-minded, creative and thoughtful ways.

✳ 10.6 Summary

➤ There is a wide variety of forms of entrepreneurship to be explored in different contexts, around the world and at different periods in history. Though we have only reviewed a few examples, it is clear that 'entrepreneurship' and the 'entrepreneur' are blanket terms, covering a great deal of diversity in terms of people, practices, processes, and outcomes. This inherent variety is obscured in popular accounts of entrepreneurship, which tend to rely on anecdotal evidence to create stereotypical images of entrepreneurs and the entrepreneurship process.

➤ There are also various types of knowledge about entrepreneurship. It is important to be clear about their potential strengths and limitations in order to make intelligent use of such knowledge to address particular problems and research questions. 'Practical' knowledge is often passed on through direct contact between 'apprentices' and their entrepreneurial mentors, or through some form of experiential learning; it is sometimes highly context-specific, so may not always be applicable to other situations. The knowledge produced by academic researchers is often (but not always) of more general relevance, but can be seen as serving a complementary role.

➤ Entrepreneurship has attracted the interest of researchers from several academic disciplines, including psychology, behavioural studies, economics, sociology, anthropology, human geography, business and management studies, and history. While each of these disciplines has brought its own preferred research methods, some of the most interesting research has been interdisciplinary in nature, examining entrepreneurship at multiple levels of analysis. These approaches are examined in more detail in the remaining Part Two chapters (Chapters 11 to 15).

➤ Entrepreneurship research is relevant to several different audiences, including students, academics, policy-makers, practitioners, and citizens. There are likely to be differences both within and between these audiences, regarding the kinds of questions that they want answered, and also the types of knowledge they find most useful. Before proceeding with the rest of Part Two, you may find it helpful to spend some time reviewing (and reflecting on) what you currently 'know' about entrepreneurship, and how this knowledge might best be combined with the material to be covered in the remaining chapters.

Case 10.4 Deconstructing Dyson: applying a network perspective

James Dyson is a successful British industrial designer, innovator, and entrepreneur, best known for his 'Dual Cyclone' vacuum cleaner. His autobiography, *Against the Odds*, is very readable and inspiring, showing how creative thinkers can succeed, even in very mature markets dominated by large incumbent corporations (Dyson 1997). Dyson's personal journey was far from easy, and his lively writing style emphasizes the importance of self-belief, courage, persistence, and sheer hard work in creating a new venture. But is this the full story? Steve Conway and Oswald Jones decided to examine the role played by other people located on the margins of Dyson's narrative. In their re-reading of the autobiography, the two researchers focused on the role played by the entrepreneur's informal or 'social' network (Conway and Jones 2006) (Sections 4.5 and 13.2). The following extracts indicate a few of the ways that network connections contributed important resources, including support, information, and knowledge.

From sea trucks to vacuum cleaners: the basic story

While studying for a Masters degree course in design at the Royal College of Art (RCA), London, James Dyson began to work for an entrepreneur named Jeremy Fry who manufactured motorized valve actuators for pipelines. Fry encouraged him to adopt a 'hands-on' (i.e. practical) approach to design rather than one based on theory. Dyson was soon working on one of his innovative ideas, the 'Sea Truck', and over the following months went on to build a prototype. He patented his idea and Fry set up a subsidiary of his company, 'Rotork', to manufacture the product. Whilst working for Rotork, Dyson and his family moved from London to a 300-year-old farmhouse in the Cotswolds. Undertaking most of the re-building work himself, he became familiar with the failings of the traditional wheel-barrow: unstable when fully laden, tyres prone to puncture, liable to sink into soft ground, and with a steel body that damaged door frames and human limbs. Having considered the problem for around a year, he hit upon the idea of reinventing the wheel-barrow by constructing it in plastic and replacing the wheel with a ball. At this point, Dyson decided to set-up his own manufacturing company. He launched the 'Ballbarrow', which soon became a commercial success. However, the idea was then stolen by a US company and Dyson's company lost the subsequent legal case. This failure led to tension between board members and Dyson was voted out by his business associates. Undeterred, he decided to investigate another problem encountered during the refurbishment of his old farmhouse: why did the performance of his vacuum cleaner decline so rapidly after fitting a new dust bag? Dyson found that it needed only a thin layer of dust inside the bag to clog the pores and reduce the suction. Experience with industrial cyclone technology, which is widely used in sawmills and to handle other powdery materials, gave him the idea for a cyclone vacuum cleaner. Using an old vacuum cleaner, cardboard, and industrial tape, he spent one evening constructing a fully working model of the world's first bagless cleaner – the prototype for the 'Dual-Cyclone'. After two years of trying to convince British and European companies of the Dual-Cyclone's potential, Dyson decided to try the US. Despite the optimism and the 'can-do' spirit of the US, which he found refreshing after the negativity he experienced in the UK, no company was willing to manufacture the Dual-Cyclone. In November 1984, after five years of trying to gain interest in the Dual-Cyclone among European and US manufacturers, Dyson received an informal approach from a Japanese company, who agreed to produce the Dual-Cyclone for the Japanese market under the 'G-Force' brand name. He then managed to set up a deal with a Canadian company, who agreed to produce the Dual-Cyclone for the US market under the 'Drytech' brand name. However, just before the product launch, Dyson discovered that Amway, a US company that had rejected the Dual-Cyclone concept several years before, had now launched their own version. Reluctantly, Dyson found himself involved in another long-running and extremely expensive legal battle. In 1991, after almost five years of litigation, Amway agreed to a deal over their patent infringement and the haemorrhage of legal fees stopped. Finally, in July 1993, 15 years after his original idea, the first 'DC01' Dual-Cyclone vacuum cleaner rolled off Dyson's own assembly line, and the innovation was successfully launched in the UK.

Friends and contacts: the story from a social network perspective

While studying at the RCA Dyson met theatrical and film impresario Joan Littlewood, who invited him to design a new theatre. Dyson created a 'mushroom-shaped auditorium built of aluminium rods'. He sought financial support for the project from British Aluminium. During his first meeting, a manager suggested that he contact Jeremy Fry; this was to be the start of a long relationship:

> I had shown Fry my model of the proposed theatre, and I think he rather liked it, if not enough to cover me with gold. What he did offer me, however, was to prove far more useful in the long run: work [at Rotork], and the first of many collaborations. (Dyson 1997: 47)

Dyson eventually left Fry's company, to establish his 'Ballbarrow' venture. This is one of several occasions where the entrepreneur acknowledges the considerable emotional and practical support provided by his wife, Deirdre:

> I still marvel at Deirdre's encouragement of me at that time. It could have meant losing everything. But she was always philosophical, and insisted that if everything failed she could paint pictures for money and I could make furniture. (Dyson 1997: 78)

Although he had made money from the Sea Truck, Dyson needed financial support to establish his company. As with many entrepreneurs, he turned to his family. These direct and indirect network ties were fundamental to the start-up, providing legal advice on company formation, plus funding to develop the Ballbarrow and to invest in production equipment:

> 'I went to see a lawyer friend of my brother-in-law . . . Andrew Phillips not only helped with the formation of the company, but fell in love with the Ballbarrow and persuaded said brother-in-law (Stuart Kirkwood) to invest in it. Stuart was the son of one Lord Kirkwood,

former chairman of the mining company RTZ. He and his brother . . . as a result, inherited some family money. Which is always nice. (Dyson 1997: 79-80)

Following his departure from the Ballbarrow venture, Dyson decided to concentrate his efforts on developing the 'Dual-Cyclone' vacuum cleaner. However, he needed finance to proceed, and thus sought a partner to invest in the setting up of the 'Air Power Vacuum Cleaner Company'. Dyson generated some capital from his own resources, but for the balance, he turned again to Jeremy Fry:

Fry . . . was always likely to be my best hope. And so it proved. With £25,000 from Jeremy, and £25,000 from me, £18,000 of which I raised by selling the vegetable garden at Sycamore House and the rest borrowed with my home as security . . . I was in the vacuum cleaner business. (Dyson 1997: 120)

Dyson eventually built around 5,000 prototypes over a three-year period, and by 1982 he had a Dual-Cyclone that was 100% efficient, but he also had debts of more than £80,000. Dyson's connection with Jeremy Fry and Rotork again proved invaluable in providing essential funding (Dyson 1997: 138). However, a key element in the ultimate success of the Dual-Cyclone was the deal he established with the Canadian company run by Jeffery Pike, a fellow British national:

[W]ith whom I had become friendly quite by chance after we sat next to each other on an aeroplane in May 1986, and both turned out to be reading the same novel by Fay Weldon. Having flunked English A-level [school examination] all those years before, my fortune looked as if it was about to be made by a novel. (Dyson 1997: 175; emphasis added)

As plans for the manufacture of the Dual-Cyclone in the UK progressed, Dyson used his connections to hire talented young design engineers direct from the RCA, just as Jeremy Fry had done previously (Dyson 1997: 192). Dyson's continuing involvement with the RCA illustrates his ability to maintain and to utilize long-standing social networks:

Round about the time I was planning the DC-02, I was at the RCA degree show – for I had since become an internal examiner on their product design course – and I went around offering one or two of the graduates jobs, as is my habitual wont. (Dyson 1997: 239)

By 1996 Dyson was considering ways in which he could extend into the increasingly global market for consumer products. After considering the attractions of Germany and France as the first step in his expansion, he eventually settled on Australia:

I got a call from a man called Ross Cameron. Cameron was an Australian who had seen a presentation of mine at Johnson-Wax in Racine, Wisconsin. 'Why not start up in Australia?' I asked. A couple of days later Ross rang back to say 'OK'. He was that sort of man, not one to mess about. (Dyson 1997: 252–3)

Yet again, Dyson's social network proved to have a major impact on the direction and fortunes of his entrepreneurial venture.

Questions

1. Using the extracts presented in the case, locate the examples of entrepreneurial networking.

2. In each case, identify: (a) the main actors, (b) the kinds of things that are flowing through the network (e.g. finance, information, influence), (c) the outcome for Dyson and his business ventures.

3. Take another example, from your own personal experience or from a secondary source (e.g. a biography or novel), and try to identify evidence of entrepreneurial networks.

4. What does a network perspective add to your understanding of entrepreneurial activity?

Sources: Conway and Jones (2006); Dyson (1997); Johannisson (2000) – original case material adapted with permission and acknowledgements.

 ## Practical activities

1. The colourful world of enterprise: Using the approach adopted in Case 10.2 as a model, search for a further THREE examples of entrepreneurship. For the purposes of this exercise, we are not overly concerned about the quality of your sources, so feel free to search the web for interesting and unusual entrepreneurial narratives of all kinds, wherever they are to be found. Good places to start include: online newspapers and magazines (NB search the archives for relevant stories); enterprise support organization sites (NB these often contain short case studies, highlighting successes and 'best practice'); campaigning organization sites (NB these may highlight cases of 'bad practice', such as unethical behaviour); entrepreneurial organizations' own sites (NB look out for pages labelled 'about us' or 'our history'); or academic research (NB focus on publications that have adopted a case-based approach). Try to find at least one example that you consider to be a fairly 'extreme' or 'marginal' case, but that you could still argue for as being 'entrepreneurial' in some meaningful way. Prepare your examples as either a two-page comparative case study, or as a four slide presentation, using visual material as appropriate. In the accompanying text, highlight what you consider to be the distinctively 'entrepreneurial' aspects of each example, and also their major differences. If you are working with other students, presentations can be followed by a discussion with the following themes: (a) What makes these examples entrepreneurial? (b) Are the extreme/marginal cases really entrepreneurial, or do they represent something different? (c) Which, if any, of these types of entrepreneurship appeals to you as a potential career path? This group exercise can be extended with students creating a 'patchwork quilt' of entrepreneurial examples, either electronically or as a large poster display.

2. The entrepreneurial knowledge bank: Re-read Case 10.1 and check for updated materials on the London Development Agency website (www.lda.org.uk) and on the Online Resource Centre. You could use an alternative piece of policy-related entrepreneurship research published by a similar organization, adapting the questions accordingly.

a. Review the findings detailed in these extracts and prepare lists of the following: (i) statements that *do* surprise you; (ii) statements that *do not* surprise you; (iii) statements that you *disagree* with, based on your own experience and prior knowledge.

b. What do you think are the likely consequences if the LDA was unable to achieve its stated aims (i.e. finding out more about entrepreneurship in London's BME communities)?

c. Using the report as a starting-point, prepare a list of what you see as the THREE most interesting questions that researchers need to be asking about this topic area. To extend the activity, add a column to the right of your list of questions, and insert your suggestions as to how these questions might be answered (i.e. what kind of research would you need to carry out?).

3. Connecting with entrepreneurship research: As with practical entrepreneurship, one of the best ways to engage with research is to make a personal connection. For this activity, you need to find someone with a direct involvement in an entrepreneurial venture – of whatever kind. The person may be a relative, friend, neighbour or even someone you do business with (e.g. the owner of a shop or restaurant). Ask your interviewee the following questions (or devise your own versions), then compare the responses with findings discussed in Chapters 12 and 13:

- Why did you set up this venture?
- How did you identify the opportunity?
- Who else is involved in the venture?
- What are your ambitions for the venture?
- Do you consider yourself to be an entrepreneur?
- What makes someone 'entrepreneurial'?
- Have other members of your family set up new ventures?
- What lessons have you learned about setting up a new venture?

 Discussion topics

1. Re-read the sections that discuss different *sources and types of knowledge* about entrepreneurship (Section 1.4 in the opening chapter and Section 10.3 in this chapter). Which sources and types of knowledge do you find: (a) most interesting; (b) least interesting? What are your reasons? If you are working in a group, compare your responses with those of other students. Why are particular sources and types of knowledge more or less appealing? Retain your notes and re-read them when you have completed Part Two.

2. Re-read the discussion about different *academic research approaches* to entrepreneurship (Section 10.4). Which approaches do you find: (a) most interesting; (b) least interesting? What are your reasons? If you are working in a group, compare your responses with those of other students. Why are particular academic disciplines more or less appealing? Retain your notes and re-read them when you have completed the other Part Two chapters.

3. Richard Swedberg suggests that social science researchers could get a better understanding of entrepreneurship by paying more attention to the 'practical knowledge' of entrepreneurs (Section 10.3). How might you achieve this in practice? To focus your discussion, you might consider one of the following: (a) researching gender differences in high technology entrepreneurship; (b) researching the impact of entrepreneurial role models on young people; (c) researching the motivations of social entrepreneurs.

Further reading guide

One of the best places to find concise overviews of entrepreneurship research is in edited books and handbooks. **Swedberg (2000)** is a collection of classic readings with an interesting introductory chapter. The *Oxford Handbook of Entrepreneurship* edited by **Casson et al. (2008)** is a substantial work with chapters covering many of the research approaches introduced in this chapter. For example, the chapter by **Ricketts (2008)** gives a historical overview of economic theory on entrepreneurship. Several other contributions to this Handbook are identified in the relevant Part Two chapters. **Acs and Audretsch (2003)** is another wide-ranging handbook with a multi-disciplinary emphasis; it addresses a number of themes covered in Part Two and has a good coverage of research methodologies. **Sexton and Landström (2000)** is an earlier handbook with several informative chapters, including **Johannisson (2000)** on entrepreneurial networking. There are several useful and accessible summaries of recent research on entrepreneurship in **Carter and Jones-Evans (2006)**, including the chapter by **Conway and Jones (2006)**, which discusses the authors' research on James Dyson (Case 10.4). Another good source is the critical literature surveys, which appear from time to time in leading journals such as *Entrepreneurship Theory and Practice*, *Entrepreneurship and Regional Development*, and the *International Journal of Management Reviews*. It is also worth comparing research evidence with other kinds of information; **Dyson (1997)** and **Dennis (2006)** are good examples of entrepreneurial autobiographies in which the authors reflect on their experience; further examples can be found in Chapter 12. **Bryman and Bell (2007)** and **Blumberg et al. (2008)** are general introductions to research methods, with an emphasis on business organizations.

 ## References

Acs, Z.J. and Audretsch, D.B. (2003) *Handbook of entrepreneurship research: an interdisciplinary survey and introduction*. Dordrecht: Kluwer.

Aldrich, H.E. and Martinez, M.A. (2001) 'Many are called, but few are chosen: an evolutionary perspective for the study of entrepreneurship.' *Entrepreneurship Theory and Development*, 25, 4: 41–56.

Audretsch, D.B., Grilo, I., and Thurik, A.R. (eds) (2007) *Handbook of research in entrepreneurship policy*. Cheltenham: Edward Elgar.

Baumol, W. (1990) 'Entrepreneurship: productive, unproductive, and destructive.' *Journal of Political Economy*, 98: 893–921.

Best, M. (2001) *The new competitive advantage*. Oxford: Oxford University Press.

Blundel, R.K. and Tregear, A. (2006) 'Artisans and factories: the interpenetration of craft and industry in English cheese-making, c1650–1950.' *Enterprise and Society*, 7, 4: 1–35.

Blundel, R.K., Spence, L.J., and Zerbinati, S. (2010) 'Entrepreneurial social responsibility: scoping the territory.' In L.J. Spence and M. Painter-Morland (eds) *Ethics in small and medium sized enterprises: a global commentary*. Dordrecht, NL: Springer.

Bornstein, D. (2004) *How to change the world: social entrepreneurs and the power of new ideas*. Oxford: Oxford University Press.

Bryman, A. and Bell, E. (2007) *Business research methods* (2nd edition). Oxford: Oxford University Press.

Blumberg, B.F., Cooper, D.R., and Schindler, P.S. (2008) *Business research methods* (2nd European edition). London: McGraw-Hill.

Bygrave, W.D. (1989) 'The entrepreneurship paradigm (I): a philosophical look at its research methodologies.' *Entrepreneurship Theory and Practice*, 14, 1: 7–26.

Carter, S. and Jones-Evans, D. (2006) *Enterprise and small business: principles, practice and policy* (2nd edition). Harlow: FT Prentice Hall

Casson, M., Yeung, B., Basu, A., and Wadeson, N. (2006) *The Oxford handbook of entrepreneurship.* Oxford: Oxford University Press.

Conway, S. and Jones, O. (2006) 'Networking and the small business.' In S. Carter and D. Jones-Evans (eds) op. cit. (305–23).

Davidsson, P. and Wiklund, J. (2001) 'Levels of analysis in entrepreneurship research: current research practice and suggestions for the future.' *Entrepreneurship Theory and Development*, 25, 4: 81–99.

Della-Guista, M. and King, Z. (2008) 'Enterprise culture.' In M. Casson et al. (eds) op. cit. (629–47).

Dennis, F. (2006) *How to get rich.* London: Ebury Press.

Dyson, J. (1997) *Against the odds: an autobiography.* London: Texere Thomson.

Fletcher, D.E. (2006) 'Entrepreneurial processes and the social construction of opportunity.' *Entrepreneurship and Regional Development*, 18, 5: 421-440.

Gibb, A. (2007) 'Creating the Entrepreneurial University: Do We Need a Wholly Different Model of Entrepreneurship?' In A. Fayoll (ed.) *Handbook Of Research In Entrepreneurship Education, Volume 1 A General Perspective.* Cheltenham: Edward Elgar (67–103).

Greene, F.J., Mole, K.F., and Storey, D.J. (2008) *Three decades of the enterprise culture: entrepreneurship, economic regeneration and public policy.* Basingstoke: Palgrave.

HEA/NESTA (2007) *Creating entrepreneurship: entrepreneurship education for the creative industries.* London: Higher Education Academy, Art Design Media Subject Centre and NESTA.

Hayek, F. von (1972 [1945]) 'The use of knowledge in society.' In *Individualism and Economic Order.* Chicago: Henry Regnery Company (77–91).

Johannisson, B. (2000) 'Networking and venture growth.' In D.L. Sexton and H. Landström (eds) *The Blackwell handbook of entrepreneurship.* Oxford: Blackwell (368–86).

Jones, C. (2001) 'Co-evolution of entrepreneurial careers, institutional rules and competitive dynamics in American film, 1895–1920.' *Organization Studies*, 22, 6: 911–44.

LDA (2005) *Re-defining London's BME-owned businesses.* London: London Development Agency/ Mayor of London.

Langley, A. (1999) 'Strategies for theorising from process data.' *Academy of Management Review*, 24, 4: 691–717.

Low, M.B. and MacMillan, I.C. (1988) 'Entrepreneurship: past research and future challenges.' *Journal of Management*, 14, 2: 139–61.

Macpherson, A. and Holt, R. (2007) 'Knowledge, learning and small firm growth: A systematic review of the evidence.' *Research Policy*, 36, 2: 172–92.

Milne, S. (2004) *The enemy within: Thatcher's secret war against the miners* (new edition). London: Verso.

Minniti, M. (2008) 'The role of government policy on entrepreneurial activity: productive, unproductive, or destructive?' *Entrepreneurship Theory and Practice*, 32, 5: 779–90.

Nicholson L. and Anderson, A.R. (2005) 'News and nuances of the entrepreneurial myth and metaphor: linguistic games in entrepreneurial sense-making and sense-giving.' *Entrepreneurship Theory and Practice*, 29, 2: 153–72.

Parrish, B.D. and Foxon, T.J. (2009) 'Sustainability entrepreneurship and equitable transitions to a low-carbon economy.' *Greener Management International*, 55: 47–62.

Porritt, J. (2006) *Capitalism as if the world matters.* London: Earthscan.

Ram, M. (1999) 'Trading places: the ethnographic process in small firms' research.' *Entrepreneurship and Regional Development*, 11, 2: 95–108.

Ram, M., Barrett, G., and Jones, T. (2006) 'Ethnicity and entrepreneurship.' In S. Carter and D. Jones-Evans (eds) op. cit. (192–208).

Reid, K. and Griffith, J. (2006) 'Social enterprise mythology: critiquing some assumptions.' *Social Enterprise Journal*, 2, 1: 1–10.

Ricketts, M. (2008) 'Theories of entrepreneurship: historical development and critical assessment.' In M. Casson et al. (eds) op. cit. (33–58).

Sexton, D.L. and Landström, H. (eds) (2000) *The Blackwell handbook of entrepreneurship.* Oxford: Blackwell.

Spear, R.G., Cornforth, C.J., and Aiken, M. (2009). 'The governance challenges of social enterprises: evidence from a UK empirical study.' *Annals of Public and Cooperative Economics*, 80, 2: 247–73.

Staber, U. (1997) 'An ecological perspective on entrepreneurship in industrial districts.' *Entrepreneurship and Regional Development*, 9, 1: 45–64.

Stiglitz, J.E. (2010) *Freefall: free markets and the sinking of the global economy.* London: Penguin.

Swaminathan, A. (1995) 'The proliferation of specialist organizations in the American wine industry, 1941–1990.' *Administrative Science Quarterly*, 40: 653–80.

Swedberg, R. (ed.) (2000) *Entrepreneurship: the social science view.* Oxford: Oxford University Press.

Volkov, V. (1999) 'Violent entrepreneurship in post-communist Russia.' *Europe-Asia Studies*, 51, 5: 741–54.

Zafirovski, M. (1999) 'Probing the social layers of entrepreneurship: outlines of the sociology of enterprise.' *Entrepreneurship and Regional Development*, 11, 4: 351–71.

11 Economic perspectives
Influences and impacts

An entrepreneur is someone who specialises in taking judgemental decisions about the coordination of scarce resources.

Mark Casson, *economist*

By pursuing opportunities that otherwise would not have been pursued by the incumbent organizations, entrepreneurship plants the seeds for entire new industries and is, thus, a driving force of industrial restructuring.

David Audretsch and Max Keilbach, *entrepreneurship researchers*

Learning outcomes

After reading this chapter you should be able to:

➤ Explore entrepreneurial activity from an economic perspective.

➤ Identify the contribution made by the main economic research approaches, and related research evidence, to our understanding of entrepreneurship.

➤ Understand the relationship between entrepreneurial activity and performance outcomes, including economic growth, innovation, and competitiveness.

➤ Recognize how entrepreneurship can become unproductive or destructive.

➤ Evaluate economics-based evidence and relate it to findings obtained from other research perspectives.

➤ Apply these insights to your own experiences of entrepreneurship.

Case 11.1 Micro-enterprise development in Pakistan

Micro-enterprises can perform a valuable economic development function, particularly in less developed regions. But how do you encourage this kind of entrepreneurial activity? Khwendo Kor (www.khwendokor.org.pk) is a non-profit, non-government, and non-partisan organization that promotes, 'the development of women and children, strong families and communities, and a progressive society.' Founded in 1993 by Maryam Bibi, it works in hundreds of villages in the most remote and politically sensitive parts of Pakistan's *Khyber Pakhtunkhwa* (formerly North West Frontier Province) and Federally Administered Tribal Areas (FATA), adjacent to the Afghan border. *Khwendo Kor* is a Pushto term, meaning 'Sister's Home', and it is based on active community involvement (i.e. 'participatory development'), rather than top-down initiatives. In this case we look at Khwendo Kor's 'sustainable livelihoods' programme, which aims to make vulnerable groups, particularly women and children, more economically self-sufficient.

Pakistan has about 4 million commercial bank borrowers in a population of 170 million, and 84% of Pakistan's population earns less than $2 a day. In FATA the average income is only half this and only 34% of households are above the official poverty level. In the rural areas of Khyber Pakhtunkhwa many farming households have to subsist on less than one acre of land. Women work the land along with men but official figures underestimate the extent of poverty among them. Poorly educated, sometimes debarred by custom from owning property, and limited in the occupations they can undertake, they are far more likely than men to be poor. These deeply engrained problems are exacerbated by the violence and political conflict, which is disrupting trading activities in the region. Maryam Bibi describes the situation:

> Political parties are banned in the tribal areas, but radical religious organizations have become very powerful. They are linked to the Taliban and get mosques and local media to spread propaganda. When we do polio vaccinations, they say we're putting stamps on the bottoms of women and children to take their bodies to America for research. The US drone attacks, which have been going on for the past year, have made local people angry and our work even harder. We've had to stop work in many villages, and our children's learning centres have been blown up. (Sunday Times 2009: n.p.)

It is against this background that Khwendo Kor has been developing its micro-enterprise and microfinance programmes for women, enabling them to acquire skills, an income and greater control of their own affairs. Like similar programmes around the world, it is based on the idea that entrepreneurial activity is one of the most effective ways of ensuring that communities can generate stable and resilient income streams. The programme helps villagers to enhance their skills, self-confidence, and entrepreneurial potential. Women are encouraged to develop micro-enterprises through the provision of micro-credit, market links and specialist training. So far, more than 900 women have been provided with credit in appropriate forms (i.e. as Islamic loans, conventional loans or less restrictive, 'soft' loans), with total advances exceeding 12 million Rupees. Khwendo Kor receives funding from several development charities, including Oxfam, the Oxfam-Novib, Action Aid, and the Friends of Khwendo Kor (www.frok.org.uk). Is providing micro-credit a cost-effective use of these financial resources? There is plenty of evidence that enterprise activity can improve economic conditions of poor rural communities. New micro-enterprises help to increase the income level of the owners, which then feeds into the local economy. Ownership of a micro-enterprise also enables women to gain direct access to economic resources, a benefit that they can extend to their children and other family members. Here are two examples of the development projects in action:

- **Peshawar district marketing study** Female entrepreneurs were finding it difficult to diversify and to develop new products that met market requirements. A research study was conducted, with the aim of reducing the gap between communities and their markets. By talking to entrepreneurs and analysing existing marketing approaches, the researchers were able to produce five business and product profiles for: poultry products, porcelain, beauty parlours, beads, and home made snacks. These are being used to increase awareness, develop marketing skills, and improve market linkages.

- **Capacity building in Karak district** Both women and men from a number of villages have been given practical training in relevant skills, including livestock management, 'tie and dye' and block printing. Female entrepreneurs were also given an opportunity to visit other micro-enterprises in order to share and learn from each other's experiences. Another programme in this district has encouraged the establishment of home-based plant nurseries. Some of these failed due to water scarcity and marketing problems, but others have prospered. Field days and awareness sessions have attracted the interest of hundreds of village women, students, teachers, and others. The aims of these events are: to mobilize communities, to market plants grown in Khwendo Kor-supported nurseries, and to identify potential new horticultural entrepreneurs.

Craft-based micro-enterprises such as weaving can generate additional income for remote rural communities

© *Khwendo Kor*

Microfinance is a relatively new but rapidly growing field. Outside Pakistan's Khyber Pakhtunkhwa and FATA regions, there are other important providers, including the Kashf Foundation (www.kashf.org), which was founded by Roshaneh Zafar following a meeting with Muhammad Yunus of Grameen Bank (www.grameen-info.org). In 2008, Kashf expanded its operations to include a full service microfinance bank (www.kmfbank.com). Around the world, innovative micro-enterprise and microfinance initiatives are having an enormous economic and social impact in poor communities. For example, microfinance is now being delivered via the Internet, with organizations such as Kiva (www.kiva.org) enabling individuals to lend directly to entrepreneurs in developing countries.

Points to consider

1. What do you see as the main *economic* and *non-economic* functions of the micro-enterprises described in this case study?

2. How would you measure the impact of this kind of entrepreneurial activity on local economies in Pakistan?

3. What *economic* and *non-economic* arguments could you make for governments and voluntary sector agencies to support micro-enterprise development?

Sources: Bibi (2010); Khwendo Kor (2010); Sunday Times (2009): Kashf (2010).

11.1 Introduction

This chapter is concerned with the economic perspectives on **entrepreneurship**. There are competing views on what economics is, or should be, concerned about. For our purposes, economics can be described, in general terms, as a branch of social science that examines how societies allocate and manage scarce resources between alternative uses. In the past, these activities have taken place under different economic systems, with varying degrees of control being exercised by political leaders (e.g. feudalism in the medieval era and state socialism in the twentieth century). Today, most of the world's resources are allocated and managed under various forms of industrial capitalism (Hall and Soskice 2001). In this chapter, we investigate the entrepreneurial function in these modern economies, including its capacity to generate wealth, employment, and economic development. The opening case illustrates how even the most modest enterprises can transform the livelihoods of individuals, families, and local communities. Over the last few decades, entrepreneurial activity has also been transforming the prospects of people in transition countries and creating new economic superpowers (e.g. Sauka and Welter 2006; Khanna 2008). The economic transformation is particularly dramatic in some of today's high technology 'hot spots' (e.g. Shanghai, Bangalore, Dubai), with massive new construction projects, vast inflows of human and natural resources, and flamboyant displays of personal wealth – the luxury yachts, private aircraft, and exclusive fashion stores (Case 10.1). The economic outcomes of entrepreneurship are often obvious. But what is going on beneath the surface? Simon Parker, an economist with a specialist interest in entrepreneurship, provides us with a concise definition of the scope of the field:

> In essence, the economics of entrepreneurship analyses how economic incentives influence entrepreneurial behaviour, and how entrepreneurial behaviour in turn affects the broader economy. (Parker 2009: 4)

As the chapter title suggests, we are paying particular attention to the second of these questions, exploring the economic impact of entrepreneurship on individuals, organizations, and geographic regions. However, we also touch on the first theme, identifying the economic pre-conditions for entrepreneurship. In particular, we consider how resource constraints influence entrepreneurial activity, and the practical ways in which entrepreneurs overcome these limitations. Some themes reappear in other Part Two chapters (e.g. Section 13.5 considers economic geography, Section 14.3 looks at the rise and fall of **industries** and regions and Case 15.2 discusses entrepreneurial behaviour in transition countries). Economics-based research has a strong influence on our understanding of entrepreneurship, which can be seen in many areas of life. For example, when analysts describe the performance, including the 'success' or 'failure', of an entrepreneurial venture, they often define the outcome in purely economic terms. The same thing happens when politicians and policy-makers talk about the outcomes of entrepreneurial activity on a larger scale. Economists can rightly claim to have originated the term, 'entrepreneur', and over the years they have built up a strong body of economic theory and research evidence. We can draw on these valuable sources to make sense of what entrepreneurial activity is, and how it works. However, economics does not have all the answers. There are still many unresolved questions within the discipline of economics, and many aspects of entrepreneurship that require the perspectives and insights of other academic disciplines (Section 10.4).

Economists have identified many different roles for the entrepreneur. These include: identifying or creating opportunities, making **innovations**, taking risks, bearing uncertainty, acting as an intermediary, allocating resources between different uses, co-ordinating resources, and leading organizations. One common theme in this varied list is a capacity to exercise judgements under conditions of risk and uncertainty (Casson 2003 [1982]). Entrepreneurs have to make (and to implement) all kinds of decisions. The quality of these judgements can have a profound impact on both the performance of the venture and its capacity to generate economic value. This is illustrated by the practical example, which identifies the main activities, and associated decision-making, in a typical start-up venture (Figure 11.1).

The chapter proceeds as follows. In Section 11.2, we review some of key insights that have been provided by economists, concentrating on the positive contribution that entrepreneurial activity can make to the economy, and on the economic factors that either promote or constrain such activity. Section 11.3 is concerned with the different ways in which the entrepreneurial function has been explained by economists, from the early pioneers to present day researchers. Section 11.4 examines how entrepreneurial activity can become economically unproductive or destructive, and opens up a debate about how these negative outcomes might be avoided. In Section 11.5, we conclude by considering the practical implications of economics-based research for individual entrepreneurs, entrepreneurial organizations, and those involved in policy-making.

11.2 Economic insights into entrepreneurship

11.2.1 Applying economic methods

The economics of entrepreneurship can be something of an obstacle course. Economic theory is often rather abstract and inaccessible to those without the necessary technical background. As a consequence, theoretical debates in economics can appear far removed from the everyday realities of creating a new entrepreneurial venture (Section 10.5). In addition, economists tend to have distinctive ways of viewing the world, which are not always clear to non-specialists. For these reasons, the next two sections of this chapter review some of the more interesting *questions* that economists have addressed, coupled with examples of *contributions* that economics has made to our understanding of entrepreneurship. It is not possible to offer a comprehensive picture of such a large and diverse research field in a single chapter. However, to give a flavour of the work that is being done, we have selected three contrasting themes, each highlighting a different set of insights that can be gained by applying economic research techniques:

- Patterns in the number of enterprises.

- Entrepreneurship, economic growth, and regional development.

- Access to finance as a barrier to entrepreneurship.

In addition, each of these research areas has a high profile in government circles. As a consequence, there is an opportunity to follow up on some of the issues raised in Chapter 15, when we examine the world of policy-making.

Figure 11.1 Decision-making in a new venture: an economic perspective

Activity	Practical example (based on a fictional start-up venture)	Commentary
Identifying or creating new opportunities	Three engineering graduates decide to establish 'EcoDry' a new venture that seizes a growing market opportunity. They have combined several existing technologies, creating a new, more environmentally friendly technique for dry cleaning textiles.	This activity is not always innovative in terms of technologies, products, or markets, but it does identify or create new opportunities to generate value. Economic value is typically measured as sales, profits, and cash flow that would not otherwise have existed. New ventures can also create social or environmental value.
Mobilizing and leveraging resources	The founders manage to secure financial resources from a number of sources, including their own family and friends. They also decide to recruit an experienced technology entrepreneur in order to increase their credibility with potential investors and business partners.	Entrepreneurs mobilize economic resources, often overcoming constraints (i.e. resource scarcity) through a combination of creativity and initiative – activities include 'financial bootstrapping', to minimize start-up finance requirements, and the use of personal contact networks to get access to valuable resources.
Appropriating and accumulating value	The founders decide to set up a commercial holding company on a franchise-based business model; they considered adopting a social enterprise model, but decided that this had the greatest growth potential. The founders accumulate wealth from the franchisees and from their own equity stake.	Entrepreneurial actors need to create suitable organisational forms to organize financial, human, intellectual, and technological resources. Their initial decisions are likely to affect the longer-term economic performance and impact of the venture. Social enterprises face similar issues, while also needing to balance social and economic value.
Redistributing and redirecting value	Once it is trading, 'Eco-Dry' is paying wages to employees, reimbursing suppliers, paying dividends to investors and taxes to local and national governments. The founders may also decide to re-invest their profits in new projects and by making donations to environmental charities.	It is also important to consider how entrepreneurs make use of the economic value they have secured. For example, is the capital re-circulated within the local economy, or taken abroad? Is it re-invested in promising new commercial and social ventures or in personal art collections?

11.2.2 Patterns in the number of enterprises

There are no simple measures of entrepreneurial activity, but researchers often use data that are based on the number of enterprises. Perhaps the simplest indicator is how the numbers are distributed between enterprises of different sizes. The differences between countries and regions can be quite striking. For example, the following table compares size-class distribution data for three European Union countries (Figure 11.2):

Figure 11.2 Comparing firm size data in three EU countries

Enterprise	EU	UK	Denmark	Czech Republic
Micro	18.04 million (91.8%)	1,383,311 (87.1%)	176,043 (87.0%)	813,700 (95.1%)
Small	1.35 million (6.9%)	171,703 (10.8%)	21,881 (10.8%)	34,180 (4.0%)
Medium	0.21 million (1.1%)	27,562 (1.7%)	3,654 (1.8%)	6,715 (0.8%)
Large	0.04 million (0.2%)	6,240 (0.4%)	668 (0.3%)	1,389 (0.2%)
SMEs per 1,000 inhabitants	40	26	37	86

European Union SME definitions

Enterprise	Headcount	Turnover (million €)	Balance sheet (million €)
Micro	<10	2	2
Small	<50	10	10
Medium	<250	50	43
Large	>=250	>50	>43

Note: The EU definition states that, in addition to headcount ceiling, an enterprise qualifies as an SME if it meets either turnover OR balance sheet ceilings.

Source: Eurostat (2008, 2009); European Commission (2005)

Among other things, the data reveals that the Czech Republic, with 86 **SMEs** per 1,000 inhabitants has more than twice the European Union average. At the other end of the scale, Slovakia has just 8 SMEs per 1,000 of its population (Eurostat 2009: 46–7), suggesting that these countries have very different economic environments. Similar differences can be found for related SME indicators, such as number of people employed and value added.

Size distributions provide a basic picture of the current 'stock' of enterprises but they do not reveal anything about their 'flow' (i.e. the numbers of new firms being created and of existing firms that cease to exist). These flows can be substantial, as indicated by the authors of an annual survey of EU enterprises:

> *Each year about 1.5 million new enterprises are established, corresponding to 9% of the total enterprise population. At the same time 1.3 million enterprises annually cease to exist, corresponding to a death rate of 8% of the stock of enterprises.* (Audretsch et al. 2009: 9)

New firm formation data are often used as an indicator of entrepreneurial activity in different geographic locations (e.g. comparing the rates between countries, regions, cities, urban and rural areas) (Section 13.5), and over time (e.g. identifying historical trends in industries) (Section 14.3). These patterns are often used as a starting-point for enquiry. For example, they have prompted researchers to look at factors that might either promote or inhibit new firm formation rates, such as the number of creative people living in a particular area (Lee et al. 2004), or to scrutinize claims that new firm formations have a positive impact on economic goals such as job creation (e.g. Van Stel and Storey 2004).

11.2.3 Entrepreneurship, economic growth, and regional development

Economists have always been interested in growth, and how it is created. In one of the earliest and most influential works in English, Adam Smith launched, *An Inquiry into the Nature and Causes of the Wealth of Nations* (Smith 2008 [1776]). Smith identified a number of reasons why some economies grew more, and hence became wealthier, than others. One of the main strands in his explanation was concerned with the ways that individual enterprises could increase productivity through the division of labour (i.e. giving workers more specialized tasks) and other economies of scale – as illustrated by Smith's well-known example of the pin factory. Another strand concentrated on the way that economic activity was co-ordinated, and here Smith argued that the 'invisible hand' of the market, or the combined effect of individuals making their own self-interested choices, was likely to be more effective than co-ordination by political leaders and other bodies, such as the medieval craft guilds. Over the years, economists developed a number of theories about the growth process, focusing to varying degrees on issues related to industrial production, technological innovation, and the role of market mechanisms. In the last two decades, a new approach known as 'endogenous growth theory' (or **'new growth theory'**) has become particularly influential (cf. Romer 1994; Solow 1994). New growth theory recognizes the role of played by technological innovation and associated 'knowledge spillovers' (Arrow 2010 [1959]) (Case 11.3). For economists, **knowledge spillovers** are a type of positive externality, in which knowledge created by scientists and other technical specialists becomes more widely available, creating new opportunities for others to exploit it:

> *[A]ny original, valuable knowledge generated somewhere that becomes accessible to external agents, whether it be knowledge fully characterizing an innovation or knowledge of a more intermediate sort. This knowledge is absorbed by an individual or group other than the originator.* (Foray 2004: 91)

What function do entrepreneurs perform in this process? Economists and economic geographers have examined a variety of ways in which entrepreneurial activity influences economic development (Section 13.5). However, one of the central findings is that commercially driven entrepreneurs keep economies moving forward by recognizing (and exploiting) opportunities to shift resources into functions that yield a higher return:

> *Entrepreneurs seek out these opportunities for personal gain and, in so doing, ensure that resources are constantly being reallocated in a manner that improves efficiency. In the absence of entrepreneurs, resources continue to be devoted to functions where the returns*

are low, leading to an ossified [i.e. fixed and unchanging] economy in which resources are under-used. (Acs and Storey 2004: 872–3)

Of course, entrepreneurs have always pursued opportunities. However, research suggests that entrepreneurs in today's innovative, technology-based industries need appropriate institutions and infrastructures, including well-established systems of intellectual property rights and networks of university-based researchers and spin-off firms, if they are to compete effectively (e.g. Van de Ven 1993; Best 2001).

11.2.4 Access to finance as a barrier to entrepreneurship

It is possible to identify a number of economic factors that can influence the level of entrepreneurial activity in different countries, regions or industries. These include broad 'macro-economic' (i.e. economy-wide) factors, such as interest rates, gross domestic product (GDP), inflation rates, taxation, and public spending, as well as narrower 'micro-economic' (i.e. market-specific) factors such as access to finance. From an economist's perspective, these financing constraints are evidence of 'market imperfections', which in turn are produced by 'information asymmetries'. In practical terms, this means that entrepreneurs are facing excessive financing costs because finance providers do not have sufficient access to information about their ventures. There are two kinds of information asymmetry:

> *First, one party to a transaction is in possession of relevant information that is not known by the other party. Specifically, entrepreneurs possess more information about their own abilities and the prospects of their firm than the provider of finance and may misrepresent this information. This creates the risk of adverse selection by the funder, which can only be mitigated by incurring the expense of a lengthy due diligence process to obtain relevant information about the entrepreneur and the business (which because of its private nature may not be available) and interpret it. This is particularly problematic in technology sectors, where it is difficult to value the firm's scientific knowledge and intellectual property, the products are likely to be new and untested in the market, and the management may lack commercial skills. Second, one party to a transaction cannot observe relevant actions taken by the other party that might influence the outcome of the investment. Dealing with this problem – moral hazard – is also costly to the investor, requiring complicated contracts that are time consuming to design and negotiate, and labour-intensive monitoring systems. Because the costs involved in investment appraisal and monitoring are fixed regardless of the size of investment, this makes small investments uneconomic for funders.* (Mason 2009: 537)

These market failures have created funding gaps for new ventures, particularly in technology-based sectors. As Colin Mason's study indicates, governments have responded to this situation by intervening in various ways, including:

- Introducing fiscal incentives, including tax relief for new start-up ventures.
- Promoting networks of '**business angel**' investors, and helping them locate new ventures.
- Reforming securities (i.e. stock market) legislation to reduce the burden on entrepreneurs.
- Building the capacity of entrepreneurs, including training delivered by business angels.

- Building the capacity of investors, by training and learning within their networks.
- Co-investing with business angels through government-financed venture capital funds.

This example of access to finance illustrates how economics-based research informs public policy, helping to shape the environment for entrepreneurship (Section 15.1). It also indicates that the interaction between entrepreneurial activity and economic growth is highly complex. In order to understand these causal relationships, researchers need to use a combination of methods, drawing on economics and other social science disciplines (Section 15.5).

In the following Researcher Profile (Case 11.2), we discuss a research study on **credit rationing** in the Netherlands, and how banks make decisions regarding the financing of relatively small start-up ventures. The research study illustrates one way in which quantitative methods can be used to study aspects of entrepreneurship, and the valuable insights that can be obtained from this kind of approach.

Case 11.2 *Researcher Profile*

Boris Blumberg, examining how credit rationing affects entrepreneurial activity

Boris Blumberg is an entrepreneurship researcher based at Maastricht University in the Netherlands. After obtaining a masters degree in business at Mannheim University in Germany, he obtained a PhD in sociology from Utrecht University in the Netherlands. His thesis looked at the management of inter-organizational partnerships between technology-based firms. Boris has research interests in social networks, small businesses, and methodological issues and has published in several journals including *Organization Studies* and *Small Business Economics*. He is also the lead author of the European edition of the textbook, *Business Research Methods* (Blumberg et al. 2008).

In this interview, Boris discusses his research on the important issue of credit rationing and business start-up ventures. He also explains some of the quantitative research methods adopted for the study, and the particular insights that they provide.

Q: Why did you want to research in this area? How did you decide on your main research questions?

New business start-ups need finance and by far the most important source for finance are bank credits. However, if you look at academic studies, venture capital is much more researched than bank credits. Howard Aldrich once commented that there are more research studies on venture capital than firms financed by it! For these reasons, we felt that bank credits were worth looking at. Then we developed the idea that getting a bank credit is a two-sided decision process. The bank decides whether the start-up gets the credit, but before they can decide they need a start-up to make an application, and some start-ups might not apply for credit because they do not expect to get finance. Taking such a two-sided perspective, we were interested in whether some start-ups did not apply for credit although they had a good chance to get it. We also wanted to find out whether some start-ups did not obtain credit asked for, although they were rather good creditors.

In a second step, we looked at the determinants of credit approval and denial and decided to look at this issue from a slightly different angle. Rather than looking at risk of a loan, we asked whether business founders or owners could reduce credit denial through giving commitments, such as collateral (i.e. securing the loan against an asset), or sending reliable signals to the banks.

Q: What methods did you use?

This study was quantitative and employs a rather unique data set of 1,140 individuals living in South Limburg (The Netherlands) who considered becoming self-employed in 1998 and 1999. This data set is based on computer-assisted personal interviews that lasted about one hour and covered various areas of the process of starting a business. One of these areas is obviously the financial area and we used the information obtained there to conduct this study. Three hundred and forty-two of the 1,140 individuals applied for a bank loan to start their business and 29% of these applications were rejected by the bank. To understand whether business starters do not apply because they expect their request to be denied we needed to analyse the loan application decision simultaneously with the loan approval decision. Wilko Letterie, my co-author, is trained in econometrics and he came up with the appropriate statistical technique to estimate the two decisions simultaneously. More specifically we estimated the chance that a bank denies a credit request conditional on the decision to apply for a credit.

Q: What were your key findings? Do they have practical implications for entrepreneurs?

We argued that a bank's decision to approve or deny a credit application should depend on commitments and signals provided by the potential entrepreneur showing the bank that the new venture's success is likely and repayment of the debt is highly probable. Our study shows that commitments in the form of own money and reliable signals play both an important role, but banks value commitment more than signals. If you are an entrepreneur needing some financial help from a bank, you are more likely to get it if you can provide collateral. In line with recent research evidence, we found that home ownership is important to acquire access to external financial resources. You are also more likely to get credit if you put some of your own money into the venture and if you make the effort to write a business plan and hire an accountant. The effects of a business plan and advice from an accountant point also to the fact that banks are more likely to grant credit if the information provided is more trustworthy and reliable and less subject to an optimistic bias of the business founder.

Just to get the perspective right, the loans we are talking about are not really huge; we are not talking about millions, but somewhere in the range, 5,000 to 20,000 Euros. As I mentioned before, banks value commitments more than signals. This becomes especially clear if we look at the earning capacity of a loan applicant. Earning capacity signals that the loan is very likely to be repaid, even if the entrepreneurial venture fails. If you are a young engineer and you secure a loan of 20,000 Euros, even if your business fails, you can earn enough in a paid job to repay the loan. However, we see that banks are more reluctant to rely on such signals, and still prefer to have collateral. This result is interesting, especially in the light of the current financial crisis and the credit crunch. On the one hand, it suggests that banks ration credit too much and neglect people with a good education, and high earning capacity, if they have not yet accumulated sufficient personal wealth. On the other hand, banks need to be cautious in providing finance to entrepreneurs, given that they are lending out money from their customers' savings accounts.

Q: Were there any particular challenges in conducting these studies?

Using the data we employed was not our first option. First, we wanted to approach banks and ask them whether we could have a look at their credit applications and approvals. But we soon discovered that no one wanted to share that information. This information is pretty sensitive. Banks are afraid that detailed knowledge about their approval criteria would create 'moral hazards' (i.e. if you know exactly what a bank is looking for, you may be tempted to fill in an application according to these criteria, rather than to reflect the real situation). As banks were not willing to provide the information, we had to approach the entrepreneurs. This proved to be a good choice, as now we were able to include those business starters that did not apply for a credit. The other challenge was the two-sided character of our model. In the first versions of the paper we analysed the two decisions separately, but reviewers and others were not convinced by that approach. Then Wilko came up with a statistical model that allowed us to estimate the two decisions simultaneously.

Q. Where do you think research in this area needs to develop in future?

I have the feeling that research on entrepreneurial finance still has a strong focus on the top 5% of the start-ups, but personally I am much more interested in the thousands of unnoticed start-ups that do not become the corporate giants (e.g. Google or SAP) of tomorrow, but will grow into sizeable companies with 50 or 100 employees. How do they get money to grow further? Another issue I am interested in is the market of private financing. From our research in Limburg we know that about 20% of the business starters got a loan from their family, friends, or a business partner. There are even websites where people can lend their money to other people. It is a little bit like transferring the concept of micro-credits in developing countries to developed countries. But, we know hardly anything about how this informal credit market operates in Europe.

Sources: Blumberg and Letterie (2008); Blumberg et al. (2008).

11.3 Economic perspectives on entrepreneurship

11.3.1 Introduction: contrasting approaches and contributions

Entrepreneurial activity comes in all shapes and sizes. At one extreme, there are the small group of highly innovative 'system builders', who are responsible for leading major structural transformations. Examples can be found in the railway, steel, and oil industries of the nineteenth century, the car manufacturing, electricity generation, and computing industries of the twentieth century. At the other extreme, there are a multitude of 'low-level' entrepreneurs trading on a relatively small scale in local markets. Is it possible to identify a common 'entrepreneurial function' shared by such a diverse group? Economists have always recognized that entrepreneurs are significant economic actors, but it has proved difficult to integrate the entrepreneur into economic theory. Over the last century, economists have continued to explore, and to argue about, the entrepreneurial function. There have been important contributions from a number of leading economists, including Frank Knight, George Shackle, Joseph Schumpeter,

Edith Penrose, Mark Casson, David Audretsch, and many others. In the following paragraphs, we review some of these contributions, and consider their practical implications. The section is written in non-technical language; economists and others with a more specialist interest in this subject will find relevant sources in the Further reading guide. We begin by looking back to some of the earliest attempts at identifying the economic function of the entrepreneur. The section concludes with some examples of the current state of play in economics-based research.

11.3.2 Pioneering contributions: Cantillon and Mill

In his *Essai sur la nature du Commerce en Generale*, the economist Richard Cantillon (1697–1734), depicts the entrepreneur as a risk-taker, who acquires labour and raw materials when the price of the end-product was still uncertain. Cantillon was writing in a pre-industrial economy and many of his examples were based on agriculture. In this English translation, his 'undertaker' (i.e. entrepreneur) is a farmer, who has to make decisions about allocating resources under conditions of uncertainty:

> *The farmer is an undertaker who promises to pay to the landowner, for his farm or land, a fixed sum of money (generally supposed to be equal in value to the third of the produce) without assurance of the profit he will derive from this enterprise. He employs part of the land to feed flocks, produce corn, wine, hay, etc. according to his judgement without being able to foresee which of these will pay best. The price of these products will depend partly on the weather, partly on the demand; if corn is abundant relatively to consumption it will be dirt cheap, if there is scarcity it will be dear. Who can foresee the increase or reduction of expense which may come about in the families? And yet the price of the farmer's produce depends naturally upon these unforeseen circumstances, and consequently he conducts the enterprise of his farm at an uncertainty.* (Cantillon 1959 [1755]: Part I, Chapter XIII.1)

Cantillon identifies three distinct types of economic actor: landowners, entrepreneurs, and what the original English translation describes as 'hirelings' (i.e. employees). Though most of his contemporaries still saw landowners as more prestigious figures, Cantillon recognized that entrepreneurs were playing a more decisive role, and one that was influencing many different aspects of economic life:

> *Cantillon's entrepreneur is someone who engages in exchanges for profit; specifically, he exercises business judgements in the face of uncertainty. This uncertainty (of future sales prices for goods on their way to final consumption) is rather carefully circumscribed. As Cantillon describes it, entrepreneurs buy at a certain price to sell again at an uncertain price, with the difference being their profit or loss.* Cantillon stressed the function, not the personality of the entrepreneur. *He generalized the function of the entrepreneur so that it embraced many different occupations and cut across production, distribution, and exchange.* (Hébert and Link 1989: 42; emphasis added)

Throughout this textbook, we are encountering examples of entrepreneurs performing this function in various contexts (e.g. social entrepreneurship (Case 10.2), technological entrepreneurship (Case 10.4), and micro-enterprises (Case 11.1)). However, it has not always been so straightforward. The political economist, John Stuart Mill introduced the term 'entrepreneur' into the English language in the mid-nineteenth century. Mill saw that handling the 'exertions of entrepreneurship demanded no ordinary skill' (i.e. distinctive capabilities). Though one person might combine entrepreneurship activities such as providing finance or managing existing businesses, economists needed to make a distinction between these functions:

> *It is to be regretted that this word, in this sense, is not familiar to an English ear. French political economists enjoy a great advantage in being able to speak currently of 'les profits de l'entrepreneur.'* (Mill 1909 [1848]: Chapter 15, note 93)

11.3.3 The disappearing entrepreneur: classical and neoclassical economics

In the late eighteenth and early nineteenth centuries, the first industrial revolution saw a new generation of entrepreneurs taking an increasingly powerful role in the economy, transforming industrial sectors such as manufacturing (e.g. cotton), transport (e.g. canals), and services (e.g. banking):

> *As rulers gradually submitted to constitutional constraints on their power, and property rights became more secure within the nation states, entrepreneurial energy was released at an unprecedented rate.* (Ricketts 2008: 37)

Paradoxically, it was during this period that economists lost track of the distinctive entrepreneurial function that had been identified by pioneering figures such as Richard Cantillon. As one leading economist has noted, 'the strange disappearance of the entrepreneur from the centre of the stage of economic debate has a long history.' (Blaug 2000 [1986]: 77) The story is complicated, but we can isolate two of the more important developments:

- **Classical political economy** The most influential figures of this school, notably Adam Smith, David Ricardo, and Karl Marx, did not separate the entrepreneurial function from that of providing finance. For example, Marx examined the relationship between suppliers of capital and labour (i.e. the 'labour process'), but did not extend his analysis to consider providers of entrepreneurial services. Important exceptions include J.S. Mill, discussed in the previous section, and the French economist, Jean-Baptiste Say (1767–1832), who attempted to reintroduce the entrepreneur into economic theory as a fourth factor of production. Say also put his ideas into practice, setting up a cotton mill in Northern France, which proved to be very profitable.

- **Neoclassical economics** From the late nineteenth century, economics became dominated by the marginal or 'neoclassical' theories of William S. Jevons, Carl Menger, and Leon Walras. Neoclassical thinkers developed a static general equilibrium model of the economy, and attempted to model economic relationships using the formal language of mathematics. The main problem of economics became that of allocating resources in an optimum way:

  > *Given, a certain population, with various needs and powers of production, in possession of certain lands and other sources of material: required, the mode of employing their labour which will maximize the utility of the produce.* (Jevons 1911: 267)

Neoclassical theory proved to be an effective tool for analysing micro-economic phenomena such as price movements and their relationship with changes in supply and demand. It has also been successfully applied within entrepreneurship. For example, Baumol (1990) used it to examine how a fixed supply of entrepreneurial talent is allocated between 'productive', 'unproductive', and 'destructive' activities (Baumol 1990) (Section 15.4). However, as economists began to explore dynamic problems, such as the processes that generate technological innovation (Schumpeter 2004 [1934]) and the growth of firms (Penrose 1995 [1959]), it became clear that neoclassical theory was insufficient:

> [T]he entrepreneur was gradually extruded from economic analysis when economists attempted more and more to emulate the physical sciences by incorporating the mathematical method. Mathematics introduced greater precision to economics, and thereby promised to increase the power of economics to predict. Yet it was a two-edged sword. Its sharp edge cut through the tangled confusion of real-world complexity, making economics more tractable and accelerating its theoretic advance. But its blunt edge hacked away one of the fundamental forces of economic life – the entrepreneur. Because there was not and is not a satisfactory mathematics to deal with the dynamics of economic life, economic analysis evolved by concentrating on comparative statics, and the entrepreneur took on a purely passive, even useless, role. (Hébert and Link 1989: 48)

In the next section, we consider two alternative theoretical perspectives that have shed new light on the entrepreneurial function.

11.3.4 The entrepreneur returns: neo-Austrian and evolutionary economics

During the twentieth century, the entrepreneur returned to mainstream economics by a number of different routes, the most significant influences being **neo-Austrian** and **evolutionary economics**. Though they are often treated as alternative perspectives on the entrepreneurial function, it is useful to see them as complementary:

Neo-Austrian economics This approach derives its name from the home country of its most well-known founding figures, Ludwig von Mises and Frederick Hayek. The tradition remains influential in economics, and is also having an increasing impact on entrepreneurship research (Chiles et al. 2010). Neo-Austrians challenged neoclassical assumptions about resource allocation. They drew attention to the many forms of economic activity that are based on 'local' knowledge, and argued that these seemingly ordinary activities should have a more prominent place in economic theory:

> [T]he shipper who earns his living from using otherwise empty or half-filled journeys of tramp steamers, or the estate agent whose whole knowledge is almost exclusively one of temporary opportunities, or the arbitrageur [i.e. intermediary] who gains from local differences of commodity prices, all are performing eminently useful functions based on special knowledge of circumstances of the fleeting moment not known to others. (Hayek 1945: 522)

Building on the ideas of Cantillon and Say, neo-Austrians argued that exploiting 'special knowledge' represents a distinctive entrepreneurial function. Entrepreneurial profits are earned when people make use of their knowledge (NB this argument contrasts with another influential research strand in economics, in which entrepreneurial profits are a reward for bearing uncertainty (Knight 1921)). Israel Kirzner has refined earlier neo-Austrian ideas, arguing that profits could be attributed to entrepreneurial 'alertness' to previously unidentified opportunities (Kirzner 1979). The typical 'Kirznerian' entrepreneur identifies opportunities to exploit price differentials, typically due to over-supply of products in one location or unsatisfied customer demand in another. By pursuing these opportunities, entrepreneurs bring markets to life, and in the process help to restore equilibrium. As von Mises recognized, these entrepreneurs were also free to make errors, which could have an impact on the economy as well as creating further opportunities for others (Swedberg 2000: 21).

---

 online resource centre 'The Enterprise Culture's Political Roots.'

Evolutionary economics This strand of economics has been primarily concerned with the way that economic systems change over time. As its title suggests, evolutionary theory addresses the three fundamental processes of selection, retention, and variation (or creativity). Evolution in the natural world operates through biological mechanisms and is essentially 'blind' (Dawkins 2006). By contrast, in evolutionary economics these processes are purposeful, being driven by conscious human actions, and entrepreneurs have an obvious role to play. Joseph Schumpeter, one of the leading figures in this tradition, was born in the Austro-Hungarian Empire in the early twentieth century. Though he admired neoclassical theorists, he developed an early ambition to replace it with a more dynamic alternative. Schumpeter's most famous statements about entrepreneurship are taken from Chapter 2 of his book, *The Theory of Economic Development*, which appeared in two German editions (1911 and 1926), and was first published in English in 1934. For Schumpeter, the entrepreneurial function is about 'innovation' (i.e. carrying the new combination into practice). Though it can involve the same people, this task requires an entirely different set of capabilities to 'invention' (e.g. creating a new technology). Innovation is also much more demanding than managing existing activities, where you can rely on established routines and experiences:

> *Carrying out a new plan and acting according to a customary one are things as different as making a road and walking along it.* (Schumpeter 2004 [1934]: 64)

Schumpeter identifies five ways in which innovative entrepreneurial activity creates variety by introducing 'new combinations' of productive means:

> *(1) The introduction of a new good – one with which consumers are not yet familiar – or a new quality of a good; (2) The introduction of a new method of production, that is one not yet tested by experience in the branch of manufacture concerned, which need by no means be founded upon a discovery scientifically new, and can also exist in a new way of handling*

a commodity commercially. (3) The opening of a new market, that is a market into which the particular branch of manufacture of the country in question has not previously entered, whether or not this market has existed before. (4) The conquest of a new source of supply of raw materials or half-manufactured goods, again irrespective of whether this source already exists or whether it has first to be created. (5) The carrying out of the new organization of any industry, like the creation of a monopoly position (for example through trustification) or the breaking up of a monopoly position. (Schumpeter 2004 [1934]: 51–2)

New combinations are important from an evolutionary perspective, because they transform the economic conditions for other entrepreneurs, disrupting existing patterns and creating new opportunities for investment, growth and employment. Researchers working in this evolutionary tradition have since discovered a great deal about the process of economic development, including the ways in which industries tend to rise and fall (Section 14.3). In his later work, *Capitalism, Socialism and Democracy*, Schumpeter describes a characteristic evolutionary pattern of innovation, boom, and recession that has been repeated many times, and which he termed '**creative destruction**':

The opening up of new markets, foreign or domestic, and the organizational development from the craft shop to such concerns as U.S. Steel illustrate the same process of industrial mutation – if I may use that biological term – that incessantly revolutionizes the economic structure from within, incessantly destroying the old one, incessantly creating a new one. This process of Creative Destruction is the essential fact about capitalism. (Schumpeter 2010 [1942]: 83)

These two contrasting perspectives have helped to reinstate entrepreneurship as a key element in economic research and policy-making. The entrepreneurial functions depicted by these researchers are often treated as opposites, with Kirzner's entrepreneur making a profit while moving the market towards equilibrium and Schumpeter's entrepreneur doing the same while creating a new *dis*equilibrium. Technical distinctions of this kind remain important to economists, even though they may be of little interest to the practising entrepreneur (Swedberg 2000: 21). In this particular case, there are signs of a move towards integration (e.g. Kirzner 2008).

Case 11.3 builds on this discussion with an example of economics-based research, which examines knowledge spillover theory (Section 11.2.3) and how entrepreneurial activity influences the development of today's globalized and knowledge-based economies.

Case 11.3 Entrepreneurship in the knowledge economy

This case is based on extracts from a recent study by three leading entrepreneurship scholars, David Audretsch, Max Keilbach, and Erik Lehmann (Audretsch et al. 2006). The case focuses on three themes that are addressed in the book: the role played by entrepreneurship in a modern knowledge-based economy; the sources of entrepreneurial opportunity in such an economy; and the idea of entrepreneurial activity as 'creative construction'.

Entrepreneurship in the knowledge economy

'The role of entrepreneurship in the economy and, in particular, the impact of entrepreneurship on economic growth and employment has evolved considerably since World War II. In the post-war economy, investments in physical capital were the driver of economic growth. Economic activity based on physical capital was most efficiently organized in large-scale operations. In the physical capital economy, there was little room for entrepreneurship and small business, at least not as an engine of economic growth. At best, small firms were tolerated for social and political values, and the ensuing inefficiency associated with small-scale production was endured as the cost of such non-economic goals. As recognition grew, both among scholars and policy-makers that knowledge was also a key factor shaping economic growth, a new set of public policy instruments for generating economic growth became prominent, with a focus on research, intellectual property, and human capital. If anything, the inclusion of knowledge as a factor of production served only to reinforce the view that small firms were anathema to economic growth. Recognition of the model of the knowledge production function seemed to mandate economic organization in large-scale enterprises in the knowledge economy, just as it had in the capital economy. In fact, small firms and entrepreneurship emerged as essential to economic growth in the 1990s. Part of this recognition came from the empirical or policy experience emanating from investments in new knowledge in the absence of entrepreneurship. Much has been made about the so-called European Paradox, wherein high levels of investment in new knowledge exist from private firms as well as public research institutes and universities. Countries such as Sweden rank among the highest in terms of investment in research, at least as measured by the ratio of R & D [i.e. investment in research and development] to GDP. Similarly, levels of human capital and education in Sweden as well as throughout many parts of Europe rank among the highest in the world. Yet growth rates remained stagnant and employment creation sluggish throughout the 1990s and into the new century. [. . .] [A] growing consensus has emerged that investment in new economic knowledge alone will not guarantee economic growth and employment creation. Rather, key institutional mechanisms are a prerequisite for such knowledge investments to become transmitted and transformed into economic knowledge, through the process of spillovers and commercialization. Entrepreneurship has emerged as a driving force of economic growth because it is an important conduit of knowledge spillovers and commercialization. Thus, as knowledge has become more important as a factor of production, knowledge spillovers have also become more important as a source of economic growth. Entrepreneurship takes on new importance in a knowledge economy because it serves as a key mechanism by which knowledge created in one organization becomes commercialized in a new enterprise, thereby contributing to the economic growth, employment, and vitality of the overall economy.' (Audretsch et al. 2006: 33)

The source of entrepreneurial opportunities

'While much has been made about the key role played by the recognition of opportunities in the cognitive process underlying the decision to become an entrepreneur, relatively little has been written about the actual source of such entrepreneurial opportunities. The Knowledge Spillover Theory of Entrepreneurship identifies one source of entrepreneurial opportunities: new knowledge and ideas. In particular, this theory posits that new knowledge and ideas created in one context, such as a research laboratory in a large corporation or a university, but left uncommercialized or not vigorously pursued by the source, generates entrepreneurial opportunities. Thus, in this view, one mechanism for recognizing new opportunities and actually implementing them by starting a new firm involves knowledge spillovers. This implies that the source of knowledge and ideas, and the organization actually making (at least some of) the investments to produce these, is not the same as the organization actually attempting to commercialize and appropriate the value of that knowledge – the new firm. If the use of that knowledge by the entrepreneur does not involve full payment to the firm making the investment that originally produced that knowledge, such as a licence or royalty, then the entrepreneurial act of starting a new firm serves as a mechanism for knowledge spillovers.' (Audretsch et al. 2006: 39)

Entrepreneurship as 'creative construction'

'We would not want to argue that the view of the youthful Schumpeter (2004 [1934]: xxvii) was wrong about "a perennial gale of creative destruction is going through capitalism." However, it does seem that twenty-first century entrepreneurship has more to do with creative construction than with creative destruction. By facilitating the spillover of knowledge investments that might otherwise remain uncommercialized, entrepreneurship takes little away from the incumbent enterprises, but instead creates alternative opportunities for employment. Rather, as we suggested [in Chapter 2], the destruction comes from the side of globalization that presents competitive alternatives to standardized production in high-cost *Standort* [i.e. a specific geographical location]. This destructive element, emanating from globalization, comes with or without entrepreneurship. The exposure of a *Standort* to global competition has less to do with its endowment of entrepreneurship capital and more to do with its traditional source for economic activity. By contrast, the construction comes from an entirely different source: the entrepreneurship capital of that *Standort*. Perhaps because he dealt with a singular closed and unglobalized economy in both his early (1911) and later (1942) writings, Schumpeter did not consider that the destructive force would actually come from opportunities coming from outside of the domestic economy. In contrast, the entrepreneurial opportunities that might not otherwise have been pursued come from within the *Standort*. Thus, rather than serving as a force for destruction of the status quo, entrepreneurship serves as a constructive force for a new economic alternative from knowledge and ideas that otherwise might have not been commercialized. To the individual, the knowledge accessed to reach the entrepreneurial decision is virtually a free good. To the firm or non-profit organization, the knowledge has no *a priori* economic value. Whereas Schumpeter's (2010 [1942]) pronouncement that innovation is becoming routinized may have been correct, the generation of entrepreneurial opportunities and their concomitant assessment by economic agents are anything but routine. Thus, entrepreneurship is a constructive force because it increases the value of knowledge and ideas that might otherwise not be pursued and commercialized.' (Audretsch et al. 2006: 191–2)

Questions

1. How has entrepreneurship changed since the mid-twentieth century?

2. How can knowledge spillovers lead to new entrepreneurial opportunities?

3. What are the practical implications of these arguments for: (a) governments seeking to defend their economies against global competition; (b) entrepreneurs seeking to make use of new knowledge?

Source: Audretsch et al. (2006): extracts reproduced by permission of Oxford University Press.

11.4 **Entrepreneurship as dysfunctional**

11.4.1 **Economically 'unproductive' and 'destructive' enterprise**

Much of the economics literature assumes that entrepreneurship is, by definition 'a good thing'. Research has indicated that increased levels of entrepreneurial activity are associated with positive economic outcomes, including more employment opportunities, less unemployment, lower prices, more rapid technological innovation, and increased rates of economic growth. While there are good reasons for this emphasis, it is also important to consider how entrepreneurial activity can become dysfunctional and inflict damage on the world's economic systems. The global financial crisis of 2007–10 was a recent dramatic example, with serious repercussions for individuals, businesses, and communities around the world (Stiglitz 2010). In a widely cited paper, the US economist and entrepreneurship researcher, William Baumol distinguished between economically 'productive', 'unproductive', and 'destructive' forms of entrepreneurship (Baumol 1990). Productive entrepreneurship has a beneficial impact (e.g. increasing incomes and employment). By contrast, unproductive entrepreneurship (e.g. 'rent-seeking' activities, such as tax avoidance) has negative effects, while destructive entrepreneurship (e.g. organized crime) can undermine an entire economy.

Baumol's historical study explores how entrepreneurial resources have been reallocated between these three roles over the centuries. This is an important, yet relatively under-researched area, which is now attracting the attention of researchers (e.g. Sobel 2009; Minniti 2008; Douhan and Henrekson 2008) and policy-makers (Section 15.3.2 and Case 15.3).

---

 online resource centre 'Unproductive and Destructive Entrepreneurship.'

11.5 **Practical implications**

Economic approaches are important in examining many aspects of entrepreneurship. But what is the practical value of economic research for prospective or practising entrepreneurs, and for others interested in entrepreneurship? Having reviewed a number of sub-fields, we have seen how economics provides insights into both the impacts of entrepreneurial activity and the factors that encourage or constrain it, such as credit rationing. The following examples illustrate how you might apply this knowledge to a new venture:

- **Evidence and patterns** Entrepreneurs can use economic data, such as new firm formation rates and firm survival rates, to guide their decisions in setting up or growing a venture. For example, you might decide to reconsider your ambitions found a new technology-based empire having seen recent data on the failure rate of new firms in that industry sector. If the economic data are more positive, you may also make use of them to support a new venture proposal, demonstrating the attractiveness of your target market or showing how your new organization is responding to recent industry trends.

- **Entrepreneurial finance** Research on the financing of entrepreneurial ventures, including the phenomenon of capital rationing (Case 11.2), is particularly relevant to new start-ups. The findings summarized in this chapter provide an important warning to new entrepreneurs, particularly those who are seeking finance in unfamiliar industry sectors, or who are attempting to fund unproven technologies, product concepts, and business models. On a more positive note, recent research in this area has also highlighted a number of practical techniques that entrepreneurs can use to deal with financial constraints.

- **Economic development** This might seem a rather low priority area for entrepreneurs preoccupied with the practical demands of creating a successful venture. However, it may be worth considering how your venture is contributing to the development of your local town, city, or region. Politicians and public officials can be important gatekeepers and in some situations, demonstrating the broader economic value of your venture (e.g. its capacity to generate local employment and income), could prove worthwhile.

- **Economics and policy-making** Economic perspectives have been particularly influential in policy terms, so it is obvious that the policy-makers need to have a good grounding in economic methods and in the research evidence that it produces. We return to this theme in other Part Two chapters, and Chapter 15 in particular.

Economics has made a major contribution to our understanding of entrepreneurship, but we have also seen some of its limitations. Some of the most influential economic thinkers on entrepreneurship, including Joseph Schumpeter, have recognized the need for **multidisciplinary** approaches. Economists can refine their theories, improve their methods, and make more sense of their evidence by interacting with researchers from other disciplines:

> [E]conomists who study entrepreneurship should in the future begin to borrow a little more freely from other disciplines where appropriate. For example, sociologists can tell us a lot about trust, and the basis for social relationships within teams. While the study of trust is beginning to make itself felt in economics, the economics of entrepreneurship is yet to incorporate it in any serious way. Other examples abound. The key point here is that the economics of entrepreneurship has nothing to lose and much to gain from occasionally looking over the fence to learn from other disciplines. (Parker 2005: 43–4)

In the following Part Two chapters, our task is to climb across this fence in order to examine entrepreneurship from the perspective of other disciplines, including psychology, sociology, geography, history, and policy studies. However, there are also opportunities to revisit economics and to see how these different insights might be combined.

✳ 11.6 Summary

> ➤ Economists have explored entrepreneurial activity from within several distinct traditions. Neoclassical theory has provided limited insights, but there have also been contributions from mainstream economics, neo-Austrians, and evolutionary theorists.

➤ Empirical studies have provided evidence on the relationship between entrepreneurial activity and specific economic indicators, notably employment creation, economic growth, technological innovation, and competitiveness.

➤ Economic theory has helped to clarify our understanding of the entrepreneurial function, but there are many unresolved issues, some of which require the application of non-economic concepts, theories, and evidence.

➤ Researchers have also examined how entrepreneurial activity can generate economically unproductive and destructive outcomes; this research field remains under-developed, but is attracting increasingly interest.

➤ Economic theory and research evidence can have practical value for prospective and practising entrepreneurs, and for policy-makers, particularly when combined with insights from other disciplines.

Case 11.4 Entrepreneurship: theory, networks, history

This case is based on a new book by the economist Professor Mark Casson, *Entrepreneurship: Theory, Networks, History* (Casson 2010). It builds on ideas introduced in his classic work, **The Entrepreneur: An Economic Theory** (Casson 2003 [1982]). Though grounded in economics, the book explores the relationship between entrepreneurship studies and other disciplines, including sociology, social psychology, international relations, management, and business history. As Professor Casson explains, the theory of entrepreneurship set out in the book was originally developed to 'plug a gap' in economic theory, including its capacity to explain how firms and markets are created:

> *Conventional economics, it is often pointed out, is inherently static; even growth is often analysed as a steady-state process. By recognizing the importance of a specific class of people dedicated to the pursuit of change, the study of entrepreneurship transforms static analysis into dynamic analysis. (Casson 2010: 372)*

Entrepreneurship research can also address another fundamental problem in economics. Because it lacks a satisfactory theory of success, conventional theory, 'does not explain fully why certain people are able to derive so much profit from the market process, nor why some small firms grow into successful large firms whilst many others fail' (Casson 2010: 372). In the following extract, Professor Casson introduces the concept of entrepreneurial judgement, and explains how it helps us to address these issues. He begins with a review of the leading traditional (or 'canonical') theories of entrepreneurship.

The theory of entrepreneurship: from Cantillon to Kirzner

It is the function of the entrepreneur that is important – 'an entrepreneur is what an entrepreneur does'. But what does an entrepreneur do? The canonical literature suggests a variety of tasks, including 'high-level' activities like innovation and risk taking, and also 'low level' activities such as spotting opportunities for arbitrage. The theory presented in this book is based on a synthesis of the principal insights set out by the canonical authors on the subject.

Cantillon and risk The term 'entrepreneur' appears to have been introduced into economic theory by Richard Cantillon (1759), an Irish economist of French descent. According to Cantillon, the entrepreneur is a specialist in taking on risk. He 'insures' workers by buying their output for resale before consumers have indicated how much they are willing to pay for it. The workers receive an assured income (in the short run, at least), while the entrepreneur bears the risk caused by price fluctuations in consumer markets.

Knight and uncertainty This idea was refined by the US economist Frank Knight (1921), who distinguished between risk, which is insurable, and uncertainty, which is not. Risk refers to recurrent events whose relative frequency is known from past experience, whilst uncertainty relates to unique events whose probability can only be subjectively estimated. Knight thought that most of the risks relating to production and marketing fall into the latter category. Since business owners cannot insure against these risks, they are left to bear them by themselves. Profit is a reward for bearing this uninsurable risk: it is the reward of the pure entrepreneur. With freedom of entry into industries, profits in one industry can exceed profits in another industry in the long run only if the uncertainties are greater in the more profitable industry – in other words, if the demands on entrepreneurship are greater in that industry.

Schumpeter and the Entrepreneur-Hero Popular notions of entrepreneurship are based on the heroic vision put forward by Joseph A. Schumpeter (2004 [1934]). The entrepreneur is visualized as someone who creates new industries and thereby precipitates major structural changes in the economy. The entrepreneur innovates by carrying out new combinations; he is not a pure inventor, because he adopts the inventions made by others, nor is he a financier, because he relies on bankers to fund his investments. The entrepreneur takes the crucial decision to commit resources to the exploitation of new ideas. An element of calculation is involved, but it is not pure calculation, because not all of the relevant factors can be accurately measured. He is motivated by profit, but not purely by profit: the other motivators include the 'dream and the will to found a private kingdom'; the 'will to conquer: the impulse to fight, to prove oneself superior to others'; and the 'joy of creating'.

Marshall and low-level entrepreneurship Schumpeter was concerned with the heroic or 'high level' kind of entrepreneurship that, historically, has led to the creation of railways, the development of the chemical industry, and the growth of integrated oil companies. A weakness of his analysis is that it leaves little room for the much more common, but no less important, 'low level' entrepreneurship carried on by small firms. Few economic histories nowadays would ignore the important role of small firms in economic development. Alfred Marshall (1919) emphasized their importance and described the role of these firms in some detail, but critically omitted them from his formal analysis of supply and demand. Given the techniques that were available to him, Marshall could only model equilibrium situations, and so could not fit entrepreneurship into his analysis. But he explicitly recognized the importance of low-level entrepreneurship.

The Austrian School and arbitrage The essence of low-level entrepreneurship can be explained by the Austrian approach of Friedrich A. von Hayek (1937) and Israel M. Kirzner (1973). Entrepreneurs are middlemen who provide price quotations as an invitation to trade.

While bureaucrats in a socialist economy have little incentive to discover prices for themselves, entrepreneurs in a market economy are motivated to do so by profit opportunities. They hope to profit by buying cheap and selling dear. In the long run, such differentials, once discovered, generate a profit for the entrepreneur. The difficulty with the Austrian approach is, however, that it isolates the entrepreneur from the organization of routine activities, which is so characteristic of a firm. It fits an individual dealer or speculator far better than it fits a small manufacturer, say, because the latter has to oversee an organization whereas the former does not. For a fuller understanding of entrepreneurship we need to clarify the link between the entrepreneur and the firm.

Judgemental decision-making

The insights of these economists can be synthesized by identifying an entrepreneurial function that is common to all approaches. This is the exercise of judgement in decision-making (Casson 2003 [1982]). Judgement is the ability to come to a sound, defensible decision in the absence of complete information. A middleman who buys before he knows the price at which he can resell must make a judgement about what the future price will be, for instance. Or an arbitrager must make a judgement about where price differentials are most likely to be found, in order to focus his price discovery effort on a suitable segment of the market. An innovator must assess whether a new product will prove attractive to consumers, or whether a new technology will really cut costs by as much as its inventor claims.

Examples of judgemental decisions include the following:

- An opportunity to exploit a new technology has been identified and a quick decision is required in order to pre-empt a rival. The investment is irreversible – i.e. the costs are sunk – so that a mistake cannot be corrected afterwards. The revenue stream is uncertain, and cannot be guaranteed by forward sales of output. Should the investment be undertaken right away?

- A new source of competition has just emerged from a firm in a newly-industrialising country. Should the dominant firm in the industry cut its price, or can it rely upon its existing customers not to switch to the rival firm? Is the rival firm producing more cheaply because of low-cost labour and/or subsidies, about which nothing can be done, or is it using more efficient techniques which ought to be imitated?

Judgemental decisions normally require the synthesis of different types of information. The high-level entrepreneur of the Schumpeterian type, for example, needs to synthesize information about new inventions with information about trends in product demand, and in the prices of raw materials, in order to determine whether an innovation is worthwhile. If the entrepreneur does not possess this information himself then he must know where to acquire it. If some of the information is confidential then it will have to be acquired through personal contact rather than from published sources. The entrepreneur therefore needs to create a network of contacts that can feed him the information that he requires.

A synthesis of information has commercial value only if it relates to a profit opportunity. If everyone recognizes the same opportunity at the same time then profits will be competed away. As rival entrepreneurs bid for up the price of inputs, and the prospect of increased supplies drives output prices down, everyone's profits will disappear. The only beneficiaries will be the customers and the suppliers. Profit opportunities arise on a regular basis when economic conditions are volatile, because the allocation of resources continually needs to be adjusted. In addition, long-term trends such as the accumulation of knowledge, the growth of population, and the depletion of non-renewable resources also create a need for change. When incentives work well, profit is the reward that the entrepreneur obtains for expediting economic adjustments and, in some cases, for making adjustments that might otherwise never occur.

If information were freely available, and could be costlessly processed, then there would be no need for judgement. Every decision would be correctly taken and no mistakes would ever be made. But in practice information is costly. It is time-consuming to make and record observations. Human memory capacity is limited. Interpretative skills are scarce. Above all, communication is an expensive process. It follows that people do not have all the information they need when taking a decision. When decision-makers cannot afford to collect all the information they need, they have to act under uncertainty. But the uncertainty faced by one person may be different from the uncertainty faced by another person. Sources of primary information are highly localized; for example, only people 'on the spot' can directly observe an event. Different people in different places will therefore have different perceptions of any given situation. They may therefore make different decisions. The nature of the decision therefore depends on the identity of the person who makes it. The entrepreneur matters because their judgement of a situation is potentially unique.

Not all information is reliable. The senses may be confused, but the biggest risk relates to information obtained from other people. The other person may be unreliable, or their message may be misunderstood. Alternatively, they may set out deliberately to mislead, so that they can extract more profit from their information for themselves. One person may check their information sources more carefully than another, and therefore stand less chance of being misled. The interpretation of information may differ too. Different people may hold different theories about the way the environment works. As any social scientist knows, it is difficult to test conclusively between rival theories because of data limitations. Thus different theories coexist because of data limitations, leading to different interpretations of similar evidence. In a business context, entrepreneurs may act differently on the basis of similar information because they interpret the situation in different ways (Harper 1996).

If a situation recurs frequently, it is worthwhile investigating it carefully in order to find the theory that fits it best. This theory identifies which information is required to make the correct decision. Arrangements can be made to collect the information on a regular basis, so that it is always to hand when required. Whenever a decision needs to be made, this information is processed using an appropriate decision rule in order to arrive at a correct decision. If some information is very costly to collect, then its costs have to be traded off against its benefits to arrive at the correct decision rule. This rule does not guarantee the correct decision; but it is optimal in economic terms, in the sense that it trades off the risk of a mistake against the saving in information cost.

Once this optimal decision rule is known there is no further need for the entrepreneur. Everyone knows how the decision rule has been specified, and so no reward can be earned by those who take the decision properly. Now consider the opposite case in which no such rule is available. This is likely to involve a novel situation. It either has no precedent, or is so unusual that it never pays to investigate it fully. Nobody knows the correct decision rule, and nobody systematically collects information on the situation. The more complex the situation, the more inadequate the theory is likely to be. There may be no theory at all, or there may be a range of rival theories which it is difficult to choose between. There may be no information, or a surfeit of information, because no one is quite sure what information is relevant and what is not. Matters are even worse if the decision has to be arrived at quickly – for example, because the situation is unstable, and will continue to deteriorate until something is done. This is the kind of situation that calls for the most intensive judgement. To improvise a decision quickly, people have to rely on the theories with which they are already familiar, and the information that they can retrieve from their memory. Differences in theories, combined with differences in memories, lead to differences in decisions. In the intermediate case, the situations are less complex, more relevant information may be available and situations less volatile. But once again, the people with the most relevant theories and the most comprehensive memories will tend to make the best decisions. These are the entrepreneurs – they possess the quality of judgement required to improvise a decision successfully when no agreed decision rule is available. Entrepreneurs – whether at a high or low level – are therefore those who exercise entrepreneurial judgement.

Questions

1. Why it is important for economists to develop a better theory of entrepreneurship?

2. What practical steps can entrepreneurs take to ensure they are capable of: (a) synthesizing different kinds of information effectively; (b) obtaining the most accurate and reliable information; (c) improvising important decisions under intensive time pressure?

3. In what ways (if any) would you expect entrepreneurial judgement to operate differently in social and commercial enterprises?

4. Search business news websites (or other case studies in this book) and identify one example of an entrepreneurial judgement that proved to be correct and one that turned out to be incorrect. How do the explanations given for the different outcomes compare to the arguments presented in this case?

Source: Casson (2010): extract reproduced by permission of Edward Elgar Publishing.

▶ Practical activities

1. Neo-Austrian school researchers have investigated how entrepreneurs identify opportunities arising from disequilibrium in a product or factor market (i.e. a temporary difference in supply and demand of raw materials, intermediate or finished goods and services). Using the illustrations in Section 11.3 as a starting-point, identify three real-world examples. How might you exploit these differences? What practical obstacles do you envisage?

2. Re-read Schumpeter's five cases of 'new combinations' (Section 11.3.4). Identify ONE real-world example of an entrepreneurial venture that is based on each of the types listed, and present as a simple table. If you are unable to identify an example, try to imagine ventures that would fit each description.

3. As an extension of Activity 2, try to identify ONE entrepreneurial venture in each of the following categories: (a) commercial manufacturing businesses; (b) social enterprises involved in manufacturing; (c) commercial service-based businesses; (d) social enterprises providing services.

Discussion topics

1. There is a continuing debate among economists over the role of entrepreneurial activity in generating employment and economic growth. Sometimes there seems to be a tension between what is good for the local economy, and what is in the national interest. Join the debate by arguing either for or against one of the following:
   - Small firms are better for the economy than large corporations.
   - Start-up ventures are better for the economy than established firms.
   - Competition between social enterprises generates more social value than co-operation.

2. Re-read the discussion about 'productive, unproductive and destructive forms of entrepreneurship' (Section 11.4). Are governments justified in taking action to encourage economically productive forms of entrepreneurial activity, and to discourage those that are economically destructive? Do your arguments extend beyond the economic sphere to cover the social and environmental impacts of entrepreneurial activity?

3. Which of the following *economic* functions do you consider to be the most important? Give the reasons for your choice:
   - To create new firms.
   - To 'grow' existing firms.
   - To make firms and industries more innovative.
   - To make firms and industries more competitive.
   - To create new employment.
   - To promote economic regeneration.
   - To generate taxable profits.
   - Other *economic* functions you have identified.

Further reading guide

Economists have written a great deal about particular aspects of entrepreneurship, but much of this literature is inaccessible to non-specialists. There are few concise yet comprehensive overviews of the research literature, which cover its different strands and often contradictory approaches.

Parker (2009) is a comprehensive text reflecting a strongly economics-based perspective on entrepreneurship. Swedberg (2000) and Birley (1998) present a selection of classic articles on entrepreneurship in either full or extracted form. Ricketts (2008) and Parker (2008) review significant contributions by economists. Greene and Storey (2010) is an up-to-date introduction to the substantial literature on the economics of small firms. Early work in the neo-Austrian tradition can be found on the website of the Ludwig von Mises Institute (mises.org) and in the *Quarterly Journal of Austrian Economics*. Chiles et al. (2010) reviews this tradition and its distinctive approach to entrepreneurship. Joseph Schumpeter was a 'larger than life' character – Swedberg (1991) and McCraw (2007) show how his ideas were formed, while Hébert and Link (2006) put his work on economics, entrepreneurship, and innovation into historical perspective. For an insight into evolutionary economics, including work in the Schumpeterian tradition, it is worth looking at articles in the *Journal of Evolutionary Economics*. Major works in this tradition include Nelson and Winter (1982) and North (2005). The chapter includes a brief discussion of 'dysfunctional' forms of entrepreneurship. Several authors have followed up on the classic statement by Baumol (1990), including Minitti (2008) and Sobel (2009). There are relatively few accounts of criminal entrepreneurship, but Mehlum et al. (2003) provides an interesting economic analysis, while Rehn and Talas (2004) and Volkov (1999) address social and institutional contexts.

 # References

Acs, Z.J. and Audretsch, D.B. (eds) (2003) *Handbook of entrepreneurship research: an interdisciplinary survey and introduction.* Dordrecht: Kluwer.

Acs, Z.J. and Storey, D.J. (2004) 'Introduction: entrepreneurship and economic development.' *Regional Studies*, 38, 8: 871–7.

Arrow, K. (2010 [1959]) 'Economic welfare and the allocation of resources for invention in the rate and direction of inventive activity.' Santa Monica CA: Rand Corporation. Available at http://www.randproject.com (accessed 21 April 2010).

Audretsch, D. B., Keilbach, M., and Lehmann, E. (2006) *Entrepreneurship and economic growth.* Oxford: Oxford University Press.

Audretsch, D.B., van der Horst, R., Kwaak, T., and Thurik, R. (2009) 'First section of the annual report on EU small and medium-sized enterprises.' Zoetermeer: EIM Business and Policy Research. Available at http://ec.europa.eu/enterprise/ (accessed 21 April 2010).

Baumol, W. (1990) 'Entrepreneurship: productive, unproductive, and destructive.' *Journal of Political Economy*, 98: 893–921.

Baumol, W. (2002) *Free market innovation machine: analyzing the growth miracle of capitalism.* Princeton: Princeton University Press.

Best, M.H. (2001) *The new competitive advantage: the renewal of American industry.* Oxford: Oxford University Press.

Bibi, M. (2010) Personal communication: interview (15 February).

Birley, S. (ed.) (1998) *Entrepreneurship.* Aldershot: Dartmouth.

Blaug, M. (2000) 'Entrepreneurship before and after Schumpeter.' In R. Swedberg (ed.) op. cit. (76–88).

Blumberg, B.F. and Letterie, W. (2008) 'Business starters and credit rationing.' *Small Business economics*, 30, 2: 187–200.

Blumberg, B.F., Cooper, D.R., and Schindler, P.S. (2008) *Business research methods* (2nd European edition). London: McGraw-Hill.

Cantillon, R.E. (1959 [1755]) *Essai sur la nature du commerce en général* [Essay on the nature of trade in general] (tr. H. Higgs). London: Frank Cass. Available at http://www.econlib.org/library (accessed 21 April 2010).

Casson, M.C. (ed.) (1990) *Entrepreneurship.* Aldershot: Edward Elgar.

Casson, M.C. (1995) *Entrepreneurship and business culture.* Cheltenham: Edward Elgar.

Casson, M.C. (2003 [1982]) *The entrepreneur: an economic theory* (2nd edition). Cheltenham: Edward Elgar.

Casson, M.C. (2010) *Entrepreneurship – theory, networks, history*. Cheltenham: Edward Elgar.

Casson, M., Yeung, B., Basu, A., and Wadeson, N. (2008) *The Oxford handbook of entrepreneurship*. Oxford: Oxford University Press.

Chiles, T.H., Tuggle, C.S., McMullen, J.S., Greening, D.W., and Bierman, L. (2010) 'Dynamic creation: extending the radical Austrian approach to entrepreneurship.' *Organization Studies*, 31, 1: 7–46.

Coase, R.H. (1937) 'The nature of the firm.' *Economica* (New Series), 4: 386–405.

Dawkins, R. (2006) *The blind watchmaker* (new edition). London: Penguin.

Douhan, R. and Henrekson, M (2008) 'Productive and destructive entrepreneurship in a political economy framework.' (IFN Working Paper No. 761). Stockholm: Research Institute of Industrial Economics.

European Commission (2005) 'The new SME definition: user guide and model declaration.' Brussels: European Commission – Enterprise and Industry.

Eurostat (2008) 'Enterprises by size class – overview of SMEs in the EU (Statistics in Focus 31/2008).' Luxembourg: European Commission.

Eurostat (2009) *European business: facts and figures* (2009 edition). Luxembourg: European Commission.

Foray, D. (2004) *The economics of knowledge*. Cambridge MA: MIT Press.

Foss, N.J. (ed.) (1997) *Resources, firms and strategies: a reader in the resource-based theory of the firm*. Oxford: Oxford University Press.

Foss, N.J. and Klein, P.G. (eds) (2002) *Entrepreneurship and the firm: Austrian perspectives on economic organization*. Cheltenham: Edward Elgar.

Greene F.J. and Storey D.J. (2010) *Small Business and Entrepreneurship*. Harlow: Pearson.

Hall, P.A. and Soskice, D. (2001) *Varieties of capitalism: the institutional foundations of comparative advantage*. Oxford: Oxford University Press.

Harper, D.A. (1996) *Entrepreneurship and the market process: an inquiry into the growth of knowledge*. London: Routledge.

Hayek, F.A. (1937) 'Economics and knowledge.' *Economica*, n.s. 4: 33–54.

Hayek, F.A. (1945) 'The use of knowledge in society.' *American Economic Review*, 35: 519–30.

Hébert, R. and Link, A. (1989) 'In search of the meaning of entrepreneurship.' *Small Business Economics*, 1, 39–49.

Hébert, R.F. and Link, A.N. (2006) 'Historical perspectives on the entrepreneur.' *Foundations and Trends in Entrepreneurship*, 2, 4: 261–408.

Henrekson, M. and Douhan, R. (2008) 'The political economy of entrepreneurship: an introduction' (with Robin Douhan). In M. Henrekson and R. Douhan (eds) *The political economy of entrepreneurship, Vol. I and II*. Cheltenham: Edward Elgar.

Jevons, W.S. (1965 [1911]) *The theory of political economy* (4th edition). New York: Sentry Press.

Kashf (2010) Kashf Foundation – 'About us'. Available at http://www.kashf.org (accessed 9 April 2010).

Khanna, T. (2008) *Billions of entrepreneurs: how China and India are reshaping their futures – and yours*. Cambridge MA: Harvard Business School Press.

Khwendo Kor (2010) Khwendo Kor – 'About', 'Projects', 'Achievements'. Available at http://www.khwendokor.org.pk (accessed 9 April 2010).

Kirzner, I.M. (1973) *Competition and entrepreneurship*. Chicago: University of Chicago Press.

Kirzner, I.M. (1979) *Perception, opportunity and profit*. Chicago: University of Chicago Press.

Kirzner, I.M. (2008) 'The alert and creative entrepreneur: a clarification.' (IFN Working Paper No. 760) Stockholm: Research Institute of Industrial Economics.

Knight, F.H. (1921) *Risk, uncertainty and profit*. Boston, MA: Houghton Mifflin.

Lee, S.L., Florida, R. and Acs, Z.J. (2004) 'Creativity and entrepreneurship: a regional analysis of new firm formation.' *Regional Studies*, 38, 8: 879–91.

Loasby, B. (1976) *Choice, complexity and ignorance*. Cambridge: Cambridge University Press.

McCraw, T. (2007) *Prophet of innovation: Joseph Schumpeter and creative destruction*. Cambridge MA: Harvard University Press.

Marshall, A.M. (1919) *Industry and trade*. London: Macmillan.

Mason, C.M. (2009) 'Public policy support for the informal venture capital market in Europe.' *International Small Business Journal*, 27, 5: 536–56.

Mehlum, H., Moene, K, and Torvik, R. (2003) 'Predator or prey?: Parasitic enterprises in economic development.' *European Economic Review*, 47, 2: 275–94

Milgrom, P.R. and Roberts, J. (1992) *Economics of organisation and management*. Englewood Cliffs NJ: Prentice-Hall.

Mill, J.S. (1909 [1848]) *Principles of Political Economy with some of their Applications to Social Philosophy* (7th edition). London: Longmans (note: an electronic version is available at http://www.econlib.org).

Minniti, M. (2008) 'The role of government policy on entrepreneurial activity: productive, unproductive, or destructive?' *Entrepreneurship Theory and Practice,* 32, 5: 779–90.

Nelson, R.R. and Winter, S.G. (1982). *An evolutionary theory of economic change.* Cambridge MA: Harvard University Press.

North, D.C. (2005) *Understanding the process of economic change.* Princeton NJ: Princeton University Press.

Parker, S.C. (2005) 'The economics of entrepreneurship: what we know and what we don't.' *Foundations and Trends in Entrepreneurship.* 1, 1: 1–54

Parker, S.C. (2008) 'Entrepreneurship, self-employment and the labour market.' In Casson, M. et al. (eds) op. cit. (435–60).

Parker, S.C. (2009) *The economics of entrepreneurship.* Cambridge: Cambridge University Press.

Penrose, E. T. (1995 [1959]) *The theory of the growth of the firm* (3rd edition with new Foreword). Oxford: Oxford University Press.

Rehn, A. and Taalas, S. (2004) 'Crime and assumptions in entrepreneurship.' In D. Hjorth and C. Steyaert (eds) *Narrative and discursive approaches in entrepreneurship.* Cheltenham: Edward Elgar (144–59).

Romer, P. (1994) 'The origins of endogenous growth.' *Journal of Economic Perspectives,* 8, 1: 3–22.

Ricketts, M. (2008) 'Theories of entrepreneurship: historical development and critical assessment.' In M. Casson et al. (eds) op. cit. (33–58).

Sauka, A. and Welter, F. (2006) 'Productive, unproductive and destructive entrepreneurship in an advanced transition setting: the example of Latvian small enterprises.' In M. Dowling and J. Schumde (eds) *Empirical entrepreneurship in Europe: new perspectives.* Cheltenham: Edward Elgar (87–111).

Sautet, F.E. (2000) *An entrepreneurial theory of the firm.* London: Routledge.

Schumpeter, J.A. (1939) *Business cycles: a theoretical, historical and statistical analysis of the capitalist process.* New York: McGraw-Hill.

Schumpeter, J.A. (2004 [1934]) *The theory of economic development: an enquiry into profits* (2nd edition, translated by R. Opie). New Brunswick NJ: Transaction.

Schumpeter, J.A. (2010 [1942]) *Capitalism, socialism and democracy.* London: Routledge.

Shackle, G.L.S. (1979) *Imagination and the nature of choice.* Edinburgh: Edinburgh University Press.

Shane, S. (ed.) (2002) *The Foundations of entrepreneurship.* Cheltenham: Edward Elgar.

Smith, A. (2008 [1776]) *Wealth of nations: a selected edition.* Oxford: Oxford University Press.

Sobel, R.S. (2009) 'Testing Baumol: Institutional quality and the productivity of entrepreneurship.' *Journal of Business Venturing,* 23, 6: 641–55.

Solow, R.M. (1994) 'Perspectives on growth theory.' *Journal of Economic Perspectives,* 8, 1: 45–54.

Stiglitz, J. (2010) *Freefall: free markets and the sinking of the global economy.* London: Allen Lane.

Sunday Times (2009) 'A Life in the Day: Maryam Bibi.' London: *Sunday Times.* Available at http://www.timesonline.co.uk (accessed 17 December 2009).

Swedberg, R. (1991) *Joseph A. Schumpeter: his life and work.* Cambridge: Polity.

Swedberg, R. (ed.) (2000) *Entrepreneurship: the social science view.* Oxford: Oxford University Press.

Van de Ven, A.H. (1993) 'The development of an infrastructure for entrepreneurship.' *Journal of Business Venturing,* 8, 3: 211–30.

Van Stel, A.J. and Storey, D.J. (2004) 'The link between firm births and job creation: is there an Upas tree effect?' *Regional Studies,* 38, 8: 893–909.

Volkov, V. (1999) 'Violent entrepreneurship in post-communist Russia.' *Europe-Asia Studies,* 51, 5: 741–54.

Westhead, P. and Wright, M. (eds) (2000) *Advances in entrepreneurship.* Cheltenham: Edward Elgar.

Witt, U. (1999) 'Do entrepreneurs need firms?: a contribution to a missing chapter in Austrian economics.' *Review of Austrian Economics,* 11, 1–2: 99–109.

Witt, U. (1998) 'Imagination and leadership: the neglected dimension of an evolutionary theory of the firm.' *Journal of Economic Behaviour and Organization,* 35, 2: 161–77.

Individual perspectives
Beyond the 'heroic' entrepreneur

The quality of entrepreneurial judgement is only partly a question of the personal characteristics or temperament of the individual.

Edith Penrose, *economist*

I was always interested in investing in people.

Arthur Rock, venture *capitalist*

Learning outcomes

After reading this chapter you should be able to:

➤ Explore individual-level perspectives on entrepreneurship, with a focus on psychological and behavioural studies.

➤ Recognize the contribution of leading psychological and behavioural research approaches (i.e. theory, concepts, methods, and empirical research) to our understanding of entrepreneurship.

➤ Evaluate the kinds of knowledge produced by psychologists and behavioural researchers, and begin to relate it to knowledge obtained through other research perspectives.

➤ Appreciate the influence of psychological and behavioural research on policy and practice.

➤ Apply these insights to your own experiences of entrepreneurship.

Case 12.1 'No more heroes?' Entrepreneurs reflect on their lives

In the following extracts, three entrepreneurs talk about aspects of themselves and their backgrounds. Each of these entrepreneurs has been extremely successful in their own fields. There are some interesting areas of common ground, and many of their achievements could certainly be described as 'heroic', yet none of them fits a simple stereotype of the entrepreneur. Their activities are also varied, ranging across the commercial and social sectors in fields as diverse as executive recruitment in Ireland, helping to build the UK's appetite for Indian foods, and championing the rights of children. The accounts and quotations are drawn from published biographical accounts; full references can be found at the end of the chapter:

Anne Heraty founded the CPL Group, a leading recruitment and human resources consultancy, based in Dublin (www.cpl.ie). CPL is organized into eight specialist recruitment companies, which place 20,000 temporary and contract candidates every year and find permanent jobs for around 9,000 more. In 2006, Anne won Ernst & Young's Entrepreneur of the Year award. She grew up in rural Ireland, where her parents ran a farm, a shop, and a bar. Her father was also the local undertaker: 'My father died when I was 16 and, from that period on, my mother ran the family business on her own, with everyone in the family pitching in to help. My mother was really very passionate about her business. She used to tell us children that we should get good, secure, pensionable jobs, but the fact is that children learn from seeing what their parents do, not from what they say, and what we saw every day was a woman who was driven, excited and passionate about her business, with an incredible work ethic. My mother was the closest I had to a role model in my early years. My first job was in 1986 as a sales executive with Xerox. Xerox offered excellent training, and I learned a great deal, especially about how to sell professionally. I worked in a number of other sales positions, and then I registered with an employment agency, looking for a new opportunity. As it happened, the agency asked me if I would be interested in working in recruitment with them and offered me training in the field. I thought about it and decided to do exactly that. I loved recruitment from the outset and had found the work that I was born to do. After a year and a half, I decided to set up my own business.' (Flannery 2008: 73)

Tony Deep is the co-founder of East End Foods (www.eastendfoods.co.uk). Today, his company employs more than 300 people and is one of the largest importers of Indian spices and condiments into the UK. It was the early 1960s when Tony Deep packed his bags and boarded the plane to Britain. He was just 18, he'd never stepped outside India, and he had a paltry £3 in his pocket. 'I was a "runaway graduate". I turned my back on my studies to come to the UK. My father had lost a lot of money and I felt it was my duty to get a job and revive the family fortunes.' Deep settled in Wolverhampton and started hunting for a job. ('There were no immigration laws back then,' he chuckles.) He did a stint as a cement mixer, then 'shunted trains' for British Rail before signing up for a secretarial course at a local college. 'My teacher thought I was only interested in the programme because there were 25 women in the class,' he says. 'She was shocked when I took the test: I typed 100 words per minute.' It was there that he met Barbara – now his wife – who helped him find a job as a door-to-door salesman, selling eggs to Asian housewives. He started to make a tidy little profit. Chatting to his customers each day, typically about the curries they were preparing for their evening meals, Deep started to realize the potential of the ethnic food trade. He decided to take the plunge and set up his own wholesale business. 'I knew a little bit about Indian food, so I thought, "Why don't I buy some spices from importers and sell them on?"' He convinced his elder brother Trilok, who had just arrived in Britain to train as a barrister, to join him. 'I told him I had a gem of an idea. He wanted to finish his training first, but I used my powers of persuasion and talked him into going into business with me.' So, in 1972, the siblings set up East End Foods. (Pritchard 2008: 25–6)

Jeroo Billimoria founded Childline, a 24-hour helpline and emergency response system for children (www.childlineindia.org.in). Founded in Bombay in 1996, it quickly branched out and currently operates in 83 cities across India, defending the rights of street children, underage labourers, and other children at risk of abuse. In its first 12 years, Childline worked with over 3 million children in need of care and protection. Jeroo grew up in a prominent Bombay family in which the dominant profession was accounting. Her father, Mehervan – an accountant in a manufacturing firm – was cautious and conservative. Her mother, Homai – a social worker who counselled low-income children in public schools – was adventurous and liberal. As an undergraduate, Jeroo studied commerce (i.e. business studies). She was leaning towards a career in accounting but her father's death, when she was 20, caused her to re-evaluate her life plans: 'My father was a very kind man. He felt very strongly that you should focus on giving of yourself. And I found that after his death, despite his being so unwell – he had a heart and lung condition – that he helped many people living on the streets anonymously. We had queues of people who came to pay their respects. Even my mother did not know that he had silently supported these people through the years.' (Bornstein 2004: 74–5)

Points to consider

1. What do these extracts suggest about each person's: (a) personality; (b) motivation; (c) approach to life's practical challenges? Are there any similarities or differences?

2. What else would you want to know, in order to more fully understand their life stories?

3. What lessons would you draw from their stories, in order to help with your own entrepreneurial journey?

Background note Anne Heraty's profile is drawn from a chapter in Pearce Flannery's (2008) book, *Grabbing the oyster: anecdotes and advice from icons of Irish business*. All profits from the sale of that book are being donated to the Irish Childline (www.childline.ie). This project has similar aims to Jeroo Billimoria's, and operates through the Irish Society for the Prevention of Cruelty to Children (ISPCC).

Sources: Bornstein (2004); Flannery (2008); Pritchard (2008).

12.1 **Introduction**

This chapter reviews established research on **entrepreneurship** that takes the individual person as its focus. We look at entrepreneurial personality, cognition, motivation, and learning, highlighting some of the most influential studies and seeing how the field has developed. Our main aims are to indicate the kinds of insights you can gain by studying entrepreneurship at this level of analysis, to consider the challenges that researchers have had to tackle, and to see how far these approaches can help you towards a better understanding of entrepreneurship. The focus on individuals opens up many opportunities to compare the research evidence with your own personal experiences: you will find some suggestions for making these connections in the Practical Activities and Discussion Topics at the end of the chapter.

For most people, 'entrepreneurship' is mainly concerned with the lives of particular entrepreneurs. As we have already seen, entrepreneurship researchers have long recognized that 'the entrepreneur' is only part of a much more complicated story (Section 10.3). However, for the time being, we will also focus our attention on these individuals, and try to find out something more about 'what makes them tick'. In the opening case, we discovered something about the lives of three successful entrepreneurs (Case 11.1). Their stories are compelling, but they also leave us with more questions than answers – for example:

- Do they share some distinctive, 'entrepreneurial' characteristics?
- Were they 'pre-programmed' to act entrepreneurially, or was it a personal choice?
- Do their minds work in different ways from those of other people?
- Can aspiring entrepreneurs learn to be like them?

Science has made great advances over the last 50 years. We now have a fairly detailed understanding of human anatomy, including the complex biological mechanisms that enable us to function. Geneticists have unravelled the mysteries of the DNA sequence, and medical technologies enable specialists to track activities within the human brain. Much has been achieved, yet despite this, we are still struggling to understand human actions, including those that we might describe as 'entrepreneurial'. So what can we say about entrepreneurship at an individual level? In order to answer this question, we have structured the rest of the chapter as a series of steps, rather in the style of a clinical investigation. Section 12.2 provides a critical review of the extensive body of research that has attempted to identify entrepreneurial personality characteristics. Section 12.3 is concerned with research on **entrepreneurial cognition**, or ways of thinking, with a particular focus on cognitive biases, opportunity recognition, and creativity. Section 12.4 builds on the preceding sections with a review of **entrepreneurial learning** research. In Section 12.5, we conclude by drawing out some practical implications. Given the individual focus of the chapter, there is also an opportunity for you to reflect on the ideas discussed, and the implications for your own entrepreneurial journey.

12.2 In search of the entrepreneurial individual

12.2.1 Isolating personality 'traits' or characteristics

A great deal of effort has been put into searching for the entrepreneurial individual. Most of this research has focused on the make-up of peoples' minds rather than their bodies. This seems surprising, particularly given that: (a) there is a close connection between mental and physical well-being; and (b) the lives of entrepreneurs can be both mentally and physically demanding.

In fact, very little academic work has been published on either the physiology or the physical health of individual entrepreneurs. A few recent studies have investigated how biological mechanisms, including body chemistry and genetics, might influence entrepreneurial behaviour. Though potentially interesting, these research strands are still in their infancy (White et al. 2006; Nicolaou and Shane 2009).

ⓤ **online resource centre** 'Do You Have the Body of an Entrepreneur?'

By contrast, there is a long history of psychological studies that have attempted to isolate the personality 'traits' or characteristics of entrepreneurs. This work forms part of a much larger tradition of personality research, which developed from the mid-twentieth century. In entrepreneurship, it developed around the observation that certain personality characteristics, such as risk-taking and need for achievement, might influence entrepreneurial performance (e.g. McClelland 1961; Brockhaus 1980). It would be very useful if you could identify the ingredients of a successful entrepreneur. As one of our opening quotations suggests, investors are often as interested in the people as they are in their venture. The 'entrepreneurial personality' is a compelling idea that is also supported by anecdotal evidence. For example, most of us can think of an individual who stands out as being particularly 'entrepreneurial', and we could probably point to several ways in which this person is distinctive. Figure 12.1 summarizes six of the characteristics that are most commonly associated with entrepreneurship. Can you identify examples of 'real-world' entrepreneurs who display one or more of these characteristics?

Figure 12.1 Individual-level entrepreneurial characteristics

Characteristic	Background and commentary	Useful references
Need for achievement	McClelland argued that people with high need for achievement (NAch) scores are attracted to open-ended entrepreneurial situations because they provided an opportunity to satisfy this need. It has become one of the best-known personality characteristics. It suggests intrinsic motivations for engaging in entrepreneurial activity. For example, people are motivated by the prospect of making a difference, or having a tangible impact of some kind. Modified versions of the NAch concept have been supported in subsequent empirical studies.	McClelland (1961), Miner et al. (1994)
Over-optimism	Another popular image of the entrepreneur is of someone who generally 'looks on the bright side', or makes positive evaluations of the future. As with locus of control and risk-taking propensity, much depends on the context in which an individual is asked to make an assessment. Empirical studies have detected evidence of entrepreneurs being over-optimistic about the prospects of their own ventures, but this does not demonstrate that over-optimism is a settled personality characteristic. More recent work on entrepreneurial cognition has provided useful insights into the relationship between a person's perceptions and the assessments they make.	Cooper et al. (1988), Hmieleski and Baron (2009)

(continued)

Risk-taking propensity	Frank Knight distinguished between risk and uncertainty, the latter characterizing many entrepreneurial decision-making situations (Section 11.3). In popular imagery, entrepreneurs are big 'risk-takers', but the belief in this personality characteristic is not supported by the research evidence. Studies have revealed a much more complex picture, in which the degree of risk-taking (or tolerance of uncertainty) depends on a variety of factors, relating to the individual (e.g. age, educational level, prior experience, cognitive biases) and to the situation in which the decision is being made.	Knight (1921), Kirzner (1979), Brockhaus (1980)
Desire for autonomy	There is some evidence that entrepreneurs, defined in occupational terms as owner-managers, value their autonomy and are resistant to external forms of control in comparison to other occupational groups. However, there is a paradoxical element to the desire for autonomy. For both owner-managers and social entrepreneurs, wanting to retain personal control becomes a barrier to the further growth of the organization. Prospective entrepreneurs may be motivated by a desire for autonomy, but this desire may also develop as a product of the experience of setting up a new venture, or of taking control of an existing organisation.	Caird (1991), Cromie (2000)
Locus of control	This concept described a person's perception of whether achieving outcomes or goals, was under their own control, or subject to external factors. In other words, 'do you make things happen in the world?' (i.e. internal locus of control), or, 'do things happen to you?' (i.e. external locus of control). Empirical testing of the concept produced inconclusive results, with some studies showing no significant differences between populations of entrepreneurs and managers. Locus of control has largely been superseded by more sophisticated concepts, notably 'self-efficacy' (Section 12.3).	Rotter (1966), Sexton and Bowman-Upton (1985), Furnham and Steele (1993)
Creativity	Successful entrepreneurs are often seen as having a distinctively creative approach to problem-solving, sometimes identified informally as 'lateral thinking', or 'thinking outside the box'. However, there is no necessary relationship between individual creativity and the success of an entrepreneurial venture. It is also evident that people can learn to become more creative, or possibly to recover an inherent creativity that has been suppressed. In practical situations (e.g. in a high technology venture), creative and entrepreneurial roles are generally shared among the members of a team. Cognitive science is now enhancing our understanding of creativity and its role in entrepreneurial activity (Section 12.3).	Whiting (1988), Amabile (1997), Ward (2004)

Characteristics-based approaches are still widely used by practitioners, teachers, and researchers. One of the commonest applications is online tests designed to diagnose or evaluate entrepreneurial potential (Practical activity 1). However, despite their considerable popularity, these approaches have become controversial, with methodologies and findings being challenged. In order to assess the value and relevance of these approaches, it is important to bear in mind three underlying assumptions. Firstly, that some individuals possess psychological characteristics that can be associated with entrepreneurial behaviour, either in the present or in the future (e.g. Carland et al. 1984). Secondly, that the characteristics are relatively stable (over time) and consistent (across different social settings). Thirdly, that researchers are able to isolate the relevant characteristics from other aspects of an individual's personality, and from the context in which they are operating. In the next section, we review the current state of play.

12.2.2 **Entrepreneurial characteristics: limitations and applications**

Arguments over the uses and limitations of characteristics-based approaches date back over more than two decades (e.g. Gartner 1989a, 1989b; Caird 1993). The main criticisms are summarized in the following review:

> *Definitional and methodological problems associated with these past psychological studies, such as non-comparable samples, bias toward successful entrepreneurs, and the possibility that observed entrepreneurial traits are* the product *of entrepreneurial experience, make it difficult to interpret the results. Furthermore, at a more fundamental level, it can be argued that the wide variations among entrepreneurs make any attempt to develop a standard psychological profile futile.* (Low and Macmillan 1988: 148)

Given the continuing interest in entrepreneurial personality, it is worth considering these criticisms in more detail. Firstly, there are problems in defining and operationalizing the concept of personality characteristics. Researchers have identified a large number of characteristics that *might* be associated with entrepreneurial behaviour but the causal relationships remain unclear. Taking 'desire for autonomy' as an example, a person may be content to take orders at one point in time (e.g. while learning a new trade), but require more autonomy at another point (e.g. once they are qualified, or have experienced a more independent way of life). In addition, it is difficult to establish a causal link between individual-level characteristics and outcomes at an organizational level. At an anecdotal level, it is easy to identify examples of successful social and commercial ventures founded by individuals who lack one (or more) of the **entrepreneurial characteristics** listed in Figure 12.1. There are plenty of people who possess many entrepreneurial characteristics, yet prove to be either unsuccessful entrepreneurs, or who apply their talents in other ways. Secondly, there are problems with the measurement of entrepreneurship as an outcome, whether this takes the form of actual behaviours, intentions, or potential. Observed behaviours are themselves a product of multiple factors, so that founding a new venture, for example, can only be explained in terms of an interaction involving a number of people in a particular context. This may be why research has shown that possessing entrepreneurial attitudes at one point in time is not, in isolation, a good predictor of a person subsequently engaging in entrepreneurial behaviours such as starting or growing a business. Lastly, much of the characteristics literature has adopted what we have termed a 'narrow' definition of entrepreneurship (Section 1.2), as the act of founding and controlling an independent, commercial business venture. There appears to be an opportunity here for researchers to consider how to operationalize a 'broader' definition of entrepreneurial behaviour that is capable of: (a) embracing the activities of social and corporate entrepreneurs; and (b) moving beyond the individual level to address the collective phenomena such entrepreneurial behaviour within a new venture team.

Researchers have continued to examine how the psychological characteristics of entrepreneurs may be related to the success, or otherwise, of their ventures (e.g. Begley and Boyd 1987; Miner et al. 1994; Miner 1997; Rauch and Frese 2007). However, following recent advances in psychology, there have been calls for entrepreneurship scholars to update the way they interpret personality. Many psychologists now agree that there are five fundamental personality dimensions, commonly referred to as the 'five-factor model' (FFM) (Goldberg 1993; Wiggins 1996). Taking each of these factors in turn, you might expect a person who is at the 'higher' end of the scale to display the following typical dispositions, and someone who is at the 'lower' end to display the opposite:

1. **Extraversion**   tends to be outgoing, sociable, and optimistic.

2. **Neuroticism**   tends to be anxious, emotionally unstable, prone to depression.

3. **Agreeableness**   is easy to get on with, widely liked by other people.

4. **Conscientiousness**   is hard-working, reliable, conformist.

5. **Openness to experience**   adopts liberal, innovative approaches to problems.

Psychologists suggest that each of these broad dimensions of personality is made up of a number of narrower traits (e.g. anxiety or gregariousness), although their exact number and nature is still hotly debated. In another important refinement of the theory, personality traits are now generally seen as 'potentialities' or 'basic tendencies' which may (or may not) be realized in the lives of particular individuals (McCrae and Costa 1996: 69). Though you might expect to inherit certain tendencies, these remain open to a variety of other influences during the course of your life. For example, aspects of your personality may be modified as a result of early childhood experiences. As a result, the FFM can only provide part of the explanation for human behaviour:

> *In itself FFM does not explain how social roles are forged in to a personal identity, or how the flow of behaviour is organised, or how attitudes are formed and changed.* (McCrae and Costa 1996: 65)

In other words, while 'the big five' factors may be influential, they are only one component in a more complex and dynamic process, which also involves interactions between the factors. The debate over personality continues to rage: is it really 'set in plaster' by the age of 30, or can it continue to change into adulthood (e.g. Srivastava et al. 2003). Though these arguments are unresolved, we can conclude that personality is only one factor amongst many that contribute to an individual's entrepreneurial behaviour.

 online resource center 'Creating Entrepreneurial Personality: A Dynamic Process?'

What are the implications of these developments for our understanding of the entrepreneurial individual? Psychological research remains important, and there are signs that the FFM framework is being applied more widely in entrepreneurship research (e.g. Ciavarella et al. 2004). However, given the complex causal relationships involved, the search for a stable, universal, and defining set of entrepreneurial traits looks increasingly like a 'dead end' (Davidsson et al. 2001: 12). By contrast, there is still a great deal to discover about the processes that help to develop an individual's entrepreneurial potential, and those that convert into concrete behaviours. Studying these processes requires alternative approaches. Our starting point is cognitive science research (Section 12.3).

12.3 **Entrepreneurial cognition**

12.3.1 **Three research areas in cognitive science**

Research on human cognition is concerned with the way individuals think (i.e. their perceptions, memory and mental processes), and its effect on their behaviour. As Mitchell et al. (2002: 96) explain, 'cognitive psychology emerged to help explain the mental processes that occur within individuals as they interact with other people and the environment around them.' So, while the focus remains at the individual level, there is also a social dimension. This research theme has become very popular in the last decade, and now comprises several sub-fields, including social cognition theory. The research is important to entrepreneurship researchers because it fills some of the gaps we have already identified between individual-level factors and **entrepreneurial activity**:

> Research in entrepreneurial cognition has investigated a very broad range of issues and topics and has generally found that cognitive factors play an important role in key aspects of the entrepreneurial process. (Baron and Ward 2004: 557)

Figure 12.2 summarizes some of the key themes in cognitive research on entrepreneurship; as with previous listings, there is some overlap between the themes (e.g. **self-efficacy** and learning). Given the breadth of the field, we have selected three themes for more detailed discussion, each of which is particularly relevant to the task of creating a new entrepreneurial venture: perceptions of **entrepreneurial opportunity** (Section 12.3.2), cognitive biases (Section 12.3.3), and **entrepreneurial creativity** (Section 12.3.4).

Figure 12.2 Entrepreneurial cognition: summary of key themes

Research theme	Commentary
Differences in cognition	Are there measurable differences between the cognition of entrepreneurial individuals and others, both in terms of content (i.e. what they think about) and process (i.e. how they think)?
Opportunity perception	How does the cognition of entrepreneurial individuals help them to be more alert to opportunities and/or more capable of exploiting them?
Cognitive biases	What kinds of cognitive biases (i.e. misinterpretations of evidence) are associated with entrepreneurial decision-making?
Creativity	How does the cognition of entrepreneurial individuals help them to be more creative, both in terms of 'creating opportunities' and in addressing entrepreneurial challenges (e.g. raising finance, gaining legitimacy)?
Perceived self-efficacy	How does a person's belief in their capacity to achieve a specific performance (e.g. setting up a new venture) influence their behaviour?
Developmental cognition	How does a person's cognition affect the way that they learn, and how can formal approaches to learning take these factors into account?

Sources: Bandura (1995); Baron and Ward (2004); Chia (2008); Mitchell et al. (2002); Simon and Houghton (2002).

12.3.2 **Perceiving entrepreneurial opportunity**

When students are considering options for a new venture creation assignment, there are often a few individuals who quickly identify several brilliant ideas, while many others struggle to find an interesting opportunity. Entrepreneurs are sometimes thought to be more 'alert' to potential opportunities than other people (Kirzner 1979) (Section 11.3). If so, how is it that their 'antennae' are pointing in the right direction, and tuned to the right frequency, to detect these messages (Shapero 1985)? Probing the subject a little deeper, there are several factors that can help to explain these differences:

- **Local knowledge** From Hayek, we are aware that the knowledge needed to identify and to create entrepreneurial opportunities is often highly localized (Section 11.3).

- **Modes of learning** Cognitive science research suggests that people learn in different ways from their experiences, and that these differences can influence how opportunities are identified and exploited (Corbett 2005).

- **Resources and capabilities** We are more able to recognize opportunities if they relate to our existing 'bundle' of resources and capabilities (Penrose 1995 [1959]).

Cognitive researchers have also looked at the mental processes involved in deciding to pursue an opportunity. Here, the concept of 'self-efficacy' (Bandura 1995), meaning a person's subjective perception that they are able to achieve a particular task, plays a significant role:

> *People with high self-efficacy believe themselves capable of successfully taking adaptive action as challenges unfold. They tend to choose to undertake more challenging tasks, and are less likely to be deterred from them.* (Wadeson 2008: 99)

There is a clear connection between perceived self-efficacy and the likelihood of succeeding in a task. However, a high level of perceived self-efficacy can also be problematic since it, 'carries the risk of over-optimism, and of escalating commitments to failing courses of action.' (Wadeson 2008: 99)

12.3.3 **Cognitive biases**

Recent work in this tradition suggests that entrepreneurs' perceptions of opportunities are often distorted by cognitive biases (Licht and Siegel 2008; Wadeson 2008). For example, cognitive research has challenged the conventional view of entrepreneurs as risk-takers:

> *Rather than risk-taking, perhaps the characteristics observed and reported in the entrepreneurship literature are actually the result of systematic differences in cognitive processes.* (Palich and Bagby 1995: 428)

In other words, entrepreneurs are not necessarily predisposed to take bigger risks. For example, imagine that two people are confronted with information from the outside world. The information is similar but their minds process it in distinctive ways. As a result, even though these people might have a similar propensity to *take* risks, they do not *perceive* risk in the same way. As a result, their decisions, and their behaviours, may differ. Several cognitive biases have been identified, which might help to explain this outcome in the context of entrepreneurial decision-making. These include over-optimism, a belief in the 'law of small numbers', an illusion of control, and reasoning by analogy (Simon and Houghton 2002). We have added practical examples that may be familiar to anyone following the new venture creation activity in Part One of this book:

- **Belief in the 'law of small numbers'** where a person relies on a limited amount of information in order to make assumptions about a much larger population (e.g. you might assume that there is demand for your product or service because a few friends tell you it is a good idea).

- **Over-optimism** where a person faced with an uncertain outcome assumes that it will be more positive than is suggested by the available evidence (e.g. you might over-estimate potential demand for your product or underestimate the response of competitors); the law of small numbers can reinforce these over-optimistic assessments.

- **Illusion of control** where a person places too much emphasis on the extent to which outcomes can be determined as a result of exercising their own skills and abilities (e.g. you assume that your personal powers of persuasion can win over a sceptical financier); this cognitive bias can be seen as showing the limits of self-efficacy (Bandura 1995).

- **Reasoning by analogy** when a person confronted by an unfamiliar situation tries to make sense of it by comparing to a familiar one, based on your existing knowledge (e.g. you promote your **social enterprise** to an entirely new kind of customer using the same approach that you used for your original market); this can lead you to ignore more effective, and sometimes creative, solutions obtained from external and less familiar sources.

What are the practical implications? The researchers conclude that by identifying the more common cognitive biases, entrepreneurs (and those who work with them) can be better prepared, and take the necessary actions to avoid making costly mistakes:

> *Although most entrepreneurs are likely to report that they are constantly seeking out everything and anything that could pertain to their interests, in truth, no one can even begin to be exhaustive in information collection. Sensitizing the entrepreneurs to the need to search for different sources of data may mitigate the effects of a particular bias. For example, entrepreneurs may need to invest more time reading statistical information, rather than talking to a few individuals, to minimize their belief in the law of small numbers.* (Simon and Houghton 2002: 118)

12.3.4 Entrepreneurial creativity

One of the most interesting areas of cognitive science is that dealing with human creativity. Entrepreneurial activity is inherently creative, but the issue of creativity is relatively unexplored, with many questions remaining. For example: How do entrepreneurs generate and develop new ideas? Why is so much entrepreneurial activity successful yet seemingly unoriginal? How can we encourage more creative forms of **enterprise** that are capable of addressing the many economic, social, and environmental challenges of the twenty-first century? Cognitive researchers are beginning to explore how we might pursue these questions:

> *Clearly, humans have the capacity to move beyond what currently exists to generate and implement new ideas. It is also clear, however, that people's attempts at creativity often reveal unnecessarily limited thinking.* (Ward 2004: 175)

One of the great paradoxes of creativity is that new ideas do not appear from nowhere – they have to come out of a person's existing knowledge. How, then, can novel ideas emerge? As cognitive researchers have suggested, there are several processes that enable creativity. We will review these briefly, and illustrate them with practical examples:

- **Combining concepts** This is perhaps the most obvious mechanism for creating new ideas, and it is well-known to entrepreneurship researchers from the work of Schumpeter (Section 11.3). You simply take two (or more) existing concepts and put them together; the resulting combination may have 'emergent features' (i.e. properties that go beyond what was available from its component parts). For example, when people had the idea of combining a surf board and a sailing dinghy, they created an entirely new sport: windsurfing. In a similar creative process, people combined skateboards and skis to produce snowboarding and a distinctive fashion culture that developed around it.

- **Analogical reasoning** We discussed this process in the previous section (Section 12.3.3) as a possible source of cognitive bias, due to an over-reliance on familiar ideas and approaches. However, people do use analogies with familiar objects as a source of creativity, often with dramatic results. For example, in the world of science, Ernest Rutherford adopted the image of the solar system as a model for explaining the structure of the hydrogen atom (Ward 2004: 180). Similarly, in an entrepreneurial setting, Gordon Roddick, John Bird, and colleagues took a very familiar idea, of selling magazines on street corners, and re-applied it to an entirely different context, that of homelessness in urban centres. The Big Issue Foundation is the concrete outcome of a creative idea, based on analogical reasoning, which was converted into a sustainable social enterprise (www.bigissue.com).

Are there some practical lessons that we can draw to enhance our creative thinking? Ward (2004) highlights one potentially useful approach. He points out that creative ideas tend to arise when people retrieve their examples at a more *abstract* level. Chia (2008) makes a related point, arguing that entrepreneurial creativity can be a product of 'peripheral vision', where people look beyond the immediate and obvious, avoid jumping to quick conclusions, and allow themselves to attend to less obvious ideas. In the following case, we explore the practical implications of these insights, by reviewing two examples of creative thinking (Case 12.2).

Case 12.2 Fuzzy logic? Creative thinking and new venture creation

This case comprises two stories of how an individual's creative thinking has led to entirely new products and businesses. Further examples and practical advice on creative thinking can be found on the online resource centre and in Chapter 3 (Section 3.3).

online resource centre 'Enterpreneurship and Creativity'

A life-saving innovation inspired by a cat

What kind of technological product could you devise that was inspired by the average domestic cat? If your thinking remained at a concrete (or specific) level, you might consider things like automatic cat flaps, odour-free litter trays, or electronic name tags. Percy Shaw's approach was more abstract, and the results were far more significant. One winter night he was driving home on an unlit road, and finding it hard to find his way. Then he noticed a cat standing at the side of the road, and was struck by the way that the car lights reflected from its eyes, making the animal stand out clearly in the darkness. Percy was a road engineer. He took this abstract idea – the reflective properties of a cat's eye – and re-applied it in order to make unlit roads safer. He designed a robust reflector that could be produced in large numbers and installed along the white lines in the centre of the road. Having patented his invention in 1934, Percy set up a company to develop the 'Catseye'®. The company is still in business and the product has helped to save countless lives around the world (www.percyshawcatseyes.com).

A popular product inspired by industrial waste

It is the Second World War, and you are living on a farm in the south-east of England making gaskets for use on tanks and other military vehicles. Some local women are working with you, cutting up thick layers of felt to make the gaskets. What would you do with all the off-cuts? Lois Allen was a designer who had studied fashion in Paris in the 1920s. She had the idea of using the off-cuts to entertain children in a crèche that the women had organized. She used the back of a table mat as a board and encouraged the children to create their own pictures by attaching the pieces of felt. After the war, Lois began to manufacture the product commercially. 'Fuzzy Felt'® became one of the UK's favourite toys, enjoyed by generations of children, and it remains popular to the present day (www. http://www.toybrokers.co.uk).

Questions

1. How were these creative ideas, and others you have identified, turned into new ventures? Analyse the accounts using the concepts discussed in Section 12.3.4.

2. What additional questions would you like to ask, in order to understand more about the creativity displayed in this account?

3. How important is it for an individual entrepreneur to demonstrate this kind of creativity?

Of course, there can be disadvantages to creativity. Many entrepreneurial ventures have failed because their ideas were either too unrealistic or simply ahead of their time. In addition, the uncontrolled exercise of creative thinking has sometimes had disastrous consequences. For example, creative thinking by specialists working in the financial **markets** resulted in a series of technical **innovations** in the way that debt was traded. These new practices de-stabilized the system and sparked the global financial crisis of 2007–10 (Section 11.4).

12.4 Entrepreneurial learning and entrepreneurship education

12.4.1 'Learning the ropes': can you learn how to be an entrepreneur?

Philippe Petit, the French high-wire artist, became famous – or perhaps infamous – for walking between the bell towers of Notre Dame, and subsequently between the Twin Towers of the World Trade Center. Petit says that he began by teaching himself the standard techniques, but then abandoned most of them in order to develop his own distinctive technique. There is a similar paradox in entrepreneurship. You might be able to learn many of the practices that we associate with successful entrepreneurship, but how do you convert this learning into practice? As a starting point, we need to recognize that learning can be particularly difficult when you are actually engaged in an entrepreneurial venture. The authors of a recent study of technological entrepreneurship have highlighted three powerful reasons for this (Ravasi and Turati 2005: 138):

- **Ambiguity** Entrepreneurs may be seeking solutions to ill-defined problems, using prototype technologies, or trying to guess which opportunities prove fruitful.

- **Multiple actors** Entrepreneurs need to secure contributions (e.g. of knowledge, skills, resources) from many different people, within and beyond their immediate team.

- **Constraints** Entrepreneurial ventures are often short of money, the entrepreneur's time is limited, and it is not possible to pay sufficient attention to all areas.

Given these obstacles, how can people 'learn' to act entrepreneurially? And if each situation has its own unique, open-ended challenges, how can entrepreneurial learning be transferred from one setting to another? The rapidly expanding literatures on entrepreneurial learning and entrepreneurship education are generating many interesting insights into these questions (e.g. Neary and Parker 2004; Kuratko 2005; Pittaway and Cope 2007). In the following sections we revisit our earlier discussion of the entrepreneurial learning cycle (Section 1.3), by examining the three most significant vehicles for entrepreneurial learning:

- Formal learning approaches associated with entrepreneurship education in schools, colleges, and universities (Section 12.4.2);

- Informal learning that takes place through direct exposure to role models and mentors (Section 12.4.3);

- The relatively neglected yet vital topic of how entrepreneurs learn from their own challenges, mistakes, setbacks, and failures (Section 12.4.4).

12.4.2 Formal learning: the role of entrepreneurship education

You often hear highly successful entrepreneurs arguing that people cannot 'learn' to act entrepreneurially (i.e. they subscribe to the view that entrepreneurs are 'born' not 'made'). In any field of activity (e.g. football, music, art), there are always a few exceptionally talented individuals, and it is clearly not possible for the rest of us to match their levels of performance, however many lessons we take. But even superstars can benefit from formal education. Returning to our previous examples, a few really great footballers, musicians, and artists are largely self-taught, but most achieved their greatness after a long apprenticeship. While it is unlikely that many of today's most successful entrepreneurs took a formal course in entrepreneurship, most acknowledge that they benefited from informal learning, often obtained through influential figures encountered during their upbringing (Section 12.2.3). More importantly, if we look away from the exceptional few, there is a much larger group of people that can benefit from entrepreneurship education. There is some evidence that educational courses, if properly structured, can help to develop and enhance entrepreneurial skills and attitudes (e.g. Binks 2005; NIRAS 2008). Formal education can, in effect, 'fill the gap' for those whose lives have not provided more informal entrepreneurial learning experiences. Structured courses of study can provide the practical skills, knowledge, and understanding that people need in order to become more effective, and possibly more reflective, as they embark on an entrepreneurial career. For example, the School for Social Entrepreneurs works with people wanting to set up social enterprises (www.sse.org.uk). Education can also help others who do not see themselves as 'entrepreneurs' to gain a better understanding. These include: scientists, engineers, or artists who may find themselves part of an **entrepreneurial team** (Section 4.2); marketing, operations, or finance professionals providing services to entrepreneurial ventures (Chapters 5, 6, 7, and 8); and policy-makers seeking to encourage new enterprises (Section 15.1). There is still a great deal of ignorance and misunderstanding surrounding entrepreneurship in its various forms. Tackling this is vital if societies are to realize their entrepreneurial potential fully, and to find ways of guiding it towards more socially and environmentally productive ends.

There is now considerable interest in entrepreneurship education, extending from school to university level. Recent publications have highlighted the fact that entrepreneurship courses are already well established in some institutions (e.g. business schools), though under-represented in others (NIRAS 2008). Formal educational initiatives need to take account of students' motivations and learning styles (e.g. Gibb 2002; Souitaris et al. 2007). The policy implications are discussed further in the final chapter (Section 15.4).

12.4.3 **Learning from others: role models and mentors**

People do not exist in a vacuum. Our beliefs, ideas, and ways of thinking are influenced by those around us, through various forms of persuasive communication and argument (Ajzen 1991: Blundel and Ippolito 2008). In the case of entrepreneurship, this kind of interaction is likely to affect people's attitudes towards the kinds of ventures they want to create, the way they approach the task and their expectations about how much it should grow (e.g. Wiklund et al. 2003). One of the most powerful influences is that exerted, often over extended periods of time, by the members of an entrepreneurial family firm:

> [A]t the level of the individual firm, shared family experience leads to shared understandings and perceptions which shape the evolution of the firm. This is not the same as saying that the development of family firms is in some way pre-determined. Instead history matters in the change and innovation process as it affects choices and informs development. (Howorth et al. 2008: 230)

Anne Heraty, one of the entrepreneurs featured in the opening case study, highlighted the way her mother became a powerful role model (Case 12.1). Anne reflects that, as a child, it was her mother's behaviour rather than her advice that proved decisive (i.e. she acquired her mother's passion for her business, and her work ethic, but disregarded her idea of going into a job that was secure and which had a good pension scheme). An entrepreneur's ethical practices can also be learned from mentors and role models, including family members and others in their social circle. For example, religious beliefs and practices can have an important influence on how a person acts entrepreneurially (e.g. Spence 2000; Valliere 2008).

In summary, it is clear that an individual's entrepreneurial self-identity, attitudes, and ways of thinking are not set in stone. To varying degrees, they remain open to the influence of other people, and can be modified by circumstances. We return to this theme in the next chapter, in a discussion of 'relational learning' (Case 13.3).

12.4.4 Learning from adversity: challenges, mistakes, setbacks and failures

Entrepreneurial learning can also occur as people deal with emerging challenges, mistakes, setbacks, and failures. All of us encounter adversity during our lifetimes. It can range in intensity from the superficial (e.g. losing your car keys), to the profound (e.g. dealing with the loss of a close relative or friend). Entrepreneurial activity is characterized by a whole series of challenges, which can begin to seem insurmountable. Some of these are inevitable. For example, it is always going to be difficult to convince people about a new technology, particularly when your team lacks a 'track record'. Even when things are going well, entrepreneurs often face hostility from vested interests, along with usual competitive pressures. Other challenges arise as a result of making judgements under conditions of uncertainty, and sometimes getting it wrong. So is there a distinctively 'entrepreneurial' approach to the problems that are bound to come your way? When it comes to making mistakes, many successful entrepreneurs would echo this insightful comment:

> With respect to mistakes made in business, my only advice is that you've just got to learn from them and move on quickly. Anyone who wants to run their own business has to get comfortable with the reality that they are going to make mistakes and even, at times, to experience failure. I learn as much from failure as success. (Anne Heraty, quoted in Flannery 2008: 74–5)

In the next case study, our profiled researcher, Jason Cope, discusses his work on the ways that entrepreneurs learn from traumatic episodes and the experience of failure.

Case 12.3 *Researcher Profile*
Jason Cope examines entrepreneurial learning from venture failure

Jason Cope was a senior lecturer based at the Hunter Centre for Entrepreneurship, University of Strathclyde. He received his undergraduate and doctoral degrees from Lancaster University and went on to work there as a lecturer until he joined the Hunter Centre in January 2009. Sadly, Jason died in November 2010, shortly before the publication of this book. However, his influence will continue through the work of friends and colleagues. Jason was interested in developing a dynamic learning approach to entrepreneurship by applying an interpretative phenomenological perspective (i.e. trying to understand lived experience and how people make sense of their experiences). His published work spans the entrepreneurship and management learning literatures. He was a contributor to an influential *Entrepreneurship Theory and Practice* Special Issue on entrepreneurial learning (Cope 2005), and has examined different contexts in which entrepreneurial learning takes place, including entrepreneurship education, SME leadership, and learning from venture failure. He co-edited a special issue of *Action Learning: Research and Practice* with Professors Richard Thorpe, Monder Ram, and Mike Pedler on action learning in SMEs, and was involved in co-editing two special issues of *Entrepreneurship and Regional Development on* entrepreneurship education and the new 'European School' of entrepreneurship. In this interview, Jason discusses his research on entrepreneurial learning from venture failure. He explained his commitment to developing an understanding of failure from the entrepreneur's perspective, and to building a deeper appreciation of how learning from failure takes place.

Q: Why did you want to research in this area? How did you decide on your main research questions?

I suppose it is unusual to hear someone state that they are passionate about failure, but in my case I'm afraid to say it is true. So many entrepreneurship studies are focused on the dynamics of opportunity recognition and new venture creation that we tend to overlook the opposite and often damaging end of the venturing spectrum – failure. To be honest, I think I was always destined to study failure as I grew up in a small business, which was forced to shut at the beginning of the last UK recession in the early 1990s. I vividly remember how hard that was and how close we came to losing our house. Perhaps this is why I have always been interested in how entrepreneurs learn from crises and arguably there is no greater crisis that an entrepreneur will face than failure. What sparked my interest in this area was that in 2001 two colleagues of mine from Lancaster – Frank Cave and Sue Eccles – were involved in some fascinating research exploring preconceived societal perceptions that in the UK failure is stigmatized, while in the US it is treated as a learning experience. I owe much to Frank in stimulating my (some might say unhealthy) obsession with failure. This inspired me to do some further research and so I took a trip to Silicon Valley in 2004 after the Internet bubble had burst and conducted some interviews there, together with interviews back in the UK. Another reason for this research was that at the time the personal and social dimensions of recovering, learning, and moving on from failure had received scant attention in the entrepreneurship literature. It seemed that almost everyone was concerned with cause and prevention at the expense of understanding the often harmful impact that failure can have on entrepreneurs and their supporters. I must also say that I was inspired by an amazing book published in 1998 by Claire Whyley entitled *Risky Business*, which is a heartbreaking account of the emotional, psychological, and financial damage that small business failure can have. Finally, there is so much rhetoric about failure being a learning experience and we often hear high profile entrepreneurs claiming that failure must be viewed in this light. I thought the time was right to examine this issue from a qualitative perspective and engage with entrepreneurs to hear their views on what and how they have learned from this exceptional experience.

Q: What methods did you use?

I would describe myself as a phenomenologist and so all my work reflects a commitment to understanding the lived experience of the subject I am studying. In this instance, the research involved unstructured phenomenological interviews with eight entrepreneurs who had directly experienced venture failure. Four of the participants were from Silicon Valley, while the remaining four were geographically spread throughout the UK. I did not have an interview guide or any specific questions that I wished to explore, I just wanted to hear their story of what happened and what impact failure had. I did not specifically ask about what they had learned, and yet this issue naturally emerged during our dialogue. My only question was 'Can you tell me about your experience of being involved in a venture that hasn't succeeded?' I was also careful not to use the term 'failure' due to the negative connotations that still seem to surround this term.

Q: What were your key findings?

I found that failure has a significant and negative impact on numerous spheres of the entrepreneur's life. Despite the obvious financial consequences, a key finding was that the powerful emotional and psychological impact of failure was inextricably linked to its complex social costs. Both professional and personal relationships, including marital relations, were strained and in need of repair. It impressed on me the rather obvious point that failure extends beyond the entrepreneur, harming the entrepreneur's family as well as employees, investors and other supporters. On a more positive note, all the participants felt that they had not suffered any long-term professional consequences as a result of failure. Put simply, recovery enabled those surrounding the entrepreneur to recognize ultimately that, while painful, failure is part and parcel of entrepreneurial life: 'some you win, some you lose'. These findings challenge the preconceived societal views of failure mentioned earlier. The study also demonstrated that failure involves a number of distinctive learning processes that foster a range of higher-level learning outcomes, proving significant in both personal and business terms. It highlighted that the lessons of failure are seen by entrepreneurs to be extremely beneficial in making them more prepared for future enterprising activity. This led me to the conclusion that failure is one of the most complex, traumatic, and yet valuable learning experiences that entrepreneurs will ever have the (mis)fortune to engage in.

Q: Were there any particular challenges in conducting this study?

People do not go around shouting about having had a failed venture. Finding participants can therefore be very tricky. In my case this was especially hard as I was trying to find participants in the US while sat behind a desk in the north of England. However, I was lucky enough to be introduced to a venture capitalist who gave me the contact details of several entrepreneurs whom he had funded and whose businesses had subsequently failed. However, my PhD student Orla Byrne, who is conducting a qualitative study into recovery from failure, is constantly bumping into people who know someone who has experienced failure and is willing to be interviewed. This is a very positive sign and perhaps the global economic downturn means that failure is so commonplace that people do not feel such a taboo associated with disclosing a failure.

Q: Where do you think research in this area needs to go in the future?

The avenues for further research into the personal and social dynamics of failure are virtually endless, we really have only begun to scratch the surface of this vitally complex phenomenon. Of course I would say this, but more qualitative research is needed to balance the largely quantitative and conceptual studies that currently dominate. I would like to see more research into the social dimensions of recovery and learning from failure, understanding not only how others (particularly the family and employees) are affected by failure but also how social support mechanisms help the entrepreneur cope with the descent into failure and subsequently facilitate recovery. I also think that research needs to engage policy-makers more effectively, informing the development of more structured and timely support mechanisms that help entrepreneurs manage, recover and learn from failure. As Orla insightfully observed, there are innumerable 'how to start your own business' programmes but no 'how to close your business' programmes!

Sources: Whyley (1998); Cope (2005).

12.5 Practical implications

In the following paragraphs, we draw out some other practical implications of the research evidence presented in this chapter.

- **Entrepreneurial characteristics** Given the limitations of earlier characteristics-based approaches to predicting entrepreneurial outcomes, it is important not to assume that the absence or presence of particular characteristics is in any way definitive. However, by combining findings from more recent personality research with insights from cognitive science and entrepreneurial learning, you can identify a number of ways to develop your own entrepreneurial potential, and that of other people. The essential truth behind the 'characteristics' debate is that, though there may not be a universal set of entrepreneurial characteristics, personal qualities can and *do* make a difference. For example, the **venture capitalist** Arthur Rock, who played a key role in launching some of the most successful Silicon Valley start-ups, from Fairchild Semiconductor to Intel and Apple, once observed that entrepreneurs needed intellectual honesty to attract investors:

  > *I'm not enough of a technologist to be able to understand what most of these entrepreneurs are about technically. The way I went about it was to spend a lot of time with these would-be entrepreneurs. The main thing is, 'are they honest?' By honest I don't mean taking money out of your pocket, but intellectually honest. Do they see things the way they are and not the way they want them to be?* (Rock, quoted in Krause 2009: A3)

  When asked about this more recently, Rock acknowledged that modern venture capitalists also needed to understand the technological aspects (Gupta 2000, Krause 2009). However, his opening quotation, 'I was always interested in investing in people', is still relevant today. Entrepreneurial activity depends on interpersonal relationships and 'first impressions' often count, particularly when you are seeking support for a new venture. However, opinions can sometimes change. One day, Rock was introduced to two 'computer geeks', named Steve Jobs and Steve Wozniak. Initially he was unimpressed, but later changed his mind while visiting a computer exhibition: 'Everybody at the show was around the *Apple* booth. I could not even get close to see them. At that point, I knew, well, maybe we had something.' (Krause 2009: A3)

- **Entrepreneurial cognition** We have seen how paying attention to the ways that people think, and to the content of their thoughts, can help to overcome potential biases that might lead to poor decision-making. We also saw how cognitive science research is helping to open up the ways in which entrepreneurs identify opportunities. Finally, we discussed how creative thinking operates, and how it relates to entrepreneurial activities, both in terms of creating new opportunities and in dealing with challenges and obstacles more effectively. These insights can be applied in practical contexts, including by entrepreneurs engaged in new venture creation activities and by those concerned with entrepreneurial learning.

- **Entrepreneurial learning and entrepreneurship education** These are rapidly developing fields, which build on many of the ideas developed by psychologists and cognitive scientists, as well as more sociological approaches. People are capable of developing their entrepreneurial capacity and potential through a combination of informal and formal methods. By discovering more about the way people learn, and the effectiveness of different methods, it should be possible to develop more effective approaches. At a more personal level, entrepreneurs can gain from a better understanding how they learn, as they will be better able to identify what support they need to develop both their own capabilities and those of other team members. Another important lesson is that learning to be a more effective entrepreneur often involves individuals working together (e.g. peer-to-peer learning); we revisit these social aspects in the next chapter (Section 13.3).

We conclude with two observations. Firstly, all kinds of people can become entrepreneurs. The management writer, Peter Drucker reflected on this insight in typically strong language:

In 30 years I have seen people of most diverse personalities and temperaments perform well in entrepreneurial challenges. Some entrepreneurs are ego-centric and others are painfully correct conformists. Some are fat and some are lean. Some entrepreneurs are worriers and some are relaxed, some have great charm . . . and some have no more personality than a frozen mackerel! (Drucker 2007 [1985]: 243)

Secondly, in the closing sections of this chapter we moved beyond the territory of the individual to see how learning can often involve families and other social relationships. In practice, the dividing line between the individual (Chapter 12) and the social (Chapter 13) is often blurred, with entrepreneurial activity being generated as a result of interactions between individuals and their social settings (e.g. Hobbs 1988; Down and Reveley 2004). What are the practical implications of this insight? Imagine you are working in a small social enterprise in a deprived urban area. You know that your organization has the potential to develop into a much larger and more effective force, generating additional income and benefiting more people. As an individual you may have the capacity to achieve something, but you can *still* be constrained by a lack of vision and energy in your management team. Can you use your high levels of 'self-efficacy' to overcome their lack of 'collective efficacy'

(Bandura 1995) (Section 12.3.2)? Will you just get frustrated and leave? There is also the question of how such an organization can overcome its entrepreneurial deficit and move forward. Individual-level explanations may shed some light on the problem, but they are not going to be sufficient to resolve it; we need to combine them with the kinds of approach outlined in the next chapter.

✳ 12.6 Summary

➤ Individual-level perspectives using a variety of psychological and behavioural approaches have enhanced our understanding of entrepreneurship.

➤ Earlier research focused on the search for distinctive entrepreneurial traits or personality characteristics. These ideas remain popular and influential, but it is important to be aware of their limitations and of subsequent advances in psychological and behavioural research.

➤ Recent research on entrepreneurial cognition provides some interesting insights in areas such as opportunity recognition. Researchers have also helped to explain cognitive biases can contribute to mistakes and the failure of some entrepreneurial ventures.

➤ There are three main vehicles for entrepreneurial learning: formal education; informal sources; and learning from direct experiences. People can acquire entrepreneurial skills and understanding from each of these sources; it is also possible, though arguably more difficult, to develop entrepreneurial attitudes and values in this way.

➤ The relationship between social interactions and individual behaviour is attracting increasing attention. Research in this area has challenged traditional assumptions in areas such as the creation of entrepreneurial self-identity and gender roles.

➤ Individual-level research findings from sub-fields, such as entrepreneurial cognition and entrepreneurial learning, have practical implications for individual entrepreneurs, entrepreneurial ventures and for policy-makers.

Case 12.4 Whose story is it anyway? Entrepreneurship's 'invisible' women

Background: researching 'invisible' women

This case is based on a research study conducted by Dr Eleanor Hamilton, Director of the Institute for Entrepreneurship and Enterprise Development, University of Lancaster. Eleanor's research challenges some of the assumptions that underpin previous studies of entrepreneurship in family firms. More specifically, it highlights the dangers of focusing on the narrative accounts (or 'stories') of individual owner-managers and either ignoring or down-playing the roles played by other members of the household. The case is based around an extended extract from an article, which was first published in the *International Small Business Journal* (Hamilton 2006).

The entrepreneurship and family business literature commonly assumes that an individual, the 'owner-manger' who is also assumed to be the entrepreneur, undertakes the processes of founding and leading a business. That individual, usually identified as male, is often the focus of research. In the literature the wives/partners/daughters/sisters of the owner-manager rarely appear. As a result of this lack of research interest the term 'invisible' or 'hidden' has been used to describe the role of women in founding and running businesses. The research was designed to illuminate complex relationships in a family business context, putting the family at the heart of the research as opposed to an individual owner manager. Eight interviews were undertaken, with two generations in three families. Interviews were conducted with a generation that founded a business and those members of the family who had taken over the business in the next generation. In some cases the interview was with an individual, some with husbands and wives together, depending on the circumstances of the interview and the wishes of the participants. The interviews were taped and transcripts produced from the tapes.

In the following paragraphs, we explore the part played by a woman in founding a family business, even though she had a career of her own. It shows very powerfully how 'family' and 'business' are difficult to separate in the founding and running of a family business. Elements of this narrative also support the explanatory power of patriarchy [i.e. the exercise of power by men over women] and paternalism in the creation of entrepreneurial masculinities. The subtle shifts in roles and power in the relationships over time, revealed by the analysis, cast some doubt that this explanation is, of itself, adequate.

The 'invisible' woman who was a driving force in the business

The role of the wife in this story represents a phenomenon that can also be found in the business history literature. The wife of the founder came from a business background. Her earning capacity and ability to borrow money supported the development of the business at a critical time. Colli et al. (2003) in a study of family firms in the nineteenth and twentieth century in Britain, Spain, and Italy look at patterns of women and inheritance. They found that women were vital sources of finance and provided access to business and family networks of trust. They point to the fact that marriage and business were inseparable and they give examples of intermarriages strengthening businesses. Women often led and developed businesses, either as widows, until a male relative could be found to take over, or while the men were away from home travelling long distances, particularly in the mercantile companies. They observe that women: 'represented a hidden resource and their participation often went unrecorded' (Colli et al. 2003: 42). The business consists of a large group of companies built up over the years, which started from humble beginnings in a village hardware shop and petrol station. The family lived above the shop. During the interview with the founder he frequently refers to his wife. This is not in itself surprising; however, what emerges is interesting in terms of her influence on the development of the business. He married what he describes as the boss's daughter. She was in fact the daughter of his father's employer who was a fireplace manufacturer.

> *Me wife was me father's boss's daughter so she'd come from a business family, they were business people, most of her mother's brothers and sisters were in business, she had a leaning towards business, I don't say she's business minded, she isn't, my wife is a, was, a head teacher.*

Despite this view of her not being 'business minded' he goes on to explain it was she who suggested he first go into business at the age of 28, buying the local petrol station and hardware shop in the village they lived in. They have since then built up a large portfolio of businesses across the UK and both of their sons work in the business. Her numerous interventions have played a key role in the life of the business. Another critical contribution came after their first business was established. The next stage of growth and development was made possible with the purchase of a nearby farm with a farmhouse, three-acre paddock, and farm buildings. As they were not selling the shop, which was their livelihood, or the flat above where they were currently living they needed to arrange a mortgage:

> We paid £14,500 for it and the trouble, the problem though, we weren't selling anything, we weren't selling a house to buy a house, and it was difficult, so me wife got the mortgage, she was a teacher, she was a head by this time and she got the mortgage.

Based on her earnings and ability to borrow capital, the business was able to expand. It was not just her ability to earn and borrow that was critical; it was her determination and powers of persuasion at the building society that made the difference. The founder explained:

> And she browbeat the building society because even then they were reluctant to let a woman have a mortgage, but she could as she was in permanent employment, good prospects and it was permanent, you know it was alright and she got the mortgage.

He joked about the fact that it was, therefore, seen as her house and that she had the power to throw him out:

> So it's me wife's house and she always says I live there under sufferance, she always says that. I daren't put a foot wrong in case she throws me out!

This is an example of the female gaining power through the business becoming economically dependent upon her. This could be interpreted as an example of conditions under which patriarchy can be resisted. He went on to make clear the importance of these events in the subsequent growth and diversification of what was to become a large group of companies:

> So now that was the making of the business because this farm with three acres of land had outbuildings, we were able then to think of stocking a little bit more stuff for the shop and selling different things. And then we started to sell Calor gas and things for camping and slowly expanding.

There are many such examples of her contribution and influence in the business, which call into question a simplistic analysis of the power relations in a family business. Although an interpretation is possible invoking strategies of patriarchy in the use of female kin's labour to support the capitalist/husband there are elements of the story that challenge a single interpretation. To marginalize her contribution to a support role, as is so often done in the literature, also seems inadequate. To understand the subtle play of their lives over time as they deal with events requires the development perhaps of some more multifaceted understanding. Through bringing exceptional resources to the business and perhaps also by maintaining her independence from her husband

and the business she resists patriarchal forces and gains power. In this same family, the younger son suffered a cerebral haemorrhage aged 17 years old. Following this tragedy, as a young man, he struggled to find suitable employment. One day as they drove past a travel agency for sale his mother suggested to his father that he buy the business and put their son to work there, creating suitable employment. The family went on to develop a chain of more than 40 travel agents.

Eleanor Hamilton's research reveals that the 'entrepreneurial family business narrative' is one crafted within complex, delicate, constantly changing relationships. Identities and notions of self are revealed as more intricate and difficult to define than suggested by the notion of a predetermined, predefined male and female identity. The stories of the families studied bring to light subtle relationships of duty, love, power, and conflict, as reflected in Kondo's (1990) work [an anthropological study of business and family relationships in a Japanese workplace]. They suggest that universal explanations, while comforting in their certainty, may not be adequate.

Questions

1. Re-read the case and try to identify examples of: (a) entrepreneurial identity; (b) entrepreneurial behaviour; (c) entrepreneurial learning.

2. What factors altered the power relationship between the founder and his wife over the course of the story?

3. What lessons would you draw from this account? (NB If you have the opportunity, it may be interesting to compare your responses with those of male and female colleagues.)

4. You are about to conduct a questionnaire survey of small entrepreneurial firms. How might the findings of this study influence your approach?

Source: Hamilton (2006); extract reproduced with permission.

 ## Practical activities

1. **My entrepreneurial personality** Re-read the arguments in Section 12.2, and try at least one of the entrepreneurial assessment tests detailed there, or on the Online Resource Center. What is your impression of the results? Do they reflect your own assessment? Were there any surprises? If possible, compare the findings with those of a close colleague or friend. (NB If these results suggest a lack of enterprising attributes do not assume that your entrepreneurial journey is over. Instead, review the various limitations of characteristics-based approaches and refer to the discussion on entrepreneurial learning, and how it can transform skills, knowledge, and attitudes.)

2. **Exploring other entrepreneurial lives** Using Cases 12.1 and 12.4 as a guide, find three examples of people talking about the factors that prompted them to act entrepreneurially. This may be establishing a social or commercial enterprise, or becoming an 'intrapreneur' in an existing organization. Compare the accounts, highlighting examples of each of the following: (a) early signs of entrepreneurial potential; (b) informal learning; (c) formal learning; (c) other influences on their

behaviour. Write a short commentary (800 words), reviewing your findings with reference to concepts discussed in this chapter. (NB In order to find your source material, try searching in biographies, autobiographies and magazine profiles. See the Further reading guide for initial suggestions.)

3. Entrepreneurial learning: your perspective Parts One and Two of this textbook, and the companion website, have been designed to encourage entrepreneurial learning. What techniques have the authors used? To consider this question, take a look through the textbook and the online resource centre, noting the kinds of resources available and how they have helped you to explore various aspects of entrepreneurship. Write a short commentary (800 words) on your thoughts and experiences in using these resources.

Discussion topics

1. The entrepreneurial personality debate Form two teams and prepare a set of arguments 'for' and 'against' the motion: 'This House believes that there is such a thing as an entrepreneurial personality.' Allow five minutes for each side, followed by a further five minutes to respond to the arguments presented. Then move to a vote. To make the debate more interesting, allocate team members so that those who disagree with the motion have to defend it, and vice-versa. The debates can also be adapted for use in a virtual learning environment.

2. The entrepreneurial learning debate Following the guidance for Discussion topic 1, organize a debate based on the motion, 'This House believes that you can teach successful social and/or commercial entrepreneurship.' Entrepreneurship tutors could take on the role of challenging the motion.

3. Encouraging 'better' kinds of entrepreneurship Many governments and governmental agencies have the aim of promoting what might loosely be termed 'better' kinds of entrepreneurial activity (e.g. more innovative, more competitive, and more socially and environmentally responsible) (Section 15.4.2). But how would you change the behaviour of an individual entrepreneur? Apply the ideas discussed in this chapter to address ONE of the following practical challenges at an individual level: (a) encouraging the founder of a struggling social enterprise, or the owner-manager of a struggling small firm, to become a more effective leader; (b) encouraging a young woman, currently studying at secondary school (i.e. high school), to develop her entrepreneurial potential in a responsible way; (c) persuading a criminal entrepreneur to move into a legitimate form of entrepreneurial activity Identify at least three actions that you would take in order to achieve your goal. Do you think your strategy would succeed? What other kinds of intervention might help?

Further reading guide

For interviews with leading social and commercial entrepreneurs, look for biographical sources such as **Flannery (2008)**, **Bornstein (2004)**, entrepreneurial autobiographies, and personal profiles in magazines such as *Real Business and Social Enterprise*. **Baron (2000)** and **Frese et al. (2000)** summarize some of the main developments in psychological research on entrepreneurship.

Chell (2008) provides a detailed account of the author's long-standing research on entrepreneurial personality, which adopts a social constructionist approach. Kets de Vries (1985, 1996) illustrates how the techniques of clinical psychology have been used to examine entrepreneurs, producing interesting (but also contentious) evidence of troubled personalities and personal backgrounds. Baron and Ward (2004) and Wadeson (2008) review recent research on entrepreneurial cognition. There are many studies examining entrepreneurial opportunity, including Foss et al. (2008), which addresses subjectivity, Krueger (2000), which makes a connection with cognition, and Corbett (2005), which focuses on experiential learning. Chen et al. (1998) examine self-efficacy and its role in entrepreneurial thinking and behaviour. For recent reviews of entrepreneurial learning and entrepreneurship education, see Cope (2005), Harrison and Leitch (2008), Neary and Parker (2004), and Pittaway and Cope (2007). NIRAS (2008) contains the results of a major European survey of entrepreneurship in higher education, commissioned by the European Union. For varied examples of empirical studies spanning the individual and the social, see Hobbs (1988), Down and Reveley (2004), Ravasi and Turati (2005), Hamilton (2006), and Essers and Benschop (2009).

References

Ajzen, I. (1991) 'The theory of planned behavior.' *Organizational Behavior and Human Decision Processes*, 50: 179–211.

Amabile, T.M. (1997) 'Entrepreneurial creativity through motivational synergy.' *Journal of Creative Behaviour*, 31, 1: 18–26.

Bandura, A. (1995) 'Exercise of personal and collective efficacy in changing societies.' In A. Bandura (ed.) *Self-efficacy in changing societies.* Cambridge: Cambridge University Press (1–45).

Baron, R.A. (2000) 'Psychological perspectives on entrepreneurship: cognitive and social factors in entrepreneurs' success.' *Current Directions in Psychological Science*, 9, 1: 15–18.

Baron, R.A. and Ward, T.B. (2004) 'Expanding entrepreneurial cognition's toolbox: potential contributions from the field of cognitive science.' *Entrepreneurship Theory and Practice*, 28, 6: 553–74.

Begley, T. M. and Boyd, D.B. (1987) 'Psychological characteristics associated with performance in entrepreneurial firms and small businesses.' *Journal of Business Venturing*, 2: 79–93.

Binks, M. (2005) *Entrepreneurship education and integrative learning.* Birmingham: National Council for Graduate Entrepreneurship.

Blundel, R.K. and Ippolito, K. (2008) *Effective organisational communication: perspectives, principles and practices* (3rd edition). Harlow: FT Prentice Hall.

Bornstein, D. (2004) *How to change the world: social entrepreneurs and the power of new ideas.* Oxford: Oxford University Press.

Brockhaus, R. (1980) 'Risk-taking propensity of entrepreneurs.' *Academy of Management Journal*, 23, 3: 509–520.

Caird, S.P. (1991) 'The enterprising tendency of occupational groups.' *International Small Business Journal*, 9, 4: 75–81.

Caird, S.P. (1993) 'What do psychological tests suggest about entrepreneurs.' *Journal of Psychology*, 8, 6: 11–20.

Carland, J.C., Boulton, F.H., and Carland, J.A.C. (1984) 'Differentiating entrepreneurs from small business owners: a conceptualization.' *Academy of Management Review*, 9, 2: 354–9.

Casson, M., Yeung, B., Basu, A., and Wadeson, N. (2008) *The Oxford handbook of entrepreneurship.* Oxford: Oxford University Press.

Chell, E. (2008) *The entrepreneurial personality: a social construction* (2nd edition). London: Routledge.

Chen, C., Greene, P., and Crick, A. (1998) 'Does entrepreneurial self-efficacy distinguish entrepreneurs from managers?' *Journal of Business Venturing*, 13, 4: 295–316.

Chia, R. (2008) 'Enhancing entrepreneurial learning through peripheral vision.' In, R.T. Harrison and C. Leitch (eds) op. cit. (27–43).

Ciavarella, M.A., Buchholtz, A.K., and Riordan, C.M. (2004) 'The Big Five and venture survival: is there a linkage?' *Journal of Business Venturing*, 19, 4: 465–83.

Colli, A., Fernandez Perez, P., and Rose, M.B. (2003) 'National determinants of family firm development?: family firms in Britain, Spain, and Italy in the nineteenth and twentieth centuries.' *Enterprise and Society*, 4, 2: 28–64.

Cooper, A.C., Woo, C.A., and Dunkelberg, W. (1988) 'Entrepreneurs perceived chances for success.' *Journal of Business Venturing*, 3, 2: 97–108.

Cope, J. (2005) 'Towards a dynamic learning perspective of entrepreneurship.' *Entrepreneurship Theory and Practice*, 29, 4: 373–98.

Corbett, A.C. (2005) 'Experiential learning within the process of opportunity identification and exploitation.' *Entrepreneurship Theory and Practice*, 29, 4: 473–91.

Cromie, S. (2000) 'Asessing entrepreneurial inclinations: some approaches and empirical evidence.' *European Journal of Work and Organisational Psychology*, 9, 1: 7–30.

Davidsson, P., Low, M.B., and Wright, M. (2001) 'Editor's introduction: Low and MacMillan ten years on: achievements and future directions for entrepreneurship research.' *Entrepreneurship Theory and Development*, 25, 4: 5–15.

Down, S. and Reveley, J. (2004) 'Generational Encounters and the social formation of entrepreneurial identity: "Young Guns" and "Old Farts".' *Organization*, 11, 2: 233–50.

Drucker, P.F. (2007 [1985]) *Innovation and entrepreneurship* (new edition). Oxford: Butterworth-Heinemann.

Essers, C. and Benschop, Y. (2009) 'Muslim businesswomen doing boundary work: the negotiation of Islam, gender and ethnicity within entrepreneurial contexts.' *Human Relations*, 62, 3: 403–23.

Flannery, P. (2008) Grabbing the oyster!: anecdotes and advice from icons of Irish business. Cork, Oak Tree Press.

Foss, N.J., Klein, P.G., Kor, Y.Y., and Mahoney, J.T. (2008) 'Entrepreneurship, subjectivism, and the resource-based view: toward a new synthesis.' *Strategic Entrepreneurship Journal*, 2: 73–94.

Frese, M., Chell, E., and Klandt, H. (eds) (2000) 'Psychological approaches to entrepreneurship.' *European Journal of Work and Organizational Psychology*, 9, 1, 3–102 (Special Issue).

Furnham, A. and Steele, H. (1993) 'Measures of Locus of Control: A critique of children's, health and work-related locus of control questionnaires.' *British Journal of Psychology*, 84: 443–79.

Gartner, W.B. (1989a) '"Who an entrepreneur?" is the wrong question.' *Entrepreneurship Theory and Practice*, 13, 4: 47–67.

Gartner, W.B. (1s989b) 'Some suggestions for research on entrepreneurial traits and characteristics.' *Entrepreneurship Theory and Practice*, 14, 1: 27–38.

Gibb, A. (2002), 'In pursuit of a new "enterprise" and "entrepreneurship" paradigm for learning: creative destruction, new values, new ways of doing things and new combinations of knowledge.' *International Journal of Management Reviews*, 4, 3: 233–69.

Goldberg, L. R. (1993) 'The structure of phenotypic personality traits.' *American Psychologist*, 48, 1: 26–34.

Gupta, U. (2000) *Done deals: venture capitalists tell their story.* Cambridge MA: Harvard Business School Press.

Hamilton, E.E. (2006) 'Whose story is it anyway?: narrative accounts of the role of women in founding and establishing family businesses.' *International Small Business Journal*, 24, 3: 253–71.

Harrison, R.T. and Leitch, C. (eds) (2008) *Entrepreneurial learning: conceptual frameworks and applications.* Abingdon: Routledge.

Hmieleski, K.M. and Baron, R.A. (2009) 'Entrepreneurs' optimism and new venture performance: a social cognitive perspective.' *Academy of Management Journal*, 52, 3: 473–88.

Hobbs, D. (1988) *Doing the business: entrepreneurship, the working class, and detectives in the East End of London.* Oxford: Clarendon Press.

Howorth C.A., Rose M.B. and Hamilton E.E. (2008) 'Definitions, diversity and development: key debates in family business research.' In Casson et al. (eds) op. cit. (225–47).

Kets de Vries, M.F.R. (1985) 'The dark side of entrepreneurship.' *Harvard Business Review*, 63, 6: 160–7.

Kets de Vries, M.F.R. (1996) 'The anatomy of the entrepreneur: clinical observations.' *Human Relations*, 49, 7: 853–83.

Kirzner, I.M. (1979) *Perception, opportunity and profit: studies in the theory of entrepreneurship.* Chicago: University of Chicago Press.

Knight, F.H. (1921) *Risk, Uncertainty, and Profit.* Boston MA: Houghton Mifflin.

Kondo, D.K. (1990) *Crafting selves: power, gender and discourses of identity in a Japanese workplace.* Chicago: University of Chicago Press.

Krause, R. (2009) 'A gem among venture capitalists. Get out front: Arthur Rock saw early that Intel and Apple were winners.' *Investors Business Daily*, 23 April, A3.

Krueger, N. (2000) 'The cognitive infrastructure of opportunity emergence.' *Entrepreneurship Theory and Practice*, 24, 3: 5–23.

Kuratko, D.F. (2005) 'The Emergence of Entrepreneurship Education: Development, Trends, and Challenges.' *Entrepreneurship, Theory and Practice*, 29, 5: 577–98.

Licht, A.N. and Siegel, J.I. (2008) 'The social dimensions of entrepreneurship.' In Casson et al. (eds), op. cit. (511–39).

Low, M.B. and MacMillan, I.C. (1988) 'Entrepreneurship: past research and future challenges.' *Journal of Management*, 14, 2: 139–61.

McClelland, D.C. (1961) *The achieving society*. New Jersey: Van Nostrand.

McCrae, R.R. and Costa P.T. (1996) 'Toward a new generation of personality theories: theoretical context for the five-factor model.' In J.S. Wiggins (ed.) *The five-factor model of personality: theoretical perspectives*. New York NY: Guilford Press (51–87).

Miner, J.B. (1997) 'A psychological typology and its relationship to entrepreneurial success.' *Entrepreneurship and Regional Development*, 9, 4: 319–34.

Miner J .B., Smith, N.R., and Bracker, J.S. (1994) 'Role of entrepreneurial task motivation in the growth of technologically innovative firms: interpretations from follow-up data.' *Journal of Applied Psychology*, 79, 4: 627–30.

Mitchell, R.K., Busenitz, L., Lant, T., McDougall, P.P., Morse, E.A. and Brock Smith, J. (2002) 'Toward a theory of entrepreneurial cognition: rethinking the people side of entrepreneurship research.' *Entrepreneurship Theory and Practice*, 27, 2: 93–104.

Neary, M. and Parker, A. (2004) *Enterprise, social enterprise and critical pedagogy: reinventing the HE curriculum*. Birmingham: National Council for Graduate Entrepreneurship.

Nicolaou, N. and Shane, S. (2009) 'Can genetic factors influence the likelihood of engaging in entrepreneurial activity?' *Journal of Business Venturing*, 24, 1: 1–22.

NIRAS (2008) *Survey of Entrepreneurship in Higher Education in Europe*. Brussels: European Commission, Directorate General for Enterprise and Industry.

Palich, L.E. and Bagby, D.R. (1995) 'Using cognitive theory to explain entrepreneurial risk taking: challenging conventional wisdom.' *Journal of Business Venturing*, 10, 6: 425–38.

Penrose, E.T. (1995 [1959]) *The theory of the growth of the firm* (3rd edition with new Foreword). Oxford: Oxford University Press.

Pittaway, L. and Cope, J. (2007) 'Entrepreneurship education: a systematic review of the evidence.' *International Small Business Journal*, 25: 479–510.

Pritchard, K. (2008) 'I'll have what Tony Deep is having.' *Real Business*, March, 25–8.

Rauch, A., and Frese, M. (2007) 'Let's put the person back into entrepreneurship research: a meta-analysis on the relationship between business owners. personality traits, business creation, and success.' *European Journal of Work and Organizational Psychology*, 16, 4: 353–85.

Ravasi, D. and Turati, C. (2005) 'Exploring entrepreneurial learning: a comparative study of technology development projects.' *Journal of Business Venturing*, 20, 1: 137–64.

Rotter, J.B. (1966) 'Generalized expectancies for internal versus external control of reinforcement.' *Psychological Monographs*. 609, 80: 1–28.

Sexton, D.L. and Bowman-Upton, N. (1985) 'The entrepreneur: a capable executive and more.' *Journal of Business Venturing*, 1, 1: 129–40.

Shapero, A. (1982) 'Some social dimensions of entrepreneurship.' In C. Kent, D. Sexton, and K. Vesper (eds) *The encyclopedia of entrepreneurship*. Englewood Cliffs, NJ: Prentice-Hall (72–90).

Simon, M. and Houghton, S.M. (2002) 'The relationship among biases, misconceptions, and the introduction of pioneering products: examining differences in venture decision contexts.' *Entrepreneurship Theory and Practice*, 27, 2: 105–24.

Srivastava, S., John, O. P., Gosling, S. D., and Potter, J. (2003) 'Development of personality in early and middle adulthood: set like plaster or persistent change?' *Journal of Personality and Social Psychology*, 84: 1041–53.

Souitaris V, Zerbinati, S., and Al-Laham, A. (2007) 'Do entrepreneurship programmes raise entrepreneurial intentions of science and engineering students?: the effects of learning, inspiration and resources.' *Journal of Business Venturing*, 22, 4: 566–91.

Spence, L.J. (2000) 'Priorities, practice and ethics in small firms.' London: Institute of Business Ethics.

Valliere, D. (2008) 'Exploring Buddhist influence on the entrepreneurial decision.' *International Journal of Entrepreneurial Behaviour and Research*, 14, 3: 172–91.

Wadeson, N. (2008) 'Cognitive Aspects of Entrepreneurship: Decision-Making and Attitudes to Risk.' In Casson et al. (eds), op. cit. (91–113).

Ward, T.B. (2004) 'Cognition, creativity and entrepreneurship.' *Journal of Business Venturing*, 19, 2: 173–88.

White, R.E., Thornhill, S., and Hampson, E. (2006) 'Entrepreneurs and evolutionary biology: The relationship between testosterone and new venture creation.' *Organizational Behavior and Human Decision Processes*, 100, 1: 21–34.

Whiting, B.G., (1988) 'Creativity and entrepreneurship: how do they relate?' *Journal of Creative Behaviour*, 22, 3: 178–83.

Whyley, C. (1998) *Risky Business: the personal and financial costs of small business failure.* London: Policy Studies Institute.

Wiggins, J.S. (ed.) *The five-factor model of personality: theoretical perspectives.* New York: Guilford Press.

Wiklund, J., Davidsson, P., and Delmar, F. (2003) 'What do they think and feel about growth?: an expectancy-value approach to small business managers' attitudes toward growth.' *Entrepreneurship Theory and Practice*, 27, 3: 247–70.

13 Social perspectives
Understanding people and places

To understand how any society functions you must understand the relationship between the men and the women.

Angela Davies, *civil rights campaigner and academic*

Without persons, no society; without society, no persons.

Thomas Hill Green, *nineteenth century philosopher*

Learning outcomes

After reading this chapter you should be able to:

➤ Explore social-level perspectives on entrepreneurship, with a focus on sociological, anthropological, and geographical approaches.

➤ Recognize the contribution of these approaches to our understanding of entrepreneurship, in terms of empirical findings, research methods, and theoretical frameworks.

➤ Consider the kinds of knowledge generated by these approaches, and begin to relate it to that obtained from other research perspectives.

➤ Appreciate the practical relevance of this research for policy-makers and practitioners.

➤ Apply these insights to your own experiences of entrepreneurship.

Case 13.1 Jackson Reece: the birth of a new venture

This story of the early stages of a new entrepreneurial venture helps to illustrate the complex mix of personal and social forces at work in business today. In this case, we meet the founders of **Jackson Reece** (www.jacksonreece.com), and hear how they came to develop an innovative and highly successful new product in a mature market dominated by powerful incumbent firms.

The founders' tale

Colin and Janet Cordner live in a small town in Northern Ireland with their two sons. In December 1999, the Cordners' first son, Jackson, was born. At this time, the couple had no intention of going into business; as Colin reflects, setting up a company, 'was the last thing on our minds!' They had a new, bouncing baby, and were both in fairly secure employment. Then, when he was eight months old, Jackson developed the skin condition, baby eczema. Doctors prescribed a steroid cream, but this made the child unwell, and his parents became concerned. This is their account of what happened next:

> Soon we discovered that the alcohol present in many baby wipes compounded the condition. Our first thought was 'there has to be a natural wipe available that doesn't contain these types of chemicals?' We explored all the leading wipes and found none that offered an alcohol free, herbal alternative. We had no choice but to return to cotton wool and water, which was neither effective nor practical. Jackson's severe blistering and bleeding from nappy rash seemed to worsen. The combination of abrasive chemicals found in baby soaps and high levels of chlorine in water were making Jackson's eczema even worse. A local water scientist informed us that the chlorine found in our water system would be just as abrasive to a baby like Jackson as alcohol. As parents we felt we had no choice but to explore developing our own wipe that would protect and soothe our baby boy's delicate skin.

Finding a solution

When Colin and Janet began their search they had neither specialist technical knowledge nor formal business training. Their first step was to visit the local library, where they searched for information on skin conditions and cleaning products. Next, having purchased a computer and a broadband connection, they began searching the web for more information. They spent more than three years

researching the subject, eventually identifying a combination of naturally occurring oils and other ingredients that would cleanse the skin without damaging side-effects. They also found that China was a major producer of baby wipes for the world market. After some time, the Cordners received an email from a Chinese company confirming that it could produce their new product. In 2003, the Cordners' second son Reece was born, and in the same year, the couple launched their new venture.

A values-driven venture

Colin describes the launch of Jackson Reece as 'a long road'. When they began the business, the couple had two small children and were also in the process of building a new house. While many larger and more established companies are adopting more environmentally responsible sourcing and manufacturing strategies, the arguments are usually expressed in less personal terms. Colin admits that, in the early stages, they were naive: 'the first [product] designs were awful'. After four years' of sourcing from China, the Cordners decided to relocate manufacturing activity back to the UK. This decision reflected both practical and ethical considerations. The packaging was not performing well, with the hard plastic lids (a standard feature in the packaging for most mass-market baby wipes), not sticking to the rest of the pack. This led to a costly recall, with more than 15,000 packs being replaced. Colin also began to work with the regional development body, Invest Northern Ireland (www.investni.gov.uk). 'They have been great', he says, supplying consultancy advice on packaging, design, and trading. Jackson Reece now sources almost all of its ingredients from European countries. Manufacturing in-house is not currently feasible, partly due to the high cost of specialist machinery. The solution is to operate in partnership with other companies. In doing so, the Cordners have made considerable efforts to minimize the company's environmental impact. For example, both the product and the packaging materials are biodegradable, the wipes are assembled by a UK-based company, and the cardboard boxes used for distribution are also manufactured in the UK. Despite Jackson Reece's strong, distinctive branding and early marketing success, it has been challenging to secure listings with some of the large multiple retailers. Though buyers have been enthusiastic about the product, any new entrant is faced with two basic issues. Firstly, it is hard for small firms to satisfy the multiple retailers' high volume requirements and to cope with their low profit margins. Secondly, retailers are reluctant to add new product lines in market segments that are already occupied by a few dominant brands; as one buyer put it, 'We don't have elastic shelves.'

Jackson Reece is now selling into nine European countries, and the market is continuing to grow, with new sales enquiries coming in from as far afield as Australia. Seven years after those initial visits to the local library, Jackson Reece is an innovative, award-winning babycare company, competing effectively in a highly competitive market.

Issues to consider

1. What does the case suggest about the process of identifying (or creating) an entrepreneurial opportunity (see also: Sections 2.1 to 2.4)?

2. What theoretical frameworks and research methods would help you to better understand the challenges of creating a new venture?

3. What lessons would you draw from this successful example of new venture creation?

13.1 **Entrepreneurship in a social context**

In this chapter, we are concerned with the ways in which **entrepreneurial activity** is influenced by the societies in which it takes place. As we saw in the previous chapter, studying **entrepreneurship** at an individual level of analysis is far from straightforward. However, in moving to a social level, researchers find themselves in an even more complicated and varied landscape. It may be tempting to avoid all this complexity and simply assume that your research is picking up some universal features of entrepreneurship. Some earlier research has since been criticized for making this kind of assumption, and as a consequence failing to grasp the sheer variety of entrepreneurship practices around the world. Zafirovski (1999: 351) points out that, 'Entrepreneurship possesses an eminently social character and is subject to the operation of definite societal processes.' As the author goes on to argue, many aspects of entrepreneurship have a culture-specific dimension. The lesson for researchers is that we should not simply assume that the motives, preferences, and values of other people are going to be similar, irrespective of their social background, or of the culture and institutions in which they operate.

In the last century, the entrepreneurship research literature was dominated by publications that examined a fairly narrow range of societies, notably those of North America and Europe. Though this period generated many valuable insights, their scope was necessarily limited. In the last two decades, this situation has seen some dramatic changes. Echoing the spread of the **enterprise culture** project (Sections 10.1 and 15.2), there has been a rapid growth in studies exploring entrepreneurship in other parts of the world. At the same time, researchers have been investigating new and previously hidden aspects of the subject. This activity has produced a lot of rich and interesting material; it has also left us with a rather complicated web of ideas, with multiple research themes, research settings, theoretical frameworks, and methodologies. The main aims of this chapter are to find a way through the web, and to indicate how the various strands can be combined. Given constraints of space, we can only present a small selection of research studies in this chapter. The Further reading guide should cover some of these gaps. In addition, some related topics can be found in the next chapter, which considers historical perspectives on entrepreneurship (Chapter 14).

The remainder of the chapter is structured as follows. In Section 13.2, we take a broad overview of how researchers explore the social dimensions of entrepreneurship then look more closely at three contrasting approaches: analysing large data sets, conducting ethnographic studies, and mapping **entrepreneurial networks**. Section 13.3 introduces some of the main social research themes, indicating the scope and the variety of studies that have been conducted. The remaining sections provide a more detailed insight into two of these research areas, gender (Section 13.4) and geography (Section 13.5). Finally, in Section 13.6, we consider the practical implications for **entrepreneurs**, entrepreneurial organizations, and those involved in policy-making.

13.2 **Social research approaches: a brief overview**

13.2.1 **Introduction and three contrasting examples**

As we have already seen, entrepreneurship researchers have adopted a variety of perspectives and research approaches in order to explore their subject (Section 10.2). Research at the individual level has been dominated by a few disciplines, most notably psychology, but with increasing contributions from other fields such as learning (Section 12.1). By contrast, research at a social level has always drawn on a much wider range of social science disciplines, including sociology, anthropology, geography, and many cross-cutting fields such as cultural studies and policy studies (NB economics-based approaches are addressed in more detail in Chapter 11; **historical research** is discussed in Chapter 14). In some cases, research designs may be based around a single approach, such as a piece of ethnographic fieldwork or analysis of questionnaire data. In others, researchers may draw on multiple sources of evidence. For example, an analysis of the start-up process may take the form of a number of detailed case studies of new ventures. This reflects a broader call for entrepreneurship researchers to examine their subject using **multi-level** approaches (Low and Macmillan 1988; Davidsson and Wiklund 2001). This means making connections between entrepreneurial behaviour at various levels, including the individual, the organization, and the social context (Zafirovski 1999: 353). Social scientists use many different research methods and sources of evidence to probe these different levels. Figure 13.1 shows some of the more widely used sources and techniques. In practice, researchers often draw on multiple sources in their research designs, and may combine quantitative and qualitative evidence:

To illustrate how these decisions are made, we have selected three contrasting research approaches from Figure 13.1 for more detailed consideration:

- Analysing and modelling of entrepreneurial activity using statistical data from surveys and official data sets (Section 13.2.2).
- Interpreting the entrepreneurial experience through ethnographic fieldwork (Section 13.2.3).
- Revealing patterns and changes in entrepreneurial relationships through social network mapping (Section 13.2.4).

We compare the different sources of evidence obtained from each of these approaches and profile some recent research studies to illustrate the kinds of questions they are able to address. Further coverage of the issues discussed, and other relevant methodological questions, can be found in research methods texts such as Bryman and Bell (2007).

13.2.2 **Statistical analysis and modelling: surveys and official data sets**

A great deal of the entrepreneurship research conducted at a social level makes use of quantitative data of various kinds. One of the most widely used sources of data is official data sets, which are generally compiled by international agencies (e.g. International Monetary Fund, World Bank), and from regional, national, and local governments. Census data, which records the 'births' and 'deaths' of businesses, is often available for researchers in the form

Figure 13.1 Potential sources of evidence for entrepreneurship researchers

Source of research evidence	Further reading suggestion
Ethnography	Johnstone (2007)
Participant observation	Bryman and Bell (2007)
Action research	Leitch (2007)
Semi-structured in-depth interview	Bryman and Bell (2007)
Verbal histories	McKenzie (2007)
Focus group	Bryman and Bell (2007)
Documentary sources (e.g. minutes, accounts)	See Chapter 14 (Section 14.2)
E-mail messages	Wakkee et al. (2007)
Structured interview	Bryman and Bell (2007)
Questionnaire survey (email, postal, face-to-face)	Bryman and Bell (2007)
Official datasets (e.g. VAT registration data)	Parker (2009)
Web-based search (e.g. media coverage)	Achtenagen and Welter (2007)

of downloadable spreadsheets. These data sets typically include several kinds of categorical and variable data, including location, industry sector, legal form (e.g. limited company), sales turnover, and number of employees. Industry surveys are another common source of published data; these are often compiled by specialist research companies and cover particular industrial sectors (e.g. food retailing, tourism, consumer electronics) and **markets** (e.g. the growing markets in organic and fair trade certified clothing). Researchers also obtain primary data, typically by conducting or commissioning their own questionnaire surveys. Some of these surveys have been run over extended periods. For example, the UK's *Quarterly Small Firms' Survey* (Blundel and Gray 2011), dates back more than 25 years, when it was established by Graham Bannock, author of the influential Bolton Report on small firms (Sections 11.2 and 15.2). These approaches have been influential in areas such as economic geography, where researchers have attempted to explain the relationship between entrepreneurial activity and regional economic development (Section 13.5). Looking back over two decades of research in that field, Acs and Storey (2004: 872) noted a significant improvement in the quality of data being used and in the sophistication of the statistical analysis. For example, whereas earlier comparative studies tended to compare regional cross-section data using ordinary least squares regressions, more recent work had access to both cross-section and time-series data. The following example indicates the kinds of research question that can be addressed using these approaches. Van Stel and Storey (2004) conducted an examination of the relationship between firm births and job creation in 60 British regions, covering the period 1980–98. The study drew on a number of sources of published data, including the VAT registration data (used as a proxy for start-ups) from the Small Business Service, population density data from the Office of National Statistics (ONS), and data on regional wage rates from the ONS's New Earnings Survey Panel Data-set. A number of technical issues were addressed to test the validity of the regression results, including efforts to test for both short- and long-run effects. For the

1980s, the researchers discovered no significant relationship for Great Britain as a whole, but a negative relationship for the north-east of England, an area which had been dominated by large industrial firms, contributing to low levels of independent entrepreneurial activity: this is the so-called 'Upas tree effect', previously identified in a study of entrepreneurial activity in Glasgow (Checkland 1976) (Section 14.3). By contrast, for the 1990s they found a significant positive relationship for Great Britain as a whole, but a negative relationship for Scotland, a country that had focused its enterprise policies on start-ups. The authors concluded by questioning current UK **enterprise policies**, which appeared to be returning to an earlier emphasis on promoting start-ups in order to promote economic development: 'The lessons from the present paper are that public policies to raise the formation of new firms, particularly in unenterprising areas, are likely to be unproductive at best and counter-productive at worst.' (Van Stel and Storey 2004: 903). Other recent examples of studies adopting this kind of approach include, Allen et al. 2008 (international comparisons of female entrepreneurship), and Blumberg and Letterie (2008) (**credit rationing** and business start-ups), and Wang (2008) (entrepreneurial orientation, learning orientation, and firm performance).

13.2.3 **Conducting ethnographic studies 'in the field'**

If you were looking for a polar opposite to researching entrepreneurship by analysing data sets, ethnography would seem a good choice. Ethnographic researchers cannot study at a distance; they get out into the field and engage directly with their research subjects. In the case of entrepreneurship, this is likely to involve periods of time spent with entrepreneurs, observing their activities and recording what takes place in real time. The approach originates in cultural anthropology, and some of the pioneering studies were conducted by researchers who travelled to unfamiliar, and often pre-industrial, societies with the aim of gaining a better understanding of their cultures and practices. For example, in the early 1960s, the Norwegian anthropologist Frederik Barth produced a classic study of entrepreneurial activity among the agricultural communities of the Jebel Marra mountain massif in Darfur (Barth 2000 [1967]). The following definition provides a useful summary of the approach:

> *Ethnography is the study of people in naturally occurring settings or 'fields' by methods of data collection which capture their social meanings and ordinary activities, involving the researcher participating directly in the setting, if not also in the activities, in order to collect data in a systematic manner but without meaning being imposed on them externally.*
> (Brewer 2000: 6)

In writing ethnographies, researchers are always caught up in a tension between subjectivity and objectivity (Johnstone 2007: 105). In other words, they need to position themselves somewhere between the 'authenticity' derived from getting very close to subjects in the field, and the 'distance' seen as necessary in order to address questions in an academic research community (Pearson 1993: xi). Based on his own experience of researching small firms using an ethnographic approach, one experienced researcher concluded, 'It could almost be argued that researchers operating in such contexts have to act in very similar ways to small business owners: both have to exploit opportunities, manage relationships and engage in a variety of negotiations with different actors.' (Ram 1999: 106) In recent years, entrepreneurship researchers have made increasing use of ethnographic approaches in order to study the cultures and practices of entrepreneurs in industrialized countries. In the introduction to her detailed study of 'Freddy the Strawberry man', an entrepreneurial strawberry dealer based in the Venezuelan Andes, the anthropologist Monica Lindh de Montoya makes a very good case for the distinctive contribution that can be made by ethnographies; her comments are worth quoting at length:

> *While economists have theorized about growth and progress and the nature of entrepreneurship within the larger economic system, they more seldom undertake concrete case studies of entrepreneurial action. And despite prevailing ideas about cold rationality and the cutthroat world of business, this world is an intensely social one the functioning of which requires shared cultural understandings and the constant cooperation of a myriad of actors. The kinds of 'bright ideas' and nascent entrepreneurial ventures that become established depend to a great extent on what is socially possible within a particular society, and issues such as trust, risk, and the relationship between individual gains and social responsibility are inherent in the process of developing a business.* (Lindh de Montoya 2000: 335)

13.2.4 Investigating entrepreneurial networks and networking

Social networks play an important role in the creation of new entrepreneurial ventures (Section 4.4). Networking is now seen as a key area of entrepreneurial activity, and has been the subject of many research studies (e.g. Johannisson 1998; Blundel 2002; Shaw 2006). One of the early findings was that entrepreneurs rely largely on *informal* sources in their personal contact network (PCN) to mobilize resources before the formation of a venture (Birley 1985: 113). The unique connections between people in the PCN play an important communication role, enabling the entrepreneur to identify opportunities that are not evident to others. At the heart of this network, there are normally a small number of 'strong' ties that provide the entrepreneur with a shelter from the opportunism and uncertainty of the market. For example, one study found that most business owners report between three and ten strong ties, primarily business associates plus a few close friends and family members (Aldrich et al. 1989). The time and energy that entrepreneurs invest in these 'pre-organizational' networks appears to be converted into future benefits for their emerging firms. This includes 'human capital', in the form of relevant experiences, skills, and knowledge, and 'social capital' (i.e. being known and trusted by others). Trust facilitates access to resources, through collaboration, and helps to overcome institutional barriers to entrepreneurial activity (e.g. local political resistance to a proposed development). However, the extensive personal ties used by entrepreneurs often lead a blurring of business and social life, with mixed consequences. For example, reliance on particular individuals can sometimes lead to sudden, unpredictable and potentially disruptive, structural changes. Furthermore, while all start-up businesses make some 'entrepreneurial' use of their personal networks, most small firms settle down into an established and fairly limited pattern of interactions. By contrast, entrepreneurs continuously develop their networks, with the more or less explicit aim of expanding existing ventures or establishing new ones.

To achieve this, they maintain a broader 'latent network', parts of which are activated when required (Ramachandran and Ramnarayan 1993). Episodes of entrepreneurial networking can also be triggered by external events, such as the liberalization of a market or the entry of new organizations into an industry (Blundel 2002). What happens to the entrepreneurial network as the venture develops? Researchers have found that entrepreneurs are active in managing the complex pattern relationships that make up their network. Despite a significant growth in research interest in networks over the last two decades, there are still gaps in our understanding of networking behaviour and its relationship to venture performance (Shaw 2006). What appears to happen is that the actions of solo entrepreneurs and **entrepreneurial teams** create a favourable 'organizing context' around the venture, in which it becomes relatively easier to deal with uncertainties and to exploit emerging opportunities (Johannisson 2000: 379).

Our next case (Case 13.2) builds on the themes of **entrepreneurial learning**, which was introduced in the previous chapter (Section 12.4), but with a particular focus on the way learning is a product of the relationships that entrepreneurs form with other actors. Founders of small entrepreneurial ventures face considerable leadership challenges, which are quite different from those working in larger firms (Davies et al. 2002; Gray and Mabey 2005; Kempster and Cope 2010). They have to take on many responsibilities (or 'wear many hats'), leaving little time to deal with their own personal development. They also have to deal with many new and unfamiliar demands, as the venture develops. At the same time, they can be quite isolated, with nobody to support them from within the organization, and often limited access to help from outside. The case discusses an innovative approach to this problem, in which leadership skills training and support is provided by bringing small groups of small business owner-managers together to share their experiences.

Case 13.2 Entrepreneurial leadership: a relational learning approach

This case study reviews some of the experiences gained during 'Leading Enterprise and Development' (LEAD) programme, a two-year project based at the Institute for Entrepreneurship and Enterprise Development (IEED), Lancaster University, and sponsored in its initial phases by the UK's North West Development Agency. LEAD was intended to support the business and personal development of small firm owner-managers (i.e. between 4 and 20 employees). The intended outcomes were: *improved leadership skills; personal and professional development; a motivated workforce; increased productivity; greater competitiveness and genuine business growth.* Seventy-two participants were divided into four cohorts (of 18). One of the selection criteria was that people could demonstrate a desire to grow and develop their businesses. The following summary is based on research conducted a member of the LEAD programme team, Dr Sarah Robinson. More detailed commentary on the programme can be found in Robinson (2006, 2007), Smith and Robinson (2007), and Kempster and Cope (2010).

Designing the LEAD programme

In designing the programme, the team drew on research evidence and on their previous experience of delivering support programmes. They identified three essential requirements: (1) formal learning (i.e. informing); (2) guided reflexive learning (i.e. applying knowledge and thinking to own context);

(3) peer interaction (i.e. enhancing and supporting learning by comparing, contrasting and affirming). These three elements were integrated into a holistic design that centred on the business and the owner-manager. The three learning processes were through several different kinds of activity:

- Masterclasses (formal learning).
- Action learning (reflexive learning/peer interaction).
- Coaching and mentoring (reflexive learning).
- Business exchanges (reflexive learning/peer interaction).
- Business support (formal learning).
- Experiential learning events (reflexive learning/peer interaction).
- Mentoring (formal learning/reflexive learning).

Participants also had access to an online forum where they could discuss and reflect on issues emerging from the different course components. The course was delivered by a mixture of academics from Lancaster University, external facilitators and professional coaches.

What did the programme achieve?

As the course proceeded, the LEAD team monitored its progress. In this section, we summarize briefly the findings on two aspects of the programme: (1) the training and development needs of the owner-managers as they joined; (2) how far their needs were addressed at the end of the course.

(1) Initial learning needs Based on their pre-course and exit interviews, it seems that participants were often facing quite serious emotional problems, lacking confidence, feeling alone and isolated, frustrated, and missing or having lost passion and direction. This is reflected in the following interview extracts: 'I need some vision for the future, I am looking for a bit of inspiration I suppose really and a bit of direction – vision, inspiration, direction'; 'I felt very alone at the start of the course lacking in confidence, running the business to survive'. There was also a feeling of personally not being of a high enough standard as a leader, or of having the knowledge and skills required to develop the business: '[I] knew that I was missing some attributes to bring the business forward.'; 'I lack confidence in the overall finance business side of things.' There were also concerns about being too preoccupied with the day-to-day running of the business, and finding it difficult to stand back and see the bigger picture. Based on these initial findings, four main types of leadership challenge were identified, relating to: 'people'; 'task'; '[strategic] thinking'; and 'implementation'.

(2) Leadership learning at the end of the course As the course progressed, participants began to share their experiences with their peers. In their subsequent review of the programme, the original leadership challenges were reconceptualized in terms of the new relationships that were being developed. This 'relational learning' became particularly apparent in the exit interviews where participants described the learning processes they had actually experienced on the course. Many of the learning processes described during the course can be categorized as four sets of relationships. The impact on each participant is bound to vary but the programme seems to have supported and strengthened these relationships:

- **Relationship with the self** This involves participants in accepting and in developing themselves as an entrepreneurial leader: '[Participating in the course has] boosted my confidence. [It] has made me recognise my own skills and ability. You are a bit isolated in your own business. You have no measure; you don't realise how good you are.'

- **Relationship with staff** This means gaining respect and leading people in a more effective way: 'I feel that I am closer and more aware of other people's feelings and this has proved effective in helping them to achieve their goals.'

- **Relationship with the business** This is where the owner-manager is able to step back from the business, in order to gain a strategic perspective and to create a vision: '[Participating in the course] gave me the tools to look at my business and find my own answers.'

- **Relationship with the wider SME community** This is where entrepreneurs start to build up a network of people in a similar situation, as a source of support and ideas: 'Since meeting my fellow [course participants], and listening to their everyday workplace problems and sharing experiences, I have returned to my company more confident and determined to make it successful, and question my own ability as the business owner and my leadership style.'

The importance and ongoing development of these relationships, and the interplay between them, was reinforced by the follow-up questionnaires, which were completed one year after the formal end of the course. This questionnaire focused specifically on the interplay between the 'relationship with self' and 'relationship with staff'. In particular, the owner-managers reported a growing confidence in themselves and in others compared with their situation before the LEAD programme. They also reported other constructive outcomes, including: being more proactive; being less interventionist/stepping back; having more patience/finding it easier to listen to others; having more communication with staff; identifying and making time for training; recognizing the link between training and the growth of the business; delegating, empowering, and generally having more trust in staff.

It appears that the LEAD programme helped the owner-managers in a number of ways. It enabled them to gain and to practise certain techniques. Coaching, for example, helped with moving thinking and processes forward, and with forward planning. Action learning was seen as important in the discussion with peers and learning from others. The masterclasses gave new ideas, but also served an affirmation purpose, leading to confidence in existing practice and giving people the courage to try out new ideas and to move forward. Learning from the experience of others, and from their 'real life case studies', was highlighted as being an especially important part of the programme. Interacting with other people in a similar situation helped to build up trust and support among the course participants. This seems to have translated itself into their businesses, with the owner-managers gaining more confidence both in their own abilities and in those of their staff. Though these entrepreneurial leaders are bound to face continuing challenges, they should now be much better placed to tackle them.

The LEAD programme illustrates how individual owner-managers can learn to become more effective entrepreneurial leaders through building more effective relationships with their peers and with other actors. The model has considerable potential but more work is needed to refine these approaches and to apply the approach to other settings (Kempster and Cope 2010).

Questions

1. What are the main obstacles faced by small firm owners in leading their businesses?

2. What can entrepreneurial leadership programmes do to address these problems?

3. How could you adapt or extend the ideas developed in this programme in order to encourage one of the following: (a) more effective leadership in a social enterprise; (b) more innovative activity in an existing corporation (i.e. 'intrapreneurship'); (c) more socially and environmentally responsible approaches to business.

Sources: Robinson (2006, 2007); Smith and Robinson (2007).

Having reviewed some of the more widely adopted research approaches, we now turn our attention to the main themes of social-level entrepreneurship research. We begin with a broad overview (Section 13.3), followed by more detailed examinations of two research themes, gender (Section 13.4) and geography (Section 13.5).

13.3 Social research themes: an overview

In this chapter, we have used the broad umbrella term, 'social perspectives', to cover many different sub-fields within the wider entrepreneurship research community. Figure 13.2 lists some of the more popular research themes. As in the preceding discussion on research approaches, a list of this kind cannot cover every research topic (e.g. entrepreneurial finance, which is discussed in Chapter 11), or distinguish the many sub-themes. For example, studies conducted under the 'family' theme, which examine issues of 'succession' (i.e. passing a business on to the next generation). Researchers also make many connections between different themes, both within entrepreneurship research and with other subject areas. For example, there are studies investigating the relationship between ethnicity and firm-level growth rates, and others looking at entrepreneurs' use of information and computing technologies (ICTs).

13.4 Research on gender and entrepreneurship

13.4.1 Exploring gender difference

Over the last 30 years, gender has moved from the margins to become one of the central themes in entrepreneurship research. It has created a dynamic research community, and has made many connections into the worlds of policy and practice. In parallel with these developments, there has been an equally dramatic growth in female entrepreneurial activity

Figure 13.2 Entrepreneurship research themes: social factors

Research theme	Example studies
Gender	Essers and Benschop (2009); Terjesen and O'Gorman (2007)
Ethnicity	Ram (1999), Dhaliwal and Adcroft (2007)
Family	Kets de Vries (1996); Janjuah-Jivraj and Spence (2009)
Ethics	Spence and Rutherfoord (2001),
Religion	Valliere (2008); Essers and Benschop (2009)
Migration	Godley (2006)
Crime and violence	Fadahunsi and Rosa (2002); Volkov (1999)
National culture	Lindh de Montoya (2000)
Social capital	Cope et al. (2007)
Organizational culture	Wang (2008)
Technological innovation	Garud and Karnøe (2003); Blundel and Thatcher (2005)
Politics and policy-making	Greene et al. (2007)
Natural environment	Parrish and Foxon (2009)
Geographic location	Henry and Pinch (1999); Greene et al. (2007)
Rural enterprise	Blundel (2002); Rønning and Kolvereid (2006)
Social enterprise	Di Domenico et al. (2010)
Information technologies	Lockett and Brown (2007)

rates, including commercial and social enterprise. Though recorded rates remain lower than for men, the differences have narrowed in many countries (e.g. Allen et al. 2008). However, it is also important to be cautious about the results of survey evidence. As we saw in the previous chapter (Case 12.4), women are often 'hidden' entrepreneurs, particularly when their contribution is as a member of a family business (Hamilton 2006). The historical development of this research theme is well documented (e.g. Brush 2008; Carter and Bennett 2006). As in other areas of entrepreneurship research, much of the early work was based on North American and European experience. The focus of this work was often on making comparisons between male and female entrepreneurs, including their personality characteristics, age and social background, and motivation for starting a business. Other studies investigated barriers faced by female owner-managers, including access to finance. Another strand examined the characteristics of female-owned businesses, including their sectoral distribution, size, and growth rates. There is still a need for descriptive studies, particularly in previously under-researched countries and sectors. However, there has also been an effort to move the field forward, with studies addressing the nature of female entrepreneurial activity, including the ways that women manage various aspects of the business (e.g. raising finance, marketing). There have also been studies investigating the performance characteristics of female-owned businesses (e.g. profitability, long-term survival prospects, social responsibility). Gender-related research has been conducted with a full range of methods, from the analysis of questionnaire surveys and financial data sets to ethnographies, and has been framed by a variety of theoretical frameworks. This can be seen by comparing recent studies, such as Di Domenico (2008) and Madsen et al. (2008): see the Further reading guide.

13.4.2 Different ways of acting entrepreneurially?

People often assume that entrepreneurs always plan their ventures in advance. However, there is also evidence that entrepreneurs sometimes act in less formal ways (e.g. Garud and Karnøe 2003; Di Domenico et al. 2010). In this sub-section, we focus on a new theoretical perspective called **effectuation** theory, which has developed in order to explore this kind of behaviour (Sarasvathy 2001). Effectuation theory provides a fresh perspective on the ways that entrepreneurs behave as they attempt to create something new, whether it be a product, an organization, or a market. In one of her initial articles, Saras Sarasvathy distinguishes between the ways that entrepreneurs make decisions using effectuation processes with a more planned 'causation' approach:

> *Causation processes take a particular effect as given and focus on selecting between means to create that effect. Effectuation processes take a set of means as given and focus on selecting between possible effects that can be created with that set of means.* (Sarasvathy 2001: 245)

This distinction can be made clearer with a concrete example. Imagine being asked to make someone a meal from scratch. If you adopted a causation approach, the process would begin with a recipe. You would use the recipe to identify a list of the ingredients, go out and buy them (or perhaps collect them from your garden), return to the kitchen, and follow the instructions in order to prepare the meal. By contrast, an effectuation process would begin with a search around the kitchen, and possibly the garden, to see what you could find by way of ingredients and utensils. In Sarasvathy's (2001: 245) words, you would then, 'imagine possible menus' and create your meal, making use of what was available. A similar thought experiment can be applied to the task of creating a new business venture. In a causation process, the entrepreneur would engage in a formal planning, starting with an analysis of potential market opportunities, with further rounds of analytical efforts to segment, target, position, and ultimately to implement the plan. By contrast, in an effectuation process the starting point for the entrepreneur would be to imagine possible ventures, building on the resources at her disposal, and adjusting her approach in response to what she discovers along the way. So how do these ideas relate to practical entrepreneurship? The point is not that one process is inherently superior to the other; people often make use of both processes in their decision-making. However, Sarasvathy argues that entrepreneurial behaviour often follows effectuation logic, rather than the causation logic that is assumed in many economics-based explanations. Her concluding remarks combine striking images with some sound practical advice about creating new ventures:

> *Human imagination and human aspirations influence each other and reshape one another continually, both directly and through economic artefacts. The swirls and eddies these interactions engender often change the shoreline and make the waters treacherous for economic shipbuilders*

and navigators. That is why destinations as well as paths are often unclear in economic decision-making. And when destinations are unclear and there are no pre-existent goals, causal road maps are less useful than effectual exchanges of information between all stakeholders involved in the journey. Bold expeditions and even one-eyed pirates rule such seas, and voyages to India effectually end up in the Americas. (Sarasvathy 2001: 262; emphasis added).

In the following Researcher Profile (Case 13.3), we return to the theme of gender and see how effectuation theory is being used by a Danish researcher in order to study the behaviour of female entrepreneurs.

Case 13.3 *Researcher Profile*
Helle Neergaard, applying effectuation theory to gender

Helle Neergaard is associate professor at the Aarhus School of Business, University of Aarhus, Denmark. She was awarded an MSc in International Business Administration and Modern Languages in 1995 and completed her doctorate in International Business in 1999. Her doctoral thesis was titled *Networks as Vehicles of Internationalization.* Helle's main research interests include: entrepreneurship and growth, human and social capital, self-efficacy, effectuation, entrepreneurial identity and gender. She sits on the editorial review board of the *Entrepreneurship: Theory and Practice; International Small Business Journal* and *International Journal of Gender and Entrepreneurship.* She has been a special issue editor for *The International Journal of Entrepreneurship and Innovation* (2006) and for *Entrepreneurship Theory and Practice* (2010). Helle is also the lead editor of *Handbook of Qualitative Research Methods in Entrepreneurship* (Neergaard and Ulhøi 2007). Since 2008, Helle has been a board member of the European Council for Small Business (ECSB), responsible for the Doctorial Programme. She has organized numerous PhD courses on qualitative methodology and successful publication.

In this interview, Helle discusses her research on effectuation theory and its role in entrepreneurship, with particular reference to gender and growth. In doing so, she raises a number of important questions about the ways that women act entrepreneurially:

Q: Why did you want to research in this area? How did you decide on your main research questions?

Sarasvathy's theory of effectuation is one of the most interesting new areas of research in recent years (Sarasvathy 2001, 2008). Sarasvathy shows that many, if not most, entrepreneurial businesses are based on principles of effectuation rather than causation, which means that instead of looking for a hole in the market to be filled, successful entrepreneurs base their businesses on who they are, what they are competent at and their existing knowledge as well on whom they know. Sarasvathy based her study on expert entrepreneurs, which she defined as individuals who had started several ventures. My work with female entrepreneurs in Denmark showed that these very often followed the five principles of effectuation even in their first attempt at founding a business.

So I was intrigued: How come that female entrepreneurs act as expert entrepreneurs? Sarasvathy identified five principles of successful venture start-ups – and we want to investigate how female entrepreneurs apply these principles in practice. Our research agenda also includes an investigation of various principles of venture growth. The issue here is that women do not grow their businesses, at least not in ways that are readily measurable statistically. The result is that their contribution to economic growth is not recognized by the Danish government. For example, Danish female entrepreneurs use what I call the 'layer-cake' principle of growth. Instead of growing their business organically, thus enlarging the cake, they tend to split the cake into smaller bites and share them with other female entrepreneurs in their network. This means that they do not hire new employees and hence do not grow on this dimension. It also means that profits have to be shared between many different one-woman businesses. Consequentially, even though the total is the same, each business grows only a little. Since the usual measures of growth are number of employees and turnover, what do you think happens? So our agenda is to develop a typology of growth. This might also assist women in choosing the right way of growing for their particular business. In my view, there is no one right recipe. However, women also effectuate in many other instances. For example, in a small pilot study, together with a colleague I investigated the impact of the Danish welfare system on female entrepreneurs and found that this is actually detrimental to female entrepreneurs (Neergaard and Thrane 2009). However, they use a strategy we call 'babystrapping'.* This strategy is also a way of effectuating because women adapt to government regulations so that they can still run their business while being on maternity leave, which in essence they are not allowed to do according to the Danish legislation.

Q: What methods are you going to use?

As is probably apparent from the above, we have not actually carried out the research yet – we are still in the preparatory phases. However, we intend to use various methods – both qualitative and quantitative – and various qualitative data collection techniques. However, most importantly is to access these women's stories about how and why they started a business, so naturally a major part will be narratives. It is impossible to address the 'why?' question underlying female entrepreneurs' actions purely with quantitative methods. Sarasvathy used what she called, 'think-aloud protocol analysis' in her study, and some form of this technique would probably be useful.

Q: What are your key findings? Do they have practical implications for entrepreneurs?

Naturally with the research in its infant stages we do not have any findings as such. However, there is no doubt that there will be practical implications for aspiring female entrepreneurs in understanding that the way they act is actually theoretically accounted for. We aim at identifying patterns of behaviour, and in showing how female entrepreneurs make choices that are crucial for venture start-up and growth, and we will be able to make recommendations with regard to producing a viable growth platform. This is important because it is a minority of female entrepreneurs who grow their business to any significant size.

---

* 'babystrapping' is a variation on the term, 'bootstrapping', where entrepreneurs get a venture started using their own financial resources (i.e. 'pulling yourself up by your bootstraps').

Q: Are there any particular challenges in conducting these studies?

The biggest challenge will probably be in identifying female entrepreneurs and get sufficient numbers to participate in the research, so that we can draw solid conclusions. Since we aim to collect various forms of growth we will probably need to use a snowball sampling strategy in combination with a maximum variation strategy (see: Neergaard and Ulhøi 2007: 253–278).

Q: Where do you think research in this area needs to develop in future?

I think that there is a vast amount of work to be done to understand the challenges of growth for small businesses better. In times of crisis, such as those we are experiencing now, businesses, which have not used external capital to support fast growth, may actually be better off. A lot of the conceptual work on growth was done in the 1970s, but times have changed so significantly in the last four decades that we need to re-conceptualize the phenomenon.

Sources. Sarasvathy (2001, 2008); Neergaard et al. (2006); Neergaard and Ulhøi (2007); Madsen et al. (2008).

13.5 The geography of enterprise

13.5.1 Exploring spatial variations in enterprise

Geography plays an important part in explaining where and how entrepreneurial activity takes place. Looking back to history, we can see how physical geography has shaped the location and nature of the activity. For example, metalworking **industries** were founded close to mineral deposits, and trading centres grew up beside navigable rivers (NB historical perspectives are addressed in more detail in Chapter 14). Economic geography also exerts a powerful influence. The location of **enterprises** is likely to be influenced by a number of socio-economic factors, including its proximity to suppliers, consumers, labour markets, and the availability of suitable physical infrastructure to support the business (e.g. railways, motorways, airports, and in some countries, reliable sources of power or fast broadband access). Researchers have looked at several sub-themes related to geography and entrepreneurship. For example, studies have examined differences between enterprise in urban and rural areas in a variety of ways. For example, several studies have looked at the kinds of people establishing new ventures in the countryside, some researchers have highlighted the role of the 'rural returner', someone who grew up in a rural location, moved away to work or study, but then came back to the countryside – often with new knowledge, capabilities, and connections, in order to establish a new venture. Another pattern involves people moving to a location as an employee, and subsequently deciding to set up a new venture in that area. Another area of social research on rural enterprise is concerned with entrepreneurial careers. Several studies have examined the way that people pursue several different enterprises at the same time (i.e. 'pluriactivity' or 'portfolio working'), sometimes combining employment with self employment (Rønning and

Kolvereid 2006). These distinctive patterns have been explained as a way of maintaining secure income streams, which can be particularly difficult for farmers due to uncertainties created by the weather and changing market conditions. At a more macro-level, economic geographers have also compared the performance of firms in different locations, both at an individual level and as firm populations (e.g. Greene et al. 2007). In the next section, we consider one of the major strands of research, which has looked at the ways that similar businesses tend to become concentrated in particular locations.

13.5.2 The structure and dynamics of clusters

Why do highly localized networks continue to emerge and prosper in an era of globalization? While it may be possible to develop a rationale for the industrial districts of the last century, contemporary **clusters** appear to present a paradox:

> [T]he principal dilemma of contemporary economic geography [is] the resurgence of regional economies and of territorial specialization in an age of increasing ease in transportation and communication. (Storper 1997: 21)

  This increase in localized networking seems to operate against the homogenizing effects of globalization. Researchers have identified several fairly straightforward explanations for the formation of clusters. For example, despite modern technologies, population mobility is limited, as people tend to become attached to particular locations. However, there are also some more general explanations of clustering. For example, Storper (1997: 181) sees spatial clusters as the result of a trade-off between localized 'territorial economies' and the 'flow' economies of global capitalism. Using a similar argument, Amin and Thrift (1995: 92) suggest that the performance of a local economy is closely linked to its capacity to 'capture' global economic flows. Research into the clustering of high technology firms can be seen as a useful test case. Anna-Lee Saxenian (1991) presented evidence from one of the best-known modern spatial clusters, Silicon Valley. She argued that Californian high technology firms had similar proximity requirements to firms in the traditional industrial districts, though the latter may have grown up over centuries (see Section 14.3):

> The proliferation of inter-firm networks helps account for the continued dynamism of Silicon Valley. While the region's firms rely heavily on global markets and distant suppliers, there is a clear trend for computer systems producers to prefer local suppliers and to build the sort of trust-based relationships which flourish with proximity. The region's vitality is thus enhanced as interfirm collaboration breeds complementary innovation and cross-fertilization among networks of autonomous but interdependent producers. (Saxenian 1991: 436)

  Evidence from Minneapolis and Cambridge, England suggests that atmosphere can be created over much shorter time frames (Lawson and Lorenz 1999). These spatially concentrated networks encourage close collaboration, and also allow shared labour markets to operate. Rapid circulation of people between organizations has been identified as an important mechanism for exchanging and developing the kinds of tacit knowledge that are required in innovative, high technology sectors (e.g. Brown and Hendry 1997; Henry and Pinch 2000). However, this is not to suggest that clusters are *easily* formed, nor that they are insensitive to location. The impressive dynamism of both the Minneapolis medical equipment cluster and the technology spin-outs clustered around Cambridge can be explained, in part, by the culture induced by the long-established, elite universities located in these cities. The distinctive structure of the firm population is also a factor:

> As with Minneapolis, a general spirit of openness has been identified by various researchers. By and large, this again has been encouraged by the open science culture in the university [. . .] but also by the existence of considerable technical overlap between firms which still compete in relatively different (often niche) product markets. (Lawson and Lorenz 1999: 314)

Contemporary clusters are fragile creatures. High-technology clusters are driven by the production, exchange, and fruitful recombination of knowledge. This requires a fine balance between co-operation and competition, which can easily be jeopardized by institutional changes. In the case of the high-technology clusters, one of the main dangers is the desire to 'protect' intellectual property. More specifically, the free flow of knowledge is likely to be constrained as universities become more 'commercial', internalizing research activity and resorting to the threat of litigation (Lawson and Lorenz 1999: 314). Ultimately, high technology clusters remain dependent on global economic flows. If national or international supply chain relationships become stronger than local ones, the spatial cluster becomes vulnerable.

13.6 **Practical implications**

There is a rich and varied literature addressing social dimensions of entrepreneurship. Some of this research, though it might be interesting and important in other ways, is unlikely to have direct implications for entrepreneurs. For example, as Richard Swedberg reflected, the pioneering contributions of Max Weber – often seen as the founder of modern sociology – are unlikely to help you to create a successful social or commercial venture:

> What are the practical implications of Weber's theories about entrepreneurship? I have to admit that in trying to give an answer to this question I feel a bit like Freud, who when someone drew his attention to the psychoanalytical significance of smoking cigars (Freud loved cigars), meekly answered: 'There are times when a cigar is only a cigar.' In other words, Weber's ideas are surely innovative and brilliant – but they do not seem to have any obvious practical implications. (Swedberg 2000: 27)

It may not be possible to draw simple lessons directly from the social research literature, but there are ways that entrepreneurs can benefit from this knowledge. Perhaps the most important of these is in helping people to become more 'reflective practitioners': The research evidence, and the approaches that we have discussed could be useful to people involved in entrepreneurial activity. Examples of the research topics and potential benefits include:

- **Gender differences** learning from the experience of other female-owned businesses and considering how these lessons might influence your own approach.

- **Rural entrepreneurs** seeing different approaches to managing an entrepreneurial career, and recognizing how geographic location can influence the performance of a new venture.

- **Entrepreneurial networks** gaining a better understanding of personal and inter-organizational networks, and their role in creating and exploiting new opportunities.

There are also practical implications for policy-makers, and for others concerned with broader questions about the kinds of entrepreneurial activity that take place, and their impact in terms of the economy, society, and the natural environment:

- **Encouraging economic development** In many countries, policy-makers are unsure how best to make their economies more competitive, innovative and capable of surviving in a globalized world. They are often lacking a detailed understanding of the entrepreneurial activity already taking place, or of what could be done to enhance its potential in the future. By making use of the full range of research approaches outlined in this chapter, governments could gain insights into both the 'big picture' (i.e. the broad patterns of activity, which can be mapped using large-scale data sets) and the fine detail (i.e. the more complex interactions between people, which can be investigated using qualitative research approaches).

- **Examining social and environmental impacts** Entrepreneurship research has tended to concentrate on the ways in which social factors exert an influence on entrepreneurial activity, rather than the other way round. Exceptions include Blackburn and Ram's (2006) study on enterprise policies and social exclusion and the growing body of research on social and sustainable entrepreneurship (e.g. Parrish and Foxon 2009). There are signs that things are changing. For example, Sarasvathy (2002: 95) has called for a new vocabulary of entrepreneurship, 'to tackle the central task of imagination in economics, i.e. to create from the society we *have* to live in, the society we *want* to live in.' As the world confronts an increasingly difficult set of environmental and social challenges over the next few years, we anticipate that these research strands will become more active and influential.

✱ 13.7 Summary

- ➤ There is a rich variety of social-level perspectives on entrepreneurship, with researchers from many disciplines adopting different kinds of theory and research method. It can be challenging to navigate a way through the research literature; review articles and chapters provide some useful signposts.

- ➤ The scope of the research is vast, ranging from micro-level interpretive studies of entrepreneurial activity using anthropological approaches to macro-level economic development studies using national and regional data sets. In combination, these approaches have increased our understanding of different aspects of entrepreneurship.

➤ It is essential to select theories and methods that are appropriate to the research area, and the specific research questions addressed. The point was demonstrated in this chapter through brief reviews of two research areas: gender and geography, illustrated with sample studies.

➤ Researchers may need to draw on several approaches in order to meet the needs of policy-makers and practitioners. For example, statistical analysis of survey evidence and official data sets can detect broad patterns and associations between variables, while more detailed qualitative methods can provide insights into subjective perceptions and underlying causal mechanisms.

➤ Research evidence can be useful to people involved in entrepreneurial activity. For example, it can help individuals to gain a better understanding of personal and inter-organizational networks, and their role in creating and exploiting new opportunities.

Case 13.4 Examining barriers to growth: a Ghanaian perspective

This case study is based on a research project conducted by Bernard Acquah Obeng, which examined barriers to growth among small businesses in Ghana, West Africa. It illustrates how survey-based methods can be used to generate useful information in a previously under-researched area. More extended coverage of this research can be found in Obeng (2007), Robson and Obeng (2008) and Robson et al. (2009). For background information on the informal sector in Ghana, see Debrah (2007).

Introduction: a gap in research and policy

Previous research into barriers to growth has focused on developed nations such as Canada, Hong Kong, and the UK (e.g. Orser et al. 2000; Moy and Luk 2003), and transition countries, such as Lithuania (Aidis 2005). There have been few studies examining the barriers and problems encountered by entrepreneurs in Africa; exceptions include Wolf (2004), Tagoe et al. (2005), and Mambula (2002). Entrepreneurs have a vital role to play in promoting economic development (McPherson 1996; Mead and Liedholm 1998), but much depends on the institutional structures established to foster and regulate enterprise. In order to support the development process, governments need a better understanding of micro, small, and medium-sized businesses, and of the challenges faced by their owner-managers. Many initiatives have been launched in order to investigate the underlying problems in Ghana and to provide institutional support for enterprise development. However, there have been few large scale research studies that would enable the government to respond more effectively to the needs of entrepreneurs.

Research approach

The research evidence presented in this case study is drawn from a survey of 500 entrepreneurs in the six regions of Ghana where approximately 91% of all businesses are located. The survey covered the manufacturing (193), services (217), and agriculture (90) sectors, the numbers in parentheses representing the number of respondents in each sector. The main criteria for selection were that the entrepreneur employed between 4 and 50 full-time workers. This range of employment was selected because they are the focus of the Ghanaian government policy and are also the businesses served by the main support organizations. In each case the entrepreneurs completed the written questionnaire, which was given to them in person by the researcher, over the period of January to June 2005. The 37 factors which could be barriers to entrepreneurs' firms achieving their objectives in the three previous years, 2002–05, covered a broad range of factors and these were categorized into the following seven groups: (i) finance, (ii) market, (iii) managerial and technical, (iv) inputs, (v) economic and regulatory, (vi) sociocultural, and (vii) other. The piloting of the survey minimized the number of factors which fell within the other group of factors. The project involved a detailed investigation of each area. The overall findings are summarized below. This case concentrates on two social themes: family and geographic location. However, before turning to these themes, we summarize the main findings of the study.

Summary of the overall findings

The component bar chart summarizes the owner-managers' responses, ranking the factors from the greatest to the least important in limiting their ability to meet their business objectives in the last three years. The research indicated that economic *factors* were perceived as the most important barriers to growth. Firstly, a *high rate of inflation* was seen by 71.4% of the respondents as an 'important' or a 'crucial' factor. This result confirmed the findings of an earlier survey of 100 businesses in the Greater Accra and the Northern regions of Ghana (Wolf 2004). Although it has been the Ghanaian government's policy to reduce the rate of inflation to a single-digit level since the beginning of the Economic Recovery Programme (ERP) in 1983, this objective has been difficult to achieve in practice. Information provided by the Bank of Ghana revealed that the rate of inflation had declined from 23.6% in December 2003 to 11.6% in January 2005. However, in March 2005, the rate jumped to 16.7%. The resulting impact on the prices of general goods could explain the importance of this factor. Secondly, high interest rates were identified by 68.5% of respondents as an 'important' or a 'critical' factor. As one person noted, 'Even [though] I went to a financial institution the previous day, the interest rates put me off to take the loan'. Thirdly, the high depreciation rate was mentioned by 63.5% of the respondents as an 'important' or 'crucial' factor. In the last five years to 2005 the Cedi (the currency of Ghana) was more stable than in the 1980s and the 1990s against the major international currencies. However, the high rate of depreciation of the Cedi in the recent past has had an adverse effect upon businesses in Ghana.

Having established that economic factors were perceived as the most important barriers, we now turn to social factors, and consider on two of these – family and location – influence the growth of Ghanaian firms.

The influence of family relationships

A family business is defined here as any business which employs one or more family members who are related to the person running the business, and it is owned by that person and their family. In other words, an entrepreneur and their family control the business and there is at least one

Factors limiting entrepreneurs' ability to meet business objectives: a summary of the overall research findings

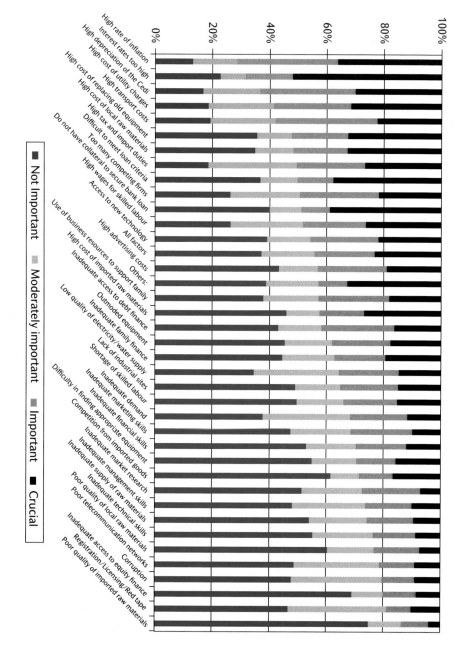

Source: Obeng (2007: Figure 6.2)

other member of the family working in the business. The contribution of family business in income generation, job creation, and the development of the economy can not be underestimated. Even in developed countries family business contributes more than a half of the total national income and a similar proportion of the labour force (Kets de Vries 1996, Morris et al. 1997). Despite their social and economic importance, there are few quantitative studies of family businesses in Ghana (Wolf 2004). In this study, 72.4% of the businesses were family businesses. In Ghana, as with many other African countries, the entrepreneurs are put under pressure to provide employment and resources for their immediate and extended family. This suggests that the people recruited on the basis of being a member of a family may not necessarily have the skills, experience, and expertise that the entrepreneur was seeking; or the entrepreneur may not have been looking to recruit, but family ties resulted in the family member being employed. The employing of a potentially less desirable, and possibly an unwanted group of workers may result in the business being less able to deal with day-to-day problems than those businesses which recruit on the basis of ability. Kotey (2005) and Sharma (2004) have also demonstrated that family businesses are more likely to face financial and managerial problems compared with the non-family businesses. Thus, it was hypothesized that family businesses were more likely to face financial problems than non-family businesses. This proved to be the case, with obligations to family members being an important constraint on growth. Growing firms were more likely to have the problem of the use of business resources to support families. This finding is consistent with the previous research of Buame (1996), Takyi-Asiedu (1993), and Kiggundu (2002) although none of these studies utilized regression techniques. The communal nature of African society and the nature of inheritance of some tribes mean that if a person becomes successful in the family he has the social obligation to cater for the other siblings who are not successful in life. Buame (1996: 197) noted that, '[n]o Ghanaian can easily do away with his or her relatives. Our traditional life is centred on kinship, I mean our relatives'.

The role of business location

Various studies in Europe have found that small businesses which were located in more 'accessible' rural areas performed better than their counterparts in the urban areas (e.g. Keeble 2003). However, similar research on urban micro and small businesses in East Africa revealed evidence to the contrary (Liedholm 2002). Thus, the role of location of the business and its impact on the performance of businesses has divided researchers. In this study, the location of the businesses has been related to three classifications, 'conurbations' (i.e. the capital, Accra, Tema and the surrounding area), 'large towns' (i.e. settlements with populations of 150,000 to 1,500,000), and small towns (i.e. settlements with populations of less than 150,000): 55.4% of the respondents were from conurbations, 21.6% from large towns, and 23.0% from small towns. There are virtually no businesses with five or more employees in the small towns. The definition of the settlements was adapted from the work of Keeble (2003), which also examined the performance and growth of small businesses by location. Closeness between firms and their customers can provide impetus for development due to the ease with which the firms can identify customer needs. Thus, it was expected that firms in conurbations would encounter fewer barriers than those in other locations. This was supported by the findings, though the picture is more complicated than it might first appear. For example, the use of business resources to support family members was identified by

42% of respondents as limiting their ability to meet their business objectives. This particular factor needs special attention because most small businesses in Africa which have collapsed or failed to grow have been due to the use of business resources to support social causes (Takyi-Asiedu 1993, Kiggundu 2002). For instance, Kiggundu (2002: 242) noted that although the African social set-up has a positive impact in the development of small business in terms of the social status of owner-managers, the overall impact has been negative. Buame (1996: 166) found in Ghana that entrepreneurs often had to relocate their businesses away from their hometowns because of the fear of the businesses becoming encumbered with family members. Location influenced the likelihood of firms encountering barriers, and the types of barriers that they faced. For example, firms in conurbations and large towns were more likely than those in small towns to experience a lack of collateral to secure bank loans, too many competing firms, and competition from imported goods. However, compared to their small town counterparts, businesses in conurbations were less likely to encounter managerial and technical constraints. This may be due to a lack of external support services in small towns, contributing to a lower capacity to absorb external knowledge (Barringer et al. 2005). By contrast, firms in conurbations, with their closer proximity to national and local government, were more likely to encounter stereotypical problems associated with Africa, including low quality electricity and water supplies, higher utility charges, higher taxation, and more bureaucratic 'red tape', though these relationships were not statistically significant. In summary, though firms in conurbations may benefit from the closer presence of a larger customer base, they can also experience overcrowding problems due to the number of firms, size of population, and an infrastructure that is struggling to cope.

Conclusion

This research study examined the problems that are encountered by firms in meeting their business objectives. We have discussed three factors in some detail. However, it is important to note that the three problems perceived as most important by the entrepreneurs surveyed were economic ones: (1) the high rate of inflation; (2) high interest rates; and (3) the high depreciation rate of the Cedi. Turning to other factors, the study also found that businesses that employed family members were more likely to face problems than the non-family businesses. This particularly applied to financial problems. These results are consistent with previous research in Africa, which has highlighted the importance of the extended family, although in the case of Ghana there was a lack of empirical research. The findings also revealed that in general firms in conurbations were more likely to encounter barriers than their small town counterparts. This underlines the need for further infrastructural improvements in Ghana if future growth and development are not to be jeopardized.

Questions

1. Why do you think these entrepreneurs perceived economic factors as the most important constraint on the growth of their ventures?

2. What do these findings suggest may be distinct about the Ghanaian context, and what factors are more likely to be found elsewhere in Africa and beyond?

3. What research approaches might you adopt in order to explore some of the issues raised by this research, including (a) family relationships in Ghanaian businesses; (b) location decisions of entrepreneurs?

Source: Obeng (2007); adapted with permission.

 ## Practical activities

1. **Comparing research approaches** Complete an online search for peer reviewed journal articles that tackle ONE of the following research themes: (a) gender; (b) ethnicity; (c) family; (d) spatial variations; (d) clusters; (e) national or organizational culture. For your chosen theme, select TWO articles that have adopted different approaches. Prepare a table, comparing their research questions, research methods, theoretical frameworks used, and findings.

2. **Effectuation in practice** Re-read the profile of Helle Neergaard (Case 13.3) and one of the recommended articles on effectuation (e.g. Sarasvathy 2001). Compare the main features of effectuation with a real-world example, using either the biography of an entrepreneur, one of the case studies in this book, or your own personal experience. Does your practical example match up with Sarasvathy's 'effectuation logic'?

3. **Learning the lessons?** Imagine that you were making ONE of the following decisions: (a) where to locate your new high technology start-up venture; (b) how to organize the supply chain for your new manufacturing venture; (c) how to encourage more entrepreneurial and innovative activity in your existing public, private or social sector organization. What research would you undertake (or commission) in order to ensure that you made a well-informed decision? Support your argument with examples.

Discussion topics

1. **What's your topic?** What would you like to know about entrepreneurship? Refer back to the opening discussion about potential social research themes (Section 13.1), and compare the themes identified (Figure 13.1) with your own favourite research topics. If you are working in a group, turn this into a 'brainstorming' exercise. Start by calling out whatever topics come to mind. Then, discuss the list you have produced and identify the three most interesting ideas. To extend the exercise, try to convert your chosen topics into potential research questions (NB this is a useful exercise to complete if you need to prepare an extended essay or dissertation as part of your course).

2. **Methods, methods, methods** Discuss the three following questions: (a) What research method would you prefer to use to explore entrepreneurship from a social perspective? (b) Why might some researchers prefer to use particular methods? (c) What reasons should guide you in selecting research methods?

3. Entrepreneurial societies Entrepreneurship researchers have tended to concentrate on the ways in which social factors exert an influence on entrepreneurial activity, rather than the other way round (Section 13.1). What kinds of questions might you ask about the influence of entrepreneurial activity on the societies in which it takes place? How might the influences you identify 'feed back' into entrepreneurial activity?

Further reading guide

The editor's introduction to Swedberg (2000) locates the various strands of social science research on entrepreneurship. Licht and Siegel (2006) review the field from an institutional economics standpoint, while Cope et al. (2007) introduces a special issue on the important theme of social capital. For a review of qualitative approaches in entrepreneurship research, see Neergaard and Ulhøi (2007); for a more quantitative, economics-based approach, see Parker (2009). Research on gender and entrepreneurship is reviewed by Brush (2008), Carter and Bennett (2006), and Greene et al. (2006). For research on ethnicity and entrepreneurship, see Ram et al. (2006), Basu (2008), and Dhaliwal and Adcroft (2007); for a review of migration studies, see Godley (2008). The family entrepreneurship field is summarized in Howorth et al. (2008) and Fletcher (2006). The entrepreneurial networking literature crosses many of the areas discussed in this chapter. Useful reviews of the field include, Conway and Jones (2006), Johannisson (2000) and Ebers (1999), which concentrates on the formation of networks. Pioneering studies include Birley (1985), Dubini and Aldrich (1991), Hansen (1995) and Johannisson and Monsted (1997). For research on the role of networking for small firms, see Shaw (2006), while Brown and Butler (1995), Jones (2001), and Blundel (2002) are examples of entrepreneurial networking in particular sectors, using a variety of research methods. The journals *Entrepreneurship and Regional Development, Environment and Planning C*, and *Regional Studies* often contain articles on the geographic dimensions of enterprise, using various approaches. For example, the special issue of *Regional Studies* edited by Acs and Storey (2004) includes several examples of quantitative studies using official data sets and survey data.

 # References

Achtenagen, L. and Welter, F. (2007) 'Media discourse in entrepreneurship research.' In H. Neergaard and J.P. Ulhøi (eds) op. cit. (193–215).

Acs, A.J. and Storey, D.J. (2004) 'Introduction: entrepreneurship and economic "development."' *Regional Studies*, 38, 8: 871–8.

Aidis, R. (2005) 'Institutional barriers to small- and medium-sized enterprise operations in transition countries.' *Small Business Economics*, 25, 4: 305–17.

Aldrich, H.E., Reese, P.R., and Dubini, P. (1989) 'Women on the verge of a breakthrough: networking in the United States and Italy.' *Entrepreneurship and Regional Development*, 1, 339–56.

Allen, E., Elam, A., Langowitz, N., and Dean, M. (2008) *Global Entrepreneurship Monitor 2007 report on women and entrepreneurship*. Wellesley MA: Babson College/Global Entrepreneurship Research Association.

Amin, A. and Thrift, N. (1995) 'Globalisation, institutional "thickness" and the local economy.' In P. Healey, S. Cameron, S. Davoudi, S. Graham, and A. Madani-Pour (eds) *Managing cities: the new urban context*. Chichester: John Wiley (91–108).

Barringer, B.R., Jones, F.F., and Neubaum, D.O. (2005) 'A quantitative content analysis of the characteristics of rapid growth firms and their founders.' *Journal of Business Venturing*, 20, 5: 663–87.

Barth, F. (2000 [1967]) 'Economic spheres in Darfur.' [Extract] in R. Swedberg (ed.) op. cit. (139–60).

Basu, A. (2008) 'Ethnic minority entrepreneurship.' In M. Casson et al. (eds) op. cit. (580–600).

Birley, S. (1985) 'The role of networks in the entrepreneurial process.' *Journal of Business Venturing*, 1, 1: 107–17.

Blackburn, R. and Ram, M. (2006) 'Fix or fixation?: the contributions and limitations of entrepreneurship and small firms to combating social exclusion.' *Entrepreneurship and Regional Development*, 18, 1: 73–89.

Blumberg, B.F. and Letterie, W. (2008) 'Business starters and credit rationing.' *Small Business Economics*, 30, 2: 187–200.

Blundel, R.K. (2002) 'Network evolution and the growth of artisanal firms: a tale of two regional cheesemakers.' *Entrepreneurship and Regional Development*, 14, 1: 1–30.

Blundel, R.K. and Gray, C. (eds.) (2011) *Quarterly survey of small business in Britain* (Vol 25, Q2, May). Milton Keynes: Open University Business School.

Blundel, R.K. and Thatcher, M. (2005) 'Explaining cluster responses to globalization: the case of volume yacht manufacturing in Europe.' *Entrepreneurship and Regional Development*, 17, 6: 405–29.

Brewer, J.D. (2000) *Ethnography: understanding social research*. Milton Keynes: Open University Press.

Brown, B. and Butler, J.E. (1995) 'Competitors as allies: a study of entrepreneurial networks in the US wine industry.' *Journal of Small Business Management*, 33, 3: 57–66.

Brush, C.G. (2008) 'Women entrepreneurs: a research overview.' In M. Casson et al. (eds) op. cit. (611–28).

Bryman, A. and Bell, E. (2007) *Business research methods* (2nd edition). Oxford: Oxford University Press.

Buame, S.K. (1996) *Entrepreneurship: a contextual perspective – discourses and praxis of entrepreneurial activities within the institutional context of Ghana*. Lund: Lund University Press.

Carter, S. and Bennett, D. (2006) 'Gender and entrepreneurship.' In S. Carter and D. Jones-Evans (eds) op. cit. (176–91).

Carter, S. and Jones-Evans, D. (eds) (2006) *Enterprise and small business: principles, practice and policy* (2nd edition). Harlow: FT Prentice Hall.

Casson, M., Yeung, B., Basu, A., and Wadeson, N. (eds) (2008) *The Oxford handbook of entrepreneurship*. Oxford: Oxford University Press.

Checkland, S.G. (1976) *The Upas tree: Glasgow 1875–1975 – a study in growth and contraction*. Glasgow: University of Glasgow Press.

Conway, S. and Jones, O. (2006) 'Networking and the small business.' In S. Carter and D. Jones-Evans (eds) op. cit. (305–23).

Cope, J., Jack, S., and Rose, M.B. (2007) 'Social capital and entrepreneurship: an introduction.' *International Small Business Journal*, 25, 3: 213–19

Davidsson, P. and Wiklund, J. (2001) 'Levels of analysis in entrepreneurship research: current research practice and suggestions for the future.' *Entrepreneurship Theory and Practice*, 25, 4: 81–100.

Davies, J., Hides, M., and Powell, J. (2002) 'Defining the development needs of entrepreneurs in SMEs.' *Education and Training*, 44, 8/9: 406–12.

Debrah, Y. (2007) 'Promoting the informal sector as a source of gainful employment in developing countries: insights from Ghana.' *International Journal of Human Resource Management*, 18, 6: 1063–84.

Dhaliwal, S. and Adcroft, A. (2007) 'Accurate portrayal or lazy stereotype?: the changing nature of the Asian business sector in the UK.' In M. Dowling and J. Schmude (eds) op. cit. (31–44).

Di Domenico, M. (2008) '"I'm not just a housewife": gendered roles and identities in the home-based hospitality enterprise.' *Gender, Work and Organization*, 15, 4: 313–422.

Di Domenico, M., Tracey, P., and Haugh, H. (2010) 'Social bricolage: theorizing social value creation in social enterprises.' *Entrepreneurship Theory and Practice*. 34, 4: 681–703.

Dubini, P. and Aldrich, H. (1991) 'Personal and extended networks are central to the entrepreneurial process.' *Journal of Business Venturing*, 6: 305–13.

Ebers, M. (ed.) (1999) *The formation of inter-organizational networks*. Oxford: Oxford University Press.

Essers, C. and Benschop, Y. (2009) 'Muslim businesswomen doing boundary work: the negotiation of Islam, gender and ethnicity within entrepreneurial contexts.' *Human Relations*, 62, 3: 403–23.

Fadahunsi, A. and Rosa, P. (2002) 'Entrepreneurship and illegality: insights from the Nigerian cross-border trade.' *Journal of Business Venturing*, 17, 5: 397–429.

Fletcher, D. (2006) 'Family and entrepreneurship.' In S. Carter and D. Jones-Evans (eds) op. cit. (209–19).

Garud, R. and Karnøe, P. (2003) 'Bricolage versus breakthrough: distributed and embedded agency in technology entrepreneurship.' *Research Policy*, 32: 277–300.

Godley, A. (2008) 'Migration of entrepreneurs.' In M. Casson et al. (eds) op. cit. (601–10).

Gray, C.W.J. and Mabey, C.L. (2005) 'Management development: key differences between small and large businesses in Europe.' *International Small Business Journal*, 23, 5: 467–85.

Greene, F.J., Mole, K.F., and Storey, D.J. (2007) *Three decades of the enterprise culture: entrepreneurship, economic regeneration and public policy.* Basingstoke: Palgrave.

Greene, P., Brush, C.G., Carter, N.M., Gatewood, E., and Hart, M.M. (eds) (2006) *Growth oriented women entrepreneurs and their business: a global perspective.* Cheltenham: Edward Elgar.

Hamilton, E.E. (2006) 'Whose story is it anyway?: narrative accounts of the role of women in founding and establishing family businesses.' *International Small Business Journal*, 24, 3: 253–71.

Hansen, E.L. (1995) 'Entrepreneurial networks and new organization growth.' *Entrepreneurship Theory and Practice*, 19, 4 (Summer): 7–29.

Hendry, C., Brown, J., and DeFillipi, R. (2000) 'Regional clustering of high technology-based firms: opto-electronics in three countries.' *Regional Studies*, 34, 2: 129–44.

Henry, N. and Pinch, S. (2000) 'Spatialising knowledge: placing the knowledge community of Motor Sport Valley.' *Geoforum*, 31, 2: 191–208.

Howorth, C., Rose, M., and Hamilton, E. (2008) 'Definitions, diversity and development: key debates in family business research.' In M. Casson et al. (eds) op. cit. (225–47).

Janjuha-Jivraj, S. and Spence, L.J. (2009) 'The nature of reciprocity in family firm succession.' *International Small Business Journal*, 27(6): 702–19.

Johannisson, B. (1998) 'Personal networks in emerging knowledge-based firms: spatial and functional patterns.' *Entrepreneurship and Regional Development*, 10, 4: 297–312.

Johannisson, B. (2000) 'Networking and entrepreneurial growth.' In D.L. Sexton and H. Landström (eds) *The Blackwell handbook of entrepreneurship.* Oxford: Blackwell.

Johannisson, B. and Monsted, M. (1997) 'Contextualizing entrepreneurial networking.' *International Studies of Management and Organization*, 27, 3, 109–36.

Johnstone, B.A. (2007) 'Ethnographic methods in entrepreneurship research.' In H. Neergaard and J.P. Ulhøi (eds) op. cit. (97–121).

Jones, C. (2001) 'Co-evolution of entrepreneurial careers, institutional rules and competitive dynamics in American film, 1895–1920.' *Organization Studies*, 22, 6: 911–44 (Special Issue on: Multi-level Analysis and Co-evolution).

Keeble, D. (2003) 'British SMEs in the 21st century: north-south and urban-rural variations in performance and growth.' In A. Cosh and A. Hughes (eds), *Enterprise challenged: policy and performance in the British SME sector, 1999–2002.* Cambridge: ESRC Centre for Business Research, University of Cambridge (87–102).

Kempster, S. and Cope, J. (2010) 'Learning to lead in the entrepreneurial context.' *International Journal of Entrepreneurial Behaviour and Research*, 16, 1: 5–34.

Kets de Vries, M.F.R. (1996) *Family business: human dilemmas in the family firm.* London: Thomson.

Kiggundu, M.N. (2002) 'Entrepreneurs and entrepreneurship in Africa: what is known and what needs to be done.' *Journal of Developmental Entrepreneurship*, 7, 3: 239–58.

Kotey, B. (2005) 'Goals, management practices, and performance of family SMEs.' *International Journal of Entrepreneurial Behaviour and Research*, 11, 1: 3–24.

Lawson, C. and Lorenz, E. (1999) 'Collective learning, tacit knowledge and regional innovative capacity.' *Regional Studies*, 33, 4: 305–17.

Leitch, C. (2007) 'An action research approach to entrepreneurship.' In H. Neergaard and J.P. Ulhøi (eds) op. cit. (144–68).

Liedholm, C. (2002) 'Small Firm Dynamics: Evidence from Africa and Latin America.' *Small Business Economics*, 18. 1–3: 225–240.

Lindh de Montoya, M. (2000) 'Entrepreneurship and culture: the case of Freddy the strawberry man.' In R. Swedberg (ed.) op. cit. (332–55).

Lockett, N. and Brown, D.H. (2007) 'Aggregation and the role of trusted third parties in SME e-business engagement: a regional policy issue.' *International Small Business Journal*, 24, 4: 379–404.

Low, M.B. and MacMillan, I.C. (1988) 'Entrepreneurship: past research and future challenges.' *Journal of Management*, 14, 2: 139–61.

McKenzie, B. (2007) 'Techniques for collecting verbal histories.' In H. Neergaard and J.P. Ulhøi (eds) op. cit. (308–30).

McPherson, M.A. (1996) 'Growth of micro and small enterprises in Southern Africa.' *Journal of Development Economics*, 48, 1: 253–77.

Madsen, M., Neergaard, H., and Ulhøi, J.P. (2008) 'The influence of roles and identity on female entrepreneurial agency.' *International Journal of Entrepreneurship and Small Business*, 5, 3/4: 358–72.

Mambula, C. (2002) 'Perceptions of SME growth constraints in Nigeria.' *Journal of Small Business Management*, 40, 1: 58–65.

Mead, C.D. and Liedholm, C. (1998) 'The dynamics of micro and small enterprises in developing countries.' *World Development*, 26, 1: 61–74.

Morris, M.H., Williams, R.O., Allen, J.A., and Avila, R.A. (1997) 'Correlates of success in family business transitions.' *Journal of Business Venturing*, 12, 5: 385–401.

Moy, J.W., and Luk, V.W.M. (2003) 'The life cycle model as a framework for understanding barriers to SME growth in Hong Kong.' *Asia Pacific Business Review*, 10, 2: 199–220.

Neergaard, H. and Thrane, C. (2009) 'The Nordic welfare model: barrier or facilitator of women's entrepreneurship in Denmark.' Paper presented at ISBE 32nd Annual Conference (4–7 November) Liverpool, UK.

Neergaard, H. and Ulhøi, J.P. (eds) (2007) *Handbook of qualitative research methods in entrepreneurship*. Cheltenham: Edward Elgar.

Neergaard, H., Nielsen, K. and Kjeldsen, J. (2006) 'State of the art of women's entrepreneurship, access to financing and financing strategies in Denmark.' In P. Greene et al. (eds) op. cit. (88–111).

Obeng, B.A. (2007) 'Business development services and small business growth in Ghana.' Unpublished PhD thesis. Durham: University of Durham.

Orser, B.J., Hogarth-Scott, S., and Riding, A.L. (2000) 'Performance, firm size, and management problem solving.' *Journal of Small Business Management*, 38, 4: 42–58.

Parker, S.C. (2009) *The economics of entrepreneurship*. Cambridge: Cambridge University Press.

Parrish, B.D. and Foxon, T.J. (2009) 'Sustainability entrepreneurship and equitable transitions to a low-carbon economy.' *Greener Management International*, no. 55: 47–62.

Pearson, G. (1993) 'Talking a good fight: authenticity and distance in the ethnographer's craft.' In D. Hobbs and T. May (eds) *Interpreting the field: accounts of ethnography*. Oxford: Oxford University Press (vii–xviii).

Ram, M. (1999) 'Trading places: the ethnographic process in small firms' research.' *Entrepreneurship and Regional Development*, 11, 2: 95–108.

Ram, M., Barrett, G., and Jones, T. (2006) 'Ethnicity and entrepreneurship.' In S. Carter and D. Jones-Evans (eds) op. cit. (192–208).

Ramachandran, K. and Ramnarayan, S. (1993) 'Entrepreneurial orientation and networking: some Indian evidence.' *Journal of Business Venturing*, 8, 6: 513–24.

Robinson, S. (2006) 'Learning to lead: developing SME leadership support for business development.' *Proceedings of the 27th ISBE National Small Firms Policy and Research Conference*, Cardiff (November).

Robinson, S. (2007) 'Relational learning: towards a model of owner-manager development.' *Proceedings of the HRD conference*, London (April).

Robson, P.J.A. and Obeng, B.A. (2008) 'The barriers to growth in Ghana.' *Small Business Economics*, 30, 4: 385–403.

Robson, P.J.A., Haugh, H.H., and Obeng, B.A. (2009) 'Entrepreneurship and innovation in Ghana: enterprising in Africa.' *Small Business Economics*, 32, 3: 331–50.

Rønning, L. and Kolvereid, L. (2006) 'Income diversification in Norwegian farm households: reassessing pluriactivity.' *International Small Business Journal*, 24, 4: 405–20.

Sarasvathy, S.D. (2001) 'Causation and effectuation: toward a theoretical shift from economic inevitability to entrepreneurial contingency.' *Academy of Management Review*, 26, 2: 243–63.

Sarasvathy, S.D. (2002) 'Entrepreneurship as economics with imagination.' *Ethics and Entrepreneurship* The Ruffin Series 3, Charlottesville, VA: Society for Business Ethics.

Sarasvathy, S.D. (2008) *Effectuation: elements of entrepreneurial expertise*. Cheltenham: Edward Elgar.

Saxenian, A. (1991) 'The origins and dynamics of production networks in Silicon Valley.' *Research Policy*, 20, 5: 423–37.

Sharma, P. (2004) 'An Overview of the Field of Family Business Studies: Current Status and Directions for the Future.' *Family Business Review*, 17, 1: 1–36.

Shaw, E. (2006) 'Small firm networking: an insight into contents and motivating factors.' *International Small Business Journal*, 24, 1: 5–29.

Smith, L. and Robinson, S. (2007) 'Leading enterprise and development: report on the design and delivery of a programme to engage and motivate small businesses in leadership and management development.' Lancaster: IEED, Lancaster University Management School.

Spence, L. J. And Rutherfoord, R. (2001) 'Social Responsibility, Profit Maximisation and the Small Firm Owner-Manager.' *Small Business and Enterprise Development*, 8, 2: 126–39.

Storper, M.J. (1997) *The regional world: territorial development in a global economy*. London: Guilford Press.

Swedberg, R. (ed.) (2000) *Entrepreneurship: the social science view*. Oxford: Oxford University Press.

Tagoe, N., Nyarko, E., and Anuwa-Amarh, E. (2005) 'Financial challenges facing urban SMEs under financial sector liberalization in Ghana.' *Journal of Small Business Management*, 43, 3: 331–43.

Takyi-Asiedu, S. (1993) 'Some socio-cultural factors retarding entrepreneurial activity in sub-Saharan Africa.' *Journal of Business Venturing* 8, 2: 91–8.

Terjesen, SA. and O'Gorman, C. (2007) 'Informal investment and venture financing in Ireland.' In H. Landström, M. Raffa, and L. Iandoli (eds) *Entrepreneurship, competitiveness and local development frontiers in European research*. Cheltenham: Edward Elgar (145–69).

Valliere, D. (2008) 'Exploring Buddhist influence on the entrepreneurial decision.' *International Journal of Entrepreneurial Behaviour and Research*, 14, 3: 172–91.

Van Stel, A.J. and Storey, D.J. (2004) 'The link between firm births and job creation: is there an Upas tree effect?' *Regional Studies*, 38, 8: 893–909.

Volkov, V. (1999) 'Violent entrepreneurship in post-communist Russia.' *Europe-Asia Studies*, 51, 5: 741–54.

Wakkee, I, Englis, P., and During, W. (2007) 'Using e-mails as a source of qualitative data.' In H. Neergaard and J.P. Ulhøi (eds) op. cit. (331–58).

Wang, C.L. (2008) 'Entrepreneurial orientation, learning orientation, and firm performance.' *Entrepreneurship Theory and Practice*, 32, 4: 635–56.

Wolf, S. (2004) 'Performance and problems of enterprises in Ghana.' Department of Agricultural Economics and Agribusiness Working Paper'. Accra: University of Ghana.

Zafirovski M. (1999) 'Probing into the social layers of entrepreneurship: outlines of the sociology of enterprise.' *Entrepreneurship and Regional Development*, 11, 4: 351–71.

Historical perspectives
The 'long view'

14

I should propose the analysis of business and economic evolution in terms of the 'disruptive, innovating energy' which over recent centuries has been a continuingly important factor in evoking change.

A.H. Cole, *business historian*

I would like to call on young people to commit themselves to activities that contribute toward achieving their long-term dreams. They have the energy and creativity to shape a sustainable future.

Wangari Maathai, *social entrepreneur and environmentalist*

Learning outcomes

After reading this chapter you should be able to:

➤ Recognize the distinctive insights that can be provided by historical research on entrepreneurs and entrepreneurship.

➤ Evaluate the knowledge gained from historical research and relate it to knowledge obtained through other research perspectives.

➤ Understand how actors create their own historical narratives, and assess their importance within the entrepreneurship process.

➤ Appreciate how entrepreneurial activity has influenced the development of organizations, communities, industries, and regions over time.

➤ Apply these insights to your own experiences of entrepreneurship.

Case 14.1 Wind energy: charting the creation of an industry

Where do successful technologies begin?

Wind energy is now a major growth industry, and the global market for turbine installations is now worth about 45 billion Euros (US$ 63 billion) (GWEC 2010). Growth is concentrated in Asia, North America, and Europe, with each installing more than 10 gigawatts (GW) of new wind capacity during 2009. China, the world's largest market, nearly doubled its wind generation capacity during that year. The Danish company Vestas Wind Systems A/S is the world's leading turbine manufacturer with an estimated 20% market share and more than 40,000 wind turbines installed around the world. Having delivered its first turbine in 1979, the company – which merged with another Danish manufacturer in 2004 – now employs more than 20,000 people (Vestas 2010). But how do particular companies, and countries, become technology leaders? In practice, success in technology entrepreneurship depends on a large cast of actors, including manufacturers, designers, technology users, evaluators, and regulators. In the case of wind energy, countries have adopted different approaches to technology entrepreneurship, and we are now able to see some of the longer-term consequences. For example, the Danish approach was distinctly low-tech and 'bottom-up', with a great deal of interaction between different groups of actors and steady improvements in the technology. By contrast, the United States took a high-tech, 'top-down' engineering-led route, in search of a more sophisticated technological breakthrough. So why were the Danes more successful, despite what appeared to be far more modest resources (Garud and Karnøe 2003: 278)?

Wind turbines

© Istock photo/Tore Johannesen

The Danish turbine story

With its large coastline, strong prevailing winds and lack of alternative sources of energy, Denmark seemed well-positioned to develop wind energy. Simple wind turbines had been used in Denmark in the early twentieth century, but today's three-blade turbine originates from a design by Johannes Juul, which operated between 1956 and 1967. Juul's ideas were revived in the early 1970s, when the global oil crisis led politicians and others to seek alternative sources of energy. Wind turbine pioneers included a number of self-builders, including amateur enthusiasts and grassroots opponents of nuclear power. Their work was promoted by the magazine *Naturlig Energie* and by the Danish Windmill Owners Association, both of which were founded in the late 1970s (Gipe 1995: 59). Other developments in this period included the founding of a small wind turbine testing station at Roskilde and government interventions to subsidize and regulate the emerging industry. At this point Vestas, a small manufacturer of farm equipment and cranes, decided to develop wind turbines. In 1979, the firm signed a licensing agreement with the self-builder, Karl Erik Jørgensen, to produce one of his new designs. Meanwhile, policy-makers in the United States identified the aerospace industry as the obvious source of expertise on turbine design (Gipe 1995: 56, 83–6). US engineers concentrated on perfecting the aerodynamic qualities of their designs, whereas their Danish counterparts focused on reliability. Danish designers were in much more regular contact with the user community, which comprised mainly small independents and co-operatives, sharing their ideas through regular 'wind meetings'. Geographic proximity, varied site conditions, and a spirit of open experimentation helped generate a rapid pace of learning, based on practical experience in the field. Danish designers were responsible for several key innovations, including brakes to slow the turbines and fibreglass blades, which had their origins in boat building. However, the overall approach was of rapid cycle incremental innovation, rather than sudden radical breakthroughs. Despite changes of government, the political coalition around wind energy was sufficient to 'steer' the industry towards maturity, with a gradual reduction in subsidies in the decade to 1989 (Garud and Karnøe 2003: 293). By contrast, government intervention in the United States, including tax credits, tended to promote building rather than operating turbines. This helped stimulate a speculative boom in California, with some installations being pursued for tax breaks rather than for power generation (Asmus 2000: 116). This was followed by a dramatic collapse in the mid 1980s when the tax credits were withdrawn; the speculative boom ended in financial failures and lawsuits, with many turbines left rusting and unused (Gipe 1995; Asmus 2000: 122).

Meanwhile in Germany . . .

Researchers studying wind energy in the German state of North Rhine-Westphalia (NRW) and the Netherlands also found a strong historical influence, with initial differences in public policies influencing subsequent entrepreneurship patterns. In the Netherlands, policies related to wind energy had favoured the large energy companies over independent entrepreneurs. Though these policies were revised in the second half of the 1990s, the German wind energy industry expanded at a faster rate. The researchers concluded that public policies had played a decisive role in this outcome: 'While in the Netherlands, the dominance of [existing energy companies] impeded the implementation capacities of other entrepreneurs, in NRW a diversity of entrepreneurs was encouraged from early on.' (Agterbosch and Breukers 2008: 645). As in Denmark, both federal and state-level policies encouraged grassroots initiatives in the early years, with farmers and small, community-owned projects being given access to the electricity grid via preferential 'feed-in' tariffs (Agterbosch and Breukers 2008: 639). After the mid 1990s, many of these locally owned initiatives were displaced by larger organizations. However, these earlier developments played an important role in helping wind energy to gain social acceptance, so accelerating the growth of the industry in this region.

Points to consider

1. Why did the 'low-tech' approach of the Danish wind turbine industry prove more successful than the 'high-tech' approach adopted in the United States?

2. What challenges would wind energy entrepreneurs in: (a) the United States; (b) the Netherlands, have faced in comparison with their Danish and German counterparts?

3. Given the current spread of wind and solar energy around the world, what practical lessons might you draw from these historical cases?

Sources: Gipe 1995; Asmus 2000; Garud and Karnøe 2003; Agterbosch and Breukers 2008; GWEC 2010; Vestas 2010.

14.1 **Introduction**

This chapter reviews established research on entrepreneurship that considers both the causes and the consequences of **entrepreneurial activity** over extended periods. This is a very broad research field, which adopts a variety of approaches. This work includes: (a) detailed biographies of individual entrepreneurs and company histories; (b) accounts of the growth and decline of particular industries, industry sectors, and industrial regions; and (c) attempts to explain industrialization and economic development (Figure 14.1). We examine

Figure 14.1 Historical research on entrepreneurship: focus and examples

Focus of study	Sample studies
(a) **Entrepreneurial individuals and organizations** (Section 14.2)	Pierre Dupont (Chandler 1971), Alfred Nobel (Fant 2007), ICI (Pettigrew 1985), John Shaw (Popp 2007, 2009b), IBM (Black 2005), Starbucks (Clark 2008)
(b) **Industries, sectors, and regions** (Section 14.3)	Oil (Yergin 2009 [1991]), Jewellery (Carnevali 2003), Motorsport (Henry and Pinch 2001), Wind energy (Asmus 2001), Engineering (Scranton 1997), Motorcycles (Wezel and Lomi 2003; Wezel 2005), Shipping containers (Levinson 2007), Outdoor clothing and equipment (Parsons and Rose 2005), Hollywood (Jones 2001)
(c) **Industrialization and economic development** (Section 14.4)	Schumpeter (2010 [1942]), Gerschenkron (2000 [1966]), Landes (2003 [1969]), Sabel and Zeitlin (1997)

each of these areas in turn, illustrating our review with relevant examples. One of the main arguments of the chapter is that 'history matters'. The opening case indicates how technology entrepreneurship can be influenced by previous policy decisions, and hinted at some deeper economic, social, and cultural influences (Case 14.1). Furthermore, entrepreneurs will be better placed to take decisions for the future, if they have a better understanding of what has happened in the past.

The chapter proceeds as follows. In Section 14.2, we review historical studies of entrepreneurial individuals and their organizations; this section builds on some of the themes introduced in Chapter 12 ('individual perspectives'). Section 14.3 examines entrepreneurial activity at the level of industries, industry sectors, and the regions in which they are located. This section is developing theories and concepts from Chapter 13 ('social perspectives'), including the network perspective. Section 14.4 is concerned with the role played by entrepreneurial activity in broader historical processes. In this section we ask why the world industrialized in the way that it did and examine the variety of 'alternatives' that have been pursued. Finally, in Section 14.5, we consider how you might apply insights from history to your own experiences. This section also looks forward to the final chapter on policy-making.

14.2 Entrepreneurial individuals and organizations

14.2.1 Introduction

People like to read about the lives of successful entrepreneurs. You will find a variety of entrepreneurial autobiographies, some written directly by the person concerned, others with the help of a 'ghost' writer. There are also many biographies, ranging from popular books about current media celebrities to more scholarly studies of historical figures. A common feature of all these accounts is that the life of the entrepreneurial individual is usually intertwined with the history of the organization, or organizations, that they helped to create. These accounts also follow a characteristic structure, with a chronological account of the person's achievements, preceded by a look back at their early years. Autobiographies tend to be interspersed with the author's reflections on what they have achieved, often linked to more general thoughts about the nature of entrepreneurship. It is important to be cautious when using biographies and autobiographies; there is a strong incentive for people to present themselves in the best possible light, so the account that you read may give a false impression of the subject. For example, authors can exaggerate their achievements and either down-play or avoid more controversial episodes (i.e. 'hagiography'). By contrast, a well-researched biography or autobiography can be very useful, providing unique insights into entrepreneurial worlds that might otherwise be difficult or impossible to access. For example, Lewis (2001) depicts life in Silicon Valley in the late twentieth century through an entertaining account of its more colourful figures, while Berlin's (2005) scholarly biography of Robert Noyce, the co-founder of Fairchild Semiconductor and Intel, provides an interesting contrast. Through a combination of interviews, direct observation, and use of documentary evidence, a good author can reveal both personal worlds (e.g. how people perceived and created opportunities in a era of rapid technological innovation), and the relationship between individuals and their broader context (e.g. how Robert Noyce and other Silicon Valley entrepreneurs made use of their social and business networks).

In the following sub-sections, we first consider how historians have written biographies of individuals, before turning to a distinct tradition of writing company histories.

14.2.2 Historical biographies

Most people's lives remain unwritten; though they may be remembered by relatives and friends, there is no published record to tell us how they lived or what they achieved. Most historical biographies tend to be written about famous, and sometimes infamous, individuals (e.g. leading politicians, artists, military leaders, social reformers, and entrepreneurs). This leaves considerable scope for writing about other entrepreneurial lives. If you have entrepreneurial ancestors, there may be an opportunity to discover more about their place in history (see Practical activity 3). Early in his career, the business historian Alfred H. Chandler wrote a biography of his great-grandfather, Henry Varnum Poor, a journalist who provided business information to the newly emerging railway industry (Chandler 1956). In common with other historical researchers (e.g. Popp 2007), Chandler found personal letters to be a useful source of evidence, which could be combined with business correspondence and published materials. He found that Henry's wife Mary, 'like many nineteenth-century New England ladies, saved nearly all the correspondence she received from her family and close friends and also collected a large number of letters that she had written to the various members of the family' (Chandler 1956: 285). Letters exchanged between Mary and her husband between 1838 and the late 1890s shed light on the couple's business and social activities. Henry was an entrepreneurial individual, and the biography shows how he developed his business, providing comment, information, and advice. The biography also provides insights into the activities of the railway entrepreneurs. For example, as the industry began to develop in the 1850s, his editorials in the *American Railroad Journal* addressed what he saw as the most pressing problems of the day, including the problem of 'over-construction' (i.e. building too many railway lines), and the need for financial and administrative reforms. Chandler discusses his ancestor's achievements, but also emphasizes his weaknesses, often referring to errors of judgement, such as placing too much confidence, 'in leading railroad and financial entrepreneurs.' (Chandler 1956: 121)

Published biographies and autobiographies can be a useful source of information in a historical study, but can be very long and complicated accounts. So how can you avoid getting lost in the details of the narrative? One answer is to focus your attention on particular research themes. For example, if you are particularly interested in individual-level factors (e.g. personality characteristics, educational background), or social factors (e.g. ethnicity, social networks), you can search the biography for evidence; you may also find that the authors of biographies have addressed your theme as part of their discussion. To illustrate this process, we can make a very brief comparison between the lives of two historical figures: (a) George Cadbury, the British entrepreneur who helped build a successful and innovative confectionery business; and (b) Alfred Nobel, the Swedish technology entrepreneur who developed a new generation of explosives, and later provided funding for the Nobel Peace Prize (Figure 14.2).

Figure 14.2 Comparing the lives of historical figures: sample starting points

Research theme	George Cadbury (1839–1922)	Alfred Nobel (1833–96)
Role of family business	Company founded by his father; worked with his brother Richard, initially including tea and coffee before focusing on chocolate and seeing more rapid growth.	Family of engineers and business people; family moved with father to St. Petersburg (1842) to set up armaments business for Tsar's army.
Religious and ethical influences	Quaker religious practice influenced entrepreneurial motivation (e.g. marketing chocolate as alternative to alcohol consumption), and practice (e.g. improving working and living conditions).	His younger brother Emil was killed in an explosion; is also thought to have been influenced by anti-war views of long-time friend, Bertha von Suttner and by contemporary depictions of him as a 'merchant of death'.
Socio-economic conditions	Cocoa could be sourced through British colonies; opportunities opened up by Gladstone's free trade budget (1860), growth in urban mass markets.	Fall in demand at end of Crimean War (1856) contributed to failure of company. Alfred and two brothers given an opportunity to restore the business.
Technological and social innovation	Company was the first to use Van Houten's new cocoa-making machine (1860s); quality product fitted new food regulations; built new factory with workers' welfare in mind (e.g. sports fields, parks), but also competitive (created French-style 'Bourneville' branding).	After many experiments, he patented a more stable form of nitroglycerine, originally invented by the Italian scientist, Ascanio Sobrero; he subsequently patented dynamite (1867). Late in life, he was responsible for several lasting social innovations, including the Nobel Peace Prize.

Sources: Bradley (2007); Fant (2007); Cadbury (2010); Nobel (2010).

There is a long and continuing tradition of writing biographies of entrepreneurs (Corley 2008). The best historical biographies place the lives of individuals in a wider context, enabling readers to see how their subjects interact with other people and with the technologies, cultures, institutions, and economic conditions in which they lived. Biographical studies can also be more useful to researchers if they are informed by relevant theoretical frameworks (Jones and Wadhwani 2008). The theoretical framing enables researchers to make comparisons between different historical studies, and even between the past and the present. By applying suitable theories and concepts, you could explore a variety of issues, based on evidence from the lives of historical figures, such as George Cadbury and Alfred Nobel (Figure 14.2). For example, with reference to the previous three chapters, we might consider the following questions:

- How did economic conditions and other factors influence their activities?

- What were the economic and social impacts of the businesses they created?

- How did their family upbringing influence their behaviour?

- Why were they able to perceive these **entrepreneurial opportunities**?

- How did ethical considerations influence their behaviour?

- What role did social networks play in the success of their ventures?

- What kinds of **entrepreneurial learning** did they undertake?

Well-researched biographies, and some of the more reflective autobiographies, provide their readers with insights into areas of entrepreneurial activity that might otherwise remain inaccessible. However, some of the more popular biographies and autobiographies can paint a rather incomplete and distorted picture of their subject. This kind of distortion is more likely in biographies of living subjects, who may still have an opportunity to influence what is written. It can be identified by comparing biographical writing with other information sources (e.g. industry data, newspaper articles, other biographies), and by reading book reviews. This kind of material can still be a useful source of evidence if you read it *critically*. For example, it could reveal how an entrepreneur wants to be perceived, or how stories are used to mould entrepreneurial self-identities (Section 12.4).

14.2.3 **Company and other organizational histories**

The lifetime of an organization is not limited in the same way as that of its human founders. While most organizations 'die young', others manage to survive for extended periods. In 2007, *Business Week* reported the failure of Kongo Gumi, a Japanese Buddhist temple builder, its assets being acquired by a larger construction company. Kongo Gumi had been founded in 578 CE and was in independent existence for more than 1,400 years (Hutcheson 2007). Other organizations, including the Scandinavian packaging and wood products company Stora Enso (www.storaenso.com), have extended lifespans, but few can compete with Kongo Gumi. The histories of such organizations, including public bodies and charities, can provide a good insight into the ways that entrepreneurial activity plays out over time. Alfred Chandler drew on his family history a second time, to write an account of Pierre S. DuPont, and the industrial **enterprise** that bears his name (Chandler and Salsbury 1971). Historical accounts may be commissioned by the organization, often to mark a significant anniversary. For example, Castronovo's (1999) history of Fiat was published in the Italian car maker's centenary year. Histories can address many aspects of organizational life, from operations management to marketing, but they usually include examples of entrepreneurial activity. The most obvious place to look is in the early years of the organization's life, but entrepreneurial activity can also be found in later periods, such as following succession in a family firm, when the younger generation gets an opportunity to introduce new ideas; both George Cadbury and Alfred Nobel illustrated this phenomenon (Figure 14.2). Larger and longer-established organizations often engage in corporate entrepreneurship (or '**intrapreneurship**') during major strategic realignments, such as acquisitions, mergers, and diversifications, though they often find it difficult to reconcile the different organizational arrangements needed to 'explore' new opportunities while also continuing to 'exploit' existing ones (March 1991).

Organizational histories can be useful sources in addressing research questions related to many aspects of entrepreneurial activity. As with historical biographies, these questions can be linked to relevant theoretical frameworks and concepts, for example:

- How did people within an organization identify or create entrepreneurial opportunities?

- How were the organization's resources and capabilities reconfigured in order to exploit these opportunities?

- What were the longer-term outcomes of an episode of corporate entrepreneurial (or 'intrapreneurial') activity?

Criticism of organizational histories has tended to focus around similar issues to those we discussed in relation to biographical writing. For commissioned histories, in particular, the main concern is that the authors might either downplay or ignore less successful, or more controversial, episodes in the life of the organization. However, while this may happen in some cases, there are also many historical studies that have addressed negative aspects of entrepreneurial activity. These range from Ida Tarbell's (2010 [1904]) pioneering 'muck-raking' investigation into the early history of Standard Oil, to more recent accounts in this tradition, which have criticized the behaviour of large corporations such as Starbucks (Clark 2008) and IBM (Black 2001). As with biographies, the better company histories do not depict their subject as though it existed in isolation. Instead, the scope of the study moves beyond the administrative boundaries of the organization, and the researchers also examine its interactions with other actors including its suppliers, customers, competitors, government agencies, and local communities (e.g. Pettigrew 1985; Whipp and Clark 1991; Casson and Godley 2007).

In the next section, we move from the level of individual organizations to consider the histories of the industries, sectors, and regions in which they are operating (Section 14.3). By way of introduction, we profile a business historian who worked with an experienced entrepreneur to write a detailed historical study. Their work charts the growth of the mountaineering and outdoor equipment industries from the mid-nineteenth century to the present day, highlighting the role played by entrepreneurs, technologists, and people who simply responded to the call of the mountains (Case 14.2).

Case 14.2 *Researcher Profile*
Mary Rose, combining technological innovation, entrepreneurship, and the call of the mountains

Mary Rose is Professor of Entrepreneurship and Director of the Institute of Entrepreneurship and Enterprise Development in the Management School at Lancaster University, UK. She specializes in evolutionary approaches to innovation and the relationships between innovation, entrepreneurship, and communities of practice. Mary has published widely on the evolution of business values, networking behaviour by family firms and the problem of leadership succession, including books, edited books, and articles in refereed journals. She has twice been president of the Association of Business Historians and was president of the European Business History Association, 2003–05. She was director of the Pasold Research Fund, a charitable trust working in the field of textile history, 1997–2006. Mary's books include, *Firms, Networks and Business Values: The British and American Cotton Industries Since 1750* (Rose 2000). She has also collaborated Dr Andrea Colli (Bocconi University, Milan) and Dr Paloma Fernandez Perez (University of Barcelona), in research on differences in the behaviour and capabilities of family firms in Britain, Italy, and Spain. In this interview, she talks about her collaborative research with Mike Parsons, former MD of the outdoor equipment company, Karrimor. The company was founded by Mike's parents in 1946, initially to make bags for bicycles; Mike joined the family firm at 18 and was instrumental in growing the company into a leading manufacturer of outdoor clothing and equipment. This historical research project has been published as, *Invisible on Everest: Innovation and the Gear Makers* (Parsons and Rose 2003), and as journal articles (Rose and Parsons 2004; Parsons and Rose 2005). The project traced the evolution of clothing and equipment for outdoor activities, from the middle of the nineteenth century to the present day. In doing so, it revealed a great deal about both the ways that entrepreneurial actors respond to social, cultural and technological developments, and the long-term impact of their activities. It also led to specialist courses and conferences serving today's dynamic global outdoor products industry (www.innovation-for-extremes.org)

Q: Why did you want to research in this area? How did you decide on your main research questions?

The outdoor industries – including design, manufacturing, and retailing of clothing and equipment for mountaineering, skiing, polar exploration, cycling, and hill walking – form an important economic sector, but in 2000, when the research began, they were under-researched. As a keen mountain walker, with an academic background in business history, this was an opportunity to carry out serious research on my hobby. I can remember vividly when I first had the idea for the book: it was in the Lake District, on a wet, windy spring weekend in 1995, having just bought some new gear, when it struck me that no one had written a history of how mountaineering clothing and equipment had developed. At the time I was struggling to finish Anglo-American book, and so the idea stayed just that for some years. Writing history is a complex process and research questions emerge and are often shaped by the research process. From the start I was interested in how the evolution of innovations in clothing and equipment shaped or were shaped by sports' users.

Q: What methods did you use?

This research began with a conventional historical methodology which places innovation in its long-term context by critically appraising archives, interviews, and secondary material. In January 2000 I made a phone call to Mike Parsons, the past owner of the outdoor brand Karrimor, asking him for an interview. Within six months that phone call had transformed the book from a conventional history to an innovative methodology. An e-mail exchange developed as I travelled round carrying out the research which convinced me that combining Mike's technical, business, and sporting knowledge with my academic experience could contribute to an unusual book. Mike's position as one of the key innovators of his generation obviously raised methodological issues relating to how to be both researcher and researched. We resolved this by adopting a holistic approach to evaluating innovations by interviewing designers, suppliers, manufacturers, outdoor journalists, and users and setting alongside a range of archival materials, including correspondence, expedition reports, and published materials.

Q: What are your key findings? Do they have practical implications for entrepreneurs?

Invisible on Everest highlights the importance of understanding user needs for successful innovation. Innovation is a social process based on combinations of knowledge often built at the boundaries of communities of practice. This is especially clear in outdoor sports and was exemplified in Mike's experience at Karrimor where his own multi–sport activity placed him in a position to devise a 'Think Tank' of lead users, including mountain photographers, polar explorers, as well as climbers and mountain guides. He met with them quarterly to brainstorm on product innovation. Throughout the book we focused on the needs of lead users, and it is worth remembering that while they may seem to be an elite niche, their needs are typically around five years ahead of the normal user. Companies developing meaningful engagement with lead users are in a better position to anticipate market needs than those relying only on conventional market research.

Q: Are there any particular challenges in conducting these studies?

The challenges of historical research are what attract me to it. It involves applying theory to the analysis of a combination of archives, secondary material, and in the case of modern studies, interviews. One of the biggest challenges may come as a surprise in an era of easy access to digitized information: there is no guarantee of the availability of archives for a particular company or organization. It was my concern that there were significant gaps in archival material for outdoor industries that actually helped build the collaborative relationship with Mike Parsons. As a result of numerous mergers and takeovers from the 1990s onwards, few outdoor companies have archives. Even when one is available, it is often no more than a jumble of public relations materials and catalogues. Part of the imagination of the historian is identifying alternative sources which help fill the gaps. While I travelled and assessed whether the project was viable I e-mailed Mike about the materials. The interactions helped build the trust and shared understanding which inspired our collaboration. One of the challenges of working with a business person to co-write research is the scepticism of colleagues that this can create rigorous research. The new research questions around the social processes underpinning innovation, and the opportunities for developing innovative practices in teaching and engagement with business, including our annual conference, 'Innovation for Extremes' were the gains.

Q: Where do you think research in this area needs to develop in future?

There has been a tendency for historical approaches to innovation and entrepreneurship to develop in entirely different silos from management studies, where much work is uninformed by history. Setting innovation and entrepreneurship in historical context helps to develop a more rounded understanding of innovation processes. This is about much more than looking at how companies or regions become 'locked in' to technologies, products, or processes. History is about change as well as continuity and this can provide the basis for combining new knowledge and skills with the traditional and develop something radically new and often unforeseen. Think about

Facebook – developed for social networking for college students and now helping transform business marketing; old and new leading to a radical process change that can only be understood in the historical context of the twenty-first century.

Sources: Rose (2000); Parsons and Rose (2003, 2005); Rose and Parsons (2004); Rose et al. (2007).

14.3 Industries, industry sectors, and regions

14.3.1 The rise and fall of industries

In the previous chapter, we discussed 'spatial' variations: how rates of entrepreneurship, and the nature of the activity undertaken, vary between geographical locations (Section 13.5). Here, we are looking at **'temporal' variations**: how entrepreneurial activity also varies in intensity and form when it is tracked across time. There are many cases of this kind of variation in our recent history. New industries have been born, sometimes during fairly dramatic bursts of entrepreneurial activity (e.g. the 'dot com' boom of the 1990s), while long-established industries have either collapsed entirely, or relocated to other parts of the world. Figure 14.3 summarizes some recent examples.

So what can historical research tell us about these longer-term changes, and how they connect with our exploration of entrepreneurship? We address these questions in two stages. Firstly, we look for evidence of trends or patterns in the way that entrepreneurial activity fluctuates over time, and ask what these changes suggest about the rise and fall of industries (Section 14.3.2). Secondly, we examine some of the mechanisms that cause entrepreneurial activity to vary over time, with particular reference to geographic **clusters** (Section 14.3.3).

14.3.2 Looking for patterns: tracking variations in entrepreneurship

Historical studies are often written up as narratives. However, there is a contrasting approach, in which researchers assemble historical data sets in order to explain patterns in entrepreneurial activity over extended periods. This is one of the aims of the Global Entrepreneurship Monitor (GEM) study, which is now collecting data on a regular basis in more than 50 countries around the world (Bosma and Levie 2010: 5). Researchers adopting this approach face several challenges, including that of identifying suitable measures. For example, Shane (1996) used a measure of entrepreneurship as the number of registered organizations per head of population to study changes in rates in the United States between 1899 and 1988. Though this measure might appear unproblematic at first sight, it has several limitations. As the author notes, it can result in the under-counting of smaller firms, which do not appear on official lists. Increases in the average size of firms can also introduce distortions (Shane 1996: 748, 777 n1). Researchers are now beginning to address these technical issues, and extending the scope of their data collection and analysis. As a result, we have access to new evidence about changes in entrepreneurial attitudes, perceptions, and activity rates over time. For example, as part of a recent GEM study, researchers compared entrepreneurial activity rates for the United States

Figure 14.3 Variations in entrepreneurial activity over time

Period	Industry/geographic location	Changes in entrepreneurial activity
1970s to 1990s	Decline of large manufacturing industries in the UK, other European countries, and the United States (e.g. steel-making, ship-building, vehicle manufacturing, consumer electronics), due to cost competition in an increasingly globalized market.	Transfer of manufacturing to Indian sub-continent and South East Asian countries created new opportunities for local manufacturers and suppliers. Some former industrial regions experienced long-term decline in activity; others have been regenerated, creating new opportunities.
1980s to date	Emerging technology-based sectors such as nanotechnologies and bio-pharmaceuticals, with geographic clusters of activity in particular locations around the world (e.g. Silicon Valley, USA; Bangalore, India; Cambridge, England; Piedmont, Italy; Cork, Ireland). Clusters are also influenced by policy initiatives such as Finland's Nanotechnology Cluster Programme (www.nanocluster.fi), and the Biopharma initiative in Belgium's Brussels-Capital Region (www.biotechinbrussels.be).	High levels of new firm formation, including 'spin-out' ventures linked to research centres in leading universities and regional outposts of major multinational corporations. Has also created many opportunities for specialist service providers (e.g. venture finance, intellectual property law, recruitment of scientists and technicians).
1990s to date	Social enterprises in European countries, the United States, and other parts of the world (e.g. Pakistan, India, South Africa), operating in a variety of sectors, including healthcare, social care, education, sports and leisure, food service, local transport, and energy generation.	Rapid increase in the number of new social enterprises in response to liberalized markets and retreat of public sector agencies. A few social enterprises have grown very large, and some have converted into commercial companies (or vice versa). Has provided opportunities to create different kinds of organization and service delivery models.
1990s to date	Public utilities and services (e.g. gas, electricity, water, transport) in European transition countries and elsewhere (NB similar changes made in some African countries as part of a World Bank 'structural adjustment' programme).	Economic liberalization and privatization of state-owned organizations created new opportunities for both local and foreign entrepreneurs (e.g. South African mobile phone companies) and social entrepreneurs (e.g. community-owned energy and transport ventures).

and Argentina over a nine-year period. They identified patterns that appeared to relate to the global economic crisis, including a decline in the 'nascent entrepreneurship' rate (i.e. a measure of the proportion of the population intending to start a new business), and an increase in the 'necessity motivation' rate (i.e. people who set up a business because they cannot find suitable employment), over the period (Bosma and Levie 2010: 37–8).

Other researchers have identified patterns and trends in data collected at an industry level, with measures such as the birth and death rates of firms fluctuating over time. The typical pattern is for an initial rush of new entrants in the early years of a new industry to be followed at some point by a 'shake-out', with some firms failing and others consolidating; though new firms may continue to be added, the population stabilizes around a smaller number of large, established firms. This strand of research, known as 'population ecology' or 'organizational ecology', can provide evidence that can be combined with the more in-depth qualitative studies discussed earlier in this chapter. For example, Figure 14.4 shows some of the data used in a study contrasting the performance of the world's leading motorcycle producer, Japan, with that of another leading country, Italy (NB the full study includes a comparison with a third country, Belgium).

The dramatic contrast in the patterns indicated by these graphs was just a starting point for the researchers, who used a range of data in as part of a multivariate modelling exercise. The aim of their analysis was to identify how the competitive advantage of a nation might be related to the dynamics of its organizational populations (Wezel and Lomi 2003: 379). Their findings suggest that one of the factors contributing to the competitive advantage of nations was the ability of organizational populations to learn from the experience of their unsuccessful members. The researchers also found 'mixed evidence' on the influence of geographical location and clustering in the countries studied and joined the call for more comparative and longitudinal studies of this factor (Wezel and Lomi 2003: 385–6). Similar approaches have been adopted to study the factors underpinning the evolution of this industry in other countries (e.g. Wezel 2005). We develop these themes further in the next section by looking more closely at the processes leading to the creation and growth of geographic clusters (Section 14.3.3).

14.3.3 Identifying causal mechanisms: the case of geographic clustering

A wide variety of mechanisms can be drawn upon to explain contrasting patterns of the kind identified in the previous section. For example, if you were interested in the ways that entrepreneurial activity could be encouraged, you might focus on mechanisms operating at an *individual* level (i.e. are we producing young people with skills, energy and ideas?), at an *organizational* level (i.e. do we have organizations of an appropriate size, with the right capabilities?), or at an *institutional* level (i.e. does our country or region have supportive rules and regulations, tax and spending regimes, or social norms?). While each of these levels of analysis is important, a common theme in much of the research on causal mechanisms is the role of social or inter-organizational networks (Sections 4.4 and 13.5). We have seen several examples in this chapter, including the opening case, which contrasts the pioneering networks of wind energy entrepreneurs and users in Denmark with those of the United States (Case 14.1); the researcher profile, which features a study of innovation networks and communities of practice in the world of outdoor sports (Case 14.2); and the closing case, which shows how English merchants in the early nineteenth century drew on their business networks in order to internationalize their operations (Case 14.4). Researchers have explored the influence of networks and networking on entrepreneurial activity in many other contexts, including religious groupings (e.g. Kirby 1993; Gilbrar 2003) and *diasporas* (e.g. McCabe et al. 2005; Osirim 2008). Since their network-related theme has its own vast literature, we have concentrated here on a single research area, geographic clustering, and one widely used mechanism, 'institutional thickness'. Given sufficient time and space, work on other topics could be developed in a similar way: see the Further reading guide for suggestions.

Figure 14.4 Motorcycle industries: two contrasting growth patterns

Italian motorcycle industry: new firms and population density

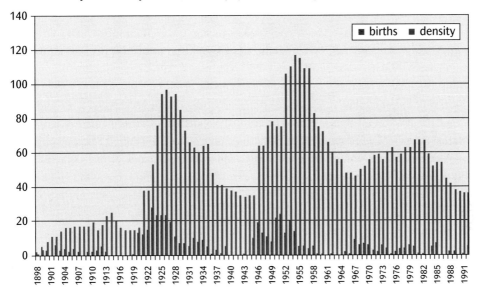

Japanese motorcycle industry: new firms and population density

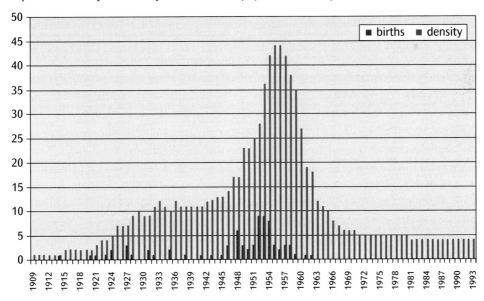

Source: Wezel and Lomi (2003: 373–4, Figures 2 and 3)

The idea of geographic clustering was originally outlined by the economist Alfred Marshall in his work on industrial districts (2010 [1920]: 222–31), and was subsequently rediscovered and refined in the late twentieth century. Researchers studying Italian regions such as Emilia-Romagna identified a link between prosperous local economies and the dense networks of independent, specialized enterprises. Many researchers investigated what Bagnasco (1977) called *Tre Italia* (i.e. the 'Third Italy'), and the idea that economic activity based on geographic clusters of smaller firms could be more competitive and flexible than either conventional **markets** or large vertically integrated corporations (e.g. Piore and Sabel 1984). We will consider two research questions from this literature, which have strong historical dimensions. Firstly, how are clusters created? Secondly, how do they survive and develop over time?

How are clusters created? From the earliest times, economic activity had a strong local flavour, with communities developing distinctive products and services which could trade with people from other areas. Perhaps the most important *initial* impetus for geographic specialization was the uneven distribution of natural resources. As Alfred Marshall observed, geological formations, soil types, plant varieties, and microclimates provided the basis for many of the traditional industrial districts:

> *Straw plaiting has its chief home in Bedfordshire, where straw has just the right proportion of silex to give it strength without brittleness; and Buckinghamshire beeches have afforded the material for the Wycombe chair-making. The Sheffield cutlery trade is due chiefly to the excellent grit of which its grindstones are made.* (Marshall 2010 [1920]: 223)

Today, the landscape or 'amenity' value of a particular location can be a significant natural resource, providing a 'quality of life' that can attract and retain 'footloose' entrepreneurs and knowledge workers. The combined effects of an attractive environment and existing institutional resources (e.g. leading research universities) can be a strong incentive for people to relocate around new clusters of high technology and knowledge-intensive enterprises (e.g. Keeble and Wilkinson 1999; Lawson and Lorenz 2000). Clusters can also be created, or encouraged to develop, through public policy interventions. Governments may seek to divert external resources to a location (e.g. by providing incentives for inward investment or in-migration), to enhance local resources (e.g. by investing in education, training, political institutions, and infrastructure), or to achieve a combination of the two. Marshall provides us with a very early example of policy-based clustering; he claimed that the 'mechanical faculty' (i.e. engineering skills) of nineteenth century Lancashire, in the north-west of England, could be traced to an eleventh century decision by the Norman duke, Hugo de Lupus, to relocate skilled metalworkers to that area. Though Marshall's claim might be open to challenge, there are many examples of long-standing local specialisms, particularly in areas such as agriculture, traditional crafts, and food production. Today's policy initiatives tend to have a rather shorter time-horizon; recent examples include the Finnish nanotechnology cluster and the biotechnologies clusters in Belgium's Brussels-Capital Region (see Figure 14.3).

How do clusters survive and develop? Whatever the initial impetus for creating a cluster, it requires other mechanisms if it is to continue to prosper. Marshall referred to this process as the creation of an 'industrial atmosphere':

> *When an industry has chosen a locality for itself, it is likely to stay there long: so great are the advantages which people following the same skilled trade get from the near neighbourhood of one another. The mysteries of the trade become no mysteries; but are as it were in the air, and children learn many of them unconsciously. Good work is rightly appreciated, inventions and improvements in machinery, in processes and the general organisation of*

the business have their merits promptly discussed: if one man starts a new idea, it is taken up by others and combined with suggestions of their own; and thus becomes the source of further good ideas. (Marshall 2010 [1920]: 225)

More recent research has greatly refined and extended Marshall's original ideas. Much of this work reflects a wider recognition that economic activity is 'embedded' in localized institutional and social relationships (Granovetter 1985) (Section 13.5). To see how this works, we can look in more detail at the widely adopted concept of 'institutional thickness' (Amin and Thrift 1995; Keeble et al. 1999; Henry and Pinch 2001). Perhaps the easiest way to grasp its meaning and significance is to picture the opposite: 'institutional thinness'. Imagine yourself in a country in the aftermath of a civil war or a major natural disaster. It is a place with very few public, private, or voluntary institutions to encourage economic activity, no effective interaction between whatever institutions exist, and no systems in place to enable knowledge to be shared or to exercise control over rule-breakers and 'rogue traders'. Consider how difficult it would be to establish a new venture in such a hostile environment, especially if you were in competition with businesses located in more favourably endowed locations. Institutional thickness is defined as a measure of the degree to which a geographic location is capable of supporting productive economic activity (Amin and Thrift 1995: 14–16). It can fluctuate over time, with obvious implications for entrepreneurial activity. For example, an assessment of the high technology cluster around Cambridge, in the East of England, concluded that until the mid-1990s, the University of Cambridge played an important yet isolated role in creating a supportive culture and initiating spin-offs. Institutional thickness has since increased with the introduction of new organizations, including an innovation centre, specialist services firms, and science parks (Keeble *et al.* 1999: 327–9). By contrast, a study of remote rural communities in Ireland illustrated how institutions can be undermined by socio-economic changes. During the 1980s, increased personal mobility, coupled with an urban shift in employment, retailing, and other services, contributed to a weakening of local economic and social institutions (Keane 1990).

Institutional thickness is not necessarily a guarantee of survival. Geographic clusters with strong, long-established institutional frameworks, cultures, and practices can find it very difficult to identify external threats, or to make the changes required in order to tackle them. The rapid decline of the Swiss watch industry in the late twentieth century is a widely cited example, where deeply embedded craft traditions and institutions (i.e. a form of 'institutional thickness') were seen as playing a negative role (Glasmeier 1994). Similarly, a number of British manufacturing regions, districts, and clusters have experienced fluctuating fortunes over time, often leading to catastrophic decline. Historians, with their long-term perspectives, are well-placed to study these dynamics (Wilson and Popp 2003; Popp and Wilson 2007; Wilson and Popp 2009). One point that emerges from this research is the necessity of considering these clusters as systems. While individual firms, or groups of firms, can make heroic efforts to resist the decline of a district, the forces involved can threaten to overwhelm even the most creative and determined of entrepreneurial initiatives. For example, between 1960 and 2002, the UK-based shoemaking firm R. Griggs created a successful international brand, *Dr Martens*, against a backdrop of widespread factory closures in a declining traditional industrial district. In 2003, the company's owners found it necessary to relocate their own production to China and Thailand, but four years later they recommenced production of a premium hand-crafted range in the original UK factory (www.drmartens.com).

In the next section, we turn to industrialization and economic development, considering the role that entrepreneurial activity might play in shaping these large-scale processes.

14.4 Industrialization and economic development: the entrepreneurial role

In the last two decades, some historical researchers have begun to challenge earlier views of economic development and industrialization, including those of Landes (2003 [1969]) and Chandler (1990). Proponents of the 'historical alternatives' approach argue that economic development takes place along different paths. Though the process may be influenced by economic drivers (e.g. resource costs, transaction costs, economies of scale and scope), and by new technologies, there is still scope for people to make strategic choices about the way forward. Recent contributions in this tradition include Sabel and Zeitlin (1997), Scranton (2000), and Carnevali (2003, 2004). The following list summarizes arguments presented by Zeitlin (2008a):

- It is wrong to assume that different countries, regions and industries are all following a 'narrow track' towards a similar model of industrialization.

- The large vertically integrated corporations and mass-production models that developed in the twentieth century are not the only ways to organize production.

- Economic actors can act strategically, adjusting to their context, considering alternative courses of action and – to varying degrees – shaping the world around them.

- One of the results of the interplay between these actors and their contexts is many 'hybrid' (i.e. mixed and combined) forms of economic organization, with their own distinctive practices.

- Much depends on the way that economic activity is organized beyond the boundaries of any individual organization; as we saw in the case of geographic clusters, inter-organizational networks and support institutions play an important role.

Following a different path into the future can have serious consequences for the people and organizations concerned. Consider, for example, the silk manufacturers of London and Lyons, who adopted radically different approaches, with equally dramatic effects. The British pursued an aggressive modernization strategy. When trade was deregulated in the mid 1820s, they opted for large-scale vertically integrated manufacturing, a model that they borrowed from the country's successful cotton industry. Their French rivals organized themselves in a different way, with dispersed, localized networks of smaller firms. By mid-century, silk manufacturing in Lyons was highly successful, with a strong export trade. By contrast, London went into a steep decline and by 1900, 90% of British consumption was imported (Cottereau 1997: 81). However, as the Dr Martens story (Section 14.3.3) illustrates, entrepreneurial actors can act strategically, anticipating and adapting in order to compete more effectively.

The historical alternatives approach suggests how entrepreneurial activity can shape economic development, helping to create different paths into the future. This process is illustrated in the following case study (Case 14.3). It charts the transformation of a traditional industry, based around craft-based methods. In the first half of the nineteenth century, English cheese-makers developed a standardized production system that became a template for industrial-scale food manufacturing, helping to create an international trade in cheese. However, their own path to industrialization proved to be rather long and winding:

Case 14.3 Big cheese: charting the industrialization of Cheddar

In the first half of the nineteenth century, English cheese-makers devised a standardized production system that became a template for industrial-scale food manufacturing and helped to create an international market in cheese. This case study looks at how a combination of entrepreneurial initiative and broader geo-political and economic factors shaped this technological innovation.

As they approached the 1850s, English cheese-makers appeared to be on the brink of a transition to full-scale industrial development. The early commercialization of the country's agricultural and food manufacturing sectors had provided the essential infrastructure, while its increasingly urbanized population created a growing demand for industrial products. Furthermore, by the mid-nineteenth century, many of the commercial English cheese-makers were engaged in scientific experimentation, their aim being to deliver increased consistency to satisfy the needs of the wholesalers and retailers. Although each of the main English regional varieties was subject to experimentation, Cheddar was the focus of attention. This can be attributed to a combination of the intrinsic characteristics of the cheese, its increasing economic significance – Cheddar was now overtaking Cheshire as the leading commercial variety on the London market – and the pioneering efforts of several leading Somerset cheese-makers. The most prominent of these was Joseph Harding (1805–76), a successful dairy farmer. Harding and his contemporaries conducted many experiments involving the precise and systematic control and monitoring of key variables such as temperature and acidity. They also invested in human capital, promoting educational programmes for cheese-makers and dairy maids, and calling for improvements in the physical condition of dairies in order to tackle quality problems. The results of these experiments were published in specialist agricultural and dairy journals, the free flow of information reflecting the new spirit of scientific enquiry. This cycle of experiment and publication contributed to the formalizing of cheese-making practices into distinctive 'systems', in effect, sets of standardized instructions or 'recipes' for the more efficient production of specific English regional varieties. The efforts of Joseph Harding and others to improve English cheese-making were motivated, to some degree, by the awareness that cheese-makers faced a potential threat from imported products. However, the nature of the knowledge being developed, and the enthusiasm with which it was disseminated, had the paradoxical effect of intensifying the competitive threat. Once formalized, Harding's Cheddar system was readily reproducible in other locations. The process of imitation was actively encouraged by leading figures in English cheese-making. Harding's own family illustrate this phenomenon, his son Henry Harding being instrumental in exporting the Cheddar system to Australia.

As experiments continued on England's commercial cheese-making farms, developments in North America were about to provide a springboard for industrial scale production. As in England, one of the primary aims was to produce a more uniform cheese for the volume market. The first cheese factory was constructed in Oneida County, New York State, in 1851, but the innovation did not catch on immediately. Furthermore, though the term 'factory' was used from the outset, production processes were essentially unchanged from those used on the farm, the main differences being that the building was purpose-built for volume production, cheese-making equipment was larger, and milk supplies were drawn from several contributing farms (McMurry 1995: 3 n6, 129). The American Civil War (1861–65) triggered a surge in factory-building and an equally dramatic increase in the export trade. The war removed men and women from the dairy farms, blocked lucrative Southern markets, and contributed to a doubling of market prices, as English importers paid for cheese in gold, which was converted into inflated paper money. In 1864, it is estimated that 205 factories were responsible for about a third of the cheese produced in New York State; by 1870 there were over 900 factories, and by 1875 one observer estimated that over 90% of the state's cheese was factory made. Given this context, it is perhaps unsurprising that visitors to Harding's cheese dairy included Xerxes A. Willard, a representative of the American Dairyman's Association, who toured England in the summer of 1866. Though modest quantities of American Cheddar had been sold in England shortly before the emergence of the first factories, Willard's visit marked a turning point for cheese-making in both countries. On his return to the United States, Willard set about promoting the essential principles of Harding's Cheddar system at dairy conventions, on factory visits, and in technical papers. These ideas were duly applied and further developed by the new generation of cheese factory managers, in conjunction with innovative mass-production technologies, such as the steam boiler and the 'gang-press', which is illustrated below.

In addition to the potential scale economies associated with the factory system, the American factories benefited from access to extensive, high quality grazing land and large, productive dairy herds. It was also unencumbered by traditional production practices and local market preferences. Exports to the United Kingdom increased tenfold, from around 5 million pounds (2,300 tonnes) in 1859 to more than 50 million pounds (22,700 tonnes) in 1863. They continued to increase over the following decade, doubling in volume by 1874. By this time, factory cheese from the United States

The gang-press: moving towards mass-production

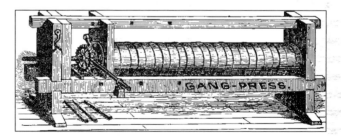

Source: Willard (1877: 369). The gang-press was one of several innovations in this period that enabled factories to process increasing volumes of cheese.

Global traders: cheese imports into United Kingdom, 1874

Country of origin	Quantity (Tonnes)	% share by volume
USA	49,296	57.2%
Netherlands	23,136	26.9%
Canada	12,820	14.9%
France	318	0.4%
Germany	254	0.3%
Sweden	182	0.2%
Other	139	0.2%
Total	86,145	

Source: Evans (1878: 156).

represented more than half of total imports and, based on contemporary estimates, more than a quarter of the English market (see above).

Questions

1. Why were entrepreneurs in the United States better positioned to develop this technological innovation, compared to their English counterparts?

2. What other social, cultural, and technological innovations would have influenced the growth of an international trade in perishable food products?

3. How would you contrast the sharing of ideas by nineteenth century dairy farmers like Joseph Harding and the actions of twenty-first century 'open source' pioneers such as Linus Torvalds (www.linux.org) and Liam Mulhall (brewtopia.com.au)?

Sources: This case is based on research conducted by Angela Tregear and Richard Blundel. For an extended version of the case, see Blundel and Tregear (2006).

14.5 **Practical implications**

There would be a strong case for historical research, even if it had no immediate practical implications (Godelier 2009; Kobrak 2009; Popp 2009; Tiffany 2009). In this chapter we have argued that history really does matter, and that historical approaches can provide valuable insights into present day entrepreneurial activity. We conclude by highlighting some of the more significant contributions:

- **Revealing patterns and trends** People tend to have very short time horizons, and pay insufficient attention to longer-term trends. One way of addressing this limitation is to collect and analyse quantitative data (e.g. entrepreneurial activity rates, firm birth and death rates) over extended periods of time. Analysis of this kind can reveal interesting patterns, such as the characteristic 'boom and bust' cycle seen in many new growth industries – such as occurred in automobile manufacturing at the dawn of the twentieth century, or web-based commerce at its end. History never repeats itself precisely, but when entrepreneurs and investors are confronted with similar patterns of activity at a future date, they could make more informed judgements by taking note of previous experience. For example, you might be able to avoid the more costly errors associated with entering an industry too early (and struggling to gain legitimacy), or too late (and finding yourself unable to catch up with the knowledge and experience gained by incumbent firms).

- **Doing justice to entrepreneurial lives** One of the biggest challenges is to reconstruct past events in ways that take account of the thoughts, feelings, and strategic judgements of the people concerned. While this is true of all areas of activity, this is a particular problem when you begin to examine the perceptions and judgements of historical entrepreneurs (Sabel and Zeitlin (1997: 29). It can be easy to forget that everyone's life is 'lived forwards'. Historical entrepreneurs did not have a crystal ball; like us, they had to rely on whatever 'local knowledge' (Section 11.3.4) was available in order to form their judgements about the future. Good historical research helps us to address this issue. By recovering archive evidence (e.g. from personal correspondence, diaries, and minutes of meetings), and in some cases through careful retrospective interviewing, researchers can find out more about the ways that people came to particular decisions. The resulting accounts are useful in two related ways. Firstly, they show us how difficult it can be to act entrepreneurially, something that is easily lost in a typical chronological summary of events (i.e. the kind of thing you find on many organizations' websites). Secondly, we can learn some important lessons from previous generations by following them through time as they tackle the uncertainties, complexities, and the inevitable pitfalls of their entrepreneurial lives (e.g. see Cases 14.1 and 14.4).

- **Uncovering hidden stories and providing fresh perspectives** By revealing previously hidden stories, and by reinterpreting what people assumed to be the case, historical research can also alter ideas in the present day. Contemporary views about the nature of entrepreneurship are based on a set of social and economic perspectives, which are themselves the product of a particular history. Until the late twentieth century, most of the scientific research on entrepreneurship was conducted by researchers based in Europe and North America, and much of the work was conducted by people who shared similar social and ethnic backgrounds. More recent historical research is bringing to our attention stories and perspectives that were not previously addressed. For example, Walker's (1986) article examines black entrepreneurship in the United States before the Civil War, while Osirim (2008) looks at the recent history of women entrepreneurs in the African diaspora.

- **Creating more informed and effective enterprise policies** Through each of these contributions, historical research can help us obtain a better understanding of entrepreneurial activity, including the different ways that it operates and its potential to contribute economically, socially and environmentally. It would also be nice to think that we could learn from past mistakes, or at least to recognize the scale of the challenge faced by people attempting to act entrepreneurially. The 'historical alternatives' approach (Section 14.5), highlights a number of practical implications for policy-makers and others who might want to influence the kind of world that we hand on to our children and grandchildren. These issues are taken up again in the final chapter (Section 15.1).

✳ 14.6 Summary

➤ There is a wide variety of historical approaches and themes, from biographies addressing the lives of particular individuals to broad historical studies concerned with industrialization processes; each of these themes provides interesting and sometimes unexpected insights into different aspects of entrepreneurship.

➤ Entrepreneurial biographies and company histories are traditional approaches, each of which remains relevant today. It is essential that studies of this kind extend beyond the boundaries of the immediate subject, in order to see how people and organizations interact with their surrounding context.

➤ The analysis of historical data sets has revealed patterns of growth and decline of industries and industrial sectors. By drawing selectively on social science concepts, historians have also examined in detail how entrepreneurial activity has developed over an extended period of time, providing many useful insights.

➤ Entrepreneurs and entrepreneurial activity feature in large-scale theoretical explanations of industrialization and economic development, but there is continuing debate over their role in these processes. The historical alternatives approach challenges deterministic accounts and highlights the capacity of entrepreneurial actors to influence social and technological innovations.

➤ Historically informed research can help to show how entrepreneurial actors 'make their own history' in a life lived forward. It can also help to shed new light on hidden and misunderstood aspects of the past, and to show how entrepreneurial activity is capable of creating alternative pathways into the future.

Case 14.4 Wolverhampton to Calcutta: Shaw and Crane's Indian 'adventure'

Introduction

In this case study, we follow two regional merchants, John Shaw and Henry Crane as they take the first steps in establishing a new enterprise in Calcutta in 1834. Despite their apparently poorly resourced and ill-equipped origins, the partners managed to establish a trading business that continued to operate until 1947. The study draws on rich archival sources, including correspondence between the partners, their families and their external contacts. This historical evidence is used to address the following questions: What motivated these entrepreneurial decisions? What factors explain the timing of the decisions and the location of the new enterprise? And what capabilities and resources was the firm able to draw upon in order to put into effect such an ambitious strategy? We focus on a short period (1827–34), in which Shaw and Crane first established a trading partnership and subsequently set up its own international business, Thompson and Co. The account is extracted from a much larger historical study, which traced Shaw's early career of as a commercial traveller in England (Popp 2007, 2009a), and the development of his Indian venture (Popp 2010).

Shaw and Crane's partnership

The roots of the partnership of Shaw and Crane were put down at some point in the first decade of the nineteenth century when farmer's son John Shaw commenced in trade as a hardware 'factor'(i.e. wholesale merchant), based in Wolverhampton in the English Midlands. This small town sat at the heart of an extensive and complex industrial district dedicated to a wide range of metal-using trades, though it was some distance from the major trading port of Liverpool. Shaw's firm distributed a myriad of metal goods to customers across the Midlands and Northern England. His customers were overwhelmingly retail businesses and ironmongers in particular. Shaw's 'journey books' (i.e. trading records) indicate that the firm had been in profitable operation for at least a quarter of a century before making its initial investment in India. In that time, it had established effective capabilities and routines (e.g. systems for managing employees, credit control and customer relations), and a deep knowledge of its domestic markets. Shaw does not seem to have drawn on his extended family or other social networks for resources. In 1813 he married the daughter of a retail customer, but there is no evidence to suggest that the marriage contributed meaningful resources to the enterprise. The partnership with Henry Crane was established in 1815.[1] The archival evidence suggests that Crane had previously worked for Shaw, with the partnership

A view of Calcutta in the early nineteenth century

VIEW OF CALCUTTA FROM THE ESPLANADE.

© Istock photo/Duncan walker

being a way of recognizing his loyal and effective service rather than as a source of financial or other resources. It also indicates that the growth of the firm was organic and by reinvesting its own profits. Though certainly successful and apparently well-run, Shaw and Crane does not appear to have been particularly entrepreneurial before 1827, and there is nothing in the archive to suggest that it was engaged in either extensive or sustained overseas trading operations prior to this date.

Starting to trade with India

Shaw and Crane's entry into trade with India came via a relatively short letter of introduction from the Sheffield merchants Joseph Rogers and Sons, who had:

> [t]he pleasure to introduce our friends Mr Rawson and Mr Holdsworth who have an establishment in Calcutta and are visiting Wolverhampton for the purpose of obtaining consignments to be sent out there. We have done some business through their hands and have always found them exceedingly punctual and attentive to our interests.[2]

Here we can see that Rogers and Sons are anxious immediately to place their recommendation in the context of their own experience of dealing with Rawson and Holdsworth, recommending their efficiency and their reliability. It stated that both men were 'highly reputable' and added that Mr Rawson had recently been, 'a Banker in Rochdale and no doubt you will recollect him,' since Shaw had connections to the business community of Rochdale through marriage.[3] In the letter, Rogers offered further advice and encouragement:

> Should you be inclined to make a treat [i.e. a commercial venture] in that Quarter we have no doubt you would find it a very profitable business if proper selections are sent out and we should be very glad to give you the advantage of our knowledge and experience in the trade as we find the amount of Sheffield manufacturers is as much as we can attend to and there is now a probability of a great increase in the demand for Wolverhampton goods.[4]

Several networks or circuits of information were in play in order to bring this opportunity to Shaw and Crane's attention. Shaw and Crane had done an extensive trade with numerous Sheffield retailers and merchants since at least 1810 and must have been well known there. Rogers and Sons, in turn, had done business through Rawson and Holdsworth, who themselves, like Shaw, had connections to Rochdale. This was clearly an extensive business network and for all the talk of 'reputable friends' it was one driven primarily by the commercial imperatives of punctuality, attentiveness and profitability. Shaw and Crane replied on 31 August 1827 with what must have been an expression of interest. Although that reply is lost, it was referred to in the next letter from Rogers and Sons, dated 4 October 1827. Rogers and Sons had been waiting to hear whether Rawson and Holdsworth had made arrangements with any other English firms:

> We have this day received a letter from them stating that they [i.e. Rawson and Holdsworth] did not make any arrangements for similar good to what you supply with any house in Birmingham or Wolverhampton. We therefore feel pleasure in recommending you to make treat and if you pursue the same plan that we have done we hope you will be equally successful.[5]

The correspondence shows how Rogers and Sons were acting as brokers of the relationship, and that Shaw and Crane were effectively competing for this entrepreneurial opportunity. Having made their recommendation 'to make treat', Rogers and Sons immediately provided detailed practical advice on how best to conduct the trade: the suggested value of initial consignments ('£300 to £400 by any one ship'), how to pack goods, what paper work was required, 'to always insure to the full amount', and how to make a selection of goods and to present that selection. Particular attention was given to charging, Rogers confiding that they, 'always reduce every article to nett cost price (as Discounts are unknown there) and we then put on an advance of fifty per cent'.[6] They also reminded Shaw and Crane of, 'the great length of time which you will be out your money and the . . . expenses which you incur . . . as well as by the exchange'.[7] In all, we can sense the more experienced Rogers and Sons instructing the novice Shaw and Crane on how to survive and prosper in the increasingly impersonalized world of international commerce (Haggerty 2006: 109).

Rawson and Holdsworth wrote to Shaw and Crane on 8 November 1827 with more practical advice, including where and when it was best to pay freight and shipping charges, the goods to be sent and the associated paperwork. Rawson and Holdsworth also offered to arrange insurance. They concluded:

> We hope the present adventure may lead to a lasting and mutually advantageous correspondence, at all events we beg to assure you that no exertion on out part shall be wanting in India to make the trade a profitable one for you.[8]

Shaw and Crane must have acted quickly, for Rawson and Holdsworth wrote again from London on 17 November 1827 enclosing an insurance policy for Shaw and Crane's first shipment (to the value of £800) along with a cover note that again expressed a desire to see their mutual interests prosper.[9] In the space of little more than two and half months, this small English hardware business was able to take the first step in the process of internationalization.

Establishing the Calcutta office

From late 1827 the Shaw and Crane archive falls silent on the subject of India, though it is apparent that the firm continued to trade internationally. Seven years later, Rawson and Holdsworth wrote to them with details of three ships sailing from Liverpool to Calcutta during October and offered to engage freight on their behalf. As the following agreement makes clear, Shaw and Crane had made another bold entrepreneurial decision; they were not merely extending the trade with India, but establishing their own base in Calcutta:

> [W]hereas the said John Shaw and Henry Crane have lately determined to open an Establishment at Calcutta in the East Indies for the sale of Ironmongery, Hardware and other goods wares and merchandise and have agreed with their late traveller Thomas Edward Thomson to manage and conduct the same as their agent who will forthwith embark with a cargo of goods for that purpose.[10]

On 11 November 1834 Thomson was writing from Liverpool to his employers in Wolverhampton to tell them that he had been ordered to be ready to board ship at seven o'clock the next morning, having, seemingly for the first time, met Mr Rawson, whom he had found to be, 'a very active man of business and also a very pleasant man'.[11] The decision over where to locate their overseas house, and when to make that move, were conditioned by the events of 1830–34 when all the established houses in Calcutta collapsed following the failure of a leading merchant, Palmer and Company.[12] This great crisis in Anglo-Indian trade created a vacuum into which a second wave of new entrants rushed, Shaw and Crane among them. Already active in Calcutta, Shaw and Crane were relatively well positioned to observe, but not be directly affected by, these cataclysmic events. By the close of 1834 they had evidently decided that this was an opportunity of which they could take advantage. Aware of their own internal resources and capabilities, bolstered by incremental processes of learning over the preceding seven years, and embedded in a wider system supplying both information and missing resources, Shaw and Crane's 'entrepreneurial vision' or 'image' shifted to incorporate this new possibility (Penrose 1995 [1959]: 31–42; Connell 2003: 103). Many of the post-crisis entrants failed during a second crisis in 1847–48 but Thompson and Co. survived, remaining in independent existence until 1947.

Questions

1. Why did Shaw and Crane decide to embark on their Indian 'adventure'?

2. What external capabilities and resources was the firm able to draw upon in order to put into effect such an ambitious strategy?

3. Why did Shaw and Crane's decisions about the timing and organization of their approach to internationalizing the business (i.e. the initial strategy of using an agent, and later decision to establish their own office), prove so successful?

4. What similarities and differences can you identify between this sequence of events, almost two centuries ago, and the internationalization efforts of twenty-first century entrepreneurs?

Notes

[1] Wolverhampton Archives and Local Studies [WALS], DB/24/A/1.
[2] Letter posted on 23 August 1827. WALS, DB/24/A/52.
[3] WALS, DB/24/A/52.
[4] WALS, DB/24/A/52.
[5] WALS, DB/24/A/53.
[6] WALS, DB/24/A/53.
[7] WALS, DB/24/A/53.
[8] WALS, DB/24/A/54.
[9] WALS, DB/24/A/56.
[10] WALS, DB/24/A/35.
[11] WALS, DB/24/A/103.
[12] WALS, DB/24/A/103.

Sources: Popp (2007, 2009a, 2010); reproduced with permission.

Practical activities

1. Comparing entrepreneurial lives Using references identified in Section 14.2 and the Further reading guide as a starting point, locate the historical biographies of two entrepreneurs. Read their life stories and summarize under suitable headings (NB the following categories are suggestions, but you may want to adjust or add to them): (a) 'family background and early childhood'; (b) 'education'; (c) 'location and travel'; (d) 'networking activity'; (e) 'venture type(s)'; (f) 'major challenges'; (g) 'how it all ended'. Write a short (500 word) commentary, comparing and contrasting these individuals.

2. Comparing organizational histories Using references identified in Section 14.2 and the Further reading guide as a starting point, locate the histories of two commercial companies or social enterprises. Read the histories and summarize using the following questions (NB these are suggested questions; you may want to adjust or add to them): (a) When, where, and by whom was the organization founded? (b) Why was it founded (i.e. what internal and external factors)? (c) What were its original aims? (d) How has it developed over time? (e) What factors have influenced its development? Write a short (500 word) commentary, comparing and contrasting these organizations.

3. Uncovering my entrepreneurial history Re-read Section 14.2 then contact members of your wider family and try to discover whether one of your ancestors was involved in entrepreneurial activity, broadly defined. If so, write an account of their life, based on whatever information you are able to collect and using the categories from Practical activity 1 as a guide. If your story includes the founding of an organization, you could also use the questions from Practical activity 2 to help organize your thoughts. If you are unable to identify an entrepreneurial ancestor, you can work with friends and acquaintances in order develop an historical narrative based on their family histories, or more recent experiences.

 ## Discussion topics

1. What 'use' is history? There is a continuing debate regarding the role and the relevance of historical research in 'practical' subjects like management and entrepreneurship; see, for example, the exchange between Godelier (2009), Tiffany (2009), Kobrak (2009), and Popp (2009b). To debate this issue, form two teams and prepare a set of arguments 'for' and 'against' the motion: 'This House believes that entrepreneurs have nothing to learn from history.' Allow five minutes for each side, followed by a further five minutes to respond to the arguments presented. Then move to a vote. To make the debate more interesting, allocate team members so that those who disagree with the motion have to defend it, and vice-versa (note: the debate format can be adapted for use in a virtual learning environment, or as an individual essay topic).

2. Adopting historical methods In Section 14.1, we considered some of the methods available to researchers who want to examine entrepreneurial activity from an historical perspective. Imagine that you were researching entrepreneurial activity in the early days of the Internet (i.e. the period 1985–2000). What methods would you select in order to discover more about this subject? What challenges would you expect to face in conducting your research?

3. Whose history? There is often a great deal of argument between historians (and others) over the factual accuracy of an account, or of how the evidence should be interpreted. For example, an entrepreneurial autobiography may give one account – perhaps emphasizing the individual's own abilities and impact – while others might argue that it was all down to luck, or to external factors. Who should you believe, and how can you be sure that the narrative you are reading is a fair representation of what actually happened?

Further reading guide

The *Oxford Handbook of Business History*, edited by **Jones and Zeitlin (2008)** provides extensive coverage, and expands on several themes introduced in this chapter; this includes **Colli and Rose (2008)** on family business, **Zeitlin (2008a)** on the 'historical alternatives' approach, **Zeitlin (2008b)** on industrial districts and regional clusters, **Graham (2008)** on technology and innovation, and **Jones and Wadhwani (2008)** on entrepreneurship. **Cassis and Minoglou (2005)** includes recent historical research on entrepreneurship and a helpful introductory essay. **Best (2001)** presents an historically informed and policy-based approach to cluster dynamics which connects firm- and inter-organizational level processes. **Levinson (2006)** is a very readable account of a decisive combination of entrepreneurship and innovation that launched the containerization industry. There are also many histories of industries, which chart the activities of entrepreneurial individuals and organizations. For example: **Yergin (2009 [1991])** is a detailed and gripping history of the oil industry; **Levinson (2006)** charts the history of shipping containers, a rarely considered innovation that helped to transform global trade in the twentieth century; and **Casson and Godley (2007)** analyse the entrepreneurial strategies of Singer, a pioneering consumer products company. For further examples of historical studies related to entrepreneurship, see the leading specialist journals such as, *Enterprise and Society, Business History, Business History Review,* and *Management and Organizational History*. Historical studies are sometimes published in more general management journals, including *Industrial and Corporate Change, Organization Studies,* and *Entrepreneurship and Regional Development*. There are relatively few historical studies of social enterprise and social entrepreneurship. **Bornstein (2004)** profiles the recent histories of some organizations and individuals, as well as famous historical figures.

References

Agterbosch, S. and Breukers, S. (2008) 'Socio-political embedding of onshore wind power in the Netherlands and North Rhine-Westphalia.' *Technology Analysis and Strategic Management*, 20, 5: 633–48.

Amin, A. and Thrift, N. (1995) *Globalization, institutions, and regional development in Europe.* Oxford: Oxford University Press.

Asmus, P. (2000) *Reaping the wind: how mechanical wizards, visionaries, and profiteers helped shape our energy future.* Washington DC: Island Press.

Bagnasco, A. (1977) *Tre Italia. La problematica territoriale dello sviluppo economico italiano.* Bologna: Il Mulino.

Black, E. (2001) *IBM and the Holocaust: the strategic alliance between Nazi Germany and America's most powerful corporation*. London: Little, Brown.

Berlin, L. (2005) *The man behind the microchip. Robert Noyce and the invention of Silicon Valley*. Oxford: Oxford University Press.

Best, M.H. (2001) *The new competitive advantage: the renewal of American industry*. Oxford: Oxford University Press.

Blundel, R.K. and Tregear, A. (2006) 'Artisans and "factories": the interpenetration of craft and industry in English cheese-making, c1650–1950.' *Enterprise and Society*, 7, 4: 1–35.

Bornstein, D. (2004) *How to change the world: social entrepreneurs and the power of new ideas*. Oxford: Oxford University Press.

Bosma, N. and Levie, J. (2010) *Global Entrepreneurship Monitor 2009 global report*. London: Global Entrepreneurship Research Association. Available at: http://www.gemconsortium.org (accessed 12 March 2010).

Bradley, I.C. (2007) *Enlightened entrepreneurs: business ethics in Victorian Britain*. Oxford: Lion Hudson.

Cadbury (2010) 'Cadbury: our story.' Bourneville: Cadbury. Available at: http://www.cadbury.co.uk (accessed 18 February 2010).

Carnevali, F. (2003) 'Golden opportunities: jewellery making in Birmingham between mass production and speciality.' *Enterprise and Society*, 4, 2: 272–98.

Carnevali, F. (2004) '"Crooks, thieves and receivers": transaction costs in nineteenth century industrial Birmingham.' *Economic History Review*, 57, 3: 533–50.

Cassis, Y. and Minoglou, I.P. (2005) *Entrepreneurship in theory and history*. Basingstoke: Palgrave.

Casson, M. and Godley, A. (2007) 'Revisiting the emergence of the modern business enterprise: entrepreneurship and the Singer global distribution system.' *Journal of Management Studies*, 44, 7: 1064–77.

Casson, M., Yeung, B., Basu, A., and Wadeson, N. (2008) *The Oxford handbook of entrepreneurship*. Oxford: Oxford University Press.

Castronovo, V. (1999) *Fiat 1899–1999: un secolo di storia Italiana*. Milan: Rizzoli.

Chandler, A.D. (1956) *Henry Varnum Poor: business editor, analyst and reformer*. Cambridge MA: Harvard University Press.

Chandler, A.D. (1990) *Scale and scope: the dynamics of industrial capitalism*. Cambridge MA: Belknap Press.

Chandler, A.D. and Salsbury, P. (1971) *Pierre S. Du Pont and the making of the modern corporation*. New York: Harper and Row.

Clark, T. (2008) *Starbucked: a double tall tale of caffeine, commerce and culture*. London: Sceptre.

Colli, A. and Rose, M. (2008) 'Family business.' In G. Jones and J. Zeitlin (eds) op. cit. (194–218).

Connell, C.M. (2003) 'Jardine Matheson & Company: the role of external organization in a nineteenth-century trading firm.' *Enterprise and Society*, 4, 1: 99–138.

Corley, T.A.B. (2008) 'Historical biographies of entrepreneurs.' In M. Casson et al. (eds) op. cit. (138–175).

Cottereau, A. (1997) 'The fate of collective manufacturers in the industrial world: the silk industries of Lyons and London, 1800–1850.' In C.F. Sabel and J. Zeitlin (eds) op. cit. (75–152).

Evans, M. (1878) 'Butter and cheese.' In G. Phillips (ed.) *British Manufacturing Industries*. London: Edward Stanforth.

Fant, K. (2007) *Alfred Nobel: a biography* (Tr. Ruuth, M.), New York: Arcade.

GWEC (2010) *Global wind energy report 2009*. Brussels: Global Wind Energy Council.

Garud, R. and Karnøe, P. (2003) 'Bricolage versus breakthrough: distributed and embedded agency in technology entrepreneurship.' *Research Policy*, 32: 277–300.

Gerschenkron, A. (2000 [1966]) 'The modernization of entrepreneurship.' In R. Swedberg (ed.) op. cit. (129–138).

Gilbar, G.G. (2003) 'The Muslim Big Merchant-Entrepreneurs of the Middle East, 1860–1914.' *Die Welt des Islams*, 43, 1: 1–36.

Gipe, P. (1995) *Wind energy comes of age*. New York: Wiley.

Glasmeier, A. (1994) 'Technological discontinuities and flexible production networks: the case of Switzerland and the world watch industry.' *Research Policy*, 20, 5: 469–85.

Godelier, E. (2009) 'History, a useful "science" for management?: from polemics to controversies.' *Enterprise and Society*, 10, 4: 791–807.

Graham, B.W. (2008) 'Technology and innovation.' In G. Jones and J. Zeitlin (eds) op. cit. (120–40).

Granovetter, M. (1985) 'Economic action and social structure: the problem of embeddedness.' *American Journal of Sociology*, 91: 481–510.

Jones, C. (2001) 'Co-evolution of entrepreneurial careers, institutional rules and competitive dynamics in American film, 1895–1920.' *Organization Studies*, 22, 6: 911–44.

Haggerty, S. (2006) *The British-Atlantic trading community, 1760–1810: men, women, and the distribution of goods*. Leiden and Boston MA: Brill.

Henry, N. and Pinch, S. (2001) 'Neo-Marshallian nodes, institutional thickness, and Britain's "Motor Sport Valley": thick or thin?' *Environment and Planning A*, 33, 7: 1169–83.

Hutcheson, J.O. (2007) 'The end of a 1,400-year-old business.' *Business Week* (16 April). Available at http://www.businessweek.com/smallbiz/content/apr2007/sb20070416_589621.htm (accessed 6 March 2010).

Jones, G. and Zeitlin, J. (eds) (2008) *The Oxford handbook of business history*. Oxford: Oxford University Press.

Jones, G. and Wadhwani, R.D. (2008) 'Entrepreneurship.' In G. Jones and J. Zeitlin (eds) op. cit. (501–28).

Keane, M.J. (1990) 'Economic development capacity amongst small rural communities.' *Journal of Rural Studies*, 6, 3: 291–301.

Keeble, D. and Wilkinson, F. (1999) 'Collective learning and knowledge development in the evolution of regional clusters of high technology SMEs in Europe.' *Regional Studies*, 33, 4, 295–303.

Keeble, D., Lawson, C., Moore, B., and Wilkinson, F. (1999) 'Collective learning processes, networking and "institutional thickness" in the Cambridge Region.' *Regional Studies*, 33, 4: 319–32.

Kirby, M. (1993) 'Quakerism, entrepreneurship and the family firm in north-east England, 1780–1860.' In J. Brown and M.B. Rose (eds), *Entrepreneurship, networks and modern business*. Manchester: Manchester University Press (105–43).

Kobrak, C. (2009) 'The use and abuse of history as a management tool: comments on Eric Gordelier's view of the French connection.' *Enterprise and Society*, 10, 4: 808–15.

Landes, D.S. (2003 [1969]) *The unbound Prometheus: technological change and industrial development in Western Europe from 1750 to the Present* (2nd edition). Cambridge: Cambridge University Press.

Lawson, C. and Lorenz, E. (2000) 'Collective learning, tacit knowledge and regional innovative capacity.' *Regional Studies*, 33, 4: 305–17.

Levinson, M. (2006) *The box: how the shipping container made the world smaller and the world economy bigger*. Princeton NJ: Princeton University Press.

Lewis, M. (2001) *The new new thing: a Silicon Valley story*. London: Penguin.

March, J.G. (1991) 'Exploration and exploitation in organization learning.' *Organization Science*, 2, 1: 71–87.

McCabe, I.B., Harlaftis, G., and Minoglou, I.P. (2005) *Diaspora entrepreneurial networks: four centuries of history* (2nd edition). New York: Berg.

Marshall, A.M. (2010 [1920]) *Principles of economics* (8th edition; abridged). New York: Cosimo.

Nobel (2010) 'Nobel Peace Prize.' Oslo: Norwegian Nobel Institute. Available at: http://nobelpeaceprize.org (accessed 18 February 2010).

Osirim, M.J. (2008) 'African women in the new diaspora: transnationalism and the (re) creation of home.' *African and Asian Studies*, 7, 4: 367–94.

Parsons, M.C. and Rose, M.B. (2003) *Invisible on Everest: innovation and the gear makers*. Philadelphia PA: Old City Publishing.

Parsons, M.C. and Rose, M.B. (2005) 'The neglected legacy of Lancashire cotton: industrial clusters and the UK outdoor trade 1960–1990.' Enterprise and Society, 6, 4: 682–709.

Penrose, E.T. (1995 [1959]) *The theory of the growth of the firm* (3rd edition). Oxford: Oxford University Press.

Pettigrew, A. (1985) *The awakening giant: continuity and change in Imperial Chemical Industries*. Oxford: Blackwell.

Piore, M. and Sabel, C. (1984) *The second industrial divide*. New York: Basic.

Popp, A. (2007) 'Building the market: John Shaw of Wolverhampton and commercial travelling in early nineteenth-century England.' *Business History*, 49, 3: 321–47.

Popp, A. (2009a) 'From town to town: how commercial travel connected manufacturers and markets in the Industrial Revolution.' *Journal of Historical Geography*, 35, 4: 642–67.

Popp, A. (2009b) 'History, a useful "science" for management?: a response.' *Enterprise and Society*, 10, 4: 831–36.

Popp, A. (2010) 'From Wolverhampton to Calcutta: the low origins of merchant enterprise.' In R. Lee (ed.) *Commerce and culture*. Aldershot: Ashgate (forthcoming).

Popp, A. and Wilson, J.F. (2007) 'Life-cycles, contingency and agency: growth, development and change in English industrial districts and clusters.' *Environment and Planning A*, 39, 12: 2975–92.

Rose, M.B. (2000) *Firms, networks and business values: the British and American cotton industries since 1750*. Cambridge: Cambridge University Press.

Rose, M.B. and Parsons, M.C. (2004) 'Communities of knowledge: entrepreneurship, innovation and networks in the British outdoor trade 1960–1990.' *Business History*, 46, 4: 606–37.

Rose, M.B., Love, T., and Parsons, M.C, (2007) 'Path dependent foundation of global design-driven outdoor trade in the North West of England.' *International Journal of Design*, 1, 3: 57–68.

Sabel, C.F. and Zeitlin, J. (eds) (1997) *World of possibilities: flexibility and mass production in western industrialization*. Cambridge: Cambridge University Press.

Schumpeter, Joseph (2010 [1942]). *Capitalism, socialism, and democracy*. London: Routledge.

Scranton, P. (2000) *Endless novelty: specialty production and American industrialization, 1865–1925*. Princeton NJ: Princeton University Press.

Shane, S. (1996) 'Explaining variation in rates of entrepreneurship in the United States 1899–1988.' *Journal of Management*, 22, 5: 747–81.

Swedberg, R. (ed.) (2000) *Entrepreneurship: the social science view*. Oxford: Oxford University Press.

Tarbell, I.M. (2010 [1904]) *History of the Standard Oil Company*. New York: McClure & Phillips. Available at http://www.history.rochester.edu/fuels/tarbell (accessed 8 March 2010).

Tiffany, P. (2009) 'Does history matter in business?' *Enterprise and Society*, 10, 4: 816–30.

Vestas (2010) 'History: 110 years of expertise, willpower and passion.' Randers: Vestas Wind Systems A/S. Available at http://www.vestas.com/en/about-vestas/history.aspx (accessed 1 March 2010).

Walker, J. (1986) 'Racism, slavery, free enterprise: black entrepreneurship in the United States before the Civil War.' *Business History Review* 60, 3: 343–82.

Wezel, F.C. (2005) 'Location Dependence and Industry Evolution: Founding Rates in the United Kingdom Motorcycle Industry, 1895–1993.' *Organization Studies*, 26, 5: 729 – 54.

Wezel, F.C. and Lomi, A. (2003) 'The organizational advantage of nations: an ecological perspective on the evolution of the motorcycle industry in Belgium, Italy and Japan, 1898–1993.' *Geography and Strategy: Advances in Strategic Management*, 20: 359–92.

Whipp, R. and Clark, P.A. (1986) *Innovation and the auto industry: product, process and work organisation*. London: Francis Pinter.

Willard, X.A. (1877) *Practical Dairy Husbandry*. New York: Excelsior.

Wilson, J.F. and Popp, A. (eds) (2003) *Industrial districts and regional business networks in England, 1750–1970*. London: Ashgate.

Wilson, J.F. and Popp, A. (2009) 'Business in the regions: from "old" industrial districts to "new" clusters.' In R. Coopey and P. Lyth (eds). *Business in Britain in the Twentieth Century: Decline and Renaissance?* Oxford: Oxford University Press (65–81).

Yergin, D. (2009 [1991]) *The prize: the epic quest for oil, money and power* (with new epilogue). New York: Simon and Schuster.

Zeitlin, J. (2008a) 'The historical alternatives approach.' In G. Jones and J. Zeitlin (eds) op. cit. (120–40).

Zeitlin, J. (2008b) 'Industrial districts and regional clusters.' In G. Jones and J. Zeitlin (eds) op. cit. (219–43).

Political perspectives
From policy to practice

15

A State which dwarfs its men [sic] in order that they be more docile instruments in its hands, even for beneficial purposes, will find that with small men no great thing can really be accomplished.

John Stuart Mill, *nineteenth century philosopher and political writer*

Entrepreneurs are the economic DNA which we need to build competitiveness and innovation in Europe.

Günter Verheugen, *European Commission Vice President*

Learning outcomes

After reading this chapter you should be able to:

➤ Explore entrepreneurship from a political perspective, with a particular focus on public policy, economic development, and innovation.

➤ Understand why governments and non-governmental organizations intervene in the entrepreneurship process, and what they seek to achieve.

➤ Appreciate the wide range of strategies and techniques used to encourage and to guide enterprise in particular directions.

➤ Critically evaluate the impact of enterprise policies, and consider how they might be adapted or developed in order to respond to contemporary issues.

➤ Make connections between policy-making and the current state of knowledge about entrepreneurship, as reviewed in the other Part Two chapters.

➤ Recognize how policies can be related to your own entrepreneurial experiences, and how they may influence your future activities.

Case 15.1 'Putting small business first': creating a new policy framework for the European Union

The European Union's SME and entrepreneurship policies have developed over an extended period, driven initially by the efforts of larger member states such as France and Germany to address a number of economic problems. By the 1980s, a new directorate (DG XXIII) was established with specific responsibilities for SMEs. However, during the 1990s, there was growing concern over the impact of European policies on SMEs: policies were being developed at two different levels (i.e. member states and EU), there was a lack of consistency in policy between member states, and firms were burdened by excessive regulatory and reporting requirements (De 1999; Sexton and Landström 2000). SME policies are now co-ordinated by a successor organization, the Directorate General for Enterprise and Industry. One of the DG's strategic objectives, and an integral element in the Lisbon strategy for growth and jobs, is: 'to promote favourable framework conditions for small and medium-sized enterprises'. Support for SMEs and enterprise is part of the DG's wider responsibility to ensuring that EU policies, 'contribute to the sustainable competitiveness of EU enterprises and facilitate job creation and sustainable economic growth'. In this case study, we focus on a new policy initiative entitled 'The Small Business Act for Europe' (SBA). The SBA has been promoted under the banner, 'Europe is good for SMEs; SMEs are good for Europe'. It was formally adopted by member states of the European Union in June 2008 and applies to all independent companies with fewer than 250 employees; that represents 99.8% out of a total of 20 million European enterprises (Eurostat 2008). Speaking at the launch of the SBA, Günter Verheugen, the European Commission Vice-President responsible for Enterprise and Industry, stressed the economic importance of SMEs:

> Now is the time, once and for all, to cement the needs of SMEs in the forefront of the EU's policy. The SBA brings the full weight of Europe behind SMEs - enlisting all the resources of Europe to help small business in their daily business and to clear the path for those that want to create more jobs and growth in Europe and beyond. (European Commission 2009)

Given their importance, the SBA represents a response by policy-makers to some of the most important problems facing SMEs across the European Union. In a recent survey for the Commission, the most commonly reported were: administrative and regulatory burdens, access to finance, taxation, lack of skills, access to public procurements, unfair/too strong competition, and labour law (European Commission 2009).

So what is the 'Small Business Act for Europe'?

The SBA comprises a set of principles which are intended to guide the conception and implementation of policies at EU level and in each member state. The overall aim is to create a 'level playing field' (i.e. similar conditions) for SMEs across the EU, to improve the administrative and legal environment in which they operate, and to generate more entrepreneurial attitudes in society. Here are some examples of what the SBA is seeking to achieve, and of specific initiatives that are intended to 'put small businesses first':

- **Creating an environment within which entrepreneurs can thrive and entrepreneurship is rewarded** With 'Erasmus for young entrepreneurs', new and budding entrepreneurs can now take advantage of cross-border mobility, as well as gaining experience and insight by spending time in an SME in a different country.

- **Designing rules according to the 'Think Small First Principle'** All new legislative and administrative proposals at European and national level should be subjected to an 'SME test' to assess their impact on SMEs. Where this impact is considered negative, member states will be able to use measures such as derogations, transition periods, and exemptions in particular from information and reporting requirements.

- **Making public administrations responsive to SME needs** The time needed to start a new company should be no more than one week. The maximum time to obtain business licences and permits should generally not exceed one month. One-stop-shops should be provided to facilitate start-ups and recruitment procedures.

- **Facilitating SMEs' access to finance** The European Investment Bank Group will increase its range of financial products offered to SMEs, particularly mezzanine finance. In addition, more funds will be made available by the Commission for microcredit and access to cross-border venture capital will be facilitated.

- **Helping SMEs to benefit more from the opportunities offered by the Single Market and third-country markets** A new statute for a European Private Company will allow SMEs to start up and operate according to the same company law provisions throughout Europe.

- **Enabling SMEs to turn the environmental challenges into opportunities** The Commission is financing a network of environment and energy efficiency experts in the Enterprise Europe Network providing advice on eco-efficient operations, markets potential, and funding opportunities for more efficient operations in particular for SMEs.

In order to support this ambitious agenda, the DG for Enterprise and Industry has also introduced a single SME portal, available in 21 different languages, which provides useful information and advice in an accessible format (http://ec.europa.eu/enterprise/sme). Overall, the SBA is an ambitious package of measures, including four legislative proposals for translating the principles into action both at EU and member state level. In order for it to be effective, the SBA will require political commitment from both the Commission and the member states, reinforced by regular monitoring of its implementation.

Points to consider

1. Why is it so important for the European Union to adopt a new small firms and entrepreneurship policy?

2. What evidence would policy-makers need in order to know whether the Small Business Act is actually working across the European Union?

3. How do you think existing or nascent entrepreneurs might make use of the EU's SME portal?

Sources: De (1999); Sexton and Landström (2000); Eurostat (2008); European Commission (2008, 2009).

15.1 **Introduction**

The environments in which entrepreneurs operate are, to a large extent, shaped by public policies, both those currently in place and earlier policies whose influence is still felt today. It is important to understand these policies and their impact on **entrepreneurial activity**. Looking to the future, it is also worth considering how changes in policy might create new challenges and opportunities for entrepreneurs. Entrepreneurial activity is a powerful force in the world. It has enormous potential to contribute to our general well-being, but it can also do widespread and long-lasting damage to our societies and to the natural world on which we all depend. Politics is also about the exercise of power, and has a similar potential for making things better or worse. This chapter concludes our exploration of **entrepreneurship** by looking at its relationship with politics and policy-making. As the editors of a special issue point out, entrepreneurship policy is still an area where we have a great deal to learn:

> While the benefits of entrepreneurship are becoming near universally acknowledged, our understanding of how and when governments intervene to assist entrepreneurs, and indeed which, if any, specific entrepreneurs should receive assistance in some shape or form, still has substantial knowledge gaps, and remains controversial. (Robson et al. 2009: 533)

We address a number of policy-related questions in this chapter. For example: Should governments be attempting either to encourage or to guide enterprise in the first place? Do policy-makers have the capacity to influence something as diffuse and 'slippery' as entrepreneurship? And what are the practical implications for entrepreneurs? The following thought experiment can be used as a starting point for thinking through these issues, and entering the peculiar world inhabited by politicians and policy-makers.

Ruling the world for a day: a thought experiment

Congratulations! Following a bloodless coup, you have just taken control of the government; you have widespread support in the general population; the Finance Ministry has granted you a substantial budget, and the legal officers have ensured that all existing enterprise policies are to be cancelled, effective from tomorrow. It seems that you have been given a 'blank sheet', and are free to decide on an entirely new set of policies to encourage and control enterprise. However, sitting at your impressive new desk, the following thoughts occur to you:

- What are my policy objectives and priorities?
- How am I going to achieve them?
- Are those approaches going to work?
- What happens if they don't?

Leading a coup against an unpopular regime was relatively easy; now you are in charge, things are beginning to look a bit more complicated. With a deep sigh, you get up from your desk and head off in search of some expert advice – and a nice cup of tea.

This scenario may seem unrealistic and extreme, but there are some strong parallels with real-world policy-making. Firstly, as you probably realized, there is really no such thing as a 'blank sheet'. Even with unlimited budgets and public support, your incoming government faces many challenges and constraints. For example, there may be large regional variations in the level of entrepreneurial activity, reinforced by geography (e.g. remote rural locations, low population densities, hostile natural environments) and historical factors (e.g. the 'Upas tree' effect of declining heavy **industries**) (Sections 13.5 and 14.3). Secondly, in order to make any decisions on policy objectives, priorities, design, and implementation, you will need to have views about what entrepreneurship is and how it works in practice. These views may be based on research evidence, anecdotal evidence, your personal opinion, or political expediency (i.e. what best fits the short-term agenda of the people in power). In reality, policy-making is often driven by a combination of these four factors. Some policy studies specialists have argued strongly for what is known as 'evidence-based' policy (e.g. Pawson 2006), coupled with a rigorous system to evaluate its outputs, impact, and longer-term outcomes. In our case, this means making better use of the research approaches discussed in previous Part Two chapters, in order to ensure that enterprise policies are well-designed and effective in achieving their objectives.

The chapter is organized as follows. In Section 15.2, we consider the political context in which recent policies have been developed, identify key features of today's policy landscape, and clarify some widely used terms. Section 15.3 asks why governments consider it necessary to become involved in the activities of entrepreneurs, distinguishing between economic and non-economic arguments for intervention. In Section 15.4, we consider the wide range of approaches that governments have adopted, and the combinations of techniques they have employed in order to pursue their chosen policy goals. Section 15.5 looks at how existing enterprise policies are evaluated and ways in which they could be enhanced in the future.

15.2 The political context

15.2.1 Shaping the entrepreneurial economy

During the last quarter of the twentieth century, many industrialized countries pursued a programme of reforms designed to create an 'entrepreneurial' economy (Audretsch and Thurik 2000) (Sections 1.1, 10.1, and 11.1). This transition is now widely recognized as being, at least in part, a political project. In other words, national and regional governments have been engaged in a conscious attempt to change existing economic and social institutions in order to encourage entrepreneurial activity. This project, and the policies adopted to pursue it, can be explained in a number of ways. From an economic perspective, they can be seen as part of a move from interventionist policies based on Keynesian economics to a 'neo-liberal' economics, which placed an increased reliance on market mechanisms. Secondly, they responded to a perceived need to reverse a decline in the population of smaller firms, and to recognize their contribution to the economy. Thirdly, they reflected a concern that big business corporations lacked entrepreneurial energy, and that large organizations of all kinds needed to recover the virtues of their smaller counterparts in order to remain innovative and to compete effectively in the future.

---

 online resource centre 'The Enterprise Culture's Political Roots.'

15.2.2 The policy landscape: scope and terminology

So far, we have been using the umbrella term 'enterprise policy' to refer to any attempt to encourage or guide entrepreneurial activity. In this section, we outline the scope of enterprise policy and clarify some of the language used in policy debates:

- **SME policies and entrepreneurship policies** These two strands of policy are at the centre of the enterprise policy landscape. Though there is considerable overlap, and the terms are often used quite loosely, researchers have noted some important differences of emphasis (e.g. Stevenson and Lundström 2002; Huggins and Williams 2009). SME policies are usually concerned with improving the short- to medium-term economic performance of existing firms. Entrepreneurship policies tend to have a wider scope and a longer-term orientation (Audretsch and Beckman 2007), and are designed to promote entrepreneurial vitality, including the encouragement of potential entrepreneurs and of new start-up ventures. This difference is also reflected in the methods adopted to drive the policy forwards. For example, in order to help existing small firms in the house building sector, you might decide to simplify regulations, reduce the tax burden, provide access to information, or subsidize current training schemes. By contrast, if your priority was to encourage more innovative entrepreneurial activity in the sector, you might decide to launch pre-start and start-up support schemes (e.g. linking university-based building technologists with external sources of venture finance and business advice), and promote networking activity among the most dynamic and technologically advanced materials, design and construction firms.

- **Other policies that influence entrepreneurship** The level and quality of entrepreneurial activity can be influenced, both directly and indirectly, by many other areas of public policy that operate alongside the policies we are discussing in this chapter. Examples might include taxation, industry regulation, international trade, and education. The influence of these related policies is bound to vary: an arts-based **social enterprise**, for example, would be affected by a different combination of policies to a biotechnology start-up venture. In some cases, their effect may be to support, or reinforce entrepreneurship and SME policies (e.g. investing in the education system could help to promote new venture creation), but there may also be tensions and conflicting objectives (e.g. groups representing small firms often complain that new government regulations increase their costs, making them less competitive against international competitors). Science and **innovation** policy, which is probably the most closely connected of these 'related' policy areas, makes an appearance later in the chapter (Sections 15.2 and 15.4).

- **Other dimensions of policy: scale and scope** We have already seen that the policy landscape contains a variety of types of policy, which can combine in different ways to influence entrepreneurial activity. Enterprise policies also operate at different geographic scales, from international policies co-ordinated by cross-national bodies (e.g. the European Union's 'Enable' Programme) to small-scale initiatives, developed at a local level (e.g. creating a farmers' market or promoting social enterprises in a small town). Policies can also vary in scope: they may be economy-wide (e.g. income tax reforms); sector-specific (e.g. industry de-regulation); or targeted at particular groups (e.g. supporting young entrepreneurs) (Section 15.4.2).

It is not possible to do justice to such a complex policy landscape in a single chapter. Rather than attempt a comprehensive review, we consider a more limited range of policies, looking at the arguments used to support them, how they were implemented, and what they have achieved.

15.3 Arguments for policy intervention

15.3.1 Economic and non-economic arguments

When people talk about entrepreneurship and enterprise, they often refer to things like 'deregulation', 'liberalization', 'autonomy', and reducing the role of government. However, in practice policy-makers have found it hard to resist the temptation to intervene in the entrepreneurship process. Intervention has taken three main forms: (1) encouraging more enterprise; (2) keeping entrepreneurial activity under control; and (3) guiding entrepreneurial activity towards particular goals. In the following sub-section, we focus on economic arguments for intervention. Social and environmental arguments are covered in Section 15.2.3.

15.3.2 Economic growth, employment, and competitiveness

The economic case for intervention has been build on the idea that governments can generate employment and stimulate economic growth, either by supporting SMEs or by promoting various forms of entrepreneurial activity (Section 11.1). Where governments have adopted SME policies, the objectives have typically been to strengthen an existing population of small firms, ensuring that they are able to compete effectively against larger firms. These interventions have often addressed specific 'market failures' that create disadvantages for small firms in relation to their larger counterparts (Audretsch et al. 2007; Huggins and Williams 2009: 21). Other SME policies have also attempted to increase the population of smaller firms in order to address issues such as economic decline or under-development in particular regions (e.g. remote rural communities or post-industrial cities). Entrepreneurship policies have taken a rather different line, focusing less on the fortunes of smaller firms, and more on the long-term development of new entrepreneurs. In some cases, governments have also attempted to guide entrepreneurial activity away from outcomes that are economically 'destructive' (e.g. involved in rent-seeking behaviour) and towards those that are more economically productive (Baumol 1990) (Section 11.4). The economic case for SME-type policies often includes some (or all) the following arguments:

- To provide employment, particularly important for communities in some locations (e.g. inner cities, remote rural areas).

- To create new economic activity, particularly important at regional and local level, where a decline in the population of firms can increase income disparities.

- To contribute to economic competitiveness at a regional and sectoral level (e.g. networks of small firms are needed to supply large manufacturing firms); despite globalization, this can also have a regional competitiveness dimension.

- Because smaller firms can pursue **entrepreneurial opportunities** that cannot readily be taken up by larger firms.

- To increase industry competition and act as a countervailing force against powerful groups of larger firms.

A common theme is that intervention is justified because SMEs are economically disadvantaged, leading to inefficiencies that cannot be corrected solely through free market mechanisms. The following examples illustrate the disadvantages you might face as the owner-manager of a small firm based in a remote rural location. How might these factors impact on your competitiveness?

- Your costs of financing the venture are higher because banks lack information on small rural firms and charge premium rates to reflect this uncertainty. You are also finding it more difficult to get information on, or access to, attractive public procurement contracts.

- Your delivery costs are higher and there is limited access to higher speed broadband due to your remote location. Administrative costs in complying with industry regulations are also proportionately higher due to the size of your organization.

- You are having difficulties in protecting intellectual property and costs are higher, in comparison to a larger firm, because you do not have access to specialist legal advice.

Underlying these 'market failure' arguments is the suggestion that there may be unequal power relationships between organizations of a different size (e.g. small shops or small food producers and large multiple retailers). One of the best ways to see these power relationships in operation is to look at the policy and campaigning activities of small business lobbying organizations, such as the UK's Federation of Small Businesses (http://www.fsb.org.uk) or Sweden's Federation of Private Enterprises, *Företagarna* (http://www.foretagarna.se).

The economic case for entrepreneurship policies is often built on similar arguments to those already discussed, the orientation is different. Instead of making the case for a particular category of organization (i.e. small- and medium-sized enterprises), arguments are based around the need to respond to major changes in the world economy, including globalization and its impact on economic growth in both industrialized and newly industrializing countries.

Policies were also shaped by the transition towards a knowledge-based economy, with entrepreneurial start-ups being seen as having a pivotal role to play in economic development:

> *Entrepreneurship takes on new importance in the knowledge economy because it serves as a key mechanism by means of which knowledge created in one organization becomes commercialized in a new enterprise.* (Audretsch and Beckmann 2007: 41)

Economic arguments for intervention are usually discussed in isolation, with economists often going to considerable effort to express them in rigorous, quantifiable terms. However, in practice, it is extremely difficult to separate the economic, social, and environmental dimensions of policy-making. Underlying the economic case, you can usually find arguments about the kind of world that people want to live in. For example, SME policies to defend small specialist retailers against the expansion of large multiple retailers may be defended in purely economic terms, with reference to market imperfections (e.g. by measuring the impact of anti-competitive, rent-seeking behaviour on consumer prices). However, the same policy could also be defended on purely social and environmental grounds (e.g. reviving local food varieties, reducing 'food miles' by local sourcing). This returns us to earlier discussions about entrepreneurial activity as generating different kinds of 'value' and efforts to make economic development economically, socially and environmentally 'sustainable' (Sections 11.1 and 11.3).

15.3.3 Social and environmental arguments

Consider four defining challenges of the early twenty-first century: climate change, the global financial crisis, international terrorism, and the 'bottom billion' of the world's population who continue to live in poverty. It is clear that governments are not capable of addressing these issues by themselves, and that entrepreneurial actors have the potential to make significant contributions in many areas (Section 10.1). For example, technology entrepreneurs are already involved in creating new, low-carbon technologies and industry sectors, and social entrepreneurs are helping to increase incomes in the poorest countries. However, as critics have pointed out, in some cases the activity of entrepreneurs is making things much worse. The problem arises when people decide to pursue economically attractive opportunities that have socially or environmentally destructive consequences. For example, the continuing boom in low-cost aviation is increasing global greenhouse gas emissions, while the exploitation of global demand for timber and palm oil is leading to the disappearance of irreplaceable rainforests. Should entrepreneurial activity be controlled, in order to minimize its more destructive effects, or guided towards more productive directions? In other words, can Baumol's (1990) distinction between productive, unproductive and destructive entrepreneurship be extended beyond the economic sphere (Section 11.4)?

- **Social arguments: combating exclusion and other problems** The world of enterprise is open to anyone, at least in principle. However, as we have seen in previous chapters, there are significant variations in the amount of entrepreneurial activity to be found in different locations and among certain social groups. If we assume, for a moment, that participation in entrepreneurial activity is a 'good thing', and capable of increasing the life chances of individuals and communities, there is a strong case for intervening to ensure that such opportunities are more widely available. This line of argument has led to a range of enterprise policies that are designed to encourage increased participation by excluded groups, including the young, older people, people with a disability, and members of some ethnic minority communities (LDA 2005; Blackburn and Ram 2006). As Blackburn and Ram (2006: 75) have noted, current thinking – at least in the United Kingdom context – is that there is an 'inextricable link' between enterprise policy and efforts to tackle social exclusion. Across Europe, social enterprises of various kinds are often seen as an effective vehicle for integrating marginalized groups into society (Spear and Bidet 2005).

- Other examples of socially oriented enterprise policies can be found in rural areas, where the objective is not simply to generate wealth, but to maintain – and in some cases to revive – local communities and cultures. Rural enterprise initiatives raise complex issues, reflecting the distinctive characteristics of rural businesses and of remoter rural areas in particular (Smallbone et al. 2002). For example, it has long been recognized that in-migrants can become a potent source of new entrepreneurial ventures, generating income and employment. On the other hand, wealthy in-migrants can distort local housing **markets**, forcing younger people to relocate to urban centres. The flow of in-migrants is also uneven, with more scenic and accessible locations (so-called 'honey-pots') drawing much larger numbers than their less attractive and more remote counterparts. There can also be tensions between encouraging the growth of new businesses and preserving heritage sites (e.g. ancient monuments) and natural resources (e.g. unique wildlife habitats). Efforts to attract inward investment can also create problems for rural areas. Large companies may be attracted to an area in response to a combination of government grants, subsidies, tax exemptions, and infrastructure investments. However, these new arrivals can prove to be 'foot-loose', relocating to other areas in response to changes in their own strategic priorities. The sudden loss of a large employer can wreak havoc on any community, but the effects can be particularly severe in rural regions, where alternative sources of employment (for local people), and of customers (for local business supplying the corporation) are few and far between (Section 13.5).

- **Environmental arguments: making enterprise sustainable** In recent years, governments have made increasing use of SME policy interventions in order to control against environmentally damaging activity, and to encourage more environmentally benign ways of operating (BERR 2009; Parker et al. 2009). The arguments for intervening are based on evidence that SMEs have been slow to adopt environmental improvements, with research evidence suggesting that this is due to a combination of internal and external barriers (BERR 2009: 4). The case for intervention echoes previously discussed economic arguments (e.g. limited resources and information). In some cases, there is also a lack of clear market signals and an inadequate 'business case' for making the necessary changes. Given the short-term pressures facing many small business owners, why should they invest time, effort, and resources to improve their performance? Since SMEs represent such a high percentage of businesses, intervention is seen as necessary for a number of reasons, including: (1) helping to address governmental targets (e.g.

reducing greenhouse gas emissions); (2) enabling larger firms and the public sector to source from environmentally sustainable suppliers; and (3) ensuring that SMEs are able to take up the new opportunities of a low carbon economy. Entrepreneurship policies in the environmental area are often linked to more conventional economic aims. Encouraging environmental technology start-ups, for example, may be presented as part of an innovation strategy, with traditional industries being transformed in order for a country or region to remain internationally competitive (e.g. UNEP 2009).

In the following case study (Case 15.2), Friederike Welter talks about her research on policy-making of transition economies (i.e. the former communist countries of central and eastern Europe), where governments are using enterprise policies to pursue economic, social and environmental objectives.

Case 15.2 *Researcher Profile*
Friederike Welter, examining enterprise behaviour in transition economies

Friederike Welter is a professor based at the Jönköping International Business School, Sweden. She received her degree ('Diplom') in economics and business administration from the University of Bochum in 1989. Her doctoral thesis was on SMEs, their strategic behaviour and SME support in Nigeria. From 1993 to 2006, she worked in the Rhine-Westphalia Institute for Economic Research (RWI), becoming deputy head of the research division, Entrepreneurship and Enterprise Performance. Friederike's main research interests are in entrepreneurship and small business development, entrepreneurial behaviour in different regional contexts, women's entrepreneurship, and support policies. She has edited books on entrepreneurship and trust, and on enterprising women in a transition context, and has co-authored a book on entrepreneurship in Central and Eastern Europe. With Candida Brush and Anne De Bruin, she was guest editor for two *Entrepreneurship Theory and Practice* special issues on women's entrepreneurship. With Frank Lasch, she also edited a special issue of this journal, featuring European entrepreneurship research. She was President of the European Council for Small Business and Entrepreneurship (ESCB) from 2007 until 2009. In this interview, Friederike discusses her research on entrepreneurship in transition countries.

Q: Why did you want to research in this area? How did you decide on your main research questions?

Initially, this was not a decision I made, but in the RWI we had acquired a large project, commissioned by the German Federal Ministry of Economics, to analyse the emergence and development of new and small ventures in Poland, Hungary, and the Czech and Slovak Republics. The topic was fascinating, in particular as little was known about SMEs and entrepreneurship in formerly planned economies at that time (1993). Moreover, for me this was a possibility to continue my research interest from my doctoral thesis. So, after this particular project finished, I looked for ways to do more research on transition economies because there were many interesting questions. Some of the research projects over the next years were financed by national governments or international organizations such as the International Labour Office or USAID. I had little to say in determining the research questions but most of these studies tackled applied, policy-related issues of SME development, which I found interesting. I also participated in, and later co-ordinated, several research projects financed by the European Union. In these cases our group could determine our own research questions which were driven by what we ('we' being a network of Western and East European researchers which had developed over time) felt were knowledge gaps in SME and entrepreneurship research. For example, one project researched women's entrepreneurship in Ukraine, Moldova, and Uzbekistan (Welter et al. 2006), a topic which is still under-researched in the context of formerly planned economies. In other projects, we studied the role of trust in relation to entrepreneurial behaviour in different contexts (cf. Höhmann and Welter 2005) or looked at innovation in small firms (Smallbone et al. 2010).

Q: What methods did you use?

All projects used a method mix. That started with desk-top research (especially where projects were government financed as in those cases we often could not fund empirical studies), secondary analysis of statistical data, and, where possible own data collection. The first project I participated in concentrated on a survey of SMEs, key expert interviews and profiles of business organizations in order to analyse the support needs of SMEs in the Ukraine, Belarus, and Moldova from different perspectives and to develop policy recommendations. In later projects, we added case studies (in-depth interviews, which were semi-structured) to our method box as those provided deep insights into the 'why' of entrepreneurial behaviour. And in the latest two projects, on cross-border co-operation and cross-border entrepreneurship, we relied on case studies only which provided very rich material.

Q: What were your key findings?

That's a huge question, asking to summarize 15 years of research! One of my key findings from all these projects sounds quite simple, namely that context matters. For example, what constitutes, at first glance, 'irrational' behaviour from an economic point of view, such as unrelated diversification or portfolio entrepreneurship by entrepreneurs who had but very few resources, emerged as rational behaviour in an environment where banks did not finance new businesses, so that entrepreneurs were using these methods to self-finance their main business. Or take 'shuttle trading' (i.e. small traders crossing borders, exporting and importing all types of goods, often illegally). At first glance, you could debate whether this constitutes genuine entrepreneurship, but in a transition context several small business owners progressed from shuttle trading, which provided them with financing, to more substantial businesses.

Q: Were there any particular challenges in conducting these studies?

Definitely! First, how to make our samples representative in those projects where we conducted surveys? There were no statistics of businesses, only outdated lists, etc. We used, again, a mix of sampling methods. Second, in the last projects on cross-border entrepreneurship we faced additional challenges, as we included petty traders in our samples. Most of those operate (partly) illegally, so interviews were conducted at border crossings, sometimes on trains or buses or at open air markets. Interviews could not be recorded, but had to be written up afterwards; and it took time to build up trust with our interviewees. Another challenge concerns data interpretation – we as researchers are also a product of our own contexts. Luckily, the close co-operation with Eastern European colleagues since the mid-1990s helped me to gain a really deep understanding of their environments – and also to question our 'Western' research concepts. We had long discussions when we started working together on seemingly simple concepts such as 'entrepreneur', 'profit' and 'management'.

Q: Where do you think research in this area needs to develop in future?

At the moment, I am particularly interested in what our research results mean for the theories and concepts we apply in entrepreneurship research. For example, how do we incorporate different contexts into our theories, and also into empirical research? Also, are theories and concepts developed for a mature market economy appropriate to explain phenomena in different environments? I don't think that we need new theories but it is important to consider the implications for 'mainstream' entrepreneurship theory. Theories of entrepreneurship need to be robust enough to accommodate the various forms of entrepreneurship that emerge in a variety of circumstances. In other words, it is about the 'embeddedness' of entrepreneurship, and this is something to be taken into account in future projects.

Sources: Höhmann and Welter (2005); Welter et al. (2006); Smallbone and Welter (2010); Smallbone et al. (2010).

15.4 How do governments intervene?

15.4.1 Intervening to encourage entrepreneurial activity

In this section, we focus our attention on entrepreneurship policies, and the methods used to pursue them. As we have already seen, policy-makers are operating in environments that are complex, variable, and often uncertain. Given these contingencies, how can they intervene to encourage entrepreneurial activity? There are three basic policy options:

> *They can try to increase the supply of potential entrepreneurs. Efforts can be made to increase the ratio of active to potential entrepreneurs. Assistance can be provided during the birth and early life of the business to increase the chances that the firm can survive.* (Mokry 1988: 23)

All three options have a role to play in entrepreneurship policy, but as the author noted, increasing the supply of potential (or nascent) entrepreneurs is likely to be the most difficult, particularly in the short to medium term, while supporting existing firms is more straightforward. Since this time, governments have conducted many different experiments in pursuit of greater entrepreneurial vitality. However, in an influential series of entrepreneurship policy studies, researchers have identified four basic levels of engagement (Stevenson and Lundström 2002, 2007). These range from what the authors term 'E-extension' policies, 'added-on' to traditional SME support measures, to more wide-ranging 'Holistic' entrepreneurship policies:

- **E-extension policy** Measures to support new firm creation and encourage other forms of entrepreneurial activity tend to be embedded within existing SME policy frameworks and implemented through existing SME programmes and services.

- **Target group policy** Measures focus on increasing the number of new firm start-ups in particular population segments. In one version, they may seek to tackle specific barriers faced by under-represented groups (i.e. unemployment, access to labour market, social inclusion). Alternatively, as part of a 'techno-entrepreneurship policy', they may encourage graduates, research scientists, and technologists to create high-growth potential ventures.

- **New firm creation policy** Measures focus on reducing barriers to business entry and exit in order to encourage new business creation. For example, they might simplify or enhance business registration, incorporation, bankruptcy, competition, and labour market policies. They might also introduce 'one-stop shops' offering easier access advice and information for entrepreneurial start-ups.

- **'Holistic' entrepreneurship policy** Measures are typically much broader and longer-term, and designed to strengthen the entrepreneurial culture and capacity of a country. The approach is more cohesive and comprehensive than other policy types. For example, they are likely to involve changes to the education system, as well as regulatory reform, better access to start-up support and financing, and strategies tailored to meet the needs of specific target groups.

As the authors emphasize, the policies adopted by national governments did not fall neatly into any one of the four categories, but there were dominant approaches, sometimes complemented by a secondary approach. For example, governments that 'added-on' an entrepreneurship focus to their existing SME support structure might offer special programmes and services to identified target groups. Though there may not be a universal model for entrepreneurship policy, Stevenson and Lundström (2007: 107–13) have argued convincingly that governments need to adopt an integrated framework comprising the following core components:

1. **Entrepreneurship promotion** This group of policies is designed to enhance the perceived value of entrepreneurial activity in society and more generally, to create greater awareness of entrepreneurs and entrepreneurship. It can be achieved in a variety of ways. For example, government departments and agencies can engage with high-profile entrepreneurs, using them to publicize and endorse their initiatives. They can also organize events, such as the European Commission's 'SME week', and awards programmes. Other organizations also have a role to play, including television broadcasters, who have been responsible for profile-raising programmes such as the BBC's *Dragons' Den* (http://www.bbc.co.uk/dragonsden).

2. **Entrepreneurship education** Governments have pursued a number of policies to promote and to integrate entrepreneurship skills, knowledge and motivation into the curricula of schools, colleges and universities. Policy measures include teacher and researcher training courses, new curriculum guidelines, sponsored business plan competitions, and support for student entrepreneurship organizations. Policies in this area are often delivered by third sector bodies, such as the UK's Princes Trust (http://www.princes-trust.org.uk).

3. **Barriers to entry and exit** The aim of these policies is to make it less time-consuming and more attractive to pursue an entrepreneurial career. They require governments to systematically review the impact of their administrative, legal, and regulatory systems on existing SMEs and new ventures, which are often disproportionately affected by these structures. Some governments have also simplified reporting requirements (e.g. for tax or employment purposes). One of the biggest challenges for policy-makers is to ensure that the potential impact of new laws and regulations is evaluated before they are introduced. In recent years, many countries have set up 'better regulation' task forces and similar initiatives in order to assess and, where possible, to reduce negative impacts on businesses. In the field of social enterprise, new legal entities, such as the UK's 'Community Interest Company' (CIC) have been introduced in order to provide a more straightforward legal structure (http://www.cicregulator.gov.uk).

4. **Start-up business support** Policies in this area aim to deliver information, advice and specialist support and networking for entrepreneurs as they move through the start-up phase. Typical measures include personalized mentoring and training, financial support for incubators (i.e. low-cost accommodation with related support services) and science parks, and supporting networks that provide an opportunity to interact with other entrepreneurs. In recent years, governments have also invested in electronic resources, such as the European Small Business Portal, which provides a single online point of access to specialist advice, information, and services in multiple European language versions (http://ec.europa.eu/small-business).

5. **Start-up and seed financing** Policies in this area are specifically directed at market failures (Section 11.3.2) and funding gaps that are experienced by some new and early-stage ventures, including those caused by lack of relevant information. Measures to address these deficiencies include the provision of microfinance (see Case 11.1), loan guarantees, and specialist 'seed capital' funds, which are designed to enable technology entrepreneurs to move beyond the prototype stage. Governments may also seek to encourage networks of **business angels**, **venture capitalists**, and venture philanthropists, the latter specializing in finance for social enterprises.

6. **Target groups** This group of policies comprises two sub-sets. The first is designed to reduce systematic barriers to an entrepreneurial career for members of under-represented groups in the population, while the second is concerned with encouraging the creation of high growth potential, technology-based start-ups. The measures required to deliver these objectives are essentially specialized versions of those identified in the previous two headings (e.g. providing specialist peer-support networks and sources of funding).

Though written more than two decades ago, the following remarks are still equally relevant today. They summarize the continuing challenge faced by policy-makers attempting to encourage more entrepreneurial activity in a particular location:

> *The easiest solution for a policy maker who wants to promote entrepreneurship is to get elected in a place where natural entrepreneurial activity is already well established. The start-up process is complex and policy tools available to influence it are few and frustratingly crude. Physical buildings, financing, information, and supportive attitudes are things that governments can offer, but these fail to reach the fundamental forces that cause entrepreneurship to come about. Policy to assist entrepreneurship will need to be flexible, targeted to gaps in market processes, proactive, and imbued with a long-term perspective that patiently waits for results. Unfortunately, the environment in which economic development policy operates rarely shares these characteristics.* (Mokry 1988: 29)

Perhaps the most important lesson learned in the intervening years is that, though there are many challenges, carefully integrated and well-targeted enterprise policies can deliver results. This was illustrated recently in the field of technological entrepreneurship, where researchers demonstrated that the combination of innovation and entrepreneurship policy can have a measurable impact on new venture creation. The study compared policies adopted by different US states in relation to nanotechnology start-ups. The researchers found that states that adopted *both* economic and innovation policies saw six times as many new firms created, compared to those that lacked this combination. While economic initiatives had a stronger effect than innovation initiatives, states with the earliest innovation policies also had relatively higher rates of new firm formation (Woolley and Rotner 2008).

15.4.2 Intervening to control and guide entrepreneurial activity

Having reviewed a number of techniques for encouraging entrepreneurial activity, we now turn to interventions that seek to control or to guide the kind of activity that takes place, revisiting the two examples discussed previously (Section 15.3.3):

- **Promoting enterprise in order to tackle social exclusion** Blackburn and Ram's (2006) review of UK polices to address social exclusion provides a good illustration of why enterprise policies need to be well thought out, with clear objectives that are grounded in a deep understanding of their subject matter. The authors conclude that social exclusion is a complex, multifaceted concept (i.e. to understand it, you need to consider both individual-level behaviours and broader social structures), and one that is contested (i.e. there is no consensus over its causes or how they can be 'cured'). In the light of this analysis, they argue that policies to encourage more commercial start-up ventures in socially excluded communities need to be reviewed:

  > *Our analysis tends to run against the latest policy 'fad' of uncritically advocating that small firms and entrepreneurship are a key route for individual and societal economic and social salvation. [. . .]* Small firms are the crucible of an economic system which both generates inequalities as well as provides a source of employment and economic well-being for individuals. *From this we argue that entrepreneurship,*

as manifested in business ownership, provides opportunities for inclusion for some people in some contexts but little scope for others. (Blackburn and Ram 2006: 85; emphasis added)

The authors also suggest that the implementation of policies needs to take more account of the needs of those they are attempting to support:

The excluded groups that we have discussed have often been sceptical of mainstream business support agencies and by their relatively non-inclusive nature are often difficult to reach. In relation to ethnic minority businesses, we have witnessed a burgeoning of ethnic-specific support agencies and groups. Young people often gravitate to more informal and fluid networks for their sources of economic and social capital. We need to explore whether these, perhaps more organic, vehicles of support are more efficacious in realizing the social inclusion agenda. (Blackburn and Ram 2006: 86)

- **Promoting sustainable entrepreneurship** Policies to promote sustainability entrepreneurship take a variety of forms. Measures designed to promote technological innovation have the highest profile (e.g. Parrish and Foxon 2009). These resemble other technology entrepreneurship measures, categorized by Stevenson and Lundström as targeted niche policies (Section 15.4.1). However, policy-makers have also supported a variety of 'social' innovations, which aim to reduce our environmental impact. For example, as part of its third sector strategy, the UK government's environment department has sponsored a number of initiatives by social enterprises, charities, and other non-commercial organizations, designed to promote pro-environmental behaviour change (Defra 2009). Environmental sustainability is often about longer-term transitions. One of the most important lessons from research in this area is that policy-makers need to design measures that take into account existing institutions. For example, our comparative case study on entrepreneurship and innovation in the wind turbine industry (Case 14.1) is a recent example of national policies producing radically different outcomes (Garud and Karnøe 2003; Agterbosch and Breukers 2008).

To summarize, policy-makers are adopting many different approaches, and experimenting with a wide variety of policy measures in order to achieve their chosen objectives. While some of these interventions are having an impact on entrepreneurial activity, others are less effective. Should poor performance be attributed to the policies, the measures, or the context in which they are implemented? We consider these questions in the concluding section, which addresses the challenge of evaluating enterprise policies.

15.5 Evaluating enterprise policies

15.5.1 Why is policy evaluation needed?

There is still considerable debate over the effectiveness of enterprise policies, and the measures they employ. In some cases, the evidence points to unintended and even counter-productive outcomes (e.g. displacement effects and increased bureaucratic hurdles), leading some critics to question whether interventions are justified (e.g. Curran 2000; Parker 2007). Governments and other organizations spend substantial amounts of money on programmes to encourage entrepreneurship. However, there is surprisingly little evidence that this funding is working (Greene et al. 2007; Greene 2009). We introduce this theme with two contrasting examples of researchers responding to the evaluation challenge (Case 15.3).

Case 15.3 Evaluating enterprise policies

This case examines two contrasting examples of research into the effectiveness of enterprise policies. The first study examines policies adopted over three decades, and in three different English regions. The second analyses the way that the World Bank measures entrepreneurial activity in fragile, post-conflict states. Though the issues are different, both of these studies raise important questions about the kinds of enterprise policies that are being implemented, the ways they are being measured, and whether these interventions can really make a difference to what happens on the ground.

1. Enterprise policies in three English regions

This research study, by Francis Greene, Kevin Mole, and David Storey of Warwick University is an important contribution to the debate on enterprise policies, and in particular those that have attempted to promote the creation and growth of new businesses in geographic regions (Greene et al. 2007). The empirical core of the study is a large data set, drawn from interviews with more than 900 'entrepreneurs', defined as owner-managers of new businesses. The study is comparative, in that it contrasts three English regions and three time periods. The regions have been selected as examples of different levels of 'enterprise performance', using the proxy measure of per capita VAT registrations. In a striking early figure, the authors indicate how relative positions of the three regions: Buckinghamshire ('high'), Shropshire ('middling'), and Teesside ('low') have remained remarkably consistent over the period 1980–2005. Teesside provides perhaps the most important and interesting theme in the study – the extent to which enterprise culture policies have influenced outcomes over an extended period. As the authors indicate, Teesside was effectively an 'experimental region' in this regard, and was subjected to successive initiatives designed to boost its economic prospects. In the Teesside data, the researchers find that businesses started by individuals who have been business owners previously are more likely to have slower sales growth than those of individuals starting a business for the first time. The authors interpret this finding as suggesting that 'most new entrepreneurs do not learn significantly from their previous business experiences and, even if they do, they are unable or unwilling to apply it to their current business venture' (Greene et al. 2007: 199). With regard to entrepreneurial finance in Teesside, the authors find that, '27.3 per cent of new businesses made use of public support in Teesside, compared to 2.3 per cent in Buckinghamshire' (Greene et al. 2007: 166). However, the authors note that it was not possible to reach clear conclusions about the impact of such funding. One of the most telling graphs compares population growth in the three regions between 1981 and 2003. While growth rates have increased consistently in Shropshire and Buckinghamshire, the Tees Valley has seen a steady decline of around 2% per annum over the study period. In their concluding remarks, the authors draw our attention back to the limits of policy interventions in the face of complex and deep-seated structural constraints.

> *What is clear is that more of the same is unlikely to enhance economic welfare of the residents of Teesside. By this we mean that efforts to raise new business formation will, if they have any effect at all, merely lead to more businesses established by individuals with low human capital, who are starting businesses in easy-to-enter industries because of a lack of alternative employment opportunities in the locality. We are also unpersuaded that the provision of public funds either to provide advisory services to such businesses, or to provide them with grants of one form or another, is likely to enhance their economic performance. The businesses themselves clearly appreciate the support, and an 'enterprise industry' has emerged to provide this support, but our evidence is that its impact is small. Whilst there have been no recent other studies of new entrepreneurs on Teesside, our view is that it is of questionable benefit for individuals to be enticed into enterprise without being made aware of the potentially considerable expected downside losses.* (Greene et al. 2007: 246)

2. Measuring the environment for entrepreneurship in fragile states

This research, conducted by Chiara Guglielmetti of the University of Trento, examines entrepreneurship support policies for 'fragile states' that are recovering from periods of conflict and civil upheaval. The primary focus of this study is the role of performance indicators, in particular the World Bank's 'Doing Business' (DB) measures. The researcher questions whether these indicators are capable of capturing entrepreneurial dynamics and of informing policy-making in an effective way. The author begins by setting out the nature and scale of the problem:

> *More than a billion people live in around 50 developing countries which have been described as 'fragile states' (Naudé et al. 2008). In fragile states, governments lack the authority, legitimacy and often the willingness to promote economic development. According to Binzel and Brück (2007: 5) fragility refers to 'the existence of persistent, systematic, significant and interrelated social, political and economic uncertainties'. Increasingly, donors and international development agencies are turning to private sector development where state capacity is lacking. Promoting entrepreneurship in fragile states, and in conflict and post-conflict situations, has therefore assumed high importance in strategies dealing with fragile states.* (Guglielmetti 2010: 1)

She also notes that fragile states face a number of distinctive challenges. For example, resources need to be reallocated away from military purposes, people need to be reintegrated into economic activities, the quality of entrepreneurship needs to be considered, and the role of women needs to be addressed. In addition, it is likely that new economic networks will have to be created, and existing ones strengthened, in order to generate flows of economic resources that can reinforce the transition towards a peacetime economy. Having conducted a detailed review of current practices, she concludes that the 'Doing Business' (DB) measures do not take such context-specific issues sufficiently into account:

DB therefore fails to stress the variety and the complexity of ways through which governments can influence the productive allocation of entrepreneurship, and does not detect fundamental inputs of entrepreneurial development. (Guglielmetti 2010: 12)

Questions

1. How do these policy issues compare with those discussed in this chapter?

2. What are the main lessons for policy-makers attempting to encourage entrepreneurial activity in: (a) regions with low levels of enterprise; (b) fragile, post-conflict states?

3. What research methods would you use to answer one of the following questions: (a) why firms started by previous business owners were more likely to have *slower* sales growth than those of first timers; (b) why a higher percentage of new businesses made use of public support in Teesside, compared to Buckinghamshire; (c) whether new networks are being created in a fragile state; (d) the potential for female entrepreneurship in a post-conflict state.

Sources: Baumol (1990); Binzel and Brück (2007); Greene et al. (2007); Naudé et al. (2008); Guglielmetti (2010).

15.5.2 Policy evaluation: approaches and implications

Different evaluation methodologies can generate radically different evidence on the outcomes and impact of enterprise programmes (Greene 2009). Traditionally, public policies have been evaluated using economic criteria, such as job creation and economic growth. Though it might be difficult to isolate the impact of particular policies, suitable statistical measures and data sets (e.g. for unemployment and GDP) were generally available, at least in industrialized countries. Today, policy-makers have a much more ambitious agenda for entrepreneurship. Policy interventions are being directed at economic, social, and environmental goals. They are also being used in a much wider range of contexts, including newly industrialized and developing countries. So what measures should we use to evaluate this new generation of entrepreneurship policy? And, at a more general level, what is the 'value' generated by entrepreneurial activity and how can we know whether it is being delivered (Section 11.1)? In an effort to develop internationally comparable measures of entrepreneurial activity, the OECD created an Entrepreneurship Indicators Programme (EIP). In their discussion of value, the OECD's researchers emphasize that the policy objectives and measures are likely to vary, depending on political considerations about the kinds of value that are being sought:

Therefore 'value' covers both monetary and non-monetary returns. These values are, naturally, identified as objectives or targets by policy makers, who will then develop policies designed to achieve these targets although clearly they are carried out by entrepreneurs and entrepreneurial firms. Some countries for example will focus on entrepreneurship's contribution to economic growth. Other countries however might focus on entrepreneurship's contribution to solving environmental problems or its contribution to social inclusion. (Ahmad and Hoffman 2007: 5).

The policy evaluation literature is still in its infancy, but many policy researchers would agree with the following conclusions about the current state of play, which introduced a recent Special Issue on entrepreneurship policy. Building on the work of several leading researchers, the Special Issue editor noted that policies needed to be more context-sensitive:

> One of the main policy implications of the previous analysis is that 'one size does not fit all.' In other words, if entrepreneurial efforts are to be allocated to productive activities, policy strategies, with respect to entrepreneurship, need to be tailored to the specific institutional context of each economic region [...] For example, the environments required for the emergence of productive entrepreneurship are likely to differ significantly between a rural area, a high-technology cluster, and a metropolitan area. Therefore, policy design needs to take account of local differences, and to adapt to the different scale and nature of existing resources, networks, and market capabilities. In spite of this need for diversity, entrepreneurship policies tend to be based on a handful of policy tools. (Minniti 2008: 708–81; emphasis added)

Evaluating enterprise policy will remain an important and challenging field. The social world is complex and dynamic, and it is often difficult to obtain the necessary evidence, and to analyse in ways that reveal the underlying causes (Pawson 2006). Enterprise policies can make a difference, and the closing case provides a striking example of this, by tracing the way that policy-making has shaped the economic development of Bavaria over the last 30 years. However, as we saw in Case 15.3, it is not always entirely clear what has happened, or whether any of the observed changes can be attributed to a particular policy intervention. What remains certain is that entrepreneurs will go on pursuing their personal visions, more or less successfully, and that the outcomes of their collective efforts will continue to shape our economies, societies and the natural world upon which we all depend.

✳ 15.6 Summary

➤ Entrepreneurial activity is a powerful phenomenon, and public policy has been used both as a vehicle for fostering more activity and for regulating its impact on society.

➤ SME policies and entrepreneurship policies overlap to some degree, but there are important differences of emphasis, and in associated policy measures.

➤ Government intervention in pursuit of SME and entrepreneurship policies has traditionally been justified on economic grounds, but the scope of policy is increasingly being extended to address broader social and environmental goals.

➤ Governments have adopted different approaches and measures in order to pursue their policy objectives. The most effective appear to be integrated policies that are also sensitive to the context in which they are implemented.

➤ Entrepreneurship policies have been criticized by some as representing an ineffective or economically inefficient use of resources and by others as reinforcing socially and environmentally unsustainable systems of production and consumption.

➤ Policies must be informed by research evidence and subject to rigorous evaluation if they are to respond effectively to today's economic, social, and environmental challenges.

➤ Existing and nascent entrepreneurs need to be aware of policies that are likely to impact on their ventures. Unexpected policy changes can create serious problems for commercial and social ventures but also new sources of opportunity.

Case 15.4 'Between laptops and Lederhosen': entrepreneurship and innovation policies in Bavaria

From the early 1990s, the southern German state of Bavaria formulated new entrepreneurship and innovation policies that drew on the advantages – and disadvantages – of the region's past. Policy-makers balanced deep-rooted, conservative traditions (i.e. 'Lederhosen') with a desire to encourage innovative, technology-based start-up ventures (i.e. 'laptops'). Initially an agricultural region that lacked large and innovative firms, Bavaria is now a leading region for biotechnology and other high technology industries, with one of the lowest unemployment rates in Europe. This case study draws on research conducted by Marcel Hülsbeck and Erik E. Lehmann of the University of Augsburg, which examined the Bavarian state's efforts to encourage entrepreneurship and innovation. In these extracts, we learn about the background to the policies, how they were introduced, and their impact on the regional economy.

Entrepreneurship policy in Bavaria (1993–2009)

The 'Free State of Bavaria' is the biggest of Germany's 16 federal states (Lander). Covering an area of 70,549 km² and roughly 12 million inhabitants (15% of all Germans), the population density of 173 inhabitants per km² is very low compared to the federal state (Land) of Baden-Württemberg (300 inhabitants/km²), which is often termed as Germanys 'model economy,' or the heavily industrialized

The entrepreneurial state of Bavaria: past and present

North Rhine-Westphalia (NRW) with its Ruhr Valley (530 inhabitants/km²). About 16% of Bavarians live in one of only three major cities (population > 250,000: Munich, Nuremberg, and Augsburg). Bavaria is a rural region, internationally renowned for its traditions and tourist attractions such as Bavarian Beer, Lederhosen, the Oktoberfest in Munich, Castle Neuschwanstein, and the Alps. Until the 1960s, Bavaria was an economically backward agrarian state, dependent on monetary transfers from other German Lander, with unemployment rates well above German average. Since then, the Free State of Bavaria has evolved into one of the economically best performing federal states. The success story started in post-war Germany. Bavaria had always been one of Germany's granaries and had been largely unaffected by the industrial revolution that transformed Lander like North Rhine Westphalia (NRW), Baden-Württemberg (BW), or Saarland (S) into industry clusters for heavy industry (NRW, S) or mechanical engineering (BW). This lack of industrial infrastructure turned out to be an advantage for Bavaria after the Second World War. Instead of investing in the rebuilding of old and existing industries, Bavaria had to invest in the settlement of new industries. At the same time, various firms from former Middle- and Eastern-German provinces were looking for new headquarters. In order to attract these possible investors and to level out the locational disadvantages, Bavarian politicians put their talents to work and used their personal networks to convince those industrial leaders to relocate their companies to Bavaria. This kind of personal networking has ever since become a tradition among Bavarian politicians, entrepreneurs and researchers, and resulted in economic growth as well as corruption scandals (e.g. the 'Amigo-Affairs'). The second strategy to overcome the infrastructural drawbacks was to promote more controversial new technologies, including those associated with nuclear power generation and the aerospace industry. Policy-makers also addressed a long-standing spatial problem in Bavaria, where a lack of urbanized and industrialized areas and a low population density had left industries geographically and sectorally dispersed. Rather than adopting 'egalitarian' policy measures that might provide additional support to its weaker regions, Bavaria encouraged the agglomeration of industry and innovation clusters by providing a regionalized research infrastructure based around 26 universities and institutes of higher education, 3 major research establishments, 12 Max Planck Institutes (basic research), and 13 Fraunhofer Gesellschaft establishments (applied research).

Institutionalizing entrepreneurship policy

Until 1993, Bavarian entrepreneurial policy was based on informal, personal networks. This ended following the resignation of the prime minister (1988–1993), Max Streibl, because of alleged bribery. The new prime minister (1993–2007), Edmund Stoiber, learned from this experience and made a number of changes that institutionalized the entrepreneurial policy. The starting point was the privatization of state-owned companies, signalling to the public that the web between politics and business was unwoven. The privatization also raised over €5 billion (1994–2004), which was invested into two frameworks supporting five goals in four key technologies in Bavarian entrepreneurship. The first framework 'Future Bavaria Campaign' has five relevant strategic goals:

1. Promotion of groundbreaking research and technology in the fields of transportation technologies, material sciences, environmental technologies, genetics/biotechnology and medicine, and medical technology.

2. Creation of effective technology transfer between science and industry.

3. Facilitation of new ventures and business start-ups.

4. Assistance for SMEs in addressing new international markets.

5. Strengthening of the position of practical orientation in education.

The second framework 'High-Tech Campaign Bavaria' aims at the same goals as the first campaign, but is meant to emphasize the importance of key technologies: life sciences (genetics, biotechnology, medicine, medical technology), energy and environment (including transportation), material sciences, and microsystems (including mechatronics). These campaigns are organized and co-ordinated by the State Ministry of Economic Affairs in co-operation with the State Ministries of Science (goal 1) and Education (goal 5), which have created three public limited companies to execute projects within the frameworks: 'Bayern Innovativ' promotes technology transfer between science and industry (goal 2); 'Bayern Kapital' supplies venture capital and financial aid for start-up companies and SMEs (goal 3); and 'Bayern International' assists SMEs in addressing new international markets (goal 4). Additional regional help comes from the Bavarian Chambers of Commerce (goal 2) and regional development assistance institutions (goal 3).

Key technologies and innovation clusters: some preliminary observations

After a decade of heavy investments, most of the privatization proceeds have been spent, and the state has already started programmes to cut down costs in higher education. The investments into entrepreneurial policy have, so far, led to impressive short-term growth and innovation rates of the Bavarian economy. Whether these achievements will persist in the future or will decline proportional to possible investments largely depends on the infrastructures of technologies addressed. One decade of policy is a rather short period of time to evaluate the success of measures taken. However, we can open up a discussion about the institutionalized innovation networks that have been created. In this case, we focus on Life Sciences Bavaria, and BAIKUM (Environmental Technology). Additional analysis is presented in Hülsbeck and Lehmann (2007), including full supporting references:

- **Life Sciences Bavaria** is the shining example of Bavaria's regionalized entrepreneurial policy. It consists of two biotechnology clusters in the Munich area and in the city of Regensburg. The Munich cluster consists of 24 biotech companies, three basic research institutes (MPIs for biochemistry, neurobiology and psychiatry), both Munich universities (LMU, TUM), which have been ranked as Germany's leading research universities in natural sciences, the National Research Centre for Environment and Health, the Institute of Agronomy and Plant Breeding, the university of applied sciences Weihenstephan (food technology), and two biotechnological research networks (immunology, prions). There are 13 specialized business services mainly offering venture capital, legal and business advice. Regarding this comprehensive structure, the Munich biotech cluster seems to be very well positioned for the future and it seems that the Bavarian government's plan to create Europe's leading biotech region has worked out quite well. Meanwhile the other Bavarian biotech cluster (BioPark Regensburg) consists of 20 biotech companies, the University of Regensburg and two business service companies (venture capital, medical technology consulting). Compared to the Munich cluster the long-term success of this cluster might be contended. But still both examples show that regional entrepreneurial policy in Bavaria has been able to create high tech clusters of new scientific-analytic technologies virtually out of nowhere.

- **BAIKUM innovation network for environmental technology** consists of firms derived from a multiplicity of industries, using analytic and synthetic knowledge. It is an eclectic industry in relation to technologies and knowledge bases with the sole communality that the field of application is environmental technology. It is a very young sector, which is not profiting from well established intra-industry networking along supply chains. The highest spatial concentration of the 35 companies in the network can be found around Augsburg (7 firms, i.e. 20%); all other firms are widely spread across Bavaria (13 locations with one to three firms). Most of the relevant research institutions are in Augsburg and Munich. Many specialized business services provide engineering consulting services, which could be interpreted as means to bring together the necessary knowledge bases. There is only little observable spatial clustering within this industry, as far as we can see in this superficial examination. This could be due to its newness, the variety of established root industries, or differing knowledge bases. It seems that the entrepreneurial policy measures undertaken have not yet led to the desired effect of creating a spatially and socially dense web of knowledge and technology transfer. The future development of these aspects will show whether managed networking activity can substitute for the lacking proximity.

Lessons and future challenges

The research summarized in this case study indicates that Bavaria is indeed a land of contrasts between laptops and Lederhosen. On the one hand, it is still the agrarian state renowned for its tourist attractions and strong traditions. On the other hand, it has managed to establish a new tradition of progress: the intuitive attempts of the post-war era to attract different industries have been translated into an institutionalized entrepreneurial policy that is yielding fruits today. The 'Bavarian model' has even been exported to other countries facing similar challenges and could prove to be useful for other economies (e.g. eastern European countries). There are four lessons to be learned from Bavarian entrepreneurial policy:

1. Policy-makers must consider the industrial history of the region concerned and must use the existing resources instead of using egalitarian approaches of spreading investments evenly across industrial sectors.

2. The spatial and infrastructural aspects (networks) should be used (and implemented) to guide investment decisions.

3. The kind of technology transfer and networking needed depends on knowledge base characteristics of the targeted industries.

4. The key question for policy-makers is not 'how much' but 'how' public financial resources are spent.

Any attempts to facilitate innovations, intra- and inter-industry co-operation should be tailored to these characteristics. However, entrepreneurship policy also depends on policy-specific variables. One key factor – regarding Bavaria and Baden-Württemberg – is political stability. Both states differ significantly from the other 14 Lander. In both states, the conservative Christian Democratic Union (CDU; in Bavaria called CSU) has run their states for more then half a century. This, however, gives an incentive for a long-term policy instead of a myopic view fixated on the next election.

Questions

1. Looking back to the mid-twentieth century, what were the main advantages and disadvantages of Bavaria as a location for entrepreneurship?

2. In what ways did policy-makers begin to address these issues prior to 1993?

3. How does the institutionalized entrepreneurial policy compare to the approaches discussed in this chapter?

4. Imagine that you are a university-based scientist with a potential spin-off venture in either biotechnology or environmental technologies. What practical lessons would you draw from this study?

Source: Hülsbeck and Lehmann (2007); adapted with permission.

Practical activities

1. Spot the policy Using the case illustrations and web links in this chapter as a starting point, search for the websites of three national or regional governments and download examples of their enterprise policies. Categorize and compare the policies using the frameworks introduced in Sections 15.3 and 15.4 of this chapter. What do your findings suggest about the way governments intervene to foster or regulate enterprise?

2. What works? Select TWO examples of policies that are being evaluated. You can begin with the case illustrations in Section 15.5 or search any of the following sources: (a) media coverage (e.g. newspaper articles, television programmes, journalists' blogs); (b) official reports (e.g. by governments and external assessors); (c) academic studies reported in books, conference papers, or journal articles. Prepare a one-page summary, addressing the following questions: (a) What policy is being evaluated? (b) What were the policy objectives? (c) How were the policy outcomes and impacts evaluated? (d) How successful has the policy been? (e) What lessons (if any) are being drawn for the future?

3. On the receiving end Find out what real-life entrepreneurs think about government attempts to foster and regulate enterprise. Search the biographies, autobiographies, public speeches, media profiles, and blogs of some well-known entrepreneurs; you can start with the people featured in case studies throughout this book. Alternatively, arrange an interview with an entrepreneur that you can contact through your friends or family. Use the discussion in Section 15.5 as a starting point. Summarize your findings as either a one-page report or as five presentation slides (NB this activity can be linked to Discussion topic 3).

▣ Discussion topics

1. Promoting technological innovation The research evidence suggests a number of different views on how best to promote technological innovation. Compare, for example, Hendry and Brown's (2006) research on opto-electronics technology firms and Henry and Pinch's (2000) findings on motor-sport technology clusters. Select one of the following technological fields and discuss what combination of policy initiatives would be most likely to support innovation.

2. Combating social exclusion: a step too far? Blackburn and Ram's (2006) review of the UK government's attempts to combat social exclusion with enterprise policies suggests a more complex and less optimistic picture than that presented by some proponents (Section 15.5): (a) Are policies to promote entrepreneurial activity capable of 'fixing' entrenched forms of social exclusion? (b) What do you see as the main lessons for policy-makers seeking to address this kind of problem?

3. What policy means to me Take one of the following roles and discuss how the policies discussed in this chapter might apply to you: (a) an existing entrepreneur, considering how best to develop her/his business; (b) a prospective entrepreneur, deciding whether to move out of regular employment and start up a new venture; (c) a small business advisor, designing courses to support existing or prospective entrepreneurs. To illustrate the discussion, you can draw on your own experiences of entrepreneurship, a new venture creation activity (i.e. Part One of this textbook), and/or material collected for Practical activity 3 (above).

▢ Further reading guide

There are a variety of views on the enterprise culture 'project' and its political context. **Audretsch and Thurik (2000)** discuss the transition towards an **entrepreneurial economy**. For contrasting perspectives, see **Della-Guista and King (2008)** and **Gray (2002)**. The current state of entrepreneurship in Europe and other parts of the world is set out in official reports, such as the **European Commission (2008)** and in research findings collected in edited books, such as **Dowling and Schmüde (2007)**. **Audretsch et al. (2007)** is a handbook on entrepreneurship policy, which contains several valuable contributions, including **Hülsbeck and Lehmann (2007)**, the study featured in Case 15.4. Research on policy-making can also be found in the leading entrepreneurship journals, including, *Entrepreneurship and Regional Development, Entrepreneurship Theory and Practice*, and the *International Small Business Journal*. They can also appear in related journals such as *Research Policy, Regional Policy, Industrial and Corporate Change*, and *Environment and Planning C: Government and Policy*. Some relevant articles include: **Minniti (2008)** and **Robson et al. (2009)**, which introduce Special Issues on the subject of enterprise policy; **Mason (2009)**, which focuses on entrepreneurial finance policies in Europe; **Mole and Bramley (2006)**, an international comparison of non-financial business support; **Smallbone and Welter (2006)**, which looks at SME policies in transition countries, and **Fritsch (2005)**, which reviews regional innovation policy.

There is a growing body of research on policy-making in relation to social enterprises, including Lyon and Ramsden (2006) and Spear et al. (2009). Pawson (2006) discusses the challenges of producing the research evidence needed to evaluate public policy. Greene et al. (2007) and Storey (2008) provide concrete examples of how enterprise policies are evaluated, and the lessons these evaluations provide.

 # References

Agterbosch, S. and Breukers, S. (2008) 'Socio-political embedding of onshore wind power in the Netherlands and North Rhine-Westphalia.' *Technology Analysis and Strategic Management*, 20, 5: 633–48.

Ahmad, N. and Hoffman, A. (2007) 'A framework for addressing and measuring entrepreneurship.' Paris: Organisation for Economic Cooperation and Development (OECD).

Audretsch, D.B. and Beckmann, I.A.M. (2007) 'From small business to entrepreneurship policy.' In D.B. Audretsch et al. (eds) op. cit. (36–53).

Audretsch, D.B. and Thurik, A.R. (2000) 'Capitalism and democracy in the 21st century: from the managed to the entrepreneurial economy.' *Journal of Evolutionary Economics*, 10: 17–34.

Audretsch, D.B., Grilo, I., and Thurik, A.R. (eds) (2007) *Handbook of research in entrepreneurship policy*. Cheltenham: Edward Elgar.

Baumol, W. (1990) 'Entrepreneurship: productive, unproductive, and destructive.' *Journal of Political Economy*, 98: 893–921.

BERR (2009) *SMEs in a Low Carbon Economy* (URN 09/574). London: Department for Business, Enterprise and Regulatory Reform/Centre for Centre for Enterprise and Economic Development Research.

Binzel, C. and Brück, T. (2007). 'Analyzing conflict and fragility at the micro-level.' *UNU-WIDER Conference on Fragile States-Fragile Groups*, Helsinki, 15–16 June.

Blackburn, R. and Ram, M. (2006) 'Fix or fixation?: the contributions and limitations of entrepreneurship and small firms to combating social exclusion.' *Entrepreneurship and Regional Development*, 18, 1: 73–89.

Casson, M., Yeung, B., Basu, A., and Wadeson, N. (2008) *The Oxford handbook of entrepreneurship*. Oxford: Oxford University Press.

Curran, J. (2000) 'What is small business policy in the UK for?: evaluation and assessing small business policies.' *International Small Business Journal*, 18, 3: 36–50.

De, D. (1999) 'SME policy in Europe.' In D.L. Sexton and H. Landström (eds) op. cit. (87–106).

Defra (2009) 'About the Greener Living Fund.' London: Department for the Environment, Food and Rural Affairs. Available at http://www.greenerlivingfund.org.uk/about/ (accessed 10 November 2009).

Della-Guista, M. and King, Z. (2008) 'Enterprise culture.' In M. Casson et al. (eds) op. cit. (629–47).

Dowling, M. and Schmüde, J. (eds) (2007) *Empirical entrepreneurship in Europe*. Cheltenham: Edward Elgar.

European Commission (2009) *The Small Business Act for Europe*. Brussels: European Commission, Enterprise and Industry. Available at http://ec.europa.eu/enterprise/entrepreneurship/sba_en.htm

European Commission (2008) *Putting small business first: Europe is good for SMEs, SMEs are good for Europe* (2008 edition). Brussels: European Commission, Enterprise and Industry.

Eurostat (2008) 'Enterprises by size class – overview of SMEs in the EU (31/2008).' Luxembourg: Eurostat.

Fagenberg, J., Mowery, D.C., and Nelson, R.R. (2005) *The Oxford handbook of innovation*. Oxford: Oxford University Press.

Fritsch, M. (2005) 'Regionalization of innovation policy – introduction of the Special Issue.' *Research Policy*, 34, 8: 1123–7.

Garud, R. and Karnøe, P. (2003) 'Bricolage versus breakthrough: distributed and embedded agency in technology entrepreneurship.' *Research Policy*, 32: 277–300.

Gray, J. (2002) *False dawn: the delusions of global capitalism* (new edition). London: Granta.

Guglielmetti, C. (2010) 'Measuring the business environment for entrepreneurship in fragile states (Working Paper 2010/14).' Helsinki: United Nations University/World Institute for Economic Development Research.

Greene, F.J. (2009) 'Assessing the impact of policy interventions: the influence of evaluation methodology.' *Environment and Planning C: Government and Policy*, 27, 2: 216–29.

Greene, F.J., Mole, K.F., and Storey, D.J. (2007) *Three decades of the enterprise culture: entrepreneurship, economic regeneration and public policy*. Basingstoke: Palgrave.

Hendry, C. and Brown, J. (2006) 'Dynamics of clustering and performance in the UK opto-electronics industry.' *Regional Studies*, 40, 7: 707–25.

Henry, N. and Pinch, S. (2000) 'Spatialising knowledge: placing the knowledge community of Motor Sport Valley.' *Geoforum*, 31, 2: 191–208.

Höhmann, H-H. and Welter, F. (eds) (2005) *Trust and entrepreneurship a West–East perspective*. Cheltenham: Edward Elgar.

Huggins, R. and Williams, N. (2009) 'Enterprise and public policy: a review of Labour government intervention in the United Kingdom.' *Environment and Planning C: Government and Policy*, 27, 1: 19–41.

Hülsbeck, M. and Lehmann, E.E. (2007) 'Entrepreneurship policy in Bavaria: between laptop and Lederhosen.' In Audretsch, D.B., et al. (eds) op. cit. (200–12).

LDA (2005) *Re-defining London's BME-owned businesses*. London: London Development Agency/Mayor of London.

Lyon, F. and Ramsden, M. (2006). 'Developing fledgling social enterprises? A study of the support required and means of delivering it.' *Social Enterprise Journal*, 2, 1: 27–41.

Mason, C.M. (2009) 'Public policy support for the informal venture capital market in Europe: a critical review.' *International Small Business Journal*, 25, 5: 536–56.

Minniti, M. (2008) 'The role of government policy on entrepreneurial activity: productive, unproductive, or destructive?' *Entrepreneurship Theory and Practice*, 32, 5: 779–90.

Mokry, B.W. (1988) *Entrepreneurship and public policy: can government stimulate business start-ups?* New York: Quorum.

Mole, K.F. and Bramley, G. (2006) 'Making choices in nonfinancial business support: an international comparison.' *Environment and Planning C: Government and Policy*, 24, 6: 885–908.

Naudé, W., Santos-Paulino, A.U., and McGillivray, M. (2008). 'Fragile States (Research Brief 3).' Helsinki: United Nations University/World Institute for Economic Development Research.

Parrish, B.D. and Foxon, T.J. (2009) 'Sustainability entrepreneurship and equitable transitions to a low-carbon economy.' *Greener Management International*, 55, 47–62.

Parker, C.M., Redmond, J., and Simpson, M. (2009) 'A review of interventions to encourage SMEs to make environmental improvements.' *Environment and Planning C: Government and Policy*, 27, 2: 279–301.

Parker, S.C. (2007) 'Policymakers beware!' in D.B. Audretsch et al. (eds) op. cit. (54–63).

Pawson, R. (2006) *Evidence-based policy: a realist perspective*. London: Sage.

Robson, P.J.A., Wijbenga, F., and Parker, S.C. (2009) 'Entrepreneurship and policy: challenges and directions for future research.' *International Small Business Journal*, 25, 5: 531–5.

Sexton, D.L. and Landström, H. (2000) *The Blackwell handbook of entrepreneurship*. Oxford: Blackwell.

Smallbone, D. and Welter, F. (2006) 'The role of government in SME development in transition economies.' *International Small Business Journal*, 19, 4: 63–77.

Smallbone, D. and Welter, F. (2010). 'Entrepreneurship and government policy in former Soviet republics: Belarus and Estonia compared.' *Environment and Planning. C: Government and Policy*, *28*, 2: 195–210.

Smallbone, D., North, D., Baldock, R., and Ekanem, I. (2002) *Encouraging and supporting enterprise in rural areas (Research Report RR009/02)*. Sheffield: Small Business Service.

Smallbone, D., Welter, F., Voytovich, A., and Egorov, I. (2010). 'Government and entrepreneurship in transition economies: the case of small firms in business services in Ukraine.' *Service Industries Journal*, 30, 5: 655–70.

Spear, R. and Bidet, E. (2005) 'Social enterprise for work integration in 12 European countries: a descriptive analysis.' *Annals of Public and Co-operative Economics*, 76, 2: 195–231.

Stevenson, L. and Lundström, A. (2002) *Beyond the rhetoric: defining entrepreneurship policy and its best practice components*. Stockholm: Swedish Foundation for Small Business Research.

Stevenson, L. and Lundström, A. (2007) 'Dressing the emperor: the fabric of entrepreneurship policy.' In D.B. Audretsch et al. (eds) op. cit. (94–129).

Storey, D.J. (2008) 'Evaluating SME policies and programmes: technical and political dimensions.' In M. Casson et al. (eds) op. cit. (248–78).

Spear, R.G., Cornforth, C.J., and Aiken, M. (2009). 'The governance challenges of social enterprises: evidence from a UK empirical study.' *Annals of Public and Cooperative Economics*, 80, 2: 247–73.

UNEP (2009) 'An introduction to the Green Economy report.' Geneva: United Nations Environment Programme/Green Economy Initiative.

Welter, F., Slonimski, A., and Smallbone, D. (2006). 'Small enterprise internationalization: national and regional aspects.' *Economic Bulletin*, 6, 33–50.

Woolley, J.L. and Rottner, R.M. (2008) 'Innovation policy and nanotechnology entrepreneurship.' *Entrepreneurship Theory and Practice*, 32, 5: 791–811.

Glossary

Balance sheet statement is a summary of the financial position of the business at a specific date, such as at a month end or the year end. It shows the balance between the assets, liabilities, and ownership equity. The difference between assets and liabilities is net worth or net assets or, simply, equity. The net worth must equal assets minus liabilities and ownership equity.

Business angels tend to be wealthy individuals who want to invest in high growth businesses. They may also be part of a syndicate with other business angels. In addition to money, they often bring with them experience, skills, and contacts. They will tend to look for opportunities in industries and sectors where they feel they have relevant experience.

Business models emerged during the 1990s as a way of understanding and comparing the plethora of new business ideas that developed around the Internet. They identify the key components, underlying assumptions, and their relationships in order to make comparisons and to identify ideas that were unique or particularly robust. In essence, business models show how a venture is going to be able to generate revenues and to make a profit from its operations.

Cash flow forecast is a financial statement that predicts the movement of cash into and out of an enterprise over a specified period (e.g. weekly, monthly, or quarterly). In the early phases of most new ventures, there is usually a negative cash flow. It is calculated by using the balance sheet and profit and loss statements together with predictions regarding significant variables such as interest rates, creditor and debtor days, stock holding, planned purchases, and sales forecasts.

Clusters are geographic concentrations of firms and other organizations (e.g. the clusters of high technology firms around places like Minneapolis, Cambridge, and Munich). New clusters can often be a focus for intensive entrepreneurial activity. See also: 'Spatial variations' and 'Temporal variations'.

Creative destruction is a term coined by Joseph Schumpeter to refer to the way that entrepreneurial activity can undermine and displace earlier business models. It is sometimes contrasted with the more recent idea of 'creative construction', in which entrepreneurial activity facilitates knowledge spillovers, which open up new opportunities for existing (or 'incumbent') businesses.

Credit rationing refers to the imbalance between demand for finance by start-up ventures and what is made available by banks and other finance providers. It has been seen as an example of a market failure, and may constrain entrepreneurial activity.

Customer relationship management (CRM) has emerged as a set of activities supported by technologies, which facilitate relationship marketing. CRM technologies support this important business process.

Effectuation theory is a new perspective on the way that entrepreneurs may behave as they attempt to create a new venture, or engage in other forms of entrepreneurial activity. It suggests that rather than conducting an initial detailed analysis of the situation and selecting the best option, some entrepreneurs adopt more informal and improvised approaches. A related concept called, 'brico-lage', has also been applied recently.

Electronic communication platforms support interactions between individuals and enterprises. New technologies, such as the Internet and 3G mobile networks, are constantly emerging and having an impact on markets and industries by creating opportunities.

Enterprise culture refers to a late twentieth century political project or initiative designed to encourage an increase in independent entrepreneurial activity and a corresponding decrease in the role of the state in regulating and intervening in the economy. Initially associated with neoliberal governments in the UK and USA, the enterprise culture has since developed in many other countries around the world.

Enterprise is an alternative term for an organization or firm, which is engaged in economic activities for financial or social gain. See also: 'Social enterprise' and 'Small and medium-sized enterprise (SME)'.

Enterprise policies is a general term that describes a wide range of initiatives to promote and guide entrepreneurial activity. These initiatives have been implemented by governments and public agencies at local, national, and international levels. They may be reinforced (or undermined) by other public policy initiatives (e.g. investments in higher education spending or changes to international trade regulations). See also: 'SME policies' and 'Entrepreneurship policies'.

Entrepreneurial activity is enterprising human action in pursuit of the generation of economic and social value through the creation or expansion of economic activity, by identifying and exploiting new opportunities for new products, processes, or markets, and by meeting outstanding social and environmental needs.

Entrepreneurial characteristics or 'traits' comprise a number of psychological concepts that have been associated with a person's entrepreneurial capabilities or potential (e.g. need for achievement, over-optimism, risk-taking propensity, desire for autonomy). Though still popular and widely used, the idea of defining characteristics has been challenged by more recent psychological and behavioural research. See also: 'Entrepreneurial cognition' and 'Entrepreneurial creativity'.

Entrepreneurial cognition is a research field that examines how people think, and the role that ways of thinking might play in entrepreneurial processes. For example, one major theme asks why entrepreneurs appear to be more 'alert' to opportunities than other people. See also: 'Entrepreneurial creativity' and 'self-efficacy'.

Entrepreneurial creativity is largely associated with the capacity of entrepreneurs and others to generate or invent new business ideas, involving new products, processes, services, or markets. For many reasons the vast majority of these ideas are not developed beyond a conceptual stage. The attrition rate is very high, but without creativity there is no innovation and without innovation there are no entrepreneurial opportunities. See also: 'Entrepreneurial cognition'.

Entrepreneurial economy is a term used to refer to a market-based economic system in which there is less reliance on the public sector and greater emphasis placed on entrepreneurial activity, which may involve both commercial and social enterprises. The term is also used to refer to an economy with a thriving population of smaller entrepreneurial firms (i.e. the economy is not dominated by large corporations). See also: 'Enterprise culture'.

Entrepreneurial learning can take place in a variety of ways, including formal learning, learning from others and learning from your own experience, all of which can help to develop your entrepreneurial thinking and practice. Learning cannot be reduced to a simple linear process (i.e. there is no 'recipe' or series of predictable steps that you can reproduce in any situation). Learning is not a one-off process but a continuous cycle, which accelerates as you begin to engage directly in entrepreneurial activity.

Entrepreneurial marketing can be contrasted with 'mainstream' marketing techniques that were developed for larger and better-established organizations. For example, in marketing a new venture, entrepreneurs tend to rely on more informal, personal, and interactive approaches. These can be used to address distinctive marketing challenges, including limited resources, lack of legitimacy and powerful competitors.

Entrepreneurial networks are created as individuals make use of their personal contacts (e.g. friends, relatives, and former colleagues) in order to obtain resources for new ventures and other forms of entrepreneurial activity. In common with other social networks, they are not based purely on economic exchange and rely on an accumulation of trust and goodwill (sometimes termed 'social capital').

Entrepreneurial opportunities are a particular type of opportunity, which could lead to the creation of self-sustaining ventures. The process is complex, and is closely related to creativity and innovation. They often arise because some people have access to potentially valuable concrete knowledge, which is not available to others.

Entrepreneurial process describes a sequence of activities from idea generation and opportunity recognition up to the point where an opportunity is exploited, or converted into a real venture. It is possible to distinguish the generation of new business ideas (i.e. creativity and innovation) from the recognition of opportunities with the potential for exploitation (i.e. evaluation and selection). However, in practice, there is usually a lot of interplay and iteration between these activities.

Entrepreneurial teams comprise, in the context of new venture creation, two or more people who are actively collaborating in the founding of a venture in which they have a direct financial and/or personal stake. Entrepreneurs rarely work in isolation, so if a new venture is to be successful, it is essential to consider both the composition of the founding entrepreneurial team, the role(s) that each team member is going to play, and how the team needs to develop once the venture begins to grow. In a wider context, they involve two or more people who are actively collaborating in entrepreneurial activity in any organization.

Entrepreneurial thinking is a mindset that is opportunity focused and draws on creative and innovative ideas to recognize and develop solutions as well as obtain the resources required to exploit or implement them. It is increasingly seen as a desirable skill in a wide range of organizations.

Entrepreneurs are people who seek to generate economic and social value through the creation or expansion of economic activity, by identifying and exploiting opportunities for new products, processes, markets, and for meeting outstanding social and environmental needs.

Entrepreneurship is the phenomenon associated with entrepreneurial activity. It involves a complex pattern of social interactions that extends beyond individual entrepreneurs to incorporate teams, organizations, networks, and institutions. It is often associated with new venture creation but can occur throughout the life of an organization. See also: 'Intrapreneurship'.

Entrepreneurship policies are usually concerned with promoting entrepreneurial activity over the longer term. They may include initiatives designed to promote new start-up ventures (e.g. in biosciences or low carbon industries), and others designed to enhance the growth and economic performance of existing organizations. See also: 'Enterprise policies' and 'SME policies'.

Equity or owner's equity is the difference between the total assets and total liabilities. The ownership equity includes the share capital and retained profit or loss. In a new commercial venture, the founding directors are normally shareholders. For potential investors, this shareholding may be seen as indicating the founders' level of commitment to the venture.

Evolutionary economics is primarily concerned with the ways that economic systems change over time through the processes of selection, retention, and variation (or creativity). Entrepreneurs influence the process in various ways, creating what Joseph Schumpeter termed, 'new combinations'.

Extended enterprise recognizes that for many new ventures interaction with external organizations is at the core of their activities. The ability to develop, facilitate, and manage these interactions is a critical ability. These entrepreneurial and commercial networks are often enabled by electronic communications platforms.

Flotation is the offering of shares on a public trading platform, such as the Alternative Investment Market (AIM) or NASDAQ. It involves an initial public listing (IPO), which results in increased investment and a subsequent opportunity for shareholders to trade shares for personal gain.

Founders, family, and friends (3Fs) are the initial funders of new ventures who play a vital but often unrecognized part in new venture creation. This initial investment is often supported by borrowing, which might be secured on a property or by a personal guarantee. 3Fs can also refer to 'family, friends, and fools'!

Historical research on entrepreneurship examines the causes and consequences of entrepreneurial activity over extended periods. It ranges from biographies and organizational histories to studies that examine the rise and fall of particular industries and regions. See also: 'Temporal variations'.

Industries (or industrial sectors) are made up of individual organizations and inter-organizational networks that supply particular categories of products or services to customers, usually in competition with others. The terminology of industries and industry sectors normally refers to commercial enterprises, but can also be applied to social enterprises. Many of these organizations also operate in competition, and sometimes in collaboration, with public and private sector counterparts.

Innovation is a process that takes various forms. For example, it may involve the introduction of new products, services, processes, markets, ways of working, or wider social practices (i.e. 'social innovation'). There is a close connection between innovation and entrepreneurial activity (e.g. entrepreneurs may be involved in promoting a technological innovation and in exploiting new opportunities that the technology creates).

Interdisciplinary research refers to new approaches and concepts that have emerged from earlier disciplines (NB sometimes termed 'neo-disciplinary' or 'transdisciplinary' research). Some of the newer approaches to entrepreneurship would fit this description.

Intrapreneurship is a term used to refer to entrepreneurial initiatives that take place within larger and more established organizations in the private, public, and voluntary sectors. These activities are also described as, 'corporate entrepreneurship'.

Key performance indicators (KPIs) are based on critical information and produced in addition to the normal financial statements. They can give an indication of how well (or not) an organization is performing. Typically these indicators have been identified by the organization as being particularly important in achieving some short-term or long-term organizational goals.

Knowledge spillover is an economic term describing the way that new ideas and innovations created by scientists and other technical specialists become more widely available, creating new opportunities for entrepreneurs (NB economists also use the broader term 'positive externality' to describe this kind of outcome).

Market segmentation is a technique of grouping customers that are sufficiently similar yet different to be characterized homogeneously. These segments need to be accessible and large enough to be profitable. Entrepreneurial marketing tends to recognize the importance of customer needs rather than simply their characteristics.

Marketing mix is a traditional and popular framework that can be used to consider the market positioning of products and services. Originally consisting of four elements (4Ps) – (1) Product; (2) Price; (3) Place; (4) Promotion – it has expanded into 7Ps to include (5) People, (6) Processes; (7) Physical evidence.

Markets are made up of customers and potential customers, which are sometimes divided up into segments, comprising product and customers that share common characteristics. Marketers often distinguish between 'business to consumer' (B2C) and 'business to business' (B2B) markets.

Multidisciplinary research draws on two or more academic disciplines (e.g. economics, geography, and sociology). Such approaches are often adopted to study aspects of entrepreneurship.

Multi-level research studies involve more than one level of analysis (e.g. entrepreneurial individuals, teams, and organizations). Entrepreneurship researchers have often been encouraged to adopt multi-level approaches.

Neo-Austrian economics challenged the assumptions of earlier neoclassical economists and emphasized the distinctive economic function performed by entrepreneurs. In doing so, they also drew attention to the 'practical knowledge' of entrepreneurs.

Neoclassical economics became highly influential from the late nineteenth century and tended to exclude the entrepreneur from economic analysis, despite some important exceptions. It can be contrasted with Neo-Austrian economics and evolutionary economics.

New growth theory is an economic theory developed in the late twentieth century. It recognizes the important role played by technological innovation and associated 'knowledge spillovers' in promoting economic growth (NB sometimes termed 'endogenous growth theory').

Opportunity business models is a technique that can help to understand the dimensions and drivers for a business idea in order to decide whether there is a genuine entrepreneurial opportunity that can be exploited. It is a way of shaping a vision, like drafting a traditional business plan or entrepreneurs expressing their 'gut feeling'. It describes both the key dimensions (Proposition, People, Place, Process, Profit) and the key drivers (Societal, Commercial, Legal, Technological) that enable and underpin new entrepreneurial opportunities.

Practical knowledge refers to the kind of specialized local knowledge that an entrepreneur might use on a day-to-day basis in order to secure a profit (NB sometimes termed 'local' or 'concrete' knowledge). It can be contrasted with 'scientific knowledge'.

Profit and loss statement (P&L) indicates the relationship between sales (revenue or turnover), cost of sales, gross profit, operating expenses, interest, tax, and net profit for a specific period (e.g. per month, quarter, or year). This is vital management information for directors, shareholders, and staff and needs to be produced in a timely nature. In other words, quickly enough after a period end so that decisions can be taken to maintain or improve the trading position.

Scientific knowledge, a term coined by Friedrich von Hayek, refers to the kind of knowledge used by academic researchers, including economists. It can be contrasted with 'practical knowledge'.

Self-efficacy refers to a person's belief in their own capacity to achieve a specific performance (e.g. setting up a new venture), and is thought to be an important influence on behaviour. An entrepreneur's perception of self-efficacy may differ depending on circumstances, and can also vary over time. See also: 'Entrepreneurial characteristics' and 'Entrepreneurial cognition'.

Small and medium-sized enterprises (SMEs) in the European Union are defined as firms that have fewer than 250 employees, annual turnover of less than €50 million or total assets less than €43 million, and is not more than 25% owned by a corporation. Simpler definitions refer to firms employing fewer than 250 people. In the EU, small enterprises have fewer than 50 employees and micro-enterprises fewer than 10. These definitions vary around the world (e.g. in the United States, small to medium-sized businesses (SMBs) employ fewer than 500 people and small businesses fewer than 100).

SME policies are usually concerned with improving the short- to medium-term performance of existing firms in this size category. They may focus on particular sectors (e.g. tourism, house building), and are likely to involve initiatives such as: simplifying regulations, reducing taxes, providing information, or offering training schemes.

See also: 'Enterprise policies' and 'Entrepreneurship policies'.

Social enterprises are trading organizations that primarily serve a social purpose. They can take a variety of legal forms, including co-operative, limited company, and community interest company. Many 'for profit' enterprises and entrepreneurs may also provide social gains, but this is normally a secondary purpose.

Spatial variations refer to differences in the quantity and type of entrepreneurial activity found in different geographical locations. These differences can be identified at various levels (e.g. between regions within a country and between different countries). See also:

'Clusters' and 'Temporal variations'.

Temporal variations refer to changes in the quantity and type of entrepreneurial activity taking place over time. For example, researchers have shown similar patterns in the birth of new industries, with many new entrants in the early years, followed by consolidation. It is also possible to identify variations in the life of a particular organization or individual.

Venture capitalists are a source of private equity capital but they usually manage larger funds than syndicates of business angels. They are also more likely to look for an exit through an initial public listing (IPO) or trade sale to a larger company.

Index